Politics in Western Europe

SECOND EDITION

Politics in Western Europe

edited by

Gerald A. Dorfman

and Peter J. Duignan

Hoover Institution Press

Stanford University, Stanford, California

Hoover Press Publication 404

First printing, 1991

97   96   95   94   93   9   8   7   6   5   4   3   2

Manufactured in the United States of America
⊚ Printed on acid-free paper

Library of Congress Cataloging-in-Publication Data
Politics in Western Europe / edited by Gerald A. Dorfman and Peter J. Duignan. — Rev. ed.
          p.   cm.
    Includes bibliographical references and index.
    ISBN 0-8179-9122-0 (acid-free)
    1. Europe—Politics and government—1945–   . I. Dorfman, Gerald Allen, 1939–   . II. Duignan, Peter.
JN94.A2P63   1991   91-2633
940.55—dc20   CIP

Contents

Preface to the 1991 Edition

This is an updated and augmented edition of *Politics in Western Europe* (1988). At the suggestion of reviewers and users we have added chapters on Ireland, Greece, and European unification efforts since 1945. A section on East Germany, including reunification, has been added to the chapter on Germany.

Preface to the Original Edition

At the end of World War II, much of Western Europe lay in ruins. The traditional European state system had broken down, so much so that all the war-torn states, except Great Britain, had lost their traditional sovereignty. A speedy revival of the European economies seemed impossible, given both the destruction incurred in wartime and the many long-standing structural weaknesses of the economies. The West European states also suffered from profound internal dissensions and, in many cases, from a profound sense of pessimism. Western Europe henceforth was to face the overweening power of the Soviet Union. Many Europeans were convinced that the future lay with the East.

Western Europe, however, confounded the pessimists' forecasts. To a greater or lesser extent, all West European countries experienced an astonishing recovery, one that would have appeared incredible in 1945. Democratic government and parliamentary institutions, gravely challenged during the 1930s, were reestablished. Western Europe passed through a new industrial revolution and through profound societal changes that left the region much more prosperous than before. Western Europe and the United States became closely linked, militarily through NATO, economically and culturally through a great variety of new associations within the Atlantic Community. Their safety and well-being turned out to be inextricably interlinked.

Nevertheless, a great deal of ignorance persists on both sides of the Atlantic concerning the partners. The striking growth of Western Europe's power in international affairs enhanced, if anything, this widespread mutual incomprehension, as evidenced by a great deal of mutual recrimination—sometimes justified, but often without adequate grounds. All too many Americans, to give just one example, remain to this day woefully ignorant of the size of NATO's defense effort, the importance of Western Europe to U.S. prosperity, or our cultural links to Europe.

In 1984, the Hoover Institution embarked on a research project entitled "West European Studies," under the general editorship of Peter Duignan and L. H. Gann, which is designed to improve American knowledge of Western Europe, to stress the importance of Western Europe for the United States, and to illustrate the reciprocal relations and mutual interdependence within the Atlantic Community. The project is interdisciplinary. The first volume is on the politics of Western Europe, and has been edited by Gerald Dorfman and Peter Duignan, both Senior Fellows at the Hoover Institution. The second volume, edited by L. H. Gann, covers the defense forces of Western Europe, including the U.S. contribution to NATO (Croom-Helm, London, is the publisher). A collaborative volume on the economies of Western Europe is being edited by Elliot Zupnick, professor of economics and director of the Institute on Western Europe at Columbia University. A volume is also planned on the societies and cultures of Western Europe.

Western Europe has rebuilt itself since 1945. Economic recovery went hand in hand with economic cooperation. Although the federal unity of the Europeanists has not been achieved, a high degree of social and political integration has been attained. Parliamentary institutions now dominate, and in much of Western Europe there is a free movement of labor. Federal union may be far off, but a custom union, an alliance system, and a common military organization now unite all of Western Europe, except the neutral states.

The West, that is the Atlantic Community, has been incredibly successful, given Western Europe's military, political, and economic impotence at the end of World War II. Today, the European Economic Community is a global giant. In 1985, its gross domestic product amounted to about two-thirds of the U.S. figure (approximately $2,700 billion as against $3,947 billion). Its population is larger (273 million as against 232 million). Its exports were larger than those of the United States ($227.20 billion as against $217.88 billion). Western Europe's economic progress over the last 40 years has been astounding—despite many setbacks during the last decade. The EEC is one of the world's great manufacturing centers; it commands a vast reservoir of scientific and technological skills. Indeed the Western powers remain the main source of technical and scientific creativity and innovation for the world at large. The EEC is a major food producer and a major donor of food aid, as well as one of the most important sources of capital and technical assistance and a huge market for the developing world. Its combined military strength could be formidable. It produces some of the world's best military equipment. Its members among them maintain as many men under arms as does the United States (2,109,000 as against 2,350,000). If the Western alliance were willing to translate its economic strength into equivalent military power, the Soviet Union would form no threat to the rest of the world.

We hope the essays in this volume will enlighten Americans about politics in Europe since 1945. Better understanding of Europe's political structure, parties, and politics should lead to greater cooperation and to the further growth of the Atlantic Community.

Contributors

Desmond Dinan is Director, European Studies, George Mason University.

Gerald A. Dorfman is Senior Fellow, Hoover Institution.

Peter Duignan is Senior Fellow, Hoover Institution.

Richard C. Eichenberg is Assistant Professor of Political Science, Tufts University.

L. H. Gann is Senior Fellow, Hoover Institution.

David Gress is Senior Research Fellow, Hoover Institution.

Richard Gunther is Professor of Political Science, Ohio State University.

Gale Irwin is Professor of Political Science, University of Leiden.

Dennis Kavanagh is Professor and Head of Politics, University of Nottingham.

Norman Kogan is Professor of Political Science, University of Connecticut.

Vincent E. McHale is Professor and Head of the Department of Political Science, Case Western Reserve University.

Roy C. Macridis is Professor of Political Science, Brandeis University.

Anton Pelinka is Professor of Politics, University of Innsbruck.

Jürg Steiner is Professor of Political Science, University of North Carolina at Chapel Hill and University of Geneva.

Politics in Western Europe

1

Introduction

to European Politics and Policies

Dennis Kavanagh

Western Europe has been the home of many of the formative experi-ences in human history, including Greek civilization, Roman law, Christianity, the Renaissance, the Reformation, the emergence of sovereign states, the French Revolution, and the rise of industrialism and liberalism. In the twentieth cen-tury it provided the battleground for two great wars and witnessed the shaping of large societies in accordance with the ideologies of Nazism and communism. Surely no other area can have been so influential in forming modern society.

But there are difficulties inherent in any study of West European states. The European states all draw on common legacies, but Europe is also enormously diverse. The states differed greatly, for example, in the manner in which they industrialized. The industrial revolution began in Great Britain and Belgium; thereafter Germany pulled ahead and became the most successful of European industrial states. The importance of social class varies from country to country; so does the role played by religion in politics. In general, religion has not played an important part in post–World War II British politics—with the exception of Northern Ireland. In Germany, Italy, and France—by contrast—parties that claimed to stand for Christian democracy evolved. All European countries dis-play striking regional differences. These may have diminished somewhat in re-cent years, but they still play an important part in countries such as Italy, where the south has remained the most backward part, and Great Britain, where the north of England and the "Celtic fringe" (Scotland and Wales) have failed to share in southeastern England's general prosperity. All the states have experi-

1

enced migration, both from rural regions to the conurbations and from abroad—but the impact of migration has varied enormously.

Generalizations become all the more difficult when we consider Europe's national diversity. Every European country must cope with transnational ideologies—socialism in various forms or the challenge of the ecological movements and feminism. All experienced a "baby boom" after World War II, followed by a striking decline in the birthrate. All have been affected to a greater or lesser extent by the commercial and cultural impact of the United States. All are concerned with the Soviet challenge—military and political. All have seen a revolution brought about by new means of electronic communications and industrial production. Foreign travel has vastly increased in scope. The religion of patriotism may have declined in fervor, compared with the first half of the present century, but the bulk of Europeans still consider themselves above all as members of a particular nation-state. Indeed, usage of the term *Western Europe*—and the assumption that there are sufficient important similarities among the states to justify the term—is a recent development. The postwar geographical and political division in Europe between the USSR and its socialist neighbors in the east (Poland, Hungary, Czechoslovakia, Romania, Bulgaria, East Germany, Yugoslavia, and Albania) and the "other" states has meant that, almost by default, the latter states are now regarded as West European.

For the purposes of this chapter, Western Europe consists of eighteen states: the five Nordic states of Finland, Norway, Sweden, Denmark, and Iceland; the eleven which are on the continental mainland (France, Italy, Germany, Switzerland, Luxembourg, the Netherlands, Belgium, Greece, Spain, Portugal, and Austria); and the island-nations of Britain and the Republic of Ireland. Some may object to the inclusion of Britain and Ireland, which are physically separate from the West European landmass. Others think of Western Europe as consisting primarily of the twelve current members of the European Community.

As of 1980, these eighteen states had a combined population of 349 million, appreciably larger than the populations of the United States or the Soviet Union. Although Western Europe is sometimes referred to as a superpower, like the United States or Soviet Union, the analogy is somewhat misleading. In contrast to these countries, Western Europe is not a sovereign state. It does not have a central government, a supreme lawmaking body, a written constitution, a head of state, a common currency or military force, or a shared history of symbols of statehood and nationality.

Western Europe is, however, a useful and meaningful term. States remain important actors, membership in international organizations is confined to states, and the loyalties of most citizens and laws of government are largely based on states. But we also talk in terms of areas—"the free world," "the West," "Anglo-American societies," and so on. Clearly we find the concept of an area transcending the state system useful and sometimes necessary. This chapter provides an introduction to the studies of the politics of a number of West European countries that follow. It examines first some common features of West European states and their progress toward political integration. Second, it discusses party systems and ideologies and, finally, major domestic and foreign policy issues.

These states all exhibit some common features. First, they are highly industrialized and affluent. In 1945 many of the states had substantial proportions of their populations working on the land; as late as 1950 a quarter of the work force in Germany and France was in the primary (agricultural) sector. But the postwar shift from the land into industry has been quite rapid. Eight states now have at least 10 percent of their work force engaged in agriculture, but only Greece, Spain, Portugal, and Ireland have more than one-fifth so employed. Interestingly, these four are the poorest states in Western Europe in terms of per capita GDP. Portugal is the poorest member-state of the European Community, but it enjoys living standards higher than those of most states in Africa, Asia, and Latin America. There is, of course, a strong interrelation between such economic features as industrialism, urbanism, and affluence and such social conditions as high levels of literacy, education, health care, private ownership of cars, and other indicators of high living standards.[1] Within the more industrialized states, like Sweden, France, Britain, and Germany, there is now a second, or postindustrial, revolution in which employment moves out of heavy industry (shipbuilding, iron and steel, coal, and engineering) into new service and high-technology occupations. In these countries more than half of the work force is in tertiary (service) occupations.

West European states are also liberal democracies. There are, of course, great differences in their national histories, party systems, and political institutions (be they parliamentary or presidential, monarchical or republican systems). Some, like Britain and Sweden, have durable histories as liberal democracies. Others, like Germany, Italy, and Austria, have had checkered records. The Netherlands, Norway, Denmark, France, and Belgium were occupied in World War II. Spain, Portugal, and Greece were under military rule until the mid-1970s and have become democracies only recently.

The relationship between socioeconomic conditions and the stability of liberal democracy merits further comment. There are exceptions (for example, Nazi Germany) to the theory that advanced socioeconomic development always produces stable democracy. Yet it is interesting that Portugal, Spain, and Greece are among the most socially and economically backward states in Western Europe and have been the slowest to move to liberal democratic institutions. The governments of these states resisted moves to greater political liberty and democracy in the nineteenth and twentieth centuries. In Portugal and Spain dictatorships were formed during the interwar years, a time when liberal democracy was retreating in Europe. The Portuguese dictatorship lasted nearly 50 years, until the left-wing army coup in 1974. In Spain the monarchy was restored after the death of General Franco in 1975, and competitive elections followed in 1977. In Greece the army has regularly intervened in politics in the twentieth century, and the military dictatorship between 1967 and 1974 was the only successful challenge to liberal democracy in postwar Western Europe. Yet all these states today are constitutional democracies. The important point is that only since the mid-1970s can one generalize about Western Europe being liberal democratic.

Liberal democratic polities are a recent development and a rarity in the world today. Only 21 states have continuously permitted competitive elections since 1945.[2] Such states also have political freedoms of speech, political organization, and assembly. Six of the 21 states are Anglo-American (Britain, the United States, Australia, New Zealand, Canada, and Ireland). Thirteen are West European (the notable exclusions from our list are Spain, Portugal, and Greece). Israel and Japan complete the list. There is much justification for regarding liberal democracy as a phenomenon that is largely geographical (West European) or cultural (Anglo-American) and located in the twentieth century.

Many of the states are relatively new. It is true that Britain, Portugal, Spain, France, Denmark, Sweden, and Switzerland were recognized as securely independent states by the seventeenth century. But Belgium, Greece, Germany, the Netherlands, and Italy only acquired formal statehood in the nineteenth century and Ireland, Austria, Iceland, Norway, and West Germany only in the twentieth century. Clearly we are dealing with a number of very old societies that are also relatively new states. War has played a major role in the continent's history. One has only to think of the Thirty Years' War between 1618 and 1648, the French revolutionary wars, and the two great conflicts of 1914–1918 and 1939–1945. Italy, France, Austria, and Germany were all on the losing side in 1945, and a number of other states were occupied by the German army. Only Britain was a combatant throughout both great wars and victorious in both. The resultant continuity of its regime makes its twentieth-century history sharply different from that of many of its neighbors, which have suffered ruptures in their recent histories.

Many of the states are relatively small in size and population. Only four (Italy, Britain, Germany, and France) have populations in excess of 50 million. These four states dominate Western Europe, but are obviously medium size (at best) in comparison to the superpowers. (American readers might note that none of these countries is as large as Texas.) Indeed, these states' awareness of their postwar loss of international influence was an important factor in promoting the formation of the European Community in 1957.

Religious rivalries have been an important cause of wars in Europe, particularly in the sixteenth and seventeenth centuries. The dominant religions in the various states today reflect the impact of the Reformation and Counter-Reformation four centuries ago. The eight states that are predominantly Roman Catholic are Italy, Spain, Portugal, France, Austria, Luxembourg, Belgium, and

Ireland; the six that are predominantly Protestant are in northern Europe. The three religiously mixed states, Switzerland, West Germany, and the Netherlands, reflect the mixed success of Catholic and Protestant forces. Before 1945 the Roman Catholic Church was suspicious of many modern political values that we associate with present-day Western Europe—liberal democracy, individualism, and secularism. Since 1945 the Catholic church has shown more willingness to accept the values of democracy and liberalism. Indeed the church's support for the new moderate-right Christian democratic parties in West Germany and Italy has been important in providing greater political stability in these two countries. At the same time, Catholics gained greatly in social and political influence. In Bismarckian and Weimar Germany, for example, Catholics had formed a self-conscious political minority. In the Federal Republic of Germany, by contrast, Catholics form nearly half the population, and many of the new industries center on Catholic Bavaria. In Belgium, Catholic Flanders—once the most backward part of the country—now forms the economically most advanced part of the kingdom. In Holland, Catholics have also enhanced their social and economic status.

The variety of political models in Western Europe presents a challenge to the student of politics. The three Scandinavian societies, for example, are among the most affluent in the world. They are also highly collectivist in their political cultures and, as a result of nearly half a century of social democratic dominance in government, rank near the top of international tables in public spending, welfare provision, and taxation. The Netherlands, Belgium, Austria, and Switzerland have attracted attention because they have combined political stability in the postwar period with social fragmentation. The societies have been divided along religious, cultural, ideological, and linguistic lines into virtually separate subcultures, with their own political parties, pressure groups, and mass media. The impressive literature on consociational democracy demonstrates how cooperation among elites has bridged differences among the grass roots.

Yet, traditionally, most academic interest has centered on the so-called great states of Britain, France, and Germany. Britain, as Gerald A. Dorfman notes in Chapter 2, has long been viewed as a model democracy. It has balanced strong central government with secure civil liberties and the rights of political opposition. For nearly a thousand years it has been free from invasion or internal collapse. England achieved internal unity under the Normans in the eleventh century and won secure borders by successively absorbing Wales and Scotland. The expansion into Ireland, by contrast, was less successful and was short-lived. The possibility of religious conflict (which plagued many other states) was effectively prevented by Henry VIII's break with Rome and establishment of a national church between 1529 and 1534. In terms of building a nation-state, England was far ahead of most of its West European neighbors. In the seventeenth century continuing disputes, and even civil war, between the supporters of the monarchy and the Parliament were resolved in favor of the latter. In contrast to the victory of monarchical absolutism on the continent, England henceforth would have limited and constitutional monarchy.

In the postwar period, however, the British experience has attracted less admiration. Its comparatively slow economic growth and relative economic decline have meant that living standards have fallen behind those of its neighbors. The decline has also sharpened ideological divisions between the two main political parties. Economic remodernization in the first industrialized society poses a continuing challenge for elites and society.

France is the home of *the* revolution, that of 1789, and has been a breeding ground for political ideologies that transcend national frontiers. The legacy of these two factors has been a record of political instability and division. The Fifth Republic functions under France's twelfth constitution since 1789; the country has experienced rule by monarchs, republicans, military dictators, and even an emperor. Historically, France's main political difficulty has stemmed from its inability to reconcile the values of strong government (long identified with the political right, the monarchy, Catholicism, and the upper class) and a popular government (long identified with the political left and a regime that gave more power to the legislature than to the executive). The former has often degenerated into outright reaction; the latter into virtual ungovernability, as under the Fourth Republic. The ideological divisions were reflected in the existence of several political parties unwilling or unable to aggregate the different groups into meaningful electoral alternatives.

The Fifth Republic has restored stability to France by combining a strong, directly elected president with a simplified party system, one that pits a left-wing "stream" (Socialists and Communists) against a right-wing stream (Gaullists and Giscardians). Moreover, the institutions of the regime now appear to be accepted by all sections of French society.

Germany, like France, until recently has been something of a negative model of liberal democracy. In the words of scholar, politician, and bureaucrat Ralf Dahrendorf, Germany has been a "faulted nation." Created in 1871 largely by Prussian military strength and bureaucratic and diplomatic skill, it was an example of a state made from above. Liberal democratic and liberal values were weak, not only in the development but also in the subsequent history of the German state. Until the 1950s Germany combined economic modernity with a degree of political and social traditionalism and authoritarianism. Germany, like Japan, found itself in the position of a political outcast, regarded by its neighbors at best with suspicion and at worst with hatred. The new West German state was created, again by force, in 1949, this time as a result of a decision of the three Western occupying powers. Today, it is probably the most successful regime in German history and is widely regarded as a model of good governance.

Today West Germany is perhaps the only case of a totalitarian society that has made the transition to liberal democracy. Its impressive economic recovery has played some part in gaining legitimacy for the regime. However, the simplification of the party system and the new constitution have also played a part in preventing a recurrence of the instability of Weimar. German economic efficiency has long been admired; what is new is that so many political commentators today regard its political system as a model liberal democracy.

This greater stability and acceptance of liberal democratic institutions in France, Italy, and West Germany provide a striking contrast to Western Europe in the interwar years. Then it was plausible to contrast the stable, democratic, consensual Anglo-American states with the divided, unstable, continental states of France, Germany, and Italy. The change is in a large part connected to the decline of political extremism in these states, partly to economic recovery, and partly to the successful moves to political integration in Western Europe.

European Unity

In the Middle Ages there was a sense, however fragile, of a Europe that transcended national boundaries. It was embodied in the Holy Roman Empire and such features as the Catholic religion, Latin, Roman law, and the great universities. At the same time dynastic, national, and other rivalries were important, and the suprastate claims of the emperor and the church were openly contested by the rulers of many states, principalities, and free cities.

This fragile sense of community was essentially destroyed by two major events in the sixteenth and seventeenth centuries. The first was the Reformation and its repudiation of the universal claims of the Roman Catholic church. The protest of Martin Luther provided a pretext for secular rulers to prescribe the religion of their populations. What eventually emerged was a predominantly Protestant northwest Europe and a predominantly Catholic central and southern Europe. As noted, the religious composition of these countries is still broadly similar today. The second event was the development of sovereign states by centralizing monarchs beginning in the seventeenth century. In their efforts to centralize authority, raise taxes, and maintain standing armies and bureaucracies, rulers repudiated external rival claims (largely from the Roman Catholic church) and internal claims (from bodies like representative assemblies, parliaments, cortes, and the estates). The development of strong states in France, Spain, and Prussia involved a weakening of the sense of international community and of the powers of local representative bodies. In Britain the centralizing claims of the Stuart monarchs in the seventeenth century were defeated, and power was shared between Parliament and the king. The European idea, however, crumbled in the face of the rise of sovereign states.

In the nineteenth century nationalism became of central importance.

Greece gained independence from the Ottoman empire in 1827 and Belgium from the Netherlands in 1830. More significant, however, was the emergence in 1870 of a united Germany under Prussian hegemony and a united Italy as a monarchy under the House of Savoy. There were also formidable nationalist movements in Britain and the Austrian empire.

Fragmentation intensified in the interwar years. Shaky liberal democratic regimes collapsed in Italy in 1922 and Germany in 1933, and fragile constitutional regimes in Spain, Portugal, and Austria were overthrown in 1926, 1936, and 1934 respectively. Democracy survived uneasily in France. Only in Britain and the Scandinavian states, countries with secure national identities, were the established political parties and political institutions able to withstand the economic and social disruption brought on by war and then economic depression.

In many respects the idea of Western Europe, and the consequent abandonment of the idea of a wider area embracing Eastern and Western Europe, dates from the end of World War II. The war resulted not just in the devastation and eventual division of Germany but also in the splitting of Europe into eastern and western zones. By the time of the communist coup in Czechoslovakia in February 1948, it was clear to most Western leaders that the seven East European states and Albania were securely within the Russian zone of influence. They became, effectively, Soviet-dominated, communist states controlled by one party, although professing a form of multipartyism. For defense and economic purposes all but Yugoslavia and Albania were eventually drawn into the Warsaw Pact and the Council for Mutual Economic Assistance. Winston Churchill spoke of an Iron Curtain having descended between Eastern and Western Europe. Some of the Western states received generous American aid under the Marshall Plan, became members of NATO (North Atlantic Treaty Organization), and joined various other cooperative bodies. But there was a greater awareness of their differences from states in Eastern Europe than of their similarity with each other.

The idea of a politically united Europe can be traced back over the centuries, at least to the time of the Holy Roman Empire. At that time the concept encompassed a Europe extending to the western borders of Russia. It became associated with militarism and later attempts by Napoleon I and Hitler to impose French and then German hegemony on other states. Since 1945 the idea has been given concrete expression with the formation of the European Community. The motives of the supporters of greater integration of West European states varied. One was a result of the apparent "lesson" of the two great wars. Rampant nationalism had not served Europe well. Indeed, the conflicts in 1914 and 1939 had spilled over and embroiled many other states. Some sort of union, it was argued, might be the answer to the long-standing Franco-German rivalry on the continent. Interestingly, the immediate postwar constitutions adopted by France, West Germany, and Italy all provided for possible future transfers of sovereignty to a united European body. A second influence was a growing awareness of the social and economic interdependence of states and the possibilities of more effective policies arising from cooperation. A subsequent claim for consolidation was that an economic union would provide a large market and perhaps enable West European states to compete with economic superpowers like the United States and Japan.

The final, and more explicitly political, motive for political unity was that, in the era of superpowers, only a unified Western Europe would have the population and resources to be influential in international affairs. The hostilities between Germany and its opponents from 1939 to 1942 (when the United States intervened) formed in a sense the last European war. The entry of the USSR and the United States into the global conflict changed the traditional balance of power forever. Thereafter, Britain, France, and Germany were all destined to remain second-rank powers.

The first step to unity was taken in 1951 when France, West Germany, Italy, Belgium, the Netherlands, and Luxembourg formed the Coal and Steel Community. In 1957 the same six states signed the Treaty of Rome, which established the European Economic Community. The treaty provided for the development of a common market in industrial and agricultural goods, as well as the free movement of people, capital, and goods in the member-states. In the same year, a treaty established an organization to coordinate nuclear energy development in the same six states. At this time, Britain, Sweden, Norway, and Denmark, though cooperating in many other West European bodies, had no wish to be part of an integrated body. Sweden, Switzerland, Finland, and Austria all pursued a policy of neutrality in foreign affairs, and Greece, Spain, and Portugal were not politically acceptable to some member-states. Although Britain's membership was eagerly sought by most of the other states, its so-called special relationship with the United States, its ties with the Commonwealth, and its sense of psychological separation (even superiority) stemming from geography and its victory in World War II all played a part in the British decision to stand aside. Most contemporary historians look back on the British decision as a missed opportunity.

The Community was enlarged in 1973 to accommodate Britain, Ireland, and Denmark, and the six become nine. In 1981 Greece was admitted and, as of 1985, Portugal and Spain have negotiated entry.

In line with the original program, tariff barriers have been lowered among member-states, and trade has greatly increased among them. The founders also hoped that economic cooperation would gradually lead to greater political integration. In many respects, however, the Community remains an intergovernmental body. Power rests with the Council of Ministers (usually foreign ministers of the states) and the appointed members of the Permanent Commission. Only in 1979 was a European Parliament directly elected, and it still lacks much power. It can enforce the resignation of the commission, debate the commission's annual report, and suggest amendments to the Community budget. The autonomous budget of the Community amounts to less than 1 percent of total member-states' GDP; much of it is spent on agriculture and little on regional or social programs. But national interests still prevail, and by tradition member-states can veto policies in the Council of Ministers. Decisions are effectively made during meetings of government leaders. The entry of Portugal and Spain, with per capita incomes of one-third and one-half respectively of the Community average, may make the evolution of common policies even more difficult in the future. Although there still remains widespread popular support for the general idea of European unity (see below), interest in the progress of the European Communities toward closer political integration has slowed.

The elections for the European Parliament in June 1984 were fought as national campaigns in the member-states. The average turnout was 60 percent, 2 percent less than for the previous elections in 1979. The more pro-EEC states like Belgium, Luxembourg, and Italy had turnouts of over 80 percent, while the more indifferent British had a derisory one of 32 percent. (See Table 1.1.)

Parties and Party Systems

The countries of Western Europe have a wide range of party systems, electoral arrangements, and political ideologies. The character of a country's party system, particularly the number of parties, ideologies, and interactions among the parties can be explained both by the political institutions and by the nature of the society. The popular election of the presidency in France (since 1962) has encouraged a reduction of the final electoral choice to one of two main candidates or political tendencies. In Britain the single-member plurality system of elections, by instituting a major hurdle to the breakthrough of third parties, has hitherto safeguarded the position of the two main parties in Parliament. In many other West European states the existence of a proportional electoral system has encouraged the perpetuation of a number of small parties. A rule-of-thumb generalization has been to distinguish the two-party contest, single-party government system (usually exemplified by Britain) from the multiparty coalition governments in many West European states. The virtues claimed for the former are clarity of electoral choice and electoral responsibility, both of which are difficult to achieve in a multiparty system. Its defects are its occasional unrepresentative outcomes (the percentages of seats a party holds in the legislature rarely equals its share of the popular vote) and its failure to represent minorities in Parliament. The old argument, however, that one-party government is more efficient or effective than coalition government is rarely heard today.

The nature of society is also important in shaping the party system. In Britain the relative weakness of divisions over language, race, agriculture, and reli-

Table 1.1   **Turnout for European Elections, 1984 (percentage)**

Belgium	89
Luxembourg	89
Italy	84
Greece	77
Ireland	64
France	57
West Germany	57
Denmark	53
Holland	51
Britain	32

gion (outside Northern Ireland) has left social class important. As one authority, S. E. Finer, pithily observed, class is important in Britain only because nothing else matters. The greater diversity of social identities in such countries as Belgium, Italy, and Denmark is reflected in a wider range of political parties. The genesis of party systems and social cleavages, or distinctive groups that vote for a particular political party, is to be sought in history. A major study by S. M. Lipset and Stein Rokkan, *Party Systems and Voter Alignments*, has noted the present-day legacy of two major historical episodes.[3] One is the so-called national revolution in each state in which an expanding, central, nation-building culture clashed with different ethnic, linguistic, and religious groupings. This gave rise to disputes between church and state and the center versus peripheral groups (for example, linguistic or subnational cultures). The second major episode was the industrial revolution, which gave rise to conflicts between landed interests and rising industrial interests. Later, as widespread industrialism was achieved, the more salient divisions between capital and labor raised issues of class conflict, distribution of wealth, and ownership of industry.

An ingenious study by Richard Rose and Derick Urwin has tried to establish the social bases of political parties in Western states.[4] Their criterion for judging whether a party was based on a social group was that at least 75 percent of its electoral constituency should have a common social attribute (class, religion, language, or region). They examined 76 parties in seventeen Western states and found that the largest group of parties (35) was based on religion. This was true for the bulk of party support in France, Belgium, Austria, West Germany, the Netherlands, Italy, and Northern Ireland. Thirty-three parties were based on social class, 20 being working-class and 13 middle-class parties. Issues of nationalism and conflicting communal loyalties remain important in Belgium, Finland,

and Northern Ireland. Interestingly, parties in the most durable democratic states, such as Britain, Ireland, and the Scandinavian states, are either class-based or heterogeneous in their electoral support.

A number of observers are impressed by the overall postwar continuity in the party systems despite the remarkable social and economic changes in Western Europe. Notwithstanding growing affluence and the embourgeoisement of the working class, electoral support for parties of the left has not declined. Although church attendance has fallen off in most states and there has been a growing secularization of values, electoral support for Christian democratic parties has not fallen. The two political traditions of socialism and center/conservative/ Christian democracy still account for over 80 percent of the vote. The socialists (including labor and social democratic parties) are first or second in electoral strength in every state but Ireland and Italy, and the Christian or conservative-liberal parties are first or second in every state. (See Table 1.2.)

The only long-term shift between 1949 and 1986 in Western Europe as a whole has been a slight growth in socialist support and a modest reduction in communist support.

Yet there have been some important changes since 1945 in the party systems of particular countries. The most obvious has been the collapse of fascist and Nazi strength in Italy and Germany. The establishment of competitive politics in Spain and Portugal in the 1970s revived organized political parties in those countries. Another change has been the rise of Christian democratic parties, in the center or right of the political spectrum, and their dominance in Germany and Italy. Other notable shifts include the spectacular rise and decline of Gaullist parties in the fourth and fifth French republics and of the antitax Justice Party in Denmark in the 1970s and the rise of the Socialists in France in the 1970s and of the Liberal–Social Democratic alliance in Britain in the 1980s. Perhaps the most significant declines have been those of the Christian parties in the Netherlands (from approximately half to less than 30 percent of the vote between the 1960s and the 1980s), of the British Labour Party (from 48 percent of the vote in 1966 to 27 percent in 1983), and of the French Communist Party (virtually halved from 1978 to 1983). More recently, in the 1980s, there have been shifts to the political right in Britain, Norway, the Netherlands, and Denmark and shifts to the left in France, Sweden, and Greece.

In France and West Germany there has been a reduction over time in the number of important political parties. More important has been the emergence in France of two broad political tendencies, the left and right, represented by the Communists and Socialists on the one hand and the Independent Republicans (RPR) and Democratic Center (UDF) on the other. There has been a similar dualism emerging in West Germany, where the Christian Democrats/Christian Social Union and the Social Democrats have been dominant, though the Free Democratic Party has played an important pivotal role in the formation of gov-

Table 1.2   Electoral Support for Main Tendencies in Western Europe (percentages)

	Communist	Socialist	Liberal/ Labor[a]	Right/ Center[b]	Extreme Right
August 1949	11.9	33.5	5.1	46.5	0.8
June 1983	8.3	36.1	4.2	47.4	1.5
Change	−3.6	+2.6	−0.9	+0.9	+0.7

SOURCE: Adapted from G. Smith, *Politics in Western Europe*, 4th ed. (London: Heinemann, 1983), pp. 332–33.
NOTES:
[a] Includes independent socialist, social democratic, and labor.
[b] Includes liberal-conservative, center-democratic, conservative, and nationalist.

ernments. Although Italy is often regarded as an extreme multiparty system, the two leading parties, the Christian Democrats and the Communists, together usually receive nearly 70 percent of the total vote. This was the proportion gained by the two leading parties in Britain in the 1983 general election, and Britain is widely regarded as a model two-party system. In Denmark and Norway the conservative parties have gained strength impressively, and bourgeois alliances have also managed to form more coherent alternatives to the traditionally dominant social democratic and labor parties.

The party system of a number of countries has fragmented. In Britain, for example, the Liberals, the new Social Democratic Party, and different nationalist parties have gained support since 1970. In general elections between 1945 and 1970, the Conservative and Labour parties together gained an average of some 90 percent of the vote. Their combined vote has steadily fallen, and in 1983 it was down to 70 percent. In Belgium the language issue has divided the major parties, Social-Christians, Socialists, and Liberals and increased the electoral followings of linguistic parties. In Norway divisions over that country's proposed membership in the Common Market in 1973 also produced a fragmentation of the party system. These changes are connected to a greater volatility among electorates. Social change—the spread of affluence, higher education, and mass media—and the weakening of traditional values and loyalties to parties and institutions have posed problems of adaptation for the parties. New issues, such as defense, nuclear energy, terrorism, and more self-expressive life-styles, cut across the old left-right economic divisions.

The degree of competitiveness, or chances of a turnover in party control of government, varies across countries. There has been a move to some kind of a balance between broad left and broad right political tendencies. Some countries have parties that clearly dominate the system. In Italy the Christian Democrats have been the dominant party in virtually all Italian coalition governments since the war and have always been the largest party in terms of popular support. Though it is the second largest party in Italy, the Communist Party has not been in the cabinet since 1947. In Sweden, Norway, and Denmark the largest parties have long been social democratic or labor and for four decades were the usual parties of government. With 40 percent or more of the vote, they were able to form coalitions with smaller, friendly parties. The fragmented nonsocialist or antisocialist parties usually found it more difficult to form alliances. But there has been a revival in the strength of the latter forces in recent years, particularly in Denmark and Norway. In West Germany the Christian Democrats have been in office for all but ten years of the post-1949 period and emerged as the largest party in all general elections except from 1972 to 1976. The political right has clearly been dominant in the French Fifth Republic since 1958, and the left came to power only in 1981. Between 1945 and 1980 the Labour and Conservative parties in Britain were in power for almost an equal number of years.

Political Ideologies

As noted, the two major political tendencies in postwar Western Europe have been Christian democracy on the center right, and social democracy on the left. Social democracy has been strongest in Northern Europe, particularly in Britain and the Scandinavian countries. Interestingly, in each of these states, which are predominantly Protestant and have had relatively smooth state-building histories, the left-wing party has been reformist rather than revolutionary. The parties of the left in Norway, Sweden, Denmark, and Austria have enjoyed long periods in power. The hegemony of social democracy has been much less assured in Southern Europe, and in France and Italy it has had to compete with significant communist parties. In these predominantly Catholic countries, where the parties had to struggle for political rights, the left for long periods has been syndicalist or extremist. In Spain and Portugal it has become the largest party since these countries have resumed competitive elections.

Social democracy pursues a number of policies. First and foremost there is a commitment to greater social and economic equality, which is to be achieved through redistributive tax and economic policies and the promotion of social security and welfare services. Most social democratic parties have also attached importance either to public ownership of major industries or to a great degree of governmental control of the economy, for purposes of planning and the redistribution of wealth. Finally, these parties accept liberal democratic institutions rather than revolution as a means of resolving political questions.

The growing affluence of the working class (particularly the spread of home and car ownership), together with its decline in numerical terms, has made appeals to working-class solidarity less electorally rewarding for parties of the left. There has been a marked decline in working-class support for the left in West Germany, Britain, and Scandinavia in recent elections.[5] In Britain in 1983 even though more than 13 percent of the work force was unemployed, nearly as many of the working class voted Conservative (37 percent) as voted Labour (38 percent). Social democracy's traditional emphasis on redistribution to the less well off has also met with a growing resistance among skilled and well-paid workers at a time of low economic growth. The parties face the problem of reconciling the promotion of equality and high public spending with the reluctance of workers to pay heavier taxes.[6]

There are several substantial Christian democratic parties in Western Europe today.[7] These parties differ from the Catholic parties of the interwar period and have distinguished themselves from the traditional right, which was discredited in 1945. In Italy, West Germany, Belgium, and Luxembourg, Christian democrats (or their equivalents) have been the normal parties of government. In the Netherlands, a Christian democratic alliance, formed in 1976 from two Protestant parties and one Catholic one, has been the usual fulcrum of Dutch governments. These Christian parties have accepted the maintenance of a high level of social welfare but rely more on the free market for economic management. They have also been influenced by the social teachings of the Catholic church. Their appeal to Catholics and Protestants, particularly in Germany, has made them something of a cross-class or catchall political party. In spite of the shift of workers from the land, the growth of secularism, and the decline in church attendance, Christian democracy remains a strong force. But the limits of that support were illustrated in Italy in 1974 when, contrary to the appeal of the Vatican and the Christian Democrats, Italians voted decisively in a referendum in favor of allowing divorce.

In Britain and France there are strong secular parties of the right. In the Scandinavian countries, however, the political right lacks the support of a powerful church and is fragmented among conservative, agrarian, and confessional parties.

The Communists have long been a minor electoral force in Western Europe, though their electoral strength is unevenly distributed across countries. In the postwar period they have been most important in Finland, France, Italy, and recently Portugal. In the mid-1970s the phenomenon known as Eurocommunism developed in Italy, France, and Spain. Economic growth and affluence continued to improve the living standards of the working class. There was little prospect of the collapse of capitalism and virtually no prospect of the communist parties winning power through elections in these countries. The easing of cold war tensions from the mid-1950s gradually made the Communists less like outsiders in Italy and France. The parties abandoned or diluted their claims that the transition to socialism required the "dictatorship of the proletariat," arguing instead that the transition could be achieved peacefully, and they loosened their ties with Moscow. In Italy there was also a realization among communist leaders that the party would probably find it impossible to govern in the face of powerful military, business, church, and parliamentary opposition. (The overthrow of the Marxist Allende government in Chile in 1973 was not lost on them.) The leadership, therefore, tried to make a "historic compromise" with the Christian Democratic Party. In France the Communists agreed on a Common Program with the Socialists in 1972. In these two countries there seemed to be a good chance of communist participation in government, and the Communists did enter the Socialist-led coalition in France in 1981.

The French Communist Party, once one of the most powerful parties in Europe, has declined—in part owing to the erosion of its working-class bastions, especially the "Red belt" around Paris and the iron and steel region of the northeast. In Italy and Spain, the Communists have also encountered growing problems. Hence Eurocommunism attracts less attention today. The term mistakenly implies something coherent and united, whereas there have in fact been important differences between the French and Italian parties. The Italian party is more supportive of the European Community and of moves toward greater integration of member-states and also accepts its country's membership in NATO. The French party has opposed all three of these policies and in recent years has moved closer to Moscow again.

Domestic Politics

West European states made a rapid and impressive recovery from the economic collapse of wartime. By 1950 most had already surpassed their 1939 figures for GDP. This recovery heralded the postwar record of full employment, low inflation, and rapidly improving living standards that prevailed until the mid-1970s. Various countries, particularly Austria, West Germany, France, and Italy, enjoyed economic "miracles." It was also an era of broad consensus on domestic policy in many countries. Most states greatly expanded their provision of welfare, encompassing old-age pensions and guaranteed incomes for people who suffered sickness and unemployment. There was also an expansion of the role of government in managing the economy. In many West European states railways, airlines, and the coal, gas, iron, and steel industries were either directly owned by the state or subject to extensive state control and regulation. The role of the state in both welfare and economic management was much more marked in West European states than in Canada or the United States.[8]

The growth of scientific thought and expertise, exemplified in Keynesian economics, appeared to weaken the appeal and relevance of the political ideologies of the left and the right. Continued affluence softened social and class polarization and narrowed policy differences between the parties of the left and the right. So-called catchall, voter-oriented political parties sought support from most sections of the electorate. Political parties came to rely more on public relations techniques at election time and played down distinctive sectional and ideological appeals. Trends in socioeconomic distribution, state intervention and provision of welfare all moved in similar directions in West European states, in spite of the different histories, party systems, and forms of government. This decline of ideology between political parties and growth of policy convergence across states prompted one observer to comment: "This ideological agreement, which might best be described as 'conservative socialism' has become *the* ideology of the major parties in the developed states of Europe and America."[9] Much of the thinking and many actual policies were more in tune with the ideas of social democracy, and in many respects the package may be referred to as a social democratic consensus. But a number of right-wing parties accepted the policies, either because of their own paternalist traditions (the French Gaullists and British Conservatives) or the need to remain electorally competitive (the Scandinavian conservative parties).

Three of the many domestic policy developments are worth some comment, not least because there has been a reaction to them in recent years. These are (1) the growth of the role of government in social and economic life, (2) the growth of the welfare state, and (3) corporatist-style bargaining between government and producer interests.

In the course of the twentieth century there has been much greater interaction between government and citizens. The expanding role of government has been attributed to many general factors—war, economic depression, economic growth, the rise of socialist parties and collectivist values, universal suffrage, and party competition to distribute welfare benefits, to name but a few. The United States, which lacks the history of central political control and paternalism of many European states and the prestige of the civil service as a high-status group, lags far behind in the interventionist role of its government.

The growing role of government may be measured along various dimensions.[10] In four countries, West Germany, Sweden, Italy, and Britain, aggregate government spending as a percentage of GDP grew from one-third in 1962 to one-half in 1982, and to over 60 percent in the cases of Sweden and the Netherlands. In the United States, by comparison, the figure rose to only 37 percent. In the same four states the proportion of the work force employed by central and local government grew to over 30 percent by 1981. In the United States it was 18.8 percent. (See Table 1.3.)

As a distributor of welfare benefits, the role of government has also grown. In the late nineteenth and early twentieth centuries Germany and Britain introduced basic welfare services. (In Germany this was an explicit ploy by Bismarck

Table 1.3   Percentage of Work Force Engaged in
            Public Employment

	1951	1980	Difference
Sweden	15.2	38.2	+23
Britain	26.6	31.7	+ 5.1
West Germany	14.4	25.8	+11.4
Italy	11.4	24.3	+12.9
United States	17.0	18.8	+ 1.8

SOURCE: Richard Rose, *Understanding Big Government* (London and Beverly Hills, Calif.: Sage Publications, 1984), p. 139.

to gain working-class support and steal the Social Democrats' thunder.) Since 1945, virtually all West European states have adopted welfare programs for old-age pensions, sickness and unemployment benefits, and a variety of other benefits. In spite of different levels of expenditure, types of benefits, and financing, the convergence in programs is remarkable. Today most West European states spend between one-fifth and one-third of their GDP on welfare benefits. At the beginning of the 1980s, approximately one-fifth of the population was receiving state-provided education, about a quarter old-age pensions, and most some form of health coverage. Finally, governments' "take" from citizens in the form of direct and indirect taxation amounts to approximately 37 percent of GDP in Western European states and actually exceeds 50 percent in the case of Sweden.

Across all four of these areas, growth was quite rapid in the 1960s and 1970s and produced what is clearly big government. The growth was particularly marked in the Scandinavian states, which had long spells of social democratic–dominated governments as well as high spending programs and high levels of taxation.

In the mid-1970s the dramatic increase in oil prices and the slowdown in Western economies signaled the end of the long postwar economic boom. There was a simultaneous increase in levels of unemployment and prices and the resulting stagflation has produced strains for the welfare consensus, as governments everywhere found it difficult to finance programs. Policies of increasing taxation, growing public expenditure, and new programs appeared to command less acceptance at the ballot box. The costs of programs were rising by an average of 7 percent per annum in the 1970s while the economy was growing by an average of only 3.5 percent. The success in California of Proposition 13 in 1978 was paralleled by similar tax backlash movements in Denmark and the swing to the right in Britain and, briefly, in Sweden. The growth rate of spending on social programs outdistanced the ability of the economy to pay for them, prompting some observers to speculate about the future bankruptcy of governments.[11]

The growing costs of welfare have been a target for more economy-minded governments in the 1980s. In recent years most governments have tried to cut or slow the growth in funding for programs or to reduce government regulation in industry. In Britain governments have gone further and sought to "privatize," or sell off existing state-owned and local government–owned services, housing, and firms. This coincided with a swing to the political right in Western Europe. Even where left-wing governments have been installed, as in Spain, Portugal, Greece, and France, they pursued right-wing social and economic policies and accorded priority to the battle against inflation even at times of high unemployment. By 1985 only Sweden was still pursuing a Keynesian-style program of government spending to maintain high levels of employment.

Another interesting postwar development was a form of corporatism (sometimes also called tripartism or social partnership), in which the government and organizations of the major producer interests negotiated economic policy packages. Government usually sought moderation in wage settlements from organized labor in return for government policies covering employment, welfare expenditure, and taxation. These arrangements worked well enough in the 1950s and 1960s in such states as West Germany, Sweden, Norway, the Netherlands, and Austria. These countries usually had centralized trade union confederations able to bargain authoritatively for their members. Many also had a strong social democratic or left-wing presence in the cabinet. The process involved some bypassing of parliaments (providing ammunition for those who mourned the decline of legislatures), as ministers and bureaucrats bargained directly with spokesmen for the interests. In the 1970s, however, under the impact of inflation and slower growth, the arrangements proved more difficult to sustain.[12]

Foreign Policies

The main features of Western Europe's foreign politics since 1945 have been its division into two different zones, east and west; the progress toward greater unity (see above); and the diminution of its influence in international affairs.

In 1945 policymakers in the United States decided that there was to be no return to the isolationism of the interwar years. Not only was the United States now the major influence in international affairs but together with the USSR it was the main arbiter of the fate of postwar Europe. With the military and economic exhaustion of Western Europe, the onset of the cold war in 1947, and the growing militancy of Communists in Italy, France, and Greece, the United

States was also the leader of the West against communism. American postwar involvement with Western Europe increased through the provision of economic aid (in the form of the Marshall Plan in 1947) and the establishment of NATO in 1949 (which eventually included Britain, West Germany, Greece, Spain, Iceland, Luxembourg, France, Belgium, the Netherlands, and Norway, from Western Europe). The signatory states committed themselves to common defense in the event of an attack on any one of them. The United States also stationed troops and missiles in Western Europe.

The Alliance has to take account of the diverse interests of members and issues that may produce differences among them. For example, Greece and Turkey are both members of NATO but at loggerheads over Cyprus. By tradition Switzerland, Ireland, and Sweden are neutral and thus have not been members of NATO, while Norway and Denmark, although in NATO, do not allow foreign troops or missiles on their soil (out of sympathy with Sweden). Under the terms of its 1955 Permanent Neutrality Act, Austria is legally obliged to be neutral and may not join any military bloc. In all of these countries government and public opinion are usually sympathetic to the West in cases of East-West conflict. For historical, political, and geographic reasons, Finland has avoided any involvement in activities that the USSR may construe as anti-Soviet.

In the late 1970s the phenomenon of Eurocommunism concerned a number of West European and American leaders. Communist parties in Italy, France, and Spain stressed their independence from Moscow and their acceptance of liberal democratic political institutions. In France between 1981 and 1984 the Communists were members of the Socialist-dominated government of François Mitterrand. The main concern of Western governments was that the entry of Communists into government would undermine support for, or the effectiveness of, NATO, which was primarily an anticommunist military alliance. In the event, the French Communists were kept out of sensitive ministerial posts, Mitterrand has been a staunch supporter of the Alliance, and communism appears to be less of a threat in Italy.

More recent concern has centered on the installation of a new generation of American nuclear weapons on West European territory. In Britain, Belgium, West Germany, and the Netherlands there has been strong opposition, largely on the political left, to installing the missiles. The opposition has viewed the installation of the weapons as a dangerous escalation of the arms race and as making their own populations more vulnerable in any East-West conflict. In Germany and Britain the right-wing governments have welcomed the weapons as a means of curbing potential Soviet aggression and as a useful bargaining counter in arms negotiations.

Since 1945, the world has probably been less Euro-centered than at any time in the past five centuries. The balance of power within Europe itself no longer matters as decisively in world affairs as in the past; in global terms, military and economic power has shifted elsewhere. An indicator of the diminished world role has been the retreat from empire by many of the European states. Britain has relinquished its overseas dependencies (starting with India in 1947) relatively peacefully. The withdrawal of France from Indochina and Algeria, of Belgium from the Congo, and of Portugal from Angola were more bloody affairs.

This chapter has tried to point to certain broad common trends in the politics of West European societies. The shift from agriculture to industry, the spread and consolidation of liberal democratic institutions, active membership in or support for NATO, and the expansion of the European Community (which, including Spain and Portugal, covers some 90 percent of the population of Western Europe) all justify our reference to West European politics. It is certainly at least as justifiable as talking of Anglo-American politics (geographically, nonsense) or Third World politics (nonsense pure and simple). There is a geographical contiguity and enough political and economic similarity to justify the idea. At the same time, we must also note the variations within states and the distinctive ways in which the trends operate.

Economic "miracles" in Italy and Germany have undoubtedly contributed to the democratic legitimacy of their regimes. In the 1980s some commentators have questioned whether economic recession and a consequent belt-tightening may promote disillusion, not only with governments but also with political systems. To date, however, there is little evidence that antisystem parties are attracting much support. Indeed, with the exception of the Italian Communist Party— and it is arguable that it is still an antisystem party—most such parties perform miserably at the polls. Opinion surveys for *Euro-Baromètre*, a European Community–wide survey organization, show that nearly four-fifths of the Community's population are still satisfied with living conditions. The apparent security of the political regimes in West European states and the peaceful relations between most of them have made the past three decades the most satisfying for their inhabitants in the twentieth century. The record contrasts favorably with the political instability and wars of the past.

Update

Postwar Western Europe has been a success story in terms of achieving rising living standards, maintaining peace on a continent whose history has been ravaged by wars and national rivalries, and taking significant steps toward greater economic and political union. The economic recession of the early 1980s has been weathered and economic growth has resumed.

Three themes seem worth discussing since this volume appeared in 1988. 1. The momentous developments in Eastern Europe in 1989 and the likely end to the 40-year-long division between the pluralist, mixed-economy West and the one-party, state-planning East. Not only was Europe divided but so were Germany and Berlin, yet the Berlin Wall was dismantled in November 1989 and free movement of populations allowed between the two Germanys. The division, a legacy of the defeat of Hitler in 1945, provided Western Europe with a stability, however uneasy at times. At the end of 1989, one can only pose questions. What will follow from this instability, the ending of the supreme role of the Communist party in many East European states and the introduction of competitive elections in East Germany, Czechoslovakia, Poland, and Hungary? What will be the impact of a united and more powerful German state, both in European politics and within the European Community? What will be the role of NATO as the Warsaw Pact takes steps to dismantle itself, and what will be the case for American troops remaining in Europe?

2. The two major streams of party politics remain the center right and social democracy. Eurocommunism, a fashion of the 1970s, appears exhausted. The Italian Communist Party, though still a considerable electoral force, is declining and has now decided to drop "Communist" from its title. In France, Communism is virtually extinct electorally. The concern over the environment has prompted growing support for Green parties. The Green movement is difficult to place on a left-right ideological continuum, but on issues of civil liberties and nuclear power it clearly belongs on the more "liberal left" end. It disproportionately attracts support from middle-class and well-educated voters. The Greens are a force in the legislatures in Austria and Germany, and in the 1989 elections in Britain they gained 15 percent of the vote. The Greens are stronger in northern Europe—with its higher standard of living—than in the south. In the northern states, political parties, governments, and business and commerce are all becoming more environmentally aware.

Social democracy is still an electoral force in spite of the growing "embourgeoisement" of society and the decline of its working-class base. However, it has retreated from the belief in economic planning and now emphasizes issues relating to the quality of life, rights of women and minorities, and social protection (welfare-state concerns). Socialists control the government in France, Spain, and Sweden, and they participate in government in Austria, Italy, Belgium, and the Netherlands. In Sweden Socialists control the government, as they have done for 51 of the past 57 years.

3. In recent years significant steps have been made to advance the cause of political unity in the European Community. With twelve member states, the EC (of 320 million people) is now a significant economic bloc, second in weight only to the United States. The Single European Act was passed in 1987 in the

member-states, providing that by 1992 there will be an end to all barriers to trade, and to the movement of goods, capital and workers between member-states. The Act also envisages a commitment to major steps of integration in agriculture, financial, and social and regional policies. The so-called Delors Plan (named for the French head of the European Commission) also plans economic and monetary union between member-states—which will provide a major stimulus to political union. Already, the key institutions have accepted majority votes on some issues. Yet a handful of states, notably Britain (still something of a maverick in the European Community, because Mrs. Thatcher had not been regarded as "communautaire") and some of the less economically developed states such as Portugal, Greece, and Ireland may not be able to proceed as quickly to economic unity. The possibility is of a two-tier Europe with France and West Germany providing the impetus.

The major challenge facing the European Community after 1992 will be to strengthen the democratic element in its constitution, that is, the elected European Parliament. A significant increase in its power of course requires the further surrender of power by the legislatures of member-states.

Notes

1. S. M. Lipset, *Political Man* (New York: Doubleday, 1960).

2. A. Lijphart, *Democracy* (New Haven, Conn.: Yale University Press, 1984).

3. S. M. Lipset and S. Rokkan, eds., *Party Systems and Voter Alignments* (New York: Collier-Macmillan, 1967).

4. R. Rose and D. Urwin, "Persistence and Change in Western Party Systems Since 1945," *Political Studies* 18 (1970): 287–319.

5. R. Dalton et al., *Electoral Change in Advanced Industrial Democracies* (Princeton, N.J.: Princeton University Press, 1984).

6. See W. Paterson and A. Thomas, *Social Democratic Parties in Western Europe* (London: Croom Helm, 1977).

7. R. Irving, *The Christian Democratic Parties of Western Europe* (London: Allen & Unwin, 1979).

8. See A. Shonfield, *Modern Capitalism* (Oxford: Oxford University Press, 1965); and A. King, "Institutions and Policies of Governments: A Comparative Analysis," *British Journal of Political Science* 3, nos. 3, 4 (1973): 291–313, 409–23.

9. S. M. Lipset, "The Modernization of Contemporary European Politics," in idem, ed., *Revolution and Counterrevolution* (New York: Doubleday, Anchor, 1970 ed.), p. 303.

10. R. Rose, *Understanding Big Governments* (Beverly Hills, Calif.: Sage Publications, 1984).

11. R. Rose and W. G. Peters, *Can Governments Go Bankrupt?* (New York: Basic Books, 1979).

12. For a sampling of a still growing literature, see G. Lehmbruch and P. Schmitter, eds., *Patterns of Corporatist Policy-Making* (Beverly Hills, Calif.: Sage Publications, 1982); and John H. Goldthorpe, ed., *Order and Conflict in Contemporary Capitalism* (Oxford: Clarendon Press, 1984).

2
Great Britain

Gerald A. Dorfman

Britain is the most familiar nation covered in this volume. Its language, legal system, traditions, institutions, culture, and history are interrelated to and embedded in those of the United States. And Britain today is certainly the United States' closest ally and friend. Each country believes the interdependence between the two nations to be critically important. What happens in Britain affects not only American strategic interests but also the functioning of the two nations' commonly rooted democratic systems.

The most widely held American perception of contemporary British life is of a proudly stable and indefinably elegant nation. This image is generally correct, but it overlooks significant political, economic, and social problems that afflict the British polity. The postwar period has been a very difficult time for Great Britain. Serious economic troubles, industrial strife, class and racial conflict, civil war in Northern Ireland, and the decline of Britain's external power, including the loss of its colonies, have all significantly threatened the political system at one time or another. This chapter analyzes some of these problems, putting them in the context of Britain's political system and exploring their consequences for the future of that system as well as for their effect on Britain's position in the Western alliance, its relations with the United States, and its place in the world.

"A Tight Little Island"

Tight Little Island, the title of a film about Britain, best describes the physical and cultural characteristics that condition British politics. The smallness of the island, the uniformity of its climate, and the relative concentration of its population in a small portion of the island—England—provide a distinctive setting.

For Americans, the smallness of Britain is quite striking. The continental United States has a territory of more than 3 million square miles. Britain has only 94,216, less than the state of Oregon. Even more startling, England, with 50,335 square miles of land, is home for more than four-fifths of the entire population. The vast majority of the British population lives in a very small area almost exactly the size of the state of New York. More than 46 million persons live in the southeastern portion of Britain; about 12 million of these live in the capital city of London.

The very "tightness" of the British island is important to its politics because now, and historically, the country has benefited from easy communications. These good communications were important in facilitating economic and social development during the past two centuries. Regional differences within England have traditionally been slight compared with differences within the United States. The differences between England and Scotland, Wales, or Northern Ireland are more pronounced, but they are not dramatic and involve only about 20 percent of the total population. Probably the best illustration of the "tightness" of Britain is the "awayday" trips offered by British Rail, the state-owned railroad. For a small fare a person can whisk away to even the most remote seaside resort or major city and return the same day. Most Americans, by comparison, could visit only a small fraction of the major resorts or cities in their own state during the same time period. In fact, some Americans living in more rural areas could not reach any major cities during a single day's journey.

The Legacy of British Historical Development

Physical tightness and geographical insularity have also influenced Britain's historical development, contributing to its remarkably durable governmental structure and the complex of favorable attitudes and values that support the political system. Protected from invasion for nearly a thousand years by the moat that is the English Channel, the British polity has been able to develop free from the wars that ravaged neighboring European states. Moreover, at almost every period of stress, change has been accomplished within the context of a continuing political system. For example, there has been no permanent scarring, nor have there been intractable social fissures of the kind that France suffers. Rather, the process of negotiated change has progressively legitimized the political system to a remarkable degree.

In broad terms political authority over the centuries has flowed from royal absolutism to power-sharing between the monarch and the nobility and clergy to, in recent centuries, a widening and deepening of mass participation. As early as the eleventh century, British monarchs had centralized their rule. The importance of the Magna Carta for the polity was that it legitimated the right of the nobility to challenge the king. The struggle between strong monarchs and a contentious aristocracy in the succeeding centuries established the rule of law and thereby placed limits on the authority of both sides.

Parliament and the courts became, over time, the institutions in which the struggle between the monarch and the nobility and clergy was played out. Only as the king relied more heavily on Parliament's support did the institution take on real importance. It was especially the king's need for revenues that gave Parliament leverage. And it was from the arguments about whether, and how, revenues should be raised that Parliament began to scrutinize what the king intended to do with the money—and subsequently to insist that the monarch hear and consider its opinions in detail on a widening number of issues.

The seventeenth century was a particularly important time in British political development. In the course of the century, the monarchy lost its battles and by the terms of each new formal and informal settlement grudgingly recognized parliamentary power. The experiences of the seventeenth century established the pattern of widening political power-sharing and change within the context of continuing political institutions. The notion of a limited monarch cognizant of, and deferential to, the rights of Parliament was established, thus creating the underpinnings for further democratization of the polity.

The modern era of British politics opened in 1832 with passage of the Reform Act, which enfranchised more than one-half million men from the upper middle class. The Reform Act was not simply a gesture of goodwill or generosity by the privileged but a very pragmatic action by those who feared that Britain would suffer violent rebellion unless it opened, at least slightly, the door to political participation. The reforms of the mid-nineteenth century replaced the rotten boroughs with a much more equitable system of constituency boundaries.

This reform of the House of Commons, coupled with successive enfranchisements of a larger electorate during the balance of the century, propelled British politics into its more contemporary pattern. Politicians began to take notice of, and appeal to, a much larger audience and, to do this job, began to recognize the value of more coherent programs and permanent party organizations.

In this century, political power in Britain has almost turned on its head compared with the time of Queen Elizabeth I. The prime minister is now the real chief executive of the British government; the monarch is the ceremonial chief of state and symbol of British sovereignty. The prime minister holds that position because she or he is leader of the political party that won the most seats in the House of Commons at the last election, not because that person holds favor with the monarch. Yet remarkably this shift in power relationships has taken place without significant formal change in the structure of government. For example, it has been only in recent years that British law has taken any formal notice of the office of prime minister.

The contribution of British history to Great Britain's political development is therefore the durability of its institutions, the long tradition of change based on compromise, and the resulting high level of consensus about basic political norms and values. A wealth of contemporary evidence demonstrates the high level of legitimacy the system enjoys.

Prime Ministerial Government

The answer to the question "Who governs Britain?" illustrates how much authoritative decisionmaking in Britain has changed while the formal structure of government has remained virtually intact. As pointed out earlier, in this century the prime minister has become the dominant authority in the British political system. More than any other office or institution, the prime ministership has gained by the development of mass suffrage, increasingly complex issues, and frequent economic and military emergencies. Not only have these changes enhanced the power of centralized decisionmaking, they have also focused political responsibility more sharply. The prime minister and the opposition leader as an alternative prime minister are now the main combatants in the continuous bidding by political parties—primarily the Conservative and Labour parties—for popular support. The office of prime minister is at the center of public administration and is the main issue and prize of the political system.

The striking rise of the prime minister and the office's role in the larger political structure is best illustrated by comparing the distribution of power in the British political system today with that of a century ago. Walter Bagehot, a political observer writing in 1867, described the governing process of his time as "cabinet government." [1] Bagehot pointed out that the unwritten English Constitution, as he called it, was divided into two parts: the "dignified parts," which "excite and preserve the reverence of the population"; and the "efficient parts," by which government works and rules. [2] The monarch, according to Bagehot, headed the dignified parts, and the prime minister the efficient parts.

Bagehot described the prime minister as a leader who was first among equals in a cabinet chosen from Parliament—both from the House of Commons and the aristocratic House of Lords—and who was both a representative of Parliament and accountable to it. The essence of Bagehot's view was that Parliament was of central importance, and it was by its delegation, not that of the electorate at large, that the cabinet and the prime minister held and exercised their power. To be sure, the prime minister and the cabinet decided policy, presented bills to Parliament, and administered the law, but they could do so only so long as they held the confidence of Parliament.

Bagehot's description of British government a century ago implied a strong Parliament as well as a strong cabinet. Rather than the prime minister, Bagehot stressed the cabinet as a combining committee that joined the legislative function of the state with the executive. The prime minister decided, he said, who was to be in the cabinet and what part they were to play, but in the broad sense, the cabinet was the board of control and included persons that the legislature knew and trusted. In contrast, Parliament was the scene of great debates, the "great engine of popular instruction and political controversy."[3] A good Parliament should include, Bagehot asserted, the various special interests, special opinions, and special prejudices in the community. Moreover, Bagehot extolled the notion of an independent member of Parliament (MP) who could vigorously defend the interest he represented, whether it be special or local in character. In fact, Bagehot stressed that first-rate men would enter Parliament only if they could hope to have an impact on policy: "To belong to a debating society adhering to an executive is not an object to stir noble ambition."[4] Bagehot praised cabinet government because it preserved competent authority: rule by the better educated, by men of substance and property, acting in what they individually believed were the nation's best interests and not in response to the "baser" demands of "uninformed" voters.[5] It was this sort of man, at each stage in the transaction of public business, who produced the high quality of government that—in Bagehot's view—Britain enjoyed.

In contrast to Bagehot's view, John Mackintosh, an academic and MP during the 1970s, described his frustration at the impotence of Parliament in our time.[6] Mackintosh complained bitterly that he found that MPs could do little to influence the conduct of government, including making decisions about what policies should be chosen and, once decided, how policies should be implemented. The prime minister and the cabinet, he complained, controlled government, including the conduct of Parliament, so completely that the executive could do almost whatever it wanted; ordinary MPs were nearly helpless. Moreover, Parliament did not, he bemoaned, have even the authority to critically assess the performance of the powerful executive.

Bagehot, in a revision of his work published in 1872, anticipated in part the changes that generated Mackintosh's complaints a century later.[7] Even then, writing five years after the first edition, Bagehot commented on the first effects of the Reform Act of 1867. He worried that the extension of the vote to nearly twice as many men would undermine the smooth working system of independent MPs who came from the "better educated classes" and used their intelligence forcefully.[8] In their place, Bagehot feared a "poor man's paradise," in which each political party would bid for the support of working men, promising anything and everything to gain their vote. He warned that Parliament was losing control of the executive to the electorate, who he felt were ill-qualified to exercise that control. Britain, he predicted, would suffer debased government.

Bagehot was correct in anticipating that reform legislation would shift power away from Parliament. He was also correct in suggesting that politicians would organize to bid for the support of the new mass electorate. He was quite wrong, however, in his pessimism that there would emerge a multiplicity of parties that would cause the executive to become weak and vacillating and generally reflective of the broad party conflict over irreconcilable interests. Instead, sharp and continuous electoral competition, and the electoral system itself, conspired to encourage a highly disciplined, stable party system—and a strong government executive.

Political parties built national organizations very quickly after passage of the 1867 Reform Act. Joseph Chamberlain, a leading Liberal, rapidly founded a party organization of 30,000 members in the major city of Birmingham. Ten years later the National Liberal Association, including 93 local groups, met for the first time. Three years after that, in 1880, Chamberlain claimed that the decisive Liberal election victory of that year was due to his highly efficient organization. In response the Conservative Party worked feverishly during the 1880s to outdo the Liberals. At the same time, the winner-take-all election system in each constituency (similar to the system used to elect members of the U.S. House of Representatives) encouraged diverse interests to join one of the two developing national political parties rather than organize many small national or regional parties.

In the late nineteenth century competition between the two dominant, organized national parties—then Liberal and Conservative and now Labour and Conservative—focused more and more on winning a majority of seats in the House of Commons. The prize was control of the cabinet and thus the reins of government. This development was important in the new system of vote bidding. The two national parties needed to win control of the cabinet to carry out their promises and lay the basis for future appeals to the electorate. Further, since new elections for the House of Commons could be called by the government at any time, unlike the American system of fixed dates, both major parties demanded, and continue to demand, constant and loyal support from their MPs. A disciplined government majority determined to pass its program of legislation confronts in the Commons a disciplined opposition concertedly seeking to discredit the government. Thus, quite contrary to Bagehot's expectations, electoral reform encouraged the development of strong governments supported by highly disciplined majorities in Parliament.

Change also enhanced personal national leadership. More than local MPs, party leaders became the rallying point for parliamentary candidates and the party faithful, as well as a visible symbol for voters at the constituency level. Gladstone and Disraeli—both fine speakers and impressive personalities—became the major symbols of liberalism and conservatism in the late nineteenth century. Voters cast ballots in the hopes that their party would form the next government under the personal leadership of one or the other of the two leaders and his senior colleagues. Once in office, or even in opposition, these leaders by their words and deeds became the personification of their parties. One man's record became the party's record and therefore the major influence in the party's prospects for continuing in office or winning office. Gradually, as political concentration progressed into the twentieth century, it was the figure of the prime minister as head of the government and leader of the majority party who became the dominant political personality. And staring across the Commons from him was, and is, the leader of the opposition—the would-be prime minister upon whose shoulders the opposition pinned its hopes of a return to office.

Political Parties

Britain's difficulties during the last twenty years have also profoundly affected its political parties. Students of British politics at the beginning of the 1960s believed, somewhat smugly, that Britain enjoyed a stable, rational, and mature party system. It seemed that the Labour Party, without question, had become the permanent, major competitor of the Conservatives in a well-defined two-party system. Moreover, it appeared that these two major parties had permanently converged in supporting a policy consensus that embraced the managed economy and the welfare state.

What commentators could not see then was how profoundly the nearly continuous economic crisis and decline in Britain would affect the parties and the system in general. Political parties, after all, are sensitive societal barometers in democratic countries. They expect to rethink and possibly refashion their policies and leadership as conditions change. In Britain, as the society suffered the strains caused by repeated crises and declines, support and even tolerance for political leaders, their policies, and their political parties declined sharply. The way was thus open for significant change, which has included the resurgence of the Liberal Party, the founding of the Social Democratic Party, and the growth of regional parties in Scotland and Wales.

The Conservative Party

The Conservative Party enjoys the dominant position in the mid-1980s. But the Conservative government of this era is quite different from its predecessors. Mrs. Thatcher and most of her ministerial colleagues reject the philosophy as well as the views of earlier, postwar Conservative leaders. Whereas prime ministers Churchill, Eden, Macmillan, Home, and Heath stressed consensual governing, Mrs. Thatcher and her colleagues stress strength of purpose and determination, disparaging what they describe as debilitating negotiations. Gone is support for the elements of the postwar policy convergence between Conservatives and Labourites. For example, this government, under Mrs. Thatcher, rejects bargaining with national trade union leaders or the continued growth of social welfare programs. Instead, it stresses the virtues of private initiative and the privatization of many of the economic enterprises that the British government has so long owned and administered. Mrs. Thatcher stresses that her Conservative government wants Britain to become competitive and innovative again. She insists that government must live within its means, both financially and in terms of its real ability (which she feels is limited) to administer society. In sum, she favors a smaller government that encourages private, rather than public, initiative.

It must be pointed out, however, that although Mrs. Thatcher's views dominate the Conservative Party at the moment, they are not unanimously accepted by a number of prominent leaders, including former prime minister Heath. In their disagreement, they argue that her policies are too harsh. Taking the more traditional approach, they insist that the Tory party must ultimately return to its more consensual past if it expects to win future elections.

The Labour Party

The Labour Party has undoubtedly suffered the most damage over the past two decades. This is not surprising, because the failure of governments to cope with the economy has been seen as the failure of Labour's ideas. It has not been forgotten by the electorate that it was a Labour government, led by Clement Attlee after World War II, that established the definition of the managed economy and welfare state as well as the structure by which the postwar economy and state have been administered. Labour's philosophy, rooted in the views of John Maynard Keynes and the experiences of the Great Depression and World War II, dominated British political life for three decades. When it came under attack during the 1960s and 1970s, it was quite understandable that the Labour Party itself would suffer internal and external damage.

Internally, the struggles within Labour were expressed in endless philosophical arguments about "how much socialism?" The resulting disagreements have led to serious personal and organizational conflicts. For many years, these quite savage struggles were papered over during moments of stress and danger, during election campaigns, or when a Labour government was in peril. But as Britain's economic crisis deepened, and especially as relations between the Labour Party and its trade union allies became more strained, the arguments within the party intensified. In 1979, the combination of a winter of serious industrial strife, the fall of the Callaghan Labour government, and finally, the Conservative election victory, propelled the party into a highly damaging split. Although a new leader, Neil Kinnock, was elected and has brought youth and energy to the party's leadership, the struggles over organization and ideology between the left and more moderate wings of the party continue even now to keep it weak and marginally viable as an alternative government.

Social Democrats, Liberals, and the Alliance

The most dramatic consequence of the difficulties within the two major parties has been the rise of alternative parties in Britain. The British election system is clearly unhelpful to third parties because it offers nothing to losers. Only candidates who win elections get seats in the House of Commons; losers (as in the United States) get nothing for a good try. Therefore, a third party trying to break into the two-party system must take the risk of expending great effort and money with only a small probability of gaining political power and representation. It is some measure of Britain's political upheaval in recent years that so many experienced politicians have been willing to take the risk and make the effort to establish a viable third party.

The founding of the Social Democratic Party is the most important example of this development. In the main, Social Democrats are former Labour Party members and leaders who have decided that leaving the Labour Party was far more attractive than continuing to fight against Labour's increasingly powerful and electorally unappealing left wing. Besides personal and organizational differences, the founders of the Social Democrats have significant policy differences from their former colleagues. They are pro-European; they are more pro-NATO; they are certainly against a more vigorous push toward state socialism.

Given these views and their leadership's sense of electoral frustration, the Social Democrats, since their beginning in 1981, have also recognized the potential advantage of linkages with the Liberal Party. The Liberals, as fortune would have it, also benefited from Britain's political and economic crisis. Although Liberal policies are not very different from Social Democratic policies, they have different historic roots. Whereas the Social Democrats have clear origins in the Labour Party, the Liberals have clear, though different, origins on the

Conservative side of the spectrum. Together, they both enjoy the advantage that neither party has had experience in government. Thus, they are free from blame for the failures of the last decades.

The two parties have agreed to cooperate electorally in what they call the Alliance. So as not to destructively contest each other, the Liberals and Social Democrats ran single candidates against the main parties in nearly every constituency during the 1983 election. What they learned, which surprised few observers, was that it is very difficult to break the hold of the main parties. Despite winning 25.4 percent of the popular vote, the Alliance won only 23 seats. This was a discouraging result, especially for the Social Democrats, who won only five of those seats. The size of the Alliance's combined popular vote, however, provides hope for the future. There are difficulties about the division of power within the Alliance; the Liberals feel they should be acknowledged as the senior partners since they have more MPs, organizational strength, and experience. There are also doubts about the long-term possibilities for success unless the election system is changed. But there is little doubt that each party enjoys its best prospects if the Alliance is kept intact.

Of prime importance is the fact that the Alliance offers a real alternative within the context of a two-party system. As long as Labour remains weak and less competitive, and the electorate remains relatively dissatisfied with the main parties, the Alliance will be an important competitor. The election system creates a significant barrier to gaining seats, but the instability in the party system in recent years suggests that a basic realignment of major proportions is still quite possible.

Contemporary Issues in British Politics

The Political Challenge of Economic Problems

The Economic Challenge. The most difficult and threatening issue in British politics is the economy. Britain is simply too small and lacking in resources to provide food and other material wants for its population of more than 56 million. Although Britain ranks only seventy-second among the world's nations in size, it is the twelfth largest in population. It can produce only a little more than half of its own food, and except for coal, some low-grade iron ore, china clay, and the relatively limited gas and oil reserves under the North Sea, Britain has few natural resources.

Faced with the reality of chronic shortage, Britain depends to a great extent on international trade. As a result, it is the fifth-largest trading nation in the world. The largest category of imports is food, and Britain is, in fact, the biggest purchaser of food in the world marketplace. To pay for its food and other goods, Britain exports large amounts of manufactured products, particularly machinery, transport vehicles such as passenger cars, and chemicals. Additionally, it sells abroad large quantities of more famous consumer items, such as whiskey and china. Since the mid-1960s, British fashions and rock music have also been visible symbols of British industry.

The difficulty for Britain in this century has been that it has not been able to sell abroad enough of its production to pay for all it has bought from other countries. Two world wars and a severe depression stripped Britain of many resources it had accumulated in the previous century. The situation of shortage contrasted strikingly with the beginning of the industrial revolution, when Britain held a substantial trading advantage over all other nations. From the end of the eighteenth century, Britain lost much of this advantage, notwithstanding its imperial splendor. British production and British exports continued to increase, but at a slower pace, and the British found themselves outstripped in many fields by newer competitors, including the United States, Germany, and later Japan. Two successive world wars and economic recessions and depression have contributed to the crises that have plagued the British economy since 1945. World War I was expensive, not just in terms of material losses. An even greater effect was its disruption of traditional British markets overseas. The war caused many of Britain's trading partners to look for new sources for many items, including such things as textiles and coal, which Britain simply could not provide during the period of hostilities. When the war ended, many traditional trading partners found that they could more inexpensively and efficiently buy from other sources or produce those items themselves. The United States, for example, greatly expanded its own production during this period and consequently not only bought less from Britain but also sold many products for export that previously could be bought only from Britain. For Britain, the problem in regaining these lost markets was that its industrial structure was considerably older and more obsolete than that of the United States. Also, during the post–World War I period the British suffered more and more from rising international prices for raw materials, which the United States could extract domestically. The result of this new, unfavorable situation was that once its industry had satisfied pent-up consumer demand from the war period, Great Britain fell into a recession that began in 1920 and, though fitfully relieved during that decade, plunged during the 1930s into a depression even more severe than the one that plagued the United States during the same period.

The rapid rearmament in preparation for World War II finally ended the depression in 1939. Production of war materials required the efforts of every ablebodied man and and woman, and British industry stretched its capacity to the maximum. However, the cost of World War II in terms of damage to industry was even more severe than that of World War I. There was little further loss of already diminished international markets, but enemy bombing and the losses inflicted on the British merchant marine by enemy U-boats gravely damaged the economy. The British vastly expanded the regulatory powers of the state. By the end of the war in 1945, Britain needed desperately to rebuild its industrial capacity but was so heavily in debt that it had neither the capital to rebuild nor the funds to pay for necessary food and supplies to support a reasonable standard of living. Only a large American loan and then Marshall Plan assistance in the late 1940s saved the country from total economic chaos.

The major challenge in the postwar era was to rebuild and revive industrial production in order to recapture a share of world export markets sufficient to finance steady improvements in the standard of living. There was a strong demand by the British electorate that government intervene in economic life on a permanent basis to ensure hoped-for prosperity and thereby prevent a return to the dismal economic deprivation of the prewar years. In 1944, just as the war was ending, all three major political parties, then members of the wartime coalition government, agreed to guarantee that any future government would undertake to manage the economy.[9] The goals would be a high, and rising, standard of living, full employment, a sound currency, a low rate of inflation, and rapid economic development.

The problem with this sweeping end-of-the-war commitment was that it was contradictory and predicated on a very high degree of success in gaining large export markets for British goods. The difficult questions were: How could Britain rebuild and modernize its industrial capacity while using funds to buy abroad the goods necessary to support a high standard of living? Further, and in the long run more important, how could British government guarantee full employment without suffering consequently irresistible demands from workers for high wages that would in turn increase the price of British goods and make them less competitive in the world marketplace? These and similar questions have plagued the British economy for the past four decades, but no satisfactory answer has been found.

The Challenge of Producer Group Politics

The British now must find a new agreement as to the extent to which the formal authoritative decisionmakers and administrators in Britain should share their power to govern with informal influential leaders, particularly those who represent particular interest or pressure groups. Put another way, should Britain's political leaders share decisionmaking with sectional leaders of such groups as unions and employer associations? The monumental struggles that have periodically paralyzed Britain's economy and produced political crises during the past decades have made this issue compelling.

The Problem. Active, interventionist, democratic government simply cannot operate in a vacuum. Its legitimacy and the efficient implementation of its policies depend on how British citizens, in whatever way, respond to and participate in governing.

At the same time, British citizens for their part have a strong interest in the work of government. A century ago, government only lightly and sporadically touched their lives. It operated primarily at the margins of society, providing physical security in the form of legal and military protection and minimal public services. Today, by contrast, government affects by its policies the lives of every citizen, constantly and thoroughly. What government does is, therefore, of keen importance to all.

Political leadership today operates in an atmosphere of high stakes. Politicians accordingly bid for office during election campaigns by promising to adopt popular programs, to administer them more humanely as well as more efficiently than their opposition, and to make government more responsive to the wishes and participation of all citizens. Once in office, these commitments stir the same political leaders to cast broadly and with sensitivity in deciding policy and the details of administration. Faced also with the sheer magnitude and complexity of governing, modern British political executives display a marked susceptibility to the most explicit as well as the most subtle influences.

Pressure groups are the most important means of interaction between authoritative political leaders and British society. Lobbies are especially influential because they represent large numbers of citizens as well as high percentages of citizens concerned with a particular subject or issue. In addition, they so focus their concerns and energies that they often offer government the very best source of information and advice. Frequently, government so needs their expertise and support that pressure groups become active participants with political executives in crucial bargaining relationships.[10]

Among those groups, unions have proved to be the most important and difficult. Needless to say, the continuous supply of effective labor is central to the management of the economy. Unions, as organizers of so large a percentage of the labor force in Britain, occupy a crucial position to influence the pattern of manpower. Their influence is strongest in a negative sense; they are capable of serious disruption by their instructions to withhold labor in strike actions. This power seems greater than their ability to direct their members to take some kind of positive action, such as restraining their demands for higher wages or agreeing to work longer hours for the same pay. Nevertheless, one significant consequence for the involvement of government in managing the economy is that it must be concerned with these questions directly and therefore must work out the most cooperative arrangement possible with unions in Britain.

The development of the union's centrally important role with government in the management of the economy follows rather strikingly the growth of government itself.[11] British unions have a long history of vigorous organization but a considerably shorter history of participation in national decisionmaking.

For producer groups, and unions in particular, the commitment of political leaders after World War II to manage the economy in order to "guarantee" economic well-being ensured for them a continuing and important role as key participants. For example, in the case of the unions, the promise to ensure full employment meant that government would (and did) place the unions in a greatly strengthened position vis-à-vis employers. Recession and depression had earlier acted to weaken the union movement because their members—those who were employed—worried about protecting their jobs while those who were unemployed worried about finding a job. Unions hardly felt in a position to press employers very strongly about wage levels or working conditions. By contrast, full employment after 1945 altered working people's concerns very drastically. Having a job was no longer such a problem; rather, employees could consider working conditions and otherwise turn the new scarcity of labor into a bargaining advantage.

For the government, the irony was that its policy after 1945 of full employment enhanced union strength to the point that government itself required union cooperation in restraining aggressiveness that might, if unchecked, damage the rest of the government's economic policies. Specifically, full employment caused pressure for wage increases that in turn raised the cost of British goods to the point that they became less competitive on world markets. Thus, the problem was that one policy, full employment, led to serious difficulties for government in managing the economy to satisfy the rest of its economic commitments.

This example of government's inescapable involvement with unions is stark testimony to the whole new relationship in most of the years after World War II. Government certainly could not, if it ever did, reach policy decisions or administer programs without broad consultation. A long consensual tradition in Britain gives legitimacy to the claims of groups affected, or likely to be affected, by government's policies. Although they are not party to the actual moments of decisionmaking—that being the prerogative of government—they have long been acknowledged to have the right to what is known as consultation. That tradition has been strong enough to cause governments serious embarrassment at times when proper consultation was not followed. But in recent decades, the example of the unions as well as other groups shows that consultation has been excessive. By its commitments, the government became involved during those years in a new relationship that in many cases has been one of actually bargaining with producer groups such as unions. The whole history of government-union relations since 1945 demonstrates this transition, which has affected nearly all governmental-societal relations.

Union-Government Relations in Practice and as a Political Issue. The actual history, since 1945, of government's relationship with the spokesgroup for British trade unionism, the Trades Union Congress (TUC), is strewn with far more disappointments than with effective cooperation.[12] Although there have been a number of very useful agreements concerning such things as safety and health, adult education, and retraining of workers who have obsolete skills, there have been few examples of success in resolving the central issue in the relationship: wage levels. Of the six attempts government made to win union cooperation in restraining or freezing wages (1948, 1956, 1961, 1964, 1972–1973, and 1975), only two were successful—those of 1948 and 1975—because union officials in both cases had become badly frightened. In 1948, leaders of the Labour government successfully convinced union leaders that there was a real danger of renewed depression and a return to Conservative rule. Memories of the two interwar decades of economic deprivation were still painfully fresh, and an electricity shortage in 1947 that caused a short but dramatic rise in unemployment reinforced that fear. In 1975, rising unemployment, serious recession, and a wild inflation of more than 25 percent combined to convince union leaders to accept, at least for a limited time, a controlled increase of about $12 per week in workers' wages.

But in the other four instances, in 1956, 1961, 1964, and 1972–1973, the efforts by government to win union cooperation were wholly fruitless. These initiatives occurred during periods of real, but less visible or dramatic, economic crises when the consequences of government's commitment to full employment were causing rises in prices and consequent falls in the competitive position of British goods on world markets. At those times, government wanted agreements to restore confidence in the pound sterling and stop the erosion of British competitiveness. But it was at just those moments that British workers, buoyed by full employment and the past successes of militant efforts to press for ever higher wages, were least inclined to restrain use of the leverage they so obviously enjoyed.

The several examples of government's failure to win union cooperation in restraining wages and increasing productivity, sorely needed to manage the economy successfully, illustrate the most serious problem attending the greatly enhanced role of producer groups in policymaking. The dilemma is that the terms of its control of the economy require government to consult and bargain with groups made powerful by its policies, but there is no assurance that those groups will find it in their interests to make and keep effective agreements. Looking just at the example of the unions in Britain, it is obvious that the unions, except in periods of fear, do not find it to their perceived advantage to reach agreements. After all, trade unions were created and exist for the express purpose of getting more money and better working conditions for their members. Unions are not institutions that exist to serve the national interest, as governments ask them to do. Rather, they are institutions established to serve the narrower interests of their dues-paying members. One can hardly expect union leaders to be readily willing to accept less money or less advantageous benefits than they know they can win by free collective bargaining. And in an era of nearly full employment such as the one that existed for 30 years from the mid-1940s through the mid-1970s, there is an acute tension between the demands by government for restraint and the demands by union members that their leaders take full advantage of their bargaining leverage. So, in sum, government needs cooperation in restraining wage inflation at just those moments when unions are least likely to be cooperative—when their bargaining strength is great and their membership comparatively more militant.

Recognition of this dilemma caused both Labour and Conservative governments during the 1960s and early 1970s to attempt, unsuccessfully, to alter their relationship with the union movement.[13] While holding to their end-of-the-war commitments, governments led first by Harold Wilson (Labour) and Edward Heath (Conservative) tried to limit by legislation the power of unions or their recalcitrant members in the factories. Both efforts failed dismally because unions used the very process, amounting to a veto power, that government leaders were attempting to change. The union-government clash in 1974, for example, which involved a severe coal miners' strike and led to a three-day workweek because of diminished power supplies, ultimately caused the electoral defeat of the Heath Conservative government. It was replaced by a Labour government, again headed by Harold Wilson, committed to restoring peace with the union movement at almost any price.

The height of union power in Britain was thus reached during the mid-1970s.[14] Yet it is ironic that at that moment of supreme union influence, with political leaders in despair, the most potent economic recession since World War II delivered the first real challenge to that power. Raging inflation, a sharp downturn in industrial production, and a serious national financial and monetary crisis all pressed policymakers. As a consequence, full employment—the real linchpin of union strength—began to slip away in 1975, which resulted in the British government beginning to embrace a different kind of economic management, which in turn eroded the basis for collectivist politics. Union power thus began to ebb in Britain at just the moment when it seemed to be getting totally out of control.

These changes did not occur suddenly or all at once. It only gradually became clear that government had improved its leverage at the expense of its union adversary. And it was only by the end of the 1970s that it was possible to speculate that collectivist politics in Britain was changing and might be changed into some unrecognizable postcollectivist form.

The election of a Conservative government led by Margaret Thatcher as prime minister formed a political watershed. Mrs. Thatcher and her colleagues were committed to pursuing the new government advantage and pressing for a significant change in the relationship with the union movement. They were determined to change the rules of economic decisionmaking so that government would no longer be so dependent on the willingness and ability of the trade union movement to deliver advice and cooperation.

The present Conservative government seems to have accomplished its goal. High unemployment has debilitated union power and with it union leverage as partner with government in economic decisionmaking. At present union leaders no longer meet with the prime minister in the Cabinet room as they did under the previous Labour government.

Political leaders of both major parties, Labour and Conservative, have come to believe that they can politically "live" on an apparently continuing basis with a rate of unemployment high enough to do serious damage to their union adversaries. The question, however, is whether this is the long-sought key to permanently changing the collectivist process.

The answer is unclear, but Britain has probably not seen the end of collectivist politics.[15] The 1984 dispute in the coal-mining industry produced a spate of opinion polls that re-emphasized the tolerance of the British electorate for pressure group activity. Political leaders were reminded once again that, although economic recession has dampened union strength, the legitimacy of its behavior is fundamentally accepted. And beyond legitimacy and public opinion polls, it is still obvious that continued government management of the economy and consequent political responsibility for that management will ensure the importance of the government–pressure group relationship. In the long run, the question of Britain's economic well-being is intertwined with the question of what role pressure groups should play in policy decisionmaking. This will continue to be a critical issue in the polity.

The Political Challenge of Social Welfare Policy

The British polity's response to economic problems has a parallel in its response to the issues of social welfare policy. Both were born in the same era of deprivation between the two world wars. In the economic sphere, Britain's political leadership recognized, and played to, the growing public consensus that government should be responsible for creating and maintaining a prosperous society. Likewise, the same leadership recognized that society increasingly viewed government's responsibilities as including a broad range of social services. In sum, government was charged by the end of World War II with the task of, and responsibility for, creating a more compassionate, protective, and prosperous Britain.

The origin of these responsibilities was the bidding process by which politicians seek to win and then to retain elected office. The most important watershed in this development was the Labour Party's overwhelming and surprising victory over Winston Churchill and his Conservatives in 1945. That victory occurred in great measure because the Labour Party spoke directly of its plans for the future. It promised that, if elected to office, it would implement a whole range of policies that collectively came to be known as the managed economy and the welfare state. That it won office and then proceeded to do just as promised not only produced an explosion of government activity but also an about-face in the policies of the opposition Conservative Party. It was, in fact, the change that the Attlee Labour government's policies pressed on the Conservative Party that ensured the emergence of a new politics in post–World War II Britain. It took the Conservatives very little time to begin to discuss what they needed to do to rebuild their electoral appeal. By 1947, they were proceeding full tilt toward adopting policy plans that had the effect of converging toward those of their Labour opponents.[16] That they did so, and did so very quickly, ensured that political competition in Britain would be organized around fundamental commitments to active, interventionist government.

The effect of this convergence in policy outlook between the two great parties is shown rather dramatically by the evidence of increased government expenditure during the past half-century or so. In 1938, for example, government expended on its programs only about one-fifth of the gross national product (GNP) that the British economy produced. Twenty years later, in 1958 with a Conservative government in office, government spent 36.5 percent of GNP. Ten years further down the road, in 1968, this figure stood at a remarkable 50.6 percent.

Just as convincing as these figures is the list of social programs and economic activities that the government took on during this period. There was extensive nationalization of the economy, including the railroads, telecommunications, steel, and coal. Government-launched free medical care under the National Health Service, pensions for all, a family allowance program, housing subsidies, unemployment benefits, and a great variety of other legislation that became part of the so-called cradle-to-grave philosophy. Government, in sum, became the nation's largest employer and its citizens' most generous benefactor.

The continuing popularity of these social welfare programs is still a powerful political force. Over the years, public opinion polls have repeatedly confirmed that the electorate is strongly supportive of the general social welfare structure that the Attlee government put in place more than 30 years ago. And if public opinion polls are not proof enough, one need only observe the behavior of politicians themselves when they address the issue of funding for social welfare programs. In Britain, as in virtually every other Western democracy, politicians are very cautious about meddling with social welfare programs, however conservative their views and their rhetoric at times.

The problem for political leaders in Britain is, however, that this strong and continuing support for social welfare programs runs smack into the same adverse economic realities that have forced government to rein in costs and restrain growth throughout the economy. In economic policymaking both Labour and Conservative governments during the past decade have moved to change their policy approaches, including abandoning commitments to full employment and a constantly rising standard of living. But in the social welfare sphere, political leaders during this same period have been much less bold in holding back spending. For example, even though Mrs. Thatcher heads a Conservative government committed to smaller and more fiscally responsible government, she and her ministers have been exceedingly cautious about their approach to social welfare reductions. Their record is not so much one of reductions as it is of holding growth to the rate of inflation in some areas while allowing significant increases in funding in others. And despite the rhetoric, very few programs have actually been ended or are likely to end in the foreseeable future.

Here then, in the social welfare area, is an example of one of the most important problems facing modern British government and its politics. On the one hand, there is obvious and enthusiastic support for compassionate, beneficial policies. On the other, there is widespread recognition that the costs of such programs are too high for the economy to support without provoking serious economic problems. The dilemma for Britain's polity is how its leaders can respond democratically to the strong support for these programs while carrying out their perceived responsibility to rebuild Britain's troubled economy.

The prospects are that this dilemma will continue to plague policy decision-making in every area of British government and that it will be especially troublesome—as it has been—in the area of social welfare. At the core, the dilemma is likely to be resolved in a democratic society only when the competing pressures change, and that is not likely to happen soon. The difficulty in this era is that popular support for social welfare programs is articulated aggressively and successfully by a great multitude of pressure groups and by bureaucrats and experts within the government structure. Although these interests recognize the larger societal imperatives, such as the consequences of unrestrained growth for the country's well-being, they have no incentive to operationalize their understanding when it comes to the specific interests they champion. They cannot see or believe that their own restraint will make the slightest difference in the broader picture, nor do they believe that such action will be of any benefit to them as leaders. Quite the contrary, leaders are seen as weak and unreliable by their constituents if they do less than press for the most resources and largest programs they can achieve.

Britain's External Relations

Important issues of external relations are almost always near the top of the list of any British government's major concerns. Britain's geographic position, its history as an imperial nation, its role in the Western alliance, and its economic vulnerability all create a comparatively great sensitivity to international relations.

It is not surprising, therefore, that the speed of economic decline has been matched by a decline in Britain's power as a great nation. The loss of empire, the emergence of the United States and the Soviet Union as superpowers, and the dramatic economic successes enjoyed by a number of countries led by Japan have all battered Britain's status. It is hard to believe that only a half century ago Britain fully qualified as a great power, whereas today it stands more in the position of an important, middle-ranking power. This is not to say that Britain is unimportant. Quite the contrary. Its traditional relations with the United States, its Western allies, and former colonial nations, although not as potent as before, are nevertheless important and influential. The difference today is that Britain stands well below the point at which it can confidently dictate the course of events with the dominance it once exercised.

Britain and the United States: The Special Relationship

It is quite revealing to spend a few minutes looking through the card catalog at the Royal Institute of International Affairs in London. The institute has a wonderful collection of books, periodicals, and other materials on international relations in general and an unrivaled collection on British external relations in particular. Yet very few of these books or articles deal exclusively with British-American relations. What little material there is concerns the few disagreements and tensions that the two allies have experienced during the past 30 years. The Suez crisis of 1956 is a notable example. Since academics, no less than their audiences, are much more interested in conflict than consensus and good feelings, the Royal Institute's card catalog is an interesting confirmation of the enduring specialness of the relationship between these two close allies.

The lack of academic material about British-American relations does not mean, however, that the relationship is unimportant. To the contrary, both countries, their allies, and the rest of the world regard the relationship as highly important. The lack of academic attention also does not mean that the relationship is dull, wholly serene, or unchanging. Although there are seldom dramatic crises, an important evolution is occurring in the relationship. Within the larger changes are important issues that do produce significant tensions and strains. And beyond the current dynamic of the relationship, important differences in outlook and position between the two countries contribute to the basic conduct of the Western alliance.

One former British ambassador to the United States points out that, at any one time, there are about a half-dozen "sore" issues between the two countries. It always seems, he said, that one or two of them are about to blow up into a major quarrel—but they hardly ever do. At this point in the mid-1980s, the landscape of British-American relations fits this description.

There are, for example, important disagreements over certain technical questions. One such recent argument has been a tax dispute. The British government, supporting its own private enterprise, has been angry that California insists on taxing British firms on the profits they make outside of California. The specific complaint is that some British firms doing business in California are required to pay taxes on their overall corporate profits even though their California-based subsidiaries may actually be losing money. What makes the matter even worse in British eyes is that the U.S. Department of State agrees with the British position but is powerless to force California to revise its tax laws. The British are not particularly happy with Washington's impotence in the area of states' rights since the British are steeped in the notion of the overriding power of the central authority in London.

A second example of a relatively narrow disagreement is the question of agricultural subsidies. Both countries are unhappy about subsidies that protect local agriculture against international competition. But at the same time, each government is torn. On the one hand, both are besieged by demands from export-oriented agricultural interests who insist that they be free to trade, without facing tariff barriers, wherever there are markets. On the other hand, each government is besieged by weaker agricultural interests who want tariff barriers erected to protect them from international competition. As a result, both the American and British governments find themselves representing, quite aggressively, both sides of the same controversy against each other. It may seem unlikely, but arguments over such issues can become quite rancorous and bitter at times—even though they rarely make for newspaper headlines.

The general condition of British-American relations is not, it should be stressed, usually assessed from a reading of these sorts of technical or narrow-subject disagreements. The health of the special relationship is measured far more by the mood and details of collaboration on vital questions related to the issues of war and peace. The fortieth anniversary commemoration of the D-Day invasion of 1944 highlighted again how remarkably close the ties between the two countries have been over the years on these matters. Yet there have been significant difficulties in recent years.

The British side has been the most unhappy. One recent example of British displeasure was the Reagan administration's mining of Nicaraguan harbors in

1983. Another example was the American invasion of Grenada, also in 1983. It was not that the British disagreed with the purpose of that invasion but rather that they objected to the American government's failure to consult them and formed the impression that the Americans were undertaking a kind of gunboat diplomacy. This was, from the British point of view, an area of the world in which they had long been involved and an island that, until 1974, was a British colony.

There was also unhappiness on the British side at the first American reaction to the Falklands crisis in 1982. The United States certainly sided with its British allies once the British initiative to recapture the islands was under way. But the British sensed an American reluctance to endorse their views about the controversy because of Washington's concern over relations with Argentina. This impression was rekindled in 1983 when the American government reacted quickly to the election of a democratic government in Argentina by lifting its ban on the sale of weapons to that country.

These recent problems have produced what can best be described as some bruising of the traditionally harmonious British-American relationship. This bruising is all the more significant because it has occurred during a period marked by an unusual ideological compatibility between the leaders of the American and British governments. In fact, Mrs. Thatcher and her Conservative colleagues have come in for withering criticism at times from the opposition Labour Party because in Labour's view the Thatcher government has been too obsequious to American views and actions. There is, and has long been, a vein of anti-Americanism in Britain. The development of so many disagreements between the two countries about important issues during the past few years, even with the Conservative government in office, has greatly stirred such feelings and made them a political force, although still a minor one. The possible return of a Labour government at some point might make these feelings more significant since the left wing of the Labour Party is most apt to indulge in anti-Americanism.

All of this points to a fundamental change in British-American relations. Britain is no longer the comparatively equal partner of the United States as a world power that it was at the time of D-Day more than 40 years ago. It is now more of an upper-middle-level power and thus far more dependent on its alliance with the United States for its national security. This position is uncomfortable for a country so long used to a role as one of the dominant nations in the world. For British-American relations, this change has meant the intrusion of a much greater sensitivity by the British about their collaboration. There is no question that there is every sign of this sensitivity in the British reaction to the irritating events of recent years. Although the consequences are not likely to lead to a serious disruption, much less a rupture of relations, they do cause considerably greater strain than the two sides have known for more than a century.

NATO, the European Economic Community and the Western Alliance

The decline of British power has an effect on British external relations that goes far beyond the question of the special ties between Britain and the United States. Another important area where this change has had a profound effect is Britain's relations with its European neighbors and its role in the Western defense community. Britain has long been a staunch member of the Western alliance. Its ties continue to be as firm as ever, and perhaps even stronger now that its own relative power is less. What has changed is Britain's economic relationship with Europe. After keeping its economic distance from Europe for two decades, Britain in the past ten years or so, realizing the decline in its economic status, has moved "into Europe" as a member of the European Economic Community (EEC).

This move into Europe has not been easy, either in its impact on Britain's relations with its European partners or within the British polity. The problem has been multifaceted, but it has focused most importantly on traditional British objections to any relationships that impinge on national sovereignty. Put starkly, the British electorate has always been unhappy, to one degree or another, with arrangements that dilute its prerogatives of self-government.

The issue of membership in the EEC has now been a primary one for more than 30 years. Nothing seems to put it to rest. Before membership was successfully negotiated in 1972 by the Conservative government led by Edward Heath, the raging national debate was about joining the EEC. The Conservative Party was generally in favor and the Labour opposition generally against—although each party had significant minorities that took opposite positions. From 1972 to 1975, when a national referendum confirmed membership, the major question was "Shall we stay in?" Once that was settled by a two-thirds majority in a referendum in 1975, the argument about the terms of British membership began. The question since that time has been whether Britain is getting a fair return for its expenditures in the community. More recently, Mrs. Thatcher's government was involved in very bitter negotiations with Britain's European partners in an effort to secure a rebate on its contribution.

In addition, important and sometimes very amusing arguments have raged between Britain and its EEC partners about the application of EEC rules to British law. Although these disagreements have sometimes seemed inconsequential compared with the struggle over Britain's financial contribution, they have been even more important because they concern the issue of sovereignty most directly. One such celebrated disagreement, for example, was the question of whether the EEC could apply its prescription for the ingredients of ice cream to Britain. The British had long been used to buying "ice cream" that includes nondairy substances. These ingredients were less expensive and made the traditional Lyons Maid and Walls "ice cream" treats cheaply available. But they clashed with EEC rules requiring the inclusion of dairy products in anything called "ice cream." The whole dispute seemed quite funny to an outsider, but it produced angry charges by many British political leaders that this sort of intrusion illustrated how the EEC would gradually destroy British sovereignty and with it democratic government.

It is within this context of reluctance and animosity that the terms of British membership in the EEC can be expected to be debated far into the future. There is little chance that Britain will soon back out of the EEC because the value of economic integration is too obvious to ignore. But its membership is likely to continue to be cranky and self-interested. It is easy to imagine, however, that a serious crisis that impinges too strongly on British sovereignty might cause serious consideration to be given to returning back across the English Channel.

The Commonweath and Developing Nations

Britain's interest in and involvement with developing nations is strong and continuing. Its ties are quite naturally strongest with its former colonies and possessions. Most of these are members of the Commonwealth. Britain keeps these ties for more than emotional and sentimental reasons. They have, in most cases, an ongoing economic and political importance.

The visitor to London begins early to appreciate the significance of these ties by simple observation. Both the people one meets in London and activities at the universities and in business suggest the magnitude of the continuing relationships. For example, many young people from Commonwealth countries still receive an advanced education in Britain, including politically important military education. In addition, London is still the hub for a great percentage of the financial activity conducted by developing nations, including both actual transactions and the saving of assets. In sum, the independence movement clearly stripped Britain of a great empire, but the importance and quantity of Britain's relationships with these new nations is very great indeed.

Although these relationships have great significance, their importance within the British polity itself has diminished over the past few decades. Independence was one of the great issues of this century, but now that the question has been settled in nearly every case, the arguments within Britain about policy toward these independent countries are much less compelling.

What does remain as an issue is the question of immigration. Britain traditionally has been very proud of its tolerance, and for many years allowed the peoples of its far-flung empire to come freely to Britain to work and live. However, once large numbers of colonial citizens began to immigrate into Britain, beginning in the 1950s, the traditional open-door policy became the subject of inflamed debate. Gradually, and then more decisively, British political leaders began to legislate what has become a very restrictive policy on immigration. This has caused both further internal debate and external friction as several Commonwealth nations have denounced Britain as racist. Since it appears that there is little probability that Britain will retreat from its restrictive policies, the question of immigration will likely continue to be a significant divisive element undermining the Commonwealth.

Future British Politics and Policies

This brief essay about contemporary British politics and issues is by no means comprehensive. It encompasses only the most primary issues and contemporary political trends. It does not deal with a great number of major issues, such as race relations, the problem of Northern Ireland, local-national government relations, relations between England and Wales, changing attitudes toward social class and accents, and perhaps a declining respect for such inherited institutions as the church, the club, the regiment, the public school.

The most visible sign of political change was the election in 1979 of Mrs. Thatcher as prime minister of a new Conservative government, the first woman to have held this office in Britain. Snobbishly assailed by many left-wing critics as a "grocer's daughter from Grantham," she stood for conservatism of a more militant kind, one that rejected the former consensus that had joined Tory paternalism with Labour commitment to the regulatory state. She and her closest colleagues had argued for several years before taking office that government needed to change its direction quite drastically. Drawing on the failures of the economy and the resulting turmoil within British society, Mrs. Thatcher, as leader of the Conservative opposition in the mid- and late 1970s, argued that government's management of the economy was a failure. She condemned both the suffocating debt that expansive government had brought down on the economy and the stifling of personal initiative, which she argued must be revived if Britain was to recover its dynamism. Once Mrs. Thatcher took office, she and her colleagues promised to revive Britain by refashioning government into a far more frugal and nonintrusive institution whose goal would be to encourage innovation and initiative.

The question of whether Mrs. Thatcher and her government have achieved these goals, or at least moved far toward their accomplishment, is the subject of considerable controversy. It is generally agreed, however, that she has pressed and articulated these goals so as to open a considerable disagreement between the two great parties (and the two "third parties," the Social Democrats and the Liberals) that compete for political office in Britain. This is a dramatic change from the profile of the political landscape for most of the years after 1945. For nearly four decades, the Labour and Conservative parties had been in fundamental agreement. They embraced Keynesian economic management and the principle of a compassionate and interventionist government seeking to develop a comprehensive social welfare program. There were differences of degree, but political scientists long pointed to the fundamental consensus within British politics about the general role that government should play in ensuring a prosperous and protective society. Now that agreement is gone, and the two parties compete with very different views about what government should be doing and how society should be structured.

The prospects are that this disagreement will continue and even intensify. There are likely to be continued debates within both major parties as the Conservatives wrestle with the question of whether they are compassionate enough and Labour wrestles with the question of what it will take to win office again. But the splits within Labour, including the breaking away of important leaders of the party's middle and right wings, make the prospect of renewed convergence between the main parties unlikely.

The Labour Party has a long history of internal dissension. Each great struggle over the years engendered predictions about the party's demise. But just when matters looked bleakest, the party pulled itself together long enough to effectively battle the Conservatives and sometimes to win and hold office. It is tempting to view Labour's recent turmoil in the same light, but the evidence is convincing that the party's troubles since 1979 are more serious. The departure of so many leaders, the establishment of the Social Democratic Party, and the continued organizational struggles within the party over the reselection of candidates for Parliament has been fundamentally damaging. This development has greatly weakened moderating influences that might otherwise influence the party and win broad support from the electorate. Barring a serious failure that would propel voters to oust the Conservatives, no matter what the alternative, it seems unlikely that the British electorate will vote for a decidedly left-wing government. Certainly, Labour's experience after 1951 is that its election victories have been won by relatively moderate and slightly left-of-center leaders and policies.

The composite view of the future of British politics posed by this situation is of the Labour and Conservative parties continuing to compete from positions that are further to the left and right than has been the pattern since World War II. Labour will undoubtedly want to do what it can to win the next election, but the prospects are that it will not be able to overcome its ideological, organizational, and personality problems sufficiently to move toward the center. Thus, for their part the Conservatives will not have to move from the right toward the center to capture votes unless Mrs. Thatcher's policies are perceived as a serious failure. This is not to say that the rumblings of discontent heard from more moderate Conservatives will be silenced. In fact, their voices could become much more influential if unemployment continues to be high. But it does seem that the election of 1979 produced a political watershed that ended the convergence between the political parties in Britain and opened an era of serious ideological disagreement.

Update

Politics in Britain is in transition. After nearly a dozen years as prime minister, Mrs. Thatcher was forced from power in November 1990 by her own colleagues in the Conservative Party. John Major, Mrs. Thatcher's chancellor of the Exchequer and close ally, was then elected to replace her as party leader. As a result, Major became prime minister.

News of this political upheaval startled and confused many around the world. Mrs. Thatcher had seemed so dominating and invincible a leader. She had enjoyed an overwhelming Conservative majority in the House of Commons. She was a strong figure in world politics. How could she fall, and how could she fall so quickly?

What had gone little noticed outside of Britain was Mrs. Thatcher's political slide into crisis. This slide had started soon after her third straight election victory in June 1987 and become quite serious during 1989. Worried senior colleagues and Conservative backbenchers had hoped against hope for months that Mrs. Thatcher would reverse her government's unpopularity, but increasingly they came to fear that she could not lead them to a fourth election victory.

Month after month, for more than a year, public opinion polls in Britain told the same story. The electorate was tired of and annoyed with Mrs. Thatcher's style of leadership and increasingly in disagreement with a number of her government's key policies. The two most contentious issues were the so-called poll tax and the role that Britain should play in the rapidly developing integration occurring in the European Community.

As it turned out, it was the European issue that provided the trigger for the rebellion against Mrs. Thatcher. It might have been just as easily the poll tax, or even some other issue, that provided the sort of explosive chemistry that caused Conservative MPs very quickly to decide that their prospects for the future looked much better in the hands of a new leader.

The poll tax issue was certainly the most visible, persistently inflammatory, and dangerous for Mrs. Thatcher during her last year. Had the European issue not triggered the leadership struggle it did in late 1990, the poll tax issue by itself might have brought down the Conservative government at the next election. It is hard to imagine an issue that could have been more broadly unpopular.

The poll tax, or "community charge" as the government described it, replaced the traditional tax on property ownership. The new tax is a "head tax" on each adult in the community, and its purpose is to pay for local government services. The amount of tax owed varies by locality and depends on how much local government intends to spend. In some cases, the tax levy is nearly $1,000 per adult per year. Since so many in Britain are renters, they did not pay the old property taxes—or rates, as they were called. Now, however, these voters are receiving large bills. Although the wealthier British adults are quite pleased to see their tax burden spread out among their fellow citizens, the rest of the electorate, including smaller property owners, is quite angry.

Mrs. Thatcher had certainly expected anger—even a great deal of anger. What she hoped, however, was that such anger would be directed at free-spending local government authorities. She expected that the electorate would crack down on local officials who legislated expensive social service programs. Government would become more accountable, she reasoned. The costs of local government would be more fairly distributed, she reasoned. May be best of all for her, those nasty Labour-dominated urban city governments such as in infamous Liverpool would be brought to heel.

What happened, instead, was that Mrs. Thatcher and her government took nearly all the heat for imposing the new tax. That tax, and then her unwillingness to consider its meaningful change, made politically tangible all the years of charges that Mrs. Thatcher was mean spirited and uncaring. Serious riots against the poll tax in London in the spring of 1990 shocked the nation and crystallized the opposition to the prime minister. Mrs. Thatcher's colleagues in the House of Commons began to worry seriously at that time that she was leading them to disaster. Only a full-scale retreat from the tax would help, but they knew, as she had said so often, that the lady was "not for turning."

It was not the poll tax that brought her down in November 1990, however. It was the issue of Britain's place in Europe. Mrs. Thatcher had vocally and persistently made her case against the surrender of "critical" aspects of Britain's sovereignty to the developing integration of Europe. Although she ultimately agreed to each step of that growing integration over the years, she did so only after protracted argument and intransigence in nearly every instance. The British polity as a whole had also long displayed its reluctance about Europe but in recent years most political leaders had come to accept that Britain could not afford to ignore the continent any longer—in fact they had come to believe that Britain needed to play an active and influential role in European affairs and in the Community. Thus, although many continued to agree with Mrs. Thatcher's views on a philosophical level, as a practical matter they condemned her behavior toward the European Community as putting the nation at risk.

The climactic event about Europe came after the European Summit in Italy in November 1990. Mrs. Thatcher told the media, in response to questions about her government's objections to the otherwise unanimous decision to develop a European bank and currency, that as far as she was concerned Britain had given up enough sovereignty. That statement was too much for her longest-serving colleague, Sir Geoffrey Howe.

Howe had served in the Cabinet at the most senior levels for the whole of Mrs. Thatcher's administration. He had stayed on in office despite a fierce disagreement with the prime minister about British membership in the European Monetary System. But her outburst on this occasion was more than he could bear. He resigned very suddenly and then in his resignation speech to the House of Commons, he electrified the nation and plunged his party into a leadership crisis by openly denouncing his prime minister.

The impact was immediate. Mrs. Thatcher found herself quickly challenged by former Defence Minister Michael Hesseltine in the annual leadership election. When she failed to defeat Hesseltine on the first ballot, it became quite clear that she faced defeat on the second. The prime minister had been too wounded politically to continue, and after some agonizing hours of consultation, she withdrew and left her two Cabinet colleagues, John Major and the foreign secretary, Douglas Hurd, to carry on the fight against Hesseltine.

Sir Geoffrey Howe had thus given worried Conservative MPs just the signal they were waiting· for. For months they had yearned for yet another Thatcher miracle which would have turned public opinion polls around. But there had been no miracles and Mrs. Thatcher was obviously not about to "buy" back her popularity by "surrender" on matters of principle. In the end, her colleagues in the House of Commons acted not on gratitude to Mrs. Thatcher for her many triumphs. Instead, they acted for what they saw as their own futures. In doing so, they behaved very much as the British electorate had in 1945 when it turned Winston Churchill out of office at the moment of his victory over Germany. The electorate at that time acted on their fears about the shape of postwar British society rather than out of gratitude to Churchill for his heroic wartime leadership.

John Major's victory in the Conservative leadership struggle that followed also suggested that it was Mrs. Thatcher's own leadership and not her ideas that they were rejecting. Major was clearly a Thatcher protégé who agreed with his former boss on most policy issues. But in his campaign for the leadership he had made it clear that he was prepared to make changes both in style and in those policies that were clearly unpopular—particularly the poll tax and the government's attitude about Europe. Those assurances were music to Conservative MP ears. Thatcherism with a human face and without Thatcher was just what they wanted.

Only a couple of years ago, when this chapter was first written, Mrs. Thatcher and her ideas looked unchallengeable. It appeared likely at that time that the prime minister would be able to keep her promise to go "on and on." The main advantage Mrs. Thatcher and her colleagues enjoyed was the lack of a real opposition. The elections of 1983 and 1987 had produced enormous Conservative victories and equally enormous defeats for the Labour Party. In particular, Labour seemed mired in a possibly irreversible political wilderness. Riddled with dissension and dominated by its left-wing and attendant politically unattractive policies, the party gained far more public scorn and derision than substantial votes.

Alienated from Labour, many in the electorate fled toward the centrist third parties, the Social Democrats and Liberals. This alternative proved to be equally disappointing as the British election system demonstrated again—as it similarly does in the United States—how unkind it can be to third parties. Despite receiving approximately one-quarter of the vote in both 1983 and 1987, these parties combined in the "Alliance" were able to produce winning margins in less than 25 seats, or only about 4 percent of the seats in the House of Commons. Since Labour continued to hold its stronghold seats in the inner cities, the Conservatives at that time could look out on the political landscape without sighting a real threat to their hold on power.

Much has now changed. One key development is the revival of the Labour Party. Neil Kinnock, its leader since 1983, has doggedly and successfully argued that Labour's only chance to regain power lies in undertaking thoroughgoing reform. By reform, Kinnock has meant both policy and structural change. The electorate, he has insisted, had lost confidence that Labour's policies were sensible or would work and doubted that its leadership was competent to govern. What Labour needed to do, he urged, was to turn its energy away from intraparty warfare and toward the development of new policies that mixed elements of Thatcher's free market economics with a renewal of compassionate social democracy and a continuation of restraints on trade union power (thus excluding a return to collectivist politics). At the same time Kinnock pressed for structural reforms that would diminish more radical influences which had so strongly undermined moderate leadership and pushed the troubled party to the left and therefore out of the political mainstream.

Despite considerable skepticism, Kinnock has been quite successful in making these changes. He skillfully tapped the anger of moderate elements who resented the ways in which the left had used party rules to create destructive domination. He also used the party's growing hunger to return to office. Even some on the hard left and militant elements in the union movements have come to recognize that the Tories—if not Mrs. Thatcher herself—will go "on and on" as she once boasted.

Kinnock's success has been translated into growing public confidence in Labour's credibility as an alternative government. Polls show some suspicion about the permanence of Labour's new image but the party now has enough credibility to profit at times when the government loses popularity. Only a few years ago such discontent mostly produced gains for the Alliance parties.

The end of the Thatcher reign, the coming to power of John Major, and the resurgence of the Labour Party as a viable, more centrist, opposition work together to raise the possibility of a new consensus in British politics about the responsibilities of government.

Mrs. Thatcher undoubtedly changed public policy and the ideology of politics in Britain for some time to come. The reform of Labour Party policies reflects this influence as Neil Kinnock and his colleagues, for example, talk far more of free market economics than they did during the days of union dominated collectivism or the still earlier period of nationalization from 1945 to 1951. At the same time, during the last months of Mrs. Thatcher's leadership and into the beginning of John Major's, the Conservative Party became anxious that its policies be more closely based on broad political support. Moreover, during their leadership fight John Major, Douglas Hurd, and Michael Hesseltine all appealed to traditional Tory support for more compassionate social policies—for a "kinder and gentler" Britain, to borrow an expression from recent American politics.

In sum, Britain's political parties show clear signs of policy convergence, though on quite different terms from before Mrs. Thatcher. What Mrs. Thatcher seems to have done in her time was to create a whole new political ground. Now both major parties are beginning to compete about differences on this new ground, just as they did when the Conservatives adjusted to the dramatic changes the Labour Government legislated beginning in 1945.

Notes

1. Walter Bagehot, *The English Constitution*, 2d ed. (Garden City, N.Y.: Doubleday, 1961).

2. Ibid., p. 63.

3. Ibid., p. 76.

4. Ibid., p. 83.

5. Ibid.; see especially "Introduction to the Second Edition."

6. John P. Mackintosh, *The Government and Politics of Britain*, 3d ed. (London: Hutchinson, 1974).

7. Bagehot, *English Constitution*, "Introduction to the Second Edition."

8. Ibid., p. 13.

9. Gerald A. Dorfman, *Wage Politics in Britain* (Ames, Iowa, and London: Iowa State University and Charles Knight, 1973 and 1974), chap. 3.

10. Samuel H. Beer, *Modern British Politics* (London: Faber & Faber, 1969), chap. 12.

11. Dorfman, *Wage Politics in Britain*, chaps. 2 and 3.

12. For an extended analysis of union-government relations in Britain, see Dorfman, *Wage Politics in Britain*; idem, *Government Versus Trade Unionism in British Politics Since 1968* (London and Stanford: Macmillan and Hoover Institution Press, 1979); idem, *British Trade Unionism Against the Trades Union Congress* (London and Stanford: Macmillan and Hoover Institution Press, 1983).

13. Dorfman, *Government Versus Trade Unionism*, chaps. 2 and 3.

14. Ibid., chaps. 3 and 4.

15. Dorfman, *British Trade Unionism*.

16. The main document that expressed the change in Conservative Party policy views was Conservative Party, *The Industrial Charter* (London: Conservative and Unionist Central Office, 1947).

Suggested Readings

Almond, Gabriel, and Verba, Sidney, eds. *The Civic Culture Revisited*. Boston: Little, Brown, 1980.

Bagehot, Walter. *The English Constitution*. 2d ed. Garden City, N.Y.: Doubleday, 1961.

Beer, Samuel H. *Britain Against Itself*. London: Faber & Faber, 1982.

Beer, Samuel H. *Modern British Politics*. London: Faber & Faber, 1969.

Butler, David, *Governing Without a Majority*. London: Collins, 1983.

Butler, David, and Stokes, Donald. *Political Change in Britain*. New York: Macmillan, 1975.

Cyr, Arthur. *British Foreign Policy and the Atlantic Area*. New York: Macmillan, 1979.

Dorfman, Gerald A. *British Trade Unionism Against the Trades Union Congress*. London and Stanford, Calif.: Macmillan and Hoover Institution Press, 1983.

————. *Government Versus Trade Unionism in British Politics Since 1968*. London and Stanford, Calif.: Macmillan and Hoover Institution Press, 1979.

Finer, Samuel. *Adversary Politics and Electoral Reform*. London: Anthony Wigram, 1975.

————. *The Changing British Party System*. Washington, D.C.: American Enterprise Institute, 1980.

Kavanagh, Dennis. *The Politics of the Labour Party*. London: Allen & Unwin, 1982.

McKenzie, R. T. *British Political Parties*. New York: Praeger, 1966.

Norton, Philip. *The House of Commons in Transition*. Oxford: Martin Robertson, 1981.

Punnett, R. M. *British Government and Politics*. London: Heineman, 1980.

Rose, Richard. *Politics in England*. Boston: Little, Brown, 1980.

————. *The Problem of Party Government*. New York: Free Press, 1974.

Walkland, S. A. *The House of Commons in Transition*. Oxford, Eng.: Oxford University Press, 1979.

Wallace, William. *The Foreign Policy Process in Britain*. London: Royal Institute of Foreign Affairs, 1977.

3

France

Vincent E. McHale

France is not only the largest country in Western Europe geographically but also one of the oldest European nation-states. Currently, its 54 million inhabitants are spread across 211,208 square miles of territory, representing an area approximately four-fifths the size of Texas. Metropolitan France also includes the Mediterranean island of Corsica. France has among the lowest population densities of the countries in the European Community (EC). Although no longer a colonial power with extensive worldwide holdings, France continues to exercise jurisdiction over five overseas departments: Guadeloupe and Martinique in the West Indies, Reunion in the Indian Ocean, French Guiana in South America, and the islands of St. Pierre and Miquelon off the coast of Newfoundland, Canada. Four additional areas are classified as overseas territories: New Caledonia, French Polynesia, the islands of Wallis and Futuna in the South Pacific, and the island of Mayotte off the coast of Africa. Both the overseas departments and territories have representation in the French Parliament as well as locally elected assemblies.

Domestic Context of Politics

French economic development in the post-1945 period has been impressive at the national level but uneven spatially and still hampered by various structural weaknesses. France has managed to shed some of the characteristics of the stalled society, a pejorative term that was widely used in the 1950s and

1960s. Throughout the 1960s and 1970s, the gross national product (GNP) rose an average of 7 percent annually. In the decade of the 1970s, industrial production increased by 33 percent. Only Japan surpassed France in economic growth during this period. The cumulative result has made France one of the world's most affluent nations and the world's fifth industrial power behind the United States, the Soviet Union, Japan, and West Germany. France has entered the 1980s as a fully diversified modern industrial economy although it remains one of Western Europe's leading agricultural producers, with about 9 percent of the total active population still engaged in agriculture (compared with 15 percent in 1968).

Foreign trade is an important part of the French economy. Energy requirements consume about 3.4 percent of the world oil supply, although imports of crude oil have fallen in the 1980s as alternate sources such as nuclear fuels have been exploited. France currently ranks as the world's fifth-largest exporting nation. Its principal trading partner has been West Germany, followed by the other members of the EC. The United States accounts for approximately 8 percent of France's imports and about 5 percent of exports.

French development has been uneven over time and space. Population growth has been erratic, with periodic swings in the birthrate traceable, in part, to France's involvement in the two world wars. Throughout the 1970s, the trend had been upward, making France the sixteenth most populous nation in the world. Two consequences have emerged from recent demographic trends. First, despite recent increases, France has had to rely on foreign labor to offset work force shortages in various branches of the economy. This condition has led to political conflict over immigration policy, problems of racial assimilation, rising xenophobia, and occasional violence. Second, a moderate rise in the birthrate has resulted in a significant expansion of the youth component of the population (under twenty years). This trend stands in sharp contrast to the other industrialized nations, many of which are now faced with the prospect of aging populations due to declining birthrates. Although this situation allows for demographic revitalization, it also has the potential for political conflict as the government is forced to respond to the policy needs of contrasting demographic cohorts. Part of the current unemployment problem in France is due to the approximately 700,000 young people who annually enter the job market for the first time.

Demographic projections for the 1990s call for a marked decline in population growth, dropping from 0.8 to below 0.4 percent in the next decade. The Mitterrand government has proposed a new family assistance program containing incentives designed to encourage families to have more than two children.

Urbanization and individual mobility have also led to certain structural imbalances across the surface of France, by drastically altering the distribution of the active population and thereby creating geographical inequities in wealth and social access. Development continues to be centered northeast of an imaginary line connecting Le Havre to Marseilles, while those regions southwest of this line have had little relief from low growth and population decline despite long-standing government efforts to rectify this historical imbalance. The problems of the underdeveloped areas of France—in particular the difficulty in reaching a common agricultural policy that would shield these regions and their products from European competition—have weighed heavily on French policy in the EC.

Since the 1950s, the urban population in France has increased about 25 percent. Approximately 13 percent of the population now lives in or around an urban area (50,000 or more inhabitants). One individual in five currently resides outside the region of his or her birth. Sharp imbalances exist at the upper and lower levels of the French urban structure. The growth of the Paris region has been phenomenal and difficult to control. With a mere 2 percent of the space, the Paris region contains one-fifth of the total population and accounts for three-fourth's of France's industrial production. It is an administrative, cultural, educational, and scientific center. The attraction of Paris as a world city and symbol of French grandeur has placed additional resource demands on the government, resulting in equity problems between the special needs of the capital and the more general needs of the rest of the country. Paris represents an important political base, and the office of the mayor of Paris may prove to be one of the most important stepping-stones for future presidential aspirants.

At the lowest level, many of France's small rural communes have remained intact and continue to serve as bastions of traditional values in the midst of modernizing change. Of the 36,395 total French communes, 87 percent have less than 1,500 inhabitants, and almost half of this number populations of 300 or below. Only 1 percent (229) of the communes had populations of 30,000 or more. Fourteen urban areas have exceeded the 300,000 level and two cities, Lyons and Marseilles, are close to the 1 million mark, but they have had little influence as poles of attraction in offsetting the pull of Paris. In this regard, France is fundamentally different from West Germany, Italy, or the United Kingdom, where regional urban-industrial centers have frustrated the emergence of an unbalanced macrocephalic structure.

The French economy is still burdened by certain historical weaknesses that have been extremely difficult to eliminate or circumvent. Although a pioneer in noncompulsory capitalist planning, France still exhibits characteristics of an overadministered society, dominated by an overcentralized elitist state bureaucracy, that has proven to be quite resistant to reform. Innovation is stymied, and capital funds for new business ventures have been scarce. Periodic political crises, real or perceived, have reduced business confidence and have led to capital flows outside of the country. This situation has forced the French government to play a greater role in business and industrial enterprises through policies of state capitalism. At present, the state-owned sector accounts for about 30 percent of France's industrial output.

Finally, when compared with the other industrialized nations, France still possesses a sizeable traditional independent middle class of retail merchants and artisans who have been opposed to certain aspects of economic modernization (for example, the opening of supermarkets). These groups continue to figure in the calculus of political power even though they have exhibited little in the way of stable political attachments. Through periodic electoral mobilization and occasional direct action, they have forced the political authorities to pay greater heed to their interests and fears.

The processes of development have created an ambiguous coexistence of modernity and tradition in French society. Because of this, the consequences of development have not been accompanied by an expanding political and social consensus over basic values and institutions but instead have led occasionally to situations of conflict that have challenged, and continue to challenge, the stability and functioning of the French polity.

History and Culture

The absence of political and social consensus has been reflected in the contours of French history. France is a country of strong political traditions that often interact with realities of the present to mold contemporary outlooks on society and politics. Culturally, France can be considered a homogenous entity although much has been written concerning the two-France image—traditional versus modern France. Superimposed on this image have been distinct and meaningful variations in religious outlook in the form of clericalism versus secularism. This two-dimensional cultural framework has been used to provide an explanation of the bases of mass political organization and patterns of electoral outcomes over the course of the twentieth century.

The effects of these cultural variations on the geography of politics in France have waned in importance in recent years, as migration and occupational mobility have eroded traditional political ties. The growth of television has nationalized politics by reducing the power of the regional press and has forced parties to construct broad-based programs. Nonetheless, distinct regional patterns of a cultural variety continue to be manifest in French mass politics. In the 1981 presidential elections, Valery Giscard d'Estaing, the incumbent conservative candidate, received strong support in the Catholic areas of Alsace and Brittany (eastern and western France respectively), while the socialist challenger, François Mitterrand, did best in the traditionally anticlerical areas of central, northern, and southern France. Electoral maps continue to display a strong correspondence between regional divisions and political traditions.

A fundamental element in the French political tradition that continues to exhibit relevance has been the uncertainty, controversy, and persistent debate over the nature of political legitimacy as it relates to the institutional structure of the regime. In the past two hundred years, France has experienced two monarchies (pre-1792, 1814), two empires (1804, 1852), five republics (1792, 1848, 1875, 1946, and 1958), and the anomalous Vichy regime (1940–1944). Since the Revolution, France has been governed by fifteen constitutions. Although the current Fifth Republic has at last outlived its predecessor, the Fourth Republic (1946–1958), it still has a long way to go to match the 65-year life span of the Third Republic (1875–1940), which itself was brought into being by a slim majority of supporters.

Although no single system of institutional arrangements has enjoyed a level of legitimacy equal to that accorded to the British system, the evidence points to a growing acceptance of the major governmental outlines of the Fifth Republic on the part of the French public. The current regime, once thought to be little more than the personalist creation of its founder, General Charles de Gaulle, has not only survived his withdrawal from politics and eventual demise but also passed through a series of institutional tests and now appears secure in the absence of any major domestic or international crises. However, the loss of a presidential majority in the National Assembly, which occurred in 1986, may well be the toughest test of all.

Prior to his election as president, Mitterrand had been an outspoken critic of many institutional aspects of the Fifth Republic, in particular the strong presidency and the single-member district electoral system, which penalized the left. He returned France to a system of proportional representation and multimember districts in 1986—moves that would greatly increase the number of parties in the National Assembly and make presidential majorities more difficult to construct and maintain. Proportional representation appeared to work against the Socialists in 1986, and the new conservative majority has promised a return to the single-member system.

Government Structure

President

The principal governing structures of the Fifth Republic consist of the president of the Republic, the Parliament, the Constitutional Council, and the Economic and Social Council. The president is the most important and stands as an arbiter above the other governing institutions. The president, who is elected for a seven-year term by universal suffrage under a two-ballot system, is charged with the responsibility of ensuring the regular functioning of the machinery of government and the continuity of the French state. This provision gives the president broad discretionary powers, both specified and unspecified. These include appointing the prime minister and cabinet and presiding over them as well; appointing other senior government officials and military officers and dismissing them, as necessary, after consultation with the prime minister; and dissolving the National Assembly (lower house) after consultation with the prime minister and presidents of both houses of Parliament. The constitution also grants to the president broad emergency powers (Article 16) should circumstances warrant such action (as in 1961 following the military revolt in Algeria), although these do not include dissolving the assembly once such powers are invoked. Various interpretations of the constitution over the course of the Fifth Republic have resulted in a strengthening of the prerogatives of the executive and a diminution of the scope of parliamentary authority.

There have been four elected presidents since the establishment of the Fifth Republic: Charles de Gaulle (1959–1969), Georges Pompidou (1969–1974), Valery Giscard d'Estaing (1974–1981), and François Mitterrand, who assumed office in May 1981. Alain Poher, president of the Senate, served as interim president in 1969 and 1974 following de Gaulle's resignation and Pompidou's death respectively.

Mitterrand's victory as the first popularly elected socialist president was a watershed in French history. With the additional victory of the Socialists in the subsequent legislative elections, the French left was firmly in power with all of the institutions of the Fifth Republic at its disposal. Mitterrand, a writer and Resistance hero, is a seasoned politician who had held several ministerial offices in the Fourth Republic. He had demonstrated his political mettle by opposing de Gaulle in the 1965 presidential elections and forcing the general into a humiliating runoff campaign. He secured 44.8 percent of the second ballot vote. Later, he was instrumental in rebuilding the Socialist party as a broadbased formation of the noncommunist left and was elected its first leader. Finally, he narrowly lost (49.2 percent) the presidency to Giscard d'Estaing in 1974.

Mitterrand's victory in 1981 was based upon growing weariness of conservative rule and Giscard's lofty monarchical style, serious problems in the economy, and embarrassing scandals involving Giscard and his family over the receipt of jewels from the former emperor of the Central African Republic, Jean Bokassa. Of major importance was the disciplined support of the French Communist Party, which when coupled with Gaullist defections, gave Mitterrand his 1.3 million vote margin on the second ballot. Polls indicated that Mitterrand's electorate was predominantly made up of males, those in the 25 to 40 age cohort, and middle-income wage earners with incomes ranging between the equivalent of one and two thousand dollars per month.

Parliament

The French Parliament is a bicameral structure consisting of a directly elected National Assembly and the indirectly elected Senate. The National Assembly is composed of 577 (491 prior to 1986) deputies who serve five-year terms unless interrupted by dissolution. Seventeen deputies represent the overseas departments and territories. France has operated under nine different legislative electoral systems over the past hundred years. Prior to 1986, the system was based upon single-member constituencies with two ballots. Proportional representation and multimember districts were introduced in 1986. Unlike the Fourth Republic, which was characterized by a high level of cabinet instability and ministerial rotation in office, deputies who accept positions in government must resign their legislative seats in favor of alternates who will serve out the remainder of their terms.

The initial alignment of political forces in the 1981 assembly gave Mitterrand a healthy presidential majority of 333 votes, which was large enough to withstand any threatened defection by Communist Party deputies. The parties in the 1981 government coalition were the Socialist Party (269), French Communist Party (44), Movement of Left Radicals (14), and six others. The opposition was dominated by the Gaullist Rally for the Republic (88), the Giscardian-centrist Union for French Democracy (63), and seven others. Pierre Mauroy served as premier between 1981 and 1984. He was followed by Laurent Fabius, who served between 1984 and 1986.

Following the 1986 legislative elections, the partisan breakdown of parliamentary seats was as follows: Socialist Party (215), Rally for the Republic (150), Union for French Democracy (127), French Communist Party (35), National Front (33), independents (14), and three others. In March 1986, Mitterrand offered the premiership to Jacques Chirac, who appointed a new rightist government.

The Senate membership was raised to 316 in 1983. Senators are elected indirectly by departmental or territorial electoral colleges composed of an assortment of local government officials. Senators serve nine-year terms with one-third of the membership being renewed every three years. The president of the Senate serves as interim president of the republic (until elections can be held) whenever this office becomes vacant. The Senate can exercise a veto over any legislation passed by the assembly, but may be overridden by a second favorable vote, should the government choose to support the measure. Because of its periodic intransigence in opposing various government policies, the Senate has been the subject of various proposed reforms that would either eliminate its legislative role or allow it to be more reflective of the political coloration of the assembly.

The power of the French Parliament has been carefully circumscribed under the constitution of the Fifth Republic and excludes the virtual totality of domestic policy concerns. The assembly has only limited control over its agenda. It must give priority to government proposals. In addition, its legislative scope of authority is restricted to certain specified areas. Unspecified areas remain the prerogative of the executive. Ordinarily, the assembly meets in two annual sessions lasting a total of 170 days.

Constitutional Council

The Constitutional Council is a nine-member judicial body charged with the responsibility of constitutional review. Its members serve nine-year nonrenewable terms. One-third of the membership is renewed every three years. Three members are appointed by the president of the republic and three apiece by the presidents of both houses of Parliament. Former presidents serve as lifetime members on the council. Its principal responsibilities are to examine the constitutionality of proposed legislation and treaties and to ensure fairness and equity in various electoral procedures.

Unlike similar institutions in the Anglo-American tradition, it cannot be accessed by individuals as an appeals court. Since the early 1970s, it has widened its role in general, especially in the matter of individual liberties. In 1983, Mitterrand appointed Daniel Mayer as the first Socialist to serve on this body since the founding of the Fifth Republic.

Economic and Social Council

The Economic and Social Council is a quasi-corporative body composed of various representatives of labor, business, and agricultural organizations. It functions as a consultative lobby ostensibly to advise the government in various legislative areas affecting the interests of its members.

Subnational Government

France is administered internally through a three-tiered system of 24 regions (22 for metropolitan France), 96 departments, and over 36,000 communes. One of the chief functions of local government in France is to serve as a conduit for the administration of various programs and policies dealing with public finance and national development planning. Under the terms of decentralization legislation that was promulgated in 1982, the formerly state appointed department prefects have lost most of their executive power. They have been replaced by directly elected local councils. Prefects have been redesignated as commissioners of the republic whose primary responsibility is the maintenance of public order.

Intergovernmental relations in France form a pattern of intricate ties and mutual interdependence, both vertically between levels and horizontally among locally elected officials and Paris-controlled career civil servants. Many locally elected officials also hold seats in the National Assembly. The complex process of decentralization remains a controversial issue in French politics.

The French Party System

The French party system gives life to the otherwise inanimate structures of government and society. Parties are a reflection of the organized political needs of their respective societies and, as such, it is reasonable to assume that in their origins, organizational makeup, and functional patterns, political parties will be conditioned by the cultural and socioeconomic setting in which they are embedded.

In France, as well as other European democracies, the nature and depth of various societal cleavages has exerted a dominant influence on the evolution and shaping of the party system. This has caused immense problems for the political system, especially in the difficulties that have arisen in adjusting a fragmented political culture to the needs of a stable political order. Although French parties have not been wholly identified with every societal cleavage, they have been highly related to them, especially in the spheres of religious differences and other ideological quarrels that have deeply divided the French since the Revolution.

Historically, French political parties have been more attuned to ideology than to the practical aspects of programmatic action. This is largely the result of circumstances surrounding party development in France, wherein most parties trace their origins to certain past ideological battles involving the nature of the regime, the role of the Catholic church, or the desirability of socialism in France. Being ideologically constrained and reflecting somewhat the varied cleavages and fissures in the political culture, the functional impact of French parties in the political system has been more one of interest representation and divisiveness rather than the broad aggregation of interests into workable policy packages.

Immobility at the electoral level has often overburdened the legislative system, where deputies, freed from the constraints of their narrow constituencies, were forced to fashion a multitude of unaggregated demands into coherent national policy. This situation contributed significantly to the stress and institutional instability that has historically characterized the French political system. Under the Fifth Republic it has been relieved in part through the development of a strong presidency and various pressures toward party regroupment.

The social turmoil growing out of the processes of developmental change in

France has often aligned one sector of the society against the other. However, it has been difficult to identify socioprofessional or class categories with the party system except in a most general way. Other societal cleavages, such as religious solidarity, have been found to blunt class appeals.

Although partisan divisions in France have not been completely congruent with divisions in the social structure, the results of survey research have demonstrated at least a tendency on the part of certain social groups to support different parties. As one moves across the French party spectrum from the Communists to the center, the proportion of working class support steadily declines, while the proportion of support by farmers, business classes, and retired persons increases. Certain middle-income elements, such as government employees, have indicated a tendency to support the noncommunist left, while the upper echelons of management in the private sector still gravitate toward the parties of the right. With few exceptions, these tendencies have remained quite stable over time.

Other socioeconomic classes have been internally divided in their political loyalties. For example, the partisan preferences of white-collar groups and the new technocratic professional classes reveal little significant variation among the parties; thus it is difficult to assess the probable impact upon the French party system as the proportion of white-collar groups continues to increase in post-industrial France. The increasing bipolarization of French political life that emerged in the late 1960s appeared to be less a clash of traditional socioeconomic interests and more a new source of tension over the continuation of conservative rule and the various implications of a growing interdependent technological order.

Post-Gaullist France continues to be characterized by a proliferation of parties representing perhaps the most complete ideological spectrum of any European polity. Most parties are very small, with narrow ideological appeals and practically no mass base. Only four major partisan formations or presidential coalitions have substantial (over 70 percent) electoral support and thus can be considered major contenders for political power. From left to right, they are the French Communist Party; the Socialist Party; the Union for French Democracy, a coalition of the center-right; and the main body of the Gaullist movement, currently known as the Rally for the Republic.

French Communist Party

The French Communist Party (PCF) has traditionally had the largest and most stable membership of all French political groups (about 650,000). The party traces its origins to a split in the socialist movement in 1920. Since its founding, the party has experienced a number of twists and turns in policy and strategy, coupled with various ideological fissures and defections. After a brief period of cooperation with other left groups in the early post-1945 period, they were excluded from the government from 1947 to 1981. The party has also alternated between moods of cooperation and intransigence with the Socialists and has often been accused of frustrating the development of a united majoritarian left in France.

Since the mid-1960s, the party has mellowed in its ideological stance and now accepts a democratic path to socialism in France, including alternation in power and the existence of opposition. The party has also given tacit acceptance to the major institutions of the EC. French Communists have occasionally demonstrated their independence from the Soviet Union, but on the major current issues, such as Afghanistan and Poland, they have supported Soviet policy. They have been less enthusiastic about the development of Eurocommunism than either their Italian or Spanish counterparts.

The French Communist Party is a highly disciplined group. They are well organized across France at the local level (particularly in the Paris suburbs), where they hold many mayoral offices and dominate local councils. Their decision to support Mitterrand on the second ballot in 1981 contributed to his presidential victory. As a gesture of unity, they were given four cabinet posts in the new Socialist government: transport, health, professional training, and civil service and administrative reform.

Policy divisions between the Communists and Socialists, which have been manifest on several occasions, have not been severe enough to rupture their participation in the governing coalition. Participation in the Mitterrand government had forced the Communists to accept some degree of responsibility for his government policies. They withdrew in 1984, creating a political dilemma for themselves in that contributing to Mitterrand's success served to raise the prestige and competence of the Socialist Party, whereas withdrawal from the government could have adverse effects on the Communist Party by forcing it back into political isolation.

The electoral fortunes of the party have varied over the course of the Fifth Republic. Mass support for the party's candidate, Georges Marchais, in the 1981 presidential elections was a little over 12 percent of the total first ballot vote. This is a significant drop from the 21 percent received by party candidate Jacques Duclos in 1969; in fact, it was the lowest vote the party had obtained since 1945. One factor contributing to Marchais's poor showing were serious allegations concerning his wartime activities and failure to take part in Resistance activities. Marchais, who joined the party in 1947, is the current secretary. The party's electoral support dropped to 9.8 percent of the vote in 1986.

Socialist Party

The Socialist Party (PS) is the oldest political party of the four major contenders, having been founded in 1879. The party has been characterized by numerous ideological fissures and disputes resulting in fragmentation and leading to the formation of splinter groups on both its right and left. The main body of the Socialists adopted a reformist stance after the 1890s, a position that led to additional breakaways by various groups that sought to maintain a revolutionary tradition. The party supported several governments in the 1920s and finally came to power in 1936 under the leadership of Leon Blum in the Popular Front.

The Socialists played a key role in the politics of the Fourth Republic by participating in and organizing many governments. They entered a period of decline in the late 1950s and were eventually swept into ineffectual opposition under the Fifth Republic. Attempts to fashion a united left in the mid-1960s started a chain of events that culminated in a new party in 1971 with new leadership under François Mitterrand. Efforts have been made to recruit new members from among the emerging middle sectors. Total membership hovers around 210,000.

Similar to the other social democratic parties in Europe, the Socialists have had difficulty in reconciling socialist ideology with the pragmatic policies of governing, a dilemma that has become more acute with their new role as a presidential party. In addition, cooperation with the Communists and other left-wing allies, such as the Unified Socialist Party (PSU), has tended to pull the Socialists leftward ideologically. The party supports nationalizations, worker self-management, planning, and increased outlays for social welfare. Although the party remains pro-Western and pro-European, it seeks an equal partnership with the United States and intends to pursue policies leading to what has been defined as a socialist Europe of workers, free of multinational capital and independent of east and west.

The political future of the Socialists depends on the ability of the leadership to maintain internal unity and to conclude supportive alliances with other moderate left-wing groups to offset communist domination. The party must also be able to retain the confidence of the French public in its ability to manage the complex interdependencies of government and society. Despite their loss of a parliamentary majority in 1986, the Socialists have maintained a respectable standing in the polls. They captured 32.8 percent of the vote in 1986.

Union for French Democracy

The Union for French Democracy (UDF) was founded in 1978 out of a diverse collection of center–right groups pledged to the support of Giscard d'Estaing's presidency. The principal constituent parties are the Republican Party (PR), the Center of Social Democrats (CDS), the Radical Party, and the Social Democratic Party. The UDF has had considerable difficulty maintaining cohesion because of the strong personal and organizational identities of the adhering groups. During the Giscard presidency, these parties were forced to rely heavily on Gaullist parliamentary support. Both groups were united in the Union for the New Majority for the 1981 assembly elections.

The core element in the UDF has been Giscard's Republican Party, which was founded in 1971. The PR traces its origins to a number of loosely organized elements known as the Moderates in the Fourth Republic. Under the Fifth Republic, this political orientation was manifested in the National Center of Independents and Peasants under the leadership of Giscard. Although pro-Gaullist on many issues, they remained a separate entity. They openly broke with the Gaullists in 1969 and passed through several name changes until 1971.

The PR espouses a type of French liberalism based on conservative economic and fiscal policies. They have been pro-European but somewhat distant from the United States. Giscard hesitated in condemning Soviet action in Afghanistan, disregarded the Olympic boycott, and has advocated an expansion of trade with the Soviet Union.

Programmatically, the UDF aspires to develop a centrist alternative to governance in France, free of Gaullist domination. Their poor electoral performance, however, coupled with a weak grass-roots organization, makes some cooperation with the Gaullists inevitable if they are to achieve majoritarian status. Debate in the coalition has focused on whether centrism should move to the left or right.

Steps were taken in 1983 to develop a new seven-point charter (the fourth since 1981) as the basis of cooperation with the Gaullists in any future action. Although most of the provisions were overly general, point six was novel in that it called for an end to state monopoly over television and radio broadcasting in France. The real issue revolves around who will become the acknowledged leader of the opposition under Mitterrand and who is best placed to challenge Mitterrand in 1988. Giscard, now serving as a departmental councilor, has attempted to reassert his role as leader of the anti-Mitterrand forces, but he faces strong challenges from Gaullist Jacques Chirac and his former premier Raymond Barre.

Gaullist Movement

The Gaullist movement, currently known as the Rally for the Republic (RPR), was founded in 1947 by Charles de Gaulle as the Rally of the French People (RPF) in the hope of reforming political life in the Fourth Republic. After some initial success, the movement eventually declined and became dormant as de Gaulle withdrew from active political life. A skeletal organization remained and was revived in 1958 as the Union for the New Republic (UNR). The Gaullists have since passed through a series of reorganizations and name changes, although the leadership, mass base, and ideology have remained remarkably constant.

The Gaullists dominated political life in France between 1958 and 1974. For the first time in French history, they were able to achieve an absolute majority based on a single party in the National Assembly (1968–1973) and held the presidency for sixteen years. They have survived both the death of their leader and the loss of the presidency, by remaining the largest party in the assembly until 1978. Presently, they are the second largest party and had been the chief opposition group prior to 1986.

The Gaullists have been successful in transforming their movement into an effective mass organization of more than a half million adherents. The party is strong at the grass-roots level. Their current leader, Jacques Chirac, is the mayor of Paris and by the mid-1980s had already been touted as a definite presidential candidate for 1988. He received 18 percent of the first ballot vote in 1981. Chirac became premier in 1986 as head of a new conservative coalition.

Like most French parties, the Gaullists have had to struggle to maintain internal unity against dissident tendencies. The most important division has been between the conservative and left-wing Gaullists, a division that extends back to the early postwar period. The left-wing Gaullists have been strongly committed to social and economic reform in contrast to the more conservative policies of the orthodox group. In recent elections, some of these elements have cooperated with groups on the left.

Recent struggles for leadership within the party have focused on the relationship with Giscard, whose Gaullist authenticity is doubted, and on which Gaullist personality is in the best position to defeat Mitterrand. The principal personalities in the RPR have been Chirac; Marie-France Garaud, former advisor to Georges Pompidou; Michel Debre, an old-line Gaullist who is regarded as the chief constitutional architect of the Fifth Republic; and Raymond Barre, former premier under Giscard between 1976 and 1981. Barre is considered a leading rightist candidate for the presidency in 1988.

Gaullist doctrine has stressed the principles articulated by the late President de Gaulle, namely, national independence, defense of the institutions of the Fifth Republic, and increased citizen participation. The new Chirac government has focused on economic recovery and denationalization as its primary policy goals.

Minor Parties

A number of minor parties dot the French political landscape and provide a type of ideological and electoral diversity unlike that of any other European polity. On the extreme left, one still finds anarchist, Trotskyite, and Maoist political formations active in France. Some have advocated revolutionary violence to achieve their ends. Most have not been electorally oriented. The principal organizations are the International Communist Party (PCI) and the Worker's Struggle (LO).

The French right has also produced a number of parties ranging from monarchists to emergent neofascist elements. The monarchists perpetuate an old tradition in advocating the restoration of a progressive monarchy in France under the count of Paris. Neofascism is a recent phenomenon, although it has deep roots reaching back to the Third Republic. The National Front (FN) led by Jean-Marie Le Pen secured 33 seats in 1986 and is now a formal parliamentary grouping. Many of these groups have attempted to build transnational links as part of a Euro-right movement. Some organizations, such as the Federation of National and European Action (FANE), have been banned by the government for engaging in violent action. Membership in neofascist organizations has been estimated at 25,000.

In recent years, France has also witnessed the emergence of various regional autonomist parties, some of which have advocated and conducted violent antigovernment action. The majority of these groups have been located in Brittany and Corsica, although other movements have emerged in southern France (the Occitan Movement, for example). In contrast to other European polities, no autonomist party has been able to secure national-level representation in France.

Between the extremes lie a number of moderate parties, special interest groupings, and political clubs. The environmentalist movement is growing in France and operates under an organization known as the Ecology Political Movement (MEP), which was formed in 1981. Brice Lalonde, their presidential candidate, captured almost 4 percent of the total first-ballot vote in 1981. The environmentalists, however, have made little progress toward unifying their diverse lines of support.

The impact of presidential politics has had two important effects on the French party system. First, it has created the need for personalized electoral machines and assembly majorities that extend beyond the bounds of a single party. Second, it has weakened the role of parties in the policymaking process. Traditional party elites now find their power ebbing, overshadowed by a new breed of presidential advisors. Proposals have been made in recent years to provide government financial aid to the political parties based upon their electoral and assembly strength. These proposals have evoked strong protest by the smaller parties, who fear they would not enjoy the benefits of such legislation.

Contemporary Political Issues

The major political problems now facing France are a direct outgrowth of economic issues that have resulted from France's adjustment to an increasingly interdependent world. Although political issues abound, three overlapping policy problems have become matters of general concern. In order of importance, they are economic performance, immigration policy, and politically motivated violence by extremist groups in metropolitan and overseas France.

Economic Performance

After 23 years of unbroken conservative rule, the Socialists were swept into power on a wave of hope and expectation in 1981. Despite years of growth and progress, economic problems began to mount amid increasing domestic and international tensions. During the latter part of the 1970s, Europe and the United States were first affected by the shock of rising world oil prices and then plunged into economic recession. Sluggish growth contributed to widespread unemployment, a sharp decline in industrial output, and higher levels of social stress. Meanwhile, the inflationary spiral continued.

Mitterrand's success in 1981 was due in large part to voter perceptions that the policies of the Giscard government were failing. Giscard and Barre had attempted to govern France through a variety of centrist policies, and ironically, in the aggregate, they were beginning to achieve a measure of success toward the end of his term. Their principal economic goals were to stabilize the franc, reduce inflation, and ease the balance-of-payments problem. Attempts were also made to reduce French dependence on imported fuels by pursuing a controversial expansion of nuclear energy, making France Europe's largest manufacturer of nuclear energy. Nine percent of France's energy needs are now supplied by nuclear power. Giscard and Barre also sought to refashion French industry around new high-technology fields and discontinued government subsidies for noncompetitive industries in decline.

By 1980, the French growth rate of 1.8 percent was still above the EC average of 1.3 percent. However, in the eyes of the electorate, Giscard's policies were seen in a negative fashion. Inflation continued to remain high, eventually reaching 14 percent. Even though a policy of indexing kept wages and prices in tandem with the inflation rate, it merely fed the spiral going higher rather than starving it. Giscard's industrial policies, although designed to make France more competitive in world markets, resulted in a sharp climb in the unemployment rate as various depressed industries and coal mines were closed. In 1982, the unemployment rate hovered at about 8 percent of the work force reaching a post-1945 high. The political significance of this situation is apparent in the figures. There were almost 2 million unemployed compared with only 400,000 during the troubled days of May 1968.

Throughout his presidential campaign, Mitterrand vowed he would solve France's economic woes through socialist policies. The challenge, however, was to pursue economic and monetary policies that would not only work domestically but also inspire confidence abroad, making France attractive for new investment ventures that would stimulate growth.

Mitterrand's first attack on economic problems followed long-standing socialist dogma. In 1982, he completed the nationalization of the banking industry (36 banks and two financial holding companies) and brought several other industrial sectors under government control. This raised the state-controlled share of the economy from 12 to 17 percent. The minimum wage was increased. New taxes on higher income brackets were imposed to finance the costs for increased social welfare benefits and allowances. Mitterrand's goal was to stimulate the French economy through increased consumption and investment.

The expected economic improvements failed to materialize, and by 1983, the policy of stimulating the economy had been reversed. New austerity policies were announced; they included a reduction in the budget deficit, wage and price controls, and efforts to reduce excessive government bureaucracy. This reversal brought charges from the opposition on both the left and right. The former accused Mitterrand of deserting the workers and reneging on his promises; the latter charged the government with incompetence and indecisiveness, pointing out that socialism would never work in France.

Although Mitterrand has yet to face any domestic or international crisis that would challenge his leadership skills, his government was shaken by French involvement in the sinking of the *Rainbow Warrior* in Auckland, New Zealand. The ship belonged to Greenpeace, an international group protesting French nuclear testing.

Economic difficulties have continued to mount. Mitterrand has had not only to fend off strong attacks from the opposition but also to endure popular frustration in the streets of Paris, as various elements vented their anger over government policies. The franc is still weak, despite devaluations and heavy borrowing in the Euromarket. Industrial modernization will continue to lead to more worker dismissals, although the Socialists have promised to cushion the adverse effects of unemployment. The growth in GNP is expected to hover around 1.5 percent annually, and France's trade balance is likely to show a substantial deficit in the years to come.

The mood of the public prior to the 1986 elections was uncertain and gloomy. National opinion polls have registered a decline in Mitterrand's popularity, and many of the French have indicated dissatisfaction with the Socialist handling of the economy. The Socialists had lost three assembly seats in by-elections in 1982 and 1983 and did not do as well as anticipated in the 1983 municipal elections. Their decline in support continued into the 1986 elections.

The difficulty is that any real attempt at dealing with the French economy treads on powerful social and political interests. The closing of inefficient coal mines in the Socialist bases of the north has been especially difficult on party morale. Middle classes and professional sectors remain highly skeptical of Socialist policies, and in September 1982, had staged a demonstration against government policies designed to reduce the social security deficit by enforcing cost-cutting plans in health care delivery. Others nourish the fear that the Socialists will eventually limit or even eliminate long-standing economic privileges. The hope is that by the late 1980s, France will be in a more competitive situation internationally, with inflation under control, reduced deficits, and unemployment at tolerable levels.

Immigration Policy

Traditionally, France has long served as a refuge for political dissidents and a haven for immigrants. Groups of foreign minorities have existed for years and had reached a level as high as 6 percent of the total pre–World War II population. The various governments had maintained a fairly permissive attitude toward immigration through the decade of the 1960s, especially in allowing foreign workers and their families easy entry. This policy was based on the generally accepted notion that the influx of foreign workers compensated for labor shortages in the economy due to the low birthrate among the native French.

By the mid-1950s, the number of foreign immigrants increased substantially as labor demand exceeded availability. A decade later, the foreign population was growing at a rate of a quarter million annually. The bulk of the immigrants in the 1950s and 1960s came from North Africa and Italy, whereas in recent years, they have tended to come from Portugal and Spain. Hostility and bitterness toward the foreign workers was already evident in the 1960s; it has grown more acute in the 1980s in the wake of economic slowdown, rising unemployment, factory closings, and increasing social and political demands on the part of the immigrant population.

The total foreign population of France is about 4.1 million or 8 percent of the population. Of this number, about 1.7 million are classified as foreign workers. In rank order, they have come from Portugal, Algeria, Spain, and Italy. Foreign labor has tended to cluster both spatially and in certain occupational categories. These factors further complicate the problem. Almost one-third of the total foreign population is located in the Paris region, and comprises one-third of the region's inhabitants. Other major concentrations are in southern France around Marseilles. One-third of all French regions have foreign populations reaching 10 percent.

In terms of occupational categories, over one-fifth of the workers in the construction and automobile manufacturing industries are foreign, while lesser proportions make up the work force in mining, steel, petrochemicals, and tourism (hotels and restaurants). Many of the low-status positions in the service sector, such as refuse collection, are almost totally staffed by foreign labor.

The social and political costs of a large permanent work force began to manifest themselves in the early 1970s. Many immigrants lived in squalid and hazardous housing, known as hostels, and often fell victim to unscrupulous landlords and employers. Crimes, such as drug peddling, domestic violence, and other social ills seemed to correlate positively with the size of the immigrant community. They were often viewed as a serious threat to social harmony and were subject to increased police surveillance.

As racial hostility flared up, it was accompanied by a resurgence of ultra-nationalistic right-wing extremism, and the issue of immigration policy assumed greater political importance. It became even more sharply defined with demands for political rights on the part of the immigrants, many of whom were now being organized into various pressure groups. These demands were initially supported by the unions and the parties of the left, but this support waned in the wake of growing racial fears at the grass-roots level. It is a position on which the Socialists and Communists are clearly divided. The Socialists have leaned toward greater toleration and understanding, whereas the Communists, especially those in the working-class suburbs of Paris, have taken a vocal anti-immigrant stand.

In 1974, Giscard d'Estaing created a cabinet-level post, secretary of state for immigration, to deal with this explosive issue. All immigration was halted as new stringent conditions for entry were devised. At the same time, several new social programs were instituted for immigrants and their families. At the end of Giscard's term, proposals had been drafted that would have allowed greater police discretion in dealing with immigrants, including expulsion. These proposals evoked considerable debate in the assembly, and resulted in a hardening of positions vis-à-vis the immigrant issue.

The Socialists have repealed some of the more oppressive aspects of immigration policy, and have pledged to follow more liberal lines in the future. The position of the Gaullists and center-right opposition has been to halt immigration completely and to engage in a policy of voluntary repatriation modeled after France's 1980 agreement with Algeria.

The immigration issue has intruded upon other policy domains, especially in the area of economic policy. A case in point was the 1983 strike by French workers at the Peugeot Talbot automobile plant at Poissy. Consistent with the government's modernization program, Peugeot attempted to cut its 17,000 work force by 4,140 by giving early retirement to 1,235 and dismissing 2,905 workers. Many of the workers scheduled for dismissal, who were foreign without French citizenship, accused both Peugeot and the government of racist tactics. Approximately 52 percent of the plant's work force was made up of immigrants, one of the highest percentages in the auto industry. They were predominantly North Africans, Turks, Senegalese, and Spaniards. In a compromise with Peugeot, the Socialist government managed to save only 1,000 jobs, with a promise of special benefits to those dismissed. The electoral success of the National Front in 1986 suggests that this issue is likely to become more important in the next few years.

Political Violence

Politically motivated violence in France has escalated sharply in recent years and, by the beginning of the 1980s, posed a serious challenge to the government authorities. The incidence of violence had nearly tripled over the decade of the 1970s and, by 1981, had come to average more than eleven attacks per week. Incidents have ranged from political murders to bombing attacks on groups of individuals and public buildings, including an attempt on the life of President Giscard d'Estaing at Ajaccio airport in Corsica in April 1981. The problem is complicated by the diversity of the perpetrators and their underlying political goals, targets, and methods of operation. Three distinct groups of perpetrators can be identified: (1) domestic extremist groups of both the left and right, (2) transnational terrorist groups who have conducted their activities on French territory, and (3) various separatist groups in metropolitan France and their pro-independence counterparts in the overseas areas.

Both the left and right extremists in France have launched sporadic attacks against each other for years. However, in recent years, their targets have changed away from each other toward ones symbolic of their political ideology. Groups on the extreme left (for example, the Direct Action Movement and the Autonomous Group for Radical Action Against Capital) have increased their attacks on public buildings and other property (such as parking meters) as well as on symbols of bourgeois society (such as fashionble Parisian shops). Threats have also been made against judicial authorities who have handed down harsh sentences against their members. The extreme left has also been involved in various industrial disturbances, clashing frequently with police whom they have accused of harboring right-wing sympathies. On occasion, they have been able to enlist the support of students and young workers in their demonstrations.

The extreme right in France has directed many of its actions against the Jewish community. One of the most spectacular incidents was the attack on the Rue Copernic synagogue in Paris in October 1980 in which four people were killed and more than twenty injured. Although it is believed that this attack was committed by elements linked to the Palestine Liberation Organization (PLO), public reaction to the bombing resulted in a massive demonstration of nearly a quarter million people in Paris and a brief nationwide strike to condemn this action. The extreme right has received renewed vigor and inspiration from the writings of the Study Group for European Civilization (GRECE), which has used sociobiology to reject equality, materialism, and the Judeo-Christian culture while stressing the inescapable influence of heredity and the superiority of the Indo-European civilization. However, GRECE has disavowed any connection with right-wing extremism or the rising incidents of antisemitic violence in France.

Many of the violent groups in France have been found to have transnational links to similar groups in other societies. France has also been the site of transnational violence by groups based outside of the country. Extremist Muslim Shiite elements have threatened action in France for its peacekeeping role in Lebanon, and other terrorists have engaged in violent action demanding a separate homeland for Armenia. Both Spanish rightists and Basque separatists have been active in France and have been suspected by the police of various shootings and political murders.

In recent years, various separatist and autonomist groups in Brittany and Corsica have employed violence to intensify their campaigns against what they refer to as internal colonialism in France. In each case, the groups have advocated greater internal autonomy for their respective regions, as well as an increased allocation of resources for social and economic development. Both groups have tended to confine their activities to their respective regions. In 1980 and 1981, several major trials were held involving Breton and Corsican separatists.

Proindependence activity has also intensified in several of the French overseas areas and has occasionally resulted in violent action. The root cause seems to be economic. Many of the overseas areas have chafed under French rule and have raised the issue of equity in economic policy. High unemployment, low wages and living standards, emigration to metropolitan France, and control over the economy by white Europeans have figured prominently in their list of grievances.

New decentralization policies promulgated by the Mitterrand government are expected to result in greater self-rule for Corsica and several of the overseas areas. The government hopes that these new structural reforms will defuse militant separatist demands and end the rising tide of violence. In 1982, in recognition of the serious problem political violence poses for France, Mitterrand created the post of secretary of state for public security to coordinate government efforts at all levels. A security and liberty law that had been promulgated in 1981 granted additional powers to the police in dealing with internal security matters. Most of the bill's provisions were rescinded after Mitterrand's election. Chirac has promised a tougher stance on law and order.

Intraeuropean Political and Economic Relations

The cornerstone of French intraeuropean policy since the founding of the Fifth Republic has been a desire to build a recognizable economic and political entity that is independent of the two superpowers while at the same time preserving French autonomy of action. This policy appears to be an immutable theme in the contemporary French spirit, for it has been reaffirmed by every president from de Gaulle to Mitterrand. The origins of this posture are rooted in the experience of the Fourth Republic in meeting the postwar challenge of regional and global interdependence.

Under the Fourth Republic, French security had shifted from decision making in Paris to the North Atlantic Treaty Organization (NATO) command, a regional security arrangement under the dominant influence of a foreign, non-European power—the United States. France soon realized that membership in NATO offered no guarantee of support by the alliance for those global aspects of French policy that lay outside of the European theater, particularly in Indo-China and North Africa. Similarly, negotiations by Fourth Republic politicians leading to the Treaty of Rome in 1957 implicitly carried with them the notion of eventual supranational integration, in which the French society and economy would dissolve into a larger European community.

De Gaulle's return to power in 1958 not only coincided with the initial implementation of the Treaty of Rome but also marked the opening up of the French economy to intense world competition and penetration by the United States. The assault on what de Gaulle perceived to be the identity and national independence of France was rebuffed by a drastic reversal of French policy toward European and Atlantic affairs. The Gaullist response was to fashion a new set of policy alternatives based on the goals of national independence, resistance to American hegemony, and the restoration of French initiative and influence in the global community. In the future, France would balance its participation in the EC and Atlantic Community with increasingly independent programs and actions in the areas of defense, industrial development, trade, and monetary policy.

De Gaulle accepted the Treaty of Rome with strict interpretations and resisted all efforts at further supranational integration. The break with NATO was inevitable after 1960, once France embarked on the construction of an independent nuclear force. France withdrew from NATO's integrated command in 1966 but continued to be a member of the alliance. Cooperation with NATO was conducted on a nonofficial basis, however, and beginning with Giscard d'Estaing's presidency in 1974, France became more involved in the operational defense apparatus of the alliance. France has continued to participate in joint exercises involving NATO forces and currently has approximately 70,000 troops stationed in West Germany.

Mitterrand has rejected any full reintegration of France into the military structure of NATO but has expressed his support of the alliance in principle, in the event of an attack on Western Europe from Warsaw Pact forces. Although expressing a desire for disarmament and the reduction of tensions in Europe, the French have steadfastly insisted that matters involving France's security arrangements must remain outside the scope of any arms reduction discussions between the Soviet Union and the United States.

The issue of national independence persists as a theme in French intra-european policy, but this issue has been compromised by all of de Gaulle's successors, who have perceived French interests in different ways. Pompidou considered European policy as a means to increase French economic growth and to sustain France as an industrial competitor in European markets. To this end, Pompidou accepted British membership in the EC as a counterweight to the growing power and influence of West Germany. He also sought to achieve greater cooperation on economic matters through discussions within the institutional framework of the EC.

Giscard was conciliatory toward Britain but attached greater importance to France's relationship with West Germany. He nourished a close personal relationship with Chancellor Helmut Schmidt, which some described as a Paris-Bonn axis in the EC. Giscard tolerated moderate growth in EC institutions by committing France to the support of direct elections to the European Parliament, in spite of Gaullist objections. However, his support for Spanish membership in the EC evoked strong protests from France's agricultural groups, which lessened Giscard's popularity in the underdeveloped areas of southern France.

As the first Socialist president, Mitterrand's policies toward Europe reflect a style and outlook distinctly different from his conservative predecessors. They are based on his personal concern with the Third World as it relates to Europe, and ideological currents within the Socialist Party. Mitterrand has rejected bilateralism, an approach favored by Giscard, in favor of multilateralism based on an equal partnership among the members. It is expected that Mitterrand will use the EC to coordinate common policies toward the Third World, based on French initiatives.

The contemporary socialist image of Europe has changed significantly from the period of the Fourth Republic. The Socialists had originally been strong advocates of a united Europe. International and domestic conditions have weakened their idealism, and they now express a cautious attitude about the future course of European unity.

Several key issues are likely to guide the Mitterrand government in its policies toward the EC. The first issue concerns institutional growth. The Socialists have not raised any strong objections to expanding the competencies of the EC institutions. However, they have advocated greater democratization in community decisionmaking, coupled with higher levels of participation by workers and consumers to counter what they consider to be the preponderant influence of multinational capital. A more active European Parliament is desirable, but its powers cannot exceed those of the national parliaments under any conditions.

The second issue is enlargement of EC membership. On this issue, the Socialists have been closely tied to domestic interests, which must be protected from what they perceive to be the adverse effects of EC expansion into the Mediterranean region. The Socialists have expressed many of the reservations voiced by the agricultural lobby in France, that inclusion of Mediterranean Europe is likely to lead to an unsalable agricultural surplus, falling prices, and a further aggravation of regional disparities in the EC.

Although the European cleavage has cut across traditional party lines in France, all of the major political formations are opposed to further integrative efforts that would diminish the scope and authority of national decisionmaking. The socialist and communist perceptions of Europe have converged in recent years, and there appear to be no major areas of conflict regarding intraeuropean policy that could rupture their current partnership.

Relationships with the Third World

The evolution of contemporary French policy toward the Third World has been an outgrowth of France's pattern of relationships with its former colonies and its efforts to pursue globalist policies independent of both the other Western nations and the communist bloc. For France, the Third World represents the future, and unless a new balance in relationships can be established between the developed north and underdeveloped south, the economies of the industrialized world are likely to suffer disastrous consequences.

France's overseas empire was created during the Third Republic, and with it, the notion of eventual assimilation of the colonial peoples into the body politic of France itself. Although the growth of nationalism destroyed this notion, a feeling of kinship remained. France has worked hard to maintain good relations with its former colonies by concluding a series of bilateral agreements on aid, security, and mutual cooperation. Such agreements have provided for extensive economic and military assistance, as well as help in the maintenance of domestic order. The operation of these policies has been most clearly demonstrated in Chad.

Mitterrand has raised the priority level of French policy toward the Third World. This concern not only reflects long-standing policies of the Socialist Party but also stems directly from Mitterrand's previous experience as minister for overseas territories (1950–1951) during the Fourth Republic. Symbolic of this new emphasis were the appointments of Claude Cheysson as minister of foreign affairs and Regis Debray as Mitterrand's personal advisor for Third World problems. Cheysson's previous duties as a commissioner in the EC involved the coordination of EC policies toward the Third World. Debray, a writer and an associate of Latin American revolutionaries, has been an outspoken sympathizer of national liberation movements, especially those directed against what he perceives as U.S. imperialistic policies.

France has always taken pride in its long history of economic support for the least developed countries and is only surpassed by the United States in terms of foreign aid as a percentage of GNP. Unlike U.S. policies, French aid has never been viewed solely as a barrier to communism but has generally been argued on the practical merits of trade advantage. Over 75 percent of French public and private aid goes to countries in the franc zone, a monetary arrangement that gives France preferential trade advantages and relieves France from paying in other hard currencies (dollars, pounds, marks, and the like). Although France pays above-market prices, the zone offers a ready outlet for French industrial products, services, and investments.

Mitterrand has pledged increased aid and investment for the Third World by doubling the percentage of France's GNP devoted to foreign aid by the end of his term in 1988. One of his major proposals calls for increased public aid to the Third World amounting to approximately 0.7 percent of the GNP of each industrial country. France is expected to continue the policy of paying above-world-market prices for certain raw materials as a means of avoiding the adverse effects of price instability that have chronically affected Third World trade.

The principal goals of French policy toward the Third World as stated by Mitterrand are threefold: (1) to assist the developing countries in achieving levels of self-sufficiency in food production and energy independence commensurate with their needs, (2) to encourage a level of industrial development consistent with each country's ability to absorb new technology, and (3) to work for greater cooperation among the industrialized nations to ease the gap between rich and poor, especially in halting the growing indebtedness of Third World countries.

In contrast to the policies pursued by Giscard, Mitterrand has moved away from unilateral intervention in the Third World toward the promotion of regional solutions to regional problems. He has encouraged closer links between the former British and Portuguese territories in Africa and has pledged French support for an African peacekeeping force.

Mitterrand has also stressed the need for greater respect for human rights worldwide. He has called for the withdrawal of Soviet troops from Afghanistan, condemned United States support for right-wing dictatorships in Latin America, and has supported Solidarity in Poland. In contrast to Giscard's openly pro-Arab policies in the Middle East, Mitterrand's policies are expected to lean more in favor of Israel.

French policies toward the Third World have not been conflict-free. Foreign aid remains a controversial issue, and France continues to be a major arms supplier. One of the fundamental weaknesses of French foreign policy has been the strain between the pursuit of extensive global interests and the limited nature of French resources. Given Mitterrand's new foreign policy emphasis, this issue is likely to become more attenuated as France attempts to balance a generous aid program against its ability to maintain a costly defense structure and cover promised increases in social welfare and public investment.

France and the Atlantic Community

The transformation of France from a weak client state in the early post-1945 period to an independent economic and military power under the Fifth Republic has had important implications for the resurgence of French nationalism as a reaction to perceived American domination, calling for the elimination of all vestiges of American dependence. Steps were taken to halt American cultural and economic penetration, and France's publicized withdrawal from NATO suggested distrust over the uncertainty of the American commitment to defend Europe. France's relations with the United States grew increasingly strained toward the end of 1960s, as France set about building its independent nuclear force and engaged in new policy overtures to the East.

Relations remained frosty throughout the Pompidou presidency, although the strident tones of Gaullist nationalism were muted somewhat following de Gaulle's withdrawal from active political life. Giscard d'Estaing's pragmatic approach to foreign policy led to a gradual improvement in relations with the United States, and was marked by a rising volume of American investment in the French economy. Giscard's pro-Arab policies, however, remained an issue of contention.

Relations between France and the United States are likely to continue to improve under the Mitterrand government, despite a lingering atmosphere of mutual suspicion. Policymakers in the United States have expressed skepticism over socialist economic policies and remain wary of communist influence in the French government. Although the French remain critical of the United States, a key element of change toward a more positive Atlantic outlook has been the emergence of strong anti-Soviet feelings in France. Recent international actions, such as the shooting down of a Korean commercial passenger aircraft, have caused the French to perceive the Soviet Union as a symbol of totalitarianism, whose sincerity and commitment to world peace are questionable.

French attitudes toward U.S. hegemony have also changed dramatically since a decade ago. The United States is no longer regarded as the dominant power but as a necessary ally against the Soviet Union. Mitterrand has been one of the strongest Atlantic supporters of the 1979 NATO decision to install Pershing II missiles in Europe. The French peace movement is weak, at best, and has not reached a level of political importance matching that of West Germany or the Low Countries.

There are still several important economic issues that divide France and the United States. These issues include steel, agricultural products, weapons sales to unstable regimes, and the Soviet gas pipeline. All are subject to negotiation, however. The possibility of a clash of interests in the Third World is likely to be more serious, especially in the troubled areas of Latin America, where U.S.

policies have been strongly criticized. The fundamental question facing the Mitterrand government is the extent to which France can still exercise a degree of absolute freedom of action in world affairs while at the same time continuing to pursue policies that lead to a closer involvement in the interdependent network of the Atlantic Community.

Update

François Mitterrand's loss of a presidential majority in the National Assembly in March 1986 led to a brief two-year period of Socialist "cohabitation" with a conservative center-right government under Premier Jacques Chirac. Almost immediately, the new conservative government began to dismantle and reverse Socialist programs that had been put in place between 1981 and 1986, in particular the controversial nationalizations. Privatization and economic reform became the rallying cry of the conservatives. The conservative goal, supported by changing public opinion, was to reduce the role of the state, and to move France toward a more competitive, capitalist economy with the potential of attracting considerable public investment. The conservative government also abolished proportional representation and reinstituted the previous two-ballot runoff system for the 1988 legislative elections.

In 1988, Mitterrand was re-elected president for a second term, after defeating Chirac by a 54 to 46 percent margin on the second ballot. Mitterrand had attempted to separate his personal campaign from that of the Socialist Party, suggesting that the presidency was to be above partisan politics. Mitterrand's opponents were weakened by personal and ideological divisions, thereby fragmenting their vote. In the legislative elections that followed, the Socialists won 277 seats as compared to 272 for the center-right group, 27 for the Communists, and 1 for the extreme right National Front. The legislative elections were characterized by a high rate of abstentionism, ranking among the highest in the past 40 years.

Although the Socialists improved their parliamentary representation by a slim majority, they did not reverse the conservative policies of the previous center-right government, nor did they embark on new radical Socialist programs. Attentive to public opinion, which had grown increasingly skeptical of the state's role in the economy, Socialist policies took on a more centrist character. The new Socialist premier was Michel Rocard—an up and coming leader reputed to have presidential ambitions.

Several important trends had become apparent as France entered the decade of the 1990s. First, although French society had grown increasingly secular, religion continued to be a source of political controversy, especially in the area of moral issues, and in accommodating the needs of France's Moslem population in the education system. Related to religious controversy was the conflict over immigration policy and racist attitudes directed at France's North African population. Although these issues were exploited for political gain primarily by the charismatic Jean-Marie Le Pen and his National Front, they touched all the political parties, including the Communists.

As a result of changes in Central and Eastern Europe, and the transformation of the French economy, communism has ceased to be an important political force in French political life. The once electorally powerful French Communist Party continues to experience a decline in public support and has been riddled with divisive tendencies, leadership splits, and political defections. Although it still manages to hold on to a small core of older adherents, overall it has ceased to attract youth and is destined to become an insignificant and indeed irrelevant force in French political life.

Important changes in French political attitudes are also apparent in opinion polls. A more highly educated and mobile electorate coupled with the communicative power of television has completed the nationalization of French political life. Evidence for this was the round of televised presidential debates between Mitterrand and his challengers, which forced them to address national and global concerns.

The transformation of French political culture is most noticeable in attitudes toward the management role of the state. The old centralized institutions of the Napoleonic state are being called into question in terms of their relevance to the needs of modern democratic society. Local control over spending public funds and greater citizen input have increased.

Although vocal extremes on the right and left continue to exert some political influence in raising issues and affecting political agendas, France has actually experienced a growing convergence between the major political forces around centrist policies. This convergence has led to the blurring of programmatic differences between government and opposition, and has lessened political antagonisms in domestic and foreign policies.

The new reality of the post-Cold War period raises important questions for France. European issues will weigh heavily on France in the 1990s as the outlines of a newly united Germany take shape. There are many unanswered questions for France. The events in Germany are likely to force France to redefine its role in the Atlantic Community and NATO, as well as suggest new relationships toward the Soviet Union and Central Europe. The march toward "Europe 1992" has been overtaken by the unfolding of German unity, and the conflict in the Persian Gulf.

In the decade of the 1990s, France will complete its transition toward a new stage of political development, with a new generation of political leadership at the helm. The next scheduled presidential election, in 1995, will be an important benchmark in this development.

Suggested Readings

Anderson, Malcolm. *Conservative Politics in France*. London: Allen & Unwin, 1974.

Andrews, William G. *Presidential Government in Gaullist France*. Albany: State University of New York Press, 1982.

Andrews, William G., and Hoffman, Stanley, eds. *The Fifth Republic at Twenty*. Albany: State University of New York Press, 1981.

Ashford, Douglas E. *Policy and Politics in France*. Philadelphia: Temple University Press, 1982.

Caron, François. *An Economic History of Modern France*. New York: Columbia University Press, 1979.

Cerny, P. G., and Schain, M. A., eds. *French Politics and Public Policy*. New York: St. Martin's Press, 1980.

Charlot, Jean. *The Gaullist Phenomenon*. New York: Praeger, 1971.

Clifford-Vaughan, Michalina. *Social Change in France*. New York: St. Martin's Press, 1980.

Codding, George A., Jr., and Safran, William. *Ideology and Politics: The Socialist Party of France*. Boulder, Colo.: Westview Press, 1979.

Cohen, Stephen. *Modern Capitalist Planning: The French Model*. Berkeley: University of California Press, 1977.

Crozier, Michel. *The Stalled Society*. New York: Viking, 1973.

Ehrmann, Henry W. *Politics in France*. 4th ed. Boston: Little, Brown, 1983.

Frears, John R. *Political Parties and Elections in the Fifth Republic*. New York: St. Martin's Press, 1977.

Giscard d'Estaing, Valery. *French Democracy*. Garden City, N.Y.: Doubleday, 1977.

Gourevitch, Peter. *Paris and the Provinces*. Berkeley: University of California Press, 1981.

Irving, R. E. M. *Christian Democracy in France*. London: Allen & Unwin, 1973.

Johnson, R. W. *The Long March of the French Left*. New York: St. Martin's Press, 1981.

Kesselman, Mark. *The Ambiguous Consensus: A Study of Local Government in France*. New York: Knopf, 1967.

Kriegel, Anna. *The French Communists: Profile of a People*. Chicago: University of Chicago Press, 1972.

Kuisel, Richard F. *Capitalism and the State in Modern France*. Cambridge, Eng.: Cambridge University Press, 1980.

MacShane, Denis. *François Mitterrand: A Political Odyssey*. New York: Universe Books, 1983.

Marceau, Jean. *Class and Status in France*. Oxford: Clarendon Press, 1977.

Mitterrand, François. *The Wheat and the Chaff*. New York: Seaver Books, 1982.

Safran, William. *The French Polity*. 2d ed. New York and London: Longman, 1985.

Serfaty, Simon, ed. *The Foreign Policies of the French Left*. Boulder, Colo.: Westview Press, 1979.

Suleiman, Ezra. *Politics, Power and Bureaucracy in France.* Princeton, N.J.: Princeton University Press, 1974.

Thomson, David. *Democracy in France Since 1870.* 4th ed. New York: Oxford University Press, 1964.

Williams, Philip M. *Crisis and Compromise: Politics in the Fourth Republic.* Garden City, N.Y.: Doubleday Anchor, 1960.

———. *The French Parliament: Politics in the Fifth Republic.* New York: Praeger, 1968.

Wilson, Frank L. "France." In *Political Parties of Europe.* Vol. 1, *Albania-Norway,* edited by Vincent E. McHale and Sharon Skowronski. Westport, Conn.: Greenwood Press, 1983, pp. 233–321.

Zeldin, Theodore. *France 1848–1945: Politics and Anger.* Oxford: Oxford University Press, 1979.

4

Belgium and the Netherlands

Galen Irwin

Probably no modern planner would draw national boundaries in the lowlands in the Rhine river delta as they have been drawn by the accidents of history. With access to survey and census data and knowledge of social science, they surely would not have created states with a social composition that would almost inevitably lead to internal conflicts. Yet states have developed neither rationally nor with regard to structural or social borders, and the forces of history (whatever they may be) have combined to produce two small countries—Belgium and the Netherlands—with built-in social cleavages that have affected the development of political systems and created as yet unresolved political conflicts.

The Romans pushed their conquests in continental Europe north to the Rhine and Meuse rivers, and although the armies of Augustus crossed the rivers to include the Frisians in the empire, they were eventually pulled back. A highway was built from Cologne through Aachen and Tongeren to Bavai in northern France and on to the sea coast. This highway proved to be the demarcation line between Roman influence to the south and Germanic influence to the north. The most lasting influence of this demarcation has been the division between Romance and Germanic languages, still dividing what is modern Belgium into French-speaking Wallonia and Dutch-speaking Flanders.

At the end of the Middle Ages, the Low Countries were not excluded from attempts to carve out larger entities that were to become the states of Europe. After a short period of Burgundian rule, the lowlands fell into the hands of the Habsburg dynasty. Upon the abdication of Charles V in 1555, the Low Countries and Spain passed to his son, Philip II. Philip, however, never received the loyalty that his father had, and local authorities became more inclined to establish their independence. When this flexing of political muscle was combined with the forces of the Reformation, revolt ensued.

Although the people of the Low Countries were known for their piety and devotion, they were aware of the excesses and faults of the Catholic church, as exposed and discussed by Erasmus and his followers. Although Lutheran and Anabaptist influences were important, Calvinism quickly became the dominant force in Protestantism in the Low Countries. Calvinists provided the backbone of the revolt against Philip, opposing the new king on political as well as religious grounds.

Leadership of the rebellion fell to William of Orange, a German count of Nassau by birth, who had fallen heir to rich properties in the Low Countries as well as the principality of Orange in southern France. Despite early difficulties, the revolution spread north, and although the Spanish regrouped under the Duke of Alva and recovered lands in the south, they were never able to crush the revolt in the north. The hostilities dragged on for 80 years. After his assassination in 1584, William was succeeded by his son Maurice. The latter successfully reorganized the army and eventually reoccupied some Flemish towns, thus securing a buffer zone to protect the province of Zeeland.

With the re-establishment of Spanish domination in the southern provinces, Catholic dominance was restored. During the ensuing years, when the northern Calvinists were carrying the brunt of the revolt, a division began to occur. By the time Maurice had recaptured lands in the south, the inhabitants (who were now solidly Catholic) were no longer viewed as equal partners in the revolt. These provinces were treated quite differently from those that had joined the Union of Utrecht in 1579. The inhabitants, for their part, resented the fact that the northern Calvinists were continually fighting on their territory.

When peace finally came in 1648, the political border was drawn to the south of the religious border. To the north the new independent republic of the Netherlands was recognized, but in the south the Habsburg reign continued. This situation was to continue throughout the remainder of the seventeenth and eighteenth centuries.

On the defeat of Napoleon at the beginning of the nineteenth century, the Congress of Vienna was convened to redraw the map of Europe. In an effort to create a buffer state between the major powers, the two areas were once again united. The enlarged Netherlands was raised to the status of a kingdom, with William I (a descendant of William of Orange) as monarch and grand duke of Luxembourg. Perhaps with patience and understanding, this William could have succeeded in undoing the effects of 250 years of separate development. However, this was not William's manner, and in his haste to establish a modern, centralized state, he quickly alienated many of his new subjects in the south. Catholics feared his Protestantism and his support of public rather than church schools. They also opposed him in his attempts to centralize authority at the expense of local interests. In contrast, liberals supported his centralizing and anticlerical tendencies but opposed his restrictions on the freedom of the press and his promotion of Dutch interests. The king favored Dutch over Belgians in his appointments and decreed that Dutch was to be the official language in the Flemish areas. After years of frenchification, the Flemish elite resented the imposition of Dutch as the official language. Despite their own differences, Catholics and liberals joined in a union of oppositions to rid the Belgians once again of foreign domination. In September 1830 the Dutch were expelled from Brussels, and on October 4 a revolutionary government proclaimed Belgium independent. The following month an elected National Congress met, reaffirmed the independence of the nation, and voted to exclude the House of Orange from the possibility of ever ascending to the throne.

After only fifteen years of unification, the Netherlands and Belgium were again separated, this time seemingly permanently. Thus the forces of history produced three boundaries through the territory at the mouth of the Rhine. Yet none of these three—the political, religious, or linguistic—corresponded with any other. The political boundary defining the two states left each with internal boundaries. Belgium, to the south, was relatively homogeneous religiously but divided into French- and Dutch-speaking areas. The Netherlands, to the north, was linguistically homogeneous (with the exception of those areas in which Frisian continued to be spoken) but divided into Protestant and Catholic areas. These sources of cleavage, together with the cleavage of social class and the ideologies of liberalism and socialism, have formed the basis for social and political conflict to the present day and have provided the roots for the political party system.

The remainder of this chapter treats these cleavages and the system of democracy and governmental institutions that have evolved to attempt to control conflict within the segmented societies. In these sections the reader may be surprised to find virtually no mention of the Belgian language conflict. This discussion precedes the examination of a selection of the most pressing problems facing the two countries—the Belgian language problem, the Dutch economy, and foreign relations.

The Pillars of Society

Both the Netherlands and Belgium are often referred to as segmented societies—lack of conjunction between linguistic, religious, and geographical boundaries produced a potential for internal division. Combined with ideological and social-economic factors, an almost unique structure emerged with the development toward mass society in the nineteenth and twentieth centuries. Important segments within the societies began to organize tightly knit systems of organizations. Emancipation movements developed entire networks of social organizations that encompassed virtually all facets of the lives of those involved. These networks extended beyond the establishment of schools and trade unions. Newspapers were founded to provide communication links within the group. In the Netherlands, when radio and, later, television were introduced, separate broadcasting organizations were founded to represent the various segments. Voluntary organizations were organized along segmental lines. Thus there were Catholic, Calvinist, and secular organizations for the Dutch for virtually every imaginable activity—from sports clubs to the well-known example of the Roman Catholic goat breeders' association—even when the activity had no immediate relationship to the basis of the societal segment. Not surprisingly, political parties were organized to defend and represent the political aims of the groups.

In the 1950s Dutch sociologists began to take notice of this somewhat unusual and unique system. The system was likened to a building with its roof held up by a number of pillars. Each pillar stands independent of the others but forms an integral part of the whole. Similarly, in society there were "pillars" that held up the whole, and the Dutch term *verzuiling* entered the sociological vocabulary to describe the system (*zuil* = pillar). Three (or four) such pillars were identified for the Netherlands—Protestants, Catholics, Socialists, and possibly Liberals.

Academic attention was later in turning to the somewhat similar situation in Belgium. Here as well, extensive systems of organizations were to be found for Catholics, Socialists, and Liberals. Although it was new to apply the term "pillars," they were already recognized as the "spiritual families" of Belgium.

Liberals

In the late eighteenth century, the ideological influences that were to produce the American and French revolutions did not leave Belgium and the Netherlands untouched. In 1789 revolution broke out in Brabant, and the first independent Belgian republic was established. In the Netherlands the Batavian Republic was established in 1795. However, the period of liberal revolution was quickly interrupted by the conquests of Napoleon.

The union of the Netherlands and Belgium that followed the Napoleonic period was short-lived, and Belgium achieved lasting status as an independent state. The Belgian constitution of 1830–1831 was strongly influenced by liberal principles and included guarantees for freedom of the press, association, and worship, as well as the right of petition and the legal equality of all citizens. Principles of responsible government were provided.

Although the ruling classes of the Netherlands had long held rather liberal attitudes, liberalism as a political philosophy was rather slow in establishing itself. Yet the middle of the nineteenth century brought numerous reforms that also introduced responsible government and outlined the contours of the modern parliamentary democracy.

Even when they disagreed among themselves on other matters, the liberals in both countries were united in their anticlericalism. They believed strongly in the separation of church and state and clashed fiercely with Catholics and Calvinists on the role of religion in the schools. One such clash in Belgium provided the impetus for the formation of the first liberal party in 1846. Lacking such a direct stimulus as that provided by the Belgian Catholic bishops and given their lack of desire for mass organization, liberals in the Netherlands were slower to organize. The Liberal Union, founded in 1885, was a loosely organized party, strongly united only in its anticlericalism.

The modern descendants are the Party for Freedom and Democracy (PLP/ PVV) in Belgium and the People's Party for Freedom and Democracy (VVD) in the Netherlands. Although both still espouse the principles of liberalism, they are regarded by most observers as moderately conservative and certainly to the right of the political spectrum in their respective party systems.

Catholics

The Counter-Reformation and the Eighty Years' War left Catholics in the two countries in quite different positions. Belgium became a Catholic country in which 90 to 95 percent of the inhabitants still describe themselves as Catholic. In the Netherlands, Catholics have never constituted more than 40 percent of the population. Dutch Catholics, concentrated primarily in the two southern provinces, were for long periods treated in many ways as second-class citizens and at times were forbidden to hold public religious services or public office.

Despite the differences in social position, there are similarities in the development of the Catholic political movements. Both allied in the early nineteenth century with the liberals, in Belgium in the "union of oppositions" to oppose the Dutch king William, and in Holland to allow re-establishment of the Catholic church hierarchy. The break with the liberals was in part encouraged by a papal encyclical of 1864 warning of the improper influence of liberalism and an accompanying *syllabus errorum* stressing the need for Catholic schools. The battle over schools continued throughout the century. In the Netherlands it was finally laid to rest with the Great Compromise of 1917, which guaranteed equal state funding for religious schools. In Belgium, however, it continued to serve as a source of conflict until the School Pact of 1958.

The organization of Catholic political parties was slow in coming, partly because parties, with their divisive tendencies, were seen as antagonistic to the ideas of unified Catholicism. However, in the Netherlands a political arm of the Catholic emancipation movement was needed, and eventually a Catholic party was established. From the introduction of universal suffrage in 1917 until 1967, the predominant Catholic party received some 80 to 90 percent of Catholic votes. In 1977 the party merged with the two dominant Protestant parties to form the Christian Democratic Appeal (CDA).

In Belgium local Catholic committees merged in 1884 to form a Catholic party. After World War II, the reorganized Social Christian Party broke its formal ties with the church and altered its form of organization. New members could now join directly in what was to become a much more progressive party.[1]

Protestants

Since the Counter-Reformation, there have been only small numbers of Protestants[2] in Belgium. In the Netherlands, however, Protestants have been in the majority and even stronger socially and politically than their overall numbers might indicate. By the beginning of the nineteenth century, much of the Protestant elite had become latitudinarian in matters of state. This produced a backlash among those appalled by the idea that political authority arose from the people and not from God. The Calvinists were "little men" who were looked down upon and discriminated against because of their social position and beliefs.

The Calvinist movement of little men became one of the strongest emancipation movements of the nineteenth century. Their leader, Abraham Kuyper, espoused views on the separation of church and state that paralleled American ideas but went further. He believed that God had organized the world in various spheres, such as family, factory, school, and nation, and that each was sovereign in its own sphere. His Anti-Revolutionary Party allied with the Catholics on the question of religious schools.

Protestants have long been susceptible to schisms, and Dutch Protestant parties have certainly not been spared. The first split came over the question of extension of suffrage, when the more conservative elements broke to form the Christian-Historical Union. These two parties, the Anti-Revolutionary Party and the Christian-Historical Union, were among the five major parties in the Netherlands until they joined with the Catholics to form the new CDA.

Minor Protestant parties have also emerged in Parliament with some frequency since 1918, the oldest being the Political Reformed Party (SGP). In 1985, four of these small parties were represented in the Dutch Parliament.

Socialists

Within the combined areas of the two countries, industrialization came first to the French-speaking region of Wallonia. Among the new working class, religion began to lose its hold, and socialist ideas took root. Because the industrial revolution was later in arriving in Flanders and Holland, socialism came later also in these areas. The actual founding of socialist parties occurred at about the same time; a social democratic party was founded in the Netherlands in 1881, and the Belgian Workers' party only four years later. The early programs of the Dutch party were heavily influenced by those of their German counterparts, whereas the Belgian party was somewhat more influenced by French socialism. Nevertheless, both parties were relatively moderate and, aside from drives for better working conditions, set as their chief political goal the achievement of universal suffrage.

The Belgian party had greater initial success in achieving this goal. A general strike in 1891 eventually led to acceptance of universal suffrage. All Belgian males received a vote, although those paying higher levels of property tax or having higher educational qualifications received one or two extra votes (so-called plural voting). Equal suffrage came only after World War I, and women gained the franchise only in 1948.

In the Netherlands universal male suffrage was part of the package agreed upon in the Great Compromise of 1917. Women were added to the electorate in 1922.

Universal suffrage did not bring the electoral majorities that the parties had expected, due largely to the success of the religious parties in gaining the allegiance of workers. The parties settled into becoming parliamentary parties. Since World War II, both parties have achieved general respectability and have participated in numerous government coalitions. Both are progressive parties of the left with little residue of their Marxist beginnings. After World War II, the Belgian party found it acceptable to label itself the Socialist Party, whereas the Dutch party attempted to broaden its appeal by dropping the identifications *social democratic* and *workers* from its name to call itself the Party of Work (that is, the Labor Party).

Consociational Democracy

An important aspect of these systems of social segmentation was the recognition given to them by the state. The state support in the Netherlands for Catholic and Calvinist schools achieved by the Great Compromise has already been noted. When radio and television were introduced, broadcasting time was allotted according to the number of members of the respective associations. As the existence of the pillars became firmly recognized, and as the role of the state expanded and more areas received state subsidies, these were also distributed proportionally among the groups. Similarly, advisory boards received representation from these segments of society.

In Belgium, although the Catholics had been unable to gain control over the state, they did succeed in getting the state to finance many of the activities they administered, including social insurance, sickness and unemployment compensation, and mortgage banks.[3]

Not only did sociological analysis of these pillars of Dutch and Belgian society produce a new term—*verzuiling*—but also the manner in which these groups interacted politically and their recognition by the state were found to warrant a new descriptive term—*consociational democracy*.[4] The two most important characteristics of this type of democracy are cooperation at the top among the leaders of the various pillars and the great degree of autonomy within each of the societal segments.[5] Two additional principles are the right of veto accorded to each segment and the principle of proportional representation.

The principle of proportional representation has been noted in the state treatment of the pillars. In political terms, both countries employ the principle in most aspects of politics, such as electoral systems, appointment of mayors, composition of municipal executive commissions, recruitment of members of the senior civil service and advisory committees in the Netherlands, and the division of the budget and the promotion of governmental personnel in Belgium.

Proportional representation is but one means of providing for the autonomy of the group. This is extended by consciously removing the principle of majority rule in areas particularly sensitive to the interests of the group.[6] Thus the groups are given consideration in matters ranging from consultation and compromise to the grant of an outright veto, a system that Arend Lijphart has compared to the doctrine of "concurrent majority."[7]

These principles help depoliticize conflict within the consociational democracy. Yet, if political questions are to be resolved, it is necessary for the leaders of the group to be able to compromise. Furthermore, recognition of the "government's right to govern" and the possibility for "summit diplomacy" is required.[8]

After the late 1960s, developments in the Netherlands led observers to conclude that the system had changed.[9] Lijphart spoke of the breakdown of the politics of accommodation and in later writings no longer lists the Netherlands as a consociational democracy.[10] Belgium, on the other hand, has consciously attempted to apply the principles of consociational democracy to the settlement of the tensions between the French- and Flemish-speaking communities and can now "legitimately claim to be the most thorough example of consociational democracy."[11]

Governmental Structures

Both Belgium and the Netherlands are constitutional monarchies. Formally the monarch has powers to appoint and dismiss the prime minister and the cabinet, dissolve Parliament, and sign legislation. However, constitutional guarantees greatly limit the actual power of the monarch. He or she may delay the signing of legislation for a short time but cannot refuse to sign, and all legislation must be countersigned by a cabinet minister. Parliament is dismissed only when a governing coalition falls and no new coalition can be formed or when it is necessary to call elections before forming a new cabinet.

Although the monarch is severely limited by political realities and must consult with political leaders, the monarch does have some discretion in the selection of the cabinet because of the balance between the parties. If matters are particularly unclear, the monarch may appoint an *informateur* to advise which coalition best reflects the voting results and has the best possibilities for receiving the support of the Parliament. Once the informateur has finished, or if such work is deemed unnecessary, a *formateur* is appointed to actually form the cabinet. In such complicated situations, where subtle differences may become crucial, the actual power of the monarch may be at its greatest. Other than this, some informal power may be exercised; merely showing interest in a particular matter or piece of legislation may cause others to be more aware and careful in their actions.

The prime functions of the monarchy are in fact to act as chief of state and to symbolize the nation. These involve almost exclusively ceremonial duties and are performed best when the royal family remains out of politics and above reproach in its actions. The Dutch House of Orange has been quite successful in fulfilling this role. Since establishment of the principle of parliamentary supremacy in the middle of the nineteenth century, it has served the country well in this fashion. Throughout the twentieth century, the three queens—Wilhelmina, Juliana, and Beatrix—have enjoyed great popularity, and the few minor scandals associated with the royal household have had little effect on the strong support for the monarchy.

The Belgian monarchy has been more controversial and more political. The crown passes to the male heirs of Leopold van Saxe-Coburg, who became King Leopold I after the separation from the Netherlands. Leopold I established a tradition of the king presiding over cabinet meetings, a tradition that continued at times until 1940. Leopold II intervened in political matters and established his own African domain, which later became the colony of the Congo. The most controversial actions of a Belgian monarch came during World War II with King Leopold III. His relation with the German occupiers was strongly criticized in many quarters, and after the war a referendum was held to determine whether he should retain his throne. Although he won the referendum, the public outcry was so great that he was forced to abdicate in favor of his son. King Baudouin has since succeeded in re-establishing public faith in the monarchy.

True executive powers in the two countries are exercised by the prime minister and the cabinet. Because of the multiplicity of political parties and the balance of strength among them, it has always been necessary in the Netherlands and virtually always necessary in Belgium to form coalition cabinets. The process of cabinet formation is quite difficult and in the Netherlands in recent years has taken as much as six months.[12]

In Belgium, the prime minister officially designates the other cabinet ministers, but he is constrained by numerous factors. Principal among these is the balance between the parties in Parliament, but since 1971, a constitutional amendment has also provided that the cabinet must consist of an equal number of French- and Flemish-speaking members. The members of the Belgian cabinet may retain their seats in Parliament; this is forbidden in the Netherlands.

In the Netherlands, the prime minister is a "first among equals," although since World War II his position has become increasingly dominant. Key ministerial posts are distributed among the parties in the coalition, and each minister has considerable influence in his or her own policy area. Second in importance to the prime minister is the finance minister, who controls the budget. The cabinet operates on the principle of collective responsibility and must agree internally on important matters.

In Belgium the cabinet must receive a positive vote of confidence from Parliament before it can begin its work. In the Netherlands such a vote is not necessary, although any vote of no confidence, or even rejection of a major governmental proposal, leads to the resignation of the government. However, in recent history in both countries, the fall of a government has occurred far more often due to internal disagreements than to lack of parliamentary support. Once a compromise has been hammered out between the parties in the cabinet, it is unlikely that the parliamentary parties will reject it and thus destroy the coalition.

Parliament in both countries consists of two chambers. In the Netherlands the Second Chamber is far more important. All legislation must be initiated here; the First Chamber may not amend, but only pass or reject, legislation that has first been passed in the Second Chamber. The Second Chamber is elected on the principle of proportional representation. A list of candidates may be presented in an electoral district if supported by the signatures of 25 voters and a deposit of 1,000 guilders. Attainment of these figures in each of the eighteen districts ensures national coverage and secures the right to an equal amount of radio and television time. In counting the votes, all the districts are treated as a single national constituency. As there are 150 members to be elected, the number of votes cast is divided by this number to determine the electoral quotient (which thus equals only 0.67 percent of the total vote). Until 1970 attendance at the polls was compulsory, and the turnout was always well above 90 percent. After 1970, levels of turnout dropped, but for parliamentary elections they have consistently been above 80 percent.

The members of the First Chamber are chosen by the provincial legislatures. However, the parties ensure that the end result of these elections differs as little as possible from the relative strength nationwide of the parties as reflected in the provincial elections. Members of the First Chamber have fewer duties than members of the Second Chamber and are often semiretired party leaders who for some reason wish to withdraw from the public eye. The chief function of the First Chamber is to provide one last check on legislation before it becomes law.

In Belgium both chambers may initiate legislation, although in both countries, legislation is in fact proposed by the government. Nevertheless, it is the Chamber of Representatives that is dominant in Belgium. Matters relating to finance and defense must first be passed by this chamber. The 212 members of the chamber are elected in 30 electoral districts. Depending on the size of the district, 200 to 500 signatures must support each list submitted, but no deposit is required. Voters are required by law to appear at the polling booth. Votes are tallied and distributed proportionally among the parties according to the vote within the district. Members of the chamber may simultaneously hold local office and are more likely than Dutch MPs to consider themselves representatives of local interests.

The Belgian Senate does not have a fixed number of members. A number equal to half the size of the Chamber of Representatives is chosen by direct election. However, only individuals who have in some fashion achieved distinction in politics, business, or some other area (qualifications are listed in the constitution) are eligible for election in this fashion. In addition, for each 200,000 inhabitants a provincial council may elect a senator, and an additional number are chosen by co-optation. Sons of the king (or royal princes if the king has no sons) are automatically members of the Senate upon reaching age 18 and may vote when they reach age 25.

A final body that must be mentioned is the Council of State. Among its functions in the Netherlands is advice to the monarch and the cabinet on intended legislation. In principle the advice of the council must be asked before legislation is submitted to the Parliament, but in recent years this has often been done at such a late date that there was no time for true consultation. In recent years the council's role in administrative appeals has been increased, making its judicial function more important. A Council of State was created in Belgium in 1946, and although its legislative sector may provide counsel on pending legislation, its major function is carried out in the area of administrative law by its judicial sector.

Political Problems

No society is devoid of political problems, and despite increased standards of living and astounding technological developments, most countries seem to be suffering from more, rather than fewer, problems. Any list would include crime (including welfare fraud), drugs, educational reform, abortion, pollution and the environment, and the position of foreign workers.

Yet, rather than giving a superficial discussion of problems in the Low Countries, which would show considerable similarity with the situation in many other countries, it seems preferable to concentrate on a few specific topics that are of some special interest. Three have been chosen for emphasis here. First, the third major cleavage in Belgian society is examined. Although the language line through the territory has existed since Roman days, only in the 1960s did it become sufficiently salient to warrant drastic action. Second, Dutch economic problems are discussed. Although both countries face major difficulties, the Netherlands is somewhat more interesting because of the extent of its social welfare provisions and its policies with respect to exploitation of natural gas. Since at least 1977, public opinion surveys show that the Dutch consider unemployment to be the greatest problem facing the country, followed by inflation and other economic problems. Finally, foreign relations are treated. Since World War II, both countries have been committed to the integration of Europe and collective security within the Atlantic Alliance. Recently, however, doubts have arisen with respect to the latter, and the term *Hollanditis* has been coined to signify a new mood in Europe.

The Belgian Language Cleavage

As was noted in the discussion of historical boundaries, the area now called Belgium has been divided since the Roman period by a language line. In the southern portion known as Wallonia, French is spoken. To the north, in the territory known as Flanders, Dutch is spoken. The language of this region is often referred to as Flemish, the name being derived from the name of the area, but the many dialects spoken are now recognized as dialects of Dutch. The Flemish people formally recognized the name of their language as Dutch. However, language is treated here as a current political problem and not as an aspect of the development of the Belgian state because language has only recently become of great importance in Belgian politics. In fact, one author writes:

> Especially in the light of recent comparative developmental analysis, which has served to emphasize the historical precedence of conflict between central nation-building elites and culturally distinctive subject-populations . . . two questions arise from the Belgian experience: Why did linguistic conflict develop so late? Why has its electoral impact remained relatively small?[13]

Yet, although that author may feel that the electoral impact has been small, the political consequences have been great.

Again, an understanding of the current conflict must begin with the histori-cal background. As mentioned, the peasants of the northern area of what is now Belgium spoke a Flemish dialect of Dutch. At the time, French was the domi-nant international language and the language of diplomacy, and the Flemish elite conformed. The nobles either became completely frenchified or were bi-lingual. Governments and kings were hardly concerned with the language spoken by their subjects.

The first attempt to institute a uniform language came from the French, who annexed the area in 1794. French was declared the national language, and a concerted effort was made to establish its dominance. In the twenty years of French domination, this policy achieved significant success, and French made great inroads among the middle classes of Brussels and Flanders.[14]

When the Dutch replaced the French in 1814, King William attempted to reverse the process and dutchify not only Flanders but also Wallonia. In contrast with the French, his only success was in uniting the opposition against him. At the time of the Belgian Revolution in 1830, there does not even seem to have been a sense of biculturalism within Belgium. The revolution was a nationalist revolution, and the division was seen as between Belgium and the Netherlands.[15]

The new Belgian constitution was a quite liberal document, and in that spirit it provided that the choice of language "shall be optional." The effect, how-ever, was to guarantee the dominance of French, as the frenchified elite chose to make French the only official language for legislation, justice, secondary and higher education, and the armed forces.[16] In public life, Flemish was utilized only in elementary education, local administration, and the village church.[17]

Economic developments complicated matters during the nineteenth cen-tury. Industrial development was far greater in Wallonia, leaving Flanders pri-marily an agricultural region with an outmoded textile industry and the port of Antwerp, which achieved importance only later. Industrialization not only brought differential prosperity but also magnified the economic advantages and disadvantages of language. The growth of industry brought numerous new mana-gerial and white-collar positions, which were filled with French speakers. Social mobility, and with it economic mobility, thus became dependent upon lan-guage. To speak Flemish was to be backward; to speak French, modern.[18]

Despite these differences, only the small beginnings of a Flemish movement can be found in the nineteenth century; the main obstacle was a lack of leader-ship. In contrast with the emancipation of Dutch Catholics, for example, there was no Flemish-speaking elite with an interest in supporting such a cause. Uni-versal suffrage (1893), albeit with plural voting, brought the first measure of po-litical influence. The census of 1890 showed that the Flemish region held a slight majority of the population, and the higher birthrate in the region began to change from an economic liability to a political asset.[19] The first parliamentary speech in Dutch was made in 1894, and in 1898 landmark legislation was passed recognizing Flemish as an official language of the kingdom.

World War I amplified the disparity between the two regions. Flemish soldiers suffered more in the trenches, not only because of their condition but also because many of their officers could not speak their language. Walloons often escaped the horrors of the trenches by being sent to work in French factories. German policies only made matters worse by encouraging Flemish separatism and "leaving a train of political booby traps for the Belgian nation after the war."[20] The collaboration of some Flemish activists with the Germans caused many French speakers to question the loyalty of the entire Flemish movement.[21]

Nevertheless, after the war the system of plural voting could no longer be considered equitable, and Flemish demands for equality were granted. This brought about a shift in the demands of the Flemish movement. If the full impact of this equality was to be felt, the one-way traffic between the two language groups had to be halted. Whereas the first generations of the Flemish movement had demanded only recognition of their language alongside French, unilingualism (a single language recognized for an area) now became the goal. This shifted emphasis from a purely linguistic discussion to a question of territory because unilingualism could only be achieved within a specified territory.[22] At this time, the first Flemish political parties submitted electoral lists.

The principle of unilingualism was first legally recognized in legislation passed in 1932; Dutch officially became the language in the north and French in the south. In the border regions a census every ten years was to ask each household to record its linguistic preference. Whatever the majority chose was to be the language of the local region. Although this legislation at least partially resolved one problem, it created another. The capital city of Brussels, originally a Flemish village and still in Flemish territory, had become an international, predominantly French-speaking metropolis. The obvious solution was to make Brussels bilingual, but with the growth of the city, French speakers began to move in and alter the linguistic composition of the suburbs. This French expansion irritated the Flemish. Moreover, the Flemish felt that the census taken in these areas was often not objective.[23]

Following World War II, the conflict between the two language groups resumed and intensified. A new Flemish party, the Volksunie, was founded in 1953, and in contrast to all other Flemish parties achieved real electoral significance during the 1960s. Aside from forces leading to a worldwide revival of nationalistic feelings in many regions, the Flemish were affected by changes in internal circumstances. After the war, industry in Wallonia was in the unusual and unfortunate position of having led too much. The factories quickly became outmoded, and new industries and capital investments shifted to Flanders. This new economic power thus reinforced the political power that Flanders retained by virtue of its greater numbers and could hardly have helped but produce a reaction in Wallonia.

As one observer has succinctly stated, "As long as Wallonia prospered and francophones ran the nation, there was no Walloon problem."[24] A small Walloon movement had begun in the 1850s, but it was more literary than political. Some political elements were added in the 1870s, following the first laws recognizing the Flemish language.[25] Nevertheless, it was not until the shift in economic fortunes brought the fear that the position of domination in the country would be lost that an important Walloon political movement emerged.

> Walloon reaction came in two forms. First, there was an accelerated "prise de conscience" in which regional feelings were far more evident than cultural and linguistic ones (e.g., "This region must survive"; "The viability of this economic entity must be safeguarded"). Second, Wallonia's resistance against Flanders's use of the rule of proportionality in the allocation of public goods intensified.[26]

Under continued pressure from the Flemish, which included organized marches on Brussels, new language legislation was passed in 1962 and 1963. The most important effect of these laws was to divide Belgium into four language areas. In addition to establishing a legal boundary between the Flemish- and French-speaking areas, Brussels became legally bilingual, and a small German-speaking area was established. The boundaries could in the future be altered only by means of specific legislation.

The new legislation did little to alleviate the problem. In Flanders, 324 French speakers brought suit against the law at the European Court for Human Rights in Strasbourg, claiming it made it impossible for them to receive public education in French. Although they eventually lost the case on all but one minor point, it demonstrated the height of feelings.[27] Other problems arose concerning border areas, in particular the area of Fourons (Voerstreek).[28] In Brussels, francophones felt hemmed in by the new legislation, which prevented the addition of new French-speaking or bilingual areas to the capital. In 1964, the Front Démocratique des Francophones Bruxellois (FDF) was founded to defend francophone interests in the city. The Flemish, on the other hand, resented the continual push of French speakers into the suburbs.

Political conflict reached new heights in the 1960s. In addition to the Volksunie and FDF, the Rāssemblement Walloon (RW) was founded in 1967. The substantial gains of these language-based parties altered the balance of power between the established parties. The latter were also directly affected by the intensification of the conflict. In 1968 the Catholics split in two over the questions of the University of Louvain and the size of bilingual Brussels.[29] The Liberals broke into three sections—Flemish, Walloon, and Brussels—although both parties established coordination of the sections at the national level. The Socialists weathered the storm the longest but, in 1978, suddenly broke into two parties with only loose national ties.[30]

Constitutional Revision The continuing deterioration of the relationship between the linguistic communities necessitated the search for new institutional structures to reduce the conflict. In 1970 the constitution was amended to attempt to meet these needs. First, the linguistic boundaries established by the 1963 law were given a constitutional status. In the future these boundaries could be altered only by special majorities in Parliament. Although the single-language character of French-, Dutch-, and German-speaking areas as well as the bilingual nature of Brussels were guaranteed, this did little to solve either the problem of extension of the linguistic boundary of Brussels or the question of the region of Fourons.

A more revolutionary constitutional amendment recognized the existence of "cultural communities" within Belgium. The distinction of "cultural communities" rather than simply regions is necessitated by the situation of Brussels.[31] In Brussels, French- and Dutch-speaking Belgians live side by side, and although regional organizations might suffice for the great majority of the two language groups, it seemed reasonable that these residents of the capital city may be regarded as part of a cultural group.

These cultural communities were not merely given constitutional recognition; political institutions were created to allow the communities greater self-determination. The legislation established cultural councils with legislative powers on such topics as fine arts, libraries, radio and television, museums, and other matters related to the cultural life of the community.[32] The membership of the councils was to be made up of those members of both houses of Parliament from the two linguistic territories. (A German cultural council was established in 1973, but with only advisory authority.)

Finally, the constitutional revision recognized the existence of three regions—Wallonia, Flanders, and Brussels. Regulations for the regions were less detailed, providing only in general terms that future legislation was to provide for regional assemblies to deal with town and country planning, economic expansion, demographic policy, and other matters related to a geographical area.

The ensuing ten years were devoted to implementation of the amendments. In 1980, new amendments finally brought the next step in the process. The cultural communities were again recognized, although now one no longer spoke of cultural communities, but simply of Flemish-, French-, and German-speaking communities. The cultural councils were replaced by community councils, composed of "chosen" representatives. Until new legislation provided otherwise, the councils would consist of the members of Parliament from the language groups. These newly reformed councils were given the right to elect executives.

The constitution now outlines three areas of authority for the community councils.[33] First, the councils regulate by decree matters dealing with cultural affairs and with cooperation between the communities. They may regulate matters connected with education, with the exception of the compromises comprising the school peace, for which the Flemish socialists apparently did not feel that the Catholic majority in the community could be sufficiently trusted.[34] A second area of authority was new for the community councils and involved the so-called personally bound matters. These are matters tied to the individual members of a group rather than the group as a whole and include family affairs, public health, and policy toward foreigners, the handicapped, and the aged. Finally, the councils were given authority to regulate questions of language in public administration, public education, and the relationship between employers and employees.

In 1980, in response to demands for regionalization, provisions were made for regional councils. The constitution recognizes three regions: Flanders, Wallonia, and Brussels, although until now Brussels has not been included in regionalization.[35] The regional councils received authority to regulate matters pertaining to an area, such as town and country planning, employment policy, economic expansion in the region, and housing. The constitution allows for the combination of the regional and community councils, and this has been done in the case of Flanders and the Flemish. The Walloons, however, maintain separate bodies. There is also a council for German-speaking Belgians, but it has delegated authority over cultural matters to the regional council for Wallonia.

The result is a rather complicated system of councils with overlapping responsibilities. For example, with respect to cultural and personal matters, the decrees of the Flemish council apply to all Flemish speakers, whether resident in Flanders or Brussels, but decrees affecting regional matters apply only to Flanders. The situation is similar with regard to French speakers and Wallonia, except that two councils are involved and there is a relationship with the German council. Brussels remains a major stumbling block, for it has not yet been included in regionalization and continues to fall under the national government.

In speaking to the Belgian Parliament concerning the 1970 constitutional amendments, Premier Eyskens stated:

> The unitary state with its structure and procedures as currently regulated by law has been superseded by the events. The communities in the regions must take their place in revised state institutions which better fit the situation of the country.[36]

Certainly no observer would disagree that the amendments of 1970 and 1980 have fundamentally altered the nature of the Belgian political system. Belgium has become an "outstanding example of the non-territorial form of federalism,"[37] or at least an example of "very elaborate decentralization."[38] Whatever label one chooses,

> the federalist idea became more attractive to more people in the 1970s not strictly for linguistic or cultural or ethnic reasons, but because it bears the promise of the ultimate achievement of socialism in Wallonia and of a sort of Catholic model of societal harmony in Flanders. If [this] interpretation of recent developments is correct, it might be said that the two dominant sources of cleavage, which in the past blocked the spontaneous maturation of communal conflicts, now accelerate it.[39]

Such acceleration is hardly impeded by the self-identifications of the Belgians themselves. Whereas "in 1830 all inhabitants proudly called themselves Belgians, even while speaking various languages," they now think of themselves as Flemings or Walloons first and Belgians second.[40] One factor holding the two together is the city of Brussels, a French enclave within Flemish territory. How the so-called Brussels question is resolved may help determine the future of Belgium.[41] Furthermore, questions of allocations of funds between the regions, the degree of political autonomy for the regions, and the social and political systems to be adopted within the regions must be resolved if the two communities are not to drift even farther apart.[42]

Problems in the Dutch Economy

At the end of World War II, the Netherlands was in an extremely weak position economically. The Great Depression had lasted longer than in other West European countries, and five years of German occupation and the tolls of war had devastated the country. Yet drastic measures and foreign assistance produced a virtual economic miracle. By 1950, industrial production had increased enormously, and the Netherlands finally became a modern industrial nation.[43] In the 1960s, the economy continued to boom, although some weaker industries began to suffer from foreign competition. Unemployment dropped at times to under 1 percent and stayed low.

Two far-reaching events went virtually unnoticed at the time. The first concerned the wage and incomes policy pursued by the government. The economic recovery had been made possible in part by consciously keeping wages low, thus strengthening the all-important Dutch export position. This policy could not be maintained endlessly, however, and in 1963, a wage explosion took place. Yearly increases far exceeded those of the early period, but most important, the government lost its grip as multiyear contracts were negotiated, often with escalator clauses. In the 1970s, these clauses were replaced by automatic price compensation clauses, making it difficult for the government to check the wage-price spiral.[44] The government even lost control over the wage increases of its own personnel by introducing the so-called trend policy, which tied salaries of government employees to those in the private sector.

The second event of major importance was the discovery in the early 1960s of large reserves of natural gas in the northern part of the country.[45] Given the prevailing views on energy consumption and the future of nuclear energy, the decision was made to exploit these new resources as quickly as possible. Virtually the entire country was converted to gas, and long-term contracts at low prices were negotiated with other countries. By the beginning of the 1970s, gas sales were beginning to assume importance in the Dutch balance of payments and contributed to the hardening of the position of the Dutch guilder on international exchange markets.

After years of suffering due to economic depression and German occupation, the Netherlands set out to provide greater protection for the populace from the uncertain and uncontrollable aspects of life and the economy. The Dutch system of social welfare has since become one of the most extensive systems existent. Government pensions, unemployment compensation, and assistance to widows and orphans were introduced in the 1950s. Child payments, a national health insurance system (administered semipublicly and privately), major medical coverage, and disability insurance were introduced in the 1960s. Under the latter, an individual unable to work receives 80 percent of the last salary earned until age 65.

These aspects of the system are organized as required insurance schemes, with premiums being paid by employees, employers, or both. In principle, the premiums are expected to cover the benefits, but in practice the government has provided supplementary funds out of general revenues.

In addition, other aspects of social welfare are provided directly out of general funds. The government has set an example to industry by providing generous benefits to its own employees who lose their jobs as well as initiating "inflation-free" pensions for government workers. Under an unusual scheme, visual artists receive financial support, in return for which they donate a certain number of their works each year to the government. And direct assistance is provided for those who are not protected by any of the insurance systems.

Needless to say, provision of such generous benefits requires money, and the amounts have increased rapidly. In 1965, expenditures in the Netherlands for these various income-transfer programs totaled 11.3 percent of the gross national product, but by 1983, this had risen to 29.6 percent.[46] Figures over the same period for the United States were only 4.6 percent and 11.0 percent.[47] By the 1980s, payroll taxes for all social security programs exceeded half of the total payroll in the Netherlands, as compared to about 35 percent for West Germany and Sweden and 20 percent or less for the United Kingdom and the United States.[48] In comparison with other countries of the Common Market, the expenditure per person is 20 to 75 percent higher in the Netherlands. (Belgium, for example, is about 26 percent lower than the Netherlands.)[49]

Several reasons account for these dramatic rises. Many benefits are tied directly to other factors and increase automatically. Disability benefits are based on the last wage earned but carry a standard-of-living guarantee and increase with inflation. A declining birthrate and better medical treatment have contributed to an increase in the percentage of the population over age 65, which has increased costs not only for pensions but also for necessary medical care and nursing homes. With more liberal definitions of disability, stress and other psychological factors have led to greater numbers receiving benefits. Moreover, because disability benefits continue longer and are more certain than unemployment benefits, there is pressure on all concerned to declare workers disabled. Some have estimated that as many as 200,000 persons are included who are in fact among the "hidden unemployed."[50]

However, perhaps the most crucial factor contributing to the rise in cost has been the increase in unemployment. After having been quite low during the 1960s, it began to rise slowly but steadily during the 1970s. In 1970 there were, on average, 44,500 registered unemployed, less than 1 percent of the working population. By 1980 this average had risen to 248,000 registered unemployed (4.6 percent), and in the next two years this figure more than doubled to 541,700 (9.6 percent). The figures have continued to rise, and those released for May 1984 show 847,000 unemployed (corrected for seasonal influences, percentage not available).[51]

Between 1960 and 1981, the percentage of the Dutch national income flowing through these social insurance programs rose from 9.1 to 25.6. In addition, the percentage for the national government rose from 13.5 to 19.9, and for other public bodies, from 13.6 to 20.6. Thus, by 1981, almost two-thirds of the national income fell under the collective sector.[52] This figure is exceeded in Sweden but is higher than those of most of the West European countries and considerably higher than those for the United States and Japan.[53]

After the oil boycott of 1973 came the institution of a new policy for the exploitation of natural gas, which tied its price to that of oil. Nevertheless, the greatly increased revenues have been insufficient to prevent increasing budget deficits. In the Netherlands, the so-called financing deficit figure receives the most attention. This figure is the difference between income and outlay, diminished by payments for long-term loans. The assumption is that these payments will be reinvested in new loans, but the remaining deficit must be financed by either new borrowing or monetary measures (printing new money).[54] Dutch economists consider a financing deficit of between 4 and 5 percent as tolerable, but the figure rose to over 10 percent in 1982 and 1983. This has meant not only that money is taken away from areas of investment but also that the burden on the budget in terms of interest payments continues to increase. Until 1979, less than 2 percent of the net national income went to interest payments on the national debt, but by 1983 this had risen to 4.4 percent (6.5 percent when the entire public sector is included), posing a severe threat to the social welfare state.

All parties are now in virtual agreement that the level of the financing deficit has become too high (although they may not agree on just how high might be tolerable). Short of simply printing more money, only two options are open; either taxes and social insurance premiums must be raised or expenditures must be cut. In the early 1970s, the Liberals (VVD) pushed for substantial tax increases to cover the then-existing deficits, but given the already high levels, this is no longer considered feasible.

Reduction of governmental expenditures remains the only option, but although agreed in principle, the parties disagree on how large the cuts must be and where they will fall. The left always looks first to defense, but the Christian Democrats and the Liberals stand strongly for honoring commitments made to NATO. Others look to the wide range of services and subsidies that the social welfare state brought. Not only did the social welfare state bring greater security against such risks as disability and unemployment, but extensive facilities were provided for all areas of social and cultural life. Armies of social workers staff social centers and assist groups of all kinds. The Ministry of Social Work, Health, and Culture has grown quite large, with a budget not substantially less than that for defense. Yet every proposal to cut back on library facilities, community centers, youth centers, and museums or to fuse a number of orchestras meets with protest from clientele. Protests before the Parliament building have become increasingly frequent. Everyone seems to be convinced of the need to cut back, but too often a "Why me?" or "You first" attitude is taken. Somewhat the same attitude is apparent with respect to education, which consumes the largest percentage of the national budget. Nevertheless, despite protests, salaries of teaching personnel from kindergarten to university were "temporarily" cut by 1.85 percent. University budgets have been cut dramatically, and a drastic reorganization plan has eliminated entire departments at some universities.

One obvious choice for trimming the collective sector is the broad area of welfare benefits. Either the number of persons receiving benefits might be reduced, or the benefits themselves might be lowered in some fashion. Yet such proposals as breaking the link between the minimum wage and the minimum benefit run into serious opposition from the trade unions and the Labor Party.

Many proposals and plans have been made, but too little has come of them. Too often they were thwarted before they could become law. Yet, with so much talk, many persons seem to feel that they have been hit harder than in fact is the case. Opposition to what seems to be yet another cut becomes even greater. Nevertheless, in 1984, the ruling Christian Democrat–Liberal coalition seemed determined to achieve some results. Governmental salaries were decreased by 3 percent at the beginning of 1984, and benefits have been reduced.

The great danger in attempting to reduce budget deficits is the growth of social unrest. In the fall of 1983, strikes by civil servants against salary cuts disrupted many areas of social and economic life. The unions have consistently threatened disruptions if the government attempts to break existing labor contracts, restrict their right to collective bargaining, or impinge upon those aspects of the welfare state that unions have worked so hard to achieve. No one is willing to let go easily of that which has been built up.

At least the possibility of radical action has also emerged. In the 1982 elections a member of the so-called Center Party was elected to Parliament. This party has found a scapegoat for the economic difficulties in the many guest-workers first brought into the country to support the boom of the 1960s. Now adherents of the Center Party feel that guest-workers are taking jobs away from Dutch workers. Ethnic and racial strife, although often exaggerated in absolute terms, has been on the rise. Others have supported the Center Party more out of a general frustration with economic difficulties that they cannot control.

Yet it hardly seems likely that any substantial proportion of the Dutch population will turn to radical solutions. Too many centuries of tolerance have preceded the present to expect any alteration in the short run. Nonetheless, the great challenge for the coming years will be to restructure and stimulate the economy and to salvage the welfare state without letting unrest get out of hand.

Foreign Relations

The location of Belgium and the Netherlands, with control over the estuaries at the mouth of the Rhine, has meant that these territories have played a greater role in international affairs than their relative size might first lead one to suspect. The Dutch utilized this strategic position to emerge as a major trading nation. Dutch trading companies founded colonies abroad that contributed greatly to the high level of prosperity. The strategic importance meant, however, that control, or at least dominance, in the area was often coveted by the surrounding major powers. Belgium, in particular, was subjected to invasions and occupations from Spanish, Austrian, French, and most recently, German forces; and the Netherlands was invaded both by Napoleon and Hitler.

When Belgium successfully revolted in 1830, it was clear that none of the major powers could afford to have it dominated by another. Thus in the treaty of 24 articles that provided for Belgian independence, the major powers included a guarantee of Belgian neutrality. Although not by force of treaty, the Netherlands voluntarily pursued a policy of neutrality from the early part of the nineteenth century until World War II.

Such neutrality did not, however, prevent Belgium from becoming a major battlefield in World War I, nor did it save both countries from being overrun by German forces during World War II. After World War II, Belgium and the Netherlands turned to a new strategy for protecting their national independence. This strategy is aimed at reduction of tensions within Europe through greater economic and political integration and collective security within the Atlantic Alliance. Integration and cooperation have become the cornerstones of foreign policy for both countries.

Since World War II, both countries have gone through the traumatic experience of withdrawing from colonial territories—the Dutch from Indonesia and New Guinea and the Belgians from the Congo. Although this process was completed only with difficulty, both countries have maintained strong interest in the Third World and are among the most generous suppliers of development aid.

Yet despite the similarities between the two, certain differences of style in foreign relations can be noted.[55] The Dutch have a more legalistic and moralistic approach to foreign affairs than the Belgians. Dutchman Hugo Grotius is regarded as the father of international law, and the Netherlands has long played an important role in this field, as witnessed currently by the location of the International Court of Justice in The Hague. The moralistic approach is perhaps related to Calvinist influence, and the Dutch often regard it as their duty to preach a strong moral stand to others. Such influence is found most recently in the Interdenominational Peace Conference (IKV), whose aim is to set an example to others by first ridding the Netherlands of nuclear weapons.[56] Belgium, on the other hand, has a far more pragmatic style of diplomacy. The Belgians are concerned less with determining what may be right and more with what may be possible. They are more willing and able to bargain to achieve a compromise.

These two styles are also evidenced in public opinion. Diplomatic bargaining is conducted more easily by those free from the prying eyes of others. Belgian leaders have had such opportunities, as foreign policy has tended to evoke little public interest. Moreover, the Belgian Parliament has been willing to grant the government freedom to maneuver. The Belgian press also devotes less space to foreign matters than does the Dutch. The greater attention of the press in the Netherlands both reflects and stimulates greater interest in such matters, and public interest in foreign policy has grown since the 1960s. Now, an international event hardly occurs before a committee is formed to take a stand. Sit-ins, discussion forums, action groups, boycotts, and the like have become commonplace. Under such circumstances, it is to be expected that the Dutch Parliament wishes to take part in making the foreign policy of the government and often attempts to assert itself.

Relations Within Europe. Within Europe, relations between the two countries themselves should be considered first. These have not always been as strong as an outsider might expect. The Dutch have long taken a rather haughty attitude toward the Belgians. The Flemish dialect is regarded as inferior, and the Belgians in general are viewed as a rather dirty and messy people. What in the United States would be Polish jokes are told of the Belgians. The Dutch are in general poorly informed concerning Belgium and could care less. The Belgians, at least the Flemish, are far more aware of the Netherlands. Especially in their cultural orientation, they have looked increasingly to their northern neighbors. Yet Belgians jealously guard their independence and continue to be aware of their revolution of 1830.

The economic position of the two countries at the end of World War II differed greatly. Belgium received little damage to its industrial capacity and enjoyed increased prosperity, whereas the Netherlands was forced to begin a long period of austerity to be able to rebuild. Nevertheless, steps that had been initiated by the governments-in-exile in London were taken toward integrating the two economies, the Belgium-Luxembourg Economic Union of 1922 serving as an example. In 1948, a customs union was agreed on, and ten years later the Benelux Economic Union was established. Within the context of Benelux, attempts have been made to extend economic cooperation into other areas, such as harmonization of law and cultural cooperation. In general, however, the importance and development of Benelux have been overshadowed by larger European developments.

Several factors motivated the desire for European cooperation following World War II. Foremost was the feeling that economic cooperation and integration would counteract the economic nationalism that had caused two world wars. Most important, this cooperation might reduce the tensions between arch-rivals France and Germany. To this was added the attempt to rebuild Europe from the ravages of the war and create new prosperity. Finally, with the emergence of the United States and the Soviet Union as new superpowers, there were the desires to retain the position of Europe in world affairs and to protect Europe from the internal as well as external threat of communism.[57]

Both Belgium and the Netherlands were leaders in the movement for European integration. After the European Coal and Steel Community and the European Community for Atomic Energy, the most important initiative came in 1957 with formation of the European Economic Community. The Benelux formed three of the original six members of the community. The Belgian Paul-

Henri Spaak was one of the architects of the union, and when the three communities came under a common council in 1967, another Belgian, Jean Rey, became the first president of the new commission.

The position of the two countries within the community has differed. In keeping with its general orientation, the Netherlands has taken more uncompromising stands. Particularly during the 1960s, it resisted the direction the French desired to take with the community. The French, especially under De Gaulle, desired a Europe separate from the United States, whereas the Dutch were more in favor of an Atlantic approach. This meant that the Netherlands strongly favored the inclusion of Britain, whereas France made this impossible at the time through its veto. In this situation, Belgium often played a mediating role, although the Belgian view of a united Europe always included Britain.

With the entrance of Great Britain, Ireland, and Denmark in 1973 and Greece in 1981, the European Community now numbers ten. With the fall of dictators in Spain and Portugal, the Netherlands has favored expansion to include these countries. Although the Netherlands continues to support the community, some reservations have begun to develop. The Dutch have continually opposed the creation of European political cooperation as a competitor for decisionmaking within NATO. Both countries have felt at times that they were unjustly left out of discussions between the larger powers. Particularly on the left, concern has arisen regarding the possibility of pursuing a progressive or socialist policy within Europe. The Dutch have also been strong in pushing for extension of democratic control within the community. The first direct elections for the European Parliament in 1979 resulted at least in part from pressure from the Dutch, who in general also favor extending the power of the Parliament.[58] Former Belgian prime minister Leo Tindemans authored a report calling for greater authority for the European Commission and the European Parliament.

Belgian and Dutch support for the community has been put to the test by the economic problems of the 1980s, although the same must be said for most of the members. Restrictions on steel production have been difficult for workers in Wallonia to accept, and restrictions on milk production have hurt Dutch dairies. Yet, although leaders and public opinion have become frustrated and impatient with British attempts to secure greater rebates, support for the community remains strong, and one may expect to see Belgian and Dutch moves to attempt to maintain unity.

The Atlantic Alliance.   World War II made clear that policies of neutrality could no longer be pursued. Both countries opted for defense within a system of collective security, joining the North Atlantic Treaty Organization (NATO) upon its founding. Both were among the strongest supporters of NATO and, in general, were willing to follow the lead of the United States in defense matters. Until

1970 the Netherlands was especially strong in its gratitude and loyalty to the United States. It was the first country to accept American nuclear weapons on its soil; it attempted to strengthen both the political and military aspects of the Alliance and maintained relatively high defense expenditures. When de Gaulle moved to eject NATO forces from France in 1966 and 1967, the Dutch and Belgians were instrumental in seeking a solution. NATO military commands were transferred to the Benelux countries, and Brussels became the new NATO headquarters.

When Joseph Luns resigned in 1970 after many years as foreign minister (to become yet another Dutch or Belgian secretary general of NATO), Dutch policy and attitudes began to change. The government publicly criticized American policy in Vietnam for the first time. New governments sought to reduce defense spending, and public opinion became less favorable toward dependence on nuclear weapons. Although a majority of the population still favors membership in NATO, the Labor Party did adopt a resolution in 1975 calling for withdrawal from NATO unless certain conditions were met, and it has continued to keep a critical eye on NATO. The smaller Radical Party went even further, calling for setting a moral example by unconditional withdrawal.

Attitudes toward NATO are strongly tied to those toward the United States. After World War II, the Dutch were extremely grateful toward the United States for its role in the liberation and for Marshall Plan assistance. Despite early disagreements over policy toward Indonesia and New Guinea, Holland was almost unconditional in its support of the United States in international affairs. The Vietnam War brought a great change in attitudes. The unswerving support of the Dutch government until 1970 may even have had a negative effect upon public opinion. The U.S. role in Chile and the Watergate affair further weakened attitudes toward the United States. More and more individuals have come to equate the actions of the superpowers, viewing U.S. actions in Latin America as equivalent to Russian actions in Afghanistan or Poland. There is increasing public fear that either superpower might trigger a new war, a fear refueled by the cold war rhetoric of President Reagan. In summing up the relationship between the United States and the Netherlands since 1945, Van Staden states, "The former marriage of the heart has broken down and turned into one of convenience."[59]

The newest strain on this relationship and the relationship within NATO has come with regard to the modernization of nuclear forces through the deployment of cruise and Pershing missiles. In 1979, the NATO ministers decided to deploy 572 of these new missiles, beginning at the end of 1983, but to attempt through negotiations in the intervening years to make the deployment unnecessary. Originally the European governments had called for this modernization, and the Dutch and Belgian governments were not opposed to deployment. However, in a well-publicized footnote, the Dutch government acknowledged agreement with the argumentation but postponed the decision on deployment until 1981. Public and parliamentary resistance has become increasingly strong. In the Netherlands the IKV has mounted a crusade against the new missiles. "Free the world of nuclear weapons, beginning with the Netherlands" has been its slogan. In demonstrations in Amsterdam and The Hague (1981 and 1983), an estimated 400,000 and 550,000 persons turned out to protest the new weapons; demonstrations in Brussels brought out between 100,000 and 200,000 participants. Public opinion surveys indicated that a majority of the populace in both countries opposed the new missiles. The term *Hollanditis*, coined to describe the new European pacifism or neutralism, is worn as a badge of honor by many.

Under this public pressure, the governments have experienced difficulties. The failure of the Geneva talks led to deployment on schedule in Britain, Germany, and Italy, thereby increasing the pressure on the Belgians and Dutch to accept the weapons. Slowly and painfully the Belgian government moved toward a decision. In the fall of 1983, the Belgian Parliament accepted the assertion of the cabinet that the decision would be reached in the cabinet and announced to Parliament. In January 1985 a preliminary decision was made to make preparations, although the decision on actual placement of the missiles was delayed. On March 15 the announcement was made to deploy the first 16 of the Belgian quota of 48. The following day it became known that the missiles were already functional. Despite protests during the weekend, the governmental parties held the line and gave the cabinet a vote of confidence.

In the face of strong public opposition, the Dutch government has maneuvered to avoid and postpone any decision. Finally, in June 1984 a compromise was reached. Parliament accepted by a close vote a governmental announcement that the Netherlands would begin deployment on November 1, 1985, *unless* at that time the Soviet Union had not increased its arsenal of SS-20 rockets. Should the superpowers reach an agreement in the meantime for a reduction in the number of such weapons, the Netherlands would accept its proportional share. It remains to be seen how this decision will be received and what the long-term consequences will be.

In conclusion one might ask what effect recent political problems may have had upon public attitudes in the two countries. For some years the European Community has conducted, in the member countries, opinion polls that provide interesting insights into such questions. For example, in April 1983 the Netherlands was the most pessimistic of the member-countries on the question of whether unemployment would disappear if the economy were to revive.[60]

Both the Dutch and the Belgians are somewhat critical of the functioning of their democratic systems. A slight majority of the Dutch (53 percent), but only 43 percent of the Belgians, were "very" or "fairly" satisfied. Figures for France,

Ireland, and Italy were lower; those for Greece, Great Britain, Luxembourg, Germany, and Denmark were higher. More important than the absolute level of satisfaction is the fact that only in these two countries (and Ireland) had the level of satisfaction decreased since 1973.

On the other hand, one should not be too pessimistic. Although levels of personal happiness have declined since 1979 in all of the countries of the community (and declined more than the average in Belgium), the Dutch most often report being very happy, and overall both countries rate near the top. Also, the Netherlands has consistently ranked next to highest on an index of general satisfaction with life. Although somewhat less satisfied, the Belgians are on the average more satisfied than Germans, French, Italians, or Greeks; but, again, they show the strongest decline in satisfaction since 1973.

The overall picture would seem to be of two basically contented peoples, who nevertheless have concerns about their way of life and the functioning of their democratic systems. How their political systems handle the problems discussed here, as well as other important problems, will be of crucial importance for the future of both countries.

Updates: The Reform of the Belgian State

Problems posed by the language cleavage continue to dominate Belgian politics, and Belgian political institutions continue to evolve in attempts to find solutions. Since 1989 Belgium may be called a federal state, although the Belgian version of federalism is in many respects unique. Most federal states were formed by sovereign entities that joined to form a union and delegated a portion of their powers to a new central government. Belgium has become a federal state from the top down by delegating powers to constituent bodies.

The three communities—Francophone, Flemish, and German-speaking— and the three regions—Wallonia, Flanders, and Brussels-Capital—continue to form the major components of the new federal structure. Although the Brussels regions were officially recognized by the constitutional revision of 1980, the actual organization of political institutions was achieved only recently. The Council of the Brussels-Capital Region consists of 75 members elected by citizens residing in one of the nineteen Brussels communes. The first elections were held on June 18, 1989. Both the Council and the executive it elects are divided clearly into French-language groups and Dutch-language groups.

The 1988 constitutional revision and subsequent legislation have expanded the powers and possibilities for the Communities and the Regions. The Communities continue to have powers in five main areas: cultural affairs, education, cooperation, so-called personally bound matters, and use of languages. It is primarily in the area of education that Community powers have been expanded. Aside from a few matters requiring national uniformity, all education matters are now in the hands of the Communities.

The Regions have responsibility for ten major areas: town and country planning, environmental protection, rural renewal and nature conservation, housing, water policy, energy policy, employment policy, and certain aspects of economic policy and of public works and transport.

To make the federal structure work and the institutions viable, the budgets for the Communities and Regions have been greatly expanded. Whereas under the 1980 system the budgets for these bodies accounted for less than 10 percent of total governmental expenditures, they now are responsible for approximately 40 percent of the total budget.

However, the federal structure is not yet complete. The Senate must still be reformed along federal lines. With the exception of the German-speaking Community Council and the Brussels-Capital Regional Council, the Community Council and Regional Council hold a double mandate and consist of the appropriate members of the national Parliament. In a future move, these bodies will also be elected directly.

Although unrelated to the language question, an incident that occurred in early 1990 also illustrated the pragmatic approach of the Belgians to pressing constitutional questions. In March both houses of Parliament passed a new law that would permit abortion in certain circumstances. However, the king, a devout Catholic, informed the government that he would be unable in good conscience to sign the law. To avoid a severe constitutional crisis, a provision of the Belgian constitution was employed by which it was declared that the king was unable to rule. On the same day that this announcement was made, the Cabinet, acting now in place of the king, signed the law into existence. The following day the powers of the king were returned and the business of government returned to normal.

The Dutch Economic Situation

At the beginning of the 1980s there was fairly broad political consensus that the public sector in the Netherlands was too large and that both the budgetary financing deficit and unemployment were too high. Two governmental coalitions of Christian-Democrats and Liberals (1982–1986 and 1986–1989), under the leadership of Prime Minister Ruud Lubbers, made it a high priority to attempt to correct these problems. By 1986 public perception of the success of the measures taken had made it possible for the Christian-Democrats to adopt an electoral slogan of "Let Lubbers finish his job" and gain 9 seats in Parliament. In

1989, after the collapse of the coalition, the Christian-Democrats seemed to feel that enough had been accomplished for the moment so that it was safe to enter a new coalition with the Labor Party.

Examination of economic statistics indeed shows that certain unwanted growth trends were reversed. Expenditures in the public sector (as a percentage of the net national income), which had risen to a high of 70.0 percent in 1983, had been reduced to 62.7 percent in 1989. Similar percentages for all social insurance and welfare programs had been reduced from a high of 32.4 percent to 29.0 percent in the same years. The all-important budgetary financing deficit, which had reached 10.6 percent in 1982, was down to 6.2 percent in 1989.

Since it was not deemed possible to raise taxes, the government attempted to limit public expenditures. Various operations were undertaken under the headings: deregulation, decentralization, reorganization, personnel reduction, and privatization. Two important measures to cut social expenditures were a reduction in the maximum benefit for disability from 80 percent of the last wage level to 70 percent, and the elimination of the "coupling" of welfare benefits to the wage index. The new Christian-Democratic/Labor Cabinet is now considering whether it is possible to reintroduce the principle of "coupling."

From a high of more than 800,000 unemployed in 1984 (over 17 percent of the work force), unemployment was reduced to 658,000 (13 percent) in 1989. At least some of the reduction has been achieved by the cooperative efforts of the employers, the unions and the government. Two important measures have been the reduction of the work force by providing opportunities for early retirement and reduction of the work week from 40 to 38 hours. In addition, provisions for part-time employment have been increased.

Although these figures all represent improvement, it should be recalled that most of the (negative) figures still are higher than comparable figures for 1980. Nevertheless, although social unrest has been minimal and no radical right backlash has occurred, these changes have not been achieved without difficulty. The current government is continuing attempts to reform parts of the system—for example, health care—but is attempting to avoid any major changes that might further upset the populace.

Foreign Affairs

The dramatic events of the late 1980s have been followed with considerable interest in Belgium and the Netherlands. Of most direct impact upon the two countries was the agreement in December 1987 on the INF treaty by the United States and the Soviet Union. By agreeing to arms reductions it became unnecessary to deploy the Pershing-2 and cruise missiles in the countries of Western Europe. This was a great relief to both countries. The Netherlands, in particular, had delayed as long as possible and was now able to stop construction at the Woensdrecht base. In the same month a separate treaty was negotiated, providing inspection in the five countries in which the Western missiles were to be deployed.

The subsequent warming of relations between the United States and the Soviet Union has been greeted positively in both countries. Proposals have been made for reductions in defense spending and in the length of compulsory military service. The once-powerful peace movements have collapsed.

The events in Eastern Europe have had a less direct impact, but have certainly received great attention. There has been some underlying apprehension concerning the unification of the two Germanys, but there has been no organized opposition and neither the governments nor the media have expressed reservations publicly. Both countries have supported public and private aid programs for Eastern Europe and visa requirements have been lifted for citizens of Hungary and Czechoslovakia.

Because of the relationship with the Boers in South Africa, events in that land have always been followed closely in the Netherlands. The release of Nelson Mandela and subsequent attempts to initiate a dialog are welcomed by the Dutch. Perhaps most indicative of Dutch support for these changes has been the visit of a parliamentary delegation, which included representatives of the left as well as the right.

Finally, both countries continue to support developments toward the integration of Europe. Until the revolutionary events of 1989 pushed the topic from the front pages, great attention was given to the potential impact of 1992. In that year, or January 1, 1993, at the latest, internal boundaries will be eliminated and trade can move unhindered between the member countries of the European Community. Although there has been some concern about drug traffic and movement of aliens, there has been little public opposition to the developments. Only a slight backlash of nationalist sentiments fearing a loss of identity with a united Europe has occurred.

Notes

1. See R. E. M. Irving, *The Christian Democratic Parties of Western Europe* (London: Allen & Unwin, 1979).

2. In this chapter the term *Protestants* applies in general to members of the Dutch Reformed Church and the Rereformed Churches (*Gereformeerden*). The term *Calvinist* is employed when referring only to the latter.

3. See L. Huyse, "Belgie, een wankele natie?" in U. Rosenthal, ed., *Politieke Stelsels, stabiliteit en veranderingen* (Alphen aan den Rijn: Samsom Uitgeverij, 1982).

4. H. Daalder, "On the Origins of the Consociational Democracy Model," *Acta Politica* 19 (January 1984): 97–116.

5. Arend Lijphart, "De theorie van de pacificatie-theorie," in J. J. A. Thomassen, ed., *Democratie: Theorie en praktijk* (Alphen aan den Rijn: Samsom Uitgeverij, 1981), p. 130.

6. L. Huyse, *Passiviteit, pacificatie en verzuiling in de Belgische politiek* (Antwerp: Standaard Wetenschappelijke Uitgeverij, 1970), p. 223.

7. Arend Lijphart, *The Politics of Accommodation: Pluralism and Democracy in the Netherlands* (Berkeley and Los Angeles: University of California Press, 1968), p. 125.

8. Ibid., pp. 122–38.

9. H. Daalder, *Politisering en lijdelijkheid in de Nederlandse politiek* (Assen: van Gorcum, 1974).

10. Lijphart, *Politics of Accommodation*, 2d ed., rev. (1975).

11. Arend Lijphart, ed., *Conflict and Coexistence in Belgium: The Dynamics of a Culturally Divided Society* (Berkeley: University of California Institute of International Studies, 1981), p. 1.

12. See R. L. Peterson, M. de Ridder, J. D. Hobbs, and L. J. McClellan, "Government Formation and Policy Formulation Patterns in Belgium and the Netherlands," *Res Publica* 25, no. 1 (1983): 49–82.

13. Keith Hill, "Belgium: Political Change in a Segmented Society," in Richard Rose, ed., *Electoral Behavior: A Comparative Handbook* (New York: Free Press, 1974).

14. J. Polasky, "Liberalism and Biculturalism," in Lijphart, *Conflict and Coexistence*, p. 40.

15. R. de Schryver, "The Belgian Revolution and the Emergence of Belgium's Biculturalism," in Lijphart, *Conflict and Coexistence*, pp. 21–25.

16. Polasky, "Liberalism and Biculturalism," p. 35.

17. de Schryver, "Belgian Revolution," p. 26.

18. L. Huyse, "Political Conflict in Bicultural Belgium," in Lijphart, *Conflict and Coexistence*, pp. 108–10.

19. Hill, "Political Change," p. 29.

20. Val R. Lorwin, "Belgium: Religion, Class, and Language in National Politics," in Robert A. Dahl, ed., *Political Oppositions in Western Democracies* (New Haven, Conn.: Yale University Press, 1966), p. 161.

21. Ibid.

22. Huyse, "Political Conflict," p. 111.

23. Frank E. Huggett, *Modern Belgium* (New York: Praeger, 1969), p. 86.

24. Lorwin, "Religion, Class, and Language," p. 194.

25. de Schryver, "Belgian Revolution, " p. 30.

26. Huyse, "Political Conflict," p. 113.

27. Th. Luykx, *Politieke Geschiedenis van Belgie 2* (Amsterdam and Brussels: Elsevier, 1978), pp. 550, 585.

28. Ibid., p. 588.

29. Ibid., p. 558.

30. W. Dewachter, "Changes in Belgian Party System," working paper, mimeo., p. 5.

31. A. Molitor, "The Reform of the Belgian Constitution," in Lijphart, *Conflict and Coexistence*, p. 143.

32. Ibid., p. 144.

33. G. Craenen and W. Dewachter, *De Belgische Grondwet van 1831 tot Heden: Nederlandse en Franse Teksten* (Leuven: Uitgeverij Acco, 1980), p. 18.

34. H. Todts, "De Belgische Staatshervorming tussen 1970 en 1980," *Kultuurleven*, no. 2 (1981): 173.

35. Craenen and Dewachter, *De Belgische Grondwet*, p. 26.

36. Todts, "De Belgische Staatschervorming," p. 171 (my translation).

37. Lijphart, *Conflict and Coexistence*, p. 7.

38. Molitor, "Belgian Constitution," p. 150.

39. Huyse, "Political Conflict," p. 124.

40. de Schryver, "Belgian Revolution," p. 32.

41. Todts, "De Belgische Staatshervorming," p. 181.

42. Huyse, "Political Conflict," pp. 125–26.

43. P. W. Klein, "The Foundations of Dutch Prosperity," in Richard T. Griffiths, ed., *The Economy and Politics of the Netherlands Since 1945* (The Hague: Martinus Nijhoff, 1980), pp. 1–12.

44. P. de Wolff and W. Driehuis, "A Description of Post War Economic Developments and Economic Policy in the Netherlands," in Griffiths, *Economy and Politics*, p. 42.

45. See R. F. M. Lubbers and C. Lemckert, "The Influence of Natural Gas on the Dutch Economy," in Griffiths, *Economy and Politics*, pp. 87–113.

46. Barbara L. Wolfe, Philip R. de Jong, Robert H. Haveman, Victor Halberstadt, and Kees P. Goudswaard, "Income Transfers and Work Effort: The Netherlands and the United States in the 1970s," *Kyklos*, vol. 37, fasc. 4 (1984), p. 613.

47. Ibid., p. 612.

48. V. Halberstadt et al., "Inefficiencies in Public Transfer Policies in Western Industrialized Democracies," Report 82.19 (Center for Research in Public Economics, Leyden University, June 1982), p. 33.

49. J. W. van Deth, M. van Giessen, W. H. van Schuur, and J. C. P. M. Vis, *Politieke Problemen in Nederland* (Leiderdorp: Stichting Burgerschapskunde, 1982), p. 178.

50. Ibid., p. 190.

51. Dutch Ministry of Social Affairs.

52. Deth et al., *Politieke Problemen in Nederland*, p. 297.

53. Ibid., p. 300.

54. K. P. Goudswaard and V. Halberstadt, "Het belang van het financieringstekort voor het financieel-economisch beleid," Report 82.27 (Center for Research in Public Economics, Leyden University, November 1982), p. 1.

55. See J. Deboutte and A. van Staden, "High Politics in the Low Countries," in W. Wallace and W. E. Paterson, eds., *Foreign Policy Making in Western Europe: A Comparative Approach* (Westmead, Eng.: Saxon House, 1978).

56. See Philip P. Everts, *Public Opinion, the Churches and Foreign Policy* (Ph.D. diss., Leyden University, 1983).

57. A. van Staden, "Nederland in internationale organisaties," in R. B. Andeweg, A. Hoogerwerf, and J. J. A. Thomassen, eds., *Politiek in Nederland* (Alphen aan den Rijn: Samsom Uitgeverij, 1981), p. 378.

58. Ibid., p. 383.

59. A. van Staden, "American-Dutch Political Relations Since 1945," in J. W. Schulte Nordholt and R. P. Swierenga, *A Bilateral Bicentennial* (Amsterdam: Meulenhoff, 1982), p. 80.

60. All figures are from "Publieke Opinie in de Europese Gemeenschap," *Eurobarometer*, no. 19 (June 1983).

Suggested Readings

Dahl, Robert A., ed. *Political Oppositions in Western Democracies.* New Haven, Conn.: Yale University Press, 1966; contributions by Val R. Lorwin on Belgium and Hans Daalder on the Netherlands.

Everts, Philip P. *Public Opinion, the Churches and Foreign Policy.* Ph.D. diss., Leyden University, 1983.

Fry, Earl H., and Raymond, Gregory A. *The Other Western Europe: A Political Analysis of the Smaller Democracies.* Santa Barbara, Calif.: ABC-Clio, 1980.

Griffiths, Richard T., ed. *The Economy and Politics of the Netherlands Since 1945.* The Hague: Martinus Nijhoff, 1980.

Huggett, Frank E. *Modern Belgium.* New York: Praeger, 1969.

Irving, R. E. M. *The Christian Democratic Parties of Western Europe.* London: Allen & Unwin, 1979.

Irwin, Galen A. "The Netherlands." In Peter H. Merkl, ed., *Western European Party Systems.* New York: Free Press, 1980.

Leurdijk, J. H., ed. *The Foreign Policy of the Netherlands.* Alphen aan den Rijn: Samsom Uitgeverij, 1978.

Lijphart, Arend. *The Politics of Accommodation: Pluralism and Democracy in the Netherlands.* Berkeley and Los Angeles: University of California Press, 1968.

Lijphart, Arend, ed. *Conflict and Coexistence in Belgium: The Dynamics of a Culturally Divided Society.* Berkeley: University of California Institute of International Studies, 1981.

Rose, Richard, ed. *Electoral Behavior: A Comparative Handbook*. New York: Free Press, 1974; contributions by Keith Hill on Belgium and Arend Lijphart on the Netherlands.

van Schendelen, M. P. C. M., ed. "Consociationalism, Pillarization and Conflict-Management in the Low Countries," *Acta Politica* 19 (January 1984).

Voorhoeve, J. J. C. *Peace, Profits, and Principles: A Study of Dutch Foreign Policy*. The Hague: Martin Nijhoff, 1979.

5

The Nordic Countries

David Gress

This chapter deals with five independent states: Denmark, Finland, Iceland, Norway, and Sweden. Their inhabitants refer to them as a unit by the indigenous term *Norden*, "the North." *Norden* is the correct name for the area under discussion, but it sounds, and is, alien in English, although some writers use it. Europeans simply translate the word, but in England "the North" is always taken to refer to the north of that country. In the United States the term is ambiguous as well. "Scandinavia" is not adequate since it correctly applies only to the Scandinavian peninsula and its immediate environs, that is, to Denmark, Norway, and Sweden. "Nordic" has now become sanctioned in English usage as applying collectively to all five countries, and I will speak of "the Nordic countries" when referring to them as a whole.

Although profoundly different in many ways, the Nordic peoples share much common history and culture, and in modern times have deliberately chosen to coordinate their domestic and foreign policies to some extent. For the American reader, their interest lies partly in their social and economic policies, as symbolized by the welfare state and its achievements and problems, and partly in their

The author wishes to thank Professor H. Peter Krosby of the State University of New York at Albany for his detailed and valuable comments on an earlier draft, and friends and acquaintances in Scandinavia who contributed information and opinions, in particular Hilary Barnes, Michael Borg-Hansen, Ingemar Dörfer, the late Niels Jørgen Haagerup, Haakon Lie, Tøger Seidenfaden, and Joachim von Braun. The responsibility for the way in which their contributions were used is mine.

geostrategic position. Bordering on the Soviet Union, they are exposed, by reason of their small size and relative weakness, to direct and indirect pressures of a sort not usually experienced by larger powers. U.S.-Nordic relations are usually cordial and uncomplicated. Only 6 to 8 percent of Nordic foreign trade is with the United States, and the prime American concern in the area has always been security.

The Nordic countries are the most northerly independent states in the world. The southern border of Denmark barely reaches below the 55th parallel, while the North Cape of Norway is at the 71st parallel, well above the Arctic Circle. If one includes Greenland and the Svalbard Archipelago, dependent on Denmark and Norway respectively, the northern boundary extends above the 81st parallel.

Thanks to the Gulf Stream, the Nordic countries enjoy a fairly temperate climate, milder in the old heartlands, for example, than the climate of the American Middle West. They differ greatly in geography, size, and density of population (for basic statistics, see Table 5.1). Denmark, the smallest, is heavily cultivated (65 percent of the land area) and was the earliest to achieve administrative unity because the sea, never further than 35 miles away from any point of the islands and peninsulas that form the country, was a connecting highway and not a barrier. Finland, Sweden, and Norway, by contrast, are among the largest countries in Europe. The first two are heavily forested (65 and 50 percent respectively). More than 65 percent of Norway is barren rock and mountains, and 80 percent of the people live within four miles of the sea. Iceland, about the size of Virginia, is a volcanic island in the mid-Atlantic. Agriculture was possible and trees grew there during the age of settlement (A.D. 860–1100), but it suffered terribly during the Little Ice Age (1350–1700). In exceptional conditions, agriculture is possible again today but is of little economic importance compared with the main industry, cod fishing.

Historical Background

Human beings have lived in the Nordic area since 8000 B.C., when hunter-gatherers followed the retreating ice into what is now Denmark. The Proto-Germanic tribes who were the ancestors of present-day Danes, Icelanders, Norwegians, and Swedes seem to have arrived during the first millennium B.C. By that time, Finnish tribes originating in Central Asia had already settled in present-day Estonia, Finland, and Lappland. Since then, no significant influx of settlers has moved into Denmark or the Scandinavian peninsula, making the present population perhaps the most ethnically homogeneous in the world; this can be seen, for example, in the dominance of genetically recessive traits, such as blue eyes and blond hair.

Until around A.D. 1100, these inhabitants spoke dialects of a common lan-

Table 5.1   Basic Nordic Statistics, 1985

	Denmark	Finland	Iceland	Norway	Sweden
Population (1,000 pers)	5.114	4.903	242	4.159	8.358
Area (1,000 sq km)	43	338	103	386	487
GDP (bill units USD currency)	57.9	54.0	2.7	57.8	99.9
Per capita GDP (1,000 units USD currency)	11.3	11.0	11.3	13.9	11.9
Value added in manufacturing industry (bill units national currency) 1985	103.1	75.2	15.9	67.3	281.0
Share in 1985, percent					
Manufacturing	100	100	100	100	100
food manufacturing	23	11.6	43	15	10
textile, wearing apparel, and leather industries	5	6.8	7	3	3
manufacture of wood and wood products	5	6.4	7	8	7
manufacture of paper and paper products	10	21.4	8	14	16
manufacture of chemicals, etc.	12	12.3	6	9	11
manufacture of non-metallic mineral products	5	4.3	5	3	3
basic metal industries	1	4.2	10	8	5
engineering industries	37	32.0	12	39	45
other manufacturing industries	2	0.8	2	1	1
Share of total world exports	1.2	0.6	0.0	1.0	1.8
Share of total world imports	1.0	0.7	0.0	1.4	1.8
Total labor force (1,000 pers)	2.810	2.437	118.0	2.064	4.315
Thousand pers employed in manufacturing industry	527	557	19	335	892
Exchange rate (November 1986)	DKK	FIM	ISK	NOK	SEK
USD	7.64	4.95	40.3	7.52	6.97

SOURCE: *Nordic Economic Outlook* (Stockholm: Federation of Swedish Industries, December 1986). Used by permission.

guage known as Old Norse. It was the North Germanic descendant of Primitive Germanic, the original common language of all Germanic tribes, including the ancestors of the English, the Germans, and the now-extinct Goths. From the eleventh century onward, Old Norse gradually split into a Western form, spoken in Iceland, the Faroe Islands, and Norway, and an Eastern form, spoken in Denmark and Sweden. By 1500, differences within these two versions had emerged, and with the Reformation and the publication of vernacular translations of the Bible, the modern written languages were born. For political reasons—namely, to support national independence—Swedish was consciously differentiated from Danish in spelling and vocabulary—more than would otherwise have been necessary. Also for political reasons—namely, Danish domination—Old Norwegian disappeared as a written language until it was resurrected in the nineteenth century. The language spoken and written by most Norwegians today is closer to Danish in grammar and vocabulary than Swedish is. With little effort, modern standard Danish, Norwegian (of both kinds), and Swedish are mutually intelligible. However, Icelandic and Faroese, and of course the wholly alien Finnish and Lapp, cannot be understood by other Nordic speakers.

Beginning around A.D. 800, a series of raids and conquests by Scandinavians, or Northmen as they came to be called, marked the Viking Age. Danish and Norwegian chieftains established their rule in England, Ireland, and northwestern France, which became Normandy. Many Swedes went east, through the Russian river network, and influenced the culture and society of the first Russian state, the Grand Duchy of Kiev. Norwegian families settled Iceland. The physical orientation of the settled heartlands of the three countries predisposed their populations to turn west or east respectively, and the resulting cultural, economic, and political orientation remained a powerful factor through succeeding centuries, with repercussions to the present day.

The material culture of the Viking Age was complex and left its mark where the Northmen settled, as did their language. The expansion, however, was a two-way process, and indeed since around A.D. 1000 the Nordic region has been a net importer of culture and of political, economic, and legal practices, although each has been transformed by the native genius. The first and most important arrival was Christianity, which spread in successive waves from the south and west in the ninth to twelfth centuries.

By the mid-eleventh century, the Viking expansion had given way to the consolidation of royal power in the homelands. During the subsequent centuries, the energies of the Nordic peoples were largely consumed in consolidating and expanding settlement at home, building towns and churches, and taking part in the general advance of culture in medieval Europe. A significant achievement was the compilation of lawbooks in the various regions of Scandinavia from the later twelfth century onward. These codifications included ancient traditional law and new royal laws designed to improve the administration of justice, and they were often inspired by the principles of the universal European canon law, which was simultaneously being developed by the church. Their effect can be traced in Nordic legislation to this day.

In 1397, partly as a result of dynastic accidents, the Danish queen Margrethe the Great was chosen as common ruler of the three Scandinavian kingdoms. By this time, Iceland had lost its original independence as an aristocratic republic and had come under the rule of Norway, and the settled portion of present-day Finland had become an integral part of Sweden. The resulting Nordic union was unstable and finally fell apart when Sweden (including Finland) gained permanent independence in 1523. Norway, along with Iceland, remained bound to Denmark and was even reduced to the status of a mere province in 1536. Although the union failed and was indeed associated in Sweden chiefly with fears of Danish dominance, it left a legacy of the idea of strength in unity. This legacy became significant in modern times, in the Scandinavist movement of the nineteenth century and in contemporary efforts at Nordic cooperation.

The Lutheran Reformation won quickly and painlessly in Scandinavia; church property was confiscated to the immense enrichment of many aristocrats, and the spiritual power of the church was annexed by the growing state. From 1520 to 1720 Denmark and Sweden fought ten bloody wars, and the early Danish predominance gave way to Swedish. In 1658 Sweden was able to annex the eastern third of Denmark (now the southern tip of Sweden) and several pieces of Norway. As a result, the Danish encirclement of Sweden was replaced with a potential Swedish encirclement of Denmark, especially as Sweden at this time also had extensive possessions in northern Germany. In a series of further wars with Denmark, Prussia, and Russia, Sweden lost its empire, and Finland was devastated. Sweden did, however, retain and assimilate eastern Denmark in one of the few examples in European history of successful integration of a territorial conquest.

Apart from a couple of insignificant interludes, Denmark and Sweden did not fight each other after 1720. In 1809 Sweden was forced to cede Finland to Russia, and in 1814 Denmark, having supported the defeated Napoleon, was forced to cede Norway to Sweden. The Norwegians, however, declared unilateral independence and gave themselves a liberal constitution. The Swedish king accepted this, and Norway's status in the resulting union, which lasted until 1905, was relatively free, although the foreign affairs of both countries were a Swedish prerogative.

The condition of the Nordic countries in the early modern period is best summarized by Stein Rokkan's conceptual map of Western Europe in the era of state building and early cultural mobilization.[1] In this grid, the regions of Europe are distributed along a south-north "state-culture" axis and a west-east "state-economy" axis (see Table 5.2). The Nordic countries, having Protestant state churches and not having been part of the medieval Holy Roman Empire,

Table 5.2

SEAWARD PERIPHERY		SUCCESSFUL EMPIRE-NATIONS		LANDWARD PERIPHERY
		Seaward:	*Landward:*	
weaker cities, once independent, later a subject territory:	stronger cities, medieval empire, later reduced to dependence:	stronger cities, continuous independence:	weaker cities, continuous independence:	weaker cities, subject territory:
Iceland	*Norway*	*Denmark*	*Sweden*	*Finland*

SOURCE: Stein Rokkan, "The Growth and Structuring of Mass Politics," in *Nordic Democracy.* Used by permission of The Danish Institute.

together make up the top tier of the south-north axis. In this dimension, they are very similar. Their differences emerge only when they are placed on the west-east, "state-economy" axis, where the decisive variables are the relative strength or weakness of towns and the independence or subjection of each country.

Other variables are the relative strengths and positions of the nobility and the peasantry. Including them, one obtains the following variation in the Scandinavian countries in the early modern period:

> Denmark—towns developed, nobility powerful, peasantry oppressed
> Norway—towns developed, no nobility, free peasants
> Sweden—towns weak, nobility powerful, free peasants

Iceland and Finland, the western and eastern periphery, share a lack of towns, but Finland, being closer and larger, was dominated by Swedish and native nobles. The 30,000 or so poor fishermen and shepherds of Iceland, however, were of little interest or concern to the distant rulers in Copenhagen. Using another of Rokkan's diagrams, the combinations can be schematized as shown in Figure 5.1.

Cultural Conflicts and the Modern Party System

The period of state building in the sixteenth through eighteenth centuries was followed in the nineteenth and early twentieth centuries by mass mobilization, the second stage of Western modernity. It has three elements: the national-democratic *political* revolution inspired by the United States, France,

Figure 5.1

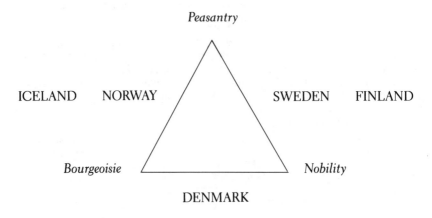

SOURCE: Rokkan, "Growth and Structuring of Mass Politics."

and Germany; the *industrial* revolution; and a *cultural* revolution involving religion, social attitudes, and group reactions to modernization, which largely determined the "cleavage structures" and party systems of our own day.[2]

The Nordic countries shared a characteristic sequence of these elements. The full impact of the third, the cultural revolution, occurred before World War I and preceded that of the second, the industrial revolution. The first, the political revolution, concerned political rights and, for the dependent regions, national independence. In Sweden, with its tradition of a free peasantry and some degree of representative rule, the extension of suffrage was gradual. In Denmark, with its absolutist heritage, the extension was sudden. The impact in the geographical periphery, Norway, Iceland, and Finland, depended on the range of mobilizing issues: cultural, social, and political. Thus, extension was gradual in Norway and Iceland, but sudden and dramatic in Finland. The polarization in Finland was indeed unique in the area and led to the only Nordic case of violent transition to mass democracy, the civil war of 1918.[3] This war, the rise of a strong communist party, the right-wing extremism of the 1930s, and the wars of 1939–1940 and 1941–1944 with the Soviet Union are atypical, indeed Central European, elements in modern Finnish history that for a time set its recent development apart from that of its Nordic brethren.

Both of the old independent states, Denmark and Sweden, remained monarchies, as did Norway after the dissolution of the union with Sweden in 1905, when the Norwegians chose a Danish prince for their king. The royal houses today are closely related by intermarriage and descent. Finland and Iceland became presidential republics in 1917 and 1944 respectively. In Denmark and Norway, the king retains vestigial authority, and his signature is necessary to give acts of parliament the force of law. As the theoretical source of legislative and executive power, he is above the law and his person is sacrosanct, but he cannot vote and must belong to the Evangelical Lutheran state church. In theory, civil servants, parliaments, and state enterprises serve at the king's pleasure; in fact, the vestigial powers, except for the signing of laws, are never exercised. The monarchy is generally felt to provide continuity and a focus of national identity, and republicanism is virtually nonexistent. In Sweden, even the vestigial powers were abolished in 1974. In daily practice, Nordic government, except in Finland, functions much as the government of West Germany or Britain, where the formal head of state is removed from the formation and execution of actual policy. In Finland the president directs foreign policy, whereas the cabinet concerns itself with domestic matters. This division of tasks and the strong presidency are reminiscent of the French system.

The fundamental cultural and economic cleavages of the later nineteenth century produced conflicts and party alignments that characterize the Nordic party system to this day. The most important cleavages were economic (socialism versus private enterprise), religious (state religion versus secular society), sociopolitical (workers versus owners), center versus periphery, moral, and linguistic.[4] Since positions on these issues were strongly correlated, however, the resulting number of parties was far smaller than the number of cleavages. In fact, in Denmark, Norway, and Sweden four parties arose, in Iceland three, and in Finland, with its special national conflict of Finnish versus Swedish and Russian, five. The division of the socialist parties following the Bolshevik Revolution in Russia increased the number of parties in the typical case to five: one communist, one social democratic, two liberal, and one conservative party. To a varying extent since the 1950s, orthodox communism has been replaced by newer forms of radical socialism to the left of the social democrats, most clearly in Denmark, Norway, and Sweden. This left the five-party system intact. In Sweden, it remains so, but in Denmark in 1973 the number of parties represented in Parliament doubled from five to ten.

A characteristic common trait of the Nordic political landscape is the coexistence of several parties in the middle ground between the socialist and conservative wings. It is customary to refer to these parties as liberal, although they in fact have represented a variety of interests arising from the cleavage structures mentioned earlier. Because cultural modernization preceded industrialization in the Nordic countries, these parties played an originally progressive, even radical, role. This role later fell to the social democrats but is far from a dead force even in these other parties, although today they are generally centrist on most issues.

In Denmark the original progressive party was Venstre, a word literally meaning "left" and confusing to present-day foreign observers because, since the

1920s, Venstre has been allied with the Conservatives, formerly known as Højre (the Right). In 1905, it split into a party of farmers and a party combining the secular, urban bourgeoisie and the poor crofters of the countryside. The Norwegian Venstre split into a Christian party, an agrarian party, and an urban liberal party, none of which has kept the old name. The Swedish liberals split on the issue of prohibition, but reunited in 1934 as Folkpartiet (The People's Party). The Swedish agrarian party, Centern, arose in the 1910s from a split in the conservative party, then known, as in Denmark, as Högern, the Right. In Iceland the split largely reflected urban-rural differences. In Finland the old progressives, as in Denmark, split into a large agrarian and an urban liberal party. The former is today's Center Party (KESK), the party of long-time president Urho Kekkonen (1956–1981), who was fond of referring to himself as a radical. The urban (progressive) liberals rejoined KESK for the 1983 and 1987 elections. The rural poor, however, had meanwhile formed their own party, the Rural People's Party (SMP).

The tension between center (capital city) and periphery crystallized a number of issues throughout modern Nordic history, particularly in Finland, Norway, and Sweden with their enormous distances and problems of regional isolation. Oslo and Stockholm became and remained bastions both of traditional liberalism (in the European sense) and of conservatism. Swedish voting patterns in particular demonstrated a surprising continuity across the great divide marked by the rise of the labor movement: the distribution of votes in the first genuinely popular election, that of 1887, between free-traders (liberals) and protectionists (conservatives) resembled that in the election of 1968 between social democrats and the center-right parties. In the 1980s, the Norwegian and Swedish conservative parties, which had to some extent assumed the ideological and cultural inheritance of the older liberalism, received more votes in Oslo and Stockholm respectively than any other party. The social democrats were strong in the medium-sized industrial cities of central and western Sweden, in the far north, and in rural Norway. In Denmark, where Copenhagen became a center of manufacturing and industry in the 1880s, the opposite was the case: the left was strong, not weak, in the capital. By the 1980s the largest party in Copenhagen was no longer the Social Democrats but the more radical Socialist People's Party.

Two other issues that were in part shaped by the center-periphery tension were language and teetotalism. In both Finland and Norway centuries of foreign domination meant that the cultural and political elite expressed themselves in a foreign language. In both countries significant numbers of the native population were native speakers of the foreign language. In Finland, moreover, the linguistic opposition between Swedish and Finnish was radical, since Finnish, together with Lapp, belongs to an Asiatic family of languages and is remotely related to other non-European tongues such as Hungarian and Turkish. While Finland was a grand duchy under the Russian tsar (1809–1917), linguistic and cultural nationalism had to contend with both the old Swedish and the newer Russian dominance. The Swedish-speaking minority of Finns, the Swecomans, eventually formed their own party (SFP). The Fennomans (Finnish-speakers) split into the liberal Young Finns and the conservative Old Finns, ancestors of the conservative National Coalition Party (KOK). The Finnish liberals became the party of the masses, opposed to the cultural and economic dominance of the conservatives, including the Swecomans, and thus were often more pro-Russian.

When Denmark took control of Norway in the late Middle Ages the languages were still so similar that the disappearance of written Norwegian and the use of Danish as the medium of expression of educated Norwegians caused no problems until the rise of modern cultural nationalism. In the mid-nineteenth century, Norwegian nationalists reconstructed a native Norwegian language from the spoken dialects of western Norway. This was opposed to the language of the capital, which, as written, was identical to Danish. Gradually, two different, mutually intelligible and not sharply defined languages emerged: a conservative Dano-Norwegian of the upper-middle classes of the Oslo area, and the New Norwegian of the west coast and towns such as Stavanger, Bergen, and Trondheim. Native Norwegian, from which New, or rather revived, Norwegian derives, was, along with Icelandic and Faroese, a West Nordic language and shared common phonetic and grammatical elements not found in East Nordic, and was far more archaic in form. Support for New Norwegian thus constituted linguistic conservatism, which, however, opposed the cultural and political conservatism of the Oslo bourgeoisie. During the past century, various reforms of spelling and grammar have made Dano-Norwegian, or *bokmaal* (book-speech), as it is called, more similar to New Norwegian. This somewhat artificially "Norwegianized" *bokmaal* is spoken today by about 70 percent of the population. New Norwegian, meanwhile, has become a symbol of the new left of regionalists, ecologists, and cultural nationalists in opposition to the conservative and liberal middle classes. This was particularly marked in the struggle over membership in the European Communities (EC) in the early 1970s. As an issue, then, language catalyzed, and was itself catalyzed by, political and cultural confrontations in two of the five countries.

Alcohol also polarized opinion in Norway and Sweden. In both countries, according to Rokkan,

> teetotalism represented a strategy of defense of status within mobile groups increasingly exposed to the opportunities and temptations of the urban *Gesellschaft* . . . a form of defensive isolation . . . in the face of the disintegration of traditional local communities. This response to the possible losses of status would be strongest in egalitarian social structures, particularly in countries with long-established traditions of freedom for the peasantry.[5]

This was also true, Rokkan continues, in countries where the capital city was less dominant than in Denmark. Denmark began taxing the local liquor, *snaps*, in 1917, not otherwise restricting its consumption, but Sweden and Norway severely curbed its sale and use by law. In Sweden, teetotalism was strongly supported not only by the lower-middle classes, politically mobilized in the old progressive party, but also by the Social Democrats (SAP), the party of the rural underclass and of the emerging urban working class. Prohibition was enforced in the 1920s and then replaced by extraordinarily high taxation combined with state control of distribution and sale. In 1982, the Ministry of Health produced an 1,100-page "White Paper on Alcohol Policy," stating total prohibition as a desirable, but unfortunately unattainable and unenforceable, goal. Among its recommendations was the suggestion that customers and their purchases should be centrally registered by computer at Systembolaget to sort out and exclude excessive drinkers from access to alcohol. Since most Swedes travel abroad at intervals, private importation up to (and above) the permitted duty-free limits is significant enough that the government, in this report, also proposed that Sweden should entirely eliminate any duty-free allowance of alcoholic beverages. Even in the absence of such regulations, the local authorities, who are the exclusive judges of what constitutes excessive buying of alcohol, can and do visit the homes of private individuals who have been visiting Systemet, as it is called, too often.

These examples of language and alcohol show how cultural and social issues dating from the nineteenth century have survived to the present. The major political development of the period after 1914 was the rise and eventual predominance in government of the socialist parties.[6] The early Norwegian, Swedish, and Finnish socialists had in common a strong base among the rural poor, whereas the Danish party was from the outset city-based, reflecting the greater relative and absolute importance of Copenhagen. Following the Bolshevik seizure of power in Russia in 1917, communist parties split from the Social Democrats in Denmark and Sweden but have remained tiny parties, gathering only a small percentage of the vote, although having some influence among intellectuals and in the trade union movement. In Norway the initial split went the opposite way, with the majority of the socialist party (DNA) joining the Communist International (Comintern) in 1919 and a reformist minority forming a social democratic party in 1921. In 1923 the Norwegian socialists rejected control by Moscow and left the Comintern, upon which a pro-Moscow minority broke away to form the Norwegian Communist Party. Finally, in 1927, the reformist social democrats rejoined the DNA. In Finland, the civil war precipitated a much larger communist party, which was outlawed from 1930 to 1944 and, partly for this reason, acted through the so-called People's Democratic Union (SKDL), which it dominated organizationally, although no communist has ever chaired the SKDL. Until 1983, when it slipped to 13 percent, it consistently got 18 to 20 percent of the vote and was thus unique in being the only communist party of any real size in northern Europe, a fascinating anomaly that can only be noted here.[7] The strength of communism in Finland also traditionally meant that the Social Democratic Party (SSP), was, with only some 20 to 24 percent of the vote, relatively weak in comparison with its three Scandinavian sister parties. In 1983 and 1987, however, the SSP obtained more than twice the votes the SKDL did, an unprecedented achievement due largely to the popularity of the current president, Mauno Koivisto. In 1986 the Communist party split, with a Eurocommunist wing remaining in the SKDL and expelling the Moscow-oriented minority, which founded its own new party, the Democratic Alternative. In the 1987 elections, the SKDL, now resembling the Swedish VpK or the Danish Left Socialists more than the Communist Party of the past, got 9.4 percent, and the Moscow-line party got 4.3 percent. The SSP got 24.3 percent and remained the most dynamic of the Nordic social democratic parties in the late 1980s. This certainly was due in part to the much lighter burden of public spending in Finland, the result of a deliberate decision in 1975 by almost all parties not to allow public sector spending to exceed 37 percent of GDP.

A parallel, if much less dramatic, manifestation of what has been called polar communism is found in Iceland, where the Communist party, called Althyðubandalagið or the People's Alliance, actually receives more votes (17 percent in 1983) than Althyðuflokkurin, the Social Democrats (12 percent).[8]

At the end of World War II, broad sympathy for the Soviet Union led to a short-lived explosion in communist strength in Denmark, Norway, and Sweden. It had subsided by 1950, and when radical socialism made itself felt again among those impatient with the welfare-state reformism of the Social Democrats, it found other outlets. In Sweden, the Communist party slid away from old Soviet loyalties and changed its tactics and its name to appeal to the New Left; in 1968, it became the Left Party of Communists (VpK). Even so, the radical socialist potential in Sweden mostly made itself felt within the SAP. In Norway, a radical left grouping, Sosialistisk Venstreparti (SV), had more, but not striking, success. Here also the radical trend of the 1960s and 1970s manifested itself more within the DNA. In Denmark the clearer distinction between radical socialists and social democrats was due, in general terms, to the divisive effects on the Left of Denmark's membership in NATO and, in concrete terms, to the efforts of one man, former communist leader Aksel Larsen, who, after being expelled for "Titoism" in 1956, founded the Socialist People's Party (SF). Under his successor, Gert Petersen, the SF became a considerable force, mustering by the late-1980s a steady 14 to 15 percent of the vote. By the mid-1980s, SF was clearly the more dynamic of the two parties, with far greater appeal to younger academics and intellectuals, and was making serious inroads among formerly safe social democratic voters. Consequently, the Danish Social Democratic Party was in the 1980s proportionally the weakest of the three central Nordic Social Democratic parties and commanded only some 30 percent of the vote compared to 41 percent for the Norwegian DNA and 45 percent for the SAP in Sweden. The more traditional and well-established character of the Danish SF compared with the VpK or the SV also meant that it has itself already been subject to several schisms, spawning in 1967 the extreme leftist party of the Left Socialists (VS), who hovered around 2 to 3 percent of the vote until internal dissensions in 1986 brought a virtual end to the party, with half of its members of parliament defecting to the SF.

With the exception of Iceland and of Finland, where Social Democrats and communists were evenly balanced until quite recently, Nordic politics were dominated by Social Democrats from the early 1920s until around 1980. The first government controlled by Social Democrats was appointed in Denmark in 1924, in Norway in 1935 (after an initial, short-lived attempt in 1928), and in Sweden in 1933. In Finland the Social Democrats joined a national unity government in 1921–1925 and returned to power in a controlling position in 1933. Social democratic dominance was indeed the characteristic feature of Nordic politics, producing a continuity unmatched elsewhere in Western Europe. Developments on the center-right were interesting reflections of cultural and economic trends, but significant on the local rather than the national level. If there is, in the 1990s, a shift of ideological legitimacy, even ascendancy, away from social democracy, it will be the most momentous development in Nordic politics since the early years of the century. Interestingly, this shift would benefit not the liberal, but the conservative, parties and to a lesser extent the radical socialists.[9] An unprecedented degree of party-political polarization took place in Norwegian politics during the struggle over membership in the EC in 1972, and this was followed through that decade by equally sharp polarization over other issues in Sweden and Denmark. This polarization was the most striking feature of Nordic politics since the mid-1970s, and was to a great extent simply a parallel to what was happening on a larger scale elsewhere in Western Europe and the United States.[10] For a listing of the active political parties in the Nordic countries and their strength as of the most recent election, see Table 5.3.

All Nordic parliaments are unicameral assemblies elected by proportional representation. Denmark, Iceland, and Sweden have a combination of direct election in multimember constituencies and distribution of additional seats on the basis of each party's national strength. This system differs from the single-member British and American system in allowing parties too small to win a constituency seat to achieve representation if the national vote exceeds a certain proportion (2 percent in Denmark and 4 percent in Sweden). Finland and Norway are divided into a few large electoral districts, within which any party with enough votes can win a seat. The election period is four years, except in Sweden, where it is three. Norway is unique among parliamentary, as opposed to presidential, democracies in that the term of parliament is fixed. Conversely, in Denmark the king (in practice this means the sitting government) can dissolve parliament at any time, and from 1966 to 1984 elections were called on average every two years. Finnish elections have not normally been held early. Another special feature of the Finnish system is that virtually all bills require qualified majorities of two-thirds or even five-sixths to pass.

Nordic Politics in the 1980s

The years since 1973 were a period of not only economic but also political, social, and cultural-psychological uncertainty. Nordic politics and policies in the 1970s and 1980s increasingly reflected a common perception that the Western economies and political systems had entered a "time of troubles," an era of sustained structural change of uncertain outcome and duration. The following account of the crucial issues of economic problems, the welfare state, and international security reflects that perception and is therefore focused as a whole on the general question of the post-1973 crisis and its effects.

The economic problems of the 1980s are treated first, even though they were in large part caused by the growth of the welfare state and social spending, the ideological background to which is outlined in a later section. This is done to give the reader an immediate feel for the problems and challenges facing the present generation of planners and leaders, before going on to describe, in a more analytical manner, the presuppositions and stages of development of the social democratic model of "politics against markets" and of comprehensive welfare.

Economic Issues

The Nordic economies were in various ways ill-prepared for the problems generated by the energy crisis and the recession that began in 1973–1974, and efficient solutions had not, by the late 1980s, been applied and maintained long enough to restore balance. Perhaps surprisingly, the most successful economy overall was Finland's, while the prize for being the greatest bungler, at least until 1983, must go to Denmark. Norway's oil helped alleviate some, but not all, problems, and Sweden, the largest of the Nordic economies, suffered from a combination of the problems plaguing them all. The economy of Iceland had its own eccentricities due to its small size and high reliance on one source of income, fish. In each case, the delay in finding appropriate solutions and, when found, the difficulties of applying them could be attributed less to honest disagreement than to the increasing polarization of political and organizational forces in "semi-corporate state[s] . . . where the real power lies with a seemingly omnipotent labor movement and a machinelike bureaucracy."[11] However, a significant degree of sometimes tacit, sometimes grudging agreement between the forces of

Table 5.3 Nordic Political Parties and Their Strength

	Denmark	Finland	Iceland	Norway	Sweden
LEFT	DKP 0.9% 0	Communists 4.3% 4		NKP 0.3% 0	
	Common Course 2.2% 4				
	VS 1.4% 0	SKDL 9.4% 16	People's Alliance 12.7% 8		VpK 5.4% 19
	SF 14.6% 27	Greens 4.0% 4	Feminists 10.0% 6	SV 4.9% 4	
	Social Democrats 29.3% 54	SSP 24.3% 56	Social Democrats 15.9% 10	DNA 37.4% 66	SAP 44.7% 159
	Greens 1.3% 0				
	Social Liberals 6.2% 11	SMP 6.3% 9	Progressives 20.7% 13	Christian 9.2% 15	Liberals 14.3% 51
	Christian 2.4% 4	SKL 2.6% 5			

RIGHT

Center Democrats 4.8% 9	SFP 5.3% 13	Citizens' 11.1% 7	Liberals 3.9% 2	
Liberals 10.5% 19	KESK/LKP 17.6% 40		Center Party 6.7% 11	Center Party 12.4% 44
Conservatives 20.8% 38	KOK 23.2% 53	*Independent Party* 28.6% 18	Conservatives 31.6% 53	Conservatives 21.3% 76
Progress Party 4.8% 9		Independent Member 0.2% 1	Progress Party 4.5% 4	
Last election: September 1987	March 1987	April 1987	September 1985	September 1985
Name of Assembly: Folketing	Eduskunta	Althing	Storting	Riksdag
Number of seats: 175	200	63	155	349

SOURCES: *Weekendavisen* (Copenhagen); *The Economist* (London).

NOTE: Parties of similar position in left-right spectrum are on the same line. Governing parties as of October 1987 are italicized.

business, organized labor, the public sector bureaucracy, and the political system had been reached by the early 1980s. In 1982, a center-right government in Denmark and a socialist government in Sweden both instituted remarkably similar strategies of economic recovery and, after the collapse of the price of oil in 1985–1986, the Norwegian government (which changed from center-right to socialist in the middle of this crisis) did the same. This shows that the basic consensus on what needed to be done in economic policy was broad. This was not so in foreign and defense policy, as we shall see in the final section.

The common, and mutually dependent, weaknesses of the Nordic economies in the 1970s can be summarized as a decline in the size of the export manufacturing sector and rapid relative and absolute growth of the public sector and of public consumption, financed by a growing tax burden and, increasingly, by deficit spending (except in Norway, where oil revenues yielded budget surpluses until 1986). The deficits, the labor market rigidities created by the weight of the public sector, and the pursuit of egalitarian wage policies combined to generate imbalances and stimulate inflationary behavior by individuals and groups that, under the post-1973 conditions of crisis, tended to aggravate the other problems.

To a greater degree than elsewhere in Europe, the Nordic economies, being relatively small, must export to survive and to provide prosperity for their citizens. The domestic markets cannot lead recoveries, sustain industrial growth, or provide the full range of resources and products required by advanced industrial societies. Together, the Nordic countries constitute almost 23 million people. However, while labor movement and economic activity is essentially free within the Nordic area, attempts to establish a common framework for economic policy (the so-called NORDEK plan) were stranded in 1971 on opposition from both Finland (deferring to Soviet wishes) and, for different reasons, from Denmark. Moreover, intra-Nordic trade only accounted, in the 1980s, for some 20 to 25 percent of the foreign trade of each country. The Nordic Council, which is the chief coordinating organ of Nordic cooperation and is composed of civil servants and politicians from all five countries, recommended in 1982 a common action plan against unemployment and a continuation of efforts to maintain the Nordic area as one domestic market. Such efforts, however, could not by themselves solve the problem, and the law of survival was clear: the revenue to pay for domestic prosperity and public spending must ultimately come from expanding markets and growing exports abroad. If market shares were lost and exports stagnated, growing domestic consumption, private or public, could only be financed on credit, which again depended on future export growth. If that growth did not materialize, the consequences could be, and were, serious.

Denmark. The characteristic problem of Denmark during the period 1974–1987 was a particularly aggravated case of deficit spending and more generally an unsatisfactory pattern of resource allocation.[12] Throughout the 1960s,

Denmark was completing the change from agricultural to industrial exports as the main source of revenue. This required large investments and, since the public sector, notably social services, expanded sharply from 1965, borrowing took place on a large scale both at home and abroad. Domestic borrowing by central and local government drove up interest rates, and wage inflation was higher than among Denmark's competitors. By 1973, the problems were getting serious. Then crisis struck.

The official reaction to the crisis was disastrous. The government allowed wage inflation to soar and, in the recession, unemployment rose fast. For this and other reasons the rate of increase of public spending took another sharp upward turn in 1976–1977. From 1977 to 1982, public spending rose by almost a third, while private consumption fell. Business investment collapsed in 1981–1982.

The government was unwilling to increase taxation sufficiently to finance the swelling budgets and ran deficits that reached 9.5 percent of the gross domestic product (GDP) in 1983. The tax burden in 1982 was 44.2 percent of GDP, fourth highest in the Organization for Economic Cooperation and Development (OECD) area, but it was not enough. The deficits had to be financed by domestic borrowing, which drove bond rates to 22 and 23 percent in 1982. Meanwhile, the number of people dependent on the public sector for their income—civil servants, pensioners, and transfer recipients—grew by 900,000 between 1973 and 1982, while private sector employment fell by 200,000—out of a total work force of 2.7 million. By 1981, industry accounted for only 19.5 percent of total employment, the result of what can rightly be called a "deindustrialization process." [13] But whereas deindustrialization was a utopian goal of ecological pressure groups and romantic philosophers elsewhere in the world, the real thing in Denmark pleased no one, least of all the radical activists.

The second oil shock, "OPEC II," and the recession of 1980–1982 added to the problems. Unemployment, already high, rose further, to 283,000 or almost 11 percent in 1983, although the actual number of long-term unemployed was closer to 60,000, the rest being persons temporarily registered between jobs, or persons, especially women, who had been employed for a while and had then voluntarily quit work but remained on the rolls as unemployed in order to collect benefits. Unemployment insurance in Denmark was perhaps the most generous in the world, since it provided benefits to anyone employed for more than three months for up to three years after loss of employment.

More serious was the rapid increase in foreign indebtedness, which rose from 27 percent of GDP in 1980 to 40 percent ($36 billion), or twice the total value of a year's exports, by mid-1986. In 1982 it was clear that matters were coming to a head. The Social Democrat government, forced by influential elements in the party to reject any policy that might increase business profitability or threaten the growth of the public sector, abdicated. A new center-right government proposed a stabilization strategy to improve the economy. During 1983–

1986, this strategy succeeded in increasing private production and employment while holding public spending flat. Business fixed investment rose sharply in 1983–1984 from its admittedly very low level of 1982 and, for the first time since 1976, private consumption in 1984 rose faster than public, by about 3 percent. GDP as a whole grew by close to 4 percent in real terms in 1984 and 1985. Automatic wage indexation, a chief source of inflation, was suspended, possibly for good.[14]

The political challenges to a sustained effort were manifested in the breakdown of the 1985 round of wage negotiations. Following a week of strikes, the Parliament imposed a settlement by law. Such a step was not unprecedented. In earlier cases, however, the Parliament had simply used the already existing arbitration proposal as a basis for its legislation; in 1985, the government imposed its own tight fiscal and incomes policy. Prime Minister Poul Schlüter took the occasion to state that "the days when the partners in the labor market—unions and employers' organizations—could be allowed to reach and impose settlements damaging to the national economy are over."[15] A clearer statement of corporatism in practice could hardly be imagined; it was ironic coming from a conservative politician who had based his career on attacking the Social Democrats for expanding the coercive powers of government.

The government, by increasing taxes and holding down public sector expansion, obtained a small surplus on the budget for 1986 (not repeated in 1987). However, the drop in interest rates and in inflation stimulated a consumer boom that resulted in a $4.7 billion current account deficit in 1986, equivalent to 4.6 percent of GDP. This deficit occurred despite the devaluation of the dollar (equal to 12 kroner in early 1985 and to 6.8 kroner in early 1987) and the 50 percent drop in the price of oil. The constant tendency for wages to outrun productivity, and the inadequate size of the export manufacturing sector and its structure prevented exports from growing nearly as rapidly as the government's stabilization strategy required. The fundamental problem for exports was, as an OECD *Economic Survey* noted, that "the commodity composition of exports has remained 'old fashioned' in the sense that 'traditional' sectors have maintained a dominant position. Denmark is running large trade deficits in high-tech products and is exporting goods produced mainly with a high input of capital and low-skilled labour . . . Moreover, the tradeable goods sector is small and appears to suffer from a certain backwardness in technological adaptation."[16] The problem had social and cultural as well as economic and political roots and was not one that could be solved in the course of a few years only.

Sweden.   The Swedish industrial structure was preeminently based on large companies. Of the twenty largest companies (private or state-owned) in the Nordic area in 1985, thirteen were Swedish, three Finnish, and two each Norwegian and Danish. In 1984, 40 percent of the manufacturing work force in

Sweden was in establishments of 500 or more employees (the comparable figure for Denmark was 24 percent, for Finland 27 percent, and for Norway 21 percent).[17] Some of these establishments dealt with the extraction and processing of Sweden's natural resources, notably iron and copper and wood products. Iron ore extraction, which took place in the Arctic north, was seriously depressed throughout the 1970s, and each ton of iron ore mined cost the Swedish government more (in wages and labor support schemes) than its market price. In 1983 this situation changed, and by 1985 iron mining was once again moderately profitable. Likewise, the wood and paper industries were recovering.[18]

Other major industries were industrial machinery, communications equipment, motor vehicles, household appliances, and services. Seven of Sweden's top ten companies were world leaders in their main products, such as L. M. Ericsson in communications equipment and Electrolux in household appliances. In some of them, the state had for some time had a stake, but in the wake of the post-1973 crisis the government adopted a deliberate policy of supporting, and then taking over, threatened industries, such as shipbuilding.

Sweden in the 1980s has been the world's most highly taxed nation, with tax receipts of 51 percent of GDP. The progressivity of the tax system and the allocation of benefits severely penalized single-income families. The incentive, and need, for both husband and wife to work reduced labor mobility and raised expectations for jobs in the public sector, which in 1982 accounted for 67 percent of the GDP. That level of spending explained in part how the number of jobs in the public sector could rise by 43 percent from 1972 to 1982, outnumbering jobs in private industry since 1978. As in Denmark, high taxes were not enough to pay for this. In 1982, the deficit was 13 percent of GDP, and the accumulated public debt in 1983 was 67 percent of GDP, the highest in the Nordic area. Foreign indebtedness reached a historic high of 24 percent.

The government's countercyclical "bridging policies" of labor support and expanded public employment in the 1970s were intended to overcome what was believed to be a short-term crisis. As recession and stagflation dragged on, Swedish industry lost competitiveness and market shares, and the level of production in 1981 was actually less than in 1973. A shrinking industrial base, falling investments and profitability, high taxes, and labor market rigidities combined, as in Denmark, in a "deindustrialization process" that ultimately threatened the foundations of Sweden's high standard of living and extensive welfare state policies.[19]

In 1976, after 44 years of Social Democrat rule, a center-right government was formed, but continued and indeed accelerated the prevailing trends toward higher deficits, more support for ailing industries, and falling investments. In 1982, the SAP under Olof Palme returned to power and began a dramatic reversal of the economic policies of the preceding decade. The opening shot in the new strategy was a 16 percent devaluation of the krona, followed over the next few years by severe cuts in the central government deficit (from 13 percent of

GDP in 1982 to 4 percent in 1987). Public spending as a whole was trimmed back from 67 percent of GDP in 1982 to 64 in 1986, still a world record. A third and equally decisive element of the strategy was the virtual abolition of subsidies to lame-duck industries. The total amount of subsidies fell from $16 billion to $5 billion in 1982–1985, but even more important was the shift from subsidizing employment in doomed industries to subsidizing research and development in new industries, high-tech investment, and regional development. The strategy resulted in a remarkable turn toward recovery. Business investments rose an amazing 20 percent in 1984, and exports grew at a 5 percent annual rate in 1983–1987. The current account swung into surplus in 1984 and 1986–1987.[20]

One of the initially most controversial moves was the introduction, in December 1983, of the so-called "wage-earner funds" to be set up, ostensibly on behalf of employees, with the revenue from extra taxes on profits and payrolls. They would then invest these funds. Although supposedly designed to provide more widespread ownership of assets and more investment capital, given that the high Swedish taxes mean that no private savings take place, the funds in fact were controlled by the government and the trade union association, which plays a dominant role in the Swedish economy and society. The funds were regarded by leading industrialists as a device to achieve complete bureaucratic control of industry and planning.

The outlook in the late 1980s was far better, both for foreign trade and for the domestic economic balance, than at any time since the early 1970s. Business profits were the highest in twenty years and inflation and unemployment were low. This performance disproved the common economic wisdom that a high level of public spending, high taxes, and strong unions lead to low growth. Sweden's growth performance of 2 percent annually in real terms over the entire period 1974–1986 was average for the OECD area, although it had higher government spending than any other country.

Although the SAP now accepted that public spending could not rise forever, the impressive achievements of 1983–1987 did not answer one fundamental question posed by the Swedish system, namely, how extensive political control of economic decisions ultimately affects a market economy. In 1986 the prominent economist and former Social Democrat Assar Lindbeck asked: "Have we in our country passed the point at which the advantages to individuals of increased public spending—in the form of public institutions and subsidized services, social security and income transfers—no longer outweigh the harm caused by the taxes required to finance the spending?"[21]

Norway. The main reason for the smooth operation of this welfare state within a market economy of the 1970s was oil. Thanks to oil and gas, which accounted for 18 percent of the GDP and 32 percent of export revenues in 1985, it was possible to maintain a positive balance of payments while conducting an industrial policy that, as in Sweden, maintained industrial employment in mainland Norway (that is, nonoil employment) at the price of losing competitiveness and market shares.[22] Oil revenues allowed Norway not only to achieve net savings on the budget and a current account surplus of 3 percent in 1984 and 2 percent for 1985, but also to repay some foreign loans. Norway's foreign indebtedness fell from 33 percent of GDP in 1980 to 21.7 percent in 1983, whereas Sweden's more than doubled during the same period.

In the early 1960s the North Sea was divided among Britain, the Netherlands, West Germany, Denmark, and Norway for the purpose of oil exploration. The Norwegians found oil in large quantities. Production began in 1966, but became significant only in the mid-1970s, just when the repercussions of "OPEC I," the first oil shock, were rippling through the global economy. Accordingly, "against the background of rapidly expanding oil revenues, economic policy . . . has been aiming at reasonable growth of real disposable incomes, high and stable employment, and more equal income distribution."[23] As in Denmark and Sweden, public sector spending, having grown at about the same rate as private consumption, took off in 1976–1977, chiefly in the form of subsidies to private industry and expansion of social services. Public sector employment grew by 180,000 from 1973 to 1981 (out of a work force of 2 million), corresponding to almost 70 percent of the total growth in employment over this period. In 1978–1984, 85 percent of all new jobs were paid for by central or local government.

Due to this policy, private consumption did not stagnate or fall, as in Denmark and Sweden, but continued to rise, albeit at a much slower pace (1.5 percent in 1984–1985). A long-standing policy, which antedated oil by far, was to resist urbanization in Oslo and the other southern towns by supporting local economies throughout the enormous country. This, combined with wage indexation and generous wage settlements, led to a steep rise in labor costs and increasing immobility of the work force. The deductibility of interest payments from taxable income had the effect of stimulating investment in housing and consumer durables far beyond what was justified by the productivity of the national economy.

The expansion of public spending was financed not only by oil revenues but also by taxation. In the 1970s, Norway became the world's second most highly taxed nation after Sweden, with a total tax burden of 50.2 percent of GDP in 1980. In the recovery of 1983–1986, this percentage dropped to 45.7.

An austerity package introduced by the Labor (DNA) government in 1980 soon foundered. At the same time, the Conservative Party—for the first time in 50 years—presented what was seen as a credible alternative and duly triumphed at the elections of 1981. The new government focused its policies on strengthening the supply side of the economy. Stimulated by these policies and by oil revenues which rose from 60 to 100 billion kroner in 1982 –1984 a recovery began in early 1983 which continued through 1986, with real GDP growth in the 4 percent range.[24]

The collapse of the world market price of oil in 1985–1986 and the uncertain prospects for a renewed rise in the immediate future affected Norway drastically. From 1985 through late 1986 oil and gas export revenues dropped from an annual rate of 80 billion kroner to about 30 billion (the krone was devalued by the incoming DNA government in 1986 to about $0.14). This was the main reason that the current account surplus of 25 billion kroner in 1985 turned into a deficit of over 45 billion kroner in 1987. Oil taxes, which had helped produce budget surpluses in 1980–1985 of up to 8 percent of GDP, also fell and helped provoke a budget deficit in 1986 and beyond. At the same time, the recovery, now driven by domestic, especially consumer, demand, was leading to bottlenecks and other symptoms of overheating, which in turn threatened the cost and price competitiveness of the private manufacturing sector.

Iceland. The peculiar problem of Iceland, due to its high dependence on imports and its main export of fish, was hyperinflation. Throughout the 1970s the inflation cycles grew shorter and the peaks higher: 50 percent in 1975 and 1978, 60 percent in 1980, and an extraordinary annual rate of 130 percent in early 1983. At that point, the new center-right government suspended wage and price indexation for two years, limited pay increases, and devalued the krona. As a result, domestic private and public consumption fell sharply, as did imports. Growth in exports depended heavily on the cod catch. The future of this mainstay of the Icelandic economy was uncertain. Over-fishing and the results of the "cod war" with Britain in the early 1970s reduced the cod harvest from 500,000 tons annually to only about 200,000 tons in 1984; however, this decline was offset by catches of other types of fish and by a relatively strong growth in nonfish exports, chiefly aluminum, marine products, and manufactures.

The GDP growth maintained at the price of hyperinflation was dramatically halted by the 1983 measures. The government hoped to keep inflation at around 10 percent for 1984, but in November of that year the strategy broke down. Public sector workers went on strike and, as a result, gained wage raises that meant that inflation in 1985 was back up to 32 percent. The government again devalued the krona (by 12 percent), and the cost of imports and foreign debt therefore again rose sharply. However, exports, both fish and nonfish, grew rapidly in 1985–1986, and this, along with the drop in the price of oil, permitted GDP to grow at 5 percent in real terms in 1986 with 2 percent projected for 1987. In 1986 there was actually a small surplus on the current account, and inflation slowed to 12 percent. With a population of 240,000 and a high degree of solidarity, the economic problems, however dramatic they may appear on paper, could not possibly have the same dimensions and long-term effects as in mainland Scandinavia.

Finland. Of the Nordic countries, Finland was the exception in the economic as well as the political picture. In regard to the economy at least, its special traits were mostly positive. Although plagued to some extent by high inflation and structural adaptation problems in the 1970s, Finland avoided the traps of extensive deficit spending, foreign borrowing, and public sector growth characteristic of the other three central Nordic economies. The size of the public sector in particular was quite comparable to the OECD average, taking in 37 percent and spending about 39 percent of GDP in 1981. Further growth was forbidden by a law of 1975. Foreign indebtedness, at 17.7 percent of GDP in 1983, was also modest by Nordic standards. Generally, Finland was able to maintain a surplus on the current account, and even the deficits of 1974 and 1975 were manageable. Compared to Denmark, which has a comparable standard of living and a slightly larger population, but none of the problems of regional support of a large and thinly settled country, Finland in 1985 spent just over half as much on central government, less than half as much on education, about half as much on health, and about a third as much on social services and welfare, including unemployment compensation—this last even though Finland did have the next highest unemployment rate in the area (7.5 percent in 1987).[25] Notably, the growth in public sector employment actually slowed in 1975–1981 in Finland, and its share of total employment, while rising, remained much less than in the other countries.

As for private versus public spending in recent years, in the Finnish case public spending also tended to rise faster than private spending, but the disparity was not nearly as marked as in the other countries and the growth curve of public spending did not show a sharp rise from 1976–1977 as in Denmark, Norway, and Sweden. Compared to these countries, the pattern of private spending was reversed in Finland: stagnation or slow growth in 1975–1978 and sustained growth from 1979 on. Exports rose sharply in 1975–1980, then slipped a bit, but rose again from 1983–1985. Fluctuations in the value of exports were determined largely by Finland's special relationship with the Soviet Union, based on the Treaty of Friendship, Cooperation, and Mutual Assistance (FCMA) of 1948. Trade between the two must be balanced; the value of goods passing from one to the other must be equal over a seven-year period. Thus, when oil prices rose in 1973–1974, the Soviet Union, as Finland's chief supplier, began receiving in return a comparably increased amount of Finnish goods. In this way Finland, unique among OECD countries, actually made up for the oil price increases by means of employment-creating exports and not through unemployment-creating domestic inflation. However, when world oil prices fell in 1985–1986, Soviet demand for Finnish goods fell by the same token, and consistent Finnish export drives in the West did not begin to outweigh this loss until 1987. In 1987, for the first time, the Soviet Union agreed to let the value of goods received from

Finland in 1980–1986 exceed the value of Soviet goods sent to Finland and to pay the difference in hard currency. Needless to say, viewing the Soviet relationship purely in the light of the trade balance is misleading, but this particular aspect of it was certainly of benefit to the Finnish economy.

The Finns did what the Norwegians tried to do, but to better effect— namely, they ran a countercyclical policy of moderate expansion at a time of international recession. The main reason for the Finnish success was the lower level of public spending and the consequently greater room for maneuver in maintaining such a policy. Even so, inflation was one area where Finland resembled its Nordic brethren. Inflation ran at about 10 percent in 1981–1983, but improved to about 3.5 percent in 1985–1987. All in all, though, there was no doubt that, in terms of purely domestic economic health, Finland scored highest of the Nordic countries.

The Welfare State

The economic problems of the Nordic countries are associated in Denmark, Norway, and Sweden primarily with the growth in state and local government spending. This growth is in turn the manifestation of the expansion of public administration and social services—in other words, of the welfare state. For many years, the image of Scandinavia abroad has been chiefly associated with this phenomenon, which is far more than a mere feature of the national economy or a set of public institutions. It is in fact the political, social, and cultural essence of modern Scandinavia. No understanding of contemporary Nordic politics or culture is either fair or complete without an evaluation of the major aspects of the welfare state, its origins and development, and the social ideology for which it has come increasingly to stand. Such an evaluation, however, is much more likely to be affected by bias, beliefs, and value judgments than would be a discussion of economics or even of security. It would be colored notably by one's view of individualism versus collectivism, of the proper, actual, or desirable relations between the individual and society, of the consequences of extensive bureaucratic control of individual behavior, and, ultimately, of one's understanding of human nature and morality.

Until Norway began a rapid expansion of the public sector in the mid-1970s, the welfare state in its advanced form was a feature mainly of Sweden, and to a lesser extent of Denmark. Most of what follows is therefore an account of Swedish and Danish developments. In the Nordic countries themselves, however, Sweden has until recently been considered a model to emulate—an attitude far from extinct even today. This traditional admiration and copying of Swedish measures and the degree to which the Swedish situation now tends to inspire fear and alarm mean that the development of Swedish society and politics in recent years is of more than merely local significance.

In its development, the welfare state in Sweden and Denmark has passed through two phases of unequal length. The first phase was that of humanitarian individualism. In this phase, the chief concern of social policy was to expand and improve the life chances of individuals in a general context of social, material, and cultural inequality. This phase lasted from the very beginnings of the "social question" in Scandinavia to sometime around 1960 and was succeeded by the second phase, ideological collectivism.

The appearance of the social question in Sweden was associated not with industrialization but with the rapid growth of a rural underclass of desperately poor, landless laborers during the late nineteenth century. There were various reasons for this, including modest advances in public health that meant, just as in parts of the Third World today, far more children survived than before. This landless proletariat was without means of support and at first emigrated in large numbers. Over a million Swedes out of a total population of between 4 and 5 million emigrated to the United States between 1860 and 1910. Others began moving to the urban areas of Sweden, especially after the beginnings of industrialization in the 1890s. There they lived in usually miserable conditions, with little education, bad health, and no certainty of employment. The rise of the Social Democratic Party (SAP) after its founding in 1881, and particularly under the leadership of Hjalmar Branting, is largely the story of the mobilization of these new groups. Furthermore, membership in the SAP was more than just a political act, it was a cultural one as well. Through its educational organization, the Workers' Educational Association (ABF), and its prohibitionist societies, it created an alternative forum for cultural mobilization and individual self-improvement to set against the perceived antisocial militarism, clericalism, and lack of concern of the ruling classes. The aim was not to work for the revolutionary overthrow of existing society or to replace traditional Swedish culture with proletarian or Marxist culture, but to change society to provide access to its material and cultural benefits for the new masses. After considerable internal debate, a similar outlook triumphed in the Danish Social Democratic Party (founded in 1871), although it differed from the Swedish party in having been based from the outset in the towns, chiefly Copenhagen.

The movement from the land to the towns in Sweden accelerated in the 1920s and 1930s, coinciding with the onset of the Great Depression and the political and financial crisis that brought the SAP to power in 1932 and destroyed the legitimacy of Högern (the conservatives) for over a generation. As in Denmark, Norway, and Finland, the depression catalyzed the determination of Social Democrats and the agrarian parties to change, improve, and expand social welfare. The characteristic traits of Nordic social democracy before 1960—the rejection of revolutionary Marxism, commitment to humanitarian individualism, and the pragmatic belief in the importance of cooperative institutions—were well expressed, in Denmark and Sweden by the two ministers for social affairs in the 1930s, K. K. Steincke and Gustav Möller, in Finland by party leader Väinö Tanner, for whom "Marxism had lost its justification when the first law for the protection of workers was enacted," and in Norway by Martin Tranmael.[26]

The typical elements of the new social legislation of the 1930s were (1) the abolition of the old notion of "poor relief" and of the civil disabilities associated with it, and (2) its replacement by legally mandated and standardized employment and health insurance and the guarantee of aid without discrimination in the case of unexpected need. Leading Social Democrats, however, clearly saw that genuine equality of life and access to higher education and hence to social mobility would not result from such elementary measures. It is precisely at this juncture, when faith in planning and the possibilities of large-scale social engineering took hold in the intellectual leadership of the SAP, that the fundamental aims and assumptions of the Swedish welfare state were established. The ideals were still those of humanitarian individualism. Contrary to the expectations of many of the founders, the long-term consequences of the decisions, during the decades of Social Democratic rule and organizational growth, led to the ideological collectivism and egalitarianism of today.

This transformation was described with particular poignancy in the autobiographical sociology of modern Sweden by the late Gunnar Myrdal, one of the early egalitarian idealists of the 1930s, who chaired the important and controversial Committee on Postwar Planning of 1944–1946. Myrdal ensured that the committee recommend economic planning and state control of the private sector. In a speech in July 1945, Myrdal announced that the "harvest time" had come for the labor movement.[27]

The "debate on the planned economy," as the late 1940s are known in Swedish political history, ended in compromise with the SAP government following the recommendations of economists Rudolf Meidner and Gösta Rehn, who both worked for the trade union congress (LO), that market forces be allowed to operate freely in the market for goods and services, while the government intervened to channel workers toward expanding industries and ensure a rising level of welfare and security. At that early date, no one on the socialist side of the political spectrum even asked Lindbeck's question, namely, "How much political control can the economy take?" That is, at what point does state power directly, by its decisions and by the role of government in the market, and indirectly, by its cost, so distort economic activity as to hinder the very task of planning itself and thus the smooth operation of the welfare state within a market economy? Rather, the Social Democratic idea was that political control of markets ("politics against markets" in Esping-Andersen's phrase) was necessary for social justice and, indeed, for better use of human and material resources.[28]

Gunnar Myrdal was perhaps the last example of the old generation of Social Democrats who combined a high ethical and moral standard with absolute faith in the beneficial results of large-scale social and economic planning. His characteristic outlook was found in an early study he wrote with his wife, Alva, on the effect of poverty on fertility. The Myrdals argued that the poverty of the majority of Swedish families in the 1930s resulted in fertility too low for the maintenance of the population and that this could and should be remedied by social engineering. As he himself put it in 1982:

> We had no doubt that the unfortunate trends could be reversed by means of social family reforms, which we considered possible in our country. We did not fear for the future of the nuclear family nor for the continued existence of marriage as a lifelong commitment.
>
> We believed that these institutions would be strengthened only if wives were better able to find work outside the home and if society took over a large part of the care of children. Moreover, the day-care centers would lead to a desirable expansion and improvement of children's development . . .
>
> I now regard our fundamental optimism as a result of our upbringing . . . for me, the core of the Enlightenment ideal was the faith that man and society can be improved by reforms.[29]

Myrdal's own highly individualistic personality and his commitment to the early humanitarian ideals of the welfare state were apparent in his belief that social welfare would strengthen family life and marriage in the long term. The link between his individualism and the ideological collectivism and political economy of the period since around 1960 was the associated assumption that "society"—that is, paid civil servants—would be better at caring for children than the parents. What happened was a twofold process. First, the entrenchment of the Social Democrats in power from 1932 to 1976 led to a gradual bureaucratization of the original institutions of the movement, especially the ABF and the LO. Second, the far-reaching economic and social planning decisions of the 1930s and 1940s led to the establishment and growth of massive bureaucracies of regulation, supervision, and control. These became a power unto themselves, where decisions affecting people's lives and welfare were made anonymously and issued, never in the name of an individual, but in that of the agency concerned. The principle that responsibility for bureaucratic decisions must finally rest with some identifiable individual, entrenched in Anglo-Saxon custom and administrative practice, was destroyed in Sweden.

Thus, in Myrdal's own words, a "corporatist society" emerged, in which the humanitarian individualism inspiring the early aims of the planners and idealists was replaced by a faceless collectivism acting always, of course, for the good of the people.[30] This has already been alluded to above in the sketch of Swedish alcohol policy. Other typical cases were child care, education, and taxation.

The original child-care policies of the 1930s were based on recommendations by the Myrdals and others whose fundamental concern was the health and survival of the family and the welfare of all its members. By the 1980s, Swedish policy in the area seemed inspired rather by a belief that children were the property of the state, which had the duty of bringing them up identically and correctly and of reducing as far as possible the influence of the family, particularly when the latter threatened to make the children nonconformist, independent, or unusual.

In the late 1960s, an SAP candidate for the Riksdag proposed that all prospective parents be made to undergo a course of instruction and that those who failed be denied the right to have children. A similar proposal was made by a radical socialist in Denmark. Both were taken to be provocative jokes. In 1982, however, 24,000 (6 percent) of all Swedish children, a world record, had been removed from their parents by decree of the local authorities. By comparison, the figure in Denmark was 710, in Finland, 552, and in Norway, 155. In one case, the staff of a government-run day-care center wanted to have the two-year-old son of a social worker admitted to a psychiatric ward for observation "because he does not cry when he falls and does not seem happy with the other children," even though the child's doctor considered him fully normal. Alarmed, the parents fled to Finland and planned to move on to the United States. Lured back by a promise that the matter would be dropped, they returned, only to have their son taken away and their appeal rejected on the grounds that their "extreme attitude" as manifested by their flight obviously indicated serious problems at home justifying the sequestration of their son, whom they have not seen since.[31]

Swedish primary and secondary education was reformed in the mid-1960s and higher education in 1975. In the former, as in similar American reforms, the aim was to reduce emphasis on grades, competition, and performance and to stress group identity and the integration of the individual in the group. Grades were to be given not according to objective criteria, but in such a way that the average of the class would always be the same and no one would fall too far from it in either direction. Diversity was discouraged. When in 1968 the heads of the last surviving private, including religious, schools, asked Olof Palme, who was then minister of education (later prime minister in 1969–1976 and 1982–1986), whether he thought the existence of an alternative to public education was a good thing, he replied, "The state does not regard alternatives to the state educational system as desirable." Tax and other benefits to private schools were withdrawn. This contrasted remarkably with the situation in Denmark, where any group of twenty parents could form their own school, subject to certain standards, and were entitled to public money in the same amount as would be spent to educate their childen in the public schools.

In the university reforms, the ancient principle of university self-government was abolished and replaced with bureaucratic rule by innumerable committees and boards made up of representatives of the students, the faculty, the technical and administrative staff, and the surrounding local community. Professors were to be judged for promotion not on their contributions to the advancement of knowledge, but on the relevance of their work to society, as shown, for example, by their ability to popularize science for public consumption. Furthermore, professors were so overburdened with administrative work in the name of "internal democracy" that they were unable to continue any basic research. One result was that basic research stagnated and there occurred a significant brain drain to the United States of many motivated researchers and professionals.

Not only was Sweden in the 1970s and 1980s the world's most highly taxed nation, but the tax authorities also assumed extensive rights of inspection and surveillance. They could legally deduct back taxes without warning from taxpayers' bank accounts and could seize the assets of relatives of delinquent taxpayers. The vast majority of Swedes rarely encounter such problems, since taxes are deducted from one's salary before it is electronically deposited in one's bank account. Moreover, in an official poll, 71 percent believed it was "not improper" for the government to merge computer files on citizens—something that is strictly illegal for private individuals or businesses—in order to verify the information given by applicants for various subsidies or to enforce the tax laws.[32]

The tentacular reach of the fiscal authorities was due in part to the vast growth of the "black," or underground, economy, which was again a result of the heavy tax burden. So great is the temptation to evade taxes when marginal rates approach or exceed 80 percent that almost any method seems worthwhile. In another of Myrdal's statements of amazement at what had happened in his native country while he was spending his career in international development, he asked why "we have become a nation of cheaters." A business research organization estimated in 1986 that the black economy comprised between 10 and 20 percent of the Swedish GDP.[33]

These privileges of the child-care and tax authorities rested not on laws passed by the Riksdag and debated by democratically elected representatives, but on anonymously issued administrative decrees. The bureaucrats involved were safe from any control or prosecution for abuse of power. The powers of the ombudsman, for years regarded as the citizen's last bulwark against arbitrary action by the authorities, were reduced in 1983. The ombudsman could no longer accept complaints of administrative error or abuse. A former ombudsman and constitutional lawyer, Gustaf Petrén, said of this: "The law in Sweden is now no more than a department of government. The magistrates see themselves as functionaries whose duty it is to defend the state against the citizens and not the other way round."[34]

Just as the pursuit of high taxes and high spending over decades raised the question of society's long-term tolerance of political control of economic decisions, so the pursuit of egalitarianism raised, finally, the question of the psychological consequences of social engineering. Assar Lindbeck writes:

Even though the effects of taxation on production are great, future observers of Swedish society in our time may emphasize a number of other traits. I am thinking in particular of four:

    1. That the position of the family in society is drastically deteriorating;

    2. That individuals have a sense of not being able to influence their own life situation ("acquired helplessness");

    3. That is has become very expensive to be honest;

    4. That politicians are forced to combat the effects of reduced honesty by means of an ever-expanding "control state"

    . . . A vast and growing apparatus of control is a necessary consequence of a system of high taxes, extensive and subsidized public services, means-tested contributions, and wide-ranging regulation of human behavior . . . As individuals find it ever more difficult to increase their income by productive work they undertake activities where they can avoid public control and hold down taxes . . . Furthermore, increased subsidies from government become ever more attractive compared to highly-taxed regular income—on the very realistic assumption that in any case others are paying for the goods. This leads politicians to increase public spending and taxes even more, which results in still more interest on the part of individuals in receiving contributions and goods from the public sector. Their interest in avoiding control by the authorities also grows, so the control apparatus must be extended still further.[35]

Only a hostile ideologue would deny that the contribution of social democracy to the prosperity and material security of the Nordic peoples today has been immense. In large, complex, and highly differentiated societies such as the German, the British, or the American, social and economic planning and engineering are indeed much more likely to have consequences unimagined by the planners or contrary to their good intentions. For a long time this was not the case in Sweden, where ethnic homogeneity, a long tradition of egalitarian individualism in the middle and lower classes, and a consequent strong sense of national solidarity and responsibility made planning both more possible and more likely to have universally beneficial results. The change came when the humanitarian impulse became an ideology of control and thus the radical vision of the 1920s and 1930s became the collectivist conformity and fear of individual independence of the 1970s and 1980s.

In *The New Totalitarians*, Roland Huntford claimed that the change simply marked a reassertion of old habits of anti-individualist suspicion and of submission to authority.[36] The reading of Swedish history on which the present sketch is based does not bear out his claim, at least not in its simple version. Perhaps the problem is only an exacerbated form of that foreseen by Tocqueville as the likely consequence of mass democracy—the people will seek, in the benevolent social state, the sense of security and confidence of self formerly provided by religion and a sharply defined social hierarchy. This may be true, but it also means that, if a serious crisis threatens the stability or prosperity of the system, the psychological consequences are likely to be more severe than in a more individualistic society. Such an assumption seems confirmed in the Nordic countries, at least if the fertility rate is an indication of the confidence of society's members in its future. In 1985 the rates of 1.45 in Denmark, 1.73 in Sweden, 1.64 in Finland, and 1.66 in Norway were well below replacement, and in 40 years a fairly swift drop in the size of the population will begin. Tiny Iceland was the Nordic exception, with a fertility rate of 2.24 until 1983; however, this fell to 1.93 in 1985.[37]

Foreign Policy and International Security

The basic decisions shaping the international political and security relationships of the Nordic countries were made in 1948. Early in that year, Stalin asked Finland for a treaty of "friendship, cooperation, and mutual assistance" (FCMA) analogous to the ones by which the Soviet Union had gained leverage and ultimate control over Hungary and Romania. Sweden was alarmed at Norway's drift toward some sort of security agreement with the Western allies, Britain and the United States, and believed that Finland might escape a total Soviet takeover if Stalin could be made to see that the Nordic area was not a threat to him. It proposed to Denmark and Norway that they join in a tripartite Nordic defense alliance based primarily on the Swedish defense forces built up during World War II, when Sweden was neutral and the other two countries were occupied by the Germans. The Norwegians, however, were already committed to a Western connection, and in view of this the Danes decided to follow them in joining the new Atlantic Alliance in 1949. Concerned that Soviet reactions might affect Finland or Sweden, however, both countries declared a policy of not accepting Allied troops or nuclear weapons on their territory in peacetime. Sweden remained neutral, but with a defense policy—the "total defense" concept—based on extensive popular mobilization and designed to present a credible deterrent to any operations aimed at Sweden in the context of a general East-West conflict in Europe.[38]

The 1948 FCMA treaty between Finland and the Soviet Union was not the prelude to a direct takeover. The Soviets, indeed, accepted the Finnish draft of the treaty, which omitted the trigger clause that could have justified Soviet intervention and which was, and is, a standard element in other such treaties. Stalin probably considered that an overt move against Finland in the still fluid situation on the USSR's northern flank in 1948 might well precipitate Sweden, with its large, mobilized army, into the Western system along with Denmark and Norway and lead to a much stronger Western presence in the area. However, if Finland remained nominally neutral, it could be used by the Soviet Union as a hostage in Nordic politics, exposed to Soviet reactions in case Sweden should show signs of drifting westward. Furthermore, the Soviet Union, to the extent that its power would exercise a gradual, but growing, influence over Finland, could use it as a conduit for political initiatives and influence in the other Nordic countries.[39]

If this was indeed the Soviet strategy, it has been extraordinarily, if not completely, successful. Its success to a large extent was based on what has become known as "finlandization," a psychopolitical process of anticipatory deference to Soviet desires. One analyst, placing Finland in what he calls the "soft sphere" of Soviet influence, notes the following elements of Finnish deference:

> The Finns have learned well the limits within which they can move without inviting the threat of Soviet sanctions; they understand the ritual of Soviet conduct toward their country. They will restrict their political relationships, purposely balance their trade for non-economic reasons, disrupt parliamentary procedures, restrict their press and political parties, and pledge themselves to fight with the Soviet Union in the event of war to accommodate Soviet interests.[40]

The furtherance of this process was the chief legacy of the long presidency of Urho Kekkonen (1956–1981). Kekkonen's policy of preliminary compliance with Soviet wishes, concealed as it was by insistence upon the beneficial nature and effects of the Fenno-Soviet relationship, should be distinguished from the original principles of that relationship as they were laid down by Kekkonen's great predecessor, Juho Paasikivi (1944–1956). The "Paasikivi line" was not a blueprint for a Finnish foreign policy serving broad Soviet interests, but the expression of a determination to preserve national independence and autonomy while facing the harsh realities of the situation of 1944 and after. However, the distinction between the ultimately firm realism of Paasikivi and the compliance of Kekkonen is denied in Finland, and this denial is itself an important symptom of finlandization, the essence of which is summarized as follows by Karen Orvik:

> [U]nder Kekkonen's tutelage, which emphasized the importance of cooperation with the Soviets, it became difficult to tell whether the Finns conformed to Soviet wishes out of a fear of repercussions or out of a developing conviction that it was in their common interest. . . What is a major political question—how to deal with the Russians—acquired in Kekkonen's time the quality of an ethical standard. A Finn does not question his nation's foreign policy. He both accepts the official policy as the only possible course and considers that it is to the good for the Finnish nation . . . The Soviets can rest comfortably in the knowledge that Finland's intentions will remain fixed. The trust the Finns wanted to create in order to strengthen their position with Moscow is in fact their major point of weakness. The Soviets have

been allowed, in effect, the benefit of a predictable pattern of response by the Finns who, when they experienced increased anxiety over their safety, showed a proportionally greater willingness to conform to Moscow's wishes.

And she concludes:

> The central point of Kekkonen's policy was that the Finns had to do whatever possible to cultivate . . . trust . . . Trust, however, is an elusive goal . . . No matter what the Finns do or refrain from doing, there is no guide nor is there an end to what the Finns must do to gain Soviet trust.[41]

Another typical expression of finlandization is found in the repeated attempts by Kekkonen to propose the formal creation of a Nordic nuclear-weapon-free zone (NWFZ), even though the Nordic countries are already free of nuclear weapons in peacetime and the only such weapons in or aimed at the Nordic area are Soviet weapons.[42] An official undertaking by the Nordic NATO countries, Denmark and Norway, never to accept nuclear weapons, not even in a time of crisis, could only serve Soviet interests. Yet Kekkonen asserted, apparently with conviction, that the plan was objectively beneficial and likely to help preserve peace. It is notable that his successor, Social Democrat Mauno Koivisto, was less willing to bring up the subject and even neatly sidestepped Soviet efforts to revive it. According to Erling Bjøl, this and other actions by Koivisto indicate that a certain de-finlandization might in fact be taking place and that the Soviets might in the future be less certain of Finnish reactions and might therefore show the Finns more respect.[43] Koivisto, however, was no less insistent than Kekkonen that Finnish foreign policy must be a presidential concern exempt from domestic investigation or criticism. The NWFZ, moreover, took on a momentum of its own in the 1980s, as it was taken over by Olof Palme and by many other Nordic Social Democrat leaders, and by parties, groups, and individuals further left.

Until 1982, the other Nordic governments never officially took Soviet or Finnish proposals for an NWFZ very seriously. These proposals and the underlying idea that the threat to peace is due to nuclear weapons in general and not to any particular nuclear power, such as the Soviet Union, had, moreover, a great deal of influence on the critical arguments against NATO and U.S. strategy and for unilateral disarmament. These arguments and the rise of neutralist tendencies in the Danish and Norwegian social democratic parties in the 1970s coincided with an unprecedented increase in overt and camouflaged political pressure by the Soviet Union against the Nordic countries and against NATO's northern flank in general.

This increase in pressure reflected not only the vast expansion of Soviet military power since the early 1960s, but also a specific concern with what, to the Soviets, was their northwestern front. The Kola Peninsula, where the Soviets have many naval shipyards and repair facilities, missile silos, and strategic installations, is directly behind the Norwegian border. From the port of Murmansk, the Soviet Northern Fleet operated and maneuvered, in every year since 1973, steadily further south into the North Atlantic through the so-called GIUK (Greenland–Iceland–United Kingdom) gap. Similarly, from Leningrad and other Baltic ports, the Baltic Fleet sent its strategic vessels through the Danish straits into the North Sea and further into the Atlantic, where they connected with units of the Northern Fleet. These naval activities, which became more frequent as well as more expertly conducted in the 1980s, "placed Norway and her Scandinavian neighbours effectively behind the Soviet front lines."[44]

Even though Norway not only refuses permanent stationing of Allied troops in peacetime but also forbids Allied maneuvers or overflights in all of the vast empty land on its side of the Soviet border (where Norway's only strength is a light regiment of 500 border guards), the Soviet Union maintains on the Kola Peninsula strong ground and air forces of up to 70,000 men equipped for arctic fighting, as well as Backfire bombers armed with nuclear-tipped cruise missiles. The Soviet Union has also been engaged for some time in the illegal military occupation of the Svalbard Archipelago in the Arctic Ocean due north of Norway. By a treaty of 1920, Norway controls Svalbard, although all signatories of the treaty have rights of access to its mineral resources. Under cover of this treaty, the Soviets have built a radar base and an airstrip prepared for heavy transport planes and bombers and have brought in attack helicopters and troop transports. Norwegian attempts to supervise Soviet behavior or control the number of Soviet personnel on Svalbard have been fruitless. The Soviets are building on Svalbard a "secret fortress inside NATO."[45]

Soviet military activities directed at the Nordic countries also include illegal trespassing in Swedish, Norwegian, and Danish territorial waters (and probably also on land), notably by submarines and most recently by a new type of minisub that is harder to detect and is able to go into shallower waters than traditional types.[46] The best-known example of such trespassing occurred in October 1981, when a full-sized nuclear-armed Soviet Whiskey-class submarine ran aground on the rocks outside the Swedish naval base of Karlskrona. There were many other incursions both before and after. In 1983, a government commission for defense against submarines published its extensive report, documenting these incursions and naming their obvious source, the Soviet Union. During and after the commission's work, a number of Swedish officers and politicians, notably the conservative defense spokesman Carl Bildt (who became leader of his party in 1986), argued that Soviet intentions against Sweden were clearly aggressive and that the decline in Swedish defense expenditure must be reversed. This infuriated Palme so much that he denounced Bildt as a "security risk" for engaging in discussions with U.S. defense specialists during a visit to Washington in 1983. Palme, who believed that the main threat to peace came from right-wing dictatorships and politicians, and whose worldview had no place for the idea of a Soviet threat, found the whole issue annoying. He was a prominent figure in the Socialist International and, in his last years, led a commission of his own, the Palme Commission, which included prominent Soviet spokesmen as members and which worked for arms control in Europe and increased aid to progressive (that is, socialist) governments in the Third World. Even before the government commission reported that the Soviet Union was engaged in a consistent policy of violation of Swedish territory, Palme, who had never insisted on any Soviet apology, decided to "normalize" relations with the Soviets. This normalization culminated in the visit of Palme's successor, Ingvar Carlsson, to Moscow in the spring of 1986. One can imagine what conclusions the Soviets drew from this seeming lack of official concern or irritation.

The Swedish public, unlike the government, was thoroughly aroused. In the mid-1980s a Stockholm publisher, Timbro, issued a series of works describing the submarine incursions and other Soviet actions against Sweden, naming all known KGB officers (with photographs) in the country, and warning that the incursions indicated that the Soviets were planning to be able, in a general European crisis, to strike quickly across the Baltic and Sweden at southern Norway to secure control of the northern region of NATO.

The submarine incursions were only part of a much broader pattern, which also included a gradual shift in the location of major Warsaw Pact maneuvers in the Baltic further westward toward Danish territorial waters. According to Wilhelm Agrell, a Swedish defense expert, the incursions were merely an expression of the fact that since the mid-1970s Sweden had "entered the Soviet security zone," namely, the geographical zone the Soviets would need to control in any conflict to protect Murmansk and secure the Baltic area. To secure the zone "it would be essential for the Soviet forces to forestall the arrival of powerful Western reinforcements by bringing about a rapid collapse of the defense of NATO's Northern Region. The most decisive way to bring about such a collapse would be the conquest of Sweden."[47] Hence the intense Soviet interest in getting as much detailed information as possible about the Swedish coastline.

The Soviets combined these military activities with a broad and sophisticated diplomatic and ideological offensive against the northern flank of NATO beginning in 1979, when NATO decided to deploy new intermediate-range missiles in Central Europe to counterbalance a much greater number of Soviet missiles. This offensive moved into high gear in 1982 and coincided with a dramatic shift in Nordic internal security policies, particularly of the Danish Social Democrats. Unlike the Soviet use of Palme, which had a global scope, these political moves were directly aimed at convincing the Danish and Norwegian governments to accept the NWFZ idea and thus, effectively, to undermine NATO's ability to deter Soviet expansion in the north.

For years, political leaders asserted their belief in "the Nordic balance," by which they meant a low level of tension and an apparent East-West equilibrium in the Nordic area that was maintained by the mutual interest of the Soviet Union, the neutrals, and the NATO countries. An essential element of this supposed balance was the foreign policies of the neutral states, Finland and Sweden, which were supposed to reassure the Soviet leaders that neither country would let itself be used by enemies of the Soviet Union. According to Kekkonen and Östen Undén, Swedish foreign minister in the 1950s, the strategy of reassurance was a realistic and reliable way to secure permanent independence. In retrospect it is clear that reassurance very easily shades into outright appeasement, as was illustrated by the Palme government's behavior following the submarine incursions. Indeed, a Soviet belief that the real reason for the Swedish policy of reassurance was Swedish fear of Soviet intentions may have helped to provoke the incursions and the new, more aggressive Soviet actions in and around Sweden. If that is so, then the results of reassurance were the opposite of what Kekkonen and Undén had hoped, and the strategy was not in fact realistic at all.[48] Nor did the Soviet Union, for its part, ever believe in any "Nordic balance." Indeed, the Soviet aim "has been a Nordic foreign policy that would eventually neutralize its entire northern periphery" and, accordingly, "the Soviets are in fact doggedly pursuing efforts which, if successful, would alter the status quo in Moscow's favor."[49]

Toward the end of the 1970s three things happened to disturb the small and tightly knit Nordic foreign policy community. First, the big NATO countries insisted that the Soviet buildup was real and needed to be opposed. Second, the character and extent of that buildup began to be all too evident in the Nordic area itself in the form of submarine incursions and other Soviet demonstrations of military force. Third, the cultural radicalism that had begun in the late 1960s and was now entrenched in left-wing parties and organizations in the Nordic countries seized upon the peace and security issue and began demanding changes in security policy.[50] The level of debate and the reasons the radical attacks were fairly successful are summarized by Swedish defense expert Ingemar Dörfer as follows:

> [T]he small size of the Nordic countries makes it difficult for a genuine "counterelite" to emerge which is both well informed and experienced enough to conduct a sophisticated debate on matters of national security. Most experts are tied in some way to their respective governments . . . The political leaders refuse to educate the public properly . . . and, deprived of orientation by the politically responsible, the public is reduced to a choice between traditional diplomatic analysis and that of the "peace movements."

Furthermore,

> the spontaneous tendency of Scandinavians is neutralist, founded on a long tradition of noninvolvement in the turbulent conflicts of Europe . . . the

underlying pretension is that these prosperous little countries on the edge of Europe are superior to the others and that the rest of the world would do well to follow their example . . . The debate is by nature social democratic, since the countries are ruled by the social democrats whatever the appearances . . . the historical inability of social democrats to understand international relations in terms of power relationships is nowhere as marked as in Scandinavia . . . in the thinking of many Nordic leaders, the very idea of an American umbrella protecting Scandinavia contradicts the idea of a small quiet corner of the world enjoying its own détente as a result of its good will and good conduct and by remaining above the conflicts of the great powers.[51]

Since the media can rely on no experts of their own and their tendency in any case is to listen with interest to the critics, the opinions of the latter are over-emphasized. This in turn affects the politicians who see "peace" as a useful and advantageous issue with which to gain possible international fame.

The conservative governments of Denmark and Norway were less inclined to give in to either Soviet or domestic pressure on security policy than were the Social Democrats they had replaced. In Norway, the DNA returned to power in 1986, but apart from a few gestures against the Strategic Defense Initiative (SDI) and U.S. policy toward Nicaragua, the government remained firmly committed to the Atlantic Alliance and generally skeptical of the NWFZ or other ideas designed to accommodate Soviet wishes. In Denmark, the center-right coalition existed on the sufferance of the small Social Liberal party, which supported the government's economic policy but voted against it on security issues. The Social Democrats, meanwhile, increasingly abandoned their loyalty to NATO, while paying lip service to continued Danish membership. By 1986 a common Social Democratic and SF platform on security policy was emerging, in which, for the first time, SF accepted NATO membership, but in such a way as to empty it of all meaning. If returned to power with SF support, the Social Democrats would be committed not only to the NWFZ and to advocating no first use of nuclear weapons in NATO (and hence to abandoning the official NATO strategy of flexible response) but also to "defensive defense," a posture that was supposed to enhance "common security" (an old Soviet phrase) by not threatening Soviet forces unless they were actually on Danish territory. Soviet spokesmen, who devoted greater attention to Danish developments in the 1980s, openly referred to Denmark as the "weak link" in NATO and looked forward to the day when Denmark would follow the Finnish model of nonalignment. The Soviets have also employed "active measures," chiefly espionage and disinformation, to considerable effect. The most important case so far is that of a high-ranking Norwegian civil servant and left-leaning Social Democrat, Arne Treholt, who was arrested as a Soviet agent in 1984. In the wake of his arrest, four senior Soviet diplomats, identified as KGB officers, were expelled from Norway.

Between 1982 and 1987, the Danish government sustained over a dozen defeats in parliament on security matters, without choosing to take any of those defeats as a vote of no confidence and thus as grounds for abdication. In consequence, Danish foreign policy was dictated by a parliamentary majority without political responsibility, and became less and less compatible with the common strategy of NATO. In neutral Sweden, the SAP, under the leadership of Olof Palme, showed consistent support for anti-Western, and especially anti-American, dictatorships, especially Cuba and Vietnam. In the 1980s, moreover, both the Danish and the Norwegian Social Democrats went on record against NATO's deployment of new medium-range missiles, while supporting Soviet proposals for the NWFZ. In 1984, for the first time, a delegation from the Danish party, composed of its leading unilateral disarmers, paid an official visit to the Soviet Communist Party, and a conference on the NWFZ was held shortly after in Copenhagen with Soviet participants. The opinions of these party activists and members of parliament, as opposed to those of the population at large, are distinctly skeptical of American policies and correspondingly willing to excuse or understand Soviet policies. [52] Unless the Social Democrats change back, which is unlikely, their eventual return to power may increase the chances of crisis in the Nordic area.

The most dramatic event of the 1980s in Nordic politics was, seemingly, wholly unrelated to international security affairs. It was the unsolved murder of Olof Palme in Stockholm in February 1986, the first assassination of a head of government in Scandinavia since 1792, when King Gustavus III of Sweden was shot at a masked ball. The crime was still unsolved a year later and no plausible motive had been found, unless one believed the speculations of an American journalist that Palme was killed because Swedish arms manufacturers had been selling arms in violation of strict Swedish laws but with Palme's connivance. According to this argument, Palme had stopped the sales to the Iranian regime of the Ayatollah Khomeini, which was at war with Iraq, and was therefore killed by Iranian hit men—or possibly by Iraqis enraged that the sales had been taking place at all. [53] The event was extraordinary and traumatic, and the botched police investigation was not without tragicomic elements. Yet it had little political significance since Ingvar Carlsson continued Palme's foreign and domestic policies unchanged, if with less panache and arrogance. The important differences emerged slowly. In Palme, Sweden had had a politician of international stature, whatever one might think of his ideology and convictions. When Carlsson took his place, Sweden reverted to a status more befitting its actual size.

The moralism to which Dörfer refers has been particularly marked in Nordic aid to the Third World. Since the mid-1960s official Swedish aid policy has favored socialist regimes, for example (North) Vietnam, Cuba, and Tanzania. Altogether, the Nordic countries in 1985 gave Vietnam $45 million (85 percent of it from Sweden, the rest mostly from Finland), Nicaragua $22 million, and Tanzania $148 million. These amounts were significantly lower than they had been in 1983, although the total amount of aid had risen, an indication that the preference for socialist regimes was perhaps weakening. It has been estimated that Nordic aid represents a third of Tanzania's GDP. In the Nordic countries themselves, the development aid bureaucracy is more costly than all other sections of the foreign ministries combined. Nor was there, until the mid-1980s, very much control over how it was spent. In 1982, a Danish volunteer worker in Tanzania, who had written critical letters home about the corruption and incompetence of the local government and about the waste of Nordic money, which was in no way benefitting the Tanzanian people, was murdered, whether as an act of deliberate terror or revenge is not clear. Her husband was jailed for the offense despite his sound alibi and plausible claims of innocence. Although forced by public opinion to make mild representations to the Tanzanian authorities for his extradition (not release), the Danish government refused to threaten to make aid conditional on its proper use or on respect for human rights by the Tanzanian government. However, by the mid-1980s there was evidence of a growing, if reluctant, recognition that, at least in the case of Tanzania, lavish aid had not promoted social or economic progress and had in fact been largely wasted in support of an inefficient and authoritarian regime. Danish government auditors went so far as to say that aid had "increased the economic problems" of the country. It was still too early to say, in 1987, whether this new realism, which was in any case confined to economic, not political, analysis, would have any lasting impact on the pattern or policies of Third World aid by the Nordic countries.

The official criterion of worthiness to receive Swedish aid is "readiness within the recipient country to use the aid in such a way that poverty and social and economic inequalities are reduced."[54] The Danes tend to stress economic growth; the Norwegians, economic self-sufficiency. Even so, the coordination of programs means that aid tends to go on to the same countries. Given the situation in some of them, moreover, it is clear that the actual degree of reduction of inequality is less important than the ideology of the regime in question. The evidence does not suggest, for instance, that the Vietnamese communist regime, the Ethiopian regime, or the Castro regime in Cuba are using Swedish aid or any other of their resources to "reduce social and economic inequalities." These and many other examples lead one to the conclusion that the criterion of worthiness to receive aid is, indeed, largely political, a conclusion reinforced by the public and private statements of leading members of the national development agencies.

The Nordic countries, in common with most of the Western world, face an uncertain future. Economic problems, the social and psychological consequences of the welfare state and its bureaucracy, and mounting political pressure from the Soviet Union and domestic critics of security policy are presenting politicians, analysts, industrial leaders, and exponents of culture with a new set of challenges. In this review of contemporary Nordic politics and culture, I have necessarily stressed the problems and the critical issues rather than the strengths and continuities that can and must serve as the sources of inspiration and renewal. I have little doubt, though, that short of some disaster striking from the outside, these ancient and strongly based cultures will recall their own past and recover their faith in the future.

Notes

1. For versions of the conceptual map, on which Stein Rokkan was still working at the time of his premature death, see his articles "Dimensions of State Formation and Nation-Building: A Possible Paradigm for Research on Variations within Europe," in Charles F. Tilly, ed., *The Formation of National States in Western Europe* (Princeton, N.J.: Princeton University Press, 1975), pp. 562–600, and "Territories, Nations, Parties: Toward a Geoeconomic-Geopolitical Model for the Explanation of Variations within Western Europe," in Richard L. Merrit and Bruce M. Russett, eds., *From National Development to Global Community* (London: Allen & Unwin, 1981), pp. 70–95. The segment used here is taken from the last completed piece he wrote, "Growth and Structuring of Mass Politics," in Folmer Wisti, ed., *Nordic Democracy: Ideas, Issues, and Institutions in Politics, Economy, Education, Social and Cultural Affairs of Denmark, Finland, Iceland, Norway, and Sweden* (Copenhagen: The Danish Institute, 1981), pp. 53–79.

2. Rokkan, "Growth and Structuring of Mass Politics," pp. 61–64. See also Neil Elder, Alastair H. Thomas, and David Arter, *The Consensual Democracies? The Government and Politics of the Scandinavian States* (Oxford: Martin Robertson, 1982).

3. Anthony F. Upton, *The Finnish Revolution, 1917–1918* (Minneapolis: University of Minnesota Press, 1980) is a thorough account in English.

4. Rokkan, "Growth and Structuring of Mass Politics," pp. 63–66.

5. Ibid., p. 68.

6. The best comparative history of the Danish, Norwegian, and Swedish social democratic parties and labor movements until the late 1970s is Nils Elvander, *Skandinavisk arbetarrörelse* (Stockholm: Liber, 1980). Gøsta Esping-Andersen, *Politics Against Markets: The Social Democratic Road to Power* (Princeton, N.J.: Princeton University Press, 1985) is excellent for background on ideology and the economic theories of Nordic socialists, and is also an articulate defense of the social democratic political economy. For the situation in the 1980s, see the chapters on the Nordic parties in William E. Paterson and Alastair H. Thomas, eds., *The Future of Social Democracy* (Oxford: Oxford University Press, 1986).

7. Erling Bjøl, *Nordic Security*, Adelphi Paper 181 (London: International Institute of Strategic Studies, 1983), p. 46 n. 43. On the Finnish Communist Party from 1918 to 1939, see also the extraordinary memoirs by the former party leader Arvo Tuominen, excerpts of which were published in English under the title *The Bells of the Kremlin* (Hanover, N.H.: University Press of New England, 1983).

8. Bjøl, *Nordic Security*, p. 46 n. 43.

9. Erling Olsen, "The Dilemma of the Social-Democratic Labor Parties," *Nordic Voices, Daedalus* 113, no. 2 (Spring 1984). Olsen, an economist, a Social Democrat, and former Danish minister for housing, attributes the crisis largely to economic causes. An evaluation in terms of cultural and political sociology remains to be carried out. On the changes in and renewal of radical socialism in the Nordic countries, see Daniel Tarschys, "The Changing Basis of Radical Socialism in Scandinavia," in Karl H. Cerny, ed., *Scandinavia at the Polls* (Washington, D.C.: American Enterprise Institute, 1977), pp. 133–53. Tarschys's paper dates from 1975 and although his analysis and predictions largely stand, his argument needs to be brought up to date. The characteristic weakness of conservative parties in Nordic politics and the more general absence of a conservative bourgeois ideology in the culture as a whole are discussed by Francis G. Castles, *The Social Democratic Image of Society* (London and Boston: Routledge & Kegan Paul, 1979), pp. 131–42. For details, see also Ib Faurby and Ole P. Kristensen, "Conservatism in Denmark: A Profile of Party Activists," in Zig Layton, ed., *Conservative Politics in Western Europe* (London: Macmillan, 1982), pp. 83–102; Sten Berglund and Ulf Lindström, "The Conservative Dilemma: Ideology and Vote Maximization in Sweden," in ibid., pp. 64–82; and Bjarne Kristiansen and Lars Svaasund, "The Conservative Party in Norway: From Opposition to Alternative Government," in ibid., pp. 103–30.

10. See Mogens N. Petersen, ed., *The Scandinavian Party Systems* (London: Francis Pinter, 1984); Sten Berglund, Pertti Pesonen, and Gylfi Gislason, "Political Party Systems," in Wisti, ed., *Nordic Democracy*; and Erik Allardt, "Representative Government in a Bureaucratic Age," *The Nordic Enigma, Daedalus* 113, no. 1 (Winter 1984), for perspective on the situation in the 1980s.

11. Matti Klinge, "Aspects of the Nordic Self," *Nordic Voices, Daedalus* 113, no. 2 (Spring 1984): 274. The Nordic countries have often been hailed (or denounced) as models of "corporatism." On this notion and its applicability, see Gerhard Lehmbruch and Philippe Schmitter, eds., *Patterns of Corporatist Policy-Making* (Beverly Hills, Calif., and London: Sage Publications, 1982), which includes chapters on the Nordic countries. See also Allardt, "Representative Government in a Bureaucratic Age," and Don S. Schwerin, "Historic Compromise and Pluralist Decline? Profits and Capital in the Nordic Countries," in John H. Goldthorpe, ed., *Order and Conflict in Contemporary Capitalism* (Oxford: Oxford University Press, 1984), pp. 231–56. An economic theory of why corporatism is growing and is likely to be particularly prevalent in countries having enjoyed long-term stability is provided by Mancur Olson, *The Rise and Decline of Nations* (New Haven, Conn.: Yale University Press, 1982). Olson's book also gives reasons why the Nordic countries might, as I termed it, learn some lessons of the crisis better than others did, such as Britain; see especially pp. 47–53. An early assessment of the problems facing Sweden, the prototype Nordic economy, was M. Donald Hancock, *Sweden: The Politics of Post-Industrial Change* (Hinsdale, Ill.: Dryden Press, 1972). Gösta Rehn, as economic advisor to LO, the trade union organization, helped design the Swedish welfare state; for an informative survey and a mildly self-critical defense of these policies, see his "Wages of Success," *Daedalus* 113, no. 2 (Spring 1984). On Norway, see Fritz Hodne, *The Norwegian Economy, 1920–1980* (New York: St. Martin's Press, 1983). For a cultural and

sociological theory of why the Nordic countries have high taxation, see the remarks on Sweden in Carolyn Webber and Aaron Wildavsky, A *History of Taxation and Expenditure in the Western World* (New York: Simon & Schuster, 1986).

12. Organization for Economic Cooperation and Development [hereafter OECD], *Economic Survey of Denmark*, May 1983, p. 7. There is some valuable information on the nature and rate of public sector growth in Denmark in Bent Rold Andersen, "Rationality and Irrationality of the Nordic Welfare State," *The Nordic Enigma, Daedalus* 113, no. 1 (Winter 1984): 130–34. Except where otherwise noted, the facts and figures in this section are taken from the most recent OECD *Economic Surveys* available, from *Yearbook of Nordic Statistics, 1986* (Stockholm: The Nordic Council, 1987) [hereafter YNS], or from *Nordic Economic Outlook* (Stockholm: Swedish Industrial Publications), December 1986.

13. OECD, *Economic Survey of Denmark*, May 1983, p. 16.

14. OECD, *Economic Survey of Denmark*, July 1984, pp. 28–31 and 43–45. On the 1985 labor conflict, see also "The Rescuing of Denmark," *The Economist* (London), April 13, 1985.

15. *Weekendavisen* (Copenhagen), March 29, 1985.

16. OECD, *Economic Survey of Denmark*, February 1986, p. 52.

17. YNS, table 82.

18. "Survey of Sweden," *The Economist* (London), October 6, 1984. See also "Sweden's Economy," *The Economist*, March 7, 1987.

19. "Survey of Sweden," *The Economist*, October 6, 1984. See also OECD, *Economic Survey of Sweden*, May 1984, pp. 9–17, and Rehn, "Wages of Success."

20. For a thorough analysis of post-1982 economic policies, see Barry P. Bosworth and Alice M. Rivlin, eds., *The Swedish Economy* (Washington, D.C.: Brookings Institution, 1987). For an overview, see "Sweden's Economy," *The Economist*, March 7, 1987.

26. Lindbeck asked the question in his book *Hur mycket politik tål ekonomin?* (Stockholm: Bonniers, 1986). Although only a sketch, this book provides the elements of a reply to Esping-Andersen's defense of socialist political control of the economy in his *Politics Against Markets*.

22. "Survey of Norway," *The Economist* (London), November 5, 1983, and OECD, *Economic Survey of Norway*, January 1986.

23. OECD, *Economic Survey of Norway*, February 1983, p. 19. See also the last two chapters of Hodne, *Norwegian Economy*.

24. OECD, *Economic Survey of Norway*, January 1986.

25. YNS, table 202.

26. Quoted in Marvin Rintala, *Four Finns* (Berkeley and Los Angeles: University of California Press, 1969), p. 64. For background on the history of socialism in Scandinavia, see works cited in note 6.

27. Myrdal's memoirs and contemporary analysis are, for those who can read Swedish, a source of capital importance for the ideological as well as political origins and present crisis of the welfare state. See Gunnar Myrdal, *Hur styrs landet?* (Stockholm: Rabén & Sjögren, 1982). For defenses of the Nordic welfare state, see Rehn, "Wages of Success,"

and Andersen, "Nordic Welfare State." An interestingly optimistic and wide-ranging survey by two Norwegian leftists, which also includes a counterattack on the critics of the welfare state, is Bernt Hagtvet and Erik Rudeng, "Scandinavia: Achievements, Dilemmas, Challenges," *Nordic Voices, Daedalus* 113, no. 2 (Spring 1984).

28. On the Committee on Postwar Planning and the "planned economy debate," see Esping-Andersen, *Politics Against Markets.*

29. Myrdal, *Hur styrs landet?* vol. 1, pp. 278–79.

30. See Klinge, "Aspects of the Nordic Self," and Hans L. Zetterberg, "The Rational Humanitarians," *The Nordic Enigma, Daedalus* 113, no. 1 (Winter 1984).

31. The example is taken from the article "Suède: le contre-modèle," *Le Point* (Paris), October 17, 1983. For a sympathetic analysis of Sweden today by the editor of Sweden's biggest daily newspaper, the independent but mostly pro–social democratic *Dagens Nyheter,* see Arne Ruth, "The Second New Nation," in *Nordic Voices, Daedalus* 113, no. 2 (Spring 1984): 53–96.

32. Zetterberg, "Rational Humanitarians," p. 87.

33. "Sweden's Economy," *The Economist,* March 7, 1987.

34. "Suède: le contre-modèle," *Le Point* (Paris), October 17, 1983.

35. Lindbeck, *Hur mycket politik tål ekonomin?* pp. 77, 86.

36. Roland Huntford, *The New Totalitarians* (New York: Stein & Day, 1972).

37. YNS, table 26. The YNS used to publish actual figures of projected population size, but stopped doing so after the 1983 edition, perhaps because they were too alarming. The total fertility rate of a given population at a given point in time is the number of children every woman in the population of child-bearing age would have if all living births were divided among them. The rate required for maintenance of the population in conditions of low infant mortality is approximately 2.12. There is an extensive literature on nonreplacement fertility in industrial societies; for a good introduction to the problem, see Mikhail S. Bernstam, Kingsley Davis, and Rita Ricardo-Campbell, eds., *Below-Replacement Fertility in Industrial Societies: Causes, Consequences, Policies,* special supplement to *Population and Development Review* 12 (1986). Also published separately (New York: Cambridge University Press, 1987).

38. Bjøl, *Nordic Security,* pp. 2–6. For general background on the origins of postwar Nordic security policies see Geir Lundestad, *America, Scandinavia, and the Cold War, 1945–1949* (New York: Columbia University Press, 1980). Haakon Lie, who, next to Foreign Minister Halvard Lange, was the most important driving force in moving the DNA and the Norwegian government toward alliance with the West, tells the full story in his *Skjebneaar, 1945–1950* (Oslo: Tiden, 1985).

39. Bjøl, *Nordic Security,* p. 6. On Finland see Roy Allison, *Finland's Relations with the Soviet Union, 1944–84* (London: Macmillan, 1985). English text of the FCMA treaty on pp. 174–75.

40. Adam M. Garfinkle, *"Finlandization": A Map to a Metaphor* (Philadelphia, Pa.: Foreign Policy Research Institute, 1978), p. 36.

41. Karen Ericksson Orvik, "Finnish Foreign Policy and the Kekkonen Legacy," *Survey,* nos. 118, 119 (Autumn–Winter 1983): 162–64. On finlandization see also Bjøl,

Nordic Security, pp. 7–16. A different judgment of the character, course, and consequences of the Kekkonen line will be found in Allison, *Finland's Relations with the Soviet Union*, and in the important study of Fenno-Soviet relations by Professor H. Peter Krosby of the State University of New York at Albany. Professor Krosby is preparing a much revised edition for publication in English.

42. On the nuclear-weapon–free zone (NWFZ) proposals see Kari Möttölä, ed., *Nuclear Weapons and Northern Europe: Problems and Prospects of Arms Control* (Helsinki: Finnish Institute of International Affairs, 1983), for a series of official and semiofficial views. See also Bjøl, *Nordic Security*, pp. 27–30; Ingemar Dörfer, "La Scandinavie ou la défense de la virginité nucléaire," in Pierre Lellouche, ed., *Pacifisme et Dissuasion* (Paris: Institut Français des Relations Internationales, 1983), pp. 127–33; and Orvik, "Finnish Foreign Policy," pp. 154–56. George Maude, "Conflict and Cooperation: The Nordic Nuclear-Free Zone Today," *Cooperation and Conflict* 18 (1983): 233–43, combines analysis of the leading proposals with strong support for the idea, based on what is in my view a fatuous faith in Soviet benevolence. The official Soviet line, that the NWFZ would promote peace and stability, is provided by L. Voronkov, *Non-Nuclear Status to Northern Europe* (Moscow: Nauka, 1984).

43. Bjøl, *Nordic Security*, pp. 42–43, but also see Orvik, "Finnish Foreign Policy," p. 164.

44. Marian Leighton, "Soviet Strategy Towards Northern Europe and Japan," *Survey*, nos. 118, 119 (Autumn–Winter 1983): 117.

45. Ibid., pp. 135–37.

46. Ibid., pp. 129–33.

47. Wilhelm Agrell, "Behind the Submarine Crisis: Evolution of the Swedish Defence Doctrine and Soviet War Planning," *Cooperation and Conflict* 21 (1986): 197–217. This article is a partial summary of the same author's *Bakom ubåtskrisen. Militär verksamhet, krigsplanläggning och diplomati i östersjöområdet* (Stockholm: Liber, 1986). See also Gunnar Jervas, "Sweden in a Less Benign Environment," in Bengt Sundelius, ed., *The Neutral Democracies and the New Cold War* (Boulder, Colo.: Westview Press, 1987), pp. 57–74.

48. Agrell, *Bakom ubåtskrisen*, pp. 188–89, 193–94.

49. Orvik, "Finnish Foreign Policy," p. 154; and Robert K. German, "Norway and the Bear: Soviet Coercive Diplomacy and Norwegian Security Policy," *International Security* 7, no. 2 (Fall 1982): 79. On the "Nordic balance" concept in general, see Arne Olav Brundtland, "The Context of Security in Northern Europe," in Paul M. Cole and Douglas M. Hart, eds., *Northern Europe: Security Issues for the 1990s* (Boulder, Colo.: Westview Press, 1986), pp. 7–18. For differing analyses of what has been happening to the "Nordic balance," see Dov S. Zakheim, "NATO's Northern Front: Developments and Prospects," *Cooperation and Conflict* 17 (1982): 193–205, and the contributions in Johan Jørgen Holst, Kenneth Hunt, and Anders C. Sjaastad, eds., *Deterrence and Defense in the North* (Oslo: Universitetsforlaget, 1985).

50. This change was most marked in Denmark which is therefore the focus of most studies of the phenomenon; see Martin Heisler, "Denmark's Quest for Security: Constraints and Opportunities Within the Alliance," in Gregory Flynn, ed., *NATO's Northern*

Allies: The National Security Policies of Belgium, Denmark, The Netherlands, and Norway (Totowa, N.J.: Rowman & Allanheld, 1985), pp. 57–112, and Michael A. Krasner and Nikolaj Petersen, "Peace and Politics: The Danish Peace Movement and its Impact on National Security Policy," *Journal of Peace Research* 23 (1986): 157–73. For background on Nordic security in the 1980s, see the contributions in Cole and Hart, *Northern Europe*.

51. Dörfer, "La Scandinavie," pp. 113–116.

52. On developments in the Danish and Norwegian social democratic parties see Nikolaj Petersen, "The Scandilux Experiment: Towards a Transnational Social Democratic Security Perspective," *Cooperation and Conflict* 20 (1985): 1–22.

53. Richard Reeves, "The Palme Obsession," *The New York Times Magazine*, March 1, 1987.

54. *YNS*, tables 208–12. The definition of "worthiness" is taken from Lars Rudebeck, "Nordic Policies Toward the Third World," in Bengt Sundelius, ed., *Foreign Policies of Northern Europe* (Boulder, Colo.: Westview Press, 1982), p. 160. Rudebeck himself believes in the criterion and in the beneficial results of aid, but see his remarks on pp. 160, 166, and 168. A better overview of the historical background and some issues of current Nordic aid policy is Nils Andrén, "The Nordic Countries and North-South Relations," in ibid. Both Rudebeck and Andrén provide full statistical details (as of 1977). The late Gunnar Myrdal, whose writings, especially *Asian Drama* (New York: Random House, 1971), did more than any other single text to stimulate the ideology of government aid in the Nordic countries in the 1960s and 1970s, claimed in the 1980s that he was misunderstood and opposed the application of any ideological criterion of worthiness. Aid should go where disaster strikes, without consideration of the real or imagined moral qualities of the regime concerned.

Suggested Readings

Allardt, Erik. "Representative Government in a Bureaucratic Age." *The Nordic Enigma, Daedalus* 113, no. 1 (Winter 1984).

Andersen, Bent Rold. "Rationality and Irrationality of the Nordic Welfare State." *The Nordic Enigma, Daedalus* 113, no. 1 (Winter 1984).

Andrén, Nils. "Five Roads to Parliamentary Democracy." In *Nordic Democracy: Ideas, Issues, and Institutions in Politics, Economy, Education, Social and Cultural Affairs of Denmark, Finland, Iceland, Norway, and Sweden*, edited by Folmer Wisti. Copenhagen: The Danish Institute, 1981.

Arter, David. *The Nordic Parliaments: A Comparative Analysis.* London: Hurst, 1984.

Berner, Örjan. *Soviet Policies Toward the Nordic Countries.* Lanham, Md.: University Press of America for the Center for International Affairs, Harvard University, 1986.

Bjøl, Erling. *Nordic Security.* Adelphi Paper 181. London: International Institute for Strategic Studies, 1983.

Bosworth, Barry P., and Rivlin, Alice M., eds. *The Swedish Economy.* Washington, D.C.: Brookings Institution, 1987.

Cole, Paul M., and Hart, Douglas M., eds. *Northern Europe: Security Issues for the 1990s.* Boulder, Colo.: Westview Press, 1986.

Derry, T. K. *A History of Scandinavia.* London: Allen & Unwin, 1979.

Elder, Neil; Thomas, Alastair H.; and Arter, David. *The Consensual Democracies? The Government and Politics of the Scandinavian States.* Oxford: Martin Robertson, 1982.

Esping-Andersen, Gøsta. *Politics Against Markets: The Social Democratic Road to Power.* Princeton, N.J.: Princeton University Press, 1985.

Flynn, Gregory, ed. *NATO's Northern Allies: The National Security Policies of Belgium, Denmark, the Netherlands, and Norway.* Totowa, N.J.: Rowman & Allanheld, 1985.

Hagtvet, Bernt, and Rudeng, Erik. "Scandinavia: Achievements, Dilemmas, Challenges." *Nordic Voices, Daedalus* 113, no. 2 (Spring 1984).

Haugen, Einar. *The Scandinavian Languages.* New York: Cambridge University Press, 1976.

Klinge, Matti. "Aspects of the Nordic Self." *Nordic Voices, Daedalus* 113, no. 2 (Spring 1984).

Lönnroth, Lars. "The Intellectual Civil Servant: The Role of the Writer and the Scholar in Nordic Culture." *Nordic Voices, Daedalus* 113, no. 2 (Spring 1984).

Nordic Economic Outlook. Stockholm: Federation of Swedish Industries. Published each June and December.

The Nordic Enigma, Daedalus 113, no. 1 (Winter 1984).

Nordic Voices, Daedalus 113, no. 2 (Spring 1984).

Organization for Economic Cooperation and Development (OECD). *Economic Surveys.* Published at approximately annual intervals for each country.

Olsen, Erling. "The Dilemma of the Social-Democratic Labor Parties." *Nordic Voices, Daedalus* 113, no. 2 (Spring 1984).

Pedersen, Mogens N., ed. *The Scandinavian Party Systems.* London: Francis Pinter, 1984.

Rehn, Gösta. "The Wages of Success." *Nordic Voices, Daedalus* 113, no. 2 (Spring 1984).

Rokkan, Stein. "The Growth and Structuring of Mass Politics." In *Nordic Democracy: Ideas, Issues, and Institutions in Politics, Economy, Education, Social and Cultural Affairs of Denmark, Finland, Iceland, Norway, and Sweden,* edited by Folmer Wisti. Copenhagen: The Danish Institute, 1981.

Sundelius, Bengt, ed. *Foreign Policies of Northern Europe.* Boulder, Colo.: Westview Press, 1982.

———. *The Neutral Democracies and the New Cold War.* Boulder, Colo.: Westview Press, 1987.

Wisti, Folmer, ed. *Nordic Democracy: Ideas, Issues, and Institutions in Politics, Economy, Education, Social and Cultural Affairs of Denmark, Finland, Iceland, Norway, and Sweden.* Copenhagen: The Danish Institute, 1981.

Yearbook of Nordic Statistics. Stockholm: The Nordic Council. Published annually.

Zetterberg, Hans L. "The Rational Humanitarians." *The Nordic Enigma, Daedalus* 113, no. 1 (Winter 1984).

6

Germany

EDITORS' NOTE

This chapter on Germany includes the chapter from the first edition of this book, "The Federal Republic of Germany (1945–1988)," as well as a new section detailing the history of East Germany from partition in 1945 to reunification in 1990.

The Federal Republic of Germany
(1945–1988)

Richard C. Eichenberg ⸻

It is often said that students of politics, like politicians themselves, tend to view other countries as more rational than their own. When attempting to understand the politics and policies of foreign political systems, we sometimes assume that they are more organized, unified, or centralized than our own. This tendency is particularly easy for Americans to fall into, for their political system is one of almost unending fragmentation, decentralization, and—it sometimes seems—confusion. Perhaps Americans can therefore be forgiven for thinking that *somewhere, somehow* other political systems have escaped the complexity of politics and public policy that characterizes the United States.

Certainly we know that many European political systems are more unified than our own. The French and British systems, in fact, are often described in terms of their historical development from distinct territories and authorities to the more centralized nation-states of the modern era, and the existence of collective, cabinet governments in Europe suggests that public policy, if not based on total agreement, is at least developed more coherently than it is in the American system of federalism and separation of powers.

It would be a mistake, however, to assume that centralization of authority is universal in Europe, and it would certainly be erroneous to assign such a pattern to the Federal Republic of Germany. West Germany—the successor state of the German empire—has descended from a political experience of fragmentation rather than centralization.[1] Indeed, from the thirteenth century on, Germany was plagued by disunity and decentralization. From the time of the Reformation

170

in the sixteenth century through the Thirty Years' War from 1618 to 1648, Germany was a "crazy-quilt pattern of competing principalities . . . an object of manipulation and conquest." [2]

The unification of the German empire did not take place until 1871 under Bismarck, and even then the identity of the former German states (such as Bavaria, Prussia, Baden, and Württemberg) was preserved in cultural, political, and religious differences. As it was, German unity was short-lived. World War I resulted in the proclamation of the first German republic (Weimar), but German democracy disintegrated under the weight of economic collapse and the victory of the Nazi Party in the 1930s. With the defeat of the German Reich in World War II, Germany was once again divided into separate states—the West German Republic and the Democratic Republic of Germany, which is in the Soviet orbit.

With this turbulent past, it is hardly surprising that the development of political unity was also late in coming to Germany. Unlike other European states, which had industrialized earlier and more slowly and had integrated the middle and working classes into a new bourgeois democracy, Germany was slow, both in economic development and in the integration of new actors into the political process. Indeed, it was the lack of a democratic consensus that contributed to the downfall of the Weimar Republic, as disparate interests representing the military, bureaucracy, aristocracy, and parties could not agree on policies for dealing with economic difficulty.

In a sense, the faits accomplis that resulted from World War II began the process of building unity and consensus—at least in the Federal Republic of Germany. Territorially, the Federal Republic was a well-defined unit, fixed in its place by the cold war that ended any hopes of the reunification of a larger Germany. Politically, the institutions of the Federal Republic contributed to consensus, for it limited the role of small, factional parties (a party must achieve 5 percent of the national vote to achieve representation in the Bundestag, or Parliament) and contributed to the development of centrist, "catch-all" parties. Whereas fourteen parties were represented in the first Bundestag elected in 1949, by 1983 this number had been reduced to four.

The centrist consensus was dominated until quite recently by three parties. The Christian Democratic Union and Christian Socialist Union (CDU/CSU) draw their major support from conservatives but also from some Catholic members of the labor movement. The Social Democratic Party (SPD) has traditionally been a working-class party, but in 1959 it shed the more socialist of its policy goals in the famous Bad Godesberger Program that announced its acceptance of a market economy and a foreign policy orientation with the West. The Free Democratic Party (FDP or "liberal" party) has traditionally been the party of small business, civil servants, and farmers, but (like the Social Democrats) it has increasingly appealed to the new service class of educated young people. In fact, given the transformation of the West German economy to a service orientation, all West German parties will probably be required to appeal to the interests of this new class of postindustrial voters.

The newest party in West Germany is the Greens, a diverse coalition of ecological and peace activists who began entering politics (in demonstrations rather than elections) in the 1970s. The Greens, who command 5 percent of the vote, base their appeal largely on environmental and peace issues and oppose many of the traditional approaches to economic policy and national security.

The electoral success of the four major parties and the breakdown of their support among major sectors of the population are shown in Table 6.1. Taken together, the figures provide a clear political history of the Federal Republic. During the economic recovery and cold war climate of the 1950s, the electoral landscape was dominated by the more conservative Christian and Free Democratic parties, while the Social Democrats suffered from suspicions about their socialist economic views and their more idealistic foreign policy orientation. After 1959, when the Social Democrats shifted their tone to a more promarket and pro-NATO stance, their electoral support improved gradually, so that by 1969 they were able to form a government with the FDP. This coalition governed until 1983, when harsh debates about the recession and government budget (described later in this chapter) combined with acrimony over nuclear weapons to force the SPD from power. Note that in the subsequent election held in 1983, the SPD suffered a clear setback, perhaps because the electorate thought that renewed international tension and economic problems required a return to conservative rule. Nonetheless, the table also reveals the emergence of the Greens, the new party that emphasizes environmental quality and disarmament. Thus, although the troubled economy and international crises of the 1980s have brought a generally conservative shift, these issues have also polarized the electoral landscape.

That polarization is also revealed in the bottom half of Table 6.1, which shows how well each party succeeds within different sectors of the electorate. Clearly, the parties have distinct identities in economic and social terms. The CDU/CSU and FDP have fewer blue-collar, union voters, whereas almost half of the SPD vote comes from union members. Somewhat surprisingly, the more radical Greens also draw much support from union members, a signal perhaps that some of the more radical members of the SPD shifted their allegiance to this new party as the economic and defense debates of the 1980s became more harsh and polarized. In any case, one thing is clear: The appeal of the Greens is greatest among the higher-educated and the young. One-third of their votes come from individuals who have completed college preparatory or actual university courses of study, and fully 90 percent of their voters are under 40 years of age.

In summary, the West German party system might be compared to a glacier. At the foundation, there is still a considerable cleavage of the older economic

Table 6.1 Electoral Performance and Social Background of West German Parties

PERCENTAGE OF VOTES RECEIVED IN ELECTIONS

	CDU/CSU	SPD	FDP	Greens
1949	31	29	12	—
1953	45	29	10	—
1957	50	32	8	—
1961	45	36	13	—
1965	48	39	10	—
1969	46	43	6	—
1972	45	46	8	—
1976	49	43	8	—
1980	45	43	11	2
1983	49	38	7	6

SOCIAL BACKGROUND OF WEST GERMAN PARTY SUPPORTERS IN 1983 (PERCENTAGES)

	CDU/CSU	SPD	FDP	Greens
Union members	25	40	28	41
Self-employed	32	5	na	na
Advanced education	8	9	12	31
Age				
Under 40	32	40	33	90
40–59	35	36	44	7
60 and over	33	24	23	3

SOURCES: Russell Dalton and Kendall Baker, "The Contours of West German Opinion," in P. Wallach and G. Romoser, eds., *West German Politics in the Mid-Eighties* (New York: Praeger, 1985), Table 3.3; and Alex Dragnich and Jorgen S. Rasmussen, *Major European Governments* (Chicago: Dorsey Press, 1986), p. 387.

issues: The conservatives and liberals are still the parties of business, while the Social Democrats remain firmly tied to their base of union workers. Nonetheless, this foundation is overlaid with change: The younger and best educated are increasingly concerned by issues of environment and disarmament, a concern that is reflected by the emergence and rise of the Green Party.

Nonetheless, although the political party system has gradually been unified under a small number of parties, it would be remiss to characterize German politics and public policy as similarly unified. One reason is that West Germany is a federal government, with authority divided among the federal government (*Bund*), state governments (*Länder*, of which there are eleven), and local governments (*Gemeinden*). Here the comparison with the United States is more useful, for the division of authority in West Germany is not unlike that in the United States. As shown in Table 6.2, the federal government controls only about 45 percent of all public spending in West Germany. In some areas its responsibilities are greater (economic services, social security), but in others control is left largely to the Länder and Gemeinden. As is the case in the United States, education and judicial functions are largely local in West Germany. However, unlike the situation in the United States, there are a fair number of uniform, national standards in West Germany. For example, the Bundestag may establish national educational standards but leave the financing and administration of those standards to the states.

Another source of decentralization in West German public policy is found in the welfare state. As shown in Table 6.3, the West German public sector constituted 43 percent of the gross domestic product in 1980, a figure that places it behind such large welfare states as Sweden and the Netherlands but ahead of the United States, Japan, and Great Britain.

Over the past decade, the division of public spending in West Germany has remained relatively stable. Social spending dominates, with a decline in the share of public resources devoted to defense and an increase in spending devoted to health, a pattern that Germany shares with other countries. But the West German welfare state is far from a monolithic example of state socialism. In fact, the programs of the welfare state are divided both in their type of administration (public and private) and in their type of financing. For example, social security pensions, the largest program by far, is divided into a number of separate programs, including schemes for white-collar workers, one for blue-collar workers, and one for miners, among others. These programs, in turn, are financed by contributions from employers, employees, and the federal government. A similar division exists for the health insurance system, with financing shared by the same three groups and with administration carried out by semiautonomous insurance funds (unlike Great Britain and Sweden, West Germany has government-mandated health *insurance* rather than a government-operated *health service*).

In addition to these programs, West Germany has legislated unemployment insurance and accident insurance. Further, there is a large program of family allowances that provides progressively generous benefits for each child after the first. There are also programs of social assistance and housing assistance for those in need and a wide variety of smaller programs, such as educational assistance and plans designed to encourage savings for housing and other projects. Finally, West Germany is among the most advanced countries in worker participation in management, with legislation providing for worker representation on the boards of all but the smallest companies.

Table 6.2   Federal Spending in West Germany

Purpose	As percentage of all public spending 1970	1975
Economic services	67	54
Social security	70	69
Research	68	75
Transport and communications	43	49
Housing	8	14
Justice and police	6	7
Health and sports	2	7
Education	5	7
Total	46	46

SOURCE: Based on Eike Ballerstedt and Wolfgang Glatzer, eds., *Soziologischer Almanach* (Frankfurt: Campus Verlag, 1979), p. 488.
NOTE: Does not include expenditures from social security funds.

Thus, although legislation has provided for coverage against almost all social contingencies, administration of the numerous programs is divided among public and private parties and federal, state, and local governments; and the financing is shared among employers, employees, and the government. The 40 percent of government spending devoted to social purposes is not found in one place but in a variety of governmental and quasi-governmental agencies, and the burden of paying for benefits is a blend of individual (worker), employer, and community responsibility.

Because the Federal Republic is a system of federated authority with a complex variety of public programs, perhaps it should come as no surprise that the policymaking process in the capital city of Bonn is also complex. This pattern emerges despite the existence of a collective, cabinet style of government designed explicitly to create a strong executive. With the federal president relegated to a largely ceremonial role, the chancellor is the real chief executive. Empowered to organize the government and appoint ministers, and with power further enhanced by a constitutional provision stating the prerogative to set overall policy guidelines, the chancellor cannot be removed through no-confidence procedures unless the opposition is capable of producing a successor with majority support. In budgetary matters, the chancellor's powers are strengthened by a provision that enables him to veto legislative or financial matters in the cabinet by siding in opposition with the finance minister. Moreover, the staff of the chancellor's office—larger than that of some ministries—mirrors the entire minis-

Table 6.3   Distribution of Public Spending

Purpose	PERCENTAGE OF TOTAL PUBLIC SPENDING	
	1970	1980
Defense	8	6
Education	11	11
Health	12	14
Social security	40	41
Total Public Spending as Percentage of GDP	33	43

SOURCE: Organization for Economic Cooperation and Development (OECD), *National Accounts Statistics of OECD Member Countries* (Paris, 1983), vol. 2, detailed tables.
NOTE: Includes expenditures of social security trust funds.

terial organization and includes staff components for planning and for budgetary matters. Nonetheless, the dominant view of observers of German politics is that the chancellor's formal powers have not been translated into a process of centralized, governmentwide priority-setting. Plain disinterest and preoccupation with foreign policy are certainly among the reasons for this, but there are also political and organizational limitations that seem to operate regardless of the officeholder.

Chief among these is the situation of mutual dependence that binds the chancellor and his ministers. Although the chancellor is technically free to appoint ministers of his choice, practical considerations often override this absolute legal privilege. In a coalition government, for example, the partner party will have a claim on some ministries. Regional, religious, economic, and political interests *within* the chancellor's party must also be balanced, both as rewards for electoral support and in anticipation of the need for assistance in passing the legislative program. Thus, it is not unusual in West German cabinets to find members of important client groups, such as unions, small businesses, and women. For practical purposes, then, a range of political and economic interests will be represented in the cabinet and have a voice in policy debates.

The West German constitution also contains a ministerial counterweight to the chancellor's competence to set overall policy—namely, the rule that ministers are personally and fully responsible for the activities of their own departments. According to one German expert, ministerial autonomy is "jealously guarded" by ministers, perhaps because they see more to be gained as successful defenders of specific programs than as supporters of general government policy: "As a consequence, cabinet members do not have a basic interest in strengthening the policy-making and policy-controlling capacities of the Cabinet as a whole and of the Chancellor's office, which might only increase outside scrutiny and intervention in departmental policies."[3]

The cabinet and the chancellor are also dependent on their majority in Parliament. The constitution does require that parliamentary increases to proposed government spending be approved by the cabinet before final passage of the budget law. In practice, governments have used this veto power sparingly because frequent disagreement between the government and its supporting majority would openly reveal an end of consensus. Indeed, a severe test of the government-Parliament balance played a major role in the downfall of Chancellor Ludwig Erhard in 1966. Facing re-election in 1965, his party—the Christian Democratic Union—passed a series of election-gift spending measures that far exceeded the budget proposed by Chancellor Erhard. Caught between an uncompromising parliamentary delegation and pressures to hold down spending, Erhard accepted the spending increases, contributing to the view that he had lost control of his party and thus of his basis for leadership.

Most chancellors have avoided such dramatic confrontations. Nonetheless, the potential for politically damaging conflict forces the cabinet and the parliamentary party to compromise. Changes to the budget, although numerous, are quite small, but these minor adjustments probably hide considerable bargaining and consultation *before* the budget is submitted for parliamentary consideration.

The give-and-take between the government and the parliamentary majority is symptomatic of an additional constraint on the chancellor and his cabinet: the need to maintain support in the party at large. Two factors make this especially important. First, the balance of regional, ideological, and economic forces within German parties makes consensus-building and leadership selection delicate tasks. Government policy, including the budget, must be formulated with an eye toward maintaining the intraparty consensus among groupings of political weight. Second, the West German federal system provides a year-round agenda of political activity, including state and local elections, party conventions, and special working groups. In formulating its policy decisions, the Bonn government must be sensitive to regional and local issues and to the effect of its decisions on local party fortunes.

Federalism is itself a major issue in German politics. Although the federal government retains authority over most types of tax legislation, expenditure of funds is undertaken autonomously by the Land and Gemeinde governments. Because tax legislation must be approved by the upper chamber of the Parliament, where Land interests are represented, debates over fiscal federalism have been among the most heated and enduring of German politics. As a rule, federal governments have found it difficult to influence the direction of fiscal policy at lower levels of government.

In summary, the West German policymaking system is less centralized than might be expected of a cabinet form of government. Constitutional and political constraints create a context in which the chancellor must build consensus from among a variety of political and departmental interests. The federal nature of the system makes it difficult to intervene directly in the budgets of state and local governments. Taken together, these constraints suggest that trade-offs among political priorities will not be made by a unified executive immune to the distractions of particularistic pressures. Indeed, the structure of the system ensures that a diversity of interests will receive a voice in the policy process.

Current Policy Issues

In West Germany, as in other countries, there are three basic societal goals that tend to preoccupy politicians, interest groups, and citizens. Perhaps the most basic is the goal of *economic growth*, a sufficient production of goods and services to provide adequate employment at stable (noninflationary) prices. But social goals do not end here. In most democratic societies, there is the further goal of *social justice*, a term that often gives rise to much debate, but a concern that is usually pursued to some extent. Finally, it has become clear during recent years that growth and justice are not enough; increasingly, citizens are concerned that economic goals not outweigh the goal of a satisfactory *quality of life*, that is, an enjoyable and lasting natural environment and the ability to develop nonmaterial values, such as self-expression.

For West Germans, the goal of economic growth has always had a special importance. Not only did many Germans experience the effect of terrible inflation during the period between the two world wars, they also suffered from the devastation wrought by World War II. For West Germany, 1945 was a zero point in economic as well as political terms, for the war had left housing and businesses destroyed. In light of this desperate starting point, the economic success of the Federal Republic since 1945 can only be called miraculous, a word often used to describe the huge success of the German economy since then—the *Wirtschaftswunder*.

In the 1950s, the German economy, aided by the Marshall Plan and the creation of a new West German currency, grew at the astounding rate of 7 percent annually after inflation. In the 1960s, this rate slowed, but it was nonetheless a healthy 4.6 percent (by comparison, American growth during the same period was 3.8 percent). During the 1970s, a decade troubled by an oil embargo and the subsequent explosion of oil prices, growth remained at 2.8 percent. Moreover, this record of economic success was accomplished with very little inflation (the lowest among advanced, industrial countries), and it brought jobs to virtually all West Germans. In fact, the Federal Republic was required during much of the postwar period to recruit workers from abroad, a group of "guest-workers" (*Gastarbeiter*) who came largely from Italy, Turkey, and Greece. In summary, for most of the period since 1945, West Germany has accomplished the goal of economic growth with huge success.

However, like all industrialized countries, West Germany now faces difficult economic times. In the recession that followed the second oil price explosion in 1979 (from 1979 to 1982), West German economic growth plunged to near zero. Inflation also increased slightly, but by far the biggest casualty of recession has been the labor force; there were still 2.4 million (9.5 percent) West Germans unemployed in 1985—the largest proportional increase among the industrialized nations during the recession. Moreover, West Germany's traditional industries, such as steel, coal, and shipbuilding, now face competition from the republic's industrialized partners as well as from newly industrialized countries of the Third World, such as South Korea, Brazil, and Taiwan. The situation is most desperate for young workers who must adjust to a new type of labor market as the traditional industries decline.

Not surprisingly, economic problems have brought political debates in their wake. In general, the ruling CDU/FDP coalition has favored policies to stimulate growth indirectly: Such proposals as tax incentives for enterprises, retraining of workers, and reduction of government deficits are seen as creating the conditions in which growth can proceed in a free-market economy. The Social Democrats, in contrast, prefer much more direct policies, such as public investment, public spending to stimulate job creation, or reduction of working hours to create new jobs.

This is not to say that one party favors a free-market approach while the other favors government intervention. In fact, all West German parties have long accepted the concept of the "social market economy," that is, a mix of government and private enterprise that operates on free-market principles but protects citizens from inevitable economic ups and downs. Indeed, the social programs just described enjoy a wide multiparty consensus as mechanisms that support, rather than supplant, the market economy. Moreover, all parties in West Germany have long accepted—indeed favored—a government role in providing services essential to the economy. Two examples are the government-owned rail and communications systems, among the largest employers in the Federal Republic.

Nonetheless, the current recession has aggravated political differences over the appropriate division of benefits (and costs) within the social market framework—the question of social justice mentioned above. This debate is nowhere more visible than in the question of adjusting the government budget to difficult economic circumstances. Recession has its most visible impact on government finances. Revenues erode as growth declines, yet the need for spending to assist the unemployed and to stimulate the economy increases. In West Germany, this situation is further aggravated by the attraction of German savings to the high-interest-rate markets of the United States, and there is the fear that continuing government deficits will exacerbate the problem as governments borrow to finance spending.

The problem of how much, and where, to cut the government budget has been the source of much political debate and turmoil in West Germany. In fact, the downfall of the SPD/FDP government of Helmut Schmidt in the fall of 1982 resulted from the inability of the two coalition parties to agree on a plan for cutting government spending. The list of competing demands is long. As we have seen, there is a large system of programs to support the aged, the sick, and the unemployed. In addition, declining birthrates mean that social programs will be supported by fewer and fewer young, working taxpayers in the coming decades. Yet the program of family allowances designed, in part, to encourage large families is among the more expensive in the federal budget. There are other competitors for public funds, such as education (expanded greatly during the 1970s) and transportation, and the international tensions of recent years, coupled with the increasing cost of weapons, also place upward pressure on the defense budget.

The conservative government of Helmut Kohl, which gained power in 1982 and was re-elected in 1983, has faced this same array of interests, but supported by a stronger coalition, it has been more successful than its predecessor in passing budget cuts. It would be a mistake, however, to view the Kohl government as a West German version of the Reagan government in the United States. Although Kohl did succeed in passing some cuts in spending (by freezing civil servants' pay, cutting some maternity and unemployment benefits, and raising some taxes), these cuts caused considerable political debate, not just with the other parties and their supporters, but *within* his own liberal-conservative coalition. In particular, the Catholic working-class component of the CDU/CSU party is sensitive to social-spending cuts, and there is little enthusiasm in any party for increases in defense spending. In summary, although the accession of a conservative government has brought some slowdown in government spending, there is no indication that more drastic cuts will be forthcoming.

If the traditional parties have dominated the debate over the goals of growth and justice, the Green Party is largely responsible for the visibility of quality-of-life issues. In the 1970s, a number of events stimulated widespread protest in West Germany over the effects of economic growth on the environment. Chief among these were protests against nuclear power (both the building of new plants and the storage of wastes) and over construction projects that threatened "green" space. These protests drew a diverse coalition, from young people with strong environmental priorities to farmers who feared the effect of nuclear power (and waste) on agriculture. Initially, the party fared poorly in national elections, although it did gain entry into some Land parliaments. But with the emergence of the issue of nuclear weapons modernization in NATO (discussed next), the Greens once again mobilized, this time with electoral success. The result has been a general rise in the environmental consciousness of all parties. In fact, it would probably be fair to say that environmental concerns will increasingly take their place as equal competitors with growth and justice issues on the agenda of *all* German parties. Beyond this arguably positive effect, the Greens have also contributed to concern about German foreign policy.

The European Community and the Atlantic Community

In addition to the domestic goals of maintaining economic growth, social justice, and quality of life, the Federal Republic of Germany has equally pressing—perhaps more pressing—security and foreign policy goals, such as maintaining the territorial security of the country and pursuing more general but equally important goals, such as improving relations with its neighbors, both East and West, and continuing the task of rehabilitating the tarnished image of Germany that resulted from World War II.

However, for West Germans it is not easy to separate purely domestic goals from foreign policy concerns. It became clear to Germans (as it had to Americans) that the satisfaction of domestic needs depends to a great extent on international relations. For example, the maintenance of a steady rate of economic growth depends on access to overseas markets for German exports (27 percent of German economic production is exported), and the German economy is dependent on fluctuations in international rates of monetary exchange and on interest rates overseas. When the German currency (the deutsche mark) is weak, it increases the cost of important overseas goods (such as oil), and when it is overly strong, the cost to others of crucial German exports increases. Yet the monetary stability necessary for healthy trade relations can be achieved only through cooperation with other countries whose economic performance and currency policies affect the Federal Republic. In a very real sense, German jobs and growth (like those of the Federal Republic's neighbors) can only be secured through international collaboration.

The same is true of quality-of-life goals. The Rhine, for example, is a major source of German drinking water, yet the river is shared with Switzerland and France, so that maintenance of clean water can only be secured through joint action with these countries. The problem of acid rain and its effects on forests poses a similar quandary, as the industrial pollution that affects the forests has its origins throughout Europe.

For West Germans, the realization that policy success depends on international cooperation is not new. Indeed, for Germans (as for all Europeans), the need for policy cooperation had been evident since before the end of World War II (if not before). During the interwar period, especially during the Great Depression, for example, economic policies were competitive rather than cooperative.

That is, the nations of Europe engaged in competitive monetary and trade policies to protect their own economies: Currencies were valued so as to minimize imports. The result, exacerbated by the effects of the depression, was to close borders to trade and increase the tensions and suspicions that already existed.

As a result, the statesmen who met to organize the postwar international system emphasized institutions and policies that would increase international collaboration and cooperation in the pursuit of economic progress. As we will see, the United States did much to foster cooperative policies internationally. For West Germany and Europe, however, the most significant outcome of this spirit was the creation of the European Economic Community (EEC) in the Treaty of Rome (1957). Although not a full-blown political community, the EEC was to become a true economic community, with free trade among its members and plans for the complete integration of currencies. Beyond these efforts, the European Community was also seen as an answer to the tragedy of past European wars: Only through regional cooperation—and perhaps eventual unification— could the animosity and conflicts of the past be put aside for good. In effect, the creation of the EEC in 1957 was a recognition on the part of European states that the domestic goals of economic progress and the international goals of security could not be met alone—they required cooperation and joint action.

Yet in the new power situation of postwar Europe, the maintenance of national security could not be achieved by Europeans, even when acting together. World War II had brought the emergence of a new European superpower—the Soviet Union, which had now mobilized a large military force and stood close to the borders of the West European nations. Soviet military and political gains had also brought them a considerable empire in Eastern Europe. Further, fears of a renascent Germany were not completely dissipated in Western neighbors, such as France, England, and the Netherlands. Finally, the West European states had been devastated physically and exhausted psychologically by two world wars in 25 years. Whereas the European Economic Community was to be the answer to the problem of economic growth, maintenance of security in the face of the Soviet (and German) threats required another institutional innovation, the creation of an Atlantic security community that included the participation of the United States in the European balance of power.

This was a major departure for the United States. Although the Americans had fought in both world wars, the governing view in the United States was that European security was a European problem that should not cause a departure from the traditional American policy of aloofness from European affairs in peacetime. In fact, the first postwar attempt by Europeans to engage the Americans in a new military alliance (the Brussels Treaty Organization) failed, in part because of traditional American isolationism but also because the United States resisted the anti-German tone of the alliance. Although the United States was increasingly concerned by Soviet actions in Europe and elsewhere, the U.S. government also believed that deterrence of the Soviet threat would require a contribution by a reformed German state (in part to lessen the need for American troops). The Americans also believed that an anti-German alliance would only repeat the mistakes committed after World War I, when the punitive conditions of the Versailles Treaty made it difficult for Germany to recover from the war.

From this brief review, it is clear that the "German problem" played a crucial role in the creation of the new, postwar Atlantic security community. On the one hand, Germany's past had raised understandable fears among its Western neighbors; on the other hand, it was clear that European security with American participation required some contribution from the new western half of the German state. It is therefore not surprising that, when it emerged in 1949, the NATO alliance carried special obligations for West Germany. By separate treaty, West Germany agreed to renounce the production of nuclear, chemical, and biological weapons as well as to accept restrictions on other categories of weapons. Although West Germany was assigned considerable obligations within NATO, including an army of 495,000 men, the German past continued to weigh heavily. In this regard, it is significant that the armed forces of the Federal Republic will be commanded, in wartime, by NATO commanders rather than by West Germans. Just as the EEC provided a forum in which West Germany could regain economic strength as a member of a wider community (and thus pose less of a threat to its neighbors), so its role in NATO has been defined—in part imposed—in community terms. West German security is NATO security.

These limitations are reinforced by restrictions imposed by the West Germans themselves. In many ways, the political culture of West German security is a culture of limits. At the psychological level, West German attitudes toward national security continue to be affected by World War II, especially by the belief that war in general results from the undue influence of the military in politics and society. In fact, it is probably not an exaggeration to assert that a latent anti-militarism continues to influence West German attitudes. Moreover, the desire to limit militarism is reflected in the constitution and laws of the Federal Republic. The constitution (Basic Law), for example, prohibits the use of German armed forces except in defense of the country. Further, in peacetime, command of the armed forces remains with the minister of defense (a civilian) rather than with the chancellor, an obvious attempt to separate political and military authority. The right to conscientious objection is constitutionally guaranteed. Finally, the outside observer of German politics may be surprised by the amount of debate over the role of the military in a democratic society, a debate that touches on the proper duties of the soldier and the relevance of military ceremony and tradition in a modern, democratic society.

To summarize, it is important to remember that, for West Germany, the pursuit of domestic and security goals is almost totally a matter of cooperation with its partners; in economic policy, as in defense policy, there is hardly anything that we might call a "German" approach. Although there are recent signs that this might be changing, German policy should be seen in community terms. In economics, German prosperity depends on the success of the European Community, and in security policy, German defense has been almost totally a matter of NATO and its reliance on the United States.

The integration of West Germany into these two Western communities was in fact the primary strategy of Konrad Adenauer, the first chancellor of the Federal Republic. That strategy has proven enormously successful; the first 30 years of the Federal Republic have seen unprecedented economic growth, and the period of peace since 1949 has been precious for a nation weary of wars.

However, the policy of Adenauer and his successors has not been without its costs. It will come as no surprise that the pursuit of economic objectives within the European Community produces political frictions because of the need to consider the policies and objectives of West Germany's partners—policies that may conflict with the maintenance of German jobs and economic growth. In addition, the building of the EEC must compete with traditional attitudes that place importance on national identity and objectives. In the security arena, membership in NATO produces friction with another important German policy goal—the reunification of the two Germanys. Because the cooperation of the Soviet Union will be crucial to reunification—in whatever form—membership in NATO and coordination of defense policy with the United States introduces a competing set of influences into German calculations. This competition has become even greater with the relaxation of international tensions during and after the years of détente in the 1970s, and it often conflicts with American views.

In light of these policy conflicts, it is all the more surprising that, among West Germans, there has been, and continues to be, a deep and continuing consensus on membership in the European Community and in NATO. As Table 6.4 shows, throughout the postwar period West Germans have been among the most supportive members of the EEC. Perhaps more significant, surveys by the European Community show that this support spans different social and political groups; from 80 to 90 percent of West Germans of all ages, levels of educational achievement, and political persuasions approve of further integration in the EEC. In fact, it may be a harbinger of the future that younger West Germans (ages 15–25) are the most supportive of the EEC. These figures suggest that, at least in economic terms, West Germans believe that their future lies with the European Community.

To be sure, there are serious economic and political issues within the European Community, and some of these involve the West German economic and political systems. Perhaps the most difficult of these involve the attempt of the EEC and its members to adjust to the recession and to increasing competition from Third World countries. The problem is most acute in the basic industries, especially coal and steel, where large numbers of jobs have been lost to the reces-

Table 6.4   **Percentage of Population Favoring Integration**

Country	1952	1962	1970	1975	1982	1984
West Germany	70	78	76	74	70	80
France	60	70	70	78	82	80
England	58	47	37	51	61	69
European average	na	72	76	74	75	77

SOURCE: Commission of the European Communities, *EuroBarometer* (Brussels), no. 22 (December 1984): table 8.

NOTE: The English figure for 1970 is from a 1973 poll; the European average is for the original six members of the European Community. The wording of the question is a variant of the following: "In general, are you for or against efforts being made to unify Western Europe?"

sion and to declining market shares abroad. Significantly, European coal and steel producers are attempting to deal with these problems together, through joint production quotas and subsidies to assist in the reduction of production capacity. Nonetheless, the cost and political problems produced by the loss of jobs in these industries will continue to produce tensions within the EEC, and as the EEC leader in steel production, West Germany will be among the most affected.

The EEC has also begun joint action to foster European competitiveness in rapidly changing information technologies. Responding to U.S. and Japanese competition and to Europe's own need to demonstrate unity of purpose, the EEC in 1983 adopted Project ESPRIT (European Strategic Program for Research in Technology) to provide EEC and industry financing for collaborative research in the fields of information processing, telecommunications, and computer-aided manufacturing.[4] Similar sentiments for an EEC role in technology development have come in positive European reactions to President Reagan's request that the NATO allies submit proposals for participation in the research phase of his "Star Wars" defense initiative.

A difficult situation exists in the agricultural sector, where the members of the EEC have implemented a Common Agricultural Policy (CAP). Put simply, the CAP was designed to support the European farmer (and ensure adequate European production) by protecting European farmers from foreign competition and by subsidizing the production of goods. However, the cost of the CAP has increased dramatically (it is the single most expensive program of the EEC), and the practice of subsidizing prices has led to the creation of huge surpluses for some products. Because the EEC budget has recently come under strain, there has been growing pressure to reform the CAP, and as the largest contributor to the EEC budget, West Germany has been increasingly visible in this debate.

Finally, the EEC, and especially West Germany, have become increasingly concerned with the lack of international monetary stability. Since its economy depends on exports, West Germany is particularly concerned that currencies remain stable in value so that international trade remains predictable. But in the late 1970s, a rapid decline in the dollar made European (and German) exports more expensive and thus uncompetitive. By contrast, in the early 1980s, the rapid rise of the dollar—coupled with high American interest rates—made exports cheaper but increased the cost of oil (which must be paid for in dollars) and hindered economic recovery (because most investors preferred higher-earning American accounts to the European accounts that would provide new capital for investment).

As a result, West Germany has been at the forefront of European countries that have attempted, within the EEC, to protect Western Europe from monetary instability. Europeans are concerned when exchange rates are either too high or too low—they prefer stability (and thus predictability) above all else. In 1979, after the decline of the dollar, Chancellor Schmidt of West Germany took the lead in the creation (actually, resurrection) of a European Monetary System (EMS) that was designed to protect European economies from monetary instability. Specifically, most of the European states pledged to maintain their currency exchange rates within fixed ranges; that is, they agreed that they would intervene (by buying and selling their currencies) to make sure that their currencies would not depart by more than a fixed percentage from each other (the American dollar was not involved). Thus, at least within Europe, traders and investors could be relatively certain that their transactions would bring a certain return, for they were protected from the wide changes in the value of money.

It is easy to see why West Germany has become a leader in monetary affairs: As a leading exporter, it is interested in maintaining the predictability of trading relationships. Nonetheless, the EMS, for all its virtues, is not without political difficulties. Like all EEC ventures, it requires occasional sacrifices in the interest of other members. For example, when the French franc declined in value in 1981, it was the West German Central Bank that provided the cash to make purchases to bring the franc back within the agreed EMS range. It is not always popular to make such loans, and West Germany's willingness to assist the French is an indication of the importance it places on monetary stability (it is also significant that the French decided to remain in the EMS rather than depart when the franc declined). Given the effect of economic change on currencies' values, this issue of monetary stability, and the role of the EMS, is likely to remain crucial for the West Germans and all Europeans.

West German participation in the NATO alliance has shown the same pattern of basic consensus interrupted by occasional turmoil that has characterized its membership in the European Community. Given the importance of NATO to the postwar West German policy of integration with the West (and the dependence of West Germany on NATO for its security), it should come as little surprise that West Germans continue to see the NATO alliance as essential to their security. Public opinion surveys show a high and consistent degree of support for NATO. This fact alone suggests that talk of neutralism in West Germany, at least as concerns the question of NATO, is unfounded. In fact, although the abstract idea of neutralism is somewhat attractive (about 30 percent of West Germans favor it when the general idea is mentioned), the number of those in favor has declined recently (from 42 percent in 1961 to 27 percent in 1981). Further, in opinion polls comparing membership in NATO with the alternatives available to West Germany, the preference for NATO becomes even clearer; in 1981, for example, 57 percent of West Germans preferred to stay in NATO versus 17 percent who favored a more European approach to defense and less than 10 percent who favored the options of a more national defense posture or of accommodation with the Soviets.

Other public opinion surveys reinforce the underlying consensus on West German membership in NATO. Further, the polls show that West Germans have overcome their postwar reservations about rearming. There was, in the early to mid-1950s, considerable resistance to rearmament, but recent surveys show that the German armed forces (the Bundeswehr), and the idea of national defense are now accepted—a fact of considerable significance, given the latent anti-militarism of most West Germans.

As was the case with membership in the European Community, however, this is not to say that a general consensus supporting NATO always translates into a consensus for specific defense policy measures. In fact, on a number of issues in the defense area, there is considerable discussion and disagreement in West Germany. Primary among these is the issue of intermediate nuclear force modernization that arose from NATO's decision (in which West Germany participated) to deploy 572 intermediate-range cruise and Pershing missiles as a counter to Soviet deployment of the intermediate-range SS-20 missiles. Although a number of surveys have yielded differing results, a review of all the polls suggests that this nuclear modernization issue has polarized West German politics: About 50 percent favor the new missiles and 50 percent oppose them, depending on the wording of the questions and the time of the survey. The polarization is more severe among the political parties; the governing CDU/CSU and FDP coalition partners continue to support the deployment, but the SPD (now in opposition) and the Greens oppose it.

One should not conclude from the current controversy that the nuclear issue is new to West German defense politics. In fact, the issue of nuclear weapons in West Germany and NATO has always been controversial, beginning with the emplacement of the first weapons in the late 1950s and continuing with the issue of the control over the nuclear "button" during the 1960s. The fact is, because of NATO strategy, tension in West Germany on the issue of nuclear weapons is inevitable.

Since the 1960s, NATO has operated under the military strategy of flexible response, a strategy that emphasizes NATO's ability to deter an attack at any level. Implicit in this strategy is the threat to escalate to the use of nuclear weapons if necessary. From the American perspective, escalation to the use of nuclear weapons should not occur precipitously, for ultimately it is American territory that will be threatened by Soviet missiles. For Europeans, and particularly for the West Germans who are located on NATO's central front with the Warsaw Pact nations, the threat to escalate should emphasize rapid escalation to convince the Soviets of the immediate costs of attack (and thus to strengthen deterrence).

When the Soviet Union acquired nuclear parity during the 1970s, the issue of nuclear strategy in Europe took on added significance, for observers—many of them American—increasingly doubted whether the United States would threaten the use of its own nuclear weapons in defense of Europe when the Soviets could respond against American territory. In fact, it was concern for the effect on Europe of the Soviet-American nuclear stalemate that led Chancellor Helmut Schmidt to be the first to raise this concern officially in a public forum, and it was Schmidt's speech that led—by a somewhat circuitous route—to the 1979 decision to deploy the missiles in Europe.

Ironically, the missiles have not had the intended effect. Although the U.S. and European governments hoped that the new development would reinforce the credibility of the U.S. commitment to Europe, many observers—including the Greens and the peace movements that have taken to the streets to resist the deployment—interpret it as a step in the direction of "decoupling" the United States from Europe by deploying missiles that might be used in a purely European exchange that would not involve the United States. Of course, one can argue that the Soviet Union is highly unlikely to see such a decoupling since the missiles are American and under total U.S. control, but skeptical observers are unlikely to be completely convinced. Moreover, talk by President Reagan and members of his administration about "limited" nuclear war made it difficult to argue that the United States did not want to limit the use of nuclear weapons to the European theater.

Thus, although the missiles have been deployed, nuclear weapons promise to remain a source of disagreement. The Social Democratic Party now opposes the deployment, and majorities of all parties remain skeptical of nuclear weapons in general. Certainly there is little support for the use of nuclear weapons, a political problem that could become serious since NATO strategy includes the possibility of using nuclear weapons first. Not surprisingly, therefore, there is increasing discussion of how the nuclear threshold can be raised, that is, how NATO can change its strategy and forces to make early use of nuclear weapons unnecessary.

Many of these proposals include discussions of expanding stockpiles of conventional weapons, but this raises a second major issue in the West German defense policy discussion: the degree of public support for additional defense spending. The issue of increasing defense budgets has in fact been on the NATO agenda since the late 1970s, when NATO adopted a program to improve conventional capabilities (the long-term defense program—LTDP). One goal of the program was for members of NATO to increase defense spending in the region of 3 percent per year.

West Germany assented to the LTDP, perhaps because it had already been increasing its spending by about that amount. In the late 1960s and early 1970s, West German defense ministers had made the final decisions to order new weapons for each of the major services, including frigates for the navy, new fighter aircraft for the air force, and new tanks and armored vehicles for the army. Thus, as the 1970s came to a close, West Germany could boast of modernized weapons for each of its major services, in addition to 495,000 men under arms.

Yet in the aftermath of the crises in Afghanistan and Iran, the United States (whose defense spending had declined during the 1970s) began increasing its defense spending just as the recession of 1979 began affecting its European partners. In West Germany, as elsewhere, the recession led to a loss of tax revenues and increased need for social spending to blunt the effects of the recession. The result was continuing deficits. Yet the currency and interest rate problems described above made it difficult to maintain such deficits in the public budget, for government borrowing can put upward pressure on interest rates that are already high.

In such an atmosphere, added spending for the defense budget is difficult to justify politically (see Table 6.5). Yet West German policymakers will soon face upward pressure on defense spending in addition to the pressure from the Federal Republic's allies. In the first place, the cost of modern weapons is increasing. New, more sophisticated weapons cost more than the weapons they replace. In West Germany, these cost increases—sometimes unforeseen—have led to controversy and even to scandal. Cost overruns for the air force's new fighter aircraft (the MRCA Tornado) led to investigations and to severe political problems for the defense minister. Yet it is clear that each new generation of weapons will cost more, putting any minister in the position of buying fewer weapons or attempting to have the defense budget increased at a time of lowered government revenues.

In addition, the population changes described earlier will also affect defense. As fewer and fewer young men are available for the draft, the government will have to decide among a number of unpopular measures, such as increasing pay to attract more personnel (cost difficulties), lengthening the tour of duty, including women in the draft, or extending the coverage of the draft laws to include resident aliens.

A third potential problem could arise from increasing pressure to expand NATO's role to include security problems outside the Atlantic area of NATO's original charter. The most likely area for trouble is the Persian Gulf, the source

Table 6.5   West German Public Opinion
                   on Defense Spending

	Decrease	Keep Same	Increase	Don't Know
1967	41	37	8	14
1968	27	35	16	22
1969	31	36	16	17
1971	38	46	12	4
1972	38	38	11	13
1973	35	39	10	17
1974	34	42	9	15
1975	38	42	10	11
1976	27	47	13	13
1977	27	50	12	11
1978	27	58	11	4
1979	27	59	10	3
1980	22	58	17	3
1981	34	52	14	1
1982	34	54	10	1
1983	35	52	12	2
1984	39	50	9	1

SOURCES: To 1979, Federal Ministry of Defense, *Hinweise für Öffentlichkeitsarbeit*, no. 7 (Bonn, September 14, 1979); after 1979, Kenneth Adler and Douglas Wertman, "Is NATO in Trouble?" (Paper presented at the 1981 annual meeting of the American Association of Public Opinion Research, Buck Hills Falls, Pa.).

NOTE: The survey question read: "Security costs money. In your opinion, does the Federal Republic spend much too much, too much, just the right amount, much too little, or too little on defense." *Much too much* and *too much* are labeled "decrease"; *just right* is labeled "stay the same"; and *much too little* and *too little* are labeled "increase." From 1979 to 1981, the surveys asked simply if defense spending "should be increased, decreased, or left at about its present level." In 1981, the question was prefaced by the phrase "bearing in mind the current international situation on the one hand and [West Germany's] economic situation on the other."

of a large portion of European energy. In West Germany, however, there are both political and constitutional limits to any role outside of the normal NATO sphere. First, the West German constitution, as previously noted, specifies that German forces can only be used in defense, and it is unclear whether this would include contingencies outside the NATO region. Certainly there are those within West Germany who would argue on legal or political grounds that it does not. Second, if European participation outside of the NATO area is seen as part of a larger American Middle East policy, there is the strong possibility that a debate would ensue, both within West Germany and within NATO, over the costs, benefits, and alternatives to the U.S. approach in the area. The cool German reaction to the U.S. strike on Libya illustrates this well.

A fourth source of potential disagreement is President Reagan's Strategic Defense Initiative (SDI); a successful defense system in the United States would raise traditional European fears of a "fortress America" isolated from Europe and its concerns. West German leaders have made clear that they are skeptical of SDI for two reasons. First, they assert that a unilateral deployment of SDI by the United States will upset deterrence because it will provide for superiority of one side. Second, deployment of SDI would cause abrogation of the 1972 ABM Treaty, and Europeans value such agreements as symbols of the arms control process. Thus it will come as no surprise to learn that the West Germans (like other Europeans) have confined their support of SDI to endorsement of research only; they state that negotiations with the Soviets would have to precede any actual deployment of defensive systems.

Finally, the nuclear missile issue has brought about a fundamental change in the way defense policies and the NATO alliance are treated in West Germany. Many people are now willing to participate in debates about security policy, and many of these new participants are now informed about alternatives to government policy. It seems fair to predict that the future will bring continuing public involvement and debate over the nature of West German security policy and alternatives to current policies. Moreover, there is concern that increased criticism by some elements of the public may endanger West Germany's primary foreign policy attachment—its alliance with the United States.

The United States and West Germany

From what has been said previously, it should be clear that for the Federal Republic of Germany, no relationship is more important than its ties to the United States. The security relationship is almost self-evident. Without participation of the United States in NATO, the security of West Germany could not have been maintained in a Europe of physical and economic exhaustion. Equally important, the economic recovery of West Germany—like that of the entire European Community—depended on U.S. assistance and policies, first through the Marshall Plan and later through jointly administered arrangements for monetary policy (the Bretton Woods System) and for trade policy (the GATT [General Agreement on Tariffs and Trade]).

West Germans viewed these ties with relief and affection. In fact, many observers have noted that the post–World War II culture of West Germany has been affected more by American culture than have the cultures of other countries, a result perhaps of the total failure of German society in the Third Reich and the consequent need for a new model. Certainly a visitor to Germany cannot but notice the gratitude for U.S. assistance in the postwar period.

This attachment to the United States continues to be reflected in opinion polls, despite increasing difficulties on such issues as nuclear weapons, defense spending, and monetary policy. For example, the polls show that overwhelming majorities of West Germans continue to express basic affection for Americans. West Germans continue to select the United States when they are asked to state which country is West Germany's best friend internationally. We have also seen that alliance with the United States in NATO continues to command majority support.

This is not to say that the U.S.-German relationship is without difficulties. Rather, it is to suggest that those difficulties that do exist are more a matter of specific policy differences than of fundamental alienation in the relationship. This makes policy coordination more difficult, but it indicates a much less pessimistic future for the alliance than is sometimes supposed.

Perhaps the greatest source of difficulty in the U.S.-German relationship is the difference of opinion on East-West relations; that is, on the question of the proper tone and content of relations with the Soviet Union and its allies. During the early 1970s, the West German government developed with the Soviet Government a series of close contacts that matched the relaxation of tensions achieved between President Nixon and General Secretary Brezhnev. Willy Brandt, the West German chancellor, accomplished a détente with the Soviet Union, Poland, and East Germany that led to increasing trade and contact between the two blocs. Most important, this détente allowed Germans in the West to greatly increase the amount of contact with their relations in East Germany—not just post and telephone contacts, but personal visits as well.

As East-West tensions have recently increased, the United States and West Germany have been increasingly at odds. Although the West German government generally supports the U.S. goal of maintaining a military balance and of meeting Soviet advances with firmness, it is also less inclined to allow the climate of relations to affect the human and economic gains of détente. Opinion surveys show that West Germans prefer to continue attempts at reconciliation with the Soviet Union, and they generally are more supportive of arms control and East-West economic trade than are Americans (or the American government). For example, in the wake of the 1979 Soviet invasion of Afghanistan, West Germans of all political parties believed that arms control negotiations with the Soviet Union should be continued (see Table 6.6). As Professor Stanley Hoffmann has observed, Europeans (and West Germans) prefer neither "collision nor collusion" in the U.S.-Soviet relationship, and they react negatively to an aggressive tone in relations with the East.

Perhaps for this reason, the recent souring of U.S.-Soviet relations has led to

Table 6.6   **West German Opinion
of Arms Control Negotiations After the
Soviet Invasion of Afghanistan
(percentage)**

	JANUARY 1980		
	Continue negotiations	*Postpone*	*Discontinue*
Overall population	63	26	11
Political parties			
CDU/CSU	55	30	15
FDP	73	24	4
SPD	70	22	8
Greens	60	31	9
Age group			
18–30	64	28	9
31–40	63	27	10
41–50	62	27	11
51–60	63	25	11
61+	68	22	10

SOURCE: Forschungsgruppe Wahlen, *Politik in der Bundesrepublik, January 1980*, mimeo. (Mannheim, 1980).

NOTE: The sample for this survey numbered 1,058 persons. The question was worded: "Recently, there have been a number of arms control negotiations between East and West. Should these negotiations be continued despite Afghanistan, should they be temporarily postponed, or should the West discontinue negotiations with the East?"

a negative turn in West German attitudes toward the United States. West Germans prefer (although by lesser margins than other Europeans) that their government steer clear of U.S.-Soviet disputes, and the general image of the United States has declined in West Germany, as elsewhere in Europe. Perhaps most telling are surveys that show a drastic decline in the early 1980s in the Germans' confidence in the ability of the United States to deal wisely in world affairs. And since the issue of nuclear weapons, the defense budget, and wider NATO problems will keep East-West relations at the forefront of the German policy agenda, U.S. policy is likely to remain a source of contention in the U.S.-German relationship.

The effect of the broader East-West climate was dramatically illustrated during the summer and fall of 1984, when both East and West Germany attempted to relax tensions between their countries and to shield them from the deterioration of relations that accompanied the deployment of INF missiles in late 1983. In fact, in addition to a number of negotiated measures (including credits from

West Germany and East German concessions on border fortifications and exit permits), East German leader Erich Honecker accepted an invitation to visit the West German capital in late 1984. However, Soviet worries about the cohesion of the Warsaw Pact and the ultimate intentions of the two Germanies led to heavy pressure on East Germany, which eventually cancelled the Honecker visit. (It should be noted, however, that the Honecker visit did finally take place in October 1987). This event showed clearly that not all problems in the East-West relationship are caused by U.S. actions. It also demonstrated that West Germany retains a strong interest in the management of détente, for their own contacts with Germans in the East are affected by superpower relations.

These complexities are aggravated by problems in the U.S.-European economic relationship. As noted earlier, the United States was a primary factor in the economic recovery of Europe, directly through the Marshall Plan and indirectly through its role in the creation of a global monetary and trading system. The European recovery is now complete, so much so in fact that the United States and Western Europe are now major competitors in many areas. Of course, this competition introduces a tension in U.S.-European relations that did not exist previously, and the tension has been aggravated by the recession. All countries on both sides of the Atlantic are suffering from lack of economic growth and jobs, and competition in steel and agriculture—to name just two areas—at times has led to serious disagreements between the United States and Europe.

West Germany has been in the thick of these disagreements, especially in the field of monetary policy, where German interests are most affected. As we have seen, it was Chancellor Schmidt who led the way in the creation of the European Monetary System. West Germans and other Europeans have strongly criticized the U.S. budget deficit and its effect on interest rates. In fact, monetary stability provided one of the most thorny issues in relations with the United States during the 1980s. As the U.S. budget deficit grew during President Reagan's term, West Germans and other Europeans became worried because the resulting increase in U.S. interest rates drove the dollar upward (increasing the amount of dollars they had to pay for oil) and drew away European investors whose capital was needed to fund economic recovery at home. Until 1985, the U.S. response was that the free market would eventually correct the dollar's rise, but after much discussion and some arguing, the leaders of the major European governments agreed with the United States to "manage" a decline in the dollar. The agreement was renewed at the economic summit in Tokyo in 1986, where the leaders also agreed that closer coordination of all economic policies would be necessary. Thus, experience with monetary policy in the 1980s provided a clear example of how the German, European, and U.S. economies were tied in a complex web that produced strains but that also called forth a common response.

In sum, both the success and the difficulty of the U.S.-German relationship results from their close partnership in the security and economic fields. West

Germany depends on the United States for its security. Precisely for this reason, it is not surprising that U.S. actions, whether in the area of nuclear weapons or defense spending, evoke a German response. Similarly, since German interests in East Germany are affected by the general tenor of East-West relations, it should come as no surprise that drastic changes in U.S.-Soviet relations (in either direction) should provoke comment and controversy in the Federal Republic. Likewise, the close partnership between the United States and Germany in the economic field produces inevitable tensions, be it over competition for markets or over the effects of changes in monetary policy. The major question is whether such natural differences in interest and perspective can be managed as they have been for the past 35 years of the U.S.-German alliance.

The Federal Republic and the Western Alliance

Developments in West Germany illustrate a paradox that is evident in all the industrial democracies of Western Europe. In all policy areas—what I have called the goals of economic growth, social justice, quality of life, and national security—it is increasingly apparent that success depends on some measure of international cooperation or harmonization. The problems of inflation, unemployment, pollution, and defense are truly international. Yet international harmonization presents difficult political problems, for often it seems that international cooperation comes at the cost of jobs at home or of compromise of important foreign policy or security interests. In an age of recession and global tensions, these disputes over domestic and defense policy are all the more difficult to manage.

In West Germany, problems with Alliance policy or European Community policy have increasingly raised the fear that the Federal Republic will adopt a go-it-alone or neutralist approach, a possibility that raises disquiet in light of Germany's past and its crucial role as an important anchor of Western defense. Our review suggests that these fears are exaggerated. Certainly the West German population continues to support the European Community as the only arena in which the German economy can continue to prosper; this support is no doubt also based on the belief that a European approach is far better than the nationalistic approaches of the past. For all its difficulties, the EEC remains a large market for German goods, and in the monetary and agricultural fields joint community policies offer the hope of continued European prosperity in an age of global economic difficulties. Another way to state this point is to say that for West Germany, as for the other European states, there may be no alternative to cooperation in the European Community.

Much the same is true of defense policy. West Germany joined the Atlantic Alliance for several reasons, chief among them being the calculation that security could best be pursued with the Western powers, who were both more ideologically attractive and more benign in their treatment of the nascent republic. An independent defense is impossible, given the predominance of the Warsaw Pact states. In sum, for both political and strategic reasons, the Federal Republic has found the NATO alliance to be the best means of ensuring its security.

This situation has changed only in tone. To be sure, the fragility of the nuclear balance—within and without Europe—has mobilized a louder German voice than has been the case in the past. Economic difficulties with the United States have aggravated a tense security situation. And unlike the past situation in which there was a German all-party consensus on NATO matters, the Greens and the Social Democrats now oppose an important NATO decision.

Does this amount to a new German nationalism? Yes, if that term means a growing willingness to articulate the German position in Western defense councils. Given its vulnerable strategic position and its large contribution to the Alliance, the Federal Republic is likely to continue its newfound role as a key European voice in nuclear and other debates. And given West Germany's major human and economic interests in Eastern Europe, it is likely to continue arguing for a less belligerent tone in relations with the Soviet Union and its East European allies.

Yet although it is clear that Alliance policies will be more controversial, it is not clear that this new West German style should be labeled neutralist. Clearly West Germany still considers the United States its most important partner. Nor do resources—or even desires—make it likely that the Federal Republic will adopt a go-it-alone posture in defense. Rather, it seems likely that the United States and the other NATO partners must accustom themselves to a more searching and skeptical German voice *within* NATO. In many ways, this represents a transformation of West Germany's status from a more or less complete dependence on its Western partners to a larger voice in Alliance strategy- and policymaking. Whereas one observer could characterize German foreign policy of the post–World War II period as the "politics of impotence," by the 1980s West Germany's economic strength, political maturity, and contribution to Alliance military strength provided a natural basis for increased participation in security debates.[5]

The addition of an influential—and sometimes critical—voice to Alliance policymaking does make the job of security cooperation more difficult. But it is not clear that it changes the Alliance fundamentally. As previous chapters in this book have shown, for example, British, and especially French, policy has at times assumed a similar tone. The difference of course, is that the Gaullist policies of other states do not carry the burden of Germany's past, with all the mistrust and suspicion that these imply. Nor do these states play the dual role of the most exposed yet most interested party in relations with Eastern Europe. For these reasons, West Germany's new role as articulator of security concerns will likely continue to raise disquiet in the West, but the permanence of these concerns guarantees that the West German voice is unlikely to fade. The question is whether Germany's partners can accept it and deal with it constructively.

Notes

1. Material in this paragraph is drawn from Joseph Joffe, "The Foreign Policy of the German Federal Republic," in Roy C. Macridis, ed., *Foreign Policy in World Politics* 5th ed. (Englewood Cliffs, N.J.: Prentice-Hall, 1975), pp. 117–20.

2. Ibid., p. 118.

3. The citation and the material in the preceding paragraph are from Renate Mayntz and Fritz Scharpf, *Policy-Making in the German Federal Bureaucracy* (New York: Elsevier, 1975), p. 43, and Renate Mayntz, "Executive Leadership in Germany: Dispersion of Power or 'Kanzlerdemokratie'?" (Unpublished manuscript, University of Cologne, 1979).

4. Pierre-Henri Laurent, "Renaissance Through Technology: The European Community Decision on ESPRIT," *Fletcher Forum* 9, no. 1 (Winter 1985): pp. 155–65.

5. Joffe, "Foreign Policy," p. 121.

Suggested Readings

Baker, Kendall; Dalton, Russell; and Hildebrandt, Kai. *Germany Transformed.* Cambridge, Mass.: Harvard University Press, 1981.

Boutwell, Jeffrey. "Politics and the Peace Movement in West Germany." *International Security* 7, no. 4 (Spring 1983): 72–92.

Capitanchik, David, and Eichenberg, Richard C. *Defence and Public Opinion.* Boston: Routledge & Kegan Paul, 1983.

Conradt, David. *The German Polity.* New York: Longman, 1982.

Deporte, Anton. *Europe Between the Superpowers.* New Haven, Conn.: Yale University Press, 1979.

German Information Service. *The Week in Germany.* Weekly newsletter available from GIS, New York.

Haftendorn, Helga, *Security and Detente.* New York: Praeger, 1985.

Heidenheimer, Arnold; Heclo, Hugh; and Adams, Carolyn. *Comparative Public Policy.* 2d ed. New York: St. Martin's Press, 1983.

Jacobs, Dan N. et al. *Comparative Politics.* Chatham, N.J.: Chatham House, 1983.

Kelleher, Catherine. "Germany and NATO." In Wolfram Harrieder, ed., *West German Foreign Policy.* Boulder, Colo.: Westview Press, 1979.

Macridis, Roy C., ed. *Foreign Policy in World Politics.* 5th ed. Englewood Cliffs, N.J.: Prentice-Hall, 1976.

Mayntz, Renate, and Scharpf, Fritz. *Policy-Making in the German Federal Bureaucracy.* New York: Elsevier, 1975.

"Schools Brief: The European Economic Community." *Economist* (London). Multipart article in issues of October–December 1982.

Stent, Angela. *From Embargo to Ostpolitik: The Political Economy of West German–Soviet Relations, 1955–80.* New York: Cambridge University Press, 1981.

Stern, Fritz. "Germany in a Semi-Gaullist Europe." *Foreign Affairs* 58 (1980): 867–88.

Szabo, Stephen. *The Successor Generation.* London: Butterworth, 1983.

Treverton, Gregory. "Managing NATO's Nuclear Dilemma." *International Security* 7, no. 4 (Spring 1983): 93–115.

East Germany:

From Partition to Reunification (1945–1990)

L. H. Gann

"Unity and right and freedom for the German fatherland" (*Einigkeit und Recht und Freiheit für das deutsche Vaterland*) run the opening lines of the Federal German Republic's (FRG) national anthem. *Deutschland, einig Vaterland*, "Germany, United Fatherland," once echoed back the national anthem of the former German Democratic Republic (GDR). German unity had not even been effectively questioned by the Allies during World War II—this despite tentative plans to break the Reich into several smaller states once Germany had been defeated. Inter-Allied arrangements, arrived at in 1944, merely provided for the division of Germany into separate zones of military occupation. In 1945 the Third Reich capitulated unconditionally, but legally Germany was not partitioned; instead a united Germany continued a shadowy existence in international law.

What exactly constituted a united Germany? History gave no clear answer. There had been the ancient Holy Roman Empire of the German Nation; then the Germanic Confederation was set up after the emperor Napoleon's fall in 1815; there had been the German Reich created by Bismarck in 1871; there had been Hitler's bloodstained Greater Germanic Empire. When this collapsed in 1945, Austria regained its independence and created for itself a new national identity. Alsace-Lorraine reverted to France and Eupen-Malmédy to Belgium. Luxembourg went back to its former status as an independent grand duchy—the longest-lived and perhaps the most successful of those small German principalities that had once made up a considerable portion of the Holy Roman Empire. The Sudetenland returned to Czechoslovakia, which expelled the Sudeten Germans.

UNITED GERMANY

What remained on the map was the territory of the Reich as it had existed in 1937. This was bisected into two portions of almost equal size. The Western half went to the Americans, British, and French, each of whom occupied a separate zone. The eastern half, roughly "East-Elbian" Germany comprising the heartland of Prussia, went to the Soviet Union. Berlin, the capital, was correspondingly divided into four sectors. In terms of counter-factual history, the Soviets might have created an East German state about as large as the three Western zones combined. Such an East German state, like Bismarck's Prussia, might conceivably have become the nucleus for a united Germany—but this time run under Prusso-Communist auspices. Stalin, however, preferred the "Polish" option. The territories east of the Oder-Neisse line went to Poland, while the Soviet Union reserved for itself the northern part of East Prussia. The German-speaking populations were expelled in the greatest enforced migration in European history. Prussia was formally eliminated as a state in 1947, the last major decision taken by the four Allies in unison, and Prussia has never since revived. The Soviet-occupied zone of Germany, popularly known as East Germany, in fact constituted no more than central Germany, as staked out on prewar maps.

In theory, the four zones of occupation were to be administered as a single economic unit under an Allied Control Council. In practice, cooperation between the Western powers and the Soviet Union soon collapsed. In 1949 the three Western zones united in the Federal German Republic (*Bundesrepublik Deutschland*) under a democratic constitution considerably influenced by U.S. concepts concerning federalism.[1] The new republic had to put up with certain restrictions on its sovereignty, but it proved stunningly successful nonetheless. During the postwar years something like fifteen million "expellees" and refugees moved from the former Eastern territories of the Reich and from the Soviet-occupied zone to West Germany; these immigrants were rapidly asorbed. West German production increased in an astonishing fashion. Between 1950 and 1974, the West German GNP increased about tenfold. West Germany joined the European Economic Community (EEC) and NATO. By the 1960s, West Germany had replaced Great Britain as the principal European ally of the United States.

In 1949 the Soviet-occupied zone of Germany likewise received a limited form of sovereignty as the Germany Democratic Republic. Unlike the Federal German Republic, the GDR was a unitary state; all effective power rested with the Marxist-Leninist ruling party, the Socialist Unity Party (SED) run by a privileged *nomenklatura*, and linked to the Soviet Union by the Warsaw Pact and many other political and economic ties. The East German state, however, continued to suffer from heavy emigration as East Germans, in Lenin's phrase, continued to "vote with their feet" against the East German variety of socialism. In 1961 the communists responded by constructing the Berlin Wall, which cut off West Berlin from all uncontrolled access to East Berlin. In addition the East Germans built a great fortified frontier zone, complete with barbed wire entanglements, mine fields, watch towers and guard posts, cutting right across Germany. *Republikflucht*, the unauthorized departure from East Germany, became a punishable offense, and only a few brave spirits continued to seek escape from East Germany by expedients daring and sometimes bizarre.

The construction of the Berlin Wall and of the great frontier zone had far-reaching effects both intended and unintended. East Germany's population drain largely ended, even though the East German population remained relatively small, about the size of the West German *Land* Rhineland-Westfalia. East Germans were forced to make the best of a bad situation. The Berlin Wall shut off East Berlin from the West—but it also shut off West Berlin from the East. The influx of East German refugees with sorry tales to tell largely ceased; instead West Berlin (a city exempt from West German draft laws) became a haven for young West Germans unwilling to serve in the *Bundeswehr*, the West German army. Many of these channeled their hopes into a revolutionary form of socialism and a utopian future. The West German youth revolt was also propelled forward by demographic factors. German manhood had been decimated in World War II, more so than that of any other Western country; thereafter Germany, like all other Western countries, experienced a baby boom. Hence young people, by the 1960s, accounted for a disproportionately large share of the German population. The great majority of the young were in no sense radicals; they paid their taxes, worked for a living, did their service in the *Bundeswehr*, and accepted the republic. An influential, highly visible, and well-educated minority, however, turned to ultraradical politics, rejected West German capitalism, and looked to a utopian revolution. As they graduated from college, their revolutionary commitment might soften, but many carried radical convictions into their subsequent jobs as teachers, university lecturers, journalists, television producers, clergymen, and the like. For them the notion of uniting Germany under Western auspices was unacceptable. Indeed there was a peculiarly German form of antipatriotism, provoked in part by the violence of the Hitler regime. (German demonstrators in 1990 would shout *Deutschland halt's Maul*, "Germany, keep your mouth shut"—a corresponding slogan would be hard to imagine in any other country.)

There was also a leftward drift in more conventional party politics. The uncompromising line pursued toward East Germany by Konrad Adenauer, the Federal German Republic's founding father, gave way to a much more conciliatory line. The new *Ostpolitik* (Eastern policy) was represented, above all, by Willy Brandt (federal chancellor 1969 to 1974), a Social Democrat far more sympathetic toward youthful leftist enthusiasts within his party than Brandt's successor, Helmut Schmidt. In 1970 Brandt visited East Germany, the first West German chancellor to do so. The Brandt government (a coalition of Social Democrats and Free Democrats) thereafter concluded a series of treaties with East Germany, Poland, and the Soviet Union. These pacts recognized the status quo in what was then called Eastern Europe (now more commonly referred to as Central Europe). The Oder-Neisse line was accepted as Germany's eastern frontier. West Germany recognized East Germany but not as a foreign country ("*nicht Ausland*," Brandt said).

West Germany abandoned its former claim that only the democratically elected government of West Germany could rightfully speak for the German people. Though the Preamble to the West German Basic Law had called on all Germans to work for national unity, this aim was given up as a national policy. Instead Brandt and his supporters, and also many conservatives, insisted on a new "realism." As they saw it, the logic of facts must be accepted; the two Germanys would coexist for a long time to come, perhaps forever. Instead, the new realists stressed the virtues of a German *Kulturnation* whose bonds derived from a common culture and a common language—not from membership in a common state. At the same time, there was rapid expansion in the number of West German tourists who visited East Germany, and—above all—in trade between the two German states. Between 1969, the year in which Brandt became West German chancellor, and 1982, when Kohl assumed office, West German exports to East Germany more than trebled; West German imports from East Germany more than quadrupled.[2]

The East German authorities, for their part, had originally hoped to unify both Germanys under socialist auspices. Walter Ulbricht, the hard-line general secretary of the SED, thus proclaimed to all and sundry in 1950 that Adenauer and his accomplices would one day be tried by a People's Court, unless they managed to escape to Latin America on a U.S. plane.[3] The SED thereafter changed its line; "peaceful coexistence" between different states (but not between different social systems) was applied to "inner-German" relations. According to the SED's revised doctrine, East Germany had taken over the best of the German past, but would go much further as the East Germans were now being fused into a new and separate nation, its identity defined by East Germany's socialist institutions, socialist class consciousness, and socialist dedication to a radiant future.

In one of the most successful public relations campaigns known to history, East German propagandists persuaded much of foreign (albeit not their own domestic) opinion that East Germans socialism was working well. East Germany supposedly had become the most efficient and productive of all the socialist countries. East Germans—so went the story—had acquired a new pride in their own state, a new socialist consciousness. Hence the division of Germany would remain permanent until such times as West Germany also turned socialist.

These views met with modified approval among many academics without the slightest sympathy for communism. Ralf Dahrendorf, a leading German sociologist, thus explained in 1965 that it was naive and dangerous to believe that the GDR merely rested on Soviet bayonets. The GDR had created a comprehensive welfare state, a new legitimacy for itself, and had indeed built "the first modern society on German soil."[4] In the opinion of Philip Windsor, an Englishman contributing to a standard work on Western Europe, published in 1986, there would be no German reunification in the foreseeable future.[5] F. Stephen Larrabee, an American writing in 1989, the year in which the GDR collapsed, argued that reunification had ceased to be a real issue.[6]

How did highly intelligent people arrive at such conclusions? There was some justification. Soviet forces brutally suppressed popular revolts in East Germany in 1953, Hungary in 1956, Czechoslovakia in 1968. Surely the Soviets would hold on to their own—come hell or high water! Both German states moreover clearly had drifted apart. In 1989 both celebrated their respective thirtieth birthdays. Both had endured longer than the Weimar Republic and the Third Reich between them. On both sides of the border there was now a new generation—men and women in their forties—who had never known a united Germany in their lifetime. East Germans had experienced forty years of communist indoctrination at school, in the youth movement, in the army, at the workplace; their very language had been modified by communist terminology. West

Germany, by contrast, had been integrated into the West—militarily, economically, culturally, politically. Particularly strong was the U.S. influence. Even the most militantly anti-American student demonstrators took their rock music, their jeans, and their jargon from America. East Germany seemed a world apart from West Germany. Surely the two would stay apart. West German businessmen and diplomats dealt with the GDR on the basis that it would last.

There were also political changes that favored peaceful coexistence between the two German states. The West German Social Democrats (whose sister party was banned in East Germany) actually joined with the SED in a "Joint Commission on Fundamental Values" (1982).[7] The SPD's object was *Wandel durch Annäherung*, to achieve "transformation by rapprochement." Willy Brandt certainly did not anticipate that the GDR would soon disappear. On the contrary, it was Brandt, the most outstanding spokesman for the new policy, who referred in 1987 to German reunification as "the living lie of the second German republic," and who dismissed as "old crusaders" those who denounced human rights violations in the Eastern bloc with excessive zeal.[8] The governing CDU was not quite that effusive. All the same it was Helmut Kohl (a federal chancellor since 1982) whose government in 1987 hosted an official visit by Erich Honecker, "red Erich," the first East German head of state to make such a call to the West.

Nevertheless, the "objective correlation of forces," in communist terminology, changed more rapidly than all experts had foreseen—barring a handful of anticommunist hard-liners. The permanent existence of the GDR as a separate state depended on certain assumptions: The Soviet Union would always be willing to defend its satellites within the Warsaw Pact against internal subversion. The Warsaw Pact states would maintain "socialist solidarity." The organs of the state, including the National People's Army, would always prove reliable. The East German economy would perform with reasonable efficiency, and so would the East German welfare services. The East German population could somehow be shielded from Western influence—despite the availability and popularity of West German television programs, the growth of tourism and, above all, the close ties of culture and kinship that continued to link Germans on both sides of the border.

By 1989, however, all these conditions suddenly ceased to apply. The full story will not be told until all relevant archives, especially the Soviet archives, are open to inspection. Apparently some time in 1988 Mikhail Gorbachev may have decided that the Soviet Union could no longer afford to back the satellite communist regimes. In August 1989, Tadeusz Mazowiecki took over as prime minister in Poland, heading the first noncommunist government set up within the Soviet sphere after the communist takeovers following World War II. Thereafter the floodgates opened. The communist systems collapsed in the same year in Hungary, Czechoslovakia, and Romania. Hungary opened its borders to the West, thereby permitting both its own citizens and East German travelers to depart freely. In 1990 the Central Committee of the Communist Party of the Soviet Union, incredibly, surrendered its constitutionally guaranteed monopoly of power.

In East Germany there was widespread agitation and huge demonstrations. These were at first led by dissident leftists who desired "socialism with a human face," intellectuals (including leftist Lutheran clergymen) united in such bodies as the "New Forum." These reformers, however, were soon left far behind by popular opinion. By now the *nomenclatura* and its allies were totally discredited by East Germany's economic failure, by the privileges enjoyed by the self-styled "vanguard of the proletariat," and by the evident mendacity of official propaganda. The *nomenclatura* itself lost heart, with many of its own members suffering from bitter disillusionment. Indeed, some highly placed former dignitaries, such as Günter Schabowski, a former member of the East German Politiburo, went further in their denunciation of communism than many a hard-line anti-communist. According to Schabowski, the entire system had been irredeemably perverted from the start since Marxism-Leninism itself rested on mistaken premises.[9] In the end only the *Staatssicherheitsdienst* (*"Stasi"* or State Security Service, an armed state within the state) would have been willing to fight. But neither the Red Army nor, apparently, the East Germany Army would intervene.

On October 17, 1989, Honecker fell from power. He was succeeded by Egon Krenz who, in turn, was replaced by Hans Modrow, both of them "reform communists" and believed to be personally untainted. By now, however, communists of any stripe could no longer master the situation. On November 9, 1989—on the very day when the Kaiser's government had signed an armistice in 1918—the East German communist government capitulated to its people by opening the Berlin Wall. On November 18 the East German authorities announced that five million of their citizens—a little less than one-third of the GDR's entire population—had applied for travel papers to West Germany. On December 1 the East German parliament got rid of the constitutional provision guaranteeing the Socialist Unity Party's leading role.

For Marxist-Leninists all over the world it was a cataclysmic event. Whatever reservations might have been held with regard to Romanian or Polish socialism, few had doubted that the countrymen of Marx and Engels had succeeded in getting socialism to work with accustomed Teutonic efficiency. But for East German communists, it was the end, as even the bulk of former party functionaries began to conceal or repudiate their own past. For the mass of East Germans, however, it was a new beginning. The East German state disintegrated with a speed that surprised, and indeed distressed, West German politicians and bureaucrats who would have preferred a more slowly paced handover.

On March 18, 1990, East Germany held free elections—the first held there since Hitler's takeover in 1933. They were among the most important held in modern German history; they would deliver the people's verdict on "real existing socialism"; they would also play a decisive part in shaping the future of a united Germany. Left-wing intellectuals such as Christa Wolf, the well-known East German writer, hoped that East Germany would wish to preserve its socialist achievements. The workers surely would now put their trust in a democratic form of socialism free from the "deformations" of the old system. These hopes were harshly disappointed.

Disappointed, too, were the expectations of academicians who considered the youth revolutions of 1968 to have formed "the great rehearsal" for subsequent risings against the status quo both east and west of the former Iron Curtain.[10] Not race, class, or gender—the issues most stressed by the heirs of 1968—played an appreciable part in the Central European revolutions of 1989 and 1990. Instead, the citizens' main concerns were national identity, freedom of speech and of religion, and a free market economy. After forty years of socialism in East Germany, 48.1 percent of the East German voters opted for the conservative Alliance for Germany, led by the Christian Democrats. The Social Democrats got 21.8 percent of the votes on an ultramoderate program that accepted a free market economy. The party of socialism, the PDS (the refurbished SED under new management), obtained only 16.3 percent of the votes, despite the party's newly found commitment to democracy and a mixed economy.

Worse still, from the left's standpoint, were the East German workers who deserted socialism—even in areas such as Saxony, once a center of proletarian militance. Of the workers, 55.4 percent voted for the Alliance, 22.2 percent for the Social Democrats, only 11.9 percent for the PDS—allegedly their very own party. The most loyal supporters of socialism were now the intellectuals. The PDS received 31.0 percent of the intellectuals' votes, the highest percentage of all occupational groups; the SPD received 22.1 percent; and the Alliance, 27.8 percent. The "new politics" represented by feminists and Greens failed to make an impact, gaining only 2 percent of the votes.[11]

According to the left-wing intelligentsia, the East German workers had permitted themselves to be lured by Western television sets and Deutschemarks—by crude consumerism. This was only a half-truth. The mass of East Germans had also voted against the former terror exercised by the *Stasi* and its thousands of informers, against *Parteichinesisch* ("party-Chinese," meaning party jargon), against the never-ending propaganda concerning a radiant future, against the privileges of the *nomenclatura* with their "special shops" and *dachas*, against the self-appointed vanguard's claim to lead the "backward masses," against forty years of incompetence, mendacity and informing. In the end, public opinion among the "toilers" proved much harder to manipulate than so many communists had assumed.

The election over, the two Germanys were now bound for reunification. Reunion would be negotiated on conservative terms, led by two conservatives, with

Helmut Kohl, the West German chancellor, very much the senior partner, and Lothar de Maizière, the East German premier, also a CDU man, very much the junior partner. The CDU also scored major successes in the now reconstituted East German *Länder* that replaced the unitary regime set up under communist auspices in East Germany. (The reconstituted *Länder* comprised Brandenburg, Mecklenburg-Vorpommern, Saxony, Saxony-Anhalt, and Thuringia.) As a result of *Land* elections held in 1990, CDU or CDU-led governments were installed in four out of the five East German *Länder*; it was only in Brandenburg that the SPD managed to win.

The military side of reunification was handled by direct arrangement with the Soviets. The combined forces of the reunited German state would not exceed 370,000 men, less than the existing *Bundeswehr* (the West German army). The East German army, the *Nationale Volksarmee*, would disappear. United Germany would remain a member of NATO. In theory, this was a partial disarmament treaty. In practice, Germany remained militarily the strongest country in Central Europe, as there was no way in which treaty limitations on the size of Germany's forces could be effectively enforced, as the Warsaw Pact disintegrated, and as the Soviet forces prepared to withdraw from their former empire over a specified number of years.

The new regime in East Germany faced an immense array of problems. Perhaps the most daunting among them were of a psychological kind. Who had truly been responsible for the failures of the past? What should happen to those who had participated in political murders, torture, and executions? Had the citizens of East Germany all been helpless victims? What of the intellectuals who had sung the praise of "real existing socialism"? How would former supporters of the regime explain their past political conduct to their own children? What of the sense of betrayal experienced by genuine idealists? What of the more practical problems of readjustment required in a country in which most citizens were unfamiliar with the working of a free market economy—and easy prey to scams? (The new government opened "citizens advice bureaus," in British parlance of World War II, to help East Germans in such matters.) What of the East Germans' poor working morale, the product of forty years of mismanagement?

There were also difficult administrative issues. Despite its reputation for efficiency, the East German state had been sketchily organized; only the SED and the *Stasi* had been well run. Now the entire administration would have to be recast, and with it the inadequate and distorted administrative codes. Particularly problematical were the questions of property rights. The SED had created for itself a huge financial empire, in part by fraudulent means. The SED's successor, the PDS, thus emerged from its political debacle with vast economic wealth—the richest political party in Europe with assets estimated at nearly two billion Deutschemarks.

Even these were minor questions compared to property relations in general. In East Germany, most farms, mines, factories—even most small-scale enterprises—had been forcibly transferred to public ownership. There was no precedent in history for dismantling a socialist state or for compensating former owners. Few if any German academicians or investigative journalists had even considered such matters, for socialism was supposedly irreversible.

Not surprisingly, the East German investment climate was full of uncertainties, with claims, counterclaims, and mutual recriminations. Bonn set up a trusteeship organization (*Treuhandanstalt*) to deal with the situation, but its task proved Herculean. So did the job of reorganizing the East German bureaucracy—huge, costly, and inefficient. (Whereas the various ministries in Bonn in 1990 employed only about 25,000 civil servants and other salaried personnel, the various ministries and agencies in East Berlin alone had 220,000 people on their respective payrolls.)

Many of these problems will not be resolved for years to come—if ever. Fortunately those bearing on foreign policy and constitutional matters proved more tractable than the most optimistic could have foreseen. In 1990 both the West and East German parliaments recognized Poland's Western frontier. Gorbachev and Kohl arrived at a major agreement whereby a united Germany would remain part of NATO, Germany would reduce the size of its military, and Soviet forces would withdraw from East Germany over a number years, in return for massive financial compensation.[12] United Germany became part of the EC. (Indeed, a surprisingly large percentage of Western respondents to a poll favored German reunification—above all in the United States, the country that had backed Kohl to a greater extent than any other.[13])

As regards "inner-German" relations, East and West Germany concluded a treaty (in force as of July 1, 1990) that created a monetary, economic, and social union. It was not a pact between two equal partners, but rather constituted the unconditional surrender of socialism, as unconditional as the capitulation of the Third Reich in 1945. West Germany's "social market economy" became the norm for united Germany. The *Bundesbank* (the federal bank of West Germany) became the central bank for all Germany, the Deutschemark became the currency for all Germany, with elaborate provisions for the exchange of "East Marks" into "West Marks."[14] The reunification treaty—900 pages long—guaranteed security for foreign investors, unified the tax laws and the legal system, and went a long way toward solving the difficult question of property rights and unifying working conditions, as well as social services. Privatization worked on West German terms.

On October 3, 1990, "Unification Day," Germany's new national day, East Germany ceded to West Germany. The German Democratic Republic disappeared into the dustbin of history. In its stead five reconstituted additional *Länder* became part of the Federal German Republic. No new constituent assembly had been convened to discuss a new constitution for a united Germany. East Germany was simply incorporated into West Germany. A new *Anschluss*, complained adherents of the *ancien régime*—but the bulk of the East German electorate was perfectly satisfied.

Under the new dispensation, the East German and the West German parliaments merged.[15] With the addition of 144 new deputies from the former East German *Volkskammer*, the total number of deputies in the *Bundestag* (the West German Lower House) rose from 519 to 663. The CDU and its allies increased their seats from 234 to 305, the SPD from 193 to 226, the Free Democrats from 48 to 57, the Greens and their associates from 42 to 59. The PDS joined with 24 members.[16] The *Bundesrat* (the Upper House) was enlarged through the accession of the five new *Länder* represented in proportion to their population. (Berlin, which previously had nonvoting representation in the German parliament, received four members, as did Brandenburg, Mecklenburg, Saxony, Saxony-Anhalt, and Thuringia, thereby increasing the number of seats in the *Bundesrat* to 69.[17] United Germany did not even adopt a new name but remained the Federal Republic of Germany. Whereas Bismarckian Germany had represented Prussian—that is, East German—predominance over West Germany, the balance of power in the new Germany had now swung decisively to the West.

The prospect of a united Germany aroused a good many political fears. Would a United Germany not revert one day to a totalitarian dictatorship? The Germans, however, had been inoculated against that particular disease. In 1945, the Nazi regime ended—not merely in defeat, but also in disgrace according to its own, self-proclaimed values. The Nazis had proclaimed themselves a heroic elite. But when the war was over the overwhelming majority of these Nordic heroes took as their role model the three wise monkeys who had seen no evil, heard no evil, spoken no evil—there was a total flight from responsibility. Exactly the same thing happened 45 years later. The former communist members of a self-described vanguard, heroes of the proletariat, for the most part disclaimed all responsibility for the past, and embarked on an unheroic struggle for jobs, pension rights, and welfare benefits. Not surprisingly, self-appointed vanguards were thereafter at a discount in Germany.

Reunited Germany faced an immense array of other problems of a kind never faced previously by any Western government. The East German economy had in large measure become obsolescent. Whereas the country had continued to do quite well in traditional industries such as the manufacture of musical instruments, toys, or gardening tools, socialism had failed in the quality of consumer goods—the East German *Trabant* was an inferior car, symbolic of East German inefficiency. Socialism had performed even worse in the latest of ongoing industrial revolutions hinging on computer science, biochemistry, ultraspecialized metallurgy, and such like. Far from being able to "unshackle the means of production" from capitalist restraints, socialism had reduced East Germany to the status of a relatively backward country whose major industrial enterprises could, for the most part, not compete on world markets.

This was not all. East Germany's ecological problems, to give another instance, were much worse even than West Germany's. (In part, East Germany's predicaments were caused by the easy availability of brown coal, a major pollutant, though not the only one.) East Germany's infrastructure—housing, railways, bridges—were in decay, as planning had made inadequate provision for repair, and as private joiners, roofers, and such like had their shops nationalized, with disastrous effects on the upkeep of buildings, roads, and drains. Heavy financial outlay would be required to deal with burgeoning unemployment in East Germany, to pay for social security, and—above all—for the modernization of industry. Modernizing the East German railway system alone was estimated in 1990 to cost 100 billion marks over the next ten years.

The total cost of unification to West Germany could not even be fully estimated. It would prove immense, and at a time when West Germany's own public-sector deficit was estimated at again over 100 billion marks. (Hence, West German plans for reducing corporate taxation had to be abandoned.) According to the terms of the Soviet-German agreement of 1990, Germany would pay to the Soviet Union a total of 15 billion marks in return for getting the Red Army to leave East Germany within four years. (The German subsidy to the Soviet Union would help to meet the cost of housing returned Soviet soldiers in the Soviet Union, of sending German farm produce to the Soviet Union, of machinery, and other assets.) In addition West Germany had incurred lesser obligations to Hungary and other countries.

Even when all this is combined, this outlay would be small compared to the total cost of rehabilitating a bankrupt, decaying socialist economy in East Germany. Adding up the total expense involved proved an attempt at futurology. The East German tax system, to give just one instance, was in a chaotic state; no expert could frame as yet even a preliminary estimate of East Germany's future revenue, once the system had been reformed. Equally uncertain were existing assessments concerning the future costs of social security, of reforming East Germany's dilapidated health services, of renewing the decrepit transport and telecommunications networks, of replacing ill-constructed and poorly maintained housing projects, of retraining East German workers. The West German finance ministry in 1990 budgeted for a total cost amounting to 4 percent of the gross national product in 1990 alone. This level of investment would have to be sustained for at least four years, according to some experts. To make matters worse, East Germany's economic hinterland in Eastern Europe was in an even more lamentable condition. (According to Miroslav Hrncir, a senior economist at the Czech Academy of Sciences, Czechoslovakia's per capita income had been ten percent above Austria's in 1939. By 1990, after more than four decades of communist rule, the Czech per capita income had sunk to 35 percent below Austria's.)[18] Pessimists therefore feared that East Germany might turn into Germany's equivalent of the Italian *mezzogiorno*, beset by heavy unemployment.

The extent of Germany's problems in this regard were widely overlooked in 1990 by those who feared that a united Germany would henceforth dominate the EC by sheer economic power and physical size. True enough, united Germany was now the second country in Europe after the Soviet Union in terms of acreage and population (nearly 80 million),[19] possibly the first country in terms of economic production though comparisons with the Soviet Union are hard to make, given the unreliability of Soviet statistics. Germany's gross national product was considerably larger than that of France, Italy, or Great Britain, yet any of these two countries combined would outweigh Germany. Moreover, the shock to the EC of being saddled with East Germany was not as great as might be anticipated. Even before East Germany's absorption by West Germany, East Germany had already entered the EC through the back door, through a variety of agreements pushed by Bonn.

At the time of this writing (November 1990), it was not as yet clear how far East Germany's adherence to West Germany would indirectly delay the achievement of a complete European Economic Monetary Union (EMU). West Germany, deeply scarred by its own past with inflation, had been the chief advocate of financial stability; West Germany was the chief economic power within the EC; the *Bundesbank* dominated the system. By the end of 1990, Helmut Kohl essentially agreed with Giulio Andreotti, the Italian prime minister, who pushed for the early beginning of "stage two" in the achievement of EMU, supported by Belgium and France. Kohl, however, insisted that there might be inevitable delays, occasioned in part by the future costs of rehabilitating East Germany. Nevertheless, at the summit conference held in Bonn in 1990, Andreotti persuaded ten heads of government, including Kohl, that stage two of EMU should start in January 1994. (Only Margaret Thatcher, the former British prime minister, had stood aloof, insisting that she would never put before the British parliament a plan for a single European currency.)[20] (For more on German reunification and the EC, see Chapter 13.)[21]

These and many other problems would continue to plague both Germany and Western Europe. All the same, the years 1989 and 1990 had proved to be miraculous, having witnessed events that few Germans had expected to see in their own lifetimes. Communism in Germany had surrendered; the Iron Curtain had been rent asunder; the two Germanys had been joined—yet not a shot had been fired, and all experts had been proved wrong. The Kaiser's Reich and Hitler's Reich had both slithered into disaster. A united Germany would get a third chance, and so, hopefully, would a united Europe.

Notes

1. The most comprehensive and up-to-date history of the Federal German Republic in English is Dennis Bark and David Gress, *A History of West Germany*: vol. 1, *From Shadow to Substance 1945–1963*; vol. 2, *Democracy and Its Discontents 1963–1988* (Oxford: Basil Blackwell, 1989). For details see the bibliographical essay in vol. 2 and the appended bibliography.

2. See Joachim Narwocki, *Relations Between the Two German States: Trends, Prospects and Limitations* (Bonn: Bonn Aktuell Gmbh., 1985), p. 126, table 7, for detailed statistics.

3. Otto Wenzel, "Es gibt nur eine Staatsangehörigkeit: Aus der Geschichte der Deutschlandpolitik der SED," *Criticon* 116 (Nov.–Dec. 1989), p. 295.

4. Ralf Dahrendorf, *Society and Democracy in Germany* (Garden City, N.Y.: Doubleday, 1969), pp. 397–411.

5. Philip Windsor, "German Disunity," in Richard Mayne, ed., *Handbooks to the Western World: Western Europe* (New York: Facts on File, 1986), p. 313.

6. F. Stephen Larrabee, "From Reunification to Reassociation: New Dimensions of the German Question," in Larrabee, ed., *The Two German States and European Security* (New York: St. Martin's Press, 1989), p. 29.

7. Bark and Gress, *Democracy and its Discontents*, p. 490.

8. Cited by Jacob E. Heilbrunn, "The House that Adenauer Built," *National Interest*, no. 20 (Summer 1990), pp. 89–94.

9. "The Man with the Big Mouth," *The Spectator*, November 10, 1990, pp. 18–19.

10. Giovanni Arrighi, Terence K. Hopkins, and Immanuel Wallerstein, "1968: The Great Rehearsal," in Terry Boswell, ed., *Revolutions in the World-System* (New York: Greenwood Press, 1989), pp. 19–32.

11. Wolfgang C. Bibowski, "Demokratischer (Neu) Beginn in der DDR: Dokumentation und Analyse der Wahl vom 18 März, 1990," *Zeitschrift für Parlamentsfragen* 1 (1990), pp. 1–18.

12. For details see "Parting Sorrows: Soviet Troops in the GDR," *Frankfurter Allgemeine Zeitung Informationsdienst* 2, Sept. 7, 1990, pp. 3–4.

13. According to *The Economist* (January 27, 1990, p. 49), 61 percent of U.S. respondents favored German reunification, 61 percent of French respondents, 45 percent of British, 41 percent of Polish; 29 percent of U.S. respondents indicated that they would worry about German predominance, 50 percent each of French and British respondents, 69 percent of Polish respondents.

14. "The New Germany—D-mark Day Dawns," *The Economist*, June 30, 1990, pp. 3–22.

15. *This Week in Germany*, October 19, 1990, p. 1.

16. *This Week in Germany*, October 26, 1990, p. 1.

17. *German Brief—Update*, October 4–11, 1990, p. 2.

18. *New York Times*, November 10, 1990, p. 1.

19. The German Democratic Republic had comprised 41,768 square miles. Its addition to the German Federal Republic gave to United Germany an area of 95,975 square miles. The GDR's population had amounted to 16.4 million inhabitants. United Germany numbers 78.7 million people. The Federal German Republic's GNP amounted to 2.2 billion Marks. The addition of East Germany's GNP would make little change, given the country's dire economic state.

20. "In Rome, Lions Are an Endangered Species," *The Economist,* November 3, 1990, pp. 55–57.

21. The most recent estimate for the cost of unification was published in *The Economist,* 29 June 1991, p. 43. To the immense costs for payments to East Germany for social security, infrastructural investment, etc. (more than 3% of all-German GNP, nearly one-quarter of the budget), were added huge additional sums, including the enormous cost of shifting the capital from Bonn to Berlin, of Soviet bills, and of coping with the East German legacy of pollution—an incalculable amount.

7

Spain and Portugal

Richard Gunther

To a casual observer, Spain and Portugal might appear as Iberian twins, marching through history in lockstep with one another. Indeed, their similarities in historical development are quite striking. Both Spain and Portugal emerged as independent states very early and by the sixteenth century had established vast overseas empires. They both underwent long periods of political decadence and economic decline and entered the twentieth century as much less modern societies than most of their West European counterparts. After brief and tumultuous interludes as democratic republics, both Spain and Portugal witnessed the establishment of conservative, authoritarian regimes that survived over four decades. Those anachronistic political regimes were replaced in the 1970s by multiparty democracies not unlike those of other West European countries. And both countries are governed today by moderate socialist or social-democratic parties that are trying to solve serious economic problems through implementation of relatively conservative short-term policies.

The differences between the economic, social, and political systems of these two countries, however, should not be overlooked. These variations greatly affect the dynamics of politics in Spain and Portugal, as well as the nature of the most serious problems they confront. Perhaps the most important of these derives from the fact that Portugal is a linguistically and culturally homogeneous nation-state, whereas the population of Spain is heterogeneous and multinational. The presence of sizable linguistic and cultural minorities in Catalunya, Euskadi (the Basque provinces), and Galicia has led to a massive restructuring of the Spanish state through processes that on occasion have posed threats to the legitimacy and viability of the new democracy. In Euskadi, these conflicts have involved much political violence, which, by early 1985, had taken the lives of over 500 persons.[1] Portugal has not had to confront micronationalist challenges during its transition to democracy. Whatever restructuring its state apparatus may undergo will take place within the context of mere administrative reform and thus not have the same destabilizing potential as conflict in Spain.

In another respect, however, Spain may be regarded as more fortunate than Portugal: its level of socioeconomic modernization is significantly higher. Spanish living standards, economic productivity, literacy rates, and degree of urbanization greatly exceed those of Portugal. Although Spain must still cope with serious short-term and structural economic problems, it nevertheless has more resources at its disposal and perhaps faces a less difficult task in the economic sphere.

One of the most striking and politically significant differences pertains to the processes by which Spain and Portugal dismantled their former political regimes and founded their current democracies. The Spanish transition was evolutionary in nature and took place under the constant guidance and legitimate authority of a single head of state. New democratic institutions were created as the product of negotiations among political representatives of all significant sectors of Spanish society and were endorsed by an overwhelming consensus. The only exceptions to this broad support for the new regime were some Basque nationalist groups and a few tiny groups on the extreme right. The transition to democracy in Portugal, by way of contrast, was initiated by military coup and was accompanied by revolutionary upheaval, political turmoil, and dissension. Even though the old regime was quickly overturned, new democratic institutions emerged by fits and starts over a rather extended period of time. Indeed, one could argue that the transition to a new democratic regime was not completed until 1982, when the nondemocratic Council of the Revolution was abolished through constitutional reforms. In the interim, Portugal experienced a great deal of social instability (in the form of purges, massive and sometimes violent demonstrations, land seizures, and abrupt policy reversals) as well as governmental instability (there were fifteen cabinet crises between July 1974 and April 1983), both of which may have damaged the Portuguese economy.

Finally, Portugal has undergone a social and economic revolution since the demise of the old regime, while Spanish society and economy have been marked by considerable continuity and stability. The Portuguese political revolution of 1974–1975 was accompanied by the nationalization of important industries and by expropriation of much of the country's arable land. Later governments reversed or modified some of these policies, but it is nonetheless clear that a significant redistribution of ownership of the means of both industrial and agricultural production has taken place. No such change occurred in Spain following the death of Franco, although taxation and government expenditure policies have altered significantly.

In many respects, one could argue that Spain and Portugal exhibited important similarities throughout much of their histories. In recent years, however, and particularly after the fall of the authoritarian regimes of Franco and Salazar, they have evolved in different ways that affect the nature of contemporary politics and society.

Social and Historical Roots of Contemporary Politics

The states of Portugal and Spain were both created as the end products of the Reconquista—that is, the reconquest of the Iberian peninsula from the Islamic peoples who had invaded in the early eighth century. By the end of that century, Moorish rulers controlled all of the Iberian peninsula except for relatively small areas near the Cantabrican mountains and in Galicia. The reconquest was completed before the end of the fifteenth century, by which time the kingdoms of Portugal and Spain had more or less assumed their present boundaries. In comparison, all of the present-day territories of Great Britain and France were not to be governed by a single ruler until the seventeenth and eighteenth centuries, respectively, and Germany and Italy did not emerge as states until the mid-nineteenth century.

What is of greatest significance for contemporary politics is that the Reconquista was undertaken not by a single group with a common language and culture, but rather by three linguistically distinct populations. Most of the interior of Spain was reconquered under the leadership of Castilian monarchs, whose tongue would serve for centuries as the official language of the Spanish state and would be exported to vast areas of the western hemisphere. The northeastern corner of Spain, however, was not reconquered by indigenous Iberians at all. Instead, what became the Kingdom of Aragón was established by groups whose origins are to be found in the French region of Languedoc. Thus, the languages of Catalunya, Valencia, and the Balearic Islands derive from medieval Occitán, a provincial dialect of French. Although the closely related Catalán, Valenciano, and Mallorquín dialects share with Castilian Spanish a Romance-language base, they are almost as different from the Spanish language as are Portuguese, Italian, and French. These linguistic differences were reflected in the emergence of two independent kingdoms—Aragón and Castile-León. The marriage in 1469 of King Ferdinand of Aragón to Queen Isabella I of Castile-León, however, joined these linguistically and culturally distinct populations together within a single Spanish state. Linguistic heterogeneity persists to the present day. Survey data gathered in 1979 indicated that 97 percent of those persons born in Catalunya claimed to speak Catalán.[2] While nearly all Catalans speak Spanish, the regional language is for many of them the maternal tongue, and in many areas Catalán is clearly the language of preference. Although in neighboring Valencia daily use of the regional language is much less common, 68 percent of the inhabitants of that region claim to speak Valenciano. An even larger percentage of the population of Galicia (86 percent) speak Galego, a dialect of Portuguese. In many rural areas of this hilly and isolated district of Spain, Galego is widely used, particularly within the home. Finally, 46 percent of those born in Euskadi claimed to speak Basque—a non-Indo-European tongue totally unrelated to the other languages of Spain.[3]

The presence of non-Spanish-speaking peoples in Catalunya (which contains 16.9 percent of the population of Spain), Galicia (containing 8.4 percent), Valencia (9.9 percent), and especially Euskadi (5.9 percent) has prevented a thorough national integration. Indeed, the emergence in Euskadi and Catalunya of micro-nationalist movements based upon these linguistic and cultural distinctions has given rise to much personal conflict and contributed to the outbreak of five civil wars over the past three centuries.

In comparison, virtually all of the population of Portugal speaks Portuguese. Regional differences in accent or dialect exist, but in no way are these comparable to the linguistic heterogeneity of Spain. This feature of contemporary Portuguese society can also be traced back to the Reconquista, which, from the mid-twelfth century onward, focused on the creation of an independent monolingual kingdom. The completion of the reconquest in 1297 established national boundaries that (except for one minor adjustment) have remained unchanged, making Portugal the oldest unitary state in modern Europe. And in sharp contrast with Spain, it is a nation-state.

Spain and Portugal are very much alike, however, insofar as their respective histories were devoid of successful experiments with democracy. The Portuguese republic of 1910–1926 and the Second Spanish Republic of 1931–1936 were both unstable and short-lived. A brief description of the weaknesses of those two regimes provides an illustration of some of the impediments to democratic competition in the past and, to some extent, identifies problems that the current political elites have had to address.

One important social cleavage that destabilized both republics involved conflict over the proper social and political role of the Catholic church. Both Spain and Portugal are (and, from the time of the Reconquista, have been) overwhelmingly Catholic. While church-state relations were subjected to occasional stress throughout the nineteenth century, the church occupied important if not privileged positions in both societies. With the demise of both the Spanish and Portuguese monarchies, however, the status of the church came under direct attack. The constitution of the Second Spanish Republic represented a clear victory of anticlerical forces in this struggle. It abruptly disestablished the church, cut off subsidies to religious organizations, secularized cemeteries, legalized divorce, confiscated Jesuit properties, excluded religious orders from participation in the educational system (which they had previously dominated), and threatened some orders with expulsion. Legislation including many of these same provisions (and some that were more extreme) was enacted by the Portuguese government shortly after the founding of the Portuguese republic. Historian Richard Robinson has argued that this legislation

> proved counterproductive in as much as it further stimulated a revival of religious feeling and brought about an increased sense of urgency among Catholics concerning the problems of building up the organizational structures of religion. Far from bringing greater unity to the nation, it divided society by reinforcing political and ideological divisions . . . The law of 1911 unnecessarily alienated a large part of the population from the Democratic Republic and played its part in stimulating a reaction against the regime.[4]

Similarly, in Spain many supporters of the church were alienated to such a degree that they backed General Franco's 1936 uprising against the Second Republic. In return, Franco fully restored the church to its former status and, for two decades, relied on it as one of the pillars supporting his regime. Following the collapse of the Portuguese republic, Antonio Salazar also reversed most (but not all) of the anticlerical legislation passed by the preceding regime and made the defense of religion a central feature of his regime's ideology, although formal separation of church and state was maintained.

The religious cleavage remains an important feature of both Spanish and Portuguese society and politics. Attitudes toward the church are clearly reflected in the political party systems in both countries, separating parties of the left from those of the right.[5] They also divide both countries geographically: religiosity is strong in the northern half of each country (particularly among the landowning peasantry) and much weaker in the south and in large urban centers. These cleavages have great significance for the dynamics of politics under the current democratic regimes. In Spain, debates over public financing and regulation of private schools, as well as over legalization of divorce, were bitter and rancorous and directly contributed to the destruction of the moderate party that governed the country between 1977 and 1982. More recently, debates over legalization of abortion have posed threats to the governing Socialist parties; in Portugal this was particularly serious, insofar as it drove a wedge between the dominant Socialist Party and its social-democratic coalition partner. In mid-1975 conflicts between the church and the revolutionary government in Lisbon were so intense that they brought the country to the brink of civil war.

Social divisions relating to class have also contributed to political instability in the past and generate issues that must be addressed by contemporary leaders. Conflict between labor and management in both Spain and Portugal gave rise to much political violence during the first decades of the twentieth century. Apart from the great tensions that arise in all societies during the early stages of industrialization, an explanation of the high degree of destabilizing labor-management conflict that characterized the republican eras in both countries concerns the ideologies and behavioral styles of the trade union leaders of that time: they often preferred maximalist rhetoric to pragmatic bargaining and sometimes opted for direct, violent action as a means of securing social and political objectives. Such behavior was consistent with the anarchist and anarcho-syndicalist ideologies of Portugal's largest union, the CGT, and the Spanish CNT—one of the two dominant labor organizations—which rejected representative democracy, favoring instead direct, violent strike action as a means of bringing about social revolution. But in Spain even the normally moderate socialist UGT shifted to maximalist political and social demands after 1933, culminating in a bloody revolt in Asturias the following year. These manifestations of conflict were rooted in the inegalitarian structure of Spanish and Portuguese societies and dismal living conditions for workers. Employers and their allies also contributed to this instability by sometimes using violence to stifle working-class dissent.

Class conflict in the agricultural sector of each country was also frequently violent and destabilizing, although one must make a clear distinction between the northern half of the Iberian peninsula and its southern half. A conservative, landowning (and religious) peasantry constitutes the agricultural work force throughout most of the northern regions of Spain and Portugal. In the south, however, the predominant pattern of landownership is latifundist. Enormous landholdings throughout Andalucía and Extremadura in Spain and the Alentejo in Portugal were usually worked by day laborers with no job security, under horrendous conditions, and with extraordinarily low incomes and living standards. Under these circumstances, radical social doctrines had great appeal. Accordingly, outbreaks of violent agrarian unrest and land seizures were common, particularly in Spain on the eve of the Civil War.

During 40 years under the authoritarian regimes of Franco and Salazar, both Spanish and Portuguese society were substantially altered as a result of economic development. The objective bases of these class conflicts, however, were by no means eliminated. Neither dictator implemented agrarian reforms to redress the problems of inequality and of inefficient utilization of land in the south. Indeed, massive emigration of surplus labor from latifundia represented the only significant change in this situation. Between 1930 and 1970 over two million workers migrated from Andalucía and Extremadura in search of employment elsewhere (mainly in other European countries and the industrial zones of Catalunya, Euskadi, and Madrid).[6] Rural Portugal also experienced considerable emigration: between 1960 and 1970 the populations of the three Alentejo districts of Beja, Evora, and Portalegre declined by 25 percent, 18 percent, and 21 percent, respectively.[7] Economic development significantly expanded employment opportunities and raised living standards in urban and industrial centers in both Spain and Portugal. Nevertheless by 1970 both Spain and Portugal remained much more inegalitarian societies than their West European counterparts. Indeed, some sociological studies revealed that the distribution of wealth in Spain was becoming progressively more unequal as economic development proceeded.[8]

Another factor that destabilized the former republican regimes of Spain and Portugal was the performance of political leaders and institutions. The elite political cultures of both countries predisposed party leaders to rancorous and intolerant behavior toward opponents and a general unwillingness to compromise.[9] Both party systems were also faction-ridden and conducive to extremely high levels of cabinet instability. In each of the three legislatures of the Second Spanish Republic, over twenty parties received parliamentary representation, with at least eleven parties in each session having ten or more seats. In none of those legislatures did a single party control more than 23 percent of the seats. Thus, broad-based multiparty coalitions were required for the formation of a government. As one might expect, this led to considerable cabinet instability: during the 25 months of the 1933–1935 Cortes session, for example, there were thirteen government crises.[10] In Portugal, factionalism within the dominant Republican Party was largely responsible for the frequent collapse of governments. Between 1910 and 1926, there were 45 different cabinets and 500 persons held ministerial office. Only one of the six presidents of the republic completed a full term of office.[11]

Two Authoritarian Regimes

In the face of deep-rooted conflicts over religion, class differences, and, in Spain, national identities, these weak democratic institutions collapsed. Two years after a coup had toppled the Portuguese republic (in May 1926), Antônio de Oliveira Salazar was appointed minister of finance by General Antônio Oscar de Fragosa Carmona. Four years later, Salazar's success in managing economic affairs led to his elevation to the post of prime minister—a position he retained until he was incapacitated by a stroke in 1968. The collapse of the Second Spanish Republic involved much more bloodshed. On July 18, 1936, General Francisco Franco broadcast an appeal to all units of the Spanish military to rise up in rebellion against the government of the republic. Rather than signaling the start of a swift coup, this plunged Spain into a tragic three-year civil war, by the end of which Generalísimo Franco had assumed full control of a new political regime. He retained the post of head of state within that regime until his death in 1975.

The regimes created by Franco and Salazar were conservative, authoritarian, bureaucratic, and corporatist. Though lacking clearly elaborated ideologies, they were both explicitly antisocialist, anticommunist, antiliberal, nationalist, and Catholic in their patterns of elite recruitment and in public utterances. The basic institutions of the two regimes were, in many respects, quite similar.

Both Franco and Salazar suppressed competitive political parties and shunned democratic elections as effective means of elite recruitment. They each created a single "political party": Franco's National Movement (which until 1958 had the catchy name, Falange Española y Tradicionalista y de las Juntas de Ofensiva Nacional-Sindicalista) and Salazar's National Union. Both organizations functioned primarily as patronage-dispensing machines. Their purpose was to increase regime support, rather than to provide ideological direction for the formulation of policy or the recruitment of elites.

The Portuguese União Nacional (UN), however, was responsible for performing a function not shared by its Spanish counterpart. Unlike in Spain, the authoritarian regime of Professor Salazar maintained a facade of democratic legitimacy; thus the UN had to ensure electoral victory for Salazar loyalists. Using the office of prime minister as his power base, Salazar could only hold office as long as he was reappointed by the president of the republic, who was (according to the 1933 constitution) to be elected every seven years. This task was made somewhat more challenging after 1945, when an expansion of the suffrage gave the right to vote to a larger segment of the Portuguese population than under the republic. Nonetheless, through monopolization of the media, use of extensive organizational and financial resources, and outright harassment of opposition candidates, Salazar supporters always won the presidency and totally controlled the National Assembly. All of this was unnecessary in Spain. Francisco was neither elected nor appointed: he was "by the Grace of God, Chief of State, Generalísimo of the Army and Caudillo of Spain and of the Crusade."

Paradoxically, maintaining a pretense of democratic freedom in Portugal appears to have required greater coercion than was normally exercised in Spain, at least after consolidation of the Franquist regime in the 1940s. The Portuguese state developed a more extensive secret police apparatus and engaged in periodic purges of public employees (for example, in universities in 1936, 1946–1947, and 1962), methods that Franco did not have to rely on. The somewhat looser rein of Franquist authoritarianism permitted a broader array of opposition parties to emerge clandestinely by the 1960s and early 1970s. In Portugal, only the closed, Stalinist Portuguese Communist Party (PCP) could establish an organizational infrastructure prior to the regime's collapse in 1974.

It would be a mistake to overemphasize the repressive nature of either the Salazar or the Franco regimes. On a world scale, these must be regarded as authoritarian and not totalitarian political systems. Neither regime attempted to penetrate totally into society, and both permitted a wide array of secondary organizations to function independently—as long as they did not engage in "political activities" or actively oppose the regime itself. Even in these cases, the authoritarian character of both regimes was rather sloppy and sometimes ineffectual. Perhaps the best illustration can be seen in the field of labor relations. In accord with Catholic-corporatist beliefs that class conflict was unnatural and inherently disruptive of the social order, horizontal trade union organizations (such as the anarchist, socialist, and communist unions that existed under the republics) were outlawed and replaced by vertical syndicates. Both labor and management were to be included within a single syndicate representing each sector of the economy (such as mining, fishing, and steelmaking). Not surprisingly, neither of these corporatist systems functioned very well. What is most noteworthy is that in both Spain and Portugal the shop floor organizations of these systems were, by the late 1960s and early 1970s, effectively infiltrated and controlled by the Communist parties of those countries (although in Spain the influence of the Communist party was not as hegemonic). Thus, paradoxically, attempts by the staunchly anticommunist regimes of Franco and Salazar to regulate labor relations through a single syndicalist organization in effect gave the Communist parties of Spain and Portugal a substantial head start over their future competitors in organizing workers.

For three decades following the end of World War II, these two authoritarian regimes remained substantially unaltered. In the context of democratic, post-industrial Western Europe they stood out as striking anachronisms. But the social and economic structures of Spain and Portugal were undergoing significant changes during this period. The process of socioeconomic modernization was much more thorough in the case of Spain (particularly after 1960), but both countries would emerge from their recent authoritarian periods as societies markedly different from those inherited by Franco and Salazar.

One of the most basic social transformations associated with modernization is the shift from agriculture to industry and the service sector of the economy. In Spain the percentage of the labor force in the primary sector (agriculture, fishing, and forestry) declined from 46 percent in 1930 to 41 percent in 1960, 25 percent in 1970, and 17 percent in 1980. Comparable figures for Portugal are 57, 43, 30, and 25 percent.[12] It is clear that the economies of both Spain and Portugal have been substantially restructured, particularly since 1960. What is somewhat less clear from these figures (which conceal important qualitative differences between Spanish and Portuguese agriculture discussed later in this chapter) is that Spanish society has become considerably more modern than Portugal.

Other indicators of modernity put this difference in sharper focus. Closely related to the shift from agriculture to the secondary (manufacturing) and tertiary (service) sectors is movement from rural areas to urban population centers. By 1970, 61 percent of the Spanish populace was residing in urban areas (with 37 percent of the total population living in cities of over 100,000 inhabitants). In that same year, only 37 percent of the Portuguese lived in cities.[13] Although that represents a significant increase over the 1960 figure of 23 percent, it certainly indicates that Portugal remained much more rural than Spain. Similarly, a comparison of per capita incomes suggests that Portuguese citizens are much poorer than their Spanish counterparts. While this indicator suggests that Spain and Portugal were about equal in terms of per capita wealth in 1960 ($274 versus $270), the rapid expansion of the Spanish economy during the 1960s and early 1970s had made Spaniards much better off by 1977 ($3,260 versus $1,840).[14] Even in comparison with other West European countries, Spain's economic advance appears impressive: its per capita income of $3,260 in 1977 was just below that of Italy ($3,530) but above those of Ireland ($3,060) and Greece ($2,950).[15] Portugal, however, clearly emerges as the poorest country in Western Europe.

Finally, one indicator directly relevant to the proper functioning of democracy—literacy—reaffirms the overall conclusion that both Spain and Portugal have made great strides in educating their populations, but Portugal still lags sadly behind. Among persons over fifteen, the literacy rate rose from 69 percent in 1930 to 93 percent in 1980 in Spain and from 32 percent to 80 percent in Portugal. While illiteracy levels in both Spain and Portugal are higher than the average for developed countries (3.5 percent in 1970), they are below the 23.6 percent illiteracy rate of Latin America and were by no means comparable to the 46.8 percent rate for Asia or the 73.7 percent rate for Africa.[16]

Different Roads to Democracy

By the late 1970s, both Spain and Portugal had established democratic regimes. They differed greatly, however, in the manner in which the former authoritarian regimes were dismantled and new democratic institutions created. The transition to democracy in Portugal (1974–1976) was tumultuous and revolutionary. The Spanish transition (1976–1978) was evolutionary (but no less complete) and utilized the basic institutions and procedures of the Franquist state to destroy that regime. Differences in the nature of the transition to democracy have had important consequences for contemporary politics in these two countries. These include various effects on the nature of the Spanish and Portuguese party systems, the degree of acceptance or legitimacy of the new democratic regimes, and the basic structure of the two economies.

The Portuguese Revolution

Antônio Salazar suffered a debilitating stroke on September 6, 1968 (he died in 1970). His successor as prime minister was Marcelo das Neves Caetano, in many respects a product of the regime, who had been closely affiliated with the União Nacional. Caetano, nevertheless, favored liberalization of the regime— "renewal in continuity" or "evolution without revolution," as he called it.[17] In the first two years of his rule, there was great expectation in many quarters that he might bring about a gradual democratization of Portuguese politics. Indeed, Caetano made some significant reforms: in 1969 the right to vote was extended to all literate males and females, the broadest suffrage in Portuguese history; the UN was relaunched as People's National Action (ANP) and was opened up to permit expressions of criticism by its liberal members (such as Francisco Sá Carneiro, who would later head the Social Democratic Party and serve as prime minister in the new democracy); other groups were permitted to form outside the ANP and criticize government policy; press censorship and regulations of labor unions were relaxed; and social welfare programs were expanded.[18]

Caetano's liberalization, however, failed to satisfy the democratic aspirations of critical sectors of Portuguese society, and his experiment was abruptly terminated by a military coup. Several factors contributed to this failure. First, Caetano was increasingly held in check by conservative segments of the ANP and by the president of the republic, Américo Tomás. In addition, it is doubtful whether he wanted ultimately to bring about a thorough democratization or merely to make minor reforms that would still preserve the basically authoritarian character of the regime. At no point, for example, did he propose significant changes in Salazar's 1933 constitution. Finally, the entire political system was destabilized by its costly and increasingly unpopular military efforts to retain the last vestiges of Portugal's overseas empire.

Unlike Britain and France (both of which, by 1958, had declared their intentions of granting independence to their former African colonies), Portugal formally regarded its overseas territories as integral portions of the Portuguese state. Thus, Portuguese governments employed military force to oppose the national liberation movements that emerged in Angola, Mozambique, and Portuguese Guinea after 1961. The eventual cost of the colonial wars was enormous. In financial terms, the segment of the state budget devoted to the military increased from 27 percent in 1960 to 46 percent in 1971. As a percentage of GNP, military spending increased from 4.5 percent to 8.3 percent during this same period.[19] (In contrast, Spanish military expenditures in 1971 amounted to only 16 percent of state spending and consumed just 1.5 percent of the gross national product.)[20] In human terms, the costs of the colonial wars were even greater. The number of Portuguese soldiers killed during the thirteen years of war in Africa was twice as high (as a percentage of total population) as American combat deaths in Vietnam.[21] To avoid conscription, thousands of young men emigrated. Military service became so unpopular that the army was incapable of replenishing its officer corps with graduates of military academies and had to resort to drafting fresh officers from the universities. This had two consequences relevant to the demise of the Salazar/Caetano regime: it introduced into the officer corps individuals with decidedly leftist ideologies, who were certainly unenthusiastic about defending an overseas empire; and it made the army much more heterogeneous politically and, ultimately, faction-ridden. In an effort to demand redress of professional grievances, many officers joined the new Armed Forces Movement (MFA) in early 1974.

On April 25, 1974, a segment of the MFA under the command of Otelo Saraiva de Carvalho toppled the old regime and sent both Caetano and President Américo Tomás into exile. While space does not permit a detailed history of the enormously complex revolutionary period that followed, an understanding of contemporary Portuguese politics requires at least some familiarity with certain key developments. For the purpose of simplifying this narrative, three phases of the revolution can be crudely distinguished. In the first (April 25 to September 28, 1974), provisional governing bodies were formed that reflected the heterogeneity of the officer corps and newly emerging political parties. The first government consisted largely of moderate military officers and representatives of the Socialist Party (PS), the Communist Party (PCP) and its allied Portuguese Democratic Movement (MDP), and the Popular Democratic Party (whose members included many from the liberal faction of the former regime's ANP, such as party leader Sá Carneiro). The first president of the republic was the colorful General Antônio de Spínola, who had played an important symbolic role in toppling the old regime, but whose political views were not greatly different from those articulated by the reformist Caetano of 1968–1971. It soon became apparent, however, that real power lay elsewhere. One important body was a coordinating committee of the MFA, which was internally divided among a pro-PCP faction under Vasco Gonçalves, a second group with more extreme leftist ideologies, and a shifting bloc of officers with other progressive views. A second center of power was a newly formed praetorian guard called COPCON, under the command of the extreme leftist Carvalho. The third center of power was to be found in the streets: popular demonstrations proved to be an effective means of influencing political events.

The second phase of the Portuguese revolution began with the departure from office of Spínola on September 30, 1974, and ended with the attempted leftist coup and moderate countercoup of November 25 of the following year. This was a period of revolutionary social and economic change and of political turmoil. It was also a period in which Portuguese democracy was nearly stillborn and replaced with a leftist-authoritarian regime.

After September 30, the political center of gravity within the MFA shifted markedly toward the left. The prime minister throughout most of this phase of the revolution was Vasco Gonçalves, who was directly supported by the PCP and its trade union allies within the Intersindical. But the direction of politics during this period was most often set in response to initiatives by mass movements whose programmatic demands were more extreme than those favored by the Communist Party. Indeed, throughout much of this period, Gonçalves and the PCP struggled to contain the excesses of what they regarded as "infantile revolutionaries." Nevertheless, under the Gonçalves government, political pluralism very nearly disappeared from the Portuguese political scene. Mobs often broke up meetings, rallies, and congresses of moderate parties. Newspapers (the most prominent was the pro-Socialist *República*) and radio stations (such as Radio Renasçença, operated by the Catholic church) were seized by workers' committees and forced to adopt prorevolutionary editorial stands. Such attacks accelerated following an unsuccessful coup by Spínola on March 11, 1975, in the aftermath of which the headquarters of three moderate parties were sacked by mobs, and some parties (including the Christian Democratic Party) were outlawed. One study has estimated that during this period there were four or five times as many political prisoners in Portuguese jails as there had been under Caetano.[22]

In spite of this harassment, elections to the Constituent Assembly on April 25 produced a massive majority for moderate parties: the Socialist Party received 38 percent of the popular vote and garnered 115 out of 247 seats; the Popular Democratic Party (PPD) of Sá Carneiro received 26 percent of the vote and 80 seats; and the center-right Party of the Social Democratic Center (CDS) received 8 percent and 16 seats. This gave the moderate parties nearly 72 percent of the popular vote, compared with the 13 percent that went to the PCP; the 4 percent of its ally, the MDP; and the less than 1 percent for the far-left People's Democratic Union (UDP). The MFA's response to this electoral outcome was to propose the creation of a "democratic" system in which parliamentary parties would be made irrelevant. A "Guiding Document" released on July 9, 1975, called for indirect elections to a People's National Assembly, which would stand at the top of a hierarchy of local, district, and regional assemblies. At the base of this pyramid, delegates would be elected by a show of hands at mass meetings within neighborhoods, factories, and military units. Leaders of the Socialist Party and the PPD immediately recognized the potential for intimidation and manipulation at the hands of the local-level organizations of leftist parties and withdrew from the governing coalition and went into outright opposition.

In the economic sphere as well, the period between September 1974 and November 1975 (particularly after March 11) was one of revolutionary change and widespread chaos. Massive land seizures by workers, often backed by COPCON troops, took place in the Alentejo and Ribatejo regions. Latifundia were expropriated and collective farms were established, often under the leadership of PCP cadres. Legislation was hastily enacted on July 29, 1975, to establish guidelines for expropriation, but in many instances they were ignored or came too late to prevent seizure of unauthorized properties. In total, more than 2.5 million acres of agricultural land were expropriated. Great change also took place in the industrial sector. Shortly after Spínola's abortive coup, the Gonçalves government began to issue decrees nationalizing banking (giving the state interests in 1,300 business firms), as well as firms in the shipbuilding, steel, cement, tobacco, fertilizer, petrochemical, paper, mining, and brewing industries. Railways, electrical generation and distribution networks, and the Portuguese air-line TAP were also transferred to public ownership. This represented a revolutionary shift in ownership of the means of production: in 1973 the public sector accounted for only 18 percent of capital investments;[23] by the end of 1975 it controlled 46 percent of gross fixed capital.[24] During this period, labor unrest was widespread and was especially intense in Lisbon, where violent demonstrations erupted. Many of these pitted workers under the leadership of extreme leftists against the policies of the Gonçalves government, the PCP, and Intersindical. Fearful that excessive strike activity could destabilize the newly emerging regime and trigger a counterrevolutionary backlash, the government and its communist supporters urged restraint. Arrayed against them were workers who demanded higher salaries, jobs, and reinflationary economic policies. In *saneamentos* (purges) throughout the country, bosses and ordinary workers were dismissed from factories, schools, trade unions, and municipal governments on political grounds. In some instances executives were replaced by workers' self-management committees.

The third phase of the Portuguese revolution began on November 25, 1975, with a successful coup by more moderate officers under the leadership of General Antônio Ramalho Eanes. The roots of this change can be seen in growing resistance to the revolution throughout the summer of 1975. Four key groups were involved in this effort. The Catholic church (which, as recently as April, had limited its political involvement to issuing an appeal to voters not to support "atheist" parties) began to intervene overtly in politics following the seizure of Radio Renascença. Speaking at rallies in the highly religious north, church leaders urged Catholics to rise up in opposition to the revolution in general and the Communist Party in particular (even though the latter had opposed the seizure of the church's radio station).[25] The second significant group was the predominantly landowning peasantry of the north, whose general conservatism on political and social matters led them to oppose the revolution and whose economic interests were harmed by enactment of an agricultural rent law on April 15. Overt opposition to the revolution after July 11 by prominent political leaders, such as the socialist Mario Soares and leaders of more conservative parties, represented a decisive shift by a third important set of actors. By midsummer political and religious leaders, as well as farmers, had turned the northern half of the country into a bastion of opposition to the revolution. Farmers sporadically blocked roads leading to Lisbon and the south. Rioting led to the destruction of nearly every communist and far left party office in northern and central Portugal,[26] and violent confrontations (resulting in some deaths) were frequent. Indeed, for some time Portugal appeared to be on the brink of civil war.

The most decisive group of actors was military officers. Reacting in part to the growing political fragmentation of the army and to an accelerating collapse of discipline within its lower ranks, moderate officers rallied to General Eanes and, following an attempted coup by extreme leftists on November 25, undertook a coup of their own. The subsequent dismissal of leftist officers from key command positions, the arrest of 150 other military officials, and the disbanding of COPCON abruptly halted the progress of the revolution. This cannot be regarded as a counterrevolutionary act since many of the changes brought about during the previous year were retained and, indeed, enshrined within a new constitution. Neither did it fully remove the military from Portuguese politics. Nevertheless, the coup of November 25 precluded further revolutionary change, reversed some of the excesses of the previous year, and set Portugal firmly on the road to representative democracy.

The revolutionary nature of the transition to democracy, however, has had a lasting impact on Portuguese politics and even on the content of policies enacted by elected governments. To preserve many of the achievements of the revolution, General Eanes and the progressive majority of officers supporting him in the military Council of the Revolution imposed constraints on the freedom of action of the Constituent Assembly elected in 1975. According to the terms of an agreement signed on February 26, 1976, by representatives of the military and the various political parties present in the assembly, the constitution would include specific provisions designed to prevent a return to the prerevolutionary past.

Unlike the constitution adopted two years later in Spain, the Portuguese constitution is not ideologically or programmatically neutral. Its preamble asserts that the new democratic institutions of government "have as their objective the assurance of the transition toward socialism through the creation of conditions for the democratic exercise of power by the working classes." Articles 9 and 10 refer to "the collective appropriation of the principal means of production." Article 82 provides for expropriation of large estates and business firms without compensation, and Article 83 flatly asserts that "all nationalizations effected since April 25, 1974, are irreversible conquests of the working classes." [27]

In order to protect these provisions from erosion by the policies of subsequent governments, the army is charged with "the historic mission of guaranteeing the conditions permitting the pluralist and peaceful transition towards democracy and socialism." Article 273 states that "the Portuguese armed forces are part of the people, and, identified with the spirit of the program of the Armed Forces Movement, ensure the continuation of the revolution of April 25, 1974." [28] This function was entrusted to a Council of the Revolution, composed of military officers, who, in conjunction with the president of the republic, were to rule on the constitutionality of legislation, play a crucial role in the appointment of governments and the dissolution of parliament, and function as supreme arbiter in all matters pertaining to the military. [29] Amendments to the constitution had to be passed by a two-thirds majority of the members of the assembly and were forbidden for a period of four years. Finally, future constitutional changes would have to respect "the rights of workers, workers' committees and trade unions." [30]

Defense of the accomplishments of the revolution was reinforced by the presence, to this time, as president of the republic of a military man loyal to the revolution, General Eanes. Elected with a majority of 61 percent in 1976 and re-elected with a 56 percent majority in 1980, Eanes steadfastly opposed efforts to enact legislation inconsistent with the basic precepts of the revolution. And the powers initially entrusted to the president in this semipresidential regime were extensive: he could veto legislation approved by the assembly, and he had considerable freedom of decision concerning the appointment and dismissal of governments and the dissolution of parliament.

The founding document of the new Portuguese democracy caused a division in the party system along ideological lines. Rather than establishing a broad consensus over essential rules of the game (as does the current Spanish constitution), Portuguese constituent elites followed the somewhat more dangerous precedent of the Second Spanish Republic—that is, the partisan document they formulated attempted to isolate the ideological and programmatic commitments from the everyday give-and-take of democratic politics. Given their majority within the Constituent Assembly and active support from the leftist Council of the Revolution, the Socialist and Communist parties were able to enshrine a commitment to socialism within a document that could be altered only with great difficulty. Given its control over coercive resources and its demonstrated willingness to use force to achieve political objectives, the army was able to create institutions within which it could continue to intervene in politics. But the votes cast in opposition to the new constitution on April 2, 1976, by representatives of the Social Democratic Center and the deep reservations expressed by Popular Democratic deputies clearly indicated that reform of the constitution would be a divisive partisan issue for years to come.

Spain: The Politics of Consensus

The transition to democracy in Spain was a pastoral symphony compared with the dissonant clashes of the Portuguese revolution. A new regime replaced the authoritarianism of the Franquist era through a relatively peaceful and evolutionary procedure. In contrast to the Portuguese transition, the leading roles were played by moderate political forces, and the dynamics of the resulting party system (except in Euskadi) induced most competitors to attempt to outdo one another in terms of moderation. All significant groups played active and positive roles in establishing new political institutions, and the constitution they produced was endorsed by a broad consensus (again, except in Euskadi). Even the economic crisis plaguing Spain throughout the constituent process provided an opportunity for opposing groups to collaborate with one another in a positive manner. As in nearly every instance of profound political change, tensions and great stress were generated, but these served primarily to produce conflict within, rather than among, parties. Although such tensions caused serious problems for some parties, these divisions did not pose as grave a threat to the stability of the new regime as would polarizing struggles among parties with distinctly different ideologies and clienteles. Only the unsolved problem of Euskadi represented a serious potential threat to the new regime's prospects for survival.

This satisfactory outcome was by no means obvious at the beginning of the transition to democracy. Prior to his death in November 1975, Francisco Franco had boasted that he would leave Spain "well tied up." Indeed, he created and staffed institutions of government in a manner that seemed to preclude evolutionary change. He had carefully picked a successor as head of state who had never publicly professed a preference for democracy. In choosing Juan Carlos I (grandson of the last Spanish king, Alfonso XIII), he skipped over the individual who should have been next in line: Juan Carlos's father, Don Juan, who had made the mistake of calling for the overthrow of Franco and establishment of a Spanish democracy shortly after World War II. In an attempt to defend the remnants of his regime, Franco circumscribed the king's freedom of action by creating an ultraconservative Council of the Realm (whose powers were roughly comparable to those of the Portuguese Council of the Revolution). Finally, the highly conservative makeup of the Cortes (parliament) seemed to rule out the prospect that legal procedures could ever be used to dismantle the Franquist regime.

Indeed, during the six months after the Caudillo's death it appeared that any change would have to be forced by the mass mobilization of segments of Spanish society. The Council of the Realm gave the king little choice but to reappoint as prime minister an old friend of the Franco family, Carlos Arias Navarro. In many respects, Arias was similar to Marcelo Caetano. Like his Portuguese counterpart, he had entered office promising to initiate political reforms. Also like Caetano, he ultimately failed to produce changes that would even minimally satisfy the democratic aspirations of most citizens. By June 1976 no significant democratization had taken place. In response, clandestine opposition parties (the largest of which was the PCE—the Spanish Communist Party—followed by the socialist PSOE—the Spanish Socialist Workers' Party) began to mobilize their supporters and organize protest activities. Demonstrations and illegal strikes (most with political rather than purely economic objectives) began to occur with ever greater frequency. The number of work hours lost through strike activity, for example, increased from 14.5 million in 1975 to 150 million in 1976.[31] In short, a significant mass mobilization of opposition forces was taking place in the first half of 1976, and a showdown with the defenders of the Franquist state seemed inevitable. Spain appeared to be going the way of Portugal.

These similarities ceased, however, with the king's dismissal of Arias Navarro and appointment of a new government in July 1976. Thenceforth, rapid progress toward democratization was made. The key to this reform process was the leadership of the new prime minister, Adolfo Suárez—a young and relatively un-known product of the National Movement, who had previously served under Franco as director general of the state-run television network and in the first post-Franco government as minister of the National Movement. In an impressive display of political skill (and in close collaboration with the king), Suárez persuaded the corporatist Cortes to commit institutional suicide by approving the Political Reform Bill of October 1976, which established procedures for future political reforms to be undertaken by a new, democratically elected Cortes. In rapid succession other crucial reforms were enacted: hundreds of political prisoners were granted pardons in July 1976 and March 1977, the National Movement was disbanded and political parties legalized, the vertical labor syndicates were abolished and replaced by independent trade unions, an electoral law that set the rules for electoral competition was negotiated with opposition political forces, and despite fierce opposition from certain sectors of the military, the Spanish Communist Party was admitted as a legitimate contender in the new political arena.

The evolutionary nature of this transition to democracy was, for several reasons, of great political significance. It contributed to the legitimacy of the new regime in the eyes of many Franquistas by initiating that political change according to formal procedures established by Franco himself. Thus, important sectors of the Franquist elite (such as former minister Manuel Fraga Iribarne) would play active roles in the reform process, rather than sitting on the sidelines as embittered opponents of change or as vengeful victims of a political purge. The evolutionary nature of the transition also ensured that change would take place within a relatively stable political and institutional environment. A prominent communist leader has pointed out that, by way of comparison, Spain's three previous experiments with democracy (as well as that of Portugal) were launched "within a common situation of an institutional vacuum, a radical break with dynastic power, a sudden irruption of important sectors of the populace into the political scene, a military crisis, and a correlation of forces favorable to those groups with the most radical transformative desires."[32] The thoroughness of Suárez's political reforms was also crucial from the standpoint of the regime's viability. The release of political prisoners and the relatively unrestricted licensing of political parties may ultimately have had some drawbacks,[33] but those decisions represented positive contributions to the new regime insofar as they brought many potential regime opponents into the democratic game of politics and encouraged them to perform as loyal and trustworthy regime supporters. Finally, the relatively gradual pace of the transition (a year and a half was to expire between the death of Franco and the first democratic election) and the comparatively unthreatening nature of the political environment permitted a large number of parties with varying ideologies to organize. The abrupt collapse of authority in Portugal, in contrast, meant that only the party that had maintained a clandestine organizational infrastructure, the PCP, would be well established. Given the disarray of its partisan opponents (resulting from their recent creation and the harassment to which they were subjected), the PCP was able to play a disproportionately influential role for more than a year after the fall of Caetano.

Some of the consequences of this evolutionary political transformation quickly became apparent. A centrist coalition surrounding Suárez emerged victorious from the June 1977 election to the constituent Cortes. The Union of the Democratic Center (UCD) received 34 percent of the popular vote and controlled 165 of 350 seats in the Congress of Deputies. On that basis, it was able to form a minority government. The second-largest party was the socialist PSOE, with 29 percent of the vote and 118 seats. The ideologically more extreme Communist Party (PCE) and Alianza Popular (AP) (founded by prominent figures from the Franquist regime) fared less well, receiving 20 and 16 seats, respectively. Thus, the new party system was one dominated by two relatively moderate political groups, the UCD and PSOE, which controlled over 80 percent of the seats in the Congress. The dynamics of partisan competition were centripetal, thus reinforcing the overall moderation characteristic of the system.

Moderation and consensus were particularly important in the first parliament because the writing of a new constitution required the new political elites of Spain to address several historically divisive issues. These included the relationship between church and state, the role of the monarchy, and the degree of political and administrative autonomy of the various regimes. It was clear that the manner in which these and other issues were addressed would have profound implications for the legitimacy and stability of the new regime. But compromise over these issues would be as difficult to achieve as it was essential. Continuation of the privileged status of the Catholic church, the bans on divorce and abortion, and criminal sanctions for cohabitation and adultery were certain to offend liberals and the left. At the same time, adoption of an anticlerical constitution could provoke the church into withdrawing its support from the regime, as it had in 1931. Similarly, rejection of appeals for regional autonomy would undoubtedly alienate Basques and Catalans, while extensive concessions to regionalists might provoke active opposition from Spanish nationalists in the military. And the continuation of antilabor statutes could lead to labor unrest and seriously damage an already sagging economy.

Differences over these issues were clearly reflected in the party system that had emerged from the 1977 election. Economic and labor-related articles of the constitution pitted the PCE and PSOE (which had their own trade unions) against the other four major parties—the UCD, the AP, and the Basque and Catalán nationalist parties (each of which received some electoral support from business groups). Concerning church-state relations and the monarchy, the traditionally anticlerical and republican PCE and PSOE initially opposed the preferences of the other major parties, although the PCE quickly adopted nonconflicted stands on both issues. Center-periphery conflicts arrayed Basque and

Catalán nationalist parties against the UCD and the intensely Spanish national-ist AP, while the Socialists and Communists shifted positions from one relevant constitutional article to the next.

The UCD, by joining its votes in the Cortes to those of the AP, could have enacted a partisan constitutional text favoring the church, business groups, and a perpetuation of a centralized Spanish state. (In doing so, it would have followed the precedent established in Portugal, in which Socialist and Communist parties joined forces to enact an explicitly socialist constitution.) Instead, the UCD chose to compromise with the parties of the left and regional nationalists in order to enact a constitution that might lay to rest those issues that had served as grounds for destructive partisan conflict in the past. In sharp contrast to their Portuguese counterparts, Spanish constituent elites rejected the notion that ma-jority parties should take advantage of their voting strength in order to maximize the interests of their respective clienteles. Instead, Adolfo Suárez defined his ob-jectives in an April 1978 speech as follows:

> During a constituent process, the government must restrict its options to those that would not produce dissensus because that is the only way to avoid what would be the gravest danger to the body politic: the lack of a concord rooted in the country and lack of respect for the basic elements of national coexistence . . . The constitution, as the expression of national concord, must be obtained by consensus.[34]

Accordingly, Spanish elites opted for a political style popularly called the politics of consensus, which shared many of the procedural characteristics of the con-sociational politics of the Netherlands, Switzerland, and Austria.[35]

The constituent process of 1977–1978 met with mixed success in addressing traditionally divisive issues. Conflicts over the position of the monarchy, legal-ization of political parties, and constitutional enshrinement of basic civil and political rights were totally resolved. Consensus over the constitutional treatment of these issues was so widespread and irrevocable that these have ceased to be objects of political controversy. Of these, the status of the monarch is the most secure: confounding PCE leader Santiago Carrillo's earlier prediction that histo-rians would refer to the king as "Juan the Brief," the decisive role played by Juan Carlos in creating (and, in 1981, defending) the current democracy has won for him the enthusiastic support of all political groups except those on the extreme right.

Compromises over religious issues, the electoral law, and economic matters (labor relations and the role of the state in the economy) are examples of what can best be described as satisfactory conflict regulation. In these cases, the major protagonists reached sufficient agreement over general principles pertaining to these matters so as to neutralize them as potential obstacles to widespread acceptance of the constitution. But while the consensus over these principles eliminated them as possible constitutional conflicts that might, by themselves, threaten the legitimacy of the new regime, implementation of these vague statements would continue to generate considerable (but so far manageable) interparty conflict. This is most obvious with regard to economic matters, over which conflict is an everyday occurrence in pluralist democracies. Unlike the Portuguese constitution, which clearly takes sides in these struggles, the current constitution of Spain has set down guidelines acceptable to both left and right. Similarly, the constitution's regulation of electoral competition in Spain did not lead any party to oppose its ratification by the Cortes or in the referendum of December 1978. Nevertheless, as elsewhere, whenever parties are disadvantaged by a particular electoral system, they will often issue demands for its reform. In these respects, Spain is no different from other democratic systems. Subsequent conflicts over implementation of constitutional articles dealing with religion, however, have been rather intense and have disrupted the stability of the party system (see below). To some extent, this was inevitable, insofar as the compromise language of the constitution functioned mainly to postpone decisions concerning such matters as legalization of divorce and abortion and state regulation of and subsidies to private education. Despite later conflicts over implementation of these general principles, the 1977–1978 constituent process must, overall, be regarded as successful in addressing these traditionally divisive issues.

Resolution of center-periphery conflict through these negotiations was more difficult to share. Considerable success was achieved in deliberations between Catalán nationalists and representatives of the Spanish state. The compromise language of the constitution was promptly endorsed by the major Catalán party and by all major Spanish parties except some segments of Alianza Popular. In an effort to satisfy regionalist and micronationalist aspirations, the constitution "recognizes and guarantees the right of autonomy of the nationalities and regions" (sharply reversing the uncompromising Spanish nationalism and centralism of the Franquist state), but balances this concession with a reaffirmation of "the indissoluble unity of the Spanish nation, common indivisible fatherland of all Spaniards." It also sets forth guidelines for the decentralization of the state and the creation of "autonomous communities" for each region (which began to come into existence in 1979, with the enactment of Autonomy Statutes for Euskadi and Catalunya). In another sharp departure from the practices of earlier regimes, the constitution establishes the co-officiality of regional languages within the respective autonomous communities. These provisions were regarded as satisfactory by Catalán nationalist parties, who voted in favor of the constitution in the Cortes and campaigned for its endorsement in the 1978 referendum. Basque nationalist parties, however, refused to support the constitutional text. The delegation of the Basque Nationalist Party (PNV), the largest Basque party, walked out of the Congress of Deputies just before that body approved the text, abstained from the final Cortes vote on the constitution, and campaigned for abstention in the constitutional referendum. Euskadiko Ezkerra (the Basque Left, then the second-largest Basque nationalist party) voted against the constitution and campaigned against its ratification in the referendum. As a result, less than half of the Basque electorate voted in that referendum (46 percent, as compared with a turnout of 68 percent throughout Spain). Only 68.8 percent of those who voted, moreover, cast favorable ballots—some 20 percent less than the national average. In Catalunya, by way of comparison, turnout was 68 percent and affirmative votes (90.4 percent) actually exceeded the national average.

Overall, the constituent process of 1977–1978 must be regarded as remarkably successful. For the first time in its history, Spain was able to launch a new democratic regime with the support of the overwhelming majority of its population and of political parties of both left and right. The ambiguity of the PNV toward the new constitution and the outright hostility of more extreme Basque nationalists, however, posed a regional challenge to the legitimacy of the new regime. This contributed, in turn, to an atmosphere of increasing tension, violence, and uncertainty about regime stability.

The Party Systems of Spain and Portugal

Consistent with the pattern observable in other spheres, the Spanish and Portuguese party systems share many superficial similarities. Until 1982 (when a significant realignment of the Spanish party system took place), they were both predominantly four-party systems, with two center to center-left parties receiving sizable majorities of popular votes cast and with two parties in each system farther from the center of the spectrum receiving less popular support (see Table 7.1). In each party system there was a communist party, a socialist party, a center to center-right party that placed greatest emphasis on attracting support from voters of the center-left, and a party located to the right of center. But in many respects, these similarities are overshadowed by differences that greatly affect the dynamics of each system.

One major difference concerns the ideologies and behavior of the Communist parties in each country. Throughout the transition to democracy, and until shortly after its substantial electoral setback in 1982, the Spanish Communist Party (PCE) was Eurocommunist in ideology and moderate in its behavior. It explicitly rejected several of the key conditions set forth by Lenin as central to communist identity. One of these is "proletarian internationalism," according to which Communist parties everywhere should collaborate closely with the Communist Party of the Soviet Union. While a minority of PCE members were intensely loyal to the USSR (about 7 percent of the delegates at the party congress of 1981 cast pro-Soviet votes, and about 25 percent of communist voters in our

Table 7.1   Percentages of Votes and Seats in National Elections

PORTUGAL

Party	1975 Votes	1975 Seats	1976 Votes	1976 Seats	1979 Votes	1979 Seats	1980 Votes	1980 Seats	1983 Votes	1983 Seats	1985 Votes	1985 Seats
MDP	4.1	2.0	—	—	⎱ 19.0	1.2	⎱ 16.9	.8	—	—	—	—
PCP	12.5	12.1	14.6	15.2	⎰	17.6	⎰	15.6	18.2	17.6	15.4	15.2
PS	37.9	46.6	34.9	40.7	27.4	29.6	28.0	29.6	36.3	40.4	20.8	22.8
PPD/PSD	26.4	32.4	24.0	27.8	⎱ 45.0	30.0	⎱ 47.1	32.8	27.0	30.0	29.9	35.2
CDS	7.7	6.5	15.9	16.0	⎰	16.8	⎰	18.4	12.4	12.0	9.8	8.8
PPM*	0.6	—	0.5	0		4.4		2.4	0.5	0	—	—
Others	10.8	0.4	10.1	0	—	0	8.0	0.4	5.6	0	6.1	0
PRD	—	—	—	—	—	—	—	—	—	—	18.0	18.0

MDP = Portuguese Democratic Movement (close to PCP)

PCP = Portuguese Communist Party (in alliance with MDP in 1979 and 1980)

PSP = Portuguese Socialist Party

PPP/PSD = People's Democratic Party, renamed the Social Democratic Party in autumn 1976 (centrist)

CDS = Party of the Social Democratic Center (right of center)

*PPM = Peoples' Monarchist Party (right of center). In 1979 includes reformers and independents, who (with PSD and CDS) made up Aliança Democratica.

PRD = Democratic Renewal Party (Eanes)

SPAIN

Party	1977		1979		1982		1986	
	Votes	Seats	Votes	Seats	Votes	Seats	Votes	Seats
PCE	9.2	5.7	10.8	6.5.	4.1	1.1	4.6	2.0
PSOE	28.9	33.7	30.5	34.6	48.7	57.7	44.1	52.6
UCD	34.0	47.1	35.1	48.0	6.8	3.4	—	—
AP	8.0	4.6	6.1	2.6	26.6	30.2	26.0	30.0
PNV	1.7	2.3	1.7	2.0	1.9	2.3	1.5	1.4
PSC/CiU	2.8	3.1	2.7	2.3	3.7	3.4	5.0	5.1
CDS	—	—	—	—	2.9	.5	9.2	5.4
Others	15.6	3.4	13.1	4.0	8.2	1.7	8.5	3.4

PCE = Spanish Communist Party (left)

PSOE = Spanish Socialist Workers' Party (left and center-left)

UCD = Union of the Democratic Center (center and center-right)

AP = Alianza Popular (right)

PNV = Basque Nationalist Party

PDC/CiU = Catalán nationalist coalitions (Pacte Democràtic per Catalunya in 1977 and Convergència i Unió in 1979 and 1982)

CDS = Social and Democratic Center (Suárez)

1982 survey preferred "friendship with the USSR" over "friendship with the United States," "neither," or "both"), the PCE leadership repeatedly asserted its independence from Moscow and strongly criticized the USSR for its invasions of Czechoslovakia and Afghanistan and for its role in the suppression of the Solidarity movement in Poland. A second major departure from orthodox Marxism-Leninism was the PCE's formal repudiation of the concept of the "dictatorship of the proletariat." It pledged itself to adhere to the democratic rules of the game and to preserve pluralist democracy even if it should come to power. There is little doubt that most PCE members (some of whom had suffered greatly under the authoritarian regime of General Franco) have come to appreciate democratic freedoms and were anxious to contribute to consolidation of the new democracy.[36]

Accordingly, the PCE and its affiliated trade union, the Comisiones Obreras, behaved in a markedly restrained and constructive manner during the transition. Both party and trade union were key supporters of the 1977 Pacts of Moncloa, according to which wage demands would be sharply limited (in order to reduce inflation) and strike activity held to a minimum in exchange for government pledges of continued political and social reforms. In the Cortes, Communist deputies were usually more consistent than their Socialist counterparts in avoiding rancorous conflicts with opponents and in reaching prompt agreement over constitutional compromises. A third departure from orthodox communism is that the PCE does not even call itself Marxist-Leninist. At its 1978 congress, the term "Leninist" was formally deleted from the party's self-description. In the aftermath of the intraparty struggles which erupted after 1982 (to be discussed below), this segment of the Spanish party system has become more fragmented and complex. But there can be no doubt that its moderation and restraint during the transition to democracy made a positive contribution to the consolidation of the new regime.

The Portuguese Communist Party is different in several respects. First, it has remained an orthodox Communist Party. In 1974 party leader Alvaro Cunhal wrote that "even the slightest deviation from the classical Leninist code would have a demoralizing effect on all aspects of the party's work and would therefore be an obstacle to the fulfillment of its historic mission."[37] Accordingly, the party has refrained from criticisms of the Soviet Union, has explicitly attacked Eurocommunism as a viable ideology for Portugal, and has not repudiated the concept of "dictatorship of the proletariat." Alvaro Cunhal flatly declared during a 1975 interview:

> We Communists do not accept the game of elections. Elections have nothing or very little to do with revolutionary dynamics. The solution to problems lies with the revolutionary dynamics. In Portugal there is now no possibility of a democracy like the one you have in West Europe. There are two options

here: either a monopoly with a strong reactionary government or the end of monopoly with a strong Communist democracy. We do not wait for the results of elections to change things and destroy the past.[38]

During the revolution the PCP behaved in accord with classical Leninist principles, taking advantage of a chaotic environment through its superior organization and internal cohesion, co-opting popular movements and seizures of agricultural lands and private businesses, and sometimes organizing *saneamentos* of opponents. It succeeded in establishing a relatively stable base of support, particularly in the latifundist zones of the Alentejo, and has consistently received between 15 percent and 18 percent of the popular vote. The greater electoral significance of the PCP, its rigidly orthodox stand, and the role it played during the revolution clearly differentiate it from the weaker, now fragmented, but predominantly moderate PCE of Spain.

A second major difference between the party systems of Spain and Portugal is to be found in the absence of openly conservative parties in Portugal. In Spain, the Alianza Popular and segments of the now defunct UCD both filled the political space to the right of center. The AP was founded by the so-called Magnificent Seven—seven prominent figures from the former regime, six of whom had held the rank of minister under Franco. Led by the cautiously reformist but conservative Manuel Fraga, the party's elite included some individuals who had acquired populist reputations (such as Licinio de la Fuente, a former minister of labor) and some (particularly those surrounding Fraga) who had pushed for a gradual democratization of the former regime. The overwhelming majority of the party's leaders, however, were right-wingers—including some of dubious commitment to democracy. Some of the more prominent leaders of the right wing of the party left the AP in 1978 (in protest over Fraga's endorsement of the new constitution), but the AP remained a decidedly conservative party, more or less of the Reaganite or Thatcherite right.

The party system that initially emerged from the 1975 Portuguese constituent assembly election was, in comparison, decidedly skewed to the left. Not only did the PS and PCP receive a larger share of the popular vote than their Spanish counterparts, but overtly conservative parties were totally absent from the political scene. This was the result of two features of the Portuguese revolution: First, during the crucial formative period between the April 25, 1974, coup and the election of the following year, centrist and conservative parties were prevented from functioning normally. Both the CDS and PPD were subjected to harassment by leftist mobs, and the more conservative Christian Democratic Party (PDC) was outlawed following Spínola's attempted coup on March 11, 1975. These disruptions impeded organizational development and campaign activities, and presumably contributed to the much poorer showing by those parties than in any subsequent election. Second, both the PPD and CDS presented themselves during the first election campaign as parties much farther to the left than their subsequent behavior would justify. In part, this was for self-preservation during a time of revolutionary upheaval. Richard Robinson argues that "the PPD sought to project a more leftist image to avoid marginalization in Lisbon and therefore survive as a national grouping offering shelter to conservatives."[39] Accordingly, it remained within the government in coalition with the PCP and PS until mid-July 1975; it applied for membership in the Socialist International (but was rejected on the grounds that the PS was Portugal's true socialist party); and it issued explicitly social-democratic programmatic appeals. Similarly, the CDS, despite its ties to the German Christian Democratic Union, its support from many right-wing *retornados* (refugees from former Portuguese colonies in Africa), and its subsequent policy stands, posed as a centrist party, supporting worker participation in industry, expanded welfare services, and state intervention in the economy.[40] Thus, party leader Diogo Freitas do Amaral only got it half right when he said, "The CDS is a party of the center which says it is, and the PPD is a party of the center which says it is on the left."[41] Over time, both parties would drift toward the right: the PPD (despite naming itself the Social Democratic Party in 1976) would emerge as a more truly centrist party; and the CDS would (despite the lack of explicit ties to the church) behave in a manner similar to the right-of-center CDU of West Germany. Nevertheless, one legacy of the Portuguese revolution remains—no electorally significant party as far to the right as the Spanish Alianza Popular exists in Portugal.

A third major difference between the Spanish and Portuguese party systems is that the latter does not contain micronationalist or regionalist parties. Indeed, it is partly incorrect to speak of Spain as if it had a single-party system: the dynamics of the two regional party subsystems existing in Euskadi and Catalunya are decidedly different from those of the rest of the country.

The combined totals of votes for all major Spanish (statewide) parties has not constituted even a plurality of votes cast in Euskadi since the first democratic contest in 1977 (see Table 7.2). Since that first election, the party system of Euskadi has been dominated by Basque nationalist groups, and in the regional elections of 1980 and 1984 the PNV was able to establish an almost hegemonic position within the newly created regional government bodies. In left-right terms the dominant PNV is moderate and centrist; its mean position on a ten-point left-right scale in 1982 was 5.4 (as compared with 3.6 for the PSOE, 6.2 for the UCD, and 8.5 for the conservative Alianza Popular). In the past it was closely tied to the Catholic church (it was a founding member of the Christian Democratic International), and it received considerable support from Basque business elites. But in terms of its commitment to Basque nationalism, the PNV is hardly moderate. As we have seen, the PNV refused to endorse the 1978 constitution, even though that document went further in the direction of political decentraliza-

Table 7.2   Election Results in Euskadi and Catalunya (Percentage of Valid Votes Cast for Major Parties)

EUSKADI

Regional Parties	1977	1979	Reg. 1980	1982	Reg. 1984	1986	Reg. 1986
PNV	30.0	27.6	38.1	32.1	41.7	28.0	23.6
EA	—	—	—	—	—	—	15.9
EE	6.5	8.0	9.8	7.8	8.0	9.1	10.9
HB	—	15.6	16.6	14.8	14.6	17.8	17.5
Total	36.5	50.6	64.5	54.7	64.3	54.9	67.9

Statewide Parties

	1977	1979	Reg. 1980	1982	Reg. 1984	1986	Reg. 1986
AP	7.2	3.4	4.8	11.7*	9.4	10.5	4.9
UCD	12.9	16.9	8.5		—	—	—
CDS	—	—	—	1.8	—	5.0	3.5
PSOE	26.7	19.1	14.2	29.4	23.3	26.4	22.0
PCE	4.6	4.7	4.0	1.8	1.0	1.2	1.0
Total	51.4	44.1	31.5	42.9	33.7	43.1	31.4

CATALUNYA

Regional Parties	1977	1979	Reg. 1980	1982	Reg. 1984	1986
PDC/CiU	17.0	16.4	28.0	22.6	46.6	32.2
ERC	4.7	4.1	9.0	4.0	4.4	2.7
Total	21.7	20.5	37.0	26.6	51.0	34.9

Statewide Parties

	1977	1979	Reg. 1980	1982	Reg. 1984	1986
AP	3.5	3.7	3.2	14.8	7.7	13.6
CC-UCD	17.0	19.4	10.7	2.1	—	—
CDS	—	—	—	2.0	—	5.1
PSC-PSOE	28.7	29.8	22.6	46.0	30.0	41.2
PSUC	18.4	17.4	18.9	4.6	5.8	3.9
Total	67.7	69.3	55.4	67.5	43.5	63.8

PNV = Partido Nacionalista Vasco (Basque Nationalist Party)
EA = Eusko Alkartasuna (schism from PNV)
EE = Euskadido Ezkerra (Basque Left)
HB = Herri Batasuna
PDC/CiU = Pacte Democràtic per Catalunya (1977); Convergència i Unió
ERC = Esquerra Republicana de Catalunya (Republican Left of Catalunya)
CC-UCD = Centristes de Catalunya-UCD
PSC-PSOE = Partit del Socialistes de Catalunya, PSC-PSOE
PSUC = Partit Socialista Unificat de Catalunya (Communist)
*UCD and AP ran in coalition in Euskadi in 1982.

241

tion, encouragement of regional languages and cultures, and recognition of the multinational character of the Spanish population than any previous constitution. Indeed, two high-ranking party leaders flatly declared (in interviews conducted by the author in 1981 and 1982) that the PNV would never endorse that document because it is a "*Spanish* constitution." The party has also maintained an ambiguous stance with regard to the ultimate objective of creating an independent Basque nation-state (composed of what are now four Spanish provinces and three French departments), and until 1985 did not take a firm and consistent stand in opposition to terrorism by ETA (Euskadi ta Askatasuna).[42]

One reason for the party's unpragmatic public posture concerning these issues is that it must compete with two more extreme Basque nationalist groups, Euskadiko Ezkerra and Herri Batasuna. The first to emerge was Euskadiko Ezkerra, a coalition of various left-wing Basque nationalist groups. In 1978 that coalition divided into the extremist Herri Batasuna and the subsequently more moderate Euskadiko Ezkerra. Herri Batasuna includes Marxist-Leninist revolutionary and ultranationalist groups and is closely tied to ETA Militar (the most intransigent branch of that organization, which has rejected the legitimacy of all representative political institutions and has relied exclusively on the armed struggle as a means of securing Basque independence). Even though it fields candidates in elections, it has refused to permit its elected representatives to participate in statewide Spanish governmental institutions and even in the regional parliament created in 1981. Instead, it emphasizes the armed struggle for Basque independence and social revolution. In sharp contrast, Euskadiko Ezkerra has adopted a much more pragmatic and moderate stance. It had been linked initially to ETA Político-militar (which sought to combine political and military methods in pursuit of Basque independence), but since the enactment of the Autonomy Statute for Euskadi in 1979, it has waged a campaign against terrorist violence as a legitimate means of struggle in the pursuit of Basque national interests. A further shift in the position of the party followed its 1981 merger with segments of the regional branch of the Spanish Communist Party. This has infused an element of Eurocommunism into the party's heterodox "ideology." Euskadiko Ezkerra has sought to present itself as a progressive, working-class, Basque nationalist alternative to the conservative, bourgeois PNV and to the insufficiently Basque PCE and PSOE. So far it has failed in its attempts to steal votes from the disruptive, antisystem Herri Batasuna.

In the aggregate, the party system of Euskadi has exhibited clear signs of the dynamics of polarization and fragmentation. Since the first democratic election, the number of Basque nationalist parties receiving significant shares of the vote has doubled. As described below, a schism within Euskadiko Ezkerra in 1978 led to the creation of the more militantly antisystem party Herri Batasuna; and in 1986 even the PNV (which had existed as an institution since the late nineteenth century) split into two parties roughly equal in size—with a new party, Basque Nationalists (EA), now competing against what remains of the PNV.

On the surface, the Catalán party system would appear to be much less affected by regionalism or micronationalism. Regional branches of Spanish statewide parties (when taken together) have received a majority of popular votes cast except on one occasion (1984), and only in regional elections does a slate of Catalán nationalist candidates win a plurality—this was the coalition Convergència i Unió (CiU) (which appeared as the Pacte Democràtic per Catalunya in 1977 and which is dominated by the Catalán nationalist party Convergència Democràtica de Catalunya). What these figures do not reveal is the extent to which the major statewide parties have been Catalanized. This is most clear with regard to the Socialist and Communist parties. In 1978 the regional branch of the PSOE merged with the Partit Socialista de Catalunya (PSC) and over the following years the leadership of the new PSC-PSOE fell increasingly under the control of former PSC elites. The principal communist party in Catalunya is the Partit Socialista Unificat de Catalunya (PSUC), which has enjoyed organizational autonomy from the PCE since the time of the Civil War. Like the PSC-PSOE and CiU, the PSUC was a strong advocate of Catalán autonomy in the constituent process. Even the two statewide parties on the right of center, the UCD and AP, noticeably adjusted their images and personnel to fit with the political environment of Catalunya. Prior to the 1979 elections the UCD entered into a coalition named Centristes de Catalunya with indigenous Catalán Christian democratic and liberal groups, and Alianza Popular, prior to the 1982 election, underwent a remarkable Catalanization of its slate of candidates for the Cortes. Thus, Catalán regionalist or micronationalist sentiments are deeply embedded within the party system of the region. But the basic nature of Catalán nationalism is markedly different from the micronationalism of Euskadi. Pragmatism and moderation are significant characteristics of elite behavior within the region. No major party (not even the highly nationalistic Esquerra Republicana de Catalunya, which advocates a switch from bilingualism to the use of Catalán as a single language within the region) has advocated independence for a Catalán nation-state. And, compared with Euskadi, political violence has been largely absent from the Catalán political environment.

In two important respects, the party systems of Spain and Portugal resemble one another. Striking similarities in the evolution of their respective Socialist parties constitute one such resemblance. Although the Spanish PSOE was founded in 1878, while the PS of Portugal did not come into existence until 1973, both parties entered the current democratic era as poorly institutionalized partisan groups with a penchant for verbal radicalism. Franquist repression had succeeded in eliminating PSOE branches from most parts of the country (to a much greater degree than in the case of the PCE). Thus, both Spanish and Portuguese Socialist leaders had, in effect, to create mass party organizations from the ground up. The influx of many young people into the rapidly expanding parties, coupled with the absence of consensus over basic decisionmaking procedures, the proper roles of militants and officials, party tactics and strategies, and even the parties' ideologies, gave rise to significant instability within both the PS and the PSOE. In addition, both parties initially staked out ideological positions rather far to the left, and explicitly condemned social democracy as inadequate for the extensive tasks of dismantling authoritarian regimes and undertaking far-reaching changes in Spanish and Portuguese societies. The PSOE, for example, officially described itself as a "class party, and therefore of the masses, Marxist and democratic." Its principal objective was stated as "the overcoming of the capitalist means of production through the seizure of economic and political power, and the socialization of the means of production, distribution, and exchange by the working class." The party rejected "any path of accommodation with capitalism or the simple reform of that system."[43] Similarly, the Portuguese Socialist Party appeared in the 1975 campaign as "Marxist and to the left of any European Socialist party."[44] Nevertheless, both parties have moved decidedly to the center in recent years and have performed in office as moderate social-democratic parties. This ideological change is most explicit in the case of the PSOE, which dropped the term "Marxist" from its self-designation in 1979, thereby returning to the more heterodox ideological stance that it had maintained for most of the first one hundred years of its existence. Both parties have also become more internally stable and firmly under the control of their respective leaders.

A second and more important similarity between the party systems of these two new democracies is that they have both experienced considerable instability. One kind of instability which they share is volatility in the voting behavior of their respective electorates. The most extreme case of high electoral volatility occurred in the Spanish parliamentary election of 1982, when the governing UCD lost 157 of its 168 seats in the Congress of Deputies and the Communist Party lost over 60 percent of its share of the vote, while the AP and PSOE gained a total of 179 out of the 350 seats in the Congress. That election's "volatility index" of 43 (which measures the sum of the vote share for new parties plus the percentage gained by parties that increased their vote shares since the last election) is, in fact, indicative of the most extensive electoral shift to be found among any industrialized democracy in the post–World War II era (the next closest is the 1947–1949 Japanese electoral turnover score of 26). The sudden emergence of former President Eanes' new Democratic Renewal Party in 1985, whose 18 percent share came largely at the expense of the Socialists, generated a volatility score of 21, which placed that Portuguese election in sixth place among the most extreme electoral shifts of the postwar era. These Spanish and Portuguese elections reflected much higher levels of volatility than is typical for Western industrialized democracies (which, between 1948 and 1977, have averaged volatility scores of 9). One source of this propensity toward extremely large electoral shifts is the low level of party identification found in these relatively new democratic systems.

Another cause of instability is the electorate's response to instability at the elite level of party politics. The nature of this instability, however, is somewhat different in the two cases. The current Portuguese regime has exhibited classic symptoms of government (or cabinet) instability. During the period between 1976 and 1983 (that is, excluding the revolutionary period of 1974–1975 and the past few years), the average government has lasted just ten months. This represents a much higher frequency of turnover than the post–World War II average for European parliamentary democracies (twenty months), and a somewhat greater degree of governmental instability than even that of contemporary Italy. Since 1983 the life span of Portuguese governments has been close to the European average, but it is still too early to determine if this represents a stabilizing and maturing of party politics in Portugal or is merely an aberration. Apart from the usual policy consequences of such instability (lack of policy continuity and ministerial expertise, an inability to undertake medium-term planning), the high frequency of collapse of Portuguese governments has had negative ramifications at the mass level of Portuguese society. Party politicians have acquired a collective image of irresponsibility. Public opinion surveys have indicated that this (coupled with the current economic crisis) has undermined popular support for the new regime. When asked which prime minister provided the best government for Portugal, fully 28 percent of respondents in a 1978 survey mentioned Marcelo Caetano.[45] The next-most-popular leader was Mário Soares (9 percent), who narrowly surpassed two rather authoritarian figures, Vasco Gonçalves (8 percent), and Antônio Salazar (7 percent). Indeed, when references to all leaders who have held office since April 25, 1974, are added together (producing a total of 21 percent) and compared to the combined total of references to Salazar or Caetano (35 percent), the lack of strong public support for leaders of the current party system becomes ominously clear. This situation has been aggravated by serious economic problems, which have led many Portuguese citizens to compare the present situation with the authoritarian past unfavorably: 39 percent of those surveyed in 1978 regarded the changes since 1974 as "for the worse," while only 18 percent said such changes were "for the better." These data have led political scientist Thomas Bruneau to lament that "a substantial part of the population look back to the non-democratic Estado Novo with a certain amount of nostalgia as they compare their memories of it to the present situation of socio-economic change and hardship."[46] Bruneau further points to a disturbing parallel between the government instability of the present regime and that of the democratic republic of 1910–1926.

The Spanish party system has not experienced this kind of instability. Indeed, Spanish governments have been rather long-lived. The first democratic government—formed by Adolfo Suárez after the June 1977 election—lasted until the end of December 1978. Its dismissal by the king was not a manifestation of government instability but, rather, a response to a request from the prime minister for early elections that might enable him to capitalize upon the widespread feeling of satisfaction over enactment of the new constitution. (This strategy was successful, and the UCD's plurality in the Congress of Deputies increased by three seats.) The first cabinet crisis cannot be said to have occurred until January 1981, when Suárez resigned in response to a breakdown of discipline within his own party (see below). While support for his successor, Leopoldo Calvo Sotelo, was anything but strong, the subsequent UCD government did survive until late summer 1982. Following a smashing victory in the October 1982 election, a Socialist government under Felipe González governed with a stable majority of nearly 58 percent of the seats in the Congress. It was re-elected with a majority of 53 percent of the seats in the 1986 election. Thus, there have really been only two significant cabinet crises during the seven years of existence of the current Spanish democracy.

An institutional factor is largely responsible for this difference between the Spanish and Portuguese party systems. Even though both Spain and Portugal have adopted the D'Hondt variety of proportional representation,[47] the substantial difference between the number of electoral districts in the two countries greatly affects the degree to which the distribution of seats is truly proportional. In Spain, a large number of districts, coupled with the overrepresentation of sparsely populated rural constituencies, substantially magnifies small pluralities of popular votes. (see Table 7.1). In general terms, the smaller the number of deputies from each district, the greater the departure from strict proportionality in seat distribution. Since 28 of Spain's 50 provinces (which serve as electoral districts) elect five or fewer deputies, small pluralities of popular votes are transformed into majorities or near-majorities of seats in the Congress. Thus, the UCD, with only 34 percent of the votes cast in 1977 and 35.1 percent in 1979, fell short of absolute majorities in the Congress of Deputies by only eleven seats and eight seats, respectively. It was therefore able to form single-party minority governments and could pick up the votes needed for passage of legislation from either the left or the right, depending upon the issue in question.[48] And even though no party has secured an absolute majority of the popular vote in any of the four parliamentary elections, single-party governments have been in office since the very founding of the democratic regime. In Portugal there are only eighteen electoral districts, which elect an average of nearly fourteen representatives each. This results in greater proportionality in party representation—which more closely conforms to abstract democratic ideals, but which also makes it somewhat more difficult to form stable governments. A wide variety of formulas have been adopted since 1976: the PS and PSD have stood alone in minority governments; there have been three "independent" governments formed under the tutelage of President Eanes; between 1979 and 1982 the CDS and PSD joined forces with several smaller groups (the People's Monarchist Party, independents, and some former Socialist deputies) to form the Aliança Democrática; in 1983 a Socialist-Social Democratic coalition was formed; and at one point, the PS leapfrogged over the PSD to form a coalition with the more conservative CDS. But, to this point, relatively unstable governments have been the most common result.

While Spain has not experienced difficulties in forming stable governments, its party system has been beset with serious instability of a different kind: intraparty conflicts have frequently assumed unmanageable proportions. The results have been schisms, resignations by party leaders, and, in the case of the UCD, the single greatest electoral disaster ever to befall a major West European political party. The first manifestation of this widespread problem was the breakup of Alianza Popular's founding elite in 1978. The more right-wing segments of the AP delegation in the Cortes refused to follow the lead of Manuel Fraga and support the new constitution. Their departure from the party somewhat weakened its infrastructure and its appeal to the most conservative elements of its electoral clientele, and at least partly as a result the AP suffered a serious defeat in the 1979 elections. This led to Manuel Fraga's temporary resignation from the party's leadership. The tremendous recovery of Alianza Popular in the 1982 election suggested that this crisis had been adequately resolved, but in 1986 the conservative coalition formed by the AP and two small liberal and Christian democratic parties collapsed. This was followed by a leadership struggle culminating in Manual Fraga's retirement from politics.

The next party to undergo an internal crisis was the PSOE. As mentioned earlier, the Socialist party initially embraced radical, ideological, and programmatic positions at its 1976 congress. But such stands and an explicit self-designation as a Marxist party came to be regarded by Felipe González and his collaborators as electoral liabilities. González's proposal to soften the radical rhetoric of the party's ideological declarations, however, encountered fierce opposition from many party cadres and militants. The ensuing struggle made readily apparent the party's low level of internal stability and its sometimes chaotic "assembly-government" deliberative style. Rather than endorsing González's proposals, a May 1979 party congress dealt him a humiliating defeat, prompting him to resign from the party's executive committee. Ultimately, González and his collaborators succeeded in adjusting the PSOE's ideological declarations to fit better the moderate image that the party wished to present to the electorate. In addition, much higher levels of internal party discipline have been imposed by a more stable and authoritative (some might say authoritarian) executive committee. More than any other party, the PSOE appears to have overcome the general propensity of Spanish parties to engage in self-destructive internal conflict.

The same cannot be said of the other principle party of the left, the PCE, which, in the two years preceding the 1982 elections, was rent by factional fights, expulsions, desertions of prominent leaders, regional tensions, and bitter attacks upon the leadership of Santiago Carrillo. The origins of these destructive internal conflicts are enormously complex and are related to the party's rather heterogeneous composition, which resulted from the recruitment of persons from vastly different backgrounds and with different political values over its extended period of organizational expansion, during which the PCE evolved from a closed, clandestine, orthodox Communist party into an open Eurocommunist party. The abandonment of Leninism, solidarity with the Soviet Union, and the traditional role of Communist parties as the "vanguard of the proletariat" ultimately alienated some older party members, many of whom remained loyal to the USSR because of its support during the Civil War. At the other extreme, moderate Eurocommunists who approved of the party's ideological revolution resented the authoritarian leadership style of Santiago Carrillo and demanded a more thorough democratization of the party. Finally, efforts undertaken by the secretary general of the Basque regional branch of the party to merge with Euskadiko Ezkerra led to intense conflict with Carrillo and triggered a massive wave of expulsions from the party. By the time of the 1982 election, the PCE had lost much of its membership base (its prime electoral resource) through resignations, expulsions, and general demoralization. Its former image of moderation, stability, and responsibility (which had enabled it to broaden its appeal in earlier elections) had been greatly damaged. Rival parties (such as Euskadiko Ezkerra and the pro-Soviet Communist Party of Catalunya) had emerged to challenge the PCE's hold on leftist voters. And the respect or admiration won by Santiago Carrillo for the constructive role he had played during the transition to democracy had been replaced by distrust and hostility. Primarily for these reasons the PCE suffered a profound setback in the 1982 election,[49] leading to Carrillo's resignation as secretary general. His departure from leadership of the party, however, did not resolve these conflicts. Instead, he engaged in almost incessant and highly divisive attacks on his successor, Gerardo Iglesias, in an effort to regain control of the party. The party was further weakened by a series of schisms: first a pro-Soviet faction of the party under Ignacio Gallego separated from the PCE, forming an orthodox Marxist-Leninist party named the Communist Party of the Peoples of Spain (PCPE). Then former PCE leader Santiago Carrillo defected from the party and founded his own Committee for Communist Unification (MUC), whose ambiguous ideological stance placed it somewhere between the PCE and the overtly pro-Soviet PCPE. In the 1986 elections, the MUC received about 1 percent of the vote, as compared with 4.6 percent received by the coalition between the PCE and the PCPE. Thus, the Spanish Communist "political family" has disintegrated, and has become electorally very weak.

The collapse of the UCD was even more startling. The centrist party had always been heterogeneous ideologically (it eclectically embraced social democracy, liberalism, and Christian democracy) and with regard to the political backgrounds of its founders (some had been members of the "moderate opposition" to the Franquist regime; others had previously served as officials within the state administration, the labor syndicates, and even the National Movement itself). Tensions among the ideological "families" that made up the party—particularly those pitting conservative Christian democrats against social democrats and Adolfo Suárez—became increasingly apparent after the 1979 elections. Intraparty conflicts over legislation regulating the education system, regional autonomy policy, and a bill legalizing divorce were especially intense. Having lost control of his parliamentary delegation, Adolfo Suárez resigned as both prime minister and head of the UCD on the eve of the party's second congress in January 1981.

Suárez did not, however, abandon hopes of returning to these positions of power. But unlike the case of Felipe González's resignation as leader of the PSOE, Suárez's efforts to reorganize his bases of support met with increasingly organized opposition within the party. The formal institutionalization of a conservative Christian democratic faction calling itself the Plataforma Moderada in August 1981 was one step toward the definitive exclusion of Suárez from the party leadership. In retrospect, it may be regarded as the first decisive step toward the disintegration of the UCD as a political party. The decomposition of the UCD accelerated in November 1981 with the departure of a small group of social-democratic deputies and their formation of the Democratic Action Party, which soon forged an alliance with the PSOE. Several months later a schism from the right wing of the party led to the formation of the predominantly Christian democratic Popular Democratic Party. Finally, in August 1982 Adolfo Suárez himself left the party, forming the center-left Social and Democratic Center Party. Lacking a working majority in the Cortes and in an effort to stem the tide of defections from what remained of the UCD, Prime Minister Leopoldo Calvo Sotelo asked the king to dissolve the Cortes and hold new elections on October 28, 1982. The result of that contest was a devastating defeat for the UCD, whose delegation in the Congress of Deputies fell from 168 seats to 12. Not even Calvo Sotelo was able to secure a seat in the new Cortes.

With the collapse of the UCD and the PCE, Spain has developed much more of a two-dominant-party system than that of Portugal. The current lineup of partisan forces will probably not last, however, and today's principal party of opposition, Alianza Popular, is unlikely to attract enough voters from the center to alternate in government with the PSOE. It is still perceived as a very conservative party, whose mean placement of 8.5 by respondents on a ten-point ideological scale in 1982 made it an unacceptable voting alternative for most voters (whose mean self-placement was a decidedly center-left 4.8). In addition, I suspect that the party's electoral appeal was dealt a serious blow by the unseemly leadership struggle which broke out in June 1986. It is likely that an effective electoral challenge to the PSOE will come from some new coalition of forces closer to the center of the political spectrum, either in alliance with the AP or standing as an independent grouping. The substantial electoral recovery experienced by Adolfo Suárez in 1986 placed him at the center of efforts to re-establish a credible party or coalition. But given the enormous reservoir of ill-will among political leaders of the center created by the collapse of the UCD, and his personal opposition to electoral collaboration with Alianza Popular, his would not be an easy task, at least over the short term. Thus, barring unforeseen developments, the PSOE could remain in power for some time to come.

Problems Facing the New Democracies

The new democratic regimes in Spain and Portugal have been burdened with extraordinarily serious problems. The economies of both countries have suffered serious short-term declines triggered by worldwide recessions beginning in 1975 and again in 1981. Both economies have structural defects that will be difficult and painful to resolve. Both are facing the economic challenge of increased competition that might result from their integration within the European Community. In addition, Spain has yet to resolve political conflicts arising out of its recent entry into NATO. Finally, both regimes have had to cope with unresolved issues held over from the transition to democracy: in Portugal, for example, the two major parties of the center and right rejected important aspects of the new constitution; and in Spain, extensive political decentralization failed to resolve regional challenges to the Spanish state.

Of all these problems, the one which posed the gravest and most immediate threat to the survival of democracy involved regional autonomy policies in Spain.[50] The seriousness of this conflict resulted not from a lack of effort to achieve compromise resolution of these issues, but from the violent conflict over these issues which pitted two potentially disruptive forces—Basque nationalist terrorism and the army—against one another. Despite the granting of extensive autonomy to Euskadi (the Autonomy Statute of 1979 gave the new regional government far more exclusive functions and fiscal resources than are under the control of American states relative to the central government), 1982 survey data suggest that 24 percent of the inhabitants of Euskadi harbor proindependence sentiments.[51] Although the overwhelming majority of the Basques regard the current structural relationship with the Spanish state as satisfactory, the existence of this separatist minority has enabled ETA to continue its campaign of violence. While it is inconceivable that a continuation of terrorist acts (at least of the magnitude experienced so far) could by itself induce a Spanish government to grant independence to Euskadi, such violence remains a very grave problem, especially because ETA terrorists have chosen as their victims military officers (some very high in rank) and policemen (who are organizationally tied to the military). ETA's strategy appears to be oriented toward destabilizing the current democracy and bringing about a right-wing military coup, which would, in turn, provoke masses of Spanish citizens to rise up in rebellion. The resulting situation of revolutionary chaos might then enable Euskadi to secede.

The first phase of this scenario came terrifyingly close to realization on February 23, 1981, when a group of paramilitary civil guards stormed into the Congress of Deputies (during the vote of investiture of a new government under Leopoldo Calvo Sotelo) and, for almost a full day, held at gunpoint virtually the entire elected political leadership of the Spanish democracy. Simultaneously, the captain general of the Valencia region declared martial law, sent his troops and tanks into the streets, and proclaimed himself head of a provisional government. Only the tireless efforts of King Juan Carlos succeeded in convincing other captains general (some apparently involved in a broader conspiracy) that they should oppose the coup and remain loyal to the existing regime. Without additional support, the coup quickly (and peacefully) failed.

Since that time the threats posed by ETA and right-wing segments of the Spanish military appear to have abated somewhat. The frequency of terrorist assassinations has declined, and increased cooperation from France (which had previously provided sanctuary for ETA terrorists) has greatly improved the effectiveness of the Spanish government's efforts to eliminate terrorism. Similarly, there is increasing confidence that the Spanish military has abandoned its interventionist tradition (which had given rise to numerous coups in the nineteenth and early twentieth centuries) and will remain loyal to the current democracy. Nevertheless, ETA retains the potential for disrupting the new regime.

In some respects relations between the Spanish government and Basque and Catalán nationalist groups have taken a turn for the worse since the departure from office of Adolfo Suárez during the constituent process and negotiations over Basque and Catalán autonomy statutes (which relied heavily upon private, bilateral negotiations between regional and Spanish government representatives) were rather successful in securing agreement among the relevant political forces concerning decentralization of the state—even the PNV and Euskadiko Ezkerra endorsed and campaigned for ratification of the Autonomy Statute of 1979. However, by decentralizing the Spanish state through separate sets of bilateral negotiations with regional representatives, inconsistencies and administrative problems were created; some regions (such as Euskadi and Catalunya) secured more extensive rights and benefits than did other regions. Thus, the PSOE and the Calvo Sotelo government joined together to formulate the Organic Law for the Harmonization of Autonomy Policies (LOAPA), which they hoped would standardize the relationships between the central government and the various regions. While the flaws in the administrative structure of center-periphery relations are widely acknowledged, the manner in which the LOAPA was formulated must be regarded, in retrospect, as a serious political blunder. Unlike the decisionmaking procedure used by Suárez (in which representatives of regional or micronationalist groups were active participants from the very beginning), regional leaders were excluded from the deliberations until a complete draft of the law had been prepared. Not surprisingly, Basque and Catalán nationalists regarded the LOAPA as an illegitimate imposition by the Spanish state that violated both the politics of consensus and the texts of the constitution and the 1979 autonomy statutes. In 1983 the Spanish Constitutional Court agreed and declared nearly every significant clause of the LOAPA unconstitutional. Thus, little lasting benefit was ever derived from the LOAPA. Instead, the principal legacy of the LOAPA appears to have been worsening relations between regional and Spanish political elites. And the uneven administrative structure and particularistic regional rights inherent in the present *estado de las autonomías* remain unreformed.

In Portugal, as well, unfinished business left over from the transition to democracy figured prominently on the agenda of the new regime. Indeed, it would not be an exaggeration to describe many such issues as "undoing the excesses of the revolution." The first to be addressed was the issue of land reform. The first constitutional government under Mário Soares moved quickly to enforce land reform legislation by evicting squatters from properties seized illegally. No Portuguese government has attempted to reverse completely the revolutionary changes that took place in the Alentejo in 1975; according to current law, about one-fifth of all arable lands will have changed hands since the fall of the Caetano regime.[52] But postrevolutionary legislation sought to balance the need for land reform against the rights of former owners. Accordingly, former latifundium proprietors may retain up to 75 acres of their former lands, as long as they work those lands themselves. In addition, properties below a certain size were declared ineligible for expropriation. As mentioned earlier, however, squatters had seized many properties that did not conform to these legal requirements. Thus, throughout the late 1970s governments faced the often unpleasant task of displacing farming cooperatives and individual squatters from unqualified lands. Violence erupted periodically.

Similar efforts were made to return certain industries and business enterprises to the private sector. The first Soares government, for example, enacted a law redefining the limits of the public sector, according to which "state intervention was to be confined to the key sector of banking and insurance, basic industries, public utilities and transport."[53] More ambitious efforts by Aliança Democrática (AD) governments to reprivatize industries, however, were frequently declared unconstitutional by the Council of the Revolution and by President Eanes. This led Aliança Democrática to push vigorously for reform of the constitution and elimination of its references to socialism, the Armed Forces Movement, and the irreversibility of nationalizations. These reform proposals also included the abolition of the Council of the Revolution and a reduction in the powers of the president. Constitutional amendments, however, required a two-thirds majority of all members of the assembly, which the AD coalition clearly lacked. An agreement with the Socialist Party was therefore the only means by which constitutional reform could be brought about. The PS was willing to eliminate the Council of the Revolution (composed of military officers who were not accountable to the electorate) and to reduce some of the functions of the president (transferring authority to appoint senior military officers to the government, for example). The PS was also willing to soften the language of the constitution's commitment to socialism and nationalizations, but was totally unwilling to alter the substance of those commitments. Thus, the constitutional reforms approved in August 1982 (with only the leftist UDP and the PCP and its MDP ally in opposition) fell well short of the changes initially demanded by the Aliança Democrática parties. They replaced the Council of the Revolution (a vestige of the MFA) with a Constitutional Tribunal (composed of judges), a Supreme Council of National Defense, and an advisory Council of State. They also slightly reduced the powers of the president. But despite the softening of some aspects of the language of the constitution, it still retains a firm commitment to socialism and the nationalizations undertaken since April 25, 1974. The Aliança Democrática government subsequently sought to reduce the scope of the public sector through ordinary legislation, but important aspects of Portuguese public policy continue to be affected by this constitutional legacy of the process by which Portugal entered the transition to democracy—the revolution of 1974–1975.

Indeed, for some observers the basic political institutions of the regime constitute problems that have yet to be resolved.[54] As mentioned above, the electoral law predisposes the party system toward fragmentation, which, in turn, contributes to cabinet instability. Many serious problems (such as restoring stability and vigor to the economy and restructuring its large and inefficient public sector) require firm and consistent government action, and yet most governments have been unstable and short-lived. Further complicating this situation is the semi-presidential structure of the regime. The president has often intervened overtly in blocking government policy initiatives and in imposing his own preferences in the appointment of cabinets. On some occasions this has given rise to disjointed policymaking or outright deadlock. Presidential intervention of this kind fueled demands for a reduction in his powers, culminating in the constitutional reforms of 1982. But at the same time, the Portuguese president is weaker than his counterpart in the French Fifth Republic: there are greater constitutional constraints on his powers, and the Portuguese president lacks comparable levels of executive or administrative authority. Thus, Portuguese democracy is faced with a paradox. On the one hand, the fragmentation and instability of the party system undermines the effectiveness of cabinet government and would seem to imply a need for a stabilizing influence, such as that which could be exerted by a president. On the other hand, the institution of the presidency lacks the full authority necessary to perform that role effectively. As a result, many of these political leaders who had been most active in pushing for the constitutional reforms of 1982 now favor a substantial strengthening of the presidency, even to the extent of converting the Portuguese regime into a fully presidential system.

Associated with these concerns is the domination of the presidency, until quite recently, by military figures: not only did a military officer (General Eanes) hold that office throughout the regime's first decade, but the top five contenders in the 1980 presidential election included three generals, a colonel, and a major. Given the frequency of presidential intervention in political matters, this undermines the democratic responsibility of the regime itself. The election as president of Mário Soares should help to resolve this problem, but perhaps not to the satisfaction of everyone: a 1978 survey indicated that 36 percent of those interviewed believed that the armed forces should play a role "at least equal" to the role they play today in politics; another 28 percent thought their political role should be more extensive; only 10 percent favored reducing the role of the military.[55] At this early stage in the Portuguese democratization process, there is no unambiguous consensus concerning the basic political institutions of the new regime.

Update: Joining Europe

Accession of Spain and Portugal to membership in the European Community on January 1, 1986, represented a watershed in the political and economic development of both countries. The two Iberian countries, often regarded as "semi-peripheral," as only half European, or as forming a "bridge" between the developed economies and societies of Western Europe and the Third World, formalized their commitments to become integral parts of the West European community. It also posed very serious challenges to the economies of both countries that reached near-crisis proportions in the mid-1980s. In the case of Spain, this profound reorientation of the country's place in the world also involved a major dispute that went unresolved for six years: the 1981 decision by the Calvo Sotelo government to join NATO represented a major shift in Spain's national security policy that embroiled the succeeding PSOE government not only in domestic partisan conflict, but also in a rancorous dispute with the United States government as well. Let us first examine the decision to join NATO, and then move on to the more complicated issues associated with economic integration with the European Community.

NATO Membership and Relations with the United States

Portugal's early entry into the Atlantic Alliance and its long-standing defense treaty with England (which dates from the fourteenth century) have accustomed the Portuguese to military interdependence. Spain, however, had a long-standing tradition of independence and neutrality: it participated in neither the First nor the Second World War, for example. Thus, the decision by Leopoldo Calvo Sotelo and his UCD government to apply for NATO membership provoked a great controversy; even his centrist predecessor Adolfo Suárez opposed the idea. Stronger opposition was expressed by the Socialist and Communist parties. Spain's actual entry into NATO in May 1982, coupled with the lack of support for such a move among Spanish voters, induced the PSOE to capitalize upon its opposition as a campaign issue later that year. The Socialist Party pledged that, should it come to power, it would hold a popular referendum on NATO membership. This opened up a whole series of defense and foreign policy issues to partisan controversy and, in light of what appeared to be widespread opposition to membership in the alliance, placed the Socialist government in a difficult position.

Spanish opposition to NATO membership was based on several factors. First, it reversed Spain's long-standing nonaligned status. Second, the security threat posed by the Soviet Union and Warsaw Pact forces seemed much less immediate than the likelihood of military conflict with Morocco—a conflict concerning which Spain would gain no benefit from its NATO alliance. (Tensions between Morocco and Spain stem largely from the latter's retention of two small vestiges of its colonial empire: the North African coastal enclaves of Ceuta and Melilla. The Moroccan government has claimed both territories as integral components of the Moroccan nation, just as Spain has claimed sovereignty over Gibraltar.) The cost of undertaking significant changes in the Spanish army to mesh with NATO forces and strategies constituted a third reason for opposing NATO membership. Until recently, the Spanish army was ill-suited for the task of waging an international war against a technologically advanced adversary. Under Franco, one of the prime functions of the army was "the preservation of the institutional order." Integration within NATO would therefore necessitate high levels of spending on modern equipment and a concomitant reduction in the size of the infantry. These efforts would place an added burden on the state budget, would marginally increase unemployment (by demobilizing many foot soldiers and shifting budgetary resources to the purchase of imported military hardware), and would entail the traditionally dangerous task of pruning down the army's overstaffed officer corps. A fourth source of opposition to NATO membership was based on widespread rejection of the notion that strengthening the military capabilities of the Western Alliance would enhance the prospects for peace. Many Spaniards, particularly those on the left, believe that great-power confrontations and the division of Europe into two opposing blocs increased the possibility of nuclear war. The aggressive foreign policy stance of the Reagan administration during its first term, morover, frightened and alienated many Spaniards.[57]

In spite of these drawbacks and his own previous stand in opposition to NATO membership, Socialist prime minister Felipe González reversed his position and decided to favor continued membership in the Atlantic Alliance. This change was related to his realization that withdrawal from NATO would seriously damage Spanish interests in other foreign policy spheres—most importantly, relations with other EC countries.

The 1982 campaign pledge to hold a referendum on NATO membership placed the González government in a very difficult situation. Survey data repeatedly indicated that, by a majority of over two to one, given a simple choice between membership and withdrawal, most Spaniards would oppose the Atlantic Alliance. A referendum outcome consistent with these findings would have placed González in a difficult position. He would have been faced with the choice between initiating withdrawal from NATO (thereby imperiling Spain's EC application), or refusing to do so (thereby inviting retaliation at the polls by an angry electorate). To escape from this predicament, he restructured the terms of the referendum. To placate antinuclear sentiments, the government declared that it would not permit its allies to station nuclear weapons on Spanish soil. In an effort to reduce fears about a loss of Spanish sovereignty, it refused to integrate its forces into the NATO command structure. And in order to capitalize upon anti-Reagan sentiments among certain sectors of Spanish public opinion, it demanded that the United States reduce its military presence in Spain by withdrawing troops and closing down bases provided for under terms of bilateral treaties first negotiated with Franco three decades earlier. Most importantly, Prime Minister González placed the considerable force of his personal popularity behind continued NATO membership. Indeed, an enormous personal effort was required just to secure backing from his own party (by a very narrow margin at its December 1984 congress) for the new policy.

The 52.5 percent majority that actually supported the government's stand in the referendum surprised everyone and rescued the PSOE government from a very difficult situation. But by no means did it lay to rest controversy over Spain's national security policy; it merely refocused the debate on the government's pledge to reduce the American military presence in Spain. Although some U.S. bases in Spain (particularly the submarine base at Rota, near the Straits of Gibraltar) were of considerable strategic significance, they were by no means of equal importance. The airbase at Torrejón, for example, was little more than a parking lot for planes whose mission was to be immediately redeployed to Turkey in the event of an escalation of tensions with the Warsaw Pact. Torrejón was also by far the most unpopular symbol of the American military presence, given its location on the outskirts of the national capital, perilously close to the flight paths for Madrid's international airport. What is most ironic is that its removal had been negotiated in 1975; it remained a U.S. base only because of confusion in the Spanish foreign ministry caused by the death of Franco and Morocco's "green wave" invasion of the Spanish Sahara. Nonetheless, the Reagan administration fought doggedly, but unsuccessfully, to retain the base. In the protracted war of words that followed, U.S.-Spanish relations were significantly damaged. The legacy of this rancorous dispute has been a significant reduction in educational and cultural exchanges between the two countries, as well as a lingering atmosphere of mutual animosity between important policy elites in the two countries.[58]

European Community Membership and the Iberian Economies

Spain and Portugal had been attempting to enter the European Common Market ever since the 1960s. The admission of these two states, however, was delayed for decades. EEC member-states first refused to consider applications submitted by the authoritarian governments of Franco and Salazar. With the completion of the transition to democracy in both countries, other more purely economic concerns posed obstacles to their admission. Finally, in March 1985, after sixteen years of negotiations, the governments of Spain and Portugal reached general agreements with the EC that provided for their entry into the community on January 1, 1986. Neither country was under the illusion that integration with the European common market would be painless. Both economies would have to be substantially restructured in order to be competitive within a free West European market in 1992. And these adjustments would be particularly difficult given the economic crises that beset both economies in the early 1980s.

Spain and Portugal were particularly hard hit by the recessions that began in 1975 and 1981. Both economies are heavily dependent upon tourism for much of their foreign exchange (in 1988 Spain, a country of 39 million people, received over 50 million foreign visitors), and international tourism is highly sensitive to economic downturns. Moreover, Spain and Portugal had previously exported surplus labor to wealthier neighboring countries; in the case of Spain this emigration amounted to 8 percent of the total labor force.[59] In response to a drop in demand for labor, other West European countries began to repatriate "guest workers." With their return, the ranks of the unemployed in Spain and Portugal swelled enormously. In Portugal this situation was exacerbated by the return to the motherland of over 600,000 refugees from former colonies in Africa that were securing their independence. Despite these unfavorable short-term economic circumstances, governments in both countries adopted more restrictive fiscal and monetary policies, and undertook bold initiatives to make their economies more competitive.

Many structural inadequacies of the Spanish economy had been inherited from the Franquist regime. Corporatist policies adopted during the 1940s and 1950s created a huge parastate industrial sector. Firms owned wholly or partly by the government often enjoyed monopoly positions within their respective economic sectors, were protected from foreign competition by high protective tariffs, and received sizeable subsidies from the state treasury when they failed to make a profit. As a result, they were often inefficient. In certain sectors, such as steel and shipbuilding, moreover, they flooded the international market with excess production for which there was no demand. Finally, corporatist features of the labor market further undermined efficiency. Policies adopted by the Labor Ministry often held wages down artificially (to the detriment of workers), but they also greatly restricted the ability of employers to dismiss or reassign workers to more productive tasks. As a result, even though Spanish labor was cheap, the rigidity of the labor market served as a serious impediment to productivity. This situation was not corrected during the first eight years following the death of Franco. The UCD government, concerned that the transition to democracy not be disrupted by a polarization of labor relations, failed to enact significant reforms. Indeed, as a means of slowing the rate of increase in unemployment during this crucial stage in the construction of a new democratic regime, it actually increased state holdings in and subsidies to inefficient industrial firms.

In the case of Portugal, considerable damage to the competitiveness of the economy resulted from the revolution itself. The massive nationalizations of the mid-1970s transferred to the public sector large numbers of industrial firms. The government was thereby locked into an enormously costly series of annual subsidies to inefficient firms, which, in turn, required substantial foreign loans. The result was worsening of Portugal's foreign indebtedness—by 1985, outstanding foreign debt amounted to 55 percent of the country's gross national product. (In this respect, Portugal contrasts sharply with Spain, which is a creditor vis-à-vis many Latin American countries, and enjoys a huge foreign exchange reserve.) The Portuguese revolution also made the labor market more rigid, through inclusion in the constitution of provisions concerning job security and the right to work that greatly impeded the ability of employers to dismiss or reassign workers.

The Spanish socialist government initiated bold intiatives to improve the competitiveness of the economy almost immediately after taking office. An "Industrial Reconversion" plan was implemented in 1983 that closed down inefficient factories and privatized many parastate firms. The loss of manufacturing jobs immediately triggered protests on the part of the country's two largest trade unions, the Socialist UGT and the Communist Comisiones Obreras. The government attempted to soften the blow somewhat by increasing social welfare spending. But not only did it not relent in the face of labor protests, it also coupled the Industrial Reconversion program with conservative monetary policies primarily oriented toward reducing inflation and encouraging saving and investment. The PSOE also took steps to liberalize the labor market by removing some of the impediments to the reassignment or dismissal of workers. One consequence of these conservative economic policies has been an increase in unemployment (eventually reaching 21.5 percent of the labor force in 1986), and a growing belief on the part of many workers that the "Socialist" government had abandoned them by implementing policies favoring a wealthy minority.

The PSOE has had to pay a heavy political price for some of these policies. The second half of the 1980s was marked by a high level of labor unrest. Indeed, tensions with the PSOE's affiliated trade union, the UGT, were so great that a rupture in relations between party and union took place in 1989. For the first time, the UGT refused to support the PSOE in the 1989 elections, and even implicitly endorsed the Communist opposition. (It is interesting to note that the PSOE's losses in the 1989 election almost perfectly mirror the increases in voting support for the Communist-led Izquierda Unida.) And in September 1989 a new "critical faction," Social Democracy, was formed inside the PSOE in opposition to the "neoliberal" policies of the González governments.

The Spanish economy, however, has grown at an impressive rate since Spain's entry into the European Community. Following closely on the heels of an investment boom that began in 1986, the annual rate of real economic growth exceeded 5 percent from 1987 through 1989—the fastest growth rate in Europe during that time period. By early 1990 the principal economic concern of the González government involved the undesirable by-products of an overheating economy: inflation and excessive demand for imported goods. Despite this improvement in Spain's economic fortunes, serious problems remained. The level of unemployment at the end of 1989 was 16.9 percent, and workers complained bitterly that they had not been permitted to share the benefits of economic expansion. Clearly, economic restructuring was not accomplished without cost.

The Portuguese government has also taken steps to improve the competitiveness of its economy. Beginning in the mid-1980s, serious efforts were made to reduce inflation, budget deficits, and foreign indebtedness—all of which met with some success. Initially, however, steps taken by the PSD governments of Aníbal Cavaço Silva to privatize inefficient public-sector firms and liberalize the labor market were blocked by a significant obstacle—the Portuguese constitution. Clauses in the 1976 constitution defining the nationalizations of the previous two years as "irreversible" and guaranteeing the job security of workers precluded far-reaching efforts at reform. Nonetheless, without economic restructuring the Portuguese economy would not be able to survive in the free market envisioned for Europe in 1992. For this reason, the PSD was able to enlist the aid of the Socialist Party in revising the constitution in June 1989.[60] Although its structural deficiencies are more serious than those of the Spanish economy, Portugal has also benefited from EC entry. Rates of real economic growth exceeded 4 percent in 1988 and 1989.

The transition to democracy has been completed in both Spain and Portugal. Indeed, both democratic regimes appear to be fully, or at least substantially, consolidated. They have remained stable even at times of severe economic distress. In the case of Spain, democracy has remained unshaken even in the face of continued high levels of terrorist violence. In light of the waves of democratization that have recently swept over Latin America and Eastern Europe, these examples of successful democratic consolidation are worthy of careful study.

Notes

1. *El País*, International ed., December 26, 1984, p. 11.

2. This survey was administered to 5,439 Spanish citizens in the late spring and early summer of 1979 by DATA, S.A., of Madrid. It was under the direction of Goldie Shabad, Giacomo Sani, and the author and was financed by the National Science Foundation under grant No. SOC77–16451. The opinions, findings, and conclusions expressed in this article, however, are those of the author and do not necessarily reflect the views of the National Science Foundation.

3. This estimate of familiarity with the Basque language is based upon self-reports by respondents and is almost certainly an overestimate of actual fluency in Euskera. The percentage of our respondents in the three provinces of Euskadi (including immigrants from other parts of Spain) who claimed to speak Euskera was 31 percent. Other estimates (based on actual language use rather than on self-reports, which are subject to exaggeration) set this figure below 20 percent.

4. Richard Robinson, *Contemporary Portugal* (London: George Allen & Unwin, 1979), p. 38.

5. See Richard Gunther, Giacomo Sani, and Goldie Shabad, *Spain after Franco: The Making of a Competitive Party System* (Berkeley: University of California Press, 1986), chap. 6.

6. Angel Carrión Garzarán et al., "La Población Española y su Territorio," in Fundación FOESSA, ed., *Estudios Sociológicos sobre la Situación Social de España, 1975* (Madrid: Editorial Euramérica, 1976), p. 70.

7. Robinson, *Contemporary Portugal*, pp. 156–57.

8. See Antonio de Pablo Masa, "Estratificación," in FOESSA, *Estudios Sociológicos*, p. 758.

9. See Robinson, *Contemporary Portugal*, pp. 35–38, and Richard Gunther and Roger Blough, "Religious Conflict and Consensus in Spain: Tale of Two Constitutions," *World Affairs* 143 (Spring 1981): 366–412.

10. Stanley Payne, *The Spanish Revolution* (New York: Norton, 1970), p. 174.

11. Robinson, *Contemporary Portugal*, p. 36.

12. For Spain, 1930–1970, Instituto Nacional de Estadística (hereafter INE), *Anuario Estadístico, 1976*, p. 53; for Portugal, 1930–1970, Robinson, *Contemporary Portugal*,

p. 136; for both countries, 1980 (Spanish figure is for 1979), *World Statistics in Brief*, UN Statistical Pocketbook, 7th ed. (New York: United Nations, 1983).

13. *Encyclopaedia Britannica*; and Gunther, Sani, and Shabad, *Spain after Franco*.

14. For 1960, Robinson, *Contemporary Portugal*, p. 140; for 1977, World Bank, *1979 World Bank Atlas: Population, Per Capita Produce and Growth Rates* (Washington, D.C.: World Bank, 1979), p. 6.

15. World Bank, *1979 World Bank Atlas*, p. 6.

16. For Portugal, 1930, Robinson, *Contemporary Portugal*, p. 159; for Spain, 1930, INE, *Anuario Estadístico, 1976*, p. 61; for Spain and Portugal in 1980, U.S. Department of Commerce, *Statistical Abstract of the United States, 1982*, p. 83; 1970 figures for the rest of the world from FOESSA, *Estudios Sociológicos*, p. 211.

17. Robinson, *Contemporary Portugal*, p. 167.

18. Ibid., pp. 167–76.

19. Ibid., p. 126.

20. Richard Gunther, *Public Policy in a No-Party State: Spanish Planning and Budgeting in the Twilight of the Franquist Era* (Berkeley: University of California Press, 1980), pp. 49 and 171. Percentage of GNP from 1973.

21. See John L. Hammond, "The Armed Forces Movement and the Portuguese Revolution: Two Steps Forward, One Step Back," *Journal of Political and Military Sociology* 10 (Spring 1982):77.

22. Robinson, *Contemporary Portugal*, p. 220.

23. Thomas C. Bruneau, "Patterns of Politics in Portugal since the April Revolution," in Jorge Braga de Macedo and Simon Serfaty, eds., *Portugal since the Revolution: Economic and Political Perspectives* (Boulder, Colo.: Westview, 1981), pp. 14–15.

24. Rodney J. Morrison, *Portugal: Revolutionary Change in an Open Economy* (Boston: Auburn House, 1981), p. 48.

25. See Robert Harvey, *Portugal: Birth of a Democracy* (London: Macmillan, 1978), pp. 64–65.

26. Robinson, *Contemporary Portugal*, p. 240.

27. Excerpts from the Portuguese constitution cited in Robinson, *Contemporary Portugal*, p. 257.

28. Ibid., p. 259.

29. Ibid., p. 260.

30. *Encyclopaedia Britannica, Book of the Year, 1977*, p. 568.

31. José María Maravall, *La Política de la Transición* (Madrid: Taurus Ediciones, 1981), p. 27.

32. Jordi Solé Tura, "La Constitución y la Lucha por el Socialismo," in Gregorio Peces Barba et al., eds., *La Izquierda y la Constitución* (Barcelona: Ediciones Taula de Canvi, 1978), pp. 19–20.

33. Among the most negative consequences of the political amnesties, for example, was the subsequent resumption of involvement in terrorist activities of some of those released from jail.

34. *Informaciones*, April 6, 1978.

35. The classic work on this variety of politics is Arend Lijphart, *The Politics of Accommodation: Pluralism and Democracy in the Netherlands* (Berkeley and Los Angeles: University of California Press, 1968). For a more detailed analysis of the application of these principles to the Spanish constituent process, see Richard Gunther, "Constitution-Making in Spain," in Richard Simeon, ed., *The Politics of Constitution-Making: Varieties of National Experience* (London: Macmillan, 1984).

36. This conclusion is drawn from over two dozen extensive in-depth interviews with PCE officials.

37. Cited by Eusebio Mujal-León, "Portugal: The PCP and the Portuguese Revolution," in David E. Albright, ed., *Communism and Political Systems in Western Europe* (Boulder, Colo: Westview, 1979), p. 177.

38. Robinson, *Contemporary Portugal*, p. 236.

39. Ibid., p. 228.

40. Ibid., p. 206.

41. Ibid., p. 254.

42. For an extensive history and analysis of ETA, see Robert P. Clark, *The Basque Insurgents: ETA, 1952–1980* (Madison: University of Wisconsin Press, 1984).

43. Partido Socialista Obrero Español (PSOE), *27th Congreso del PSOE* (Barcelona: Avance, 1977), pp. 115–16.

44. Robinson, *Contemporary Portugal*, p. 234.

45. These and the following Portuguese survey data from Thomas C. Bruneau, "Patterns of Politics in Portugal since the April Revolution." A more extensive analysis and discussion of these data may be seen in Thomas C. Bruneau and Alex MacLeod, *Politics in Contemporary Portugal: Parties and the Consolidation of Democracy* (Boulder, Colo.: Lynne Rienner Publishers, 1986).

46. Ibid., p. 1.

47. For explanations of this proportional representation system, see Gunther, Sani, and Shabad, *Spain after Franco*, chap. 6; or Douglas Rae, *The Political Consequences of Electoral Laws* (New Haven, Conn.: Yale University Press, 1967).

48. Cabinet stability in Spain is further reinforced by the constitutional requirement that governments can be toppled by a "constructive vote of no-confidence." This provision, borrowed from the Basic Law of West Germany, would have meant that the Suárez government of 1977, for example, could only have been overturned (except in the case of a breakdown of UCD internal discipline) by a voting coalition among all the major parties in the Congress of Deputies, which, at the same time, would install in office a succeeding government. Needless to say, the probability that the Communist Party and the right-wing Alianza Popular could reach agreement on such a matter was very slight.

49. For a preliminary analysis of voting behavior in the 1982 election, see Richard Gunther, "Un Análisis Preliminario del Realineamiento del Sistema de Partidos Políticos en España," *Revista de Estudios Políticos* 45 (May–June 1985):7–41.

50. For a more thorough survey of current developments pertaining to regionalism in Spain, see Goldie Shabad and Richard Gunther, "Spanish Regionalism in the 1980's," in

Stanley G. Payne et al., eds., *Europe in the Eighties: A Comprehensive Assessment of Politics, Economics, and Culture*, (Princeton, N.J.: Karz-Cohl, forthcoming).

51. These data are derived from a postelection survey (conducted by DATA, S.A., of Madrid, under the direction of the author in collaboration with Juan Linz, Hans-Jurgen Puhle, José Ramón Montero, Giacomo Sani, and Goldie Shabad) of 5,463 interviews throughout the country, with oversamples drawn in Euskadi, Galicia, Catalunya, and Navarra. The study was financed with the generous support of the Stiftung Volkswagenwerk of West Germany.

52. "Portugal: A Survey," *The Economist*, May 28, 1977, p. 19.

53. Robinson, *Contemporary Portugal*, pp. 265–66.

54. These conclusions were drawn from extensive discussions with two former Portuguese government ministers and a former prime minister held in October 1984.

55. Bruneau and MacLeod, *Politics in Contemporary Portugal*.

56. "The New Spain: A Survey," *The Economist*, April 2, 1977.

57. A public opinion poll published by the influential daily, *El País*, in June 1983, for example, revealed that almost 40 percent of the Spanish population regarded nuclear war as "probable," and by a two-to-one margin believed that such a war would be started by the United States rather than the Soviet Union.

58. It should be pointed out that responsibility for this deterioration in relations did not lie exclusively with the U.S. government. The Spanish foreign minister, Francisco Fernández Ordóñez, often leaked details of the negotiations to the press—thereby precluding concessions and compromises on key issues—and demagogically used the dispute to enhance his own reputation as a patriotic defender of Spain's national interests. In this respect, his behavior was consistent with the role he played in the destruction of the UCD in the late 1970s and early 1980s.

59. Gunther, *Public Policy in a No-Party State*, p. 106.

60. It is interesting to note that a discussion with two former PSD ministers and a former prime minister in 1984 indicated that one of the reasons why politicians of the center and the center-right were pushing so hard for EC entry was that it would be useful in dislodging the aforementioned socialist provisions from the constitution. They fully admitted that neither Portuguese industry nor agriculture could successfully compete with other EC economies, and stated that a major benefit of EC membership would be to subject inefficient Portuguese firms to the sometimes dire consequences of market discipline. Thus, in order to survive economically it would be necessary to become efficient, which would, in turn, require revising the 1976 constitution.

Suggested Readings

Bermeo, Nancy Gina. *The Revolution Within the Revolution: Workers' Control in Rural Portugal*. Princeton, N.J.: Princeton University Press, 1986.

Braga de Macedo, Jorge, and Serfaty, Simon, eds., *Portugal since the Revolution: Economic and Political Perspectives*. Boulder, Colo.: Westview Press, 1981.

Bruneau, Thomas C. *Politics in Contemporary Portugal: Parties and the Consolidation of Democracy.* Boulder, Colo: Lynne Rienner Publishers, 1986.

Carr, Raymond, and Fusi, Juan Pablo. *Spain: Dictatorship to Democracy.* London: Allen & Unwin, 1979.

Fields, Rona M. *The Portuguese Revolution and the Armed Forces Movement.* New York: Praeger, 1976.

Gunther, Richard. *Public Policy in a No-Party State: Spanish Planning and Budgeting in the Twilight of the Franquist Era.* Berkeley: University of California Press, 1980.

Gunther, Richard; Sani, Giacomo; and Shabad, Goldie. *Spain after Franco: The Making of a Competitive Party System.* Berkeley: University of California Press, 1986.

Harvey, Robert. *Portugal: Birth of a Democracy.* London: Macmillan, 1978.

Linz, Juan. "Early State-Building and Late Peripheral Nationalism." In Stein Rokkan and S.N. Eisenstadt, eds., *Building States and Nations.* Beverly Hills, Calif.: Sage, 1973.

———. "Europe's Southern Frontier: Evolving Trends Toward What?" *Daedalus,* Winter 1979.

———. "From Primordialism to Nationalism." In Edward A. Tiryakian and Ronald Rogowski, eds., *New Nationalisms of the Developed West: Toward Explanation.* Hemel Hempstead, Eng.: Allen & Unwin, 1983.

———. "The New Spanish Party System." In Richard Rose, ed., *Electoral Participation.* Beverly Hills, Calif.: Sage, 1980.

Livermore, H. V. *Portugal: A Short History.* Edinburgh: Edinburgh University Press, 1973.

Mailer, Phil. *Portugal: The Impossible Revolution.* London: Solidarity, 1977.

Morrison, Rodney J. *Portugal: Revolutionary Change in an Open Economy.* Boston: Auburn House, 1981.

Payne, Stanley G. "Catalan and Basque Nationalism." *Contemporary History* 6 (1979).

———. *A History of Spain and Portugal.* 2 vols. Madison: University of Wisconsin Press, 1973.

Porch, Douglas. *The Portuguese Armed Forces and the Revolution.* Stanford: Hoover Institution Press, 1977.

Robinson, Richard. *Contemporary Portugal.* London: Allen & Unwin, 1979.

Shabad, Goldie, and Gunther, Richard. "Language, Nationalism, and Political Conflict in Spain." *Comparative Politics* (July 1982).

Vicens-Vives, Jaime. *Approaches to the History of Spain.* Berkeley: University of California Press, 1967.

8

Italy

Norman Kogan

Italy is an old nation but a young state. Its current political regime and constitution are even younger, dating from the end of World War II. The lengthy history of the Italian people still affects contemporary behavior and culture, including political culture and political behavior. From pre-Greek and pre-Roman eras through the classical age and the medieval and Renaissance centuries, the physical remains of millennia are visibly and psychologically present in the Italian consciousness.[1] The old Greek and Roman skepticism is renewed in current political attitudes of suspicion toward the political process and pessimistic assumptions of what can be expected from government.

The Italian state as we know it today was created in the wars of the Risorgimento in the mid-nineteenth century and came into existence in 1861. Its creators for the most part were young, liberal, educated aristocrats and professionals; the peasant masses of the peninsula remained indifferent and unknowing, rooted in their local communities. In the words of Massimo D'Azeglio, one of the heroes of the Risorgimento, "We have made Italy, now we have to make Italians." The success of this second duty is still limited. Even today only about 40 percent of the population routinely and normally speaks standard Italian. Local and regional identifications run strong. Northerners look on southerners as a drain on society and the economy. Southerners see northerners as arrogant exploiters. In recent times there have been vast migrations of people inside, as well as outside, the nation, from the countryside to the city, from the south to the center and north. Periodically movements erupt to "send them back where they came from." The movements rarely get far politically, but they foster resentment. Only since the 1950s has substantial national progress been made in bringing large numbers of people into an awareness of the wider national community. The impact of the migrations has been reinforced by national radio and television networks. The legal country and the real country are finally merging into one.

Between unification in 1861 and the advent of fascism from 1922 to 1925, Italy was governed by what many historians have labeled a "liberal oligarchy." Some have written off this period as a failure because it ended in a fascist dictatorship. The writer Giustino Fortunato noted that fascism was a revelation, not a revolution, implying that fascism merely revealed the true nature of its predecessor. Other historians have seen the liberal period as a preparation for fascism; still others, as the gradual development of modern democracy, a development cut short by the strains of World War I and the postwar economic collapse.[2] In that pre–World War I age political participation slowly expanded to encompass universal manhood suffrage by 1912. The economy grew, bursting into a first industrial revolution in the decade after 1896. The foundations of an overseas empire were laid, and nominally Italy was recognized as a great power. As the weakest great power it pursued a strategy of shifting alliances and acquired a reputation for undependability. Benito Mussolini continued this strategy during the fascist period. The reputation continues to haunt Italy today, but with little justification.

The enthusiasm generated by unification gave way to cynicism fostered by corruption. In the last decades of the nineteenth century domestic politics became a series of maneuvers to build parliamentary majorities with the instruments of patronage and the spoils system. In Italian history these decades are identified as the age of transformism, when political principles and ideals were abandoned in the chase for material gains and social honors. The fascist period extended these deleterious practices, for the regime's survival depended on taking care of the people who could threaten it. Fascism was a failure as a totalitarian system. The masses of the population never became true believers, though neither did they become committed antifascists. They were never converted into the new fascist man, *homo fascistus*, because they never lived up to Mussolini's precepts. They did not, to cite the Duce's famous slogans, "believe, obey, fight"; they did not think it was "better to live one day as a lion than a hundred years as a sheep"; they did not agree that "Mussolini is always right." So the Duce had to make deals and compromises with the Italian elites: the monarchy, the Roman Catholic church, the armed forces, the bureaucracy, and Confindustria, the organization of the northern big businessmen. The elites came to terms with the regime, but never became absorbed into it. They collaborated until the fascist dictatorship went down to defeat in World War II, then they got rid of it. Mussolini was overthrown on July 25, 1943, by a military coup carried out by generals on instructions from King Victor Emanuel III, who had brought the Duce to power 21 years earlier. The king, like most of the Italian people, was neither fascist nor antifascist. Only a small minority of Italians were one or the other, and it was a dedicated group of antifascists, composing several political parties, on whom fell the task of rebuilding the country from the ruins of defeat.

Governmental Structures

The founders of the post–World War II republic were the surviving leaders of the prefascist parliamentary monarchy, backed by a younger generation of antifascists whose opposition to the dictatorship had crystallized in the late 1930s. The monarchy had been abolished in a popular referendum on June 2, 1946. These leaders represented a spectrum of political forces that had flourished in the early 1920s before being suppressed by fascism in 1925. The constitution of the Italian republic that they produced and that came into force on January 1, 1948, contained a mixture of Catholic, Marxist, and liberal democratic principles reflecting the compromises worked out in the Constituent Assembly. The major parties in the assembly were the Christian Democratic (DC), Socialist (PSI), and Communist (PCI) parties; they remain the major parties today. A myriad of smaller parties was also present, but liberals, predominant in the politics of the decades before World War I, were numerically weak and divided. Their influence depended, and still depends, on individual leaders of stature and the absorption of liberal doctrines by the mass parties. The three or four small lay parties hold the balance in multiparty coalition governments since none of the large parties can win a majority of votes on its own.

The constitution provides for a parliamentary democracy and recognizes the modern welfare state with its costly variety of economic, social, and cultural functions. It encourages a multiparty system by providing for election machinery based on large multimember electoral districts. Candidates chosen from party lists are elected by proportional representation plus a preference vote. The preference vote, which permits the elector to select four or five choices from the party list, encourages internal party factionalism because each election consists of two contests: the competition among the parties and the rivalry within each party for the preference vote. In some of the big parties, particularly the DC but not the PCI, factionalism has reached pathological proportions. Each faction is tightly organized under national leaders and regional and provincial officers, with its own press service, its own journals, its own headquarters, and, finally, its own national and local conventions.

The organization of the government is fairly standard for a parliamentary democracy. The national legislature is bicameral; the Senate and the Chamber of Deputies have identical powers. Though the systems for electing the members of the two houses differ, the results of the elections produce an almost identical distribution of party strength in each chamber. Parliament has the powers customary in a parliamentary system, with one exceptional provision: except for major acts specified in the constitution, bills can come into law by being passed in the appropriate committees of the two houses and then going to the president of the republic for signature without ever being debated or passed by the full houses. Over 80 percent of Italian legislation is never acted on by Parliament as a whole.

The executive branch consists of the standard tripartite division: the president of the republic, the cabinet, and a vast national bureaucracy. The cabinet is composed overwhelmingly of deputies or senators. Occasionally it may include a nonparliamentary technician. It begins functioning after receiving a vote of confidence from Parliament and leaves office by resigning. The cabinet resigns when it loses a vote of confidence in Parliament or when Parliament is dissolved for new elections. But the most important reason by far that cabinets resign in postwar Italy is internal disagreement, occurring when the parties directly or indirectly supporting the governments fall out or when the factions within the parties do likewise. The average life span of Italian governments has been about ten months.

Nevertheless, the instability of Italian governments is more apparent than real. The Christian Democratic Party has dominated all postwar governments. From December 1945 to July 1981 every prime minister was a Christian Democrat. Even after 1981 Christian Democrats have held most of the key cabinet posts. On paper, alternatives to Christian Democratic rule are possible; in fact, there is no way of forming a government without the DC.

The president of the republic fulfills the usual symbolic functions of a head of state in a parliamentary system, but in Italy he does something more. Not all of his actions are controlled by the government; he has a modicum of independent authority. He can express his personal opinions in public statements, not just the opinions of the government then in power. He has a limited scope for making independent appointments to a few positions in public life; he can veto bills, which then must be passed or rejected by Parliament in a special vote. Behind the scenes, he can put pressure on politicians. His most important role is forming a new government. Since Italy does not have a majority party with a clear leader, the president has to play politics in the formation of cabinet coalitions and the choice of the cabinet ministers. He can continue to play politics after a government is formed unless there is a dominant prime minister to keep him in his place. Since the early years of the republic when Alcide De Gasperi was the head of government, there has been no dominant prime minister, and Italian presidents, depending on their inclinations, have had opportunities for maneuver and intervention in political processes.

The Italian bureaucracy is big and inefficient—in its upper ranks, even arrogant—and is often charged with bias and corruption. Short of qualified professionals at the higher levels, it is overstaffed at the menial custodial and clerical levels where such posts often attract people who seek only a secure lifetime stipend, for public employees are never fired. Italian governments have routinely used the bureaucracy to absorb surplus labor and coincidentally to reduce unemployment figures. Northerners complain that it is loaded with southerners. The public claims that bureaucrats act only when improperly influenced or bribed. The bureaucracy has a poor reputation in Italy, a reputation reduced further by numerous strikes, often wildcat in nature, that disrupt public services. To get anything done requires long periods of waiting in line, the filling out of numerous documents, and endless patience. A large percentage of government employees moonlight on other jobs to keep up with inflation, neglecting their major duties in the process.

The structures and tables of organization of the bureaucracy were inherited from predecessor prefascist and fascist regimes. They have not been really modernized, just expanded. Although Italy is a modern welfare state committed to providing the full panoply of services demanded in the contemporary world, the bureaucratic roles remain primarily regulatory and record-keeping. Large amounts of money appropriated by Parliament for government remain unspent because the bureaucracy is unable to organize itself to implement programs effectively. Positive efforts at accomplishment are overwhelmed by the amount of time consumed and the number of people engaged in checking on others. Nevertheless, things get done, and the system works for those who know the right people in the right places. A recommendation from an influential personage is the key to action, however slow. During the 1980s, the quality of public services has worsened, the resentments of government employees concerning their status have grown, and the annoyance of the general public has increased.

The Italian judicial system is also an inheritance from an earlier age. The judges are civil servants who enter a judicial career by competitive examinations after completing law school. Few Italians, however, really believe that this process is aboveboard. Most are sure that the victors used influence. They have the same conviction about the outcomes of examinations for entry into any branch of the public service. The public no more believes in the objectivity and disinterest of judges than it does of other civil servants. In the course of a career, judges will also serve as investigators, prosecutors, and administrators in the Ministry of Justice. Assignments and promotion will depend on seniority, on performance, and on having the correct political attitudes. Italian judges are bitterly divided into associations identified with radical, moderate, or conservative judicial and political philosophies. They are often accused of deciding cases on the basis of political and cultural biases. In the meantime there are too few judges for the growing caseload; the dockets are backed up for years.

The Italian judicial hierarchy is structured on the traditional French model, with the Court of Cassation at the top. Beyond the hierarchy is the one postwar innovation, a special Constitutional Court with the power of judicial review. Its fifteen justices, who serve staggered twelve-year terms, are selected by a process of appointment and election: five are appointed by the president of the republic, five are elected by judges of the higher court system, and five are elected by Parliament in joint session. Party deals and bargaining are involved. As a consequence, the justices are identified with various sectors of the political spectrum. Over the years, this court has thrown out many laws left over from the fascist period. It has on occasion declared parliamentary acts unconstitutional and overturned judicial interpretations by the regular court system. The Constitutional Court also has jurisdiction in disputes between the national and regional governments. Its overall record clearly indicates a pronational bias. Its record also indicates a strong defense of civil rights and liberal democratic principles.[3]

Political Parties

Italy has been called a "parties state." The label indicates that the leaders in control of the party apparatus, not the holders of government office, make the basic decisions. Frequently these are the same people, but most of their power comes from the party. This is particularly true of the Communist Party, which, though very much present in Parliament, has not been in the national government since 1947. Inside Christian Democracy, governmental office is significant because the DC has dominated the government throughout the postwar period. A leading businessman once described his way of dealing with the government: on tactical issues he went to the chairmen of the parliamentary committees or to directors general in the ministries; on strategic issues he went to the party secretaries.

All the parties are organized on the classic Marxist model, even those with no Marxist heritage. At the national level the top body is the party congress, which meets every two or three years. The congress elects a central committee to supervise party affairs between congresses; the central committee chooses an executive committee (*direzione*), other committees, and the party secretary general and deputy secretaries, who control the organization on a day-to-day basis. The Socialist Party recently changed its rules to provide for direct election of the secretary general by the party congress. Decisions by the party congress are presumably binding on party members, including parliamentarians, cabinet ministers, and undersecretaries. The leadership normally gets its way unless intense factional disputes block policy choices.

Regional, provincial, local, and sectional party organizations usually reflect the national model. The key subnational body is the provincial federation, and the struggle for control and nominations is located there. Regional governments in Italy are relatively new and only recently institutionalized, so the same can be said of the regional party organizations. They have not, and may never, become important party organizations in their own right.

Italy has numerous political parties. The DC, PCI, and PSI have been the dominant parties throughout the postwar period. In the 1983 parliamentary election, the vote for the Chamber of Deputies was distributed as follows: the DC received almost 33 percent of the total, the PCI almost 30 percent, and the PSI 11 percent. The smaller parties shared the remaining 26 percent. Table 8.1 not only shows these results in more detail but also serves to emphasize the many political parties in Italy today. Party strength can be measured in other ways also; for example, in the number of card-carrying members. Under this criterion the DC and the PSI rank second and third respectively. The PCI, with approximately 1.8 million members, is at the same time the largest of the Italian parties and the world's biggest nonruling Communist party. Historically the parties have relied on major voting support from subcultural blocs: the Catholics, the Marxists, and the numerically smaller laic bourgeoisie. Parties have always appealed to voters beyond their core support groups, and in recent times it can be said that, in varying degrees, the three largest parties have become catchalls. The tendency of the DC and PCI to squeeze out the smaller parties reached a peak in 1976; but since then both parties have declined, and the smaller ones have gained strength. Although traditional labels are inadequate, they can be used to categorize the smaller parties into three groups: the neofascists (MSI) on the right; the Liberals (PLI), Republicans (PRI), and Social Democrats (PSDI) in the moderate center along with the DC and PSI; and the Radicals (PR) and Proletarian Democracy (DP) located to the left of the PCI. The largest of these parties is the neofascist MSI, which in 1983 received about 7 percent of the vote. The Republicans followed with 5 percent. The small parties, along with the PSI, provide the extra support necessary to create and sustain a cabinet, or to permit a minority DC government to function.

Another classification distinguishes between the parties within and the parties outside the constitutional arch. Within the arch are those parties that endorse the existing constitutional order based on the principles of parliamentary democracy. They are presumably available for inclusion in parliamentary majorities and are potential members of a government. Only the antisystem parties, currently identified as the MSI, the PR, and the DP, are outside the arch.[4] There are the Italians who reject the legitimacy of the PCI's inclusion, nevertheless, and certainly since the mid-1970s, the Communists have been treated by the other parties as members of the constitutional arch. Between 1976 and 1979 the PCI, indirectly and later directly, was part of the majority in Parliament that supported the DC minority cabinets. It claimed, although it did not receive, membership in the cabinets. It did receive important posts in the parliamentary machinery: committee chairmanships and deputy chairmanships. Since 1976 a Communist has been the speaker of the Chamber of Deputies. The party has

Table 8.1   Election Results for the Chamber of Deputies, 1979 and 1983

Party	1979		1983		DIFFERENCE	
	Percentage	Seats	Percentage	Seats	Percentage points	Seats
Christian Democracy (DC)	38.3	262	32.9	225	-5.4	-37
Italian Communist Party (PCI)	30.4	201	29.9	198	-1.9	-9
Democratic Party of Proletarian Unity (PDUP)*	1.4	6				
Italian Socialist Party (PSI)	9.8	62	11.4	73	+1.6	+11
Italian Social Democratic Party (PSDI)	3.8	20	4.1	23	+0.3	+3
Italian Republican Party (PRI)	3.0	16	5.1	29	+2.1	+13
Italian Liberal Party (PLI)	1.9	9	2.9	16	+1.0	+7
Italian Social Movement—National Right (MSI)	5.3	30	6.8	42	+1.5	+12
Radical Party (PR)	3.5	18	2.2	11	-1.3	-7
Proletarian Democracy* (DP)	—	—	1.5	7	+1.5	+7
South Tyrol People's Party (SVP)	0.6	4	0.5	3	-0.1	-1
Others	2.0	2	2.4	3	+0.4	+1

SOURCE: *Il Popolo*, June 29, 1983.

*In 1979 the Democratic Party of Proletarian Unity was in an electoral coalition with a number of extraparliamentary left groups who together won six seats. In 1983 it split with the others and joined with the Communists. The others ran under the Proletarian Democracy label and won seven seats.

been proclaiming its commitment to democracy throughout the postwar period, and since 1956 has repeated the slogan, "The Italian way to socialism is the democratic way to socialism." Although numerous Italians do not trust the PCI's proclamations, there is no question that its presence can be found in all areas of Italian life. Several regional governments, more than 40 percent of the provincial governments, and many of the largest Italian cities are controlled by coalitions in which the PCI is the leading party.

Contemporary Political Issues

Testifying before a parliamentary committee at the end of January 1984, Giovanni Spadolini, secretary general of the Republican Party and prime minister in 1981–1982, identified three major calamities of contemporary Italian life: inflation, terrorism, and corruption. Behind each of these is a variety of contributory elements, serving to aggravate the issues and the atmosphere in which they are fought out.

In 1949–1950, after a few years concentrated on reconstruction, the Italian economy entered two decades of boom that constituted a veritable second industrial revolution. The "economic miracle," as it was called, literally transformed the country. In 1946 about 45 percent of the labor force was still in agriculture, forestry, and fishing. By 1981 this figure was down to about 12 percent, and in 1987 the majority of the work force was engaged in tertiary services. Italy is now the seventh industrial power of the Western world. During the 1950s the country had the second most rapid rate of real growth in that world, exceeded only by Japan; in the 1960s West Germany moved into second place.

The year 1970 witnessed the end of the miracle when a slowdown began that has continued sporadically until 1987. In subsequent years there have been periods of stop and go, recession and recovery, almost full employment, and high youth unemployment. Beginning in 1973 double-digit inflation became standard; the peak rate was 21.2 percent in 1980. In 1984 inflation was approximately 11 percent, and a 4 percent inflation rate was forecast for 1987.

The gains in the good years were not distributed equally, either by economic category or by geographic location. Industry and financial services plunged ahead while agriculture lagged behind. The rich prospered, the number of well-to-do families increased greatly, and the poor were fewer and were less poor, but the gap between the poor and the others did not shrink. Italy is often called a dual economy, comprising an advanced north and center and a backward south. This is an oversimplification. In fact Italy is divided into many more economic regions than the dualism argument accepts. Within the south there are substantial differences in economic levels, particularly between coastal zones and the mountainous interior. The other major areas also vary widely. Parts of Italy have a general level of well-being that compares favorably with the prosperous zones of northwestern Europe.

A growing phenomenon has been the expansion of the submerged, or underground, economy. In many parts of Italy this development has revived cottage industries, small shops, and artisan combinations. Underground entrepreneurs escape the burdens of taxes, fringe benefits and social costs, and high wage rates. Their flexibility enables them to adjust to new market conditions. They avoid government and trade union regulations. The vitality of the submerged sector has kept the Italian economy competitive and responsive to changing market conditions. Some economists believe it produces from 20 to 30 percent of the gross national product, which official statistics consistently underestimate. All the political forces of the country have deplored the phenomenon but do nothing about it, for they have had no wish to destroy the mechanism that has been helping to keep the country solvent.

The high rate of inflation, however, has created a major political crisis. Italy is open to European and world markets; over 50 percent of its GNP is derived from foreign trade. The nation has little in the way of basic natural resources; it must import over 80 percent of its energy, many foodstuffs, critical raw materials, and much advanced technology. To pay for these imports it must export, and the consistently higher rates of inflation compared with those of its European and extra-European competitors threaten Italian competitiveness. In counteraction the government has devalued the lira to keep Italian products cheap abroad, but devaluation only raises import costs at home and becomes a further stimulus to inflation.

Italy has relatively little control over import costs since they are determined by world market prices or by European Community regulations. In any case these costs are only a minor cause of inflation. The two major causes are spiraling production costs and the enormous government expenditures that generate public deficits in the neighborhood of 16 percent of GNP. (Compare this with the U.S. deficit of about 5 percent of its GNP.) The major political struggle over economic policy in the 1980s revolves around these issues. The *scala mobile*, an indexing formula based on the consumer price index and guaranteeing workers 100 percent indexing of their wages every three months, also guarantees high labor costs and thus high production costs. In addition the trade unions negotiate collective bargaining contracts that raise wages above the guaranteed automatic increases. To maintain labor peace in the 1970s the government endorsed the formula revision that produced the current arrangement. Now the government is trapped since it controls many of the large firms as well as most of the banking assets of the country. Close to 40 percent of Italy's GNP is the result of government-controlled operations. Furthermore, all social welfare payments benefit from *scala mobile*.

In 1982 the Confindustria, representing the large private firms, announced that beginning with 1983 it would no longer accept the current formula. It argued that high labor costs would drive Italian firms out of business. The trade unions responded that the *scala mobile* was untouchable. In January 1983 the minister of labor, Vincenzo Scotti, negotiated a contract settlement that turned out to be a travesty since each side claimed it had been misinformed and had never agreed to its terms. After a year of tense truce the battle was rejoined in January 1984. The five-party government, led by Socialist prime minister Bettino Craxi, was divided on what to do. The Communists, who in 1977 and 1978 when they were supporting an earlier DC cabinet preached austerity to their followers, in 1984 as the leading opposition party backed union resistance to the hilt. The three major union federations, each loosely linked to one of the mass parties, are divided among themselves. Furthermore, the labor movement has been weakened in recent years. Its combative capacity is limited by defections, hostile public opinion, and undisciplined strikes. Consequently employers may well believe that the 1980s are the decade for the showdown. No one expects the elimination of indexing; what is at stake is a revision of the formula to make it less inflationary. The established formula, moreover, has contributed to the expansion of the submerged economy and to increased unemployment as firms compensate for high labor costs by becoming more capital intensive or contracting out parts of their operations. The cabinet in the meantime preaches that it is now time to move toward an incomes policy that would, in the long run, link wages to productivity rather than prices.

The major drain on the government treasury was the expenditures of the modern welfare state, which became another key political issue. Two aspects of this issue were subsidies to deficit operations and transfer payments. The government pours out huge subsidies to government-owned firms and industries to cover their deficits and to keep their workers on the payroll. No firm of any size is permitted to fail. Private employers, too, have received indirect subsidies to cover operating losses. By 1983, however, this policy had reached crisis proportions. The public deficit was approaching 16 percent of GNP. Domestic and international pressures were growing to have aged plants closed down. For example, the European Community, in the face of a lengthy international steel crisis, imposed production quotas on its members that required Italy to terminate steel operations in Genoa or Naples, or in both cities. The political parties, the trade unions, and the local politicians and business associations of these metropolitan areas were exerting counterpressures to keep the plants open. With an official national unemployment rate close to 10 percent, the government was searching for an escape from the dilemma.

Equally critical was the issue of the tremendous welfare burden. The huge costs of the pension programs and the national health services were draining the public treasury. These payments are all fully indexed and, under the standard formula, were increasing annually at a rate equal to or more than the rate of inflation. A large part of the population was feeding at the public trough. More Italians were receiving disability pensions than were receiving old age pensions. In the autumn of 1983 the government announced some cutbacks in a variety of welfare payments, as well as a reduction in the level of grants given to regional and local governments that would force those subnational governments to reduce services. Not surprisingly, political pressures quickly built up to resist welfare reductions.

Alternatives were not easily available. Cuts in other parts of the national budget could not provide resources. Italy has had the second lowest defense budget of the NATO countries for most of the postwar period, so the defense budget could not be raided. Even though taxes could be collected more efficiently, Italian collection procedures have improved so substantially in recent years that to gain further large increases in tax revenues would require destroying the submerged economy, which nobody really wanted to do. In the fall of 1983 the government introduced bills to create new taxes on income-producing real estate, both rental apartments and office space, and to pardon those who had failed to pay taxes in previous years on illegal construction if they made a one-time payment. Both bills were blocked in Parliament at the end of 1983, the second on the ground that it penalized the honest by condoning illegality and immorality, and the first because it would further discourage construction and thereby prolong the recession.

Some Italian politicians proposed eliminating the income tax exemption on the interest paid on Treasury bonds. The exemption, however, is what makes the bonds attractive. Without it the government's borrowing requirements would be harder to satisfy. More money would have to be printed, and inflationary pressures would increase. Italian parliamentarians were trapped. They knew that current or improved welfare programs would have to be paid for by the Italian people. They also knew that the Italian people wanted the programs but did not want to pay the price.[5] This predicament is hardly unique to Italy.

Most Italian regimes since unification have not been popular. The distinction between the "legal country" and the "real country" goes back to the nineteenth century. There is a long tradition of being "against the government"—any government. In the late nineteenth century the Catholic and Marxist movements claimed to represent the real country against the "liberal oligarchy" that controlled the legal country. Since World War II, Catholic and Marxist parties have dominated the state, but the hostility to the political system remains. It is especially focused against the parties. Its extreme expression is terrorism.

The terrorist movement is the outgrowth of the student movement that swept continental Europe in 1968 and 1969. Originating as an effort to reform the universities, the student movement escalated into an attack on society as a whole. It was a rejection of the modern welfare state with its materialistic consumer values, its complacency, and its enjoyment of the rewards of the economic miracle. The students were enamored of the exploits of the Third World revolutionaries. Their heroes were Che Guevara, Ho Chi Minh, Mao Zedong, and the Chinese cultural revolutionists of those years. In Italy the students closed the universities for months, stimulating and contributing to the "hot autumn" of 1969 when workers' uprisings took place in many parts of the country. The movement's real accomplishments were few, some university reforms of doubtful value. During its heyday it had escaped completely from the control of the official youth organizations of the political parties. After a time it subsided, leaving a residue of committed terrorists, not large in numbers but dedicated to violence. They were former utopian Catholic Action youth leaders or utopian Marxists who shared a sense of betrayal. With a number of terrorists from the neo-Fascist youth movement, they organized the terrorist bands of the 1970s. Most famous was the Red Brigades, led by ex-Catholic youth leader Renato Curcio, who had received training in Czechoslovakia in 1972.

The double goal of the terrorist groups was to destabilize the state and undercut the Communist Party, which was accused of betraying the revolution by its strategy of seeking the democratic way to socialism. From the terrorist perspective, the PCI had succumbed to the old Italian vice of transformism, selling out principles in return for a share of power. Not surprisingly the two largest parties—the DC, which dominated the state, and the PCI, the leader of the loyal opposition—suffered the most from the terrorists. During the first part of the 1970s the attacks were primarily against property. From 1975 on they were increasingly directed against people. Terrorists' victims were not only politicians; they included businessmen, trade union leaders, journalists, judges, and police officials. The most famous victim was Aldo Moro, president of the Christian Democratic Party and five times prime minister of Italy. The Red Brigades kidnapped and then killed him in the spring of 1978, just after he had negotiated an agreement of PCI support for the DC cabinet.

The country has survived the terrorist assault without destroying democracy in the process, although tightened security regulations could, if abused, wipe out the civil rights of the citizens.[6] After 1981 the terrorist threat subsided, though it was far from dead. New recruits still replaced convicted terrorists who received long prison sentences. Financial support and weapons came from foreign terrorist organizations in Europe and the Mideast, as well as from foreign governments.[7]

In recent years links between terrorist groups and traditional organized crime have been confirmed, so that concern over the spread of organized crime has exacerbated preoccupation with political terrorism. The Sicilian mafia, the Neapolitan *camorra*, and the Calabrian *n'drangheta* have dominated the headlines, and their activities have moved far beyond original zones. The number of deaths resulting from interfactional and intergang warfare has escalated, as has the frequency of attacks on police officials and investigating judges. The drug traffic, with its lucrative profits, was the major, though by no means the only, area of criminal involvement. The growth of nonpolitical crime was not limited to the major organized crime families. Increased rates of kidnapping, theft, and burglaries have heightened the sense of insecurity of people living in large cities.

Italian security forces have expanded their operations against criminal gangs. There have been major roundups of crime figures, and suspected gang leaders have gone into hiding. Nevertheless, while statistics on the number of arrests were impressive, the number of convictions was much lower. Meanwhile, charges of protection have been leveled against the political parties. The DC has been especially vulnerable since it is the leading party in the major crime-infested areas. Police raids against the Neapolitan camorra in the week preceding the June 1983 parliamentary election were interpreted as an effort by the DC to demonstrate its opposition, not linkage, to criminal gangs. Even though most Italians have not been direct victims of either terrorist or criminal activities, they have been affected psychologically because of the attention the mass media pay to acts of violence.

The ties between crime and politics are one aspect of the larger problem of corruption. Italians suspect corruption even where it does not exist. There is a historical "distrust of government, indifference to politics, lack of belief in the honesty and capacity of bureaucrats and politicians, and, on the other hand, instrumental participation for personal benefit, and gross pragmatism."[8] In 1978 Giovanni Leone, president of the republic, resigned from office to avoid charges in connection with the Lockheed bribery scandal. Two former cabinet ministers were indicted; one was convicted and jailed.

The news media exaggerate all the scandals, and the public cannot escape the barrage. Even so, there are enough real outrages to make cynics of even the most naive. Two prominent scandals of the early 1980s involved a secret Masonic lodge named Propaganda 2 and the Banco Ambrosiano. In Italy, unlike the United States, secret organizations are illegal. Among its membership the lodge in Italy included parliamentarians, cabinet ministers, top-level businessmen, journalists, senior bureaucrats, and commanding officers of the armed forces. When it was exposed, Licio Gelli, the lodge president, was charged with financial corruption, but what was worse, with plotting the overthrow of the parliamentary regime. The plots were alleged to have begun in 1976 when the DC government was dependent on the abstention of the PCI and PSI. Gelli escaped from Italy and later from a Swiss jail. The exposure of the secret membership lists brought down a cabinet and produced a political crisis that weakened the DC party even though it was not the only party implicated.

The Banco Ambrosiano, linked to many arms of the Catholic church and to the Vatican itself, was the largest private bank in Italy. Its unexpected failure in 1982, followed by the mysterious death of its president, Roberto Calvi, who was also a member of Propaganda 2, brought severe financial damage to its Italian depositors and to foreign banks that had invested large sums in some of its overseas affiliates. Many dubious loans had been given to Central American dummy companies on the basis of "letters of patronage" from Archbishop Marcinkus, who was in charge of the Vatican bank. Italian officials demanded repayment by the Vatican, which denied any legal responsibility. The Bank of Italy is compensating Italian depositors but rejects responsibility to foreign debt holders. In February 1984 the Vatican indicated its readiness to make a partial payment to foreign banks. The whole affair hurt the DC because of its political identification with the church.

It has been argued that corruption and scandals have had no effect on voting behavior, and indeed party support has remained remarkably stable throughout most of the postwar era. The sharp decline in DC votes in the 1983 election, however, may indicate a change in people's political attitudes. With the erosion of subcultural cohesion and solidarity and the decline of the Catholic bloc under the impact of secularization, opinion voting may be growing in importance. Negative opinions toward corruption constitute one of the probable causes of Christian Democracy's losses.

The secularization of Italian society has proceeded steadily for decades but had cumulative impact in the 1970s and 1980s. Substantial sections of the population have rejected fundamental principles of Catholic doctrine concerning church attendance, birth control, marriage, divorce, and abortion. Church attendance has dropped. In the early postwar years two-thirds of the population were regular churchgoers. By 1980 the figure was down to one-third. The birthrate has been dropping steadily since the early 1960s. Demographers forecast that by 1990 Italy could reach population stability at approximately sixty million people. Although the number of civil marriages is still small, it is increasing steadily and church weddings are declining. In a national referendum held in 1974, 60 percent of the people voted to uphold the divorce law against attempts to repeal it. In another national referendum in 1981, the voters supported a liberal abortion law against its opponents' attempts at repeal by a margin of 68 percent to 32 percent.

The DC has always received its major popular support from the Catholic faithful, those who viewed the party as the secular arm of the church. Supplementing this core bloc are the voters beholden to the DC for jobs, favors, patronage, or the hope of obtaining these perquisites. In addition are those who backed the party out of fear of communism, both domestic and foreign, and who saw the church and the DC as the only effective bulwarks against its dangers. And issue voters have supported the party for policy reasons, according to their opinions on domestic and foreign policy issues. By the 1983 election the fear of communism appeared remote and hardly entered into the campaign. Unlike earlier campaigns, active church electioneering for the party was minimal. Those policy issues the DC pushed—austerity as a means of battling inflation, reform of the party and the government as a means of fighting corruption—evidently gathered little support. A number of former DC voters apparently had no taste for austerity, whereas others, particularly among the young voters, did not believe the party had reformed, or could reform, itself. The voters the DC appears to have lost in 1983 are the opponents of austerity and the supporters of reform. Those it retained are the core bloc of the faithful and the beneficiaries of its largesse.

The absence of any significant anticommunist crusade in the 1983 campaign was a product of changing numbers and the changing nature of the PCI. After growing steadily in the postwar period, the communist vote peaked in the 1976 parliamentary election when the party obtained 34.4 percent of the vote for the Chamber of Deputies. The party had once been a battalion in an international army commanded by Moscow,[9] but from the early 1950s it had been gradually establishing its independence. By the 1970s it was the leading Eurocommunist party, formally proclaiming its commitment to parliamentary democracy, democratic socialism, and Western values. The PCI rejected the Soviet Union as a political model and the command economy as an economic model. It proclaimed the existence of a third way that lay between social democracy and East European dictatorship, one it called democratic socialism, which would go further than social democratic efforts to patch up and improve the mixed economy of the welfare capitalist state. In violent reaction to the imposition of martial law in Poland in December 1979, the Italians, blaming the Russians, announced that the principles of the October Revolution had run their course and could no longer provide any basis for the further development of the workers' movement.

These changes cost the party the support of more traditionalist party faithful who were attached to the Soviet myth and orthodox Marxist doctrine. At the same time the absence of a definitive split with the Soviet world left others unconvinced. How would the third way differ from a wavering and unstable mixed economy? How independent of emotional attachment to the East were the communist rank and file? The same question could be asked about some of the leaders. By 1983 some commentators were claiming that Eurocommunism was a waning strategy in Italy and elsewhere. They were forecasting at least a partial return to orthodoxy, if for no other reason than that Eurocommunism had not paid off politically. It had not gained votes and had not brought the PCI into the government. Communist leaders, however, continued to uphold Eurocommunism as the only type of communism appropriate to a modern, advanced, developed society.

Throughout the postwar years communist strategy has sought to avoid isolation. A second and complementary strategic goal has been to make the communist presence felt in all sectors of social, economic, cultural, and political life. Party members have been present and active wherever possible, with the aim of penetrating society rather than remaining segregated in party or front organizations. Originally, one mass trade union confederation was established in the last year of World War II, the Italian General Confederation of Labor (CGIL). Communists, Christian Democrats, and Socialists shared the leadership. The CGIL split in 1949 under the impact of the cold war, and two additional confederations emerged: the Catholic-led Italian Confederation of Free Syndicates (CISL) and the Social Democratic–Republican Italian Union of Labor (UIL). In the different atmosphere of the late 1960s there began a movement toward reunification that in 1972 culminated in the establishment of a confederation of the confederations, CGIL-CISL-UIL. Party domination of the respective confederations had declined over the years, and a condition for reunification was union independence from party control. The degree of cohesion within the CGIL-CISL-UIL has been reduced since the early 1970s, and by the 1980s the strains among and inside the confederations were substantial. In addition there exist independent unions unaffiliated with any confederation. Since the early 1970s the trade union movement in general has weakened, in response to the vagaries and fluctuations of the economy and the growth of the submerged economy. For the Communists the CGIL was a means of maintaining contact with and influence over broad sectors of the labor movement outside the party's direct influence. Today this role is less effective than it was in earlier years.

At the political level, during the war the Communists forged the Pact of Unity of Action with the Socialists. The pact was a revival of an antifascist alliance that dated from the 1930s' Popular Front in exile. Between 1943 and 1947 all the antifascist parties had collaborated in the Committees of National Liberation, but communist efforts to maintain a coalition of the three mass parties in the cold war years collapsed with the DC refusal. The pact with the Socialists ended in 1959. Although without allies at the national level, the Communists continued to have Socialist allies in local and provincial governments and made a point of playing an active role in parliament as the leading opposition party. In 1973 the Communists relaunched their attempt to come to terms with the DC and the Catholic church. The "historic compromise" proclaimed by PCI Secretary General Enrico Berlinguer was rejected by the Vatican and the DC. Nevertheless, from 1976 to 1979 the DC found it useful to accept PCI support in Parliament to keep its governments going, while resisting PCI claims for membership in cabinet coalitions.

In 1979 the PCI insisted, "Either in the government or in the opposition," thus guaranteeing its return to the opposition. The Communists then began to court the Socialists, who in the early 1970s had indicated a renewed interest in an alliance of the left. But by 1979, under the leadership of Bettino Craxi, Socialist interest in a national alliance with the PCI was waning, just as the Communists were rediscovering its virtues. As a result the PCI has been isolated at the national level in the 1980s, neither the historic compromise nor the left alternative being available to it. At subnational levels, however, the Communist party continued to participate in many governments in coalition with, or supported by, other leftist or centrist parties, except for the DC.

During the 1970s the Communists pursued a strategy of moderation and caution. They became the hated targets of the left extremists, who accused them of abandoning their revolutionary principles and betraying the working class. The terrorists, to make matters worse, were calling themselves the true Communists. In reaction the PCI became a firm defender of law and order, opposing any concessions to terrorists or indulgence of violence. In economic policies the PCI wrestled with the immediate crises of the times, recognizing the connections among indexing, inflation, unemployment, and the growth of the underground economy. In the late 1970s the Communists issued calls for austerity and fiscal responsibility. They discovered, however, that their trade union base would not follow its leaders and would accept neither a revision of the indexing formula nor a restructuring of industry that would involve the elimination of jobs and the flood of governmental subsidies. So austerity went by the board. After returning to the opposition, PCI concern for fiscal responsibility, industrial restructuring, and wage restraint disappeared. It was much easier to attack these government policies and defend the claims of every social group to a share of the public treasury. By 1984 the Communists again were calling strikes to oppose any readjustment of indexing formulas or elimination of surplus industrial capacity. Against a coalition government led by a Socialist prime minister, the PCI could accuse the PSI of betraying the proletariat.

The Communists present a contradictory image to the public. The PCI proclaims its commitment to reformist means on the one hand and revolutionary goals on the other. In some respects it is a bulwark of the status quo, and in others its enemy. The party plays parliamentary politics at all levels of government, yet is viewed as a threat to parliamentary democracy. In the central Italian regions of Emilia Romagna, Tuscany, and Umbria, the PCI is the establishment and behaves accordingly. Businesses owned and controlled by the party operate like other businesses; its cooperatives, which in many cases are big businesses, do likewise. The number of Italians who consider the PCI to be beyond the pale has declined considerably in recent years, yet there are still those who exclude it from eligibility as an acceptable political actor or coalition partner. By 1984 its voting support was as large as that of the DC; nevertheless, it is still rejected, both inside and outside Italy. As a result, the de facto choices of Italian politics remain confined to variations on a formula centered around the DC. As Christian Democratic strength has declined, its maneuverability has been restricted by the growing assertiveness of its smaller allies, who have been, nevertheless, unable to substitute for it. The continued durability of this state of affairs is difficult to foresee.

Dissatisfaction with the political inadequacies of the situation, with the apparent inability of Italian governments to make hard choices and coherent policies, has led to numerous recommendations for reform of the political system.[10] Most of these would have only marginal political effects. Some would modify the procedural rules of Parliament to accelerate the legislative process. Others would abolish the Senate, which is considered an unnecessary duplicate of the Chamber of Deputies. Proposals to change the electoral system range from the establishment of a single-member-district system to establishment of a mixed system in the German style. Some suggest establishment of a constructive vote of no confidence, as in West Germany, to prolong the life of a cabinet. Others propose the direct election of the prime minister. It has been suggested that Parliament be dissolved automatically after two cabinet crises. All the proposals focus to a greater or lesser degree on two types of change: One is to reduce the number of parties, the other to strengthen the executive. Most drastic is the plan to shift to a presidential republic on the French model. Since all the proposals that involve serious change would damage many of the existing political forces, the chances of their adoption are minimal. Minor reforms of parliamentary machinery would not deal with the causes of dissatisfaction. From time to time during the 1960s and 1970s, Italian generals were alleged to be promoting military takeovers. The scandal over Propaganda 2, the Masonic lodge, also included a charge of plotting for a coup d'etat. None of these plots came to anything, and the parties and Parliament have continued politics as usual.

Foreign Relations

Before World War II Italy thought of itself as a great power and was formally recognized as such in international affairs. Its wartime defeat brought an end to that illusion, and no postwar government has demonstrated any such pretensions. Foreign policy has been an instrument of domestic politics, manipulated for internal purposes. In 1963 I wrote, "The key objective of Italian foreign policy is to protect the domestic social structure from internal dangers."[11] The assertion holds true today. Foreign policy is used to keep the domestic parties of the left from coming to power and transforming the political and social order. In 1949 both the PCI and PSI opposed Italy's membership in NATO. In the early 1950s they attacked Italy's participation in the European Coal and Steel Community. But by the late 1950s the Socialist position was changing, and the PSI abstained in the parliamentary ratification of Italy's entry into the European Economic Community. When the PSI entered the center-left coalition governments in the 1960s, its endorsement of Italy's integration into Western Europe and participation in NATO was complete.

The Communists delayed but eventually followed the Socialist evolution. In 1957 the PCI opposed the EEC; by 1963 it had reversed its opposition. By 1969 Communists were active members of the Italian delegation at Strasbourg. At about the same time they gradually and circumspectly began to revise their opinion of NATO. The Soviet destruction of the "Prague Spring" in August 1968 was a lesson to the Italian comrades on the chances of survival of the Italian way to socialism in a Soviet-dominated Europe. By 1974 the PCI openly accepted NATO, and by 1976 its secretary general, Enrico Berlinguer, could publicly say, "I feel safer on this side." [12] In 1977 the Communists participated in the drafting of a major document of government foreign policy that identified NATO and the European Community as the cornerstones of Italian foreign policy.

The shifts in the domestic and foreign policy positions of the two major left parties might have appeared to the center parties to remove the necessity of using foreign policy as an instrument of internal conservation. Yet ambiguities about the Communists' true intentions served to nurture the suspicion of anti-PCI forces at home and abroad. The United States never accepted the PCI conversion as real and opposed its every attempt to enter the cabinet. During the middle and late 1970s, the Communists engaged in substantial efforts to establish close relations with social-democratic, socialist, and labor parties in Western Europe. They also made the same effort with the United States, only to be rebuffed regularly. After 1979 when the PCI returned to the opposition, its public antagonism toward the United States increased, and its endeavors to come to terms with the United States came to an end. The party still remains active in European affairs and has not repudiated NATO, although it regularly urges a more independent European policy within NATO with less subservience to U.S. strategic and security policies.

Although Italy has remained a loyal and consistent supporter of NATO and the European Community, its role in both organizations has been passive. In the mid 1950s it did propose that NATO's role be expanded to encompass an economic community. The suggestion was never developed, and the establishment of the EEC put an end to the idea. Italy's importance to NATO has grown over the years because of its location rather than because of the strength of its armed forces, for Italy has one of the smallest defense budgets of all the countries in the Alliance in proportion to gross national product. But as the eastern Mediterranean zone has become more and more unstable, as Greece and Turkey have become more and more unreliable, the Italian bases, especially those for the U.S. Sixth Fleet, have become important. Italy has accepted the emplacement of new intermediate-range nuclear missiles in Sicily, over the protests of the peace movement and antinuclear activities. The PCI opposed the government's commitment, but at the same time it refused to endorse the Soviet policy. It straddled the issue. The Socialists voted for the missile bases in 1979, and in 1983 a Socialist prime minister lived up to the obligation, siding with President Mitterrand of France, but splitting with Socialists in West Germany, Great Britain, and other smaller European states.

Italy has probably gained more from the European Community in imports and exports and jobs for its workers than almost all of the other members. It has frequently tried to play the role of mediator in disputes among various members, with greater or lesser success depending on the issue. Much as in domestic politics, Italians have been good at devising international formulas that evade or postpone, rather than confront, problems. The government regularly passes resolutions calling for further integration of Europe, but these go nowhere. Italy has been hurt by the Common Agricultural Program of the EEC, yet it calculates that the gains from other Community policies outweigh the losses in agriculture.[13] When national interests are at stake, it can be as nationalistic as France, at the same time preaching more unity. Public opinion, though really uninterested, remains generally favorable to the EEC. The first postwar generation saw in European unification a panacea for Europe's ills, but as in other countries, later generations have lost the enthusiasm and hopes that led to the EEC's creation. There is no evidence of a growing European identity among the Italian people.

Italians have said much about their responsibility to the nations of the Third World. Apart from words, however, little has happened. In comparison with those from other advanced, developed states, Italian contributions to development programs abroad have been minor, almost as small as Japan's. This fact should not be surprising, for Italy has within its own territory large undeveloped zones that can legitimately claim higher priority. The situation is different when it comes to trade and investment. Though most of the country's trade is with its European partners and with advanced developed democracies, Italy must import large amounts of raw materials, particularly petroleum, and pay for them with exports. Italians are very active in business with Third World countries, especially the OPEC nations. Italian firms are also major construction contractors in many parts of the world, competing successfully to build plants, roads, dams, and infrastructure projects. Italian multinationals are active in many underdeveloped areas, especially in the Mediterranean world. The Italians have spoken frequently of a "Mediterranean vocation" and have adduced a particular role for their nation among the countries bordering that sea, a role based on history, on cultural and racial tolerance, on a religious missionary tradition. They conveniently forget the negative image cast by their imperialist past. For most of the postwar period the vocation was little more than a rationalization for commercial ambition. Political activity has been minimal. In the last few years, however, the government has been more active, sending Italian troops to participate in the international contingent enforcing the Egyptian-Israeli peace settlement in the Sinai peninsula. Italian public opinion grew increasingly hostile to the military presence before the pullout. As the peace collapsed and American, British, and later French troops were withdrawn, so were the Italian troops.

It can be expected that Italy will remain a loyal partner in NATO and in the

European Community, neither upsetting any arrangements nor taking any risks. Its relatively low profile in international affairs will reflect the continuing pre-occupation with internal political and economic difficulties. Italy is not likely to engage in foreign adventures to divert popular attention from domestic problems.

Conclusions

Former Prime Minister Spadolini's list of the major evils affecting Italy in 1984—inflation, terrorism, and corruption—might cause some debate among students of contemporary Italian life. The rate of inflation, though still in double digits, was declining. Terrorist violence had abated, though common criminal violence was on the increase. Corruption continued more or less as usual, with the media seeking out new scandals to dramatize. These evils, how-ever, were more consequences than causes of the Italian malaise. They reflected weaknesses of the economy and of political institutions, as well as the inade-quacies of the political culture.

Italian economists were fearful that Italy was becoming uncompetitive with two different groupings of countries simultaneously. It was falling behind its de-veloped partners in innovation and in new investment. Along with other Euro-pean industrial states, Italy feared growing backwardness in the new high-tech communications, information, and bioengineering revolutions forging ahead in the United States and Japan. Italian investment in research and development was low, but in February 1984 it joined with its Common Market partners in sponsor-ing a new research institute in these futuristic fields. At the same time Italy was facing increasing competition from the newly developing nations of the Third World, which were invading traditional export markets where Italy had had a comparative advantage in the past.

In fact, Italy's economy was not as badly off as official figures indicated. Price, income, and employment statistics have always been suspect. People were more prosperous than they admitted. The GNP was higher than announced. Many people counted as unemployed were working. Illegal immigrants from Third World countries were doing the menial jobs that Italians formerly did themselves, an ironic situation in a country that has historically been an exporter of labor. Some economists believed that the submerged economy and flourishing cottage industries would lead the way to a new industrial order based on a loose federation of "high technology cottage industries."[14] If this were to come to pass, Italy would move out in front of its advanced neighbors.

Through January and the first two weeks of February 1984, the trade union confederations and Confindustria negotiated for a new labor contract. The nego-tiations broke down when the Communist-dominated CGIL rejected any revi-sion of the *scala mobile* formula. On February 15 the government issued four decrees that transformed the dispute. The first decree imposed modifications of the formula, slightly reducing the benefits of indexing. The other three decrees froze the rent control formula for 1984, slightly increased allowances to families with children, and set price controls and administered prices on a number of items while fixing rates on various transactions. Examples were gasoline prices, electric utility rates, and interest rates. The government controls large sectors of the economy. The goal was to limit inflation to an annual rate of 10 percent for 1984. Private industry was requested to keep within this limit also. The intention of the total package was to compensate consumers for smaller increases in money income. The decrees had to be approved by Parliament within sixty days.

The Communists and the unions they influence rejected the package and launched political attacks in Parliament and demonstrations in the country against the Socialist-led government. The non-Communist union confederations, CISL and UIL, temporarily withdrew in protest from the alliance with CGIL, which had been established in 1972. The Socialist minority within CGIL threatened to walk out of the organization in the second week of March, which would leave it completely dominated by Communists. The PCI called for a vote of no confidence in Parliament in the third week of March. In connection with the vote the CGIL proclaimed a general strike and mobilized its activists to descend on Rome. The other union confederations urged their members not to participate. The cabinet met the challenge, and on March 23, 1984, Craxi's government handily won the vote.

The communist challenge was not yet over. In Parliament the PCI engaged in a lengthy filibuster that prevented approval of the decrees within the 60-day limit. The cabinet issued them again, with marginal changes in wording to make them technically new decrees. The second time around they passed within the time limit. The PCI then circulated petitions in the country for a referendum to repeal the laws. At the same time elections to the European Community Parliament scheduled for June 1984 turned the spring into an electoral campaign period. As in other countries, the campaign centered on domestic, not European, issues. A few days before the election Enrico Berlinguer, secretary general of the PCI, died of a stroke suffered during a campaign speech. His death produced an emotional wave of sympathy, and between one and two million people attended his public funeral in Rome a few days later.

The election resulted in a Communist victory. The PCI received 33.3 percent of the vote, compared to the 29.9 percent won in the national parliamentary election of the previous year. The DC received 33.0 percent, compared with 32.9 percent in 1983, and the PSI won 11.2 percent, compared with 11.4. The smaller parties trailed behind. For the first time in postwar Italian history, the PCI led the DC. The Communist newspaper, *L'Unità*, trumpeted, "We are number one!"

Though the results had no effect on party strength in the Italian Parliament, they had a psychological effect on politics. The campaign, after all, had emphasized Italian, not European Community, issues. The Communists chose Alessandro Natta, the deputy secretary general, to succeed Berlinguer. Under Natta's leadership, the strains and divisions between the PCI and the government parties began to moderate. The isolation of the Communists was reduced. The socialist trade unionists finally did not walk out of the CGIL. The CGIL-CISL-UIL superconfederation did not formally split, though relations among the three confederations remained tense. At provincial and municipal levels, local government alliances between the PCI and other parties survived. There was a good possibility that the referendum on the spring decree laws might be dropped. By the end of 1984 the hostilities of early spring had been tempered. A reviving economy that produced a real increase of 3.0 percent in the gross domestic product in 1984 helped moderate the atmosphere.

The spring decree laws had been marginal in their economic significance. Employer organizations pointed out immediately that the new *scala mobile* would provide little reduction in labor costs. It was the political consequences that were significant. The myth of the untouchability of the *scala mobile* that had been cultivated by the unions had been destroyed. The communist claim that Italy can be governed without the Communists but not against them had been challenged. A comparatively weak Italian state was not brought down. It had shown unexpected decisiveness. Its governing coalition had survived the challenge to its economic policies, policies that deprived a large part of the population of the full rewards of an existing entitlement.

Although Italy has had its share of political utopians, the Italian people have never expected much from governments. Terrorism has been rationalized as a reaction to the absence of effective rule. It is hardly likely, however, that any effective reforms within the limits of parliamentary democracy would satisfy the terrorists or their sympathizers. This is not to argue against reform; it is a warning not to expect harmony from a nation that thrives on contention.

A succession of public opinion polls taken during recent years has clearly indicated the unhappiness of the Italian people with the state, the parties, political and nonpolitical elites, and many aspects of their own lives. The younger generations, bearing the brunt of economic uncertainties, were the most disillusioned.[15] In a sense the evidence overstated the case. Italians are notorious naysayers; they knowingly denigrate their institutions and their fellow compatriots. The fragmentation of the society and its culture could be, and has been, exaggerated. Certainly both the elites and leading counterelites of the political order have recognized that they have a stake in the maintenance of that order, even if not in all of its aspects. The enemies of the system have been isolated and kept to the margins. The broad Italian public might respond negatively to pollsters, but in 1978 when the system suffered its major terrorist blow, the kidnapping and subsequent murder of Aldo Moro, and when, a few months later, the system had to endure the extreme disgrace of the resignation of President Giovanni Leone, who faced charges of corruption, the people rallied to their state. In expressions of outrage, through tangible and intangible manifestations of solidarity they demonstrated by a large majority that they preferred Italian parliamentary democracy, with its defects, to a leap into the dark.

Update

With agreements between the United States and the Soviet Union dealing with arms control and arms reduction likely to be supplemented, and with the demands for troops and supplies in the Persian Gulf action, the U.S. presence in, and perhaps the U.S. commitment to, Europe is quite likely to be reduced. Italy, like its European partners, will have to take steps to maintain its security under different conditions. There is little evidence that the Italians are seriously thinking about or planning for such a future.[16]

The rate of inflation had begun to decline in the early 1980s. By the mid-1980s it was in the single digits, and in the late 1980s it averaged 4 or 5 percent per year. This was not much different from the rates in other advanced developed states, though still higher than the inflation rates for West Germany and Switzerland. The causes for the decline were various; linking the lira to the mark through the European Monetary System was one. In 1981 the Bank of Italy was released from the obligation to monetize the public debt; then the world prices of some key raw materials, particularly petroleum, began to decline. The U.S. dollar softened. All these developments lessened the pressure on prices in Italy, in spite of the continuing rise in the public debt. By 1989 the cumulative national debt equaled the gross national product.

The slowdown of the Italian economy that had characterized the early 1980s came to an end in the latter part of 1983, and by 1984 a miniboom had begun, a business revival that picked up speed and brought Italy into a new wave of economic expansion. People were making and spending money. The prosperity continued to benefit from the vitality of the submerged economy that had erupted in the 1970s. But there were additional factors. A restructuring of big business in the 1980s revived profits, especially among the private firms. Even the public corporations began to make money, or at least to cut their losses. The firms, both private and public, adopted the latest scientific and technological advances. They reorganized and streamlined their operations and embarked on a strategy of mergers and takeovers—national, European, and worldwide in scope. As in other developed countries, a process of privatization emerged. Public sector firms were sold to private industry. The most spectacular act of privatization occurred at the end of 1986 when the Alfa-Romeo auto company was sold to Fiat. The atmosphere of the times supported these policies. A government led by a Socialist prime minister made the sale without objection from the Communist opposition.

The service sectors exploded in the 1980s, particularly financial services. Italian family savings were invested in new financial instruments such as mutual funds, investment funds, or private pension funds. The stock market boomed. Italy has a way to go to catch up with the financial markets of its major European partners, but it has made good progress. In manufacturing and marketing it has already arrived. By 1986 Italy had become the fifth economic power of the modern world, surpassing Great Britain. Some economists forecast that Italy will overtake France in a few years.

Unfortunately, not all Italians benefited. The boom was concentrated mainly in the north and center of the country, not the south. The gap between these areas widened. Unemployment increased in the south, particularly among the young, while the north suffered labor shortages. The country was participating in a high-tech revolution that had no place for underqualified young people. The unemployment problem and the huge public debt are potential dangers for the country when the European Economic Community completes its scheduled economic and financial unification at the end of 1992. Southerners are forecasting that whatever gains might accrue to Italy would be concentrated in the north, while the south will fall even further behind.[17]

There has always been strong generic support in Italy for the EEC, though most Italians know little of its operations. The Italian government in 1985 endorsed the movement toward further EEC unification because Italy had done well since 1958. The Italian financial community, especially the bankers, were worried about their ability to compete after 1992 with the big German, French, and British banks. Italian public administration was much less efficient than the bureaucracies of the European partners. Italian manufacturers and traders were confident of the capability to build on their past successes. The business community, on the whole, ended the 1980s pleased with the country's dynamic economy and faced the post-1992 future optimistically.

Politically, the atmosphere was different. The government was involved to a great extent in internal infighting, though it did succeed in 1984 in delivering a political defeat to the Communist Party. In February of that year the cabinet decreed a change in the indexing law, the *scala mobile*, that automatically increased wages to match the rate of inflation. The particular formula, in use from 1975 to 1984, contributed to the inflationary spiral. The government's change of formula reduced the inflationary effect slightly and was welcomed by business interests. The CGIL, however, opposed the change under the stimulus of the Communist Party, which used the issue as a weapon against the government parties. Over Communist opposition in Parliament the decree became law. The PCI then circulated petitions and obtained sufficient signatures to force a referendum on repealing the law. When the referendum was held in 1985, a majority of voters upheld the government's policy. Although the economic effect of the new indexing formula was marginal, the political effect was not. The union slogan that "the *scala mobile* is untouchable" had been successfully challenged. The old Communist claim that Italy could be governed without the Communists but not against them had been exploded.

The late 1980s witnessed a continuing reduction in the strength of the union movement. The *scala mobile* issue further divided the Christian Democratic and Socialist unions from the Communist-dominated CGIL. In the nation, overall union membership declined. The high rate of unemployment weakened union militancy and discipline. In an era of technological change, jobs were being eliminated by automation and robotization. Fiat reduced its work force by 130,000 over the decade while producing more vehicles than ever. The unions were finding it difficult to orient their members' political choices and voting behavior. And their political psychology was changing. Whereas in the "hot autumn" of 1969 workers had struck to overthrow the profit system, they were now striking to participate in company profit-sharing plans.

Political rivalries between the two largest parties in the cabinet coalition limited the government to more or less routine administration. A succession of clashes between the Christian Democrats and Socialists finally led to the dissolution of Parliament and new elections in 1987. The results showed a moderate increase for the Christian Democrats, significant advances for the Socialists, and notable losses for the Communists. A new party, the Greens, won some seats in its first parliamentary election. The postelection cabinet was a repetition of the preceding five-party coalition, but it was a weaker government because the top party leaders stayed out. In the fall of 1987 the voters passed two referenda: One eliminated peaceful nuclear power plants, the other imposed civil liability on judges who were subsequently shown to have made important errors. The first result was a consequence of the 1986 Chernobyl accident in the Ukraine, which affected northeastern Italy. The second was a consequence of well-publicized criminal cases where initial guilty verdicts were later reversed on appeal to higher courts. In the meantime the victims had spent years in jail, lost income and livelihood, and perhaps their future opportunities. After the referendum the government arranged to have the state, rather than the judge, pay the liability in cases where gross mistakes were proved. Dissatisfaction with the court system was widespread. In 1989 a new code of criminal procedure came into effect. It broke sharply from the traditional judicial process. Inquisitorial methods were replaced by an Anglo-American-style adversarial process. It would take time for prosecutors and judges to get accustomed to the new system.

There has been much talk in Italy about instituting major political reforms but by the end of the 1980s little had been done. The secret ballot in Parliament was eliminated except for moral questions such as divorce or abortion.

The potentially more important political change involves the future of the Communist Party. It is still the second-largest party in spite of voting declines. It has been seeking for several years to formulate a "new course," but it is difficult to find out what the new course involves. The PCI has long since dropped its Marxism and now emphasizes family issues, ecology, feminism, illegal drugs— the topics of postmaterialist politics. It eliminated the commitment to democratic centralism and denies the existence of an international communist movement. It claims membership in a "European Left," but that is mainly Social Democratic.[18] The PCI would like to be admitted to the Second International but so far it has been blocked by the PSI and the PSDI.

Events of 1989 outside Italy made the Italian Communist Party's search for a new identity more urgent. The Chinese crackdown on the students in Tienanmen Square led to a vigorous denunciation of the Chinese party by the PCI. But even more significant were the events of the summer and fall that witnessed the crumbling of most of the Communist regimes in Eastern Europe. Although up to now Italian Communist voters have appeared to be little affected by the dramatic changes beyond the Italian borders, the long-run decline of Communist ideologies and political systems cannot but have an impact on Italy. Following the lead of some of the East European parties, the Central Committee of the PCI voted in November 1989 to change the name of the party. A party congress scheduled for the spring of 1990 will have to ratify the decision and settle on a new name. In the meantime the weakening of the PCI paradoxically makes it available as a safer government partner since there is no chance it can subvert the political-economic system for something else that has been so discredited. The Communists may now have more room for future maneuver, for playing off the two other large parties against each other.

Of the major evils listed by former Prime Minister Giovanni Spadolini— inflation, terrorism, and corruption—only the last was a significant challenge by 1990. Terrorist acts occasionally occurred; they were sporadic and no longer a threat to the political system. Inflation was at a moderate level, comparable to that in other developed countries. But corruption was widespread. The struggle against organized crime produced some spectacular trials of Mafia gangsters and Camorra mobsters but no real diminution of criminal activity. The public administration was inefficient and unreliable, but no government seemed capable of improving the operations of the post office, the telephone network, the health services, or the schools. Traffic was semiparalyzed in the urban centers (a problem that reaches far beyond Italy, of course). The public complained loudly about these insufficiencies but continued to vote for the parties that seemed incapable of remedying them.

By 1990 the country was far different from the one that emerged from World War II. It is even much different from the Italy of the student riots and the "hot autumn" at the end of the 1960s. Italy is a freer, more mobile, and wealthier society. Women especially benefit from the increased freedom and flexibility of contemporary attitudes. Popular behavior is more liberal and secular. In economic terms the country ranks among the world's leaders. In political terms, however, the relative instability of cabinets, the penetration by the parties into so many private as well as public sectors, the pettiness and byzantine nature of so many political activities disgust the public and reduce the impact of Italy on the wider European and world scenes. Inside Italy the defective public administration and distasteful political maneuvering feed hostility to the state and the parties. By a wide majority the Italian people are committed to the principles of democratic politics, but this does not translate into a commitment to the Italian state. Though life is good for many of them, they are not ready to acknowledge that their state and government play an important role in what has been achieved.

The system, nevertheless, has survived difficult tests with remarkable resilience. The leaders have avoided intransigent extremist behavior. The people, despite their grumbling, have demonstrated more patience and understanding than they are willing to admit. Italy is an unwilling success story.

Notes

1. A classic historical survey of the Italian people can be found in Luigi Salvatorelli, *A Concise History of Italy from Prehistoric Times to Our Own Day*, trans. Bernard Miall (New York: Oxford University Press, 1940). The standard history of the unitary Italian state is Denis Mack Smith, *Italy: A Modern History*, rev. ed. (Ann Arbor: University of Michigan Press, 1969). A recent history of the postwar period is found in Norman Kogan, *A Political History of Italy: The Postwar Years* (New York: Praeger, 1983).

2. See A. William Salomone, *Italy in the Giolittian Era: Italian Democracy in the Making* (Philadelphia: University of Pennsylvania Press, 1960).

3. There is no up-to-date book in English on the Italian government. Somewhat dated descriptions can be found in P. A. Allum, *Italy—Republic Without Government?* (New York: Norton, 1973); Raphael Zariski, *Italy: The Politics of Uneven Development* (Hinsdale, Ill.: Dryden Press, 1972); and Norman Kogan, *The Government of Italy* (New York: Crowell, 1962).

4. Although the professed principles of the Radical Party are not contrary to parliamentary democracy, the frequently disruptive behavior of its parliamentary delegation is calculated to discredit the democratic system.

5. Gabriele Calvi and Maurizio Cecchi, "I valori dei parlamentari e degli elettori: Una prima comparizione," *Rivista italiana di scienza politica*, August 1982, pp. 307–22.

6. For example, people can be arrested and held incommunicado for a long time on mere suspicion of involvement with terrorists.

7. In December 1982 Sandro Pertini, the president of the republic, said in a television speech that foreign governments were backing terrorist groups. He did not name any. Four weeks later the Soviet ambassador delivered a protest to the Foreign Office.

8. Dante Germino and Stefano Passigli, *The Government and Politics of Contemporary Italy* (New York: Harper & Row, 1968), pp. 88–89.

9. The phrase is from the late communist leader Giorgio Amendola.

10. Examples of this dissatisfaction can be found in the titles of two books: Giuseppe Di Palma, *Surviving Without Governing: The Italian Parties in Parliament* (Berkeley: University of California Press, 1976); and Allum, *Italy—Republic Without Government?*

11. Norman Kogan, *The Politics of Italian Foreign Policy* (New York: Praeger, 1963), p. 136.

12. *Il Corriere della Sera*, June 15, 1976.

13. F. Roy Willis, *Italy Chooses Europe* (New York: Oxford University Press, 1971); and Primo Vannicelli, *Italy, NATO and the European Community* (Cambridge, Mass.: Harvard University, Center for International Affairs, 1974).

14. Charles F. Sabel, *Work and Politics: The Division of Labour in Industry* (Cambridge, Eng.: Cambridge University Press, 1982).

15. Robert D. Putnam, Robert Leonardi, and Raffaella Y. Nanetti, "Polarization and Depolarization in Italian Politics, 1968–1981" (1981, mimeo.); Carlo Mongardini, ed., *Realtà e immagine della politica estera italiana* (Milan: Giuffre Editore, 1980); and *Public Opinion*, July–August 1978, p. 21.

16. Norman Kogan, "Italy in the International Arena" (Paper presented to a conference at the Woodrow Wilson Center, Smithsonian Institution, Washington, D.C., February 1–4, 1988).

17. Silvano Andriani, "Unification of the European Markets and the Mezzogiorno of Italy," *Journal of Regional Policy* (July–September 1988): 357–65.

18. Achille Occhetto, "Policies and Ideals of the Italian Communist Party—New Venues," *Italian Journal* (March–June 1989): 9–13. (Achille Occhetto is the new general secretary of the PCI.)

Suggested Readings

Banfield, Edward C. *The Moral Basis of a Backward Society*. New York: Free Press, 1958.

Barnes, Samuel H. *Representation in Italy: Institutionalized Tradition and Electoral Choice*. Chicago: University of Chicago Press, 1967.

Blackmer, Donald L. M., and Tarrow, Sidney, eds. *Communism in Italy and France*. Princeton, N.J.: Princeton University Press, 1975.

Di Palma, Giuseppe. *Surviving Without Governing: The Italian Parties in Parliament*. Berkeley: University of California Press, 1976.

Di Scala, Spencer. *Renewing Italian Socialism—Nenni to Craxi*. New York: Oxford University Press, 1988.

Galli, Giorgio, and Prandi, Alfonso. *Patterns of Political Participation in Italy.* New Haven, Conn.: Yale University Press, 1970.

Hughes, H. Stuart. *The United States and Italy.* 3d ed. Cambridge, Mass.: Harvard University Press, 1979.

Kogan, Norman. *A Political History of Italy: The Postwar Years.* New York: Praeger, 1983.

———. *The Politics of Italian Foreign Policy.* New York: Praeger, 1963.

Lange, Peter. *Studies on Italy, 1943–1975.* Turin: Fondazione Giovanni Agnelli, 1977.

LaPalombara, Joseph. *Democracy Italian Style.* New Haven: Yale University Press, 1987.

———. *Italy: The Politics of Planning.* Syracuse, N.Y.: Syracuse University Press, 1966.

Mack Smith, Denis. *Italy: A Modern History.* Rev. ed. Ann Arbor: University of Michigan Press, 1969.

Penniman, Howard R., ed. *Italy at the Polls: The Parliamentary Elections of 1976.* Washington, D.C.: American Enterprise Institute for Public Policy Research, 1977.

———, ed. *Italy at the Polls, 1979.* Washington, D.C.: American Enterprise Institute for Public Policy Research, 1981.

Putnam, Robert D. *The Beliefs of Politicians: Ideology, Conflict and Democracy in Britain and Italy.* New Haven, Conn.: Yale University Press, 1973.

Ranney, Austin, and Sartori, Giovanni, eds. *Eurocommunism: The Italian Case.* Washington, D.C.: American Enterprise Institute for Public Policy Research, 1978.

Salvatorelli, Luigi. *A Concise History of Italy from Prehistoric Times to Our Own Day.* Translated by Bernard Miall. New York: Oxford University Press, 1940.

Silj, Alessandro. *Never Again Without a Rifle: The Origins of Italian Terrorism.* New York: Karz, 1979.

Tarrow, Sidney. *Peasant Communism in Southern Italy.* New Haven, Conn.: Yale University Press, 1967.

Tökés, Rudolf L., ed. *Eurocommunism and Détente.* New York: New York University Press, 1978.

Zariski, Raphael. *Italy: The Politics of Uneven Development.* Hinsdale, Ill.: Dryden Press, 1972.

9

Switzerland

Jürg Steiner

Switzerland—positive or negative model for the world? The answer depends on one's perspective and values. Most people around the world have a very positive image of Switzerland, but there are some who view Switzerland negatively. Why are there these differing views about Swiss politics and society? This essay deals with both the strengths and the weaknesses of the Swiss political system. Because I have for many years divided my teaching time between an American and a Swiss university, I am able to write from what is perhaps a unique vantage point of familiarity with and detachment from Swiss life.

From my American students I almost always hear good things about my native country. For them Switzerland is beautiful, clean, and peaceful, the country of cheese, chocolate, watches, and the Matterhorn. According to opinion surveys, this positive image holds for the American public at large. Of all foreign nations, Switzerland is usually ranked at the top. Not only the masses but also the elite around the world hold Switzerland in high esteem. A Gallup poll asked 200 leading statesmen in 40 countries, "Other than your own country, what country do you consider the best governed?" Switzerland ranked first among all choices.[1]

Given this positive view of Switzerland, it is not surprising that many foreign observers have tried to draw lessons from the Swiss experience. Nineteenth-century French writer Victor Hugo once wrote that in history Switzerland will have the last word.[2] The late Norwegian political scientist Stein Rokkan considered Switzerland a microcosm of Europe and argued that "anyone seeking to understand the structure and dynamics of European politics will do well to immerse himself" in the study of Swiss politics.[3] Consociational theory attempts to learn from Switzerland how internal harmony and stability can be achieved in a culturally diverse country.[4] The theory then applies these lessons to world trouble spots, such as Lebanon, Northern Ireland, and South Africa. Most Swiss enjoy this attention from foreign observers and agree that their country has a special mission in the world. They are proud that Switzerland uses the popular referendum more than any other country in the world. They also see a humanitarian mission for Switzerland, most vividly exemplified by the International Red Cross founded in 1864 in Geneva by Henri Dunant.

But there is also a negative viewpoint. For some, Switzerland renders a disservice to the world with its banking laws that allegedly allow tax evaders, criminals, and dictators to hide their huge fortunes in a safe haven. It is also criticized for exploiting its foreign workers as, for example, in the Italian movie *Bread and Chocolate*. Quite a few Swiss intellectuals and artists find their country too narrow-minded and insufficiently open to new ideas. One of them, writer Max Frisch, spends most of his time in New York, which he finds more appealing than his native Zurich. Then there is the much-discussed "Sprayer of Zurich," a man who at night sprayed peculiar figures on the walls of the city. Caught by the police, he was convicted for public disturbance but escaped to Germany where he is celebrated for his "art." In recent years, there have been some large-scale, sometimes even violent, demonstrations by Swiss young people expressing a diffuse kind of dissatisfaction with their country. They find their lives dull and unexciting and claim that they have no influence. One of their typical slogans is "No Future."

Is making money and being rich a positive goal? Are cleanliness, punctuality, and tranquility values for which one should strive, or do they merely contribute to dullness and monotony? These questions are not answered here. The purpose of this essay is rather to provide sufficient information to allow the reader to make a judgment.

History

Switzerland is already making preparations for celebrating the seven hundredth anniversary of its independence in 1991. In 1291 it liberated itself from the domination of the Austrian Habsburg dynasty. This event is commemorated every year on August 1, National Independence Day. For the modern Swiss, liberation from the Habsburgs has an emotional meaning much like that which Americans attach to their own success in gaining independence from the British. There is, however, one major difference in the historical context of the two events. Whereas the United States immediately became an independent nation in the modern sense of the word, this was not the case for Switzerland in

1291. At that time the Swiss were part of the Holy Roman Empire and owed allegiance to its emperor. The Habsburgs ruled Switzerland in the name of the emperor. The Swiss, who resented this intermediate level of domination, wished to deal directly with the emperor, to be free within the empire and not subjugated by an intermediate authority. The Swiss stressed their loyalty to the emperor, to whom they promised to remain faithful. They argued that in earlier times they had been free within the empire, and it was to those ancient freedoms that they wanted to return. Thus, the movement for independence in 1291 was backward-rather than forward-looking. Switzerland's success in 1291 did not mean any basic changes in the internal structures of Switzerland. The customary inequalities remained—"free" citizens enjoyed full political rights, but serfs did not. Thus, 1291 did not yet mean the beginning of a modern democracy based on the principle of one man, one vote. It was different for the United States, where independence from Britain also meant the introduction of a modern democratic constitution. (We should remember, however, that these democratic principles did not yet apply to either slaves or women.)

Although the Swiss remained in the Holy Roman Empire after 1291, they were to some extent able to run their own affairs because the emperor was far away and growing progressively weaker politically. After about 1500 the Swiss had practically full independence, and after 1648 their ties to the empire and the emperor were formally dissolved.

Today Switzerland's cultural diversity includes four languages (German, French, Italian, and Romansch), two major religions (Catholicism and Protestantism), and strong regional differences between high mountain and flat areas. The Swiss who liberated themselves in 1291 were located in a small, self-contained, homogeneous area. The rebellion against the Habsburgs took place in the three small, German-speaking, Catholic, mountain cantons of Uri, Schwyz, and Unterwalden. All three were rural and farm-oriented, with similar economic and social structures and no large cities. It is important to note this early homogeneity, which contrasts, for example, with Belgium and Canada, both of which were bilingual at the beginning of their national development. This difference may partly explain why Belgium and Canada today have greater difficulty in resolving their linguistic conflicts than Switzerland does. The Swiss were able to adjust over centuries to increasing heterogeneity. They first learned how rural and urban people could live together when Lucerne, Zurich, Bern, and other urban cantons joined the rural cantons in the Swiss Confederation. This was a difficult adjustment, and it took the Swiss time to accept the fact that urban and rural cantons could have very different interests. Only with great effort was open warfare between the rural and urban cantons prevented in 1481. The mediator was a monk by the name of Brother Klaus who, through his successful mediation, became a symbolic figure in Swiss history. He is warmly remembered in Swiss textbooks as having taught the Swiss that conflicts should be negotiated and not turned into armed struggles. It was important for the development of Swiss nationalism to have had a nonmilitaristic mediator as a hero so early in Swiss history.

But this spirit of mediation did not prevent civil war during the Reformation, when some cantons turned Protestant and others remained Catholic. No fewer than four times Catholics and Protestants engaged in bloody fighting from the sixteenth through the eighteenth centuries. But even during these religious wars, there was an episode of accommodation, which is now prominently featured in Swiss textbooks. Once, during a break in the fighting, Catholics and Protestants drank milk out of the same bowl. It took a long time in Swiss history for Catholics and Protestants not only to share a bowl of milk but also to recognize each other as equal partners in the Swiss Confederation.

Linguistically, Switzerland developed very slowly into a multilingual society. It was, for example, only in 1815 that French-speaking Geneva, which already had loose ties with some of the cantons, became a canton of the Confederation. Once again relations were not always smooth. During World War I, for example, one spoke of a "trench" between French- and German-speaking Swiss because the former sympathized with France and the latter with Germany.

In the first centuries of its existence, the Swiss Confederation was chiefly a military alliance. On domestic political issues each canton acted more or less for itself. There were custom duties between cantons and every canton had its own currency and postal service. There were no central Swiss governmental structures except for an assembly (Diet) where delegates from the cantons met. Only unanimous decisions could be implemented, and when the issue was defense against the repeated Habsburg attempts to reconquer Switzerland, they were relatively easy to reach. The Swiss fought their battles against the Habsburgs in a highly unconventional, but very successful, manner. In medieval times it was the custom for opposing armies to meet on an open field and formally announce the beginning of the battle. The Swiss ignored this formality; for example, in the battle of Morgarten, they hid in the wooded hills above a lake until the Habsburg army passed below, then rolled rocks down the hills, panicking the Habsburgs and their horses, drowning many of them in the lake. Also contrary to the generally accepted military conventions of the day, the Swiss refused to take prisoners and commonly killed even surrendering enemies. As a consequence of this unorthodox behavior, the Swiss had a negative image at European courts, one that can be likened to that of contemporary terrorists or guerrillas.

The development of Swiss behavior on the international scene over the centuries throws an interesting light on the perennial question of the influence of "nature" and "nurture." In current debates one sometimes hears the opinion that certain nations are by nature violent, wild, and unwilling to follow international laws. Swiss history is an intriguing example of a change in a nation's behavior. Today the Swiss put great emphasis on the importance of international law. This behavior certainly does not correspond to an inner nature of the Swiss, because different circumstances centuries ago nurtured the Swiss to violate in a gross way the standards of international behavior. At that time they were poor mountain "have-nots"; today they have struck it rich and become "haves," which may partly explain the change in their behavior.

Having defeated the Habsburgs, the Swiss felt so secure militarily that they began an expansionist policy. They turned in particular to northern Italy, south of the Alps, for fruitful new lands to conquer. This change from a defensive to an offensive foreign policy put great strains on the Confederation. The interests of the cantons were often so divergent that it was impossible to reach a consensus at the Diet. Again it was Brother Klaus who gave wise advice. He warned his fellow Swiss to make the fence around their country "not too wide." This phrase is often cited as a basis for the idea of keeping Switzerland a small state. Brother Klaus's advice gained more and more followers after 1515 when the French defeated the Swiss in northern Italy at the battle of Marignano. The French had an enormous technological advantage with their newly developed firearms, and the Swiss were too poor to keep up in this arms race. Marignano was the last Swiss offensive battle, and from then on neutrality slowly developed as a device for Swiss foreign policy. The advantages of being neutral were vividly demonstrated when the Swiss stayed out of the general European religious conflict of 1618 to 1648 known as the Thirty Years' War. The Swiss managed to stay out of all foreign wars between 1515 and the French Revolution.

Within the Swiss Confederation this period was characterized by growing political inequities. There had always been a distinction between free citizens and serfs, but now a few free citizen families took more and more power for themselves and limited the access of others to power. The situation varied from canton to canton, but the overall picture was the same: a few ruling families placed themselves far above the rest of the population. In the canton of Bern, for example, the ruling families, called patricians, ran the canton from the city of Bern and the many castles spread around the countryside. They imitated the luxurious life-style of the nobility of the major European courts, and like the French kings, they even began to claim a divine right to their power and privileges. Financially, they exploited Swiss mercenaries, whom they auctioned off to the highest bidder among the other European rulers. Because one had to be rich to afford Swiss mercenaries, the saying "No money, no Swiss" became current at that time. Despite many heroic tales, the life of most Swiss mercenaries was miserable. They were underpaid, and most of the money paid for their hire went to their canton's ruling families. It is no wonder that during these times the ruling families had to crush some bloody peasant revolts.

When, in 1798, the armies of the French Revolution invaded Switzerland proclaiming the ideas of Liberty, Equality, and Brotherhood, they were welcomed by the many Swiss who had felt oppressed by the regime of the ruling families. The old regime, as it was called, crumbled without significant resistance. Under French tutelage, Switzerland was for the first time made into a unified country with central authorities. The revolutionary idea of one man, one vote was introduced, and all the basic individual freedoms were written into a constitution. After the defeat of Napoleon, however, the Congress of Vienna in 1815 generally restored the old regime, with control and privilege in the hands of a small group of families.

But the fundamental situation had changed, because the people had become aware of the new ideas of the French Revolution. Political parties were not allowed, but the progressive forces organized themselves in student fraternities and in associations of singers, marksmen, and gymnasts. The first half of the nineteenth century was a restless period with progressive and conservative forces clashing not only with words but also, sporadically, with arms. Finally, the progressive forces won a decisive military victory and in 1848 established a constitution for a modern unified Switzerland. Which is older—Switzerland or the United States? Switzerland, if we place its birth in 1291; but the United States, if we say that Switzerland only began to function as a unified country in 1848. The question may be an issue of national pride, but it cannot be answered in an unambivalent way.

The Swiss constitution of 1848 was strongly influenced by the American example. Like the United States, Switzerland established a federal structure, but its member-states were called cantons. Like the U.S. Congress, the Swiss Parliament consists of two chambers. In the National Council, corresponding to the House of Representatives, the cantons are represented according to population. The Council of States is analogous to the Senate, with each canton having two representatives. Also as in the United States, bills have to pass both chambers. The biggest difference between the two constitutions is in the organization of the executive. Switzerland has an executive council of seven members of equal status. This body, called the Federal Council, is not elected by the people but by the Parliament. Each federal councillor heads a department. For practical purposes it was necessary to establish the office of presiding chairman of the Federal Council. This office rotates according to seniority among all federal councillors on an annual basis. During his term as presiding officer, a federal councillor has the title of Swiss president. But this title is not at all comparable to that of the American president. During his year as Swiss president, he has no more power than any other federal councillor and continues to head his particular department.

In addition to establishing central authorities, the constitution of 1848 brought consolidation in many fields. Switzerland received a single currency for the entire country, and postal service was made a federal responsibility. Trade between the cantons was facilitated by the abolition of cantonal custom duties.

The most important development of 1848 was the implementation of the principle of one man, one vote (women were not yet included). This made

Switzerland the world's second oldest (after the United States) continually functioning democracy. France also had a democratic revolution in 1848 but soon established the Second Empire under Napoleon III. Great Britain had made democratic progress, but in the middle of the nineteenth century, its franchise system still excluded many poor people from electoral participation. In other European countries, such as Prussia and Austria, democratic progress was even slower. Thus, once again, the Swiss took a progressive stance. In 1291 they very early gained their freedom within the Holy Roman Empire, and in 1848 they became the first permanent modern European democracy. Again there were complaints from European courts that the rebellious Swiss endangered the established order. There were even diplomatic, but not military, efforts by some of the major European powers to crush the development of Swiss democracy. Today the Swiss are often considered cautious and conservative, but not much more than a hundred years ago they were viewed as progressive and adventuresome. The Swiss political system developed under the constitutional framework of 1848 and Switzerland evolved from a progressive to a more conservative position.

Armed Neutrality

In 1848, neutrality was already such a predominant feature of Swiss foreign policy that it was written into the new constitution as a guiding principle. As we have seen, neutrality began to develop slowly after the French defeat of the Swiss in northern Italy in 1515. At the Congress of Vienna in 1815, Swiss neutrality was formally recognized by the major powers and, in the context of the Treaty of Versailles, a document was signed in 1920 that stated that Swiss neutrality was in the interest of world peace.

Since the Napoleonic wars, Switzerland has been able to stay out of international wars, in particular the two world wars. Was this thanks to its neutrality? The answer cannot be given in a straightforward way because other small European countries were invaded despite their declared neutrality. Why not Switzerland? Sheer luck can never be excluded as a historical explanation. But perhaps it was more than luck—namely, the fact that a strong national defense worked as a deterrent. Many of my American students smile in disbelief when I begin to talk about the Swiss army because they are not aware that Switzerland has an army at all. But there is a strong tradition among the Swiss that their neutrality has to be defended if it wants to be credible and respected. The constitution of 1848 contains the principle that every Swiss male has to serve in the army. Only sickness and absence abroad are excuses for not being drafted. The current system is that military service begins at the age of 20 with seventeen weeks of basic training. Until the age of 50, soldiers are not merely in the reserve but in a stage of permanent readiness. For the first few years after the age of 20, they must spend three weeks of every year participating in military exercises. After about the age of 30, these exercises become shorter and less frequent, but the older soldiers must also be ready to be mobilized. They keep their uniforms and their automatic rifles with live ammunition at home and are responsible for maintaining their equipment in a state of readiness. As a consequence of these measures, Switzerland can mobilize, relative to its total population, a huge armed force in a short period of time.

The danger of being invaded was particularly great during World War II when Hitler's Germany stood to the north, Mussolini's Italy to the south, German-annexed Austria to the east, and Germany-dominated France to the west. Was it military preparedness that saved Switzerland? The Swiss strategy was to retreat into the mountains into redoubt positions. It would certainly not have been easy for the fascist forces to defeat the Swiss in these mountain fortresses, but it is also true that Switzerland made important concessions and that these concessions almost certainly helped maintain Swiss independence. Although Switzerland took in many refugees from Nazi Germany, there were occasions when refugees, in particular Jews, were prevented by the Swiss from crossing their borders. It was in this context that one of the federal councillors said that the Swiss "boat" was full. The Swiss government also permitted German and Italian war material to be transported in locked trains through the Alpine tunnels. In the case of an invasion, these tunnels and all important bridges would have been blown up. Thus, the Fascists may have preferred to collaborate with the Swiss and to keep the railway system open rather than to risk through an invasion the destruction of this essential transportation link through the Alps. Even today the discussion continues in Switzerland whether the Swiss were courageous enough in opposing Hitler and Mussolini.

What chance has Switzerland today to defend its neutrality militarily? An analysis has to begin with its location west of the Iron Curtain. In many ways the Swiss are part of the Western alliance although they are not a member of NATO. When they buy sophisticated war material, they always do it in the West, often from NATO countries. For example, the newest Swiss fighter plane was bought from the United States and the newest tank from the Federal Republic of Germany. It is clear that for all practical purposes the Swiss expect a potential enemy to come from the east. What strategy would they use to defend themselves? In the early 1960s there were some officers who advocated that a future war should be fought with small mobile units that would use chiefly guerrilla tactics and profit from the mountainous terrain. But the argument prevailed that fast advancing enemy tanks protected by air cover could not be stopped in this way. The current strategy is that an enemy should be met in open field battles. There is certainly no expectation that the Swiss armed forces could actually stop a full-fledged Warsaw Pact attack. But the Soviets and their allies may anticipate that their advance could be so much delayed that they would prefer to choose a route north or south of Switzerland to reach the Atlantic. This is the deterrent effect that the Swiss are planning on.

The military effort of Switzerland has big advantages for NATO. Because neutral Austria to the east of Switzerland has only a weak army, if Switzerland's armed forces were also weak, then the Warsaw Pact armies could break through in the center of Europe and separate the northern and southern NATO forces. Thus, in practical terms, Switzerland is protecting the bridge between the northern and southern flanks of NATO. For some Swiss, this implicit support of NATO strategy goes too far. These Swiss are mostly part of the European-wide peace movement, and they argue that Switzerland should reduce its military effort. Some supporters of the peace movement refuse to be drafted into the Swiss army. These individuals are sentenced by military courts to serve prison sentences because the Swiss constitution does not allow for conscientious objectors. The basis for this position is that the Swiss army is purely defensive and that it would never engage in any offensive war. There is also an old Swiss tradition that the dual roles of citizen and soldier are inseparable. The view that every citizen should also be a soldier is much less commonly accepted today than it was during World War II.

Although there is increasing debate over the extent to which neutrality should be militarily defended, the principle of neutrality itself is still almost universally accepted. But there is also greater discussion of the question of whether this neutrality should be combined with a more active Swiss role in world affairs. Some Swiss advocate a cautious inward-looking position best symbolized by a hedgehog. According to this view, Switzerland is too small a state to have any significant influence on the world. At most, it may play a humanitarian role, in particular with the International Red Cross. Other Swiss find this position selfish and egotistical. They argue that Switzerland should speak much more for justice in the world and do something to alleviate injustices. They refer to neutral Sweden in particular as a model. While the Swiss government remained silent, the Swedish government criticized the United States over Vietnam. The Swedes are also much more active than the Swiss in their assistance to developing countries. And sometimes Sweden makes spectacular gestures in international affairs—for example, when the Swedish prime minister tried, although without success, to mediate the war between Iran and Iraq.

It is true that the Swiss are not so cautious that they always remain silent about world affairs. Here a distinction must be made between the Swiss government and Swiss citizens. Swiss neutrality does not limit the free expression of opinions by private citizens or the mass media. Hitler was often unwilling to make this distinction, and this led to shrill protests when Swiss newspapers criticized him or his government. Today one finds a wide variety of views expressed in Swiss newspapers, ranging from support of communism to strong anticommunism. Neutrality is a concept that applies only to actions of the government.

According to its Latin root word, neutrality means "with neither side." During World War II, the Swiss government took this meaning in a very literal way and was afterward blamed for not having spoken out against the injustices of the Hitler regime. Today the Swiss government is still restrained but does raise its voice when it sees gross injustices in the world. It has, for example, protested both the suppression of the Solidarity movement in Poland and the abuses of the Chilean right-wing dictatorship.

Should the Swiss government become even more active? This issue is raised most conspicuously in the debate over whether Switzerland should join the United Nations. It is the only country in the world that, although it belongs to special UN organizations such as UNESCO, is voluntarily not a full member of the United Nations. In 1920, Switzerland joined the League of Nations but had an unpleasant experience when the League imposed economic sanctions against Italy because of its invasion of Ethiopia. It was only with great difficulty that Switzerland was allowed to withdraw from these sanctions against its southern neighbor. It was chiefly this experience that led Switzerland after World War II to abstain from joining the United Nations. But today, it becomes more and more difficult to explain this abstention in a plausible way, and many otherwise well-informed foreigners are unaware that Switzerland is not a UN member. The three other neutral nations of Europe, Austria, Sweden, and Finland, all belong to the world organization where they play a prominent role—a Swede and an Austrian have each held the important post of secretary general of the United Nations. Given this active role of the other European neutrals it is hard to justify to, say, a diplomat from Africa, why Switzerland remains so passive. There is, however, an intriguing but subtle argument why Switzerland should stay out of the United Nations. A case can be made that Switzerland does more for world peace by remaining outside it. The logic is that by taking positions in the United Nations, Switzerland would necessarily make enemies for itself. As a consequence, the task of the International Red Cross could be made more difficult. Sometimes the International Red Cross has been able to intervene when the United Nations has not, and one may argue that such cases could become rare if Switzerland began taking sides in the UN General Assembly. Another harmful development could be that Geneva would be less available as a conference site for peace and disarmament negotiations because one side or the other might be offended by a Swiss vote in the United Nations. Furthermore, other international missions of Switzerland, such as representing the interests of countries when diplomatic relations are broken, might be damaged. For instance, Swiss diplomats look after U.S. interests in Cuba and Iran. According to this view, the world needs a country that interprets its neutrality in a very strict sense and is thus available for special tasks outside the United Nations.

There is currently a fierce debate in Switzerland over whether this is a sufficiently convincing argument for staying out of the United Nations or whether it is interpreted by the world as an excuse for a selfish refusal by the Swiss to accept their legitimate responsibilities (pay their dues) in the modern world. Paying their dues could, for example, mean providing troops for UN peacekeeping forces as other neutral countries do. The decision about Swiss membership in the United Nations will be made in a popular referendum.

How might Swiss neutrality serve as a model for Europe at large, especially if the neutral area included the Eastern European countries? There is much discussion these days about the possibility (or the danger) that Europe should take a more neutral position between the superpowers. Is the location of Europe between the Soviets and the Americans similar to how Switzerland was located in the past between Catholics and Protestants and later between Germany and France? Would it be reasonable to say that European neutrality is in the interest of world peace, as was said about Swiss neutrality in the Treaty of Versailles? In this context it is interesting to note the distinction between *neutrality* and *neutralism*, with the latter term having a more negative connotation.

The Popular Referendum

More than half of all the national referenda that have ever been held in the world have taken place in Switzerland. Thus, Switzerland has developed furthest the notion that citizens should elect representatives and also decide some matters directly. Switzerland is to a large extent not only a representative democracy but also a direct one. When the Swiss speak of the sovereign, they do not refer to a monarch but rather to the people themselves. After a referendum, it is often said that the sovereign has spoken.

This notion of direct citizen involvement has its roots deep in Swiss history. In medieval times, the pastures high up in the mountains were communal property, and decisions about these pastures were made in a communal way. All co-owners assembled under the open sky and decided, for example, what day the cows should be brought down to the valley so they would not be trapped by the first snow. When modern Switzerland was established with the constitution of 1848, its founders could go back to these ancient traditions. In a mystical way, the Swiss spoke in the nineteenth century of reviving the old democratic freedoms. They certainly remembered Old Switzerland much too idealistically, forgetting, for example, that there were also many serfs who did not share the communal pastures. But however imperfect the historical reality was, it was crucially important that the founders of modern Switzerland in the nineteenth century could cite democratic traditions that they were trying to restore. Combined with the revolutionary ideas of the Enlightenment, these old democratic traditions led the Swiss to introduce the popular referendum into the constitution of 1848.

At the beginning, the referendum was limited to constitutional amendments decided by the federal Parliament. All such amendments had to be accepted by the people before they were considered valid. Later in the nineteenth century, the people themselves got the right to propose constitutional amendments. All that was needed was the collection of a certain number of signatures. Currently, 100,000 signatures are required to launch a constitutional initiative. Such initiatives are debated by the federal Parliament, which formulates a recommendation of acceptance or rejection, but the ultimate decision lies with the people. The optional referendum about legislative bills was also introduced in the nineteenth century. Here the people can demand with a certain number of signatures, currently 50,000, that a bill passed by Parliament must be submitted to the voters.

This broadening of the range of questions open to the referendum process has had the consequence of giving the people the power to decide almost any issue they wish. At the present time, however, financial appropriations for war material are not subject to a referendum. But through a constitutional amendment the people could extend the right of referendum to this area, and there are efforts now under way to do so. This example illustrates how far-reaching the Swiss referendum is: There is literally no limit to the issues the voters can decide if they so desire.

When the referendum was introduced, it was expected that its effect would be innovative. The founders of modern Switzerland wished to overcome the inaction of the old regime and its dominance by a few ruling families. They anticipated that the voters would be more open to change, but the opposite happened—the referendum has often had a delaying effect. The best example is probably the introduction of female suffrage. Parliament was ready much earlier than the male voters were to grant women the right to vote. Several times referenda defeated amendments to the constitution that would have established female suffrage. The margin of defeat, however, got smaller each time, and finally, in 1971, women were given the right to vote. This example is typical in the sense that it shows that it often takes a long time to convince people to accept a new idea. Another new idea currently under discussion is Swiss membership in the United Nations. The Federal Council supports the idea, but opinion polls indicate that a majority of the people are opposed. The main popular argument against Swiss membership is that it is a waste of money. The voters need to be convinced that the benefits will be greater than the costs, and such convincing will require time and energy. Sometimes the voters cannot be convinced, and it could very well be that Switzerland will never join the United Nations.

Generally speaking, it is not always negative to delay a decision. This may represent the making of precipitous decisions that are regretted in retrospect. As time goes by, there has been an increasing number of cases in which the people were wise not to move as quickly as their leaders desired. In the 1970s there were, for example, some negative referenda outcomes that prevented Switzerland from expanding its higher education system as quickly as West Germany had done. Today there is general agreement that these votes had the positive result that today relatively few Swiss university graduates are unemployed.

Although the referendum has generally had a delaying effect, one should not neglect the occasions when, thanks to a referendum, new ideas have been brought into the public debate. After the Arab oil embargo in 1973, some students had the original idea of making one Sunday every month traffic-free on Swiss roads. This would not only have saved energy but would also have brought some calm to everyday life. Once a month the highways would have been opened for strolls and bike riding. The students collected the necessary signatures, and the proposal had to be submitted as a constitutional amendment to a referendum. Although some exceptions (such as for ambulances) were planned, all major parties and special interest groups found the idea well-intended but impractical. Although the students received broad popular support, their proposal was still narrowly defeated. Despite this ultimate defeat, this is a good illustration of how the referendum can help to bring unorthodox ideas to public attention.

How egotistical are Swiss voters when they participate in a referendum? Is there not a danger that they simply vote for their narrow selfish interests? Is there not in particular the threat that the interests of minorities are neglected? There is, or course, always the possibility of a tyranny of the majority. And yes, there are cases in Swiss history when minorities suffered from the results of a referendum. The worst case happened at the beginning of this century when a constitutional initiative was accepted that prohibited the killing of animals according to Jewish (kosher) rites. On the surface the proposal was presented as an animal protection measure, but its real intent was clearly anti-Semitic. The referendum allowed anti-Semitic feelings to be expressed in the secrecy of the voting booth. Didn't such an amendment contradict the religious freedom guarantee of the constitution? One would assume so. But if the people themselves decided that the two parts of the constitution are compatible, then no challenge is possible. The people themselves interpret what is constitutional, and no court can overrule their decision because the people are the highest authority in the land. The anti-Semitic amendment is still part of the constitution because of a fear that a new referendum to abolish the article might reawaken anti-Semitic feelings. Rather than confront the issue again, the Swiss prefer to let sleeping dogs lie, and they simply do not enforce the amendment too strictly. It is, for example, easy to import kosher meat.

A current conflict over minority rights concerns conscientious objectors. Parliament would be willing to allow them to serve the country outside the army, but all attempts to change the constitution in this direction have failed in referendum. These two examples show the worst side of the referendum. But there are many other cases in which the referendum revealed great consideration for minority rights. Most illustrative of this positive side are several referenda on the issue of foreign workers in the 1970s. During the economic boom of the 1960s, Switzerland admitted so many foreign workers that they came to number more than 1 million in a total population of 6 million. This foreign presence was felt in many sectors of Swiss society: There were school classes where foreign children outnumbered Swiss children, and railway stations in the evening and on weekends became gathering places for foreigners. Many Swiss no longer felt at home in their own country and began to refer to the "foreignization" of Switzerland. Politically an antialien movement developed that demanded a severe reduction in the number of foreigners allowed in Switzerland. This movement launched several constitutional initiatives that would have forced hundreds of thousands of foreigners to leave the country almost immediately. There was a great temptation for Swiss voters to accept these constitutional initiatives, especially because the economic boom was over and Switzerland gave the impression of being overcrowded, with too much traffic on the highways and a severe housing shortage. To be sure, all major political parties and special interest groups recommended rejection of the constitutional amendments proposed by the antialien movement because it would be morally wrong to treat a defenseless minority in such a harsh way. But there was the obvious danger that frustrated voters would let loose their antiforeign prejudices. No rational justification was necessary, only a mark on a secret ballot. The constitutional amendments received broad popular support but were defeated each time, although sometimes quite narrowly. The leading newspapers printed editorials applauding the maturity of Swiss voters. It must indeed be recognized that in these referenda a majority of Swiss voters were willing to protect the rights of a weak minority. As a qualification it must be added, however, that the federal government itself took some vigorous steps to limit the number of foreigners in Switzerland. Thus, the majority of the voters preferred the milder policy of the government to the harsher measures of the antialien movement.

The foreign worker issue was a very difficult test for the notion that a direct democracy is able to protect minorities. When the minorities are Swiss citizens, and not as marginal as Jews and conscientious objectors, they usually have a good chance of having their special rights protected. It is even a good argument in a referendum that a proposal would benefit small minorities such as Italian speakers or mountain farmers.

How does the Swiss voter reach a decision in a referendum? Is the Swiss citizen the wise sovereign who is well informed and weighs carefully all arguments for and against a proposal? The referendum has certainly had an educating effect and has raised the level of political information, but the Swiss citizen should not be viewed as being completely idealistic. Propaganda is an important feature in referendum campaigns. Much more than in other elections, the views of the citizens can be molded in referenda. In other elections, most voters have a long-standing party loyalty that is difficult to change, but in a referendum the voter may be unfamiliar with the issue and consequently more open to propaganda effects. Money and organization are therefore important weapons in the winning of a referendum. However, a costly campaign may backfire by creating sympathy for the financially weaker side.

The main purpose in a referendum campaign is not to convice the adversary but to mobilize one's own troops, which is often not easy. Voter turnout is often shamefully low; often more than half of the voters stay home. This is of great concern, especially because the trend has been downward since the 1950s. Many explanations have been offered by scholars and other commentators. Is it too often to call on the voter to cast a ballot four times a year on the average? Have the issues become too complicated? Is it, for instance, too difficult for the average voter to evaluate what benefit and costs Swiss membership in the United Nations would bring not only to Switzerland but also to the world at large? Or are the causes deeper, a retreat into a more private life, for example, or a mistrust of politics? The explanation of the decreased turnout probably has to do with a combination of these and many other factors.

Should it be recommended that other countries use the referendum as the Swiss do? There has indeed been an increased use of the referendum in the Western world. Great Britain was for a long time the foremost example of a pure representative democracy. Yet recently the British have used referenda to decide membership in the Common Market and local autonomy for Scotland and Wales. Sweden and Austria have used the referendum as a means of tackling the thorny problem of nuclear power, and Italy resolved the divorce issue in a national referendum. In the United States the referendum gains importance in many states and local communities, and there are even some members of Congress who play with the idea of introducing the referendum at the national level. Has the time come to take the concept of democracy as rule by the people more seriously and to give a bigger role to the referendum in the democracies of the world? Switzerland provides a good basis on which to judge the merits of the referendum because the Swiss experience reveals both strengths and weaknesses of this institution of direct democracy. The most serious weakness is probably that unconventional minorities may not be sufficiently protected from possible abuses of their rights. The greatest strength of the referendum is the legitimacy it gives to political decisions. And it is precisely the lack of legitimacy of many political decisions that is an increasing problem in modern democracies. Thus, it may be a good idea to transfer more political responsibilities from politicians and bureaucrats to the people. If the results of a decision are mostly negative, then the voters must share at least part of the blame.

Federalism

To foreign observers, the most striking thing about Swiss society is often how smooth the relations among the four language groups of the country seem to be. About 70 percent of the Swiss speak German, 20 percent French, 10 percent Italian, and not quite 1 percent Romansch. The predominant position of one language causes severe problems in other countries, for example, in Canada where the English speakers outnumber the French speakers. Why does the predominant position of German speakers not cause similar problems in Switzerland? Or do the problems perhaps exist, but more subtly and therefore less noticeably? Could it be that the relations among Swiss language groups are not as smooth as they appear at first sight? The answer is complex. There is always the potential that the German speakers could dominate the linguistic minorities, but usually the federal structure of the country would prevent this from happening.

Federalism is a crucial feature in the Swiss political system. The Latin root word, *foedus*, means a tie or a bond. A federal structure consists of autonomous parts tied together within one country. For Switzerland the building blocks of federalism are not the four linguistic groups but rather the 26 cantons. This is important to understand how Swiss federalism functions. Most of the Swiss cantons have a long and proud history during which they have developed a strong cantonal identity. Cantonal flags have great symbolic value. The canton of Geneva, for example, still calls itself with great pride the Republic of Geneva. Historically speaking, the cantons came first and *they* made Switzerland—a confederation of cantons. It is not the other way around, as in France where the nation was built from a center at Paris. Due to its historical development, Switzerland has no clear center. To be sure, Bern is the center of the federal administration with the parliament building and the offices of the federal councillors. But even the federal administration is somewhat decentralized, with the supreme court, for example, located in French-speaking Lausanne and the Swiss National Accident Insurance Institute in Lucerne. Bern is only the fourth-largest city in Switzerland, with Zurich, Basel, and Geneva each having more inhabitants. Bern is also not the business center. For bank dealings, for example, one would go to the larger cities. From a cultural perspective also, other cities are more important than Bern.

The absence of a dominant center is significant for Swiss federalism. Much of Swiss political life takes place within the individual cantons. This is particularly true for educational and cultural affairs. And for these matters it is important that 22 of the 26 cantons are linguistically homogeneous. In the canton of Geneva, for example, French is the only official language, and schools teach only in this language. French speakers control educational matters in Geneva and are able to organize their schools according to their own cultural preferences.

They begin their school year, for example, in the fall, whereas other cantons begin in the spring. Leaving educational and cultural matters to the linguistically most homogeneous cantons alleviates a thorny problem for a multilingual country. For example, the Swiss do not have to fight at the national level over which textbooks should be used in schools.

The autonomy of the cantons is firmly rooted in Swiss tradition. According to the federal constitution, the cantons have priority to deal with an issue. The federal level can intervene only if it has been given the explicit right to do so. And it is not easy to shift responsibilities from the cantonal to the federal level. In all cases, a change in the constitution would be necessary, and such constitutional changes require approval by a majority of both the voters and the cantons. Therefore, the more numerous smaller cantons have a potent weapon and cannot be outvoted by the few large cantons. The small cantons are also protected in the Council of States, the chamber of the federal Parliament where each canton, regardless of size, has two representatives.

Despite the importance of the cantons, blocs of cantons could form along linguistic lines so that the language cleavage would still have great political importance. There is always the possibility that the two largest language groups in particular could confront one another as blocs of French- and German-speaking cantons. This happened recently when the French-speaking cantons bitterly complained that the representatives of the German-speaking cantons in the federal Parliament favored the airport in Zurich over the one in Geneva. Fortunately, such head-on confrontations between French- and German-speaking cantons are relatively rare. One reason is that the border between French- and German-speaking Switzerland occurs in three bilingual cantons, which blurs the distinction between linguistically based blocs of cantons. More important, neither the German- nor the French-speaking parts of Switzerland are internally homogeneous. Important cleavage lines cut across the linguistic borders. Therefore, for certain issues some German speakers have more in common with some French speakers than they do with other German speakers. This is often true from an economic perspective. The location of the tourist industry, for example, in all four linguistic areas leads to a close cooperation across these language borders. It would be very different if the tourist industry was concentrated in only the French-speaking area. In such a case, economic and linguistic interests would reinforce each other. Many other industries, such as watchmaking and cheesemaking, are also located in at least the two largest language areas. Thus, the interests of these industries are not represented by a single language group.

It is also significant for Swiss federalism that the cleavage between Catholics and Protestants cuts across the border between German and French speakers. Some German-speaking cantons are predominantly Catholic, others Protestant; the same division can be found among the French-speaking cantons. If the religious cleavage were the same as the linguistic one, it would be much more likely that coherent blocs of cantons would confront one another in Swiss politics. But with linguistic, economic, and religious cleavages cutting across each other in a very complex way, politics in Switzerland is characterized by constantly shifting coalitions. On one issue a German-speaking mountain farmer may have common interests with other German speakers, on another issue with other Catholics irrespective of language, and on still a third issue with other mountain farmers without regard to language or religion. Due to these shifting coalitions, no single group is a permanent majority. Every group risks being in the minority on at least some issues.

The absence of coherent language blocs also has a consequence that identity with one's language is not always of prime importance. To be sure, there are issues in Swiss politics, such as the subsidies to the airports of Zurich and Geneva, where language affiliation becomes a key consideration, but at other times cantonal, religious, or occupational identities are more important. In this context, it is important to add that German speakers in Switzerland have a great number of distinctive dialects and identity with a dialect may also be of great significance.

Given all this complexity, German speakers rarely function as a unified and dominant bloc in Swiss politics. But there is always the danger that such a situation could occur and threaten the interests of the linguistic minorities. In recent years the apprehension of the linguistic minorities over possible German-language domination has somewhat increased. It is in particular the economic power of Zurich that has begun to be a problem for the complex and subtle balances in Swiss society. There have been many complaints in French-speaking Switzerland that the headquarters of more and more of the largest companies are moving to Zurich. The country has to guard against the possibility that the linguistic minorities would feel exploited by a powerful economic center located in the German-speaking area. There are other aspects about which German speakers also have to be careful. For example, there has recently been some criticism that French-speaking federal officials are overly occupied with translating documents written originally in German. Influential voices from French-speaking Switzerland are suggesting that more of the original drafts should be written in French, thus giving more influence to the perspectives of this linguistic minority.

Unlike the United States, Switzerland did not seek to become a melting pot in which all citizens spoke a single language. Whereas the United States tried to advocate a single American way of life, the Swiss allowed the various parts of the country to continue their own life-styles. In recent years, the United States has once again become aware of its cultural diversity, and there have even been efforts to have Spanish accepted as a second national language. The largest American cities in particular have today a great cultural and linguistic diversity.

It would be interesting to see whether, and in what respects, they could profit from the Swiss experience. Lessons from multilingual Switzerland may also be drawn for the Common Market, which currently has seven official languages.

Elections and Appointments

In a country as culturally diverse as Switzerland the central authorities must work to balance the conflicting interests of many groups. In Switzerland this task is eased by the federal structure, which permits the central government to ignore certain issues recognized as the responsibility of the cantons or localities. The principle of neutrality in foreign policy also enables the central authorities to disregard some potentially divisive questions. For example, although opinion polls indicate that French speakers often have different views on world affairs than German speakers, most of these differences do not have to be resolved. Federalism in domestic affairs and neutrality in foreign affairs lessen the scope of the federal authorities' responsibilities, but many issues still confront the federal authorities, and the number of these issues is increasing. Economic questions in particular must be resolved more and more often at the national level. How are the officials who deal with these issues for the country as a whole elected and appointed? The basic Swiss principle is "proportionality," which contrasts sharply with the American principle of "winner take all." In the United States, politics resembles a sporting event: Either you win or you lose. In Switzerland you can win and lose to different degrees. Even if you are not the first over the finish line, you can still get a certain share of the prize (power). In principle, the power you get corresponds to your numerical strength. If the support of your group is, say, 10 percent, you should get 10 percent of the spoils.

With regard to the language groups, this principle of proportionality was applied at the foundation of modern Switzerland in 1848. In the first Federal Council there were five German, one French, and one Italian speakers. Thus, the linguistic minorities had exactly proportional representation. Since 1848 the German-speaking majority has never had more than five federal councillors and at times only four, which has been an overrepresentation of the linguistic minorities. There are currently five German- and two French-speaking federal councillors. There is now no Italian-speaking federal councillor, but this will probably change in the future. As a minority of 10 percent, Italian speakers have no claim to permanent representation in the federal executive.

The principle of proportionality with regard to language is applied not only to the Federal Council, but also to the federal administration as a whole. For example, it applies to the top positions in the army, the federal railway system, and the federal postal service. For American readers, it is important to note that the principle of proportional representation by language is not put in legal terms and is thus not enforceable by the courts. It thus differs from American affirmative action programs in regard to race and sex. In Switzerland, the right of the linguistic minorities to a proportional share of governmental positions has developed as an unwritten rule. Deep-rooted social norms, not the courts, make sure that these rules are upheld.

Whereas modern Switzerland has always used the principle of proportionality in regard to linguistic groups, this has not been true for political parties. In the struggle to establish modern Switzerland, liberals and conservatives confronted each other, with the former advocating a more centralized, the latter a more decentralized, solution. The liberals decided the issue in their favor with a military victory. In writing and applying the constitution, the victorious liberals used the principle of winner take all. Elections for Parliament based on this principle resulted in a comfortable majority for the liberals. This majority was used to elect only liberals to the Federal Council. For almost half a century the conservatives lost election after election, both for Parliament and the Federal Council. In 1891, an important change occurred when the first conservative was elected to the Federal Council. The liberals still held a parliamentary majority, but they no longer insisted on the principle of winner take all for Federal Council elections. After World War I the liberals took another step toward proportionality when they allowed the conservatives a second seat on the Federal Council. The liberals and the conservatives continue to exist today, with the liberals using the name Free Democrats and the conservatives, Christian Democrats. Each party holds two seats on the Federal Council, and this corresponds exactly to their electoral strength. Another two seats are held by the Social Democrats, who did not have significant electoral strength until early in this century. The development of the Social Democrats was assisted by the passage of a national referendum after World War I that changed the parliamentary election system from winner take all to proportional representation. This change ended the Free Democrat (liberal) majority in Parliament, and since then no single party has held a parliamentary majority. Despite their newly gained electoral strength in Parliament, no Social Democrat was elected to the Federal Council. The other parties viewed the Social Democrats, especially after their participation in a bloody general strike in 1918, as insufficiently trustworthy for such an important office. It was only during World War II that the bourgeois parties were willing to elect a Social Democrat as a federal councillor, and it was not until 1959 that they elected a second councillor, thus achieving proportional representation. The fourth largest party is currently the Swiss People's Party, which split from the Free Democrats after World War I and represented chiefly agricultural interests. Today the party is enlarging its electoral base, and the one seat it holds on the Federal Council corresponds to its current electoral strength. The formula of 2:2:2:1 for the four largest parties is often called the "magic formula"; it mirrors exactly the numerical strength of these four parties in the electorate. This formula has remained unchanged since the Social Democrats won their second Federal Council seat in 1959. There are some other parties represented in the Swiss Parliament, but none of them are strong enough to claim representation in the federal executive.

With this background it is understandable that Swiss parliamentary elections have become unexciting. The election of October 1983 is only the most recent example. As Table 9.1 indicates, the changes from the previous election were only slight.

Before and after the election of October 1983, the three largest parties each had a numerical claim to two Federal Council seats. There was also no question that the seventh seat still belonged to the Swiss People's Party. The minor parties gained about 4 percent over the 1979 results, but no one of them received as much as 5 percent of the total vote.

Given this stability in voting behavior, it would require a political earthquake to change the composition of the Federal Council. As could be expected, the same coalition of the four largest parties will continue to hold all of the executive council seats. Parliament elects the federal councillors for the entire legislative period of four years, and they are usually re-elected for at least another term or two. They tend to step down only when they reach retirement age. After the 1983 election, both a Free Democrat and a Social Democrat who were in their mid-sixties decided not to seek another term. (The Social Democrat unfortunately died a few days after announcing his retirement.)

When a federal councillor retires, the replacement process resembles the completion of a jigsaw puzzle. A successful candidate (usually a member of Parliament) must combine a particular set of characteristics in order not to upset the careful balance among the federal councillors. In 1983, the retiring Free Democrat was French-speaking and therefore his replacement had to be French-speaking also; the retiring Social Democrat was a German speaker and had to be replaced by another one. In addition, it is necessary to maintain a balance between Catholic and Protestant councillors and to rotate Federal Council membership among the various cantons.

For Swiss political insiders it is a favorite game to discuss the jigsaw puzzle of Federal Council replacements. For the voters, this game is much less interesting, and they have little input into it. This is strikingly different from the American process for electing a chief executive. U.S. presidential elections are a spectacular competition where the voters have the ultimate say. There are some Swiss political commentators who advocate a more competitive style for Federal Council elections. This would require that the magic formula be given up and that at least one of the three largest parties go into opposition. At present this would most likely be the Social Democrats. They could then try, perhaps together with other small leftist parties, to elect a parliamentary, and then a Federal Council, majority. A few Social Democrats support this idea, but the party as a whole is

Table 9.1   Party Strength in National Council Elections (percentage)

	1979	1983
Free Democrats	24.1	23.4
Social Democrats	24.4	22.8
Christian Democrats	21.5	20.2
Swiss People's Party	11.6	11.1
Minor parties combined	18.4	22.5

unwilling to adopt this electoral strategy. They argue that the stability of the Swiss electorate would not give them a parliamentary majority in the foreseeable future and that they would therefore be placed in permanent opposition. With the formula now in use, it is virtually impossible to change the membership of the Federal Council in any significant way. A federal councillor who is not making serious mistakes can anticipate remaining in office for eight or twelve years. This contrasts sharply with most other democracies, where the members of the executive are constantly faced with the problem of re-election. Is the latter situation all good? One can argue that in this way an executive always has to watch how public opinion develops, but this preoccupation may prevent the executive from taking a sufficiently long-term perspective on events. A Swiss federal councillor, on the other hand, can use job security to do some long-range planning, which may ultimately be beneficial to the country.

Decisionmaking

The principle of proportionality ensures that all groups are represented according to their numerical strength. Such representation, however, does not necessarily give power in decisionmaking. Minority groups may still be outvoted when decisions are made. Thus, it is important to study not only the participants in the decision process but also the process itself. How are political decisions typically made in Switzerland? We must distinguish preparliamentary, parliamentary, and referendum phases in the process.

Bills are usually not drafted by Parliament but rather by expert committees in a phase preceding any parliamentary deliberations. To understand Swiss decisionmaking, it is important to grasp the complex composition and working of these expert committees. In this context, to be an expert usually means to be a representative of a special interest group. The notion is that these committees need an expertise about the various special interests in society and that this knowledge is best procured by people representing these interests. When a bill has to be drafted about highway construction, representatives of the automobile associations will sit on the expert committee. Other special interests will be represented as well; for example, environmentalists who are interested in limiting the damage that the highway does to the environment. For a bill about hospitals the medical profession and the health insurance industry will certainly be represented. A few broadly defined interest groups, such as the business community, trade unions, and organizations of farmers and artisans, participate in almost all expert committees. In addition to these groups, expert committees always contain a few top-level federal bureaucrats. Furthermore, the cantons are almost always represented. Finally, there are always a few true experts who have special technical knowledge in the field being legislated.

Expert committees are appointed by the Federal Council, which, however, usually does not have much leeway in making the appointments. There are many written and even more unwritten rules on how expert committees for particular issues should be composed. For a bill about a highway issue, for example, it is simply a must for the Federal Council to appoint representatives of the automobile associations. These associations may even tell the Federal Court beforehand whom they would like to have appointed—for an important bill probably the president of the association, for a less important bill perhaps the vice president or secretary.

Deliberations of expert committees always take place behind closed doors. But some research knowledge has now accumulated on how these committees make their decisions. In most cases, the goal is to reach a consensus among all participants. Quite frequently, this goal is achieved. Such labels as amicable agreement, concordance, accommodation, and consociationalism have been attached to this pattern of decisionmaking. Sometimes the consensus is of an implicit rather than an explicit nature. This happens in particular at the end of a discussion when the chairman summarizes the sense of the meeting and in doing so counts not only heads but also the political status of the individual committee members and the intensity with which they advocate their position. This decision pattern has also been called decision by interpretation. Its main characteristic is that it remains unclear whether all committee members agree with how the chairman interprets the sense of the discussion in his summary. There are all kinds of political and psychological reasons why someone does not wish to say that he has changed his opinion and now agrees (or that he continues to disagree). These decisions by interpretation can have a manipulative element and can be used by a shrewd chairman in an autocratic way.

The voting mechanism also plays an important role in decisionmaking by expert committees. An explicit consensus in the sense of amicable agreement may not be attainable. The chairman may be challenged when he tries to interpret a decision in his summary, or the chairman may not even try to interpret the sense of the meeting. In such cases, which are not uncommon, Swiss expert committees rely on majority rule.

Expert committees report to the Federal Council, which then forwards the draft bill to Parliament. At this stage, the Federal Council may extend the process of consultation by inviting written opinions from an even larger number of special interest groups. The role of the Federal Council is particularly important if no consensus has been reached in the preparliamentary phase. In such cases the Federal Council must decide which proposal should be submitted to Parliament.

For the deliberations in Parliament it makes a big difference whether a consensus has been reached in the preparliamentary phase. If it has, then Parliament will tend to approve the consensus. To understand this pattern, it is important to know that many of the interest group representatives who participate in the preparliamentary phase also are members of Parliament. This is in sharp contrast to the American system, where the place of special interest groups is to lobby Congress. These groups are invited to testify at special congressional hearings, but they are supposedly not represented in Congress itself. In Switzerland it is considered appropriate and even useful that the president of the farmers' association, for example, have a seat in Parliament. He is elected as a member of a particular party, but everyone knows that he is serving in Parliament chiefly as spokesman for the interests of farmers.

If no consensus is reached in the preparliamentary phase, it is up to Parliament to make a decision among the competing positions, and in these cases very close votes may occur. The various political parties each take an official position, but party discipline is usually quite low in the Swiss Parliament. This is mainly due to the federal structure of the country and to characteristics of the parliamentary election system. The parties have their strongholds in the individual cantons and are only loosely organized at the federal level. Quite often cantonal sections of the same party may take different positions on an issue, which is then also reflected in the voting behavior in Parliament. As noted previously, parliamentary elections are based on proportional representation. In the present context it is important to add that the ranking of candidates on the election lists is done by the voters rather than by the parties. In most other countries using this system, the party determines in what rank order its candidates are allowed to enter Parliament. In Switzerland the party simply submits the names of its candidates, and the voters can then rank-order them by writing some candidates twice and crossing off others. The voter is even allowed to write in candidates from other parties. This system obviously takes power away from the parties. They have neither the carrot of giving a good rank to a candidate nor the stick of giving a bad rank to another. This weakening of the parties gives increased power to special interest groups, which can tell their members which candidates to write twice. The teachers' association, for example, can tell its members which candidates across all party lists are most sympathetic to the interests of teachers.

Following parliamentary debates only superficially, one gets the impression that the political parties are the major actors because their positions are widely publicized and seem to be dominant. But behind the scenes the positions of the cantons and the special interest groups are usually much more important. Thus, it is understandable that divisions in Parliament often do not closely follow party lines.

Losers in Parliament may continue the battle in a national referendum. Here again the special interest groups are in a stronger position than the political parties, because they are better organized and have more financial resources at their disposal. Referendum campaigns are often the battlefield for interest groups rather than for political parties, which usually play a secondary role.

The typical Swiss decision process from an expert committee through Parliament to a referendum does not correspond to the classic pattern of a party-based parliamentary democracy. Parliament is not the ultimate decision arena, and the political parties are not the sole actors. Parliament is only one of several arenas, and parties are sometimes overshadowed by other, more important groups. The most striking feature of the Swiss decision process is the existence of a relatively small group of persons who accumulate key roles in various groups and institutions. It is a common pattern that a member of Parliament, which is not a fulltime position, has leading roles in his party and several interest groups. Most likely he also has important positions in his canton and is perhaps a colonel in the army. It is also possible that he does some parttime teaching at a university and is therefore an expert in some special field, such as law or economics. A recent study estimated that only about 300 persons belong to this exclusive group of key decisionmakers.[5] These people meet each other in a multitude of meetings, and over the years they usually get to know each other personally as well.

Some Swiss critics speak of a closely knit elite cartel that they claim rules the country. These same critics also complain that membership in this cartel is particularly biased against giving power to the working class and women. Others see more positive aspects in how the Swiss organize their decision process. One American scholar speaks of democratic corporatism in describing the Swiss decision process and argues that the close collaboration at the elite level makes Switzerland economically more competitive on the world market.[6]

How great is the influence of the individual citizen? The individual's major weapon is the ability to say no in a referendum. However close the agreement within the elite group, it needs the support of citizens in the referenda. And as we have seen, this support is often not easy to get. There are many cases in recent Swiss history where the people as sovereign said no, although practically the entire elite recommended acceptance of a proposal. Thus, in a negative way the citizens have a great amount of power. But they cannot bring about major changes; they are in particular unable to replace one set of leaders with another: Membership in the elite changes only very slowly. In most other democracies the citizen is the referee who decides which group of leaders will hold power. In Switzerland the essential game is played between an elite group on the one hand and the people on the other. The elite group can govern, but the citizens always have the option of pulling the brake if they disagree with the direction in which the elite is taking the country.

Can the Swiss experience be considered a success? The answer is certainly positive if economic wealth is an indicator of success. If we neglect some oil-rich nations of the Middle East, Switzerland often has the highest GNP per capita (the values fluctuate with the currency exchange rates) in the world. Unemployment in Switzerland is minimal, inflation rates are low, and there are no poverty-ridden slums in Swiss cities. This bright economic picture is all the more surprising because Switzerland was for centuries a very poor country. It lacks the natural resources, such as oil and coal, on which wealth could easily be built. The economic success story of Switzerland is closely linked to its political development. The country overcame its internal divisions and established a high level of political stability, which provided the basis for successful economic development. On the labor front, for example, strikes are very rare now; this is in sharp contrast to the situation earlier in this century. It is also true that influence can move in the opposite direction, with the Swiss economic success helping promote political stability. Because the large Swiss economic pie provides plenty to distribute, there are few of the bitter confrontations that often come about when resources are limited.

Today the Swiss are aware of their privileged position. A recent study found that the Swiss are more likely to trust their government to do the right thing than the citizens of any other Western democracy surveyed, including the United States.[7] Are the Swiss also happy? Happiness is an elusive term that can be defined in many different ways. Traveling in Switzerland, one sees some grim-looking faces that do not seem to indicate a great deal of happiness. There is criticism, especially among the young, that most Swiss put too much emphasis on hard work and material goods and not enough on spontaneity and enjoyment of life. Maybe a certain stuffiness is simply the other side of political stability and economic wealth.

Notes

1. Gallup Poll, "World Leaders Say Swiss Are Best Governed People," *International Herald Tribune*, June 27–28, 1970.

2. Quoted in J. R. DeSalis, *Switzerland and Europe: Essays and Reflections* (London: Wolff, 1971), p. 79.

3. Stein Rokkan, "Foreword," in Jürg Steiner, *Amicable Agreement Versus Majority Rule: Conflict Resolution in Switzerland* (Chapel Hill: University of North Carolina Press, 1974).

4. The consociational theory is most extensively treated in Arend Lijphart, *Democracy in Plural Societies: A Comparative Exploration* (New Haven, Conn.: Yale University Press, 1977).

5. Hanspeter Kriesi, *Entscheidungsstrukturen und Entscheidungsprozesse in der Schweizer Politik* (Frankfurt/M.: Campus Verlag, 1980).

6. Peter Katzenstein, *Corporatism and Change: Austria, Switzerland, and the Politics of Industry* (Ithaca, N.Y.: Cornell University Press, 1984).

7. Dusan Sidjanski, "Turnout, Stability and the Left-Right Dimension," in Howard R. Penniman, ed., *Switzerland at the Polls: The National Elections of 1979* (Washington, D.C.: American Enterprise Institute, 1983), p. 135.

Suggested Reading

Barber, Benjamin R. *The Death of Communal Liberty: A History of Freedom in a Swiss Mountain Canton*. Princeton, N.J.: Princeton University Press, 1974.

Bonjour, Edgar. *A Short Hisory of Switzerland*. Oxford: Clarendon Press, 1952.

Codding, George Arthur. *The Federal Government of Switzerland*. Boston: Houghton Mifflin, 1961.

Hughes, Christopher. *The Parliament of Switzerland*. London: Cassell, 1962.

———. *Switzerland*. London: Ernest Benn, 1975.

Katzenstein, Peter. *Corporation and Change: Austria, Switzerland, and the Politics of Industry*. Ithaca, N.Y.: Cornell University Press, 1984.

Kerr, Henry H. *Switzerland: Social Cleavage and Partisan Conflict*. Beverly Hills, Calif.: Sage, 1974.

Luck, J. Murray. *Modern Switzerland*. Palo Alto, Calif.: Society for the Promotion of Science and Scholarship, 1978.

McRae, Kenneth D. *Conflict and Compromise in Multilingual Societies*, vol. 1, *Switzerland*. Waterloo, Ontario: Wilfrid Laurier University Press, 1983.

Penniman, Howard R., ed. *Switzerland at the Polls: The National Elections of 1979*. Washington, D.C.: American Enterprise Institute, 1983.

Rabinbach, Anson. *The Crisis of Austrian Socialism: From Red Vienna to Civil War, 1927–1934*. Chicago: University of Chicago Press, 1983.

Riedelsperger, Max E. *The Lingering Shadow of Nazism: The Austrian Independent Party Movement Since 1945*. New York: Columbia University Press, 1978.

Schlesinger, Thomas O. *Austrian Neutrality in Postwar Europe: The Domestic Roots of a Foreign Policy*. Vienna: Braumüller, 1972.

Schmid, Carol L. *Conflict and Consensus in Switzerland*. Berkeley: University of California Press, 1981.

Stadler, Karl R. *Austria*. London: Ernest Benn, 1971.

Steiner, Kurt. *Politics in Austria*. Boston: Little, Brown, 1972.

————, ed. *Modern Austria*. Palo Alto, Calif.: SPOSS, 1981.

Steiner, Jürg. *Amicable Agreement Versus Majority Rule: Conflict Resolution in Switzerland*. Chapel Hill: University of North Carolina Press 1974.

Steiner, Jürg, and Dorff, Robert H. *A Theory of Political Decision Modes: Intraparty Decision Making in Switzerland*. Chapel Hill: University of North Carolina Press, 1980.

Sully, Melanie A. *Parties and Elections in Austria*. London: Hurst, 1981.

————. *Continuity and Change in Austrian Socialism: The Eternal Quest for the Third Way*. New York: Columbia University Press, 1982.

Ziegler, Jean. *Switzerland: The Awful Truth*. New York: Harper & Row, 1977.

10

Austria

Anton Pelinka

The Historical Setting:
From the First to the Second Republic

In 1918 the Austro-Hungarian Empire collapsed. It had been a multilingual empire, the second biggest European country in size and the third largest in population. A small part of the empire, inhabited mainly by the German-speaking Austrians, became one of the smaller European countries—the Republic of Austria, inhabited by 7 million people. This republic—the First Republic—which lasted until 1934, lacked most of the characteristics that the Second Republic, founded in 1945, has established.[1]

1. The First Republic had a deficiency in national consciousness, a kind of inferiority complex implying the idea of annexation to Germany. The Second Republic is based on a widely accepted idea of a specific Austrian nation in the center of Europe with a specific national as well as international role between the superpowers and their blocs.

2. The First Republic lacked a democratic consensus, which tended in combination with other factors to destroy the democratic constitution. This happened in 1933 and 1934 when the cabinet of Engelbert Dollfuss gradually established a semifascist dictatorship. The Second Republic is a stabilized democratic system: All indicators demonstrate a highly developed consensus among the elite groups of all important political parties.

3. The First Republic failed to achieve economic stability. Inflation, unemployment, and—as a result—social tension and social unrest characterized those

years. The Second Republic still enjoys remarkable economic success, including, for example, an economic growth rate above the European average, an inflation rate below the European average, and a strike rate below the average of all West European democracies.

The lack of self-confidence was expressed in November 1918 upon the abdication of the emperor by the declaration of the Provisional National Assembly that Austria was part of the German Republic. But this annexation (*Anschluss*) was not permitted by the Entente powers, which forced Austria—against its will—to remain independent of Germany. The Republic of Austria became a state before it became a nation.

The constitution worked out and accepted by the Constituent Assembly elected in 1919 reflected the consensus of the two major political parties—the Social Democrats and the Christian Socials, both linked by the coalition behind the provisional government. But in 1920, the Social Democrats went over to the opposition, bringing about a situation typical of the First Republic: the Christian Socials, cooperating with some smaller parties from the right, held power; the Social Democrats seemed to be imprisoned in the role of permanent opposition.

Nevertheless, the Christian Socials—influenced strongly by antiparliamentary tendencies in other European countries, mainly in Italy—began to leave the constitutional consensus in the late 1920s. In 1933 and 1934, democracy and parliamentary rule were eliminated step by step. The government established the "authoritarian regime" and won a short but bloody civil war in February 1934 against the opposition on the left. The "corporate state" between 1934 and 1938 was in reality a one-party system led by the Christian Socials in the Patriotic Front (Vaterländische Front).

In March 1938 Germany occupied Austria. Foreign pressure from the German National Socialist dictatorship and domestic pressure from the Austrian Nazi Party caused the collapse of the regime. German troops invaded Austria, and Austrian independence was annulled. Austria became a German province. Democratic and patriotic forces—on the left as well as on the right—were persecuted.

In 1943, the Allied powers declared re-establishment of an independent Austria one of their political goals. During the last months of World War II, Allied troops liberated Austria. In contrast to the situation in 1918, Austrians were much more optimistic about the chances for an independent Austria. A democratic coalition formed a "provisional government" and organized free elections. The Austrian experience with dictatorship and occupation had strengthened both their belief in democracy and their belief in Austrian independence. The preconditions for an Austrian nation had been formed.

The coalition between the two major parties was not only the base of reconciliation but also the base of certain patterns of compromise decisionmaking that became the most typical characteristics of the political system. The People's Party

(ÖVP) represented the winners of the civil war in 1934; the Socialist Party (SPÖ) spoke for the losers, for the victims of "Austrofascism." Both sides had been the victims of the Nazi dictatorship between 1938 and 1945, and both now agreed on a model of political and economic cooperation. This model constitutes the principal consensus concerning all major questions of Austrian politics.

Backed by an overwhelming majority of the people, the coalition government decided two fundamental issues in the years between 1945 and 1955. Despite the presence of Soviet, American, British, and French troops, the Austrian political system should be a Western one. That meant free competition between political parties and a common front against the Communist Party, which—as many Communist parties did in other European countries—left the coalition government in 1947. The second important decision was that in spite of the Western political system, Austria would be permanently neutral in international affairs. Western in the field of domestic politics; neither Western nor Eastern in the field of foreign politics—that was the outcome of the first decade of the Second Republic.[2]

The occupation by the four Allied powers ended in 1955 with the signing of the Austrian State Treaty. The Allies could leave the country convinced that Austria would not join any military bloc. Austria got back full sovereignty. After the withdrawal of all foreign troops, the Austrian National Council declared Austria permanently neutral.

The fundamental consensus survived the end of the occupation and the end of the grand coalition. After 1955, one main argument in favor of the coalition between the two major parties became obsolete. It was no longer necessary to demonstrate national unity toward the Allied powers and their double role as liberators and occupiers. Some other factors became less important. Austrian independence was now self-evident for the international as well as the domestic community; the traumatic experience with civil war became history for most Austrians, replaced by the reality of a democratic process; and economic stability became more and more the rule—not the exception.

The end of the grand coalition in 1966 after the victory of the People's Party in the general elections was an example of self-elimination by success. The two decades of coalition were decisive in overcoming the deficiencies of the First Republic. The coalition had done its duty and was allowed to dissolve.

The People's Party was in power between 1966 and 1970. The shadows of the First Republic were gone. There was never a chance that the demise of the coalition could have brought developments similar to those of 1920, when the first grand coalition ended. In 1966, consensus outlived coalition without difficulty.

The proof came in 1970. The Socialist Party won the general elections, and the Kreisky era started. The change from conservative to socialist rule, from an

ÖVP cabinet to a SPÖ cabinet, was the first democratic transition within the constitutional rules. Nobody really worried about the possible dangers to democracy. Democratic behavior had become normal.

The Socialists stayed in power for thirteen years. After the loss of majority in the 1983 elections, the SPÖ—still the largest party in Parliament—created the "small coalition," a cabinet consisting of the SPÖ and the (comparatively) small Freedom Party (FPÖ). This change, too, was effected without drama. To be in government or to be in opposition seemed to be part of ordinary political life. The era when the same political forces now dealing with political challenges in a normal, professional way had once fought each other in a bloody civil war seemed far distant.

In many respects, Austria has joined the community of Western democracies. But even in this stabilized system of liberal democracy, some elements cannot be explained without regressing to the past. Most of the factors that deviate from the model of Western democracy are products of the past. The Second Republic can be called an antithesis to the First Republic. But this antithesis demonstrates the great impact of history.

Government Structures: Variations on Parliamentary Rule

The Austrian political system is characterized by a combination of factors—some of them completely normal for a Western system, some of them quite specific.[3] First, the constitution combines parliamentary with presidential elements, but political practice has demonstrated the dominance of parliamentarism over presidentialism. Second, parliamentary dominance in policy making is strongly overshadowed by the role of extraparliamentary actors, including the executive, the bureaucracy, the political parties, and economic pressure groups. Third, the constitution divides legislative as well as executive powers between the republic (*Bund*) and the provinces (*Länder*), but for legal and political reasons this division is biased distinctly in favor of the republic.

The Austrian constitutional system is based on the 1929 version of the Federal Constitutional Law of October 1, 1920. Power to change the constitution lies in general with the Nationalrat (National Council), which can pass constitutional laws (including laws to change the constitution) if certain conditions are met (quorum of 50 percent present, approval by at least two-thirds of the deputies). Any change in the basic principles of the constitution—by common consent the principles of democracy, the rule of law, and the federal system—can, however, be done only through a nationwide referendum.

The Austrian governmental system is a mixed type, combining elements of a parliamentary system with the elements of a presidential system, but in political practice the parliamentary elements predominate. The Austrian system is parliamentary because the government must basically enjoy the confidence of a majority of the National Council. It is also presidential because the federal president appoints and dismisses the government. A change in the constitution in 1929 gave the governmental system—originally purely parliamentary—a head of state with far-reaching powers. Since then the federal president has been elected directly by the people under an absolute majority system for a term of six years; re-election for one further term is possible.

The federal president possesses two main powers beyond those normally enjoyed by a head of state in a parliamentary system: he can dissolve the National Council (only once, however, on the same grounds); and he appoints (and dismisses) the federal chancellor and also, on the latter's proposal, the other members of the federal government. But the federal government also needs support of a majority of the National Council since it has the power to pass a vote of no confidence. It is possible, therefore, for there to develop between the federal president and the National Council a conflict that could prevent the government from governing. In practice this possibility is avoided, however, because the federal president refrains from exercising his powers in this respect. All federal presidents so far have always appointed governments with a majority behind them in the National Council, even when the majority was politically oriented differently from the federal president, as for instance in 1966, when Federal President Franz Jonas—a Socialist—appointed Josef Klaus—a member of the Austrian People's Party—who had an absolute parliamentary majority behind him. Jonas also appointed a cabinet consisting exclusively of Austrian People's Party members.

The federal government—the cabinet—consists of the federal chancellor, the vice-chancellor (until 1966 without a portfolio of his own), the federal ministers, and the secretaries of state (deputy ministers). Although the Austrian constitution does not contain a "chancellor principle" stipulating that the federal chancellor lead the federal government, the federal chancellor does have a definite superiority in ranking compared with the other members of the government. The extent of this superiority depends, however, on whether the chancellor heads a coalition cabinet (as was the case until 1966 and again after 1983), in which case he shares his superiority in ranking with the vice-chancellor, or whether he leads a one-party cabinet. Since 1966 a de facto "chancellor principle" has developed in political practice, based on the federal chancellor's leadership of his own party.

The Austrian Parliament consists of two chambers, the National Council (Nationalrat), elected directly by the people, and the Federal Council (Bundesrat), which is made up of representatives of the individual federal states (Länder). Since a reform in the voting system in 1971, the Nationalrat has 183 members, and the Bundesrat (on the basis of the population census of 1981) has 64 members. The Nationalrat is elected for a period of four years. There are no such time limits on the Bundesrat since, like the U.S. Senate, part of its membership is changed periodically. These partial renewals occur after a state legislative election (Landtagswahl) or after a population census requires a change in the number of members in the Federal Council.

The Federal Constitutional Law requires that the Nationalrat shall be elected "on the basis of the equal, direct, secret, and personal voting right of men and women . . . according to the principles of proportional representation." Since 1971 the "principles of proportional representation" have taken the concrete form of making each of the nine Länder a voting constituency in which the voters vote for one party list.

In the distribution of parliamentary powers, the constitution gives a clear priority to the Nationalrat. In case of disagreement, the Bundesrat possesses a right of veto, but only in questions that directly concern the Länder. On all other questions, the Bundesrat possesses either delaying powers or no veto powers at all. Since the constitution allows the Bundesrat to consider bills only after the Nationalrat has approved them, the predominance of the directly elected chamber is clear. This predominance is reinforced by the exclusive right of the Nationalrat to pass a vote of no confidence in the federal government—that is, only the majority in the Nationalrat has any influence on the composition of the government.

The dominant position of the Nationalrat in legislation has, as in other parliamentary systems in which political parties play a vital role, been progressively undermined. The balance of power in the present decisionmaking process has shifted toward the federal government, which—supported by an expanding civil service apparatus—de facto prejudges issues before they are considered by the Parliament. Most laws in Austria derive from proposals by the government, which are either not amended at all by the Parliament or amended only in unessential ways. Only in exceptional cases does the initiative actually stem from Parliament.

The dominant position of the executive is made possible by the actual parliamentary character and the pronounced political party basis of the Austrian governmental system. Since the government and the parliamentary majority are politically identical and since the parliamentary parties in Austria are unusually disciplined and close-knit, government and Parliament are closely interlinked, with the center of decisionmaking located within the government.

Austria's federal structure necessitates a division of administrative activity between the federal government and the Länder. The Länder also administer certain affairs of the federal administration, functioning in these cases simply as subordinate authorities ("indirect federal administration"). The lowest level of administration in Bund and Land matters is the Bezirk (county), each Bezirk administration being headed by an appointed Bezirkshauptmann.

Legislative authority is also divided between the Bund and the Länder, but not the judiciary authority, which is exclusively a federal matter. The constitution lists the areas for which the Bund is responsible. In comparison with other federal states (the United States, Federal Republic of Germany) the position of the Länder is not particularly strong, and this is brought out even more clearly by the weak position of the Bundesrat.

The government system of the Länder is, with the exception of Vienna and Vorarlberg, characterized by a proportional system: the Länder constitutions stipulate that the parties represented in the various state parliaments (Diets, Landtage) are to participate in the state government according to their respective strength. The state parliaments are all single-chamber systems. Each state parliament is headed by a Landeshauptmann.

The Constitutional Court is of some importance for the political system. This court has very wide powers. The members of the Constitutional Court are appointed by the federal president, partly on the recommendation of the Parliament and partly on the recommendation of the cabinet. In practice the Austrian Socialist Party and the Austrian People's Party have tacitly agreed that membership on the Constitutional Court shall be divided equally between judges with Socialist Party leanings and those with People's Party leanings.[4]

The Party System: Continuity and Concentration

The Austrian party system is still very much influenced by the social and religious cleavage that developed in the late nineteenth century. The present party system is the direct successor of a system established within and reflecting the conditions of the Austrian empire on the threshold to this century. The Austrian party system is one of the most traditional party systems in Europe.

The Austrian party system has another, almost unique quality: despite proportional representation, which usually favors deconcentration, the number of parties with significant impact is very limited. No other European party system with free competition and proportional representation has excluded new parties so consistently for decades.

The most remarkable attributes of the Austrian party system are continuity and concentration. The present parties are directly (in the case of the SPÖ) or indirectly (in the case of the ÖVP and the FPÖ) the heirs of parties born out of the social, cultural, religious, and ethnic fragmentation that characterized the late empire. The two major parties dominate and control the central political process. They permit the FPÖ some limited influence but exclude all other parties from influence on the national as well as on the provincial level.

Continuity and concentration are especially important for the deep involvement political parties have not only in the political system but also in the social, cultural, and economic spheres. In Austria, the "party state," the identity between political parties and all kinds of authority, seems to be almost perfect. The party state can be observed, for example, in (1) education: the public school system, especially career patterns of teachers, is strongly dependent on parties' functioning as a clientele system, mainly at the provincial level; (2) the mass media: the electronic media (state-owned, as in most European countries) reflect the power balance between the two major parties, and the print media are influenced—to a lesser extent—by economic interest groups (chambers of commerce, unions), which are traditionally linked with political parties; and (3) industry: as a result of the direct or indirect (through nationalized banks) nationalization of a large part of Austrian industry, the management of nationalized industry is also part of the political clientele system established by the parties.

The chief feature of this stable and concentrated party system is the presence of three "camps." These camps, or political "pillars," have created parties with various names in the past century. A common feature of the parties representing the three camps has been personal and programmatic continuity as well as continuity in relative strength.

The constancy in relative strength justifies the term *two-and-a-half party system* or *limping three-party system*. The parties of the two largest camps—the socialist camp (today represented by the Sozialistische Partei Österreichs, SPÖ) and the Christian social-conservative camp (today represented by the Österreichische Volkspartei, ÖVP)—are accompanied by the party of the third, smaller, German-national camp (today represented by the Freiheitliche Partei Österreichs, FPÖ). At least until 1979, there was also a gradual tendency favoring an increase in support for the two major camps.

The continuity in the party system is also underlined by the lack of success of fourth parties. The Austrian Communist Party (KPÖ), the only party able for a short time after 1945 to play a part in political life alongside the three traditional camps, was never able even during its best period to reach a figure above 5 percent. This continuity and concentration in the development of the party system has worked not only in favor of the parties of the two large camps but also against all parties attempting to operate outside the three traditional camps.

The trend toward concentration reached a zenith in the 1970s. The general elections of 1983 resulted in a significant increase for fourth parties. The background of this new development is the beginning of the rise of ecology groups—

in 1983 organized in the centrist Vereinte Grüne Österreichs (VGÖ, the Greens) and in the leftist Alternative Liste Österreichs (ALÖ, the Alternatives) (see Table 10.1).

The slight decrease in concentration could be the beginning of a long-term deconcentration process. Favored by proportional representation and by the de-ideologization of the electorate, the minor parties can expect a possible decline of voters' alignment with traditional parties, with the camps.

The Socialist Party of Austria is the most successful party in a competitive political system with an industrialized economy. No other party in Europe has won not only a majority of seats in Parliament but also a majority of votes in three successive general elections—as the SPÖ did in 1971, 1975, and 1979. During the 1970s, the Kreisky era, the SPÖ became a model for all other European socialist and social democratic parties. More successful in the field of party competition than the British Labour Party, the German Social Democratic Party, or the Swedish Social Democrats had ever been, the SPÖ enjoyed a leading role within the Socialist International.

The successes of the SPÖ were the result of different factors. The SPÖ has been an almost perfect combination of an old-style workers' party and a modernized catchall party. The party was (and, to a lesser extent, still is) able to enjoy the advantages and avoid the disadvantages that characterize these two party types. A large majority of the Austrian labor force identifies with the SPÖ. During the last years of the empire, the Social Democratic Workers' Party, founded in 1889, organized most of Austrian labor. As the heir of the Social Democrats, the SPÖ still enjoy almost a guarantee of most of the labor vote—that is, almost 40 percent of the electorate.

But after 1945, and especially after 1970, the SPÖ became more attractive to voters outside the traditional socialist camp. The Socialist vote, mainly blue-collar workers, was enlarged significantly by a white-collar constituency. By winning minority shares of the Catholic or other vote, or with the German-national camp, the SPO gained 50 percent or more of the vote.

Part of being a workers' party is the dense organization of the SPÖ. Its 700,000 members (30 percent of the Socialist electorate) and about 70,000 party officers (*Vertrauensleute*) constitute the traditional communication link between party leaders and party sympathizers. For a party with direct, individual membership only, this organization (with the entire membership of certain trade unions among its members) is still the leading one in Western Europe.[5]

Part of being a catchall party is the importance of the marketing techniques the SPÖ uses. The party has its own electoral research institute, its own party academy, its own professional staff. The SPÖ uses all the campaign methods developed in the United States. The significance of Bruno Kreisky's image as party chairman between 1967 and 1983 cannot be overestimated. The SPÖ exploited the "personality factor" fully.

Table 10.1   General Elections, 1945–1983

Year	SPÖ Percentage	SPÖ Seats	ÖVP Percentage	ÖVP Seats	VdU/FPÖ Percentage	VdU/FPÖ Seats	KPÖ Percentage	KPÖ Seats	Others[a] (percentage)	Parties in the government
1945	44.6	76	49.8	85	—	—	5.4	4	0.2	ÖVP, SPÖ, KPÖ[b]
1949	37.7	67	44.0	77	11.7	16	5.1	5	0.5	ÖVP, SPÖ
1953	42.1	73	41.3	74	11.0	14	5.3	4	0.4	ÖVP, SPÖ
1956	43.0	74	45.9	82	6.5	6	4.4	3	0.1	ÖVP, SPÖ
1959	44.8	78	44.2	79	7.7	8	3.3	0	0.1	ÖVP, SPÖ
1962	44.0	76	45.4	81	7.1	8	3.3	0	0.0	ÖVP, SPÖ
1966	42.6	74	48.4	85	5.4	6	0.4	0	3.3[c]	ÖVP
1970	48.2	81	44.8	79	5.5	5	1.0	0	0.5	SPÖ
1971	50.0	93	43.1	80	5.5	10	1.4	0	0.0	SPÖ
1975	50.4	93	43.0	80	5.4	10	1.2	0	0.1	SPÖ
1979	51.0	95	41.9	77	6.1	11	1.0	0	0.1	SPÖ
1983	47.7	90	43.2	81	5.0	12	0.7	0	3.5[d]	SPÖ, FPÖ

[a]None of these parties ever held a seat.
[b]The KPÖ left the cabinet and went over to opposition in 1947.
[c]Democratic Progressive Party, led by former Socialist Franz Olah.
[d]VGÖ (Greens) and ALÖ (Alternatives).

As a monopolistic umbrella organization, the Austrian Trade Union Federation (ÖGB) has to demonstrate independence, but the linkage between social democracy as a party and social democracy as a union is still very important for the SPÖ. Within the ÖGB, which represents about 60 percent of Austrian labor, the Socialists are backed by a significant majority. The ÖGB and thirteen of its fifteen industrial unions are dominated by the Socialist faction (Fraktion Sozialistischer Gewerkschafter), and the Socialist union faction has significant influence on recruiting Socialist members of Parliament, members of the cabinet, and holders of other governmental positions.

Social democracy as a party—the SPÖ—and Social Democracy as a union—the Socialist faction within the ÖGB—are still "Siamese twins," as Viktor Adler, the first chairman of the party in 1889, once defined the division of roles. The interconnection between party and union permits a synchronization that is especially important for Austrian consociationalism.

The Austrian People's Party is one of the most successful and best organized Christian-democratic and conservative parties in Europe. Since 1945, the party—succeeding the Christian Social Party, founded in the 1880s—has always gathered between 40 and 50 percent of the votes in general elections. Combining different social and economic constituencies—agriculture, business, white-collar labor—the party is still heavily influenced by its Catholic background. About 84 percent of the Austrian population is Roman Catholic. Most Catholics regularly attend church and are traditionally affiliated with the People's Party, as the present representative of the Christian social-conservative camp.

Active Catholics, being only a minority within the Austrian Catholic church, are not numerous enough to guarantee the present strength of the ÖVP. Despite its defeats during the Kreisky era and the opposition role the party has had to play on the national level since 1970, the ÖVP dominates six of the nine provinces. The strength of this party results from the coexistence of old and new factors. The traditional element of "political Catholicism" has expanded to become an umbrella organization of different subparty organizations: (1) the Austrian Peasants' League (Österreichischer Bauernbund); (2) the Austrian Workers' and Employees' League (Österreichischer Arbeiter- und Angestelltenbund); and (3) the Austrian Business League (Österreichischer Wirtschaftsbund). These three subparties divide all important party positions according to a certain power-sharing formula. Three other subparties in the ÖVP—the Youth Federation, the Women's League, and the Seniors' League—are of minor importance.[6]

The subparties play an especially important role in establishing institutionalized contacts between the ÖVP and economic interest groups. The Österreichischer Arbeiter- und Angestelltenbund and the Faction of the Christian Unionists (indirectly linked with the ÖVP) represent the ÖVP's interests within the Chambers of Labor and the Austrian Trade Union Federation; the Österreichischer

Wirtschaftsbund is the leading group within the Chambers of Commerce; and the Österreichischer Bauernbund dominates the Chambers of Agriculture.

The ÖVP, active within international Christian democratic and conservative umbrella organizations (like the European Democratic Union), has demonstrated a remarkable ability to organize a large membership. Its membership, usually organized by subparty, is about 800,000, exceeding that of the SPÖ and breaking the usual rule in Europe that right-of-center parties are less well organized than left-of-center parties.

The ÖVP, for the first decades of the Second Republic identified as the "chancellor-party" (its successive chairmen, Leopold Figl, Julius Raab, Alfons Gorbach, and Josef Klaus were also federal chancellors), has easily survived the long period of abstention from power on the federal level. The deep roots this party has within social subsystems, defined by cultural (religious) and economic interests, and its strong position at the state level have secured the ÖVP's position as the main opposition to the Social Democrats.

The Freiheitliche Partei Österreichs (FPÖ), representing the German-national camp, is the successor of various party formations established in the late nineteenth century mainly to defend the position of the German-speaking population. During the First Republic, the two smaller parties continuing that tradition—the agricultural Landbund (Country League) and the urban, bourgeois Grossdeutsche Volkspartei (Greater German People's Party)—were mostly junior partners in the coalition led by the Christian Socials after 1920. In the 1930s, most of their voters and activists left these two parties and joined the National Socialists (NSDAP).

In 1945, the former members of the NSDAP were excluded from the franchise. It was impossible before 1949, when former NSDAP members regained the right to vote, to form a political party out of the heritage of the German-national camp. The Verband der Unabhängigen (VdU, League of Independents) and, beginning in 1955, the FPÖ claimed with some success to express the interests of the third camp—now reconciled to the independence of Austria and abstaining from any pan-German propaganda.

Over the long run, the German-national camp has declined for various reasons. The exclusion from executive power for many decades, the decreasing attractiveness of German nationalism (without annexation), and the search for a new profile reduced the electorate of the FPÖ. The party carefully switched to a more liberal image, repressing more and more its old German-national appearance.

As a result, the FPÖ was accepted in 1979 as a member of the Liberal International. And despite its losses in 1983 (the party's vote share fell to 5 percent for the first time in the history of the German-national camp), the FPÖ managed to escape its isolation from power by becoming the junior partner in the "small coalition" led by the SPÖ.

Domestic Political Issues and Consociationalism

The political process in the Second Republic has been characterized by a lack of controversy. The political elites have successfully established a pattern of compromise in most of the fields of political decisionmaking. Two main factors permit this kind of "consociational democracy."[7] First, the Parliament from 1945 to 1966 was completely controlled by the coalition, which prevented any open disagreement between ÖVP and SPÖ in Parliament. Since 1966, there has been an overwhelming trend toward unanimous voting behavior. Most of the bills passed by the National Council are discussed informally behind the scenes and adapted to the mutual interests of all parties, in the government as well as in opposition, before they can be discussed openly on the floor (see Table 10.2). Second, neocorporatism, consisting of different institutions run by the basic economic interest groups and dominating especially economic issues, prevents open disagreement. Neocorporatism as expressed, for example, by the Joint Commission on Wages and Prices (founded in 1957), works on the principle that labor and capital (represented by interest groups) can veto any decision.

Consociationalism at the parliamentary level is based on various techniques outside as well as inside Parliament to promote the convergence of different viewpoints and to integrate different interests. There are formal techniques established by law, such as the right of provincial governments and economic interest groups to be informed and consulted about bills drafted by the administration before the Parliament itself has to be informed. And there are informal techniques established by custom, such as the personal links among party leaders, especially those in Parliament.

Consociationalism at the neocorporatist level is built on various kinds of cooperation between (national and state) government, capital, and labor.[8] A network of advisory bodies and executive committees helps integrate the powerful interest groups: mainly the Austrian Trade Union Federation, the Diet of the Chambers of Labor, the Federal Chamber of Commerce, and the Presidents' Conference of the Chambers of Agriculture—the first two under the guidance of the Faction of Socialist Unions and the last two dominated by the subparties in the People's Party.

The Joint Commission on Wages and Prices as a nonconstitutional institution has given further power to economic interest groups. The four main interest groups cooperate to gain control over wages and prices. The participation of the government has been reduced to a token. The four interest groups have been guaranteed that each of them has to agree to every decision. The Joint Commission has also established the Council of Social and Economic Advisers, which consists of the leading experts employed by the interest groups and functions as

Table 10.2 Voting Behavior in the National Council, 1975–1983

| | Percentage of actions passed | | | | | | | |
| | Unanimously | | SPÖ | | With majority of SPÖ + ÖVP | | SPÖ + FPÖ | |
	1975–1979	1979–1983	1975–1979	1979–1983	1975–1979	1979–1983	1975–1979	1979–1983
Bills	79.3	75.3	9.3	14.6	8.3	6.2	3.2	3.9
State treaties, international agreements, etc.	99.3	97.0	0.7	1.0	0.0	1.0	0.0	1.0
Reports of the cabinet	83.7	74.6	8.9	13.8	0.0	1.5	7.3	10.0
Suspensive veto of the Federal Council	—	—	78.6	72.7	—	—	21.4	27.3

SOURCE: Data supplied by the Directorate of the Austrian Parliament.

the leading brain trust not only for the Joint Commission itself but sometimes also for the cabinet and for the Parliament.

A significant example of an issue strongly influenced by parliamentary and neocorporatist consociationalism is the decisionmaking process preceding the Arbeitsverfassungsgesetz (Labor Relations Act) of 1973. This bill was especially important for the extension of codetermination—the joint determination of business policy by labor and management at the plant level.

In accordance with manifestos of the SPÖ and principal declarations expressed by the ÖGB, the Socialist administration drafted a bill to establish workers' codetermination at the plant level and to subsume various existing regulations. Rudolf Häuser, the minister of social affairs, was responsible for the draft. He was not only a member of the Socialist government, he was also vice president of the ÖGB and chairman of the strongest union, the Union of Private Employees. The People's Party, especially its business wing—the Austrian League of Business—opposed the draft, especially some newly established prerogatives for shop stewards, but it did not oppose the principle of codetermination itself.

The SPÖ could have passed the bill in the National Council, using its overall majority, but such a step would have violated vital interests of those groups that enjoy an informal guarantee that the status quo will be preserved. As a result of strong opposition expressed by the Federal Chamber of Commerce, the Associations of Austrian Industrialists, and the People's Party, the SPÖ did not avail itself of its legal right to pass the bill. The National Council decided that a committee outside Parliament should try to find a compromise. This committee, which consisted of representatives of the ÖGB, the Chambers of Labor, the Federal Chamber of Commerce, and the Association of Industrialists, succeeded. The National Council approved the compromise—which gave workers' representatives one-third of the seats on the boards of directors of medium- and large-size corporations—completely, unanimously, and almost without discussion.

The resolution of this issue is significant not only because of the procedure involved but also because of the substance consociationalism implies. The one-third solution would not fulfill the programmatic aspirations of most European unions. But usually the unions are not influential enough to reach their goals of "workers' self-management" or parity codetermination. The Austrian union federation seemed strong enough to get more—one of its leading representatives was in a key position within the cabinet, the parliamentary majority was doubtless in favor of far-reaching union strategies, and the constitution clearly did not prevent parity codetermination—but the ÖGB, the SPÖ, and the Parliament did not take advantage of the situation.

The strength of social democracy in Austria is at the same time a guarantee of moderation. Social democracy—party and union—is strong because it is moderate, and because it is moderate it is strong.

But there are limits to consociationalism. An example is the legalization of abortion during the first three months of pregnancy. The SPÖ passed a new Criminal Law Act in 1973—over the votes of ÖVP as well as the FPÖ. Their opposition was not directed against the bill itself since compromises concerning almost all original disagreements had been worked out. The abortion question itself did not allow unanimity.

The differences between the Labor Relations Act and the Criminal Law Act arose for various reasons. First, labor relations touch vital interests of labor and capital; abortion is not a major concern of economic interests. Second, labor relations are open to compromise—as soon as there is an agreement that workers should participate in management, the two sides can compromise about the degree of participation. Abortion is not open to compromise—if someone (like the Catholic church) considers it murder, the question of sanction can only be answered yes or no. Third, labor relations are a comparatively low concern of the Austrian public. They were (and still are) handled mainly by functionaries. Abortion, however, raises emotional issues on both sides.

The main opponent of legalizing abortion was not the ÖVP but the Catholic church. Catholic groups started a campaign to revise the legalization immediately after passage of the 1973 act. In 1976, a popular referendum was held, and almost 1 million voters called for revision. But the Socialist majority in Parliament declined to change its position.

Consociationalism possibly leads to petrification of the status quo. An issue exemplifying this impact is the Austrian school system. In 1962, when the grand coalition was already facing increasing difficulties, the ÖVP and the SPÖ agreed on a far-reaching compromise about school organization. Part of this agreement was the rule, established by constitutional law, that any change in school organization had to be approved by a two-thirds majority of Parliament—that is, only by a compromise between the two major parties.

The SPÖ, which favors a more unified school system (comprehensive school), was unable to use its majority between 1971 and 1983 to reorganize the school system. The ÖVP used its veto power. As a result of this balance, the school system has always been an important political issue. Since no party has ever been strong enough to realize its goal in this area, each party can emphasize school policy without risk. Despite the general trend toward deideologization in Austrian politics, the school system has become a very ideological issue during the past few years.

The SPÖ stresses the value of equality and declares that a unified school for all pupils between the ages of six and fourteen would improve the chances of lower-class children. The ÖVP stresses the value of talents and their promotion and defends the present, diversified school system.

The paradox of consociationalism is the overthrow of majorities. It is always the weaker party—in Parliament, the minority—that is mainly interested in keeping consociationalism alive. And if consociationalism works, it works in favor of the small, who are granted a veto power to balance the power of the big. The final consequence of consociationalism is the end of *majority* and *minority* as key terms and key positions in a democratic decisionmaking process.

Foreign Political Issues and Neutrality

Austrian neutrality is a legal obligation as well as a political concept. Following the Swiss pattern, which was declared a model for Austria in the Moscow Memorandum of April 15, 1955, Austria was interested in establishing its neutrality by the terms of constitutional and international law. Therefore, the Austrian National Council passed on October 26, 1955 (the day later became an Austrian national holiday), a constitutional law—the Permanent Neutrality Act. The act was opposed by the VdU (which became in that very year the FPÖ), but was backed by the ÖVP, SPÖ, and KPÖ. This law, now part of the Austrian constitution, consists of the following obligations:[9]

> 1. For the purpose of the continual affirmation of its external independence and for the purpose of maintaining the inviolability of its territory, Austria voluntarily declares its perpetual neutrality. Austria will maintain and defend its neutrality with all means at its disposal.
> 2. To secure these goals for all future time, Austria will join no military alliances and will permit the establishment of no military bases on its territory.

The Neutrality Act was accepted directly or indirectly by all nations of the world and so became part of international law. The four Allied powers, which had to leave Austria after signing the Austrian State Treaty on May 15, 1955, formally recognized Austria's permanent neutrality.

But the Neutrality Act focuses only on military matters—Austria guarantees that it will abstain from joining any military bloc. To add political instruments for implementing neutrality in nonmilitary matters, Austria had to work out the concept of the politics of neutrality. The political concept of Austrian neutrality includes two elements.

First, there are clear distinctions between domestic and foreign policies and between obligations of the Austrian government and the (lack of) obligations of Austrian citizens. This distinction does allow a political, social, economic, and cultural system that is indisputably Western.

Second, the political conditions necessary to permit Austria to abstain from military alliances are carefully considered. So Austria has always been and still is interested in good and friendly relations not only with all of its neighbors but also with the great powers, East and West.

There is no contradiction but some tension between these two aspects of neutrality. Not only is Austria—domestically—Western, but Austrian public opinion is strongly pro-Western, pro-American, and anticommunist in all matters of the East-West conflict. Austrian foreign policy had never been equidistant between East and West but nevertheless is not completely integrated with Western foreign behavior.

One indicator that illustrates the consequences of this tension is Austrian voting behavior in UN organizations. Austrian voting behavior is not only very similar to that of the other European neutrals in the United Nations—Sweden and Finland—but also similar to that of the smaller European like-minded countries with links to NATO—Norway, Denmark, the Netherlands, and Belgium. There is no clear difference between "soft" Western behavior and neutral behavior—with, of course, the very important exception of military matters.

Austrian neutrality has created a permanent foreign policy issue: the relationship between Austria and the European Community. When in 1957 the European Economic Community (EEC) was founded, Austria decided not to participate. Instead, in 1958 Austria joined the European Free Trade Association (EFTA) even though EEC countries—especially Germany—have been and still are Austria's leading trade partners. The reason for that decision was the EEC's long-term objective of not only economic but also political integration. Since all founding members of the EEC were members of NATO, Austria considered participation in the political integration of NATO-Europe inimical to neutrality and Austria's task of maximizing independence.

From the beginning of the European integration process, the coalition government tried to find a way that would maximize Austrian economic integration without political integration. The supranational character of the EEC was the obstacle. The EFTA had no political orientation and no supranational institutions; it was aimed at free trade only. Though agreeing on the need to avoid political integration, the two major parties disagreed about the steps necessary to reach an economic agreement with the EEC. The ÖVP criticized the SPÖ, whose foreign minister was responsible between 1959 and 1962 for the conduct of negotiations with the EEC, for hesitating to obtain an agreement with the EEC short of full membership. In the general elections of 1962, the ÖVP claimed it could negotiate better with the EEC; the SPÖ argued that this was a delusion.

The outcome of the elections in 1962 resulted in a shift within the great coalition: responsibility for negotiations with the EEC came to the ÖVP. Nevertheless, no breakthrough came until 1972, when Austria—along with the other European neutrals—signed a special treaty with the EEC (now the EC) in the form of a free trade agreement. This agreement allows the free flow of goods between Austria and the EC countries, with some exceptions, but does not subordinate Austria to any EC institution.

Austrian neutrality is the result of the East-West conflict. But the North-South conflict has challenged neutrality, too. When most of the Third World countries started the nonaligned movement, beginning with the Belgrade conference in 1961, Austria had to define its position toward this new pattern of non-partisanship in the East-West conflict. In 1970, at the Lusaka nonaligned summit, Austria became a "guest" of the movement, indicating common interests but also differences between neutrality and nonalignment. The ÖVP criticized the Socialist cabinet for this decision, but when the other European neutrals—including Switzerland, sometimes still considered a model for Austria—joined the nonaligned movement as guests, this status ceased to be an issue.[10]

An example of the possibilities and the limits of neutrality is the active role Austria has tried to play in the Conference for Security and Cooperation in Europe, both before and after the Helsinki summit in 1975. Together with the other neutrals and the European nonaligned countries (especially Yugoslavia), Austria established the "N and N" (neutrals and nonaligned) group as a permanent mediator between East and West. As a consequence of this activity, the follow-up conference in 1986 (after the follow-ups in Belgrade and in Madrid) took place in Vienna.

Austrian neutrality is a concept for dealing with the East-West dimension and with multilateral relations. But Austrian foreign policy has to face some bilateral problems that cannot be solved by reference to neutrality. The most important issues are disputes with Italy concerning the German-speaking minority in northern Italy (South Tyrol) and disputes with Yugoslavia concerning the Slovene-speaking minority in southern Austria (Carinthia).

The Treaty of St. Germain (1919) gave not only the Italian-speaking parts but also the German-speaking parts of Tyrol south of the Brenner Pass to Italy. During the fascist period, Italy denied any political or cultural autonomy for South Tyrol. In 1946, Italy and Austria signed an agreement granting the German-speaking population autonomy within the Italian borders. But implementation of this guarantee did not satisfy the South Tyroleans. After some attempts to cause an international incident by terrorist attacks against Italian installations, Austria—dissociating itself from the use of violence—brought the matter to the United Nations in 1960 and 1961. Italy had to accept the necessity of finding solutions better fitting South Tyrolean interests and to accept Austria as a legitimate representative of South Tyrol. In 1969, after years of negotiations, Italy and Austria signed an agreement much more precise than that of 1946.

The solution was accepted by the South Tyrolean People's Party, which represents the overwhelming majority of German-speaking South Tyroleans. It was also accepted by the Austrian National Council—over the opposition of the SPÖ and FPÖ—as well as by the Italian Parliament. Since 1969, political, economic, and cultural conditions have improved significantly in South Tyrol. The issue of South Tyrol is still alive in Austria, but less controversial than before.

The Treaty of St. Germain and the State Treaty of 1955 included guarantees for the Slovene and the Croat minorities. The situation of the Croats in Burgenland, the easternmost province of Austria, is a source of much less controversy than the situation of the Slovenes in Carinthia. In 1920, the southern parts of Carinthia decided in a plebiscite by a majority of about 60 percent to stay with Austria. Austria emphasized its intention to respect ethnic, especially linguistic, traditions of the minority. During the years of Nazi occupation, the Slovenes were oppressed.

After 1955, Slovene organizations claimed that promised rights had not been realized. In fact, the possibility of getting a Slovene education in school had deteriorated after 1955, and the possibility of speaking Slovene in court or in government offices remains undeveloped. But in Carinthia, the established parties are anxious to demonstrate their resistance to Communist Yugoslavia. It is the international weakness of the Slovenes' position that is one of the reasons that they still have many claims concerning minority rights. Yugoslavia as a communist country representing Slovene interests provokes strong anticommunism rather than understanding for Austrian Slovenes. Yugoslavia sometimes seems hesitant to push the Slovene question due to its own internal ethnic problems—for example, the issue of Albanians in the Yugoslav province of Kosovo.

The Helsinki Final Accords (1975) included the formal acceptance of present borders in Europe. So Austria has, once more, accepted the border with Italy, and Yugoslavia has accepted the border with Austria. The frontiers are undisputed, but the emotional questions about the autonomy of ethnic minorities are still not fully resolved.

New Developments:
A Farewell to Predictability?

There are some indications that the Austrian political system is on the eve of a significant transformation. First, voting behavior is becoming more flexible. Especially at the local and provincial levels, swings between the traditional parties, the success of new parties, and abstention from voting have been increasing. Second, a generation gap is evident for the first time since 1945. Attitudes toward politics and democracy correlate clearly with age. Younger voters are more skeptical about the established political process.[11] Plebiscites now play a role unknown 20 years ago. Popular referenda and plebiscites seem to be increasingly favored by the public, influencing Parliament, the bureaucracy, and neocorporatist institutions.

The Austrian political system has been considered one of the most stable Western systems. Stability remains comparatively high, but some changes are jeopardizing the traditional system of consociationalism. Three issue-oriented groups, or "movements," overlap the "camps," the deeply rooted identifications of the populace.

First, protection of the environment is for many Austrians antagonistic to the usual way and the usual outcome of political decisionmaking. Quality instead of quantity, zero growth instead of maximized growth—the ecological creed especially challenges the economic creed represented, for instance, by neocorporatism.

Second, an increasing minority of women—especially the younger and the better educated—feel discriminated against despite the high standard of legal equality. The small percentage of women in leading political, commercial, academic, and other positions supports the argument of de facto discrimination against women in Austria. The struggle to liberalize abortion has been and still is a highly emotional issue for the feminist movement.

Third, given the comparatively small size of Austrian forces, most subgroups constituting the Austrian peace movement are concerned with foreign issues. Specifically Austrian issues are cases of arms exports to countries known for their poor record in human rights (Chile, for example). Despite the tradition of pro-Americanism, Austrians criticize both NATO and the Eastern bloc, creating for the first time a balanced attitude concerning foreign policies.

Ecology, gender, and peace are issues more for young people than for their parents, more for the well-educated than for blue-collar workers or farmers. A dramatic example of the combination of all these variables and their impact on the roles of the government and of the opposition was the decision of November 5, 1978. The first nationwide democratic plebiscite in Austrian history decided by a very small margin to forbid the opening of Austria's first nuclear power plant. Following this expression of opinion, the Austrian National Council passed a bill strictly prohibiting any peaceful, commercial use of nuclear power—a decision unique in the world.

Nuclear power is an important example of new issues beyond the limits of the traditional camps. An analysis of voting behavior concerning the plebiscite of 1978 and of public opinion data from later polls shows clearly that there is no correlation at all with party identification. Groups usually bound to one of the major parties, such as blue-collar workers and farmers, are either more in favor of nuclear power or uninterested in this issue. Constituencies without significant links to a specific party, such as public or private white-collar employees, are more inclined to oppose nuclear energy for reasons of principle. Social status (in combination with education) and age are the variables explaining the existence of this issue.

This and some other specific issues resulting from the new awareness of ecological or feminist or peace problems indicate the decline of the party state. If the traditional parties are unable to canalize and to integrate new issues, the impact parties have on the decision-making process will be reduced. There is also an indication of the retreat of the corporatist state. If the network of institutionalized compromises between the basic economic interests is not able to overcome popular opposition expressed in plebiscites, the importance of neocorporatism will diminish.

An example of this trend was the public reaction to construction of a dam on the Danube River near Hainburg in Lower Austria in 1984–1985. The administration expressed its clear intentions by felling trees and sacrificing a water meadow for the dam. Some thousand demonstrators protested and occupied the building site. Police were called, but after the first clash the federal cabinet yielded. It did not capitulate to the opposition (the ÖVP did not have a clear position at all) or to an outspoken majority within the electorate. The cabinet, especially the SPÖ, simply did not want to risk a potentially increasing gap between its policy and the minority of flexible "Green," ecology-minded voters, who are necessary to win a majority from a number of different minorities. The dam near Hainburg was cancelled.

New issues not integrated into the established demand and support structure tend to create new procedures, making it necessary to change that structure (the camp, articulated by the party state and by the corporatist state). The new procedures can be summarized by the trend towards more competitiveness. Electoral results are more and more open; plebiscites challenge administration and Parliament; the political elites can no longer guarantee a certain output. The new procedures developing in Austria are part of a long-term process of Westernization. Austria is becoming more normal and losing its deviant characteristics like the party state and corporatism.

Of course, the transition has just started, and it will last, not years, but decades. The Austrian political system has begun to lose one of its most praised qualities—stability. But it has begun to win a new quality—openness.

Update

The general elections of 1986 were characterized by a dramatic decline of the two major parties: Their common proportion of voters went down from 90.9 percent (1983) to 84.4 percent. The SPÖ managed to be once again the strongest party—in spite of heavy losses: 43.1 percent of the votes (1983: 47.6 percent) and 80 seats (1983: 90). The ÖVP got 41.3 percent of the votes (1983: 43.2 percent) and 77 seats (1983: 81).

The reason for this downfall was the success of the FPÖ as well as of the Greens. The FPÖ, with a new chairman (Jörg Haider) following an opposition-style strategy against the two major, "old" parties despite the FPÖ's role as minor partner in the "small coalition" with the Socialists, got 9.7 percent of the votes

(1983: 5.0 percent) and 18 seats (1983: 12). The Greens, more or less united, received 4.8 percent (1983; the two separated Green parties together received 3.3 percent) and entered the federal parliament as newcomers with 8 seats.

The electoral outcome resulted in the re-establishment of the "grand coalition" under the Socialist Franz Vranitzky as federal chancellor. This comeback of the SPÖ-ÖVP-coalition did not strengthen consociationalism. Elections on both regional and local levels since 1986 demonstrated the same pattern: losses for the two major parties and gains for the FPÖ and the Greens. Even consociationalism on the corporate level is in crisis—the organizational strength of the union is also slightly in decline, and some preconditions of the Austrian neo-corporatism (like the obligatory membership within the chambers) are more and more criticized.

The trend of the party system has already eroded the limping three-party system. The Austrian party system at the beginning of the 1990s is more and more a pluralistic party system similar to the systems typical in other smaller European democracies. This trend leads Austria toward Westernization.

1992: Redefining Neutrality?

In July 1989, the Austrian government—at that time the "grand coalition" of SPÖ and ÖVP—officially applied for membership in the EC. After three decades of stressing the incompatibility of permanent neutrality and EC membership, the two major parties have more or less reversed their understanding of Austrian neutrality. Neutrality still is—according to the official wording of the formal application—the general and central value of Austrian foreign policy. But neutrality is now, almost suddenly, considered compatible with EC membership.

The main reason for this rather new attitude, at least officially, is the coming European single market. Austria, and especially Austria's export-oriented economy, fear being excluded from the dramatic step toward more economic integration. The single market is seen as a new barrier for all trade coming to the EC from non-EC countries. The free trade agreement from 1972 is considered not efficient enough for balancing economic and political interests.

Another factor influencing Austria's new perception of her permanent neutrality is the developments in Eastern Europe. The erosion of the communist bloc and the real possibility of the Cold War's fading away have had a strong impact on the Austrian concept of neutrality, which mainly developed out of the framework of the Cold War. Nevertheless, Austria has left the common ground the other European neutrals have defined, especially in the 1960s and 1970s: Sweden and Finland and, of special importance, Switzerland have declared openly that they will not apply for EC membership despite the advantages of the single market.

Waldheim: Reshaping the Past?

The presidential elections of 1986 had a political factor not known before: The role of the federal president, in reality a ceremonial head of state, became (during the campaign) and still is a divisive factor of Austrian politics. The decline of consociationalism is reflected and stimulated by the fragmenting "Waldheim case."

Kurt Waldheim, former Austrian foreign minister (1968–1970) and former secretary general of the United Nations (1971–1981), was elected president as a candidate of the ÖVP. For the first time since 1945, the Socialists lost this position to a (although independent) conservative. But this shift by itself was not important; the internationally induced discussion about Waldheim's past and about Austria's past became the dominating issue for months and years.

Waldheim was never a Nazi himself; he served as an officer of the Greater German Wehrmacht in the Soviet Union and in several Balkan countries. After 1945, some of his formal declarations gave the impression that he wanted to hide his function as an intelligence officer in the Balkans.

Waldheim has been judged as the typical Austrian: before 1938, a student, a follower of the semifascist, authoritarian, Catholic regime; between 1938 and 1945, neither a Nazi nor a resisting anti-Nazi; and after 1945, speaking for the first victims of Hitler's aggressive foreign policy, for Austria, but not mentioning the high proportion of Austrians participating both voluntarily and involuntarily in Hitler's war and death machinery.

There is a strong tendency to defend Waldheim and, by defending the president, to defend Austria's role as a victim. This is the dominant tendency within the ÖVP and the FPÖ. There is another strong tendency, to criticize through Waldheim the traditional Austrian attitude beginning in 1945 to cover up the specific Austrian responsibility for Nazism and Nazi crimes. This is the view among Socialists and especially among the Greens.

The perception of the past is now a strong dividing factor in Austria—no longer between (former) Nazis and (former) anti-Nazis, but between right and left, between old and young, between representatives of the traditional values (stability) and representatives of the new social movements.

Notes

1. The most representative secondary sources for the First and Second Republics (up to 1970) are Erika Weinzierl and Kurt Skalnik, eds., *Österreich, 1918–1938: Geschichte der Ersten Republik* (Graz: Styria, 1983), 2 vols., and Erika Weinzierl and Kurt Skalnik, eds., *Österreich: Die Zweite Republik* (Graz: Styria, 1972), 2 vols.

2. For an analysis of the First and the Second Republics from the viewpoint of comparative politics, see Rainer Nick and Anton Pelinka, *Bürgerkrieg-Sozialpartnerschaft: Das politische System Österreichs. 1. und 2. Republik—Ein Vergleich* (Vienna: Jugend und Volk, 1983).

3. For a history of constitutional development, see Ludwig K. Adamovich and Bernd-Christian Funk, *Österreichisches Verfassungsrecht: Verfassungslehre unter Berücksichtigung von Staatslehre und Politikwissenschaft* (Vienna: Springer, 1982).

4. Manfried Welan, "Der Verfassungsgerichtshof: Eine Nebenregierung?" in Heinz Fischer, ed., *Das politische System Österreichs* (Vienna: Europaverlag, 1974), pp. 271–315.

5. For the development of the SPÖ, see Fritz Kaufmann, *Sozialdemokratie in Österreich: Idee und Geschichte einer Partei, von 1889 bis zur Gegenwart* (Vienna: Amalthea, 1978).

6. For the development of the ÖVP, especially its comparative aspects, see Rainer Nick, *Schwesternparteien: CDU, CSU, und Österreichische Volkspartei—Ein Vergleich* (Innsbruck: Innverlag, 1984).

7. The term *consociational democracy* follows the concept developed by Lijphart (and others); see Arend Lijphart, *Democracy in Plural Societies: A Comparative Exploration* (New Haven, Conn.: Yale University Press, 1977).

8. See Anton Pelinka, *Modellfall Österreich: Möglichkeiten und Grenzen der Sozialpartnerschaft* (Vienna: Braumüller, 1981), and Bernd Marin, *Die Paritätische Kommission: Aufgeklärter Technokratismus in Österreich* (Vienna: Internationale Publikationen, 1982).

9. For the historical background, see Gerald Stourzh, *Kleine Geschichte des österreichischen Staatsvertrags* (Graz: Styria, 1975).

10. Paul Luif, *Die Bewegung der blockfreien Staaten und Österreich* (Laxenburg: Austrian Institute for International Affairs, 1981).

11. Summary information can be found in Roland Deiser and Norbert Winkler, *Das politische Handeln der Österreicher* (Vienna: Verlag für Gesellschaftskritik, 1982), and in Fritz Plasser and Peter A. Ulram, *Unbehagen im Parteienstaat. Jugend und Politik in Österreich* (Vienna: Boehlau, 1982).

Suggested Readings

Bader, William B. *Austria Between East and West.* Stanford: Stanford University Press, 1966.

Birnbaum, Karl E. and Neuhold, Hanspeter, eds. *Neutrality and Non-Alignment in Europe.* Vienna: Braumüller, 1982.

Bluhm, William T. *Building an Austrian Nation: The Political Integration of a Western State.* New Haven, Conn.: Yale University Press, 1973.

Carsten, Francis L. *Fascist Movements in Austria.* London: Sage, 1977.

Diamant, Alfred. *Austrian Catholics and the First Republic: Democracy, Capitalism and the Social Order, 1918–1934.* Princeton, N.J.: Princeton University Press, 1960.

Edmonson, C. Earl. *The Heimwehr and Austrian Politics, 1918–1936.* Athens: University of Georgia Press, 1978.

Gulick, Charles A. *Austria from Habsburg to Hitler.* Berkeley: University of California Press, 1948. 2 vols.

Klemperer, Klemens von. *Ignaz Seipel: Christian Statesman in a Time of Crisis.* Princeton, N.J.: Princeton University Press, 1972.

Luza, Radomir. *Austro-German Relations in the Anschluss Era.* Princeton, N.J.: Princeton University Press, 1975.

Matzner, Egon. *Trade Between East and West: The Case of Austria.* Stockholm: Almqvist & Wiksell, 1970.

Parkinson, F. (ed.) *Conquering the Past. Austrian Nazism Yesterday and Today.* Detroit: Wayne University Press, 1989.

Pauley, Bruce F. *Hitler and the Forgotten Nazis: A History of Austrian National Socialism.* Chapel Hill: University of North Carolina Press, 1981.

Pauley, Bruce F. *Hitler and the Forgotten Nazis: A History of Austrian National Socialism.* Chapel Hill: University of North Carolina Press, 1981.

Powell, G. Bingham, Jr. *Social Fragmentation and Political Hostility: An Austrian Case Study.* Stanford: Stanford University Press, 1970.

Rabinbach, Anson. *The Crisis of Austrian Socialism. From Red Vienna to Civil War, 1927–1934.* Chicago: University of Chicago Press, 1983.

Riedelsperger, Max E. *The Lingering Shadow of Nazism: The Austrian Independent Party Movement Since 1945.* New York: Columbia University Press 1978.

Schlesinger, Thomas O. *Austrian Neutrality in Postwar Europe: The Domestic Roots of a Foreign Policy.* Vienna: Braumüller, 1972.

Stadler, Karl R. *Austria.* London: Ernest Benn, 1971.

Steiner, Kurt. *Politics in Austria.* Boston: Little, Brown, 1972.

———, ed. *Modern Austria.* Palo Alto, Calif.: Sposs, 1981.

Sully, Melanie A. *Parties and Elections in Austria.* London: Hurst, 1981.

———. *Continuity and Change in Austrian Socialism: The Eternal Quest for the Third Way.* New York: Columbia University Press, 1982.

11

Ireland

Desmond Dinan

The words "peripheral" and "marginal" are frequently used to describe Ireland's position in Western Europe. In the geographical sense, those adjectives will always be apt. Ireland is cut off from the continent of Europe by two bodies of water on either side of another, larger island. That neighboring island will soon be physically connected to the continent by the Channel Tunnel, an engineering accomplishment unlikely ever to be emulated under the Irish Sea. Regardless of regular plane and ferry connections to Britain and the continent, Ireland will forever be romantically remote, a stunningly beautiful wind- and waveswept Atlantic island off the northwest coast of Europe.

In every other sense, however, Ireland is far from peripheral or marginal. In the past thirty years, four distinct developments have caused the country to change dramatically. First, the advent of television in the early 1960s opened Irish eyes to a bewildering wider world, and broke down social, cultural, and psychological barriers more formidable than those that ordinarily ought to exist in a country with Ireland's geographical characteristics. Second, a radical reversal of Ireland's economic policy set the country on the road to European Community (EC) membership. Ireland's accession to the EC in January 1973 marked a profound turning point in every aspect of Irish life: from education and entertainment to employment and emigration. Third, the explosive growth of Dublin's population—one-third of the Republic's 3.5 million people now live in the greater-Dublin area—spawned a cosmopolitan metropolis barely able to cope with its attendant social problems, sundered the hitherto harmonious relationship between town and country in Ireland, and compounded the Republic's already excessive centralization of government. Finally, and no less importantly, the outbreak of the current round of "troubles" in the north of Ireland fueled an incessant, intense debate in the south on the nature of Irish nationalism and the issue of Irish identity.

Despite these developments, Ireland is still recognizable to those who knew it thirty years ago. Institutions and structures remain intact, although their form and content have been altered to one degree or another. The 1937 constitution has been amended but not rewritten. The political party system is the same as before, dominated by Fianna Fail, Fine Gael, and Labour. The electoral system of proportional representation by the single transferable vote continues to befuddle outsiders, and turn constituents into clients of their TDs (*Teachta Dala*, Member of Parliament). As formulators of national policy, TDs themselves are as ineffectual as ever, with the Dail (lower house of Parliament) completely controlled by the cabinet. Personalities tower over Irish politics, as much today as when Michael Collins and Eamon De Valera split the country over the terms of the Anglo-Irish Treaty of 1921, and sowed the seeds of the Fine Gael and Fianna Fail parties. Emigration is still pervasive, although more Irish people now seek a new life in other EC countries than in the United States. The Catholic church remains influential socially and to a lesser extent politically, and a large majority of people in the Republic regularly attend Sunday mass.

Regardless of structures and institutions, the Irish character, personality, and temperament seem impervious to change. Gossip, backbiting, and begrudgery are national pastimes. Pride in things Irish with an international reputation—from Aer Lingus and Waterford glass to race horses and Lebanon hostage Brian Keenan—is undiminished. Passion for sports—from Gaelic and "foreign" games to the Olympics and general elections—is unbridled. Charity for victims of accidents and disasters is boundless. Religious conservatism is ingrained. Anglophobia is endemic. The perpetuation of these peculiarly Irish traits at a time of spectacular social, political, and economic change makes contemporary Ireland a fascinating subject of study.

Political Parties and Government

Of the three main political parties in Ireland, only the Labour Party's name is pronounceable and revelational to non-Irish ears. Indeed, Labour is a social democratic party that supposedly champions working class causes. Other than that, Labour has little in common with its British and continental European counterparts. By the early twentieth century, Ireland had a small and vibrant urban working class. Organized by the radical trade unionist Jim Larkin and the socialist revolutionary James Connolly, the Irish working class channeled its energy into the struggle for Irish independence. Born during the turbulent years of the liberation movement, the Labour Party decided not to split the nationalist vote by contesting the formative 1918 election—the first general election in eight years, the first election with thousands of newly enfranchised voters, and the first general election after the surge of Irish separatism in the wake of the 1916 rebellion. By standing outside the fray, Labour missed the chance to rally its working class constituency, which mobilized instead on the issue of Irish independence during the Anglo-Irish War of 1919–1921, and subsequently along pro- and anti-Treaty lines during the civil war of 1922–1923.

Thereafter Labour became the "half" party in a "two-and-a-half" party system. With small but faithful electoral support and consequently a small parliamentary representation (an average of fifteen members), in independent Ireland Labour's lot has been either perpetual opposition or minor partnership in coalition government. In the 1960s and 1970s, Labour enjoyed a renaissance as the party of choice for Irish intellectuals, with Conor Cruise O'Brien being the most conspicuous recruit. An influx of intellectuals probably scared away much of the working class support that Labour still retained, but brought with it some middle class voters.

With Fianna Fail not wanting or needing a partner in government, a Fine Gael-Labour coalition offered both parties their only prospect of ever getting into power, and offered the Irish electorate their only prospect of ever driving Fianna Fail out of power. In 1973, after sixteen years of uninterrupted Fianna Fail government, a majority of the electorate and both opposition parties were poised for change. At first glance Labour and Fine Gael seemed strange bedfellows. With its socialist rhetoric and working class origins, Labour looked far removed from the right-of-center, Christian Democratic Fine Gael Party. Yet Labour's lack of radicalism, Fianna Fail's anti-intellectualism, and Fine Gael's social welfarism made the 1973 coalition more than a marriage of convenience. Although many rank-and-file Labour Party members resented the affiliation with Fine Gael, most of the party hierarchy seemed at home in the three Labour-Fine Gael coalition governments of the 1970s and 1980s. The party leader, Michael O'Leary, even abandoned Labour to join Fine Gael in 1982. The demoralized Labour Party is still trying to regain its self-respect.

In the early 1980s a new political party emerged to cater to the urban working class. Appropriately named the Workers' Party, its origins lie in the most recent split within the divisive Irish Republican movement. When the Irish Republican Army (IRA) split in 1970 into the Provisionals and Officials, Sinn Fein, the IRA's political wing, similarly split into Provisional Sinn Fein and Official Sinn Fein. Reflecting a rejection of IRA violence as well as a strong lurch to the doctrinaire socialist left, Official Sinn Fein gradually and painfully transformed itself into the Workers' Party.

At first the Workers' Party appeared to have a bright future. In the cold economic climate of the early 1980s, with record high unemployment and renewed emigration, the viability of the party system came into question. Disillusionment with the establishment parties was especially high in Dublin working class districts. Strong leadership and strict discipline gave the Workers' Party added advantages. Moreover, with neither Fianna Fail nor Fine Gael–Labour able to command a large majority in the Dail, and three general elections being waged in as many years, the emerging Workers' Party seemed ideally placed to hold the balance of power. In the event, the party's prospects had been overrated. The shadow of the gun in its recent past discomfited too many Irish voters. More important, the party's extreme socialism alienated much potential support. Lavish praise for communist regimes in East Germany and Czechoslovakia came back to haunt the party's leadership during the revolutions in Eastern Europe in 1989 and 1990. Ultimately, however, the resilience of the party system consigned the Workers' Party to the margins of Irish politics. For all the electoral fluctuations and "instability" of the early 1980s, the large parties had never really been in danger of disappearing.

For that reason also, the Progressive Democrats (PD) had little chance of breaking the mold of the durable party system. In a dispute over policy compounded by personality, Desmond O'Malley left Fianna Fail in 1986 to launch the PDs. At issue was the opportunism and populism of Charles Haughey, the Fianna Fail leader. O'Malley resented Haughey's playing of the Republican and religious cards for short-term political advantage, at a time when the country seemed in urgent need of forward-looking, resourceful policies and leadership. Despite his idealism, O'Malley had little to offer Irish politics by way of imagination or innovation. His small, solidly middle class party espoused the usual platitudes that substitute for policy in Irish politics, and made little dent in Fine Gael or Labour strongholds, let alone in Fianna Fail's loyal following. Inasmuch as they represented the "New Right" in Irish politics, the PDs counterbalanced the "New Left" of the Workers' Party. Paradoxically, the PDs entered into coalition with Fianna Fail in 1987, putting Haughey and O'Malley together again at the cabinet table.

Forming a coalition with the PDs, however small the number of defections to their ranks, caused deep disquiet in the Fianna Fail Party. Since its inception in 1926, Fianna Fail has been the largest political party in the state. In office for 40 years between 1927 and 1987—twice for continuous sixteen-year periods—Fianna Fail had never before shared responsibility in government. Taking for granted their party's complete hold on power, Fianna Fail supporters used the term "coalition" to refer disparagingly to those odious occasions of aberrant Fine Gael–Labour government. Fianna Fail partisans were profoundly shocked when Haughey not only formed a coalition after the inconclusive 1987 general election, but did so with the renegade O'Malley.

Fianna Fail fury over the 1987 coalition decision was the culmination of a simmering resentment against Haughey's leadership of the party. First elected to the Dail in 1957, Haughey quickly rose to ministerial rank, an ascent that some people ascribed as much to his marriage to the daughter of Sean Lemass, then Fianna Fail leader and Taoiseach (Prime Minister), as to his undoubted aptitude and ability. What promised to be a stellar political career almost came to an end in 1970, when Jack Lynch, Lemass's successor, dismissed Haughey for alleged IRA gun-running. Although acquitted at his subsequent trial, suspicion of having been involved in arming the IRA, and in bringing the Provisionals into being, continued to cling to Haughey.

Under the circumstances, Haughey's political rehabilitation was remarkable. Thrown out of ministerial office in 1970, nine years later he ousted Jack Lynch to become party leader and Taoiseach. In the meantime, he had remorselessly reworked his way through the party ranks. Having been the personification of a party insider, Haughey now cultivated the image of an outcast and underdog. He traveled the country from constituency to constituency, building valuable support in the parliamentary party and among the rank-and-file membership. As Minister for Health and Social Welfare in the late 1970s, he demonstrated a genuine concern for the common man. When the opportunity arose to challenge Lynch's leadership over a poor Fianna Fail showing in the 1979 European Parliament elections and in two subsequent by-elections, Haughey seized it brilliantly. Sensing Lynch's disinterest in remaining in office, Haughey capitalized on his grass roots popularity and swept the other contenders aside.

The manner of Haughey's succession was as controversial as his subsequent leadership of the party and of the country. He was only the fourth leader of Fianna Fail. In 1959 De Valera, the party's founder, had passed the leadership to Lemass, by then his heir apparent. When Lemass resigned in 1966, Jack Lynch emerged as a compromise candidate to avert a bitter leadership election between Haughey, then making an early bid for the top job, and George Colley, a cabinet colleague. Haughey was especially pleased to become leader not only by ousting the unassuming and self-effacing Lynch, but also by defeating Colley in the leadership contest.

Once in office, Haughey was never able to do what Fianna Fail supporters had come to expect, or at least to hope, of their leaders: win general elections resoundingly and keep the party in power perpetually. Under Haughey's leadership, in the course of four general elections in the 1980s, Fianna Fail failed to win an absolute majority of seats in the Dail. As a result, the party had to take the unusual and, for some of its members, unseemly step of haggling for small-party support. In that, at least, Haughey proved unsurpassable. Whether it involved negotiating with the Workers' Party, PDs, or irascible Independents, Haughey excelled at making deals and striking bargains. Nor did he allow himself to be seriously threatened for the party leadership. Having survived the personal and political vicissitudes of the past two decades, including the 1987 coalition controversy, Haughey is more secure than ever before as he leads Fianna Fail into the 1990s.

In many respects, Haughey is an archetypical Fianna Failer. As a self-made man who fought tooth and nail to get to the top, he is seen by some as a role model for the post-1960s era of Irish "gombeenmen," the successor generation of Yeats's fumblers in a greasy till. These people, and their country cousins energetically exploiting the EC's Common Agricultural Policy, are the direct descendants of a core group of Fianna Fail's original followers. Whereas Fine Gael catered to the complacent urban middle class and prosperous large farmers, Fianna Fail was a haven for the have-nots in early-independent Ireland.

That crude socioeconomic characterization of the two main parties' initial adherents ties in with their original positions on the "national question." Britain's proposal to end the War of Independence in 1921 by granting the 26 counties of southern Ireland free state status within the Commonwealth split Irish nationalists. War-weary, but hopeful of a future diplomatic reversal of the unpopular option of Commonwealth membership, a majority of Irish elected representatives ratified the treaty. An intransigent minority, led by Eamon De Valera but dominated by "die-hard" gunmen, rejected the treaty and provoked a civil war, which they lost.

For the victorious civil war side—the forerunner of the Fine Gael Party— the treaty soon became an end in itself, rather than a means by which the Free State government could maneuver diplomatically within the Commonwealth to establish the coveted Republic. Realizing the futility of not recognizing the Free State, in 1926 De Valera broke with his erstwhile IRA allies and founded the Fianna Fail party. From the outset, Fianna Fail stood for a revision of the constitutional and political status quo. Socially and economically, too, Fianna Fail represented a challenge to the poverty, immobility, and high emigration endemic in independent Ireland. Although on the losing side in the civil war, De Valera nonetheless rallied a large number of Irish people who, having refused to fight with him against the treaty, were more than willing to support his political assault on the Fine Gael/Free State government.

De Valera first came to power in 1932 and overshadowed Irish politics for the next thirty years. During his first term in office he skillfully dismantled the treaty. His 1937 constitution in effect brought Ireland out of the Commonwealth, although De Valera refrained from using the sacred word "republic" in the constitution in deference to northern sensitivities. Ironically, it was John A. Costello, the Fine Gael Taoiseach, who took the final step of officially proclaiming a republic in 1949. In the meantime, De Valera's declaration of neutrality during World War II was the clearest possible expression of Irish sovereignty and independence. To be more precise, it was the clearest possible expression of *southern* Irish sovereignty and independence, for its impact on British and northern unionist opinion was to guarantee partition.

As for social and economic conditions, Fianna Fail did little to improve the lot of the average Irishman. Disaffection over that, and over the perpetuation of partition, gave rise to a new party, Clann na Publachta, in 1948. Just as the Workers' Party and the PDs failed to make a substantial impact on the party system in the 1980s, the Clann was equally unavailing in the 1940s and 1950s. Fianna Fail and Fine Gael were too deeply entrenched. Having mobilized the electorate primarily along pro- and antitreaty lines, both parties monopolized political discourse and continued to articulate issues in terms of the "national question." Allegiance to one or the other party, first given in the aftermath of the civil war, became a matter of fierce political partisanship, carefully transmitted from one generation to the next.

Today, the civil war has nothing directly to do with why people vote for Fianna Fail or Fine Gael, although history, loyalty, and habit are indirectly determining factors. On the "national question"—partition and Anglo-Irish relations—the parties differ only in their oratory. True to its antitreaty tradition, Fianna Fail spouts irredentist and republican rhetoric. By contrast, Fine Gael takes a more measured and moderate tone. In the heat of an election campaign, when tempers become testy, Fianna Failers accuse Fine Gaelers of being pro-British, while Fine Gaelers accuse Fianna Failers of being pro-IRA. When in office, the parties pursue similar policies toward the north. For all his criticism while in opposition of the Anglo-Irish agreement, once in government Haughey faithfully abided by its terms.

On social and economic issues, differences between the parties are equally slight. Both support or oppose the welfare state, depending on economic circumstances or electoral fashion; both encourage foreign investment; both advocate full Irish participation in the EC; both believe in centralized government. Style, more than substance, sets them apart. To caricature: Fianna Fail is brash, assertive, unintellectual, and uncouth; Fine Gael is polite, reticent, ineffectual, and cultured. In keeping with the personalization of Irish politics, those distinctions were especially marked between 1979 and 1987, when Haughey and Garrett FitzGerald overlapped as leaders of their respective parties.

The greatest challenge to the two parties' monopoly of Irish politics came in the 1960s, when the last of the civil war generation of politicians departed, and Ireland embarked on enormous social and economic change. Yet the parties were catalysts, not victims, of that change. It was Fianna Fail's Sean Lemass who spearheaded the switch in Ireland's economic policy from protectionism to free trade, and Jack Lynch who led Ireland into the EC. Subsequently, it was Fine Gael's Garrett FitzGerald, first as Foreign Minister and later as Taoiseach, who fashioned most of Irelands's EC policy. Both parties have done as much as possible to shape the momentous events and developments that have affected Ireland in the past thirty years, rather than allowing those events and developments to shape the parties.

Elections and the Oireachtas (Parliament)

Since the establishment of the Free State, Ireland has used a system of proportional representation by the single transferable vote (PR-STV). The fears of some politicians that PR-STV would produce weak government and political instability have proved unfounded. Critics of PR argue that the electoral history of the 1980s, when neither Fianna Fail nor Fine Gael-Labour won an absolute majority and the country went to the polls four times in six years, makes their point. It does nothing of the sort. Indeed, PR-STV made it possible for the electorate to be indecisive, but did not cause the electorate to be indecisive. In other words, the electorate chose not to give either Fianna Fail or Fine Gael-Labour an absolute majority. The electorate's ability to do so shows their extraordinary sophistication in utilizing the complex PR-STV system, and strengthened their already deep attachment to it.

The politicians who dislike PR-STV most are those who benefit from it least: Fianna Fail parliamentarians. As the largest party in the state, Fianna Fail would be far better off with a British-style, first-past-the-post system. With such a system, as the electorate knows only too well, Haughey could possibly have had an uninterrupted decade in office. Revelling in their ministerial roles, senior members of his parliamentary party would have enjoyed far more security of tenure, with their junior colleagues savoring for a longer time the spoils of government. Fianna Fail's concern about PR-STV is long-standing. In 1959, and again in 1968, Fianna Fail governments attempted to abolish PR-STV. On each occasion, the electorate endorsed its retention in a referendum.

All Dail deputies have another reason to resent PR-STV: It forces them at election time to compete not only against members of rival political parties, but also against members of their own party. Political parties typically nominate more candidates in a constituency than are likely to be elected. In a five-seat constituency, for instance, a party with a reasonable expectation of taking two seats will nominate at least three candidates, in the hope of picking up an extra seat. Candidates win marginal seats because of the way votes transfer during successive counts. By marking their preferences in front of each candidate's name on the ballot paper, voters determine both the distribution of a candidate's votes if that candidate is eliminated during the count *and* the surplus votes of a candidate who is elected after surpassing the quota.[1]

Going door-to-door in a constituency before an election, each candidate will ask the voter to give him a first-preference vote (to be marked #1 on the ballot). The candidate will then ask for the voter's next preferences to be given to the candidate's party colleagues. Voters are predisposed in any case to group their first preferences by party. However, the order in which they cast those preferences for a party's candidates can be crucial, and is unaffected by party loyalty. It depends on the candidate's popularity and usefulness. Popularity can be evaluated in any number of ways, but usefulness is measured entirely by what the candidate can do directly for the voter and for the constituency.

This scenario highlights a further drawback of PR-STV. Although endemic in any political system, clientelism is pervasive in Ireland in part because of the electoral process. Voters have little interest in a candidate's ability to understand and analyze weighty national or international issues, but care mostly about his skill in accomplishing things close to home. Thus TDs not only spend too much time in constituency clinics, but also bolster brokerage by convincing their constituents that elected representatives alone can resolve problems locally, by contacting the right people nationally. One consequence of this, not surprisingly, is that TDs strongly oppose government decentralization, lest their role as brokers with the bureaucracy be diminished.

Such a situation frustrates bright, ambitious TDs, and discourages equally capable people from standing for election. Even those TDs who nonetheless make an effort to debate national issues, and to help formulate policy, find little opportunity or encouragement in the Dail. Policy is the preserve of the cabinet, which initiates legislation and imposes strict voting discipline to ensure its enactment. Committees are weak, and by no means encompass the entire legislative agenda. The civil service is correspondingly strong. Because of the dearth of parliamentary talent, and the relatively large number of ministerial openings, an able TD in one of the establishment parties at least has a reasonable chance of promotion. Even as a government minister, however, a TD must always keep in close touch with his constituency, and constantly satisfy his voters' demands.

The Irish Senate (upper house) and presidency—the other parts of the Oireachtas—are politically unimportant. Debate in the Senate occasionally soars due to the exceptional ability of some of its members. Free of the bondage of brokerage, either because they are elected by panels representing corporate interests rather than by the electorate at large, or because they are appointed by the Taoiseach, senators have a chance to rise above the parochialism that pervades the lower house. On the other hand, the Senate's use as a holding pen or dumping ground for failed TDs leavens the sometimes stellar caliber of its members. A celebrated dispute in 1990 between the Senate chairman, a Fianna Fail politician who had already scandalized the party and country by his mismanagement of the Justice Ministry in the early 1980s, and an eminent Independent member graphically illustrated the contrasting quality of Senators, and brought the House into considerable disrepute.

The presidency is almost exclusively ceremonial. Only once, when a government minister publicly expressed indignation over a president's decision to refer constitutionally doubtful legislation to the Supreme Court, did controversy surround the office. Although a presidential term is limited to seven years, collusion between the political parties spared the country the expense, and denied voters the fun, of a presidential election in the 1970s and 1980s.

Conclusion

The 1990s are likely to be every bit as changeful as the preceding three decades. The EC's single market is well on its way to completion, bringing with it new economic challenges and opportunities for the twelve member-states. As a small, open economy, Ireland is especially vulnerable to developments inside and outside the Community. For Ireland more than for larger Western European states, much depends on the outcome of the single market program, the Uruguay Round of the General Agreement on Tariffs and Trade, and the Gulf crisis. Even the most optimistic forecasts, however, posit high unemployment in Ireland through the end of the decade. Down to 16 percent in 1990 from a record-high 20 percent in the mid-1980s, unemployment is unlikely to dip below 10 percent in the foreseeable future. As a result, emigration will continue to be a lamentable fact of Irish life.

With the single market program overtaken by events in the Soviet Union and Eastern Europe, the EC is on the threshold not only of economic and monetary union, but also of political union. Whereas a federal United States of Europe is still far in the future, undoubtedly the 1990s will see greater democratic accountability of EC institutions, and closer political and foreign policy cooperation among the member-states. Moreover, the EC's pitiable response to Iraq's invasion of Kuwait in August 1990 thrust defense cooperation onto the proposed program of Community reform. As a neutral state, Ireland opposed efforts in the 1980s to include the military aspects of security in European Political Cooperation (EPC), the Community's foreign policy coordinating mechanism. The end of the cold war renders many of Ireland's proneutrality arguments obsolete, and has robbed the country of confederates in the Community who had also opposed incorporating defense into EPC. Alone in the Community, Ireland may not be able to prevent defense policy's being put on the EC agenda. At the same time, Irish people have a growing attachment to the notion of neutrality, whatever it means in practice. Thus, in its foreign as well as in its domestic politics, Ireland could continue to be unique in the 1990s. Like Fianna Fail, Fine Gael, Labour,

PR-STV, the Oireachtas, and a host of other quaint Irish customs and institutions, neutrality might well survive the twentieth century.

Note

1. For a thorough explanation of PR-STV, see Basil Chubb, *The Government and Politics of Ireland*, 2d ed. (Longman, 1982), pp. 350–350.

Suggested Readings

Chubb, Basil, *The Government and Politics of Ireland*, 2d ed. London: Longman, 1982.

Lee, J. J., *Ireland, 1912–1985: Politics and Society*. Cambridge, Eng.: Cambridge University Press, 1989.

Laver, Michael, et al., eds., *How Ireland Voted: The General Election, 1987*. Dublin, Ireland: Poolbeg, 1987.

Mair, Peter, *The Changing Irish Party System: Organization, Ideology and Electoral Competition*. London: Frances Pinter, 1987.

Political Studies Association of Ireland, *Irish Political Studies*. PSAI Press, annually.

12

Greece

Roy C. Macridis

The story is often told that in the days of the Creation God discovered, after His work had been done, a few rocks left in His bag and scattered them over the land that is now Greece. It is a small mountainous area of some 130,000 square kilometers. Less than 25 percent of the land is arable and only a small part can be used for year-round crops such as corn and wheat. Water is scarce and natural resources are scant (bauxite, marble, lignite). Sixty-five percent of the ten million inhabitants live in congested urban areas—4 million in greater Athens—without proper amenities of urban transports and public services. There are a total of two thousand islands—most of them barren. Yet the Greek mainland and the islands are, from a strategic point of view, of great value. Ever since its independence in 1827, Greece has been coveted by all the great powers. The one that controls it dominates the southeastern Mediterranean.

The Greek economy cannot support its people. Greece has had to rely on proceeds from shipping, tourism, and remittances from the many Greeks who emigrated and, invariably, on borrowing from abroad to balance its accounts. It continues to import goods almost twice the value of its exports. The per capita income is about $4,500; the GNP was equivalent to about 46 billion U.S. dollars in the 1980s. After Portugal, Greece remains the poorest country in the European Common Market that it joined in 1981. Its total exports in 1983–1984 amounted to barely six billion dollars, and its imports to over $12 billion; its external debt has risen steadily and is expected to reach $25 billion in 1991. Inflation has averaged in the past decade about 12–14 percent, and is expected to reach about 20 percent in 1991; unemployment stood at about 11 percent in the 1980s;

domestic investment has been negligible and during the years that PASOK, a self-styled Marxist party, was in power (1981–1989), foreign investment was virtually nil.

The major employer remains the state. Under the Socialist government, most of the major services—air and rail transport, telephones and telecommunications, electricity and energy in general, tourism, banking, many extractive firms in metals and bauxite, imports and exports—had come either under the direct ownership and management of the state or under stringent controls by the state. Health services and hospitals, as well as education, were virtually monopolized by public agencies. Greece's huge bureaucracy employs more than 35 percent of the active population and absorbs about one half of all government expenditures. The state began to dominate society. Public spending increased accordingly. Huge subsidies by the European Common Market (amounting to about one billion dollars a year), by the American aid program and outright advances and borrowing from the European Bank and the World Bank failed to bring about any improvement.

Background—the Civic Culture

History has not been any more generous to the Greeks than God was. It has shaped and ultimately bequeathed the modern Greeks a complex of conflicting values. What we normally call the civic culture—the attitudes, perceptions, values, and cognitions that individuals have about political life, about the state and their role—is like a broken mirror, in which each Greek sees different images that evoke different aspirations, values, and attitudes. This reality accounts for an identity crisis.

Identity Crisis

Who is a modern Greek? A descendant of "Ancient Hellas"? An heir to the glories of the Christian Byzantium? Heir to the almost thousand years of barbarian invasion and Turkish rule? Identification with the ancient Greeks suggests democracy, rationality, and a cultural mantle second to none, commanding the respect of everyone in the world. But it also creates anxiety, frustration, and a clear sense of inferiority as the modern Greeks live in the shadow of the ancient Greek temples and the political discourse they pretend to emulate. Modern Greek language is different from ancient Greek—more so than Chaucer is for the English, just as different as Latin is for the modern Italians.

Byzantium (A.D. 413 to 1453) spells the glory of an empire straddling the straits of Bosphorus with the whole of Asia Minor and the Balkans, including of course Greece, administered by a highly centralized bureaucracy and governed by an omnipotent emperor and the patriarch head of the Greek Orthodox church in Constantinople. Byzantium carries two powerful messages: (a) religious orthodoxy and identity, and (b) nationalism—the hope that sometime the empire will be restored to its greatness. This is the "Maegahli Idea" (the Exalted Idea) that has nourished Greek nationalism for many centuries and continues even today. Centralization, religious conformity, and imperial despotism are the heritage of the Byzantine Empire. It is at odds with the secular, freedom-loving, democratic spirit of many of the ancient Greek city-states—especially Athens.

With the fall of Byzantium and the spread of the Ottoman Empire, new cultural patterns developed over the centuries from the fourteenth to the early nineteenth, with a direct impact on present-day politics: familialism, clientelism, and personalism.

Clientelism became a political form of expression to deal with the Turkish administrative officials. A kind of manipulative form of political coexistence between the indigenous elite groups and the Turkish officials developed, based on the sharing of benefits. The Turks had their Greek clients, who in turn were surrounded by theirs, in well-organized networks with clear gradations of wealth, status, and power. The church itself, from the Patriarch down, benefited from a symbiosis with the Ottoman Empire that allowed it some measure of autonomy and benefits in return for its subservience.

Familialism—both narrow and extended—was a defensive posture for every family or village. It accounts even today for "parochial," that is, narrow and selfish, attachments. Greeks continue to identify with the family; they derive their position and status from the family; they share benefits with the family. Family attachments limit the sense of loyalty to the political and national community. Personal and family obligations and personal and family "honor" remain for the Greeks above corporate and community obligation. Virtue—"civic virtue"—is identified in terms of family loyalties rather than civic ones.

Personalism, another ingredient of political culture associated with clientelism and familialism, is the personal attachment to a patron, a notable, a benefactor. Political groupings and political parties have been deeply associated with and identified with political patron saints. Political office, wealth, and patronage remained in the family, passed on from father to son. Parties and their organization often were based on family and clientelistic ties with strong local and regional identities.

Familialism, clientelism, and personalism are patterns that have prevented the emergence of collective and communitarian politics. They both atomized and individualized political behavior. Politics became but an expanding web of personal ties linked to personal benefits. This is the key to the proverbial Greek *individualism*—the lack of deep-seated civic obligations. But it also accounts for the unpredictability and volatility of Greek politics: The beneficiary or client easily shifts positions from one patron to another, depending on the benefits offered.

This is particularly so with the state, which is generally viewed as a source from which individuals and families derive benefits; it becomes the "patron state," with a "patron leader," who hands out benefits in return for loyalty and support. The legitimacy of the state as a result has been traditionally very low.

Dependence

History played yet another trick on the Greeks that encouraged them to distance themselves from the state, to disregard it and often to defy it. It never became *their* state; it always depended on outside powers and forces. Greek independence itself was made possible in 1827 only by the intervention of the then three major world powers—Russia, France, and England. They became known as the "protectors," and they virtually controlled the destinies of the country, with England gradually gaining the upper hand in the nineteenth century and until 1940. But it was a control exercised in alliance with indigenous elites that solicited it. They relied upon it until the "protection" offered was taken for granted and became a fixed pattern of Greek political life. The habit of "dependence" linked the Greek ruling groups with foreign powers and focused their attention on their relations with such powers to the detriment of developing solid popular roots and seeking popular support.

Since political power came from abroad, the political elites did not attempt to secure it from within. This was the case even when, at the turn of the nineteenth century and the beginning of the twentieth, the country began to modernize with a growing rate of urbanization, a network of communications, a national educational system, economic improvement, and in general the growth of a middle-class primarily engaged in trade and manufacturing. Modernization, however, never led to the development of a broad consensus either on political goals or political means.

This cultural and historical profile helps us follow the institutional arrangements of the Greek state—from the moment it gained its independence in a small territory on the mainland to World War I and to World War II, when finally all ethnic Greeks found themselves within the borders of the fatherland—to include Epirus in the late 1880s, Macedonia and Thrace in 1911–1913, the Aegean Islands in 1920, and finally Rhodes and the Dodecanese Islands in 1946.

Regime Instability

Throughout Greek history, and until very recently, three major forces battled over political dominance: (1) the *monarchy*, supported by conservative forces, including the church and the military, sometimes with constitutional limitations and parliamentary government (1864–1911), but more often

Table 12.1   **Greek Political Regimes since Independence**

1821	Proclamation of independence and the First Republic
1830	Absolute monarchy
	Uprising, 1843
	First parliamentary election, 1844
	Uprising, 1862; deposition of king
1863	Constitutional monarchy
	Revolt of military, 1909
	Accession of King Constantine, 1913
	Political and military uprising; king forced into exile, 1917
	Return of Constantine, 1920
	Military coup; second exile and abdication of the king, 1922
1924	Second Republic
	Military coup, 1925
	Military dictatorship, 1925–1926
	Attempted military coups, 1933, 1935
1935	Constitutional monarchy
	George II becomes king
1936	Dictatorship under General Metaxas
1941–1944	Military occupation by Germany
1944–1945	Regency of Archbishop Damaskinos
1946	Constitutional monarchy
	Referendum and return of George II
	Civil war, 1946–1949
	King Paul succeeds George II, 1951
	Death of King Paul and accession of King Constantine, 1964
1967	Military junta; exile of king
1974	Junta collapses; monarchy abolished by referendum
1974–1981	Third Republic
1981–1989	Parliamentary democracy with dominance of Marxist-Socialist Panhellenic Socialist Movement
1989–April 1990	Deadlock

governing directly; (2) the *army*, which gave its full support to the monarchy until the end of the nineteenth century when it began to waver in favor of democratic and liberal reforms; and (3) the *democratic* and *liberal* forces, appealing to farmers and manufacturers, artisans and tradesmen, but also to members of the enlightened bourgeoisie and the emerging proletariat. Communists, as a political force, remained negligible until World War II, when at the head of the resistance against the German-occupying forces, they managed to establish control over the countryside. They were dislodged first by the British and later by American aid, only to re-emerge in 1974. Table 12.1 shows the fortunes of the various regimes since Greece became independent.

The overall political legacy has been one of regime instability; sharp division between Monarchists and Democrats; intermittent military interventions and military dictatorship, similar to the Latin American model. Party fragmentation and political instability, even at Parliament and cabinet levels, became the norm of political life; ideological confrontations and intense internal civil strife became endemic.

The Constitution of 1974

The political system established by the constitution of 1974 is a republican form of parliamentary democracy. It has many similarities with the governments of other southern and western European countries. The president of the Republic acts as "head of state." The Greek president is relatively powerless, in much the same way as the presidents of Italy and the former Federal Republic of Germany.

As a parliamentary democracy, the power of the government resides in the cabinet under the direction of the prime minister, who acts as "head of government." The prime minister and his team of ministers are accountable to the Parliament. This government remains in power as long as it holds the confidence of a majority of the Parliament. The Parliament—the Vouli—is the center of legislative activity. Besides electing the prime minister, it must pass all important legislative acts, is the center of debate on governmental bills, and provides the opposition with the opportunity to criticize government policy.

As in most European democracies, parliamentary and all other political activity in Greece is generally carried out through the political parties. However, the Greek party system was fragmented, as was that of Italy. This party fragmentation not only led in the past to governmental instability during periods of democracy, but also to regime instability. Greece has attempted to remedy this. One way has been through the use of an electoral system that often excludes smaller parties from representation in the Vouli. The electoral system of proportional representation penalized, until 1985, parties that received less than 17 percent of the national vote. In 1989, however, the system was modified to allow for the representation of small parties.

The Political Forces Since 1945

There are three major stages in the post–World War II political history of Greece, and party politics as well as electoral politics share common characteristics in each of them.

Counterrevolution and Restoration

The first stage began with the Battle of Athens, in December 1944, to dislodge the Communists; it extended virtually until 1961. The first years were almost wholly devoted to dismantling the Communist-led National Liberation Front (EAM), and its fighting arm, the National Liberation Army (ELAS). It was a period in which the king returned; when foreign powers—England until 1947 and the United States thereafter—intervened in the most unqualified terms; when the notables and leaders of the political parties assumed control of the state machinery and rewove their web of influence and control based on family, local contacts, and personal favors; during which the king and his entourage reasserted their personal prerogatives over the army and foreign policy. It was also a period of rapid economic reconstruction, thanks to massive aid from the United States.

In the first election after World War II, held in March 1945 under a simple proportional system, the so-called United Front of the National Minded (*Ethnikofronon*) won a sweeping victory with 59 percent of the vote and an absolute majority in the Vouli. The centrist groups won about 32 percent. In the next election (1951), the right-wing groups under General Alexander Papagos received 44 percent of the vote, while the group headed by another general, Plastiras, managed 23.5 percent. The two generals had a majority in the Vouli but they could not agree. A new election had to be held in 1952, this time by a majority system. General Papagos won. He received 49.2 percent of the vote and seated 240 deputies out of a total of 300.

In brief, this first period was one in which a small oligarchy, consisting of the army, the crown, and the conservative political notables, governed with U.S. support and economic aid. The forms of democracy were respected, but in substance the system was oligarchic.

The Opening

The second phase began with the legislative election of 1956, in which women voted for the first time. This phase was characterized by the restructuring of the party system, with two major parties vying for control. Some parties were led by newcomers. Constantine Karamanlis assembled the various fragments of the right—to form a new party, the National Radical Union. It won 47.5 percent of the vote and 165 out of 300 deputy seats. The centrists, on the other hand, and all the leftists joined forces in one formation, the Democratic Union, to win 48.2 percent of the vote, but under the electoral system they gained only 132 seats in the Vouli. Karamanlis and his party maintained their strength and their majority in the subsequent elections of 1958 and 1961. Votes of the left and the center, however, continued to represent almost half the electorate.

The "opening" led to the electoral victory of the liberal center under George Papandreou in 1964, with 53 percent of the vote. The liberal center was now in a position to control the state, shape foreign policy, and subordinate the army. But it was pitted against the monarchy, which was supported by the military. The latter intervened in April 1967 to establish a military dictatorship that temporarily arrested this trend in the direction of liberalization.

The Military in Power (1967–1974)—An Interlude

The "opening" was interrupted by the military dictatorship that took over in April 1967 and remained in power until the end of July 1974. The military junta comprised no more than about fifty officers. It remained throughout its reign true to its origins. It did not form a party; it did not aspire to a new political ideology or try to appeal to any given social class; it never attempted to *mobilize* the masses; it hardly even tampered with the basic Greek institutions—the village, the church, the business community, the upper bourgeoisie, or the army. It developed no popular roots. Instead, it relied on force. The manner of its collapse was itself an indication of its artificiality. The conspirators simply fell apart and asked the old political leaders to take over. The political exiles came back or out of jail; civil freedoms were restored; newspapers of all political colorations mushroomed; political prisoners were released; political parties and political leaders made their triumphant return to Athens. If the junta left any lasting effect, it was in the way in which the Greeks now looked upon the United States. The vast majority blamed the United States for the military regime.

The Restoration of Democracy

The real test of the viability and legitimization of democratic institutions—the real opening—came after the fall of the junta. In the 1974 referendum, the monarchy was set aside. Two-thirds of the electorate (69.2 percent) voted in favor of a presidential democracy and against the king's return.

In this third phase of Greece's recent political history, genuine constitutionalism and liberalization under the constitution of 1974 became the rule. Civil rights were fully guaranteed and protected; freedom of the press, speech, and association were staunchly upheld, and elections were untainted by governmental intervention or fraud. The army, too, came progressively under civilian control. Only small factions among the military, and virtually none of the important political leaders, advocated a change in the republican regime or a return to the monarchy. In short, there seemed to be a legitimization of the regime, or at least the formation of a broad consensus supporting it.

Elections

Between 1974 and 1981 there were three legislative elections. Those of October 1974 and November 1977 maintained the dominance of the center-right groups. Nea Democratia, a new party formed in September 1974 under the leadership of Constantine Karamanlis, managed to develop contacts rapidly throughout the country. The Center Union, which had won a majority in 1964, continued to rely upon its traditional local and provincial leaders, but in the seven years of the junta many had abandoned their political strongholds. The left was represented by the Communists, who, if united, expected to receive the support of 10 percent of the faithful, and by the Panhellenic Socialist Movement (PASOK) founded by Andreas Papandreou in the first week of September 1974. It was the latter that attracted attention. Papandreou chose to appear as a new man and he promised socialism overnight. He promised again to secure the "independence" of Greece by cutting all ties with its protector, the United States, and also by eschewing any integrative ties with Western Europe and the Common Market. He urged the drastic purging of the Greek army. He also went far to the left by advocating broad measures of socialization in industry, health, education, and even trade.

The electoral campaign of 1974 was a model of self-restraint and dignity, and the results were also an expression of moderation, perhaps even of conservatism. Karamanlis and Nea Democratia swept the country with almost 55 percent of the vote, gaining 220 seats in the 300-member legislative assembly. The Center Union party, with about 20 percent of the vote, came in a very poor second. PASOK came in third with 13.6 percent of the vote, gaining only 12 seats in the legislative assembly as compared to 60 for the centrists. The Communists held on to almost 10 percent of the vote; they won only eight seats in the legislative assembly. But after 35 years of repression and persecution (eased only in the 1960s and then resumed with unmitigated vigor under the military junta), the party showed remarkable strength.

The Election of 1977

The election of November 20, 1977, three years later, virtually reproduced the basic left-right voter alignment. Nea Democratia, under the same leadership, won a plurality and suffered a decline of 13 percentage points. In fact, however, about half of these defectors went to a conservative right-wing party, which cooperated with Nea Democratia. The total strength of the center-right in 1977 amounted to about 55 percent. On the left the most noticeable phenomena were the stability of the Communist vote (around 10 percent) and PASOK's gains from

13.6 percent to 25.3 percent. The combined vote of PASOK, the Communists, and the other leftists rose to about 35 percent, from 25 percent in 1974.

Basically, the issues before the electorate in 1977 were the same as those in 1974. PASOK and the Communists refused to cooperate with each other, but they both harped on the same powerful nationalist slogans; they both exploited dissatisfaction with the United States and NATO; and they both argued strongly against Greece's entry into the Common Market scheduled for 1981. They both brandished the Turkish threat. Nea Democratia stood on its record: prosperity, full employment, democracy, and political and social tranquility. The European vocation of Greece, Nea Democratia claimed, was consistent both with the nation's traditions and with its future orientation.

When a new presidential election was held in April 1980, Karamanlis was the only candidate. The constitution requires that a presidential candidate obtain the votes of two-thirds of the 300-member Vouli to be elected. Failing this, the candidate needs a minimum of 180 votes in a third ballot; otherwise, a new legislative election is called. Karamanlis was elected with 183 votes on the third ballot. PASOK and the Communists abstained.

The Election of 1981: The Turn to the Left

Between 1974 and 1981, democracy functioned better than perhaps at any previous time in Greek history. Political and individual freedoms were protected, elections took place without accusations and counteraccusations of fraud, and critical decisions were made involving constitutional reform, the electoral system, important educational and social reforms and—most important of all—the entry of Greece into the Common Market in June 1981. Parliamentary institutions worked well. It was against this background that the third electoral contest took place—a contest that involved, as the Socialists continued to gain momentum, fundamental choices about the government, the economy, and the society.

What were the major issues before the electorate? First, national independence. Papandreou remained hostile to the Atlantic Alliance and NATO and promised to hold a referendum on Greece's membership in the Common Market. The time had come, so Papandreou asserted, for full Greek independence in domestic affairs and in foreign policy. It was a call for independence addressed against Turkey, the United States, Europe, and the Common Market.

The second component of the platform was socialism; PASOK claimed to be a Marxist party, committed to the socialization of the economy. Details were never clearly spelled out, but the party clearly envisioned nationalization of parts of trade, industry, and mineral wealth. PASOK, however, insisted on its attachment to democracy and parliamentary government.

Only matters of emphasis separated the Communist Party of Greece (KKE) from PASOK. The KKE appeared more radical in matters of foreign policy, asking for the immediate, definitive, and complete withdrawal of Greece from NATO, the withdrawal of U.S. forces from Greece, the closing of all U.S. military bases, and the withdrawal of Greece from the Common Market, so that "the national interests of Greece would not serve imperialism." With regard to the economy, on the other hand, the KKE appeared more moderate than PASOK. It called for the democratization of publicly owned and controlled enterprises.

Nea Democratia ran on the platform of "renewal" (*ananeossis*). Without their popular and charismatic leader, Constantine Karamanlis, who had been elected president of the republic, and plagued with dissension among its top leaders, Nea Democratia continued in substance as a party of notables and bosses. Despite many efforts, it had failed to develop an organization. It stood on its record. During seven years in office the party's leadership had scrupulously maintained constitutional liberties, kept Greece to the lowest unemployment rate in Europe, promoted modernization of the economy, and brought Greece into the European Economic Community as a full member.

The Election of 1981: The Results

The election of October 18, 1981, amounted to an unprecedented victory for the Greek left. The Pro-Soviet Communist party (KKE) won 10.9 percent of the vote while the Euro-Communist party received a mere 1.4 percent. PASOK won 48 percent of the vote. Thus the combined left received 60 percent of the total vote cast. The combined vote of the various centrist factions totaled only 3.5 percent. Nea Democratia received 36 percent of the vote, a loss of almost 13 percent.

PASOK gained 172 of the 300 members of the Vouli. All parties other than PASOK, Nea Democratia, and the Communist party failed to gain any representation.

Papandreou's motto was *allaghi* (change). The new government proceeded to legislate on some long-overdue problems. Civil marriage was introduced; divorce was made easier; the dowry was abolished; women's rights were strengthened; a liberal pension policy was extended to farmers and to women; health care was extended and expanded; and the crime of adultery was removed from the penal code. In the spirit of reconciliation, the Greeks who had left, willingly or unwillingly, during the Civil War—mostly Communists—were allowed to return.

Papandreou had also mentioned the prospects of fundamental constitutional changes, raising again the possibility of conflicts about the constitution. No such changes were undertaken until 1985. President Constantine Karamanlis and Papandreou seemed to agree on the interpretation of the constitution. The prime minister, with the support of the legislature, is, as we noted, in charge of the government and is responsible for policymaking, while the president exercises only the powers granted to him by the constitution—notably the right to dissolve

Parliament under certain conditions, to call a referendum on key national issues, and to use emergency powers.

In March 1985, after declaring his support for President Karamanlis for a second five-year term, Papandreou changed his mind and declared that he planned to revise the constitution to transfer all the president's constitutional powers to himself. Karamanlis resigned. In the ensuing presidential election, in order to prevent any further defections from PASOK (whose strength had dwindled to 167, but with only 13 Communist votes the required minimum of 180 in the Vouli for the election of the president could be attained), Papandreou insisted that the vote be public and not secret as the constitution prescribed. A new president, handpicked by Papandreou, won with the minimum required 180 votes. Subsequently, the constitution was revised to give *all* the powers of the presidency to the prime minister. Thus conflicts about the constitution were introduced.

PASOK's Re-election, 1985

The general election of June 2, 1985, was virtually a repetition of that of 1981. PASOK leaders stressed the same themes of socialism and nationalism. They warned voters that defeat would usher in turmoil and a rightist dictatorship. New Democracy, as the center-right and major opposition party, had Constantine Mitsotakis as its new leader. It urged modernization in the context of economic freedom and private enterprise, the reduction of the state-controlled sectors of the economy, and a vigorous program of investments with proper guarantees to private and foreign investors.

The election continued the trend toward a sharp bipolarization in Greek politics. The two major parties, PASOK and New Democracy, together received almost 87 percent of the total vote. The Center Union party ceased to exist and its leaders, and other centrists and independents, moved to join the two major parties. The Communist party was the only other party to survive, although it received less than 10 percent of the vote. This continued and growing bipolarization threatened to put a heavy strain on democracy, given the intense ideological chasm that separates them.

PASOK's second consecutive electoral victory gave it the opportunity to consolidate its governmental position. The Socialists gained in the countryside but did not do as well in the cities as previously. In Greece as a whole, they received almost 46 percent of the vote—only 2.5 percent less than in 1981. New Democracy, on the other hand, improved from about 36 percent in 1981 to almost 41 percent. These results translated into a parliamentary majority for PASOK. PASOK held a safe majority in Parliament—161 of the 300 seats. New Democracy held 126 seats; the Communist party, 12.

Deadlock

After the election of 1985, the economic situation worsened while ideological and societal strife intensified. Inflation began to rise. The public debt rose to almost 40 percent of the gross national product. Greece had become the poor man of the European Community. At the same time the Socialist-Marxist ideology, propounded by the leadership of PASOK, whetted the rising expectations of Greeks. They took the form of defiant demands for higher wages and pensions and more public spending. But a reaction also set in. Efforts to "nationalize" the land owned by the church backfired. Professional organizations among lawyers, doctors, and even in universities began to resist the heavy hand of the state whose public sector (and the number of public servants) kept growing. "Public scandals" began to undermine the position of PASOK and its leader. They were symptomatic of many of the cultural traits of the Greek society discussed earlier. The leaders began to dispense favors and use the public monies for their own (and their families') private gain. Outright cases of fraud were discovered, implicating the top PASOK leadership. Public opinion began to waver and PASOK began to lose ground. Opinion became sharply polarized between the left and the right—and not even the weakening of communism, both as an ideology and a form of political and societal organization in Eastern Europe and even the Soviet Union, seemed to affect the Greek left.

Three elections were held between June 1989 and April 1990. The first two produced no majority. Nea Democratia showed renewed strength, and under the old electoral system would have won a majority of seats in Parliament. Before the elections were held, however, the system was modified in the direction of greater proportionality, allowing small parties with 1 to 2 percent of the votes to be represented in Parliament and making it difficult for a majority to emerge. It was only in the election of April 8, 1990, that with 46.93 percent of the popular vote Nea Democratia won half the seats of Parliament (150)—needing the support of one independent conservative to form a government. The composition of Parliament hardly budged in three elections. The system had become deadlocked.

International Position

As we have seen, after the end of World War II, Greece came under the "protection" of the United States. First the Truman Doctrine (1947) provided for massive military aid to the country (and to Turkey as well) to defend itself against Communist insurgence that amounted to a civil war (1947–1949). Subsequently Greece benefited from Marshall Plan aid that lasted well into the mid-1950s. In 1951 Greece became a member of the Atlantic Alliance and its armed forces were integrated into NATO. Its geographic position, as we noted earlier, was, especially in conjunction with Turkey, of paramount strategic importance in denying Soviet naval forces access to the Mediterranean. In the early 1960s, the country became an associate member of the European Economic Community, and it became a full member in 1981. Thus, until PASOK came to power, Greece seemed to be firmly within the Western bloc and the Atlantic Alliance. U.S. military bases had been estalished, including air bases and homeporting facilities for ships. It was this Atlantic and European arrangement that Papandreou assailed after he returned to Greece in 1974 and when in power after the election of 1981—only a few months after Greece had officially become a member of the European Common Market.

Papandreou's early pronouncements presaged, as we noted, a break with Greece's traditional allies. He promised to close American military bases, to break with NATO, and to extricate Greece from European entanglements. Presumably Greece was to return to its "natural allies" in the Middle East and the Balkans and cultivate close relations with the other Mediterranean powers. Like France's president, Charles de Gaulle, Papandreou denounced Yalta and the division of Europe into two camps. Greece would strengthen relations with East Europe and the Soviet Union and would reach out to the Arab world.

The constant use of nationalist themes served three objectives: to attract votes, to obscure or divert the attention of the public from difficult social and economic problems, and to appease the Communist party and the PASOK activists, whose anti-Americanism and pro-Sovietism were pronounced.

Rhetoric and symbolic gestures abounded. Demonstrations against the U.S. military bases (the "bases of death") were organized regularly by Communists and PASOK activists, and were encouraged by party leaders; there were defiant statements about the position of Greece in the Common Market and pronouncements against NATO; contacts with the Soviet Union and the Eastern European Communist regimes became frequent. Papandreou endorsed the Warsaw Pact proposal for a nonaggression treaty with NATO and spoke in favor of a nuclear-free zone in the Balkans—along the lines suggested by the Soviet leadership.

Rhetoric had to be qualified by realism, however. Papandreou's government renegotiated the future of the U.S. military bases. The new agreement (concluded by the end of 1983) provided for the "termination" of the bases in five years, by December 1988. According to the Greeks, the bases were to be closed automatically on a Greek request; but according to U.S. officials, a Greek request would require renegotiation. This was particularly important because in the same agreement there are provisions for technical cooperation with the United States, for the development and procurement of weapons (including F-16 planes) and for the continuation of U.S. aid to Greece on the basis of $7 for Greece for every $10 for Turkey. The bases were not closed and negotiations continued until Papandreou lost the election in 1989.

With regard to the Common Market, realism seemed also to prevail. The early pledges to hold a referendum on Greece's membership or to demand special status for Greece in the community were shelved. Economic considerations seemed to overshadow rhetoric. In addition to the economic benefits, the European Community, in its high-level meetings, gave the Greek leader the opportunity to publicize his views. Papandreou tried to be a mediator. He spoke for the Middle East and the Arab world and for the Palestinians and their cause; at times, he spoke on behalf of the Balkans; he used his position to criticize Turkey. He arranged a meeting in Crete between the French president and the Libyan leader, providing his good offices to both.

After 1981, contacts with the Arab world multiplied. Papandreou visited most Middle Eastern capitals, excepting Tel Aviv and, of course, Ankara. Trade agreements were signed, and every effort was made to isolate Turkey and gain Arab support for the Greek position with regard to Cyprus. Although no ltate recognized the self-styled independent Turkish state on Cyprus, there were few other benefits for Greece.

All efforts to "isolate" Turkey have failed. Greece itself has been isolated and is more vulnerable to Turkish threats. No effort was made to engage Turkey in a dialogue in order to improve military, defense, trade, and tourist relations. In fact, the Greek government intervened to prevent the Greek government on Cyprus from using the good offices of the United Nations secretary-general to pursue a dialogue about the future political organization of the island. Turkey remains the rock on which Greeks vent their nationalism. Without the United States, however, the rock might be catapulted upon Greece.

Greek ideology and rhetoric pointed in one direction, tactics and *realpolitik* in the other. The landmarks of Greek foreign policy remain what they were in 1981. In the meantime precious time was lost and economic progress was delayed.

Issues and Prospects

Basic economic, societal, political, and international issues confront the Greek polity today, as they did after World War II—and as they have always. But the society and the political groups seem to be more deeply divided.

In some eight years of PASOK rule, the economy seems to share some of the same problems facing Eastern Europe—stagnation and statism. The Marxist rhetoric of PASOK brought investments, both domestic and foreign, to a standstill. The major task facing a government today, supported by a very slim majority, is to redress the situation by introducing an austerity program: cutting down public spending, privatizing the state-owned concerns and, above all, encouraging both domestic and foreign investment.

Political problems are equally serious. What is needed is the restoration of the authority of the state—to arrest terrorism, to collect taxes, and to restore civil order.

Societal changes needed are even more critical—and the government may not be strong enough to bring them about. The university was the target and the victim of efforts to impose a Marxist ideology; the students have been highly politicized; the public hospitals have been in disarray; public, especially urban, transport is inadequate; as in Eastern Europe, urban pollution is spreading into the countryside, marring some of the most beautiful landscapes of the world and undermining tourism—the country's major source of hard currency; agricultural "collectives" have been used by PASOK to assert its leadership and control in the countryside rather than to promote growth and improve marketing. The task is enormous—not different from the tasks facing the new leadership in many of the Eastern European countries.

As the political crisis continues, the system appears deadlocked. Instability may continue and may bring about a genuine political crisis unless the European Community manages, as it moves in the direction of greater economic and political integration, to intervene. After all, protection has been, as we noted, one of the ingredients of the Greek political history. It may still be needed.

There are some signs, however, that the turbulent decade of the 1980s and the ensuing deadlock of 1989–1990 may be coming to a close. First, the revolutionary Marxist rhetoric does not appear any longer as mobilizing and convincing as it was; second, the prospects of aid from the Soviet bloc have virtually vanished; third, the nationalist battle-cries of anti-Americanism and the evocation of the Turkish threat are losing their appeal; and finally, domestic, economic, and social problems need immediate attention and foreign capital, just as is the case with most Eastern European countries. Symbolic gestures are likely to give place to realistic policies. Realism may at long last prevail—as it has in other Mediterranean countries such as Portugal and Spain. Signs of moderation are also in the air; one of the most significant ones was the election of Constantine Karamanlis, at the age of 83, as president of the Republic. After having served as prime minister and president of the Republic between 1974 and 1985, the most widely respected figure in contemporary Greek politics appealed once more for democracy, moderation, and national unity—and he was heard.

Suggested Readings

Campbell, J. S., and Sherrard, P., *Modern Greece*. New York: Praeger, 1968.

Clogg, Richard, *Parties and Elections in Greece*. Durham, N.C.: Duke University Press, 1987.

———, and Yannopoulos, G., *Greece Under Military Rule*. New York: Basic Books, 1972.

Couloumbis, Theodore, and Iatrides, John O., eds., *Greek-American Relations*. New York: Pella Publishing Co., 1980.

Featherstone, Kevin, and Katsoudas, Dimitrios K., eds., *Political Change in Greece: Before and After the Colonels*. London: Croom Helm, 1987.

Iatrides, John O., *Greece in the 1940s: A Nation in Crisis*. Hanover, N. H.: University Press of New England, 1981.

Legg, Keith R., *Politics in Modern Greece*. Stanford, Calif.: Stanford University Press, 1969.

Macridis, Roy C., *Greek Politics at the Crossroads: What Kind of Socialism?* Stanford, Calif.: Hoover Institution Press, 1981.

Tzannatos, Zafiris, ed., *Socialism in Greece*. Hants, Eng.: Gower, 1986.

Vatikiotis, P. J., *Greece: A Political Essay*. Beverly Hills, Calif.: Sage, 1974.

13

European Unification,

1944–1992: An Overview

Peter Duignan and Lewis H. Gann

Determined to lay the foundations of an ever-closer union
among the peoples of Europe . . .

Resolved to ensure the economic and social progress of their
countries by common action to eliminate the barriers which
divide Europe . . .

—Treaty of Rome, 1957, creating the European Economic
Community

"Nineteen ninety-two" has already passed into common European speech: The French speak of *quatre-vingt-douze*, the Italians of *novanta due*, the Germans of the *Binnenmarkt* (the internal market). The prospect is astounding. The twelve nations that now make up the European Community (EC) will form a market with more than 337 million people (compared to 240 million in the United States, and 130 million in Japan). The EC's economy will have a gross domestic product equivalent to that of the United States, and double that of Japan. By 1989 the EC was already the world's greatest commercial bloc. Its external exports by 1989 formed 20 percent of world exports, as against 15 percent for the United States, and 9 percent for Japan. The EC had likewise become a major exporter of capital. By 1986, European direct investments in the United States totaled $125 billion, as against U.S. investments of $100 billion in the EC. An economic giant was in the making, a huge agglomeration of vital interest to the United States. By 1987 U.S. exports of goods and services to the EC had risen from 19 percent overall exports to 24 percent. U.S. direct investments in the EC had jumped from 15 percent to 40 percent of U.S. direct investments abroad.[1] No wonder that all Central and Eastern European states have come, since 1989, to look toward association with this new Europe. Given the manifold economic and social problems facing the United States, given also the Soviet Union's apparent disarray, European optimists predict that the twenty-first century will become in the future what the nineteenth century was in the past—the age of Europe. A forecaster predicting such developments fifty years earlier would have been called a visionary or a fool.

The United States has repeatedly played a major role in movements toward European unification: the first time in the decade following World War II, and the second when a new generation of American leaders encouraged a united Europe during the Bush presidency. American efforts helped to unite quarreling and competing European states into peaceful, cooperating communities, linked to each other and to North America.

Early Efforts at European Unity

A partially unified Europe had existed under Charlemagne (A.D. 774) and then under the Holy Roman Empire until its decline at the end of the eighteenth century. During the Middle Ages, Dante, in *De Monarchia*, had called for a united Europe under one sovereign. These aspirations were frustrated by wars of nationalism in the nineteenth and twentieth centuries. World War I, for example, led to the breakup of the Habsburg empire into several weak, unstable states. Fear of another world war led the Pan-European Union in the 1920s to work toward a united, peaceful Europe. Aristide Briand, a French statesman, made the most stirring call for union in 1930. Briand wanted an economic or customs union. He observed that security was related to economic union but also required political union with supranational institutions and political structures. With great foresight, he predicted a European "common market."

World War II gave a new impetus to the movement for a united Europe. The various resistance movements in the occupied countries looked to a new Europe in which traditional national hatreds would disappear. Many pan-Europeanists, such as Robert Schuman of France and Walter Hallstein of West Germany, spent the war years in the United States and became converted to American federalism, its open borders and free trade throughout the country. Union proponents such as Jean Monnet, later known as the "father of Europe," Paul-Henri Spaak, a Belgian political leader who was to author the report for setting up the European Economic Community (EEC), Winston Churchill, and Charles de Gaulle all spoke out for a federation of Europe. The U.S. role was important after the war, however, in getting Europeans to work together peacefully for their mutual benefit.

American-European cooperation was most evident in World War II in military and diplomatic affairs; after 1944, cooperation focused on security and economic affairs. This cooperation was in stark contrast to relations after World War I when isolationist factions dominated in the United States. The U.S. concern for Europe was not inevitable and resulted primarily from the determination of American leaders such as President Truman, Secretary of State Marshall, State Department officials George Kennan and Dean Acheson, and others such as W. Averell Harriman to keep peace in Europe by ending economic rivalry and to contain the Communist threat to a weak and demoralized continent.

The Atlantic Community

The Atlantic Community grew out of wartime cooperation and dependence. The Atlantic Charter (1941) called for global cooperation, postwar security, economic progress, and freer trade. Economic aid through Lend-Lease (1941) also led to economic cooperation, freer trade, and tariff reductions. These aspirations were given concrete force in the Bretton Woods Agreement (1944), which set up the International Monetary Fund (IMF) for monetary matters and the World Bank to finance reconstruction and development. Later, in 1947, the General Agreement on Tariffs and Trade (GATT) was born when the United States and twenty-two other countries met in Geneva to cut tariff rates for industrial goods, with subsequent trade conferences ("Rounds") held thereafter. The resulting tariff reductions were modest, primarily geared toward rebuilding the wartorn European economies; but they did promote cooperation between the United States and the industrialized countries of Western Europe in a variety of ways.

The postwar security system was worked out in wartime conferences at Potsdam, Teheran, and Yalta where the United States and its European allies planned the division of Europe and partitioned Germany, initially with the intention of keeping her disarmed, weak, and under Allied control. The West European countries recovered slowly, faced as they were with rebuilding after wartime destruction, and with having to confront the Soviet menace. Given these challenges, the United States, in 1947, proclaimed the Truman Doctrine, thereby permanently abandoning prewar isolationism, and instituted the Marshall Plan, named after Secretary of State George C. Marshall.

World Wars I and II, then, created the Atlantic Alliance and, after 1945, the Atlantic Community, and thus furthered Western European unification. In both these wars the United States, the greatest outside power, had intervened to prevent the domination of Europe by Germany. The two wars had taught both European and American statesmen two fundamental lessons: that Europe could no longer solve its problems by war between its member-states; and that U.S. (and indeed, global) economic welfare and growth depended on the postwar recovery of Western Europe and its economic prosperity.

European Approaches to Unity

World War II produced three guidelines for achieving unity: the confederal approach, through intergovernmental agencies (represented by Winston Churchill); the functionalist approach (economic and military cooperation) such as the European Coal and Steel Community of supranational authorities under technocrats (Jean Monnet); and the federalist approach (favored by many resistance groups, and later by the governments of France, Italy, and West Germany). Throughout its history, the European unification movement wavered between functionalism and federalism. The Italian Altiero Spinelli embraced the dream of a United States of Europe, while the Frenchman Jean Monnet pushed the functional approach, although he, too, at times appeared to want a federal Europe. Monnet's approach dominated well into the 1980s; but Spinelli and the federalists gained influence, especially while Spinelli was a member of the European Parliament (1976–1986). By the end of the 1950s, the essential characteristics of the community had been built.[2]

European leaders were to use all these approaches. The intergovernmental approach called for union by consultation and cooperation among national governments, heads of state, and ministers, but without permanent organizations and no federation. All decisions were to be unanimous. Functionalists called for economic and social cooperation and integration in common tariffs, social policies, banking, and investment. Political union, it was believed, gradually would follow economic and social integration. Political union was advocated by only a few; they called for supranational political organizations. They looked to a confederal system and some, like Monnet, foresaw a United States of Europe. The "Single European Act of 1986" was the culmination of all three types of unity espoused after World War II. Since 1986, the European Community institutions have been strengthened, and they are slowly evolving into something more like the U.S. system, with three branches of government: legislative, executive, and judicial. A real federal structure might develop late in the 1990s.[3]

When the war ended, much of Europe lay in ruins. Britain emerged as the only remaining European power. The British might have taken the lead in creating a united Europe, but they preferred to remain benevolent outsiders. The Tories specially looked toward the Commonwealth; Labour put its trust in building democratic socialism at home. Both parties stressed Britain's special relationship with the United States, with a legacy of aloofness toward continentals in general. "Fog in Channel: Europe Cut Off," an apocryphal newspaper headline would have it.

Not that Britain retreated into isolationism. In 1947 Britain concluded the Treaty of Dunkirk with France as a guarantee against possible German aggression. In 1948 Britain joined France and the Benelux countries (Belgium, the Netherlands, Luxembourg) in the Brussels Treaty, which led to the creation of an organization known as the "Western European Union" (WEU), or the "Brussels Treaty Organization." (This body was enlarged in 1954 through the accession of West Germany and Italy.) The WEU played a useful part in improving relations between its member-states. For example, WEU played an important role in negotiations that transferred the Saar region from French to West German control in 1955. As a military and political instrument, however, WEU remained subject to serious limitations. The same reservation applied to the Council of Europe, set up in 1949 in Strasbourg with an original membership of ten: Belgium, Denmark, France, Britain, Ireland, Italy, the Netherlands, Luxembourg, Norway, and Sweden—subsequently expanded to twenty-two (twelve EC, six European Free Trade Area states plus Cyprus, Liechtenstein, San Marino, and Turkey). The Council was a consultative body concerned with protecting human rights, but could make no binding decisions. The Council was not a mere talking shop, however; it favored some form of European integration; it sponsored human rights, and issued over 120 instruments such as the Convention for the Protection of Human Rights and Fundamental Freedoms (1950). There is a European Commission of Human Rights and a European Court of Human Rights, which developed out of the 1950 convention.

NATO

In functional terms, infinitely greater importance attached to the North Atlantic Treaty Organization (NATO), set up in 1949 by the North Atlantic Treaty signed in Washington by the foreign ministers of the United States, Britain, France, Belgium, the Netherlands, Luxembourg, Italy, Portugal, Denmark, Norway, and Canada. "NATO was created to keep the Americans in, the Russians out, and the Germans down," went a saying at the time. NATO was indeed born of common apprehensions—dread of Russia (especially after the Berlin blockade, and the Prague coup in 1948), fear of possible German resurgence, and concern that isolationism might revive in the United States. The NATO alliance entailed functional cooperation between its Western allies, as well as West German rearmament. Above all, the alliance spanned the Atlantic, with the United States by far its most powerful member from the economic,

NETH = NETHERLANDS
BEL = BELGIUM
LUX = LUXEMBOURG
SWITZ = SWITZERLAND

Member of NATO
(France a military member 1949-66)

ICELAND

Atlantic
Ocean

FINLAND

North
Sea

NORWAY

SWEDEN

USSR

SCOTLAND

NORTHERN
IRELAND

DENMARK

UNITED
KINGDOM

REPUBLIC OF
IRELAND

ENGLAND

WALES

NETH.

EAST
GERMANY

POLAND

BEL.

WEST
GERMANY

CZECHOSLOVAKIA

LUX.

FRANCE

SWITZ.

AUSTRIA

HUNGARY

ROMANIA

Black
Sea

ITALY

YUGOSLAVIA

BULGARIA

PORTUGAL

SPAIN

ALBANIA

GREECE

TURKEY

Mediterranean Sea

NORTH AFRICA

NATO MEMBER COUNTRIES

military, and diplomatic standpoint.[4] Imbalance seemed to be built into the very structure of the alliance—just as the "dollar gap" (the European balance of payments deficit with regard to the United States) was supposed to remain a permanent feature of the global economy.

Contrary to legend, NATO was not forced on the Western European allies by a bellicose United States. On the contrary, European (especially British) and Canadian diplomacy played a vital part in getting the United States permanently involved in Western Europe. The United States joined neither the Brussels Treaty of 1947 nor the Western European Union. Thereafter, attempts were made to set up a European Defense Community (EDC) in 1954, but the project was rejected by the French National Assembly, which opposed the creation of integrated and supranational military formations. The truly effective security force for Europe was NATO; it became the most successful peacetime venture in Western cooperation ever undertaken. It has lasted longer than expected; it has kept the peace in its area; and it drew the United States into the defense of Western Europe. With the ending of the cold war and German reunification in 1990, NATO must find other reasons for its continuing existence and for an American role in Europe.

NATO was conceived as a purely defensive alliance for protecting Western Europe against the Soviets. It called for cooperation in arms production, military training, and strategic planning. NATO is run by two committees (defense, military) and the North Atlantic Council of the foreign ministers of member-states. NATO was a historic watershed; it was the first time the United States had agreed to a permanent military and political alliance with Western Europe. This guarantee gave hope to Europe and released its energies for economic recovery. West Germany was integrated into NATO in 1954, reducing her neighbors' fears of a rearmed, revived, and independent Germany, and ensuring at the same time that NATO could draw for its defense on the newly organized and well-equipped *Bundeswehr*. It was U.S. pressure that forced the French, in 1950, to accept West Germany as a rearmed partner in the defense of Europe. The form of participation was not settled until 1954, when Germany was accepted as a full member of NATO and of the Western European Union.

The Korean War (1950–1953) consolidated the Western Alliance and NATO. The United States, after its experience with Soviet-inspired war in Korea, feared the Soviets would attack West Germany. Because the French army was largely tied down in Indochina and then Algeria until 1962, the French were not much help. The British were weakening; hence the United States favored West German rearmament, especially after the Berlin blockade (1948) and the North Korean attack (1950). The United States and its allies decided on a forward defense in West Germany. A new West German army was built and integrated into NATO and became the core (50 percent) of NATO's defense in Central Europe. The United States returned its manpower to Europe (352,000 by 1953) and rearmed NATO. In effect, Western Europe became secure largely because of U.S. planning, manpower, and funds but, above all, because of the reliance after 1954 on nuclear weapons instead of on conventional forces. The continental Europeans spent proportionately less on their defense and therefore were financially freed to develop their economies and expand the welfare state.

The Allies had to coordinate policies and strategy through a supranational organization. To meet these problems, they set up an organization of considerable complexity. The council served as the supreme organ of the alliance, with permanent representation from each member government. The council was responsible for implementing the provisions of the treaty; its work was organized by the secretary-general who directed its secretariat and its five divisions: political affairs, defense planning and policy, defense support, infrastructure, logistics and council operations, scientific affairs. The council's chief administrative officer was the secretary-general. The first incumbent was Lord Ismay, a British general who had made his reputation as chief of staff to the British minister of defense during World War II; Ismay held the post until 1957 when he was succeeded by Paul-Henri Spaak, like Eisenhower a chairman to the manner born.

The council was assisted by a host of specialized committees and agencies that dealt with matters as diverse as the press services and economics. NATO's military direction lay with the military committee composed of the chief of staff of each member-state. Subordinate to the military committee were the major commands and planning groups: Supreme Command Europe (SACEUR), Supreme Allied Commander Atlantic (SACLANT), Allied Commander-in-chief Channel (CINCHAN), Canada–United States Regional Planning Group (CURSPG); and a number of other military agencies. Supreme headquarters were first in Paris, and later shifted to Brussels. (Here NATO's impact, however, was much smaller than the EEC's. By 1990 there were still fewer than 2,300 NATO officials in Brussels, as opposed to 14,000 Eurocrats.) Subordinate agencies were located in Paris, Bonn, and Rome.

NATO was, however, more than a military alliance. It developed an extensive system of committees dealing with subjects as varied as political collaboration; the settlement of intra-alliance disputes; consultation on foreign policy; economic, scientific, technical, social, and cultural cooperation. The secretary-general of NATO, who headed its international staff, became almost as powerful as the SACEUR leader (Supreme Allied Commander Europe). The alliance united policymakers and executives of many different nationalities in a common task. No other alliance in history had comprised such a diversity of partners, cooperated on such a broad range of subjects, nor lasted as long. (By the early 1980s, NATO included Belgium, Canada, Denmark, France, Greece, Iceland, Italy, Luxembourg, the Netherlands, Norway, Portugal, Spain, Turkey, the

United Kingdom, the United States, and West Germany—enlarged briefly in 1990 by the accession of East Germany, with a special status within NATO.)

Problems within NATO

NATO was not without its problems. The alliance was a partnership of unequal partners. The United States contributed far more resources, both in absolute and relative terms, than did its allies. The United States controlled the bulk of NATO's nuclear weapons. Often there were severe tensions between the United States and its European allies. (In 1966, for example, France withdrew from NATO's military command as a result of General de Gaulle's disagreements with Washington.) There were dissensions between the European countries. (From 1974 until 1980 Greece pulled out of NATO's military affairs because of the Turkish invasion of Cyprus.) There were clashes of opinion within the respective ruling establishments of each individual ally. (For instance, the French Ministry of Defense remained "Atlanticist" in orientation even during the height of de Gaulle's Franco-centric policies.)

These varying disputes were expressed in many ways, even in shifts of military strategy. At a time when the United States held a massive superiority in nuclear weapons, NATO stood committed to the doctrine of "massive retaliation." Soviet advances in nuclear armaments, combined with intra-alliance politics, brought about a change in strategy toward the idea of "flexible response," officially enunciated in 1967. U.S. leadership within the alliance came under increasing criticism during the latter part of the Vietnam War when the United States withdrew many of its best officers and NCOs from Europe, and when its military morale strikingly declined. In 1969 a "Euro-Group" was established with NATO itself to facilitate cooperation with NATO's European partners.

Other disagreements within NATO and the EEC hinged on wider questions of policy toward the Soviet Union, as Europeans and Americans accused one another of being capricious or unreliable in their respective allegiances. For example, when the Berlin Wall was built in 1961, President Kennedy disappointed the West Germans by doing too little. The ranks of the disillusioned included Willy Brandt, then lord mayor of West Berlin, who thereafter became converted to a conciliatory *Ostpolitik*, which in turn offended the Americans. Throughout the 1970s, Bonn pursued a policy of détente (cooperation with the Soviet Union), but then again it was Chancellor Helmut Schmidt of West Germany who in 1977 put pressure on the United States to defend Western Europe adequately, and to respond to the buildup of Soviet SS-20 missiles that could reach all of Europe. Such quarrels continued, as Western Europeans and Americans alike remained ambivalent about the unequal relationship, which compelled Europeans to rely on a U.S. nuclear "umbrella" while the Europeans supplied the bulk of NATO's conventional manpower.

Despite all these quarrels, NATO's achievements remained remarkable. NATO built a formidable army, for forward defense. (By 1988, the NATO forces amounted to a million men in North and Central Europe, and another million in Southern Europe. The combat formations in North and Central Europe, the most exposed sector of NATO, in 1989, stood at 18 armored divisions, 23 mechanized divisions, and 6 infantry and airborne divisions.)[5] Given the existing weaknesses in the Warsaw Pact armies, and given especially the unreliability of the Soviet allies within the pact, NATO had managed to build a defensive system of unexpected excellence. NATO's strength had facilitated further European integration and helped restore legitimacy to Germany and Italy, the defeated powers.

Wellsprings of Europe's Unity

European unification also drew strength from other sources. There was the common experience of defeat, suffered by all European countries except Britain, the Soviet Union, and a handful of neutrals. There was also the common legacy of resistance, which had united patriots of all political stripes against the German occupiers and their collaborators. Men and women of the resistance had looked not merely to the liberation of their own respective countries, but also to a new Europe where social justice would prevail, and age-old national hatreds would be forgotten. Even in defeated Germany, there was a strong desire for a new start. The European idea was in the air. The main opponents to closer association came from the extreme left and the extreme right; the Communists draped themselves in their respective national flags, determined that the new Europe would not be rebuilt on capitalist lines. Many trade unionists opposed the formation of NATO and later of the EEC, especially in Germany where labor leaders believed that European integration would militate against the nationalization of heavy industry and against the unionists' demand for *Mitbestimmung* (workers' codetermination in the running of major enterprises). The extreme right, as ever, distrusted internationalism of any kind. The extreme left rejected any form of European unity built on capitalist foundations.

Real power in Western Europe as a whole accrued to the moderates. It was the men of the middle—reformist-minded conservatives, Christian Democrats (particularly Catholics), liberals, moderate Socialists—who dominated the postwar governments in Western Europe. Whatever their manifold differences, they openly or tacitly cooperated in the common task of rebuilding the European economies and establishing democratic governments based on the rule of law.

Europe was also fortunate in other ways. Before World War II, parliamentary democracy had widely been associated with the rule of the weak by the Nazis and Fascists. (Hitler had referred to those Western statesmen he had met at Munich as "little worms.") No one would have described Charles de Gaulle in such terms. No one would have applied such an epithet to powerful personalities such as Konrad Adenauer and Alcide de Gasperi, both practicing Catholics, Christian Democrats, architects respectively of the German Federal Republic and the postwar Italian Republic. No one would have styled as a weakling Jean Monnet, one of the chief planners of the new Europe. Anthony Sampson, a British journalist, likened Monnet to Hercule Poirot, the Belgian sleuth of Agatha Christie's detective novels. De Gaulle jokingly referred to Monnet as "a great American," but this did not prevent the general from appointing Monnet as France's first *Commissaire au Plan*, charged with the postwar modernization of France. Supremely able, equally skilled as a businessman, diplomat, and propagandist, left of center in politics, Monnet became one of the makers of the new transnational Europe.

The European Recovery Program

Of major importance to the recovery of Europe was the Marshall Plan (proposed by General George C. Marshall in 1947). The Marshall Plan was more than just an economic assistance program. It represented a massive transfer of resources from the New World to the Old, and symbolized American commitment to rebuild and defend Western Europe. The plan (technically known as the European Recovery Program, ERP) provided loans, food, fuel, and machinery for wartorn Europe. Europeans also benefited from American technological, financial, and marketing expertise—this at a time when the United States was the world's leading economic power. Equally influential was the U.S. premise that peace, consumerism, welfare, and profits went hand in hand. (The Marshall Plan ended in December 1951, and the ECA was replaced by the Mutual Security Agency in January 1952. Aid stopped and military assistance began.)

Marshall and his planners wanted to promote economic integration, supranational organizations to achieve integration, and liberal trade policies similar to those that operated in the United States. American officials tried to export the American way: management, technology, labor relations, and especially methods of getting business to work with labor and government to increase prosperity. Most American leaders were not really hopeful of creating a United States of Europe by economic unification; they worked primarily to revive Europe's economies, push economic cooperation, reduce trade barriers, and reconcile France and Germany.

Marshall Plan officials such as Lincoln Gordon, however, were full of idealism, dedicated to public service and confident that Keynesian economics could direct the revival of Europe. A new agency was created to disburse aid (the European Cooperation Administration, ECA); a central coordinating office was established in Paris (the Office of Special Representative in Europe); there were special missions in each country and a coordinating organization of Europeans to decide how aid was to be spread (the Committee for European Economic Cooperation, later to become in 1948 the OEEC). It was W. Averell Harriman as special representative in Europe who suggested that the Europeans decide who got what. Hence Europeans had to negotiate in unison and transcend narrow national interest. The skill of the secretary-general of the OEEC, Robert Marjolin, was crucial in getting the cooperation of the various national delegates.

Psychologically, Europeans benefited from the American sense of optimism—this at a time when Europe seemed in despair, and Jean-Paul Sartre's gloomy philosophy was in high fashion. The Marshall Plan created a great network both of intra-European and trans-Atlantic linkages among businessmen, civil servants, planners. Above all, the Marshall Plan was designed to push Europeans toward political and economic cooperation. Aid was administered through the Organization of European Economic Cooperation (OEEC, replaced in 1960 by the OECD, or Organization for Economic Cooperation and Development). OECD began with 20 members and by 1973 had grown to 24, the number today.

The OECD (with its headquarters in Paris) has served basically as a research institute and data bank for advanced industrial democracies. It has loaned not money, but expertise. OECD's most important role has been in opening up economies to market forces by offering advice, doing studies, and providing statistics. The organization operates through a committee structure of experts from member-governments. It has developed a wide range of expertise on diverse subjects of microeconomics. (The IMF, on the other hand, is concerned with macroeconomics.) The OECD became the leader in providing statistics for Western nations—its predecessor OEEC had developed the system of national accounts. All of this makes the OECD a likely candidate for playing a leading role in the transition during the 1990s from Socialist to market economics in Eastern Europe.

In terms of a narrowly conceived *Realpolitik*, or policies to advance national interests, the United States might have benefited more from dealing separately with its European allies in a strictly bilateral fashion. In practice, the United States looked toward a new Western European association. OEEC created a complex network of transnational committees to deal with specialized questions. New agencies came into being. These included the European Payments Union (EPU, set up in 1950). This was, essentially, a central bank and clearinghouse for intra-European trade and payments. (By 1959 the European currencies had become largely convertible, and the EPU was replaced by the European Monetary Agreement.)[6]

European Coal and Steel Community (ECSC)

Despite Western Europe's unprecedented economic recovery, neither OEEC nor the Council of Europe took effective steps toward the political unification of Europe. Instead, functional cooperation in the economic field proved a more viable alternative. The French and West German iron and steel industries were in many ways complementary; German and French magnates had always cooperated (as evinced by bodies such as the International Steel Cartel formed after World War I). De Gaulle, for all his imperial demeanor, personally got on extremely well with Adenauer. Italy joined, in part for economic advantages, in part because the Christian Democrats generally saw eye to eye with Christian Democratic policymakers in France and West Germany. (One of the main reasons why the ECSC was constructed so readily was the strong representation of Christian Democratic parties in all six governments in the early 1950s.)

Belgium, Holland, and Luxembourg had already pioneered an economic association through the creation of Benelux (initiated as a customs union in 1947). The British would not join; but the six Western European continental states in 1952 went further and successfully established the European Coal and Steel Community (ECSC, operational in 1953) with Monnet as the first president of the governing body, the High Authority. (Monnet has been called "the architect of the European Community" and "the master builder of the European union.") Another great Europeanist, Walter Hallstein, was appointed by Adenauer in 1950 to head the German delegation in the negotiations that led to the ECSC. Hallstein looked and acted like the typical Central European professor—aloof, courteous, bespectacled, very much the proper *Rektor* of his university. Hallstein also was a hard bargainer, however, a lawyer familiar with every legal complexity. Later, Hallstein took a leading part in the creation of the European Economic Community (EEC), and in 1958 he became its first president. The real founding fathers of the European Union, however, were Robert Schuman, Alcide de Gaspari, and Konrad Adenauer.

The foreign ministers of the ECSC met at Messina, Sicily, in 1955 to discuss additional means of economic cooperation. Further negotiations in 1956 led to the signing of the Treaty of Rome (March 25, 1957), which set up the Common Market (EEC) and the European Atomic Energy Community, or Euratom. In 1957, the ECSC merged with Euratom and the Common Market to form the European Community.

Until 1965 the three organizations (ECSC, EEC, and Euratom) had distinct governing bodies but by a Merger Treaty (in force July 1967), a single executive body was set up, although each group kept its independent legal status. The ECSC had established institutions that later were incorporated into the EEC:

High Authority (Commission), representatives of individual states (Council of Ministers), the European assembly, which became the Parliament, and a Court of Justice.

European Economic Community

The creation of the European Economic Community (EEC) was a historic occasion for Europe. The Soviet invasion of Hungary in 1956 had re-emphasized the Soviet strength. (Also many gifted intellectuals had transferred their loyalties from their respective parties to Community institutions.) The failure of the Anglo-French Suez venture (1956) had re-emphasized Western European weakness vis-à-vis the United States. At the same time, the United States continued to serve both as a model and as a lobbyist for European unification.

The EEC (operational in 1958) was more than a mere customs union. Its members were committed—at least in theory—to the free movement of labor and capital; they would cooperate in ending restrictions on trade and investment; they would work toward cooperation in welfare policies, and toward political co-ordination. The EEC was run by a Commission of nine members, chosen by the national governments but pledged to independence. Paralleling the Commission was the Council of Ministers, the organ of the national governments, responsible for coordinating community and national policies. (In theory the Council could decide by a majority vote. In practice, the French in particular refused to subordinate to a majority what they regarded as their vital national interests. The dispute was partially settled in 1966 through the so-called Luxembourg compromise, which required consensus on all major decisions.) The third major body was the Parliamentary Assembly, chosen by the national parliaments by proportional representation. (Direct voting for the European Parliament (EP) was only introduced in 1979.) A new Court of Justice served the EEC, as well as ECSC. (In 1965 treaty arrangements were further simplified by providing for a single Commission and Council for all three bodies—the first major constitutional change since 1957.)

France wielded the greatest political influence within the EEC, especially after the disastrous Algerian imbroglio had come to an end in 1962. West Germany, by contrast, had the greatest economic say, corresponding to its position as Western Europe's leading economic power, and its role as chief paymaster of the EEC. The British again stood aloof. Instead, they created an association of their own, a league of outsiders, the European Free Trade Area (EFTA), established in 1959, operational in 1960, composed of Austria, Britain, Denmark, Norway, Sweden, Portugal, and Switzerland.

Even for the "core states" of Western Europe, the difficulties involved in closer association were immense. They comprised enormous regional disparities, both between and within the member countries (for instance, as between Italy's developed north and backward south, the *mezzogiorno*). There were striking divergencies in wages even within the same industry.[7] There were great national differences in buying habits, consumer goods, managerial methods, legal and bureaucratic traditions; there were entrenched national interests. The technical intricacies involved in many questions under dispute boggled the imagination. Given the extent of these problems, the EEC did a remarkably good job. Long-existing customs barriers disappeared; the process was completed in 1968. Intra-Community trade was gradually freed of quota restrictions. The EEC went a long way toward assuring the free movement of workers within its boundaries. (Community workers were assured of equality of treatment in terms of employment, wages, and other working conditions.) Labor unions as well as capitalists discovered the merits of transnational cooperation. The major unions joined to form a European Trade Union Confederation, ETUC, with its headquarters in Brussels.[8] (By 1984, ETUC had 34 affiliates representing 43,000,000 workers.) The Community tried to develop a comprehensive policy with regard to science, technology, nuclear power, and space research. This was done through bodies such as ESPRIT, European Strategic Program for Research and Development Technology; ESA, European Space Agency; ENA, European Nuclear Agency, Euratom, and others.

Problems within the EEC

Not all went well with the EEC, however—despite a remarkable expansion of trade between its members, steadily rising rates of production, and improvements in living standards during the prosperous 1950s and 1960s. There were political problems, made more apparent by massive labor migration from the Mediterranean periphery (Portugal, Spain, southern Italy, Yugoslavia, Turkey) to the industrialized north. There were unresolved party issues. The Christian Democrats, for instance, stood accused by liberals and Socialists of wielding disproportionate influence. From the very start, the German reunification question loomed in the background. (In endorsing the EEC treaties, the West German SPD insisted that they would only accept the agreements on the assumption that they would not make more difficult the unification of Germany.) Above all, agricultural politics in Western Europe remained nationalistic and protectionist after 1957.

The EEC did not solve these difficulties; it may even have made them worse. Whereas some countries (the Netherlands and Denmark) were aggressively for free trade, others (Germany, Belgium, and Britain) were protectionist in agriculture. The Common Agriculture Policy (CAP) aimed at rationalizing agricultural policies. This proved a hard assignment, given the profound sociological differences between highly urbanized countries such as Britain, endowed with an efficient, highly mechanized farming industry, and countries such as France, West Germany, Italy, and Spain, where small farmers remained numerous and influential in politics (especially in the Christian Democratic parties). Helped by protection, or by guaranteed prices much higher than those prevailing on the world markets, European farmers produced mountains of surplus grain, grapes, butter, and beef. Tension increased among the states of the EEC, and also with the outside world. CAP promoted bureaucratic growth—96 percent of EEC regulations came to deal with agriculture. The key weakness of the EEC's agricultural system was its price policy, which encouraged a massive rise in production of unnecessary farm products. These problems of overproduction became even more acute after the 1960s. So did trade difficulties derived from the association of the "overseas territories" of EEC members with the Treaty of Rome—tackled only in part by the Treaty of Jaunde in 1962.

More seriously, the EEC lacked broad popular support, and even public interest. There was little appeal to the Europeans' imagination. (As late as 1977, according to an opinion poll, less than half the respondents had ever heard or read anything about the European Parliament; public awareness thereafter slowly increased.)[9] Officials of the EEC would usually serve in Brussels for many years. They went home on holidays, but inclined to mix among their own kind. Their Brussels became almost a separate city, with something of Washington's or Canberra's rarefied atmosphere. Their supranationalism failed to catch on among their respective compatriots; it lacked the color, the sense of devotion that only traditional nationalism seemed to evoke. Youthful hikers continued to pin to their rucksacks their own national flags, rather than a European symbol. Football crowds went on cheering (or at times committing mayhem) for their national teams. Men and women might still be willing to die for Britain or for France— but none of them would risk his or her life for the EEC. Europe remained—as de Gaulle had both hoped and anticipated—l'Europe des États.

Businessmen, especially those running small firms, remained hostile to the EEC—as did of course Communists and militant right-wingers of all stripes. The Community developed a large, impersonal bureaucracy of its own, accused by the respective national critics of "going native" in the new Euro-world. The agencies of the new Europe centered in cultural borderlands. (Strasbourg, seat of the European Parliament, and Luxembourg, where the Court of Justice met, were situated where German and French cultures fused; Brussels, where the Commission and Council met, was the capital of a binational French and Flemish state.) The doings of international civil servants seemed remote, even incomprehensible, to the man and the woman in the street. Certain groups seemed to gain unreasonable benefits (especially the farmers). The expansion of international bureaucracies moreover promoted the further growth of national bureaucracies, as member governments appointed more civil servants of their own to deal with their opposite numbers within the EEC.

There was also the British question. The British at first stayed out. (Even after the Treaty of Rome had been signed in 1957, the Foreign Office regarded the Common Market issue largely as a trade question, to be left to the Treasury, and the treaty was not even properly translated into English.)[10] In 1961, the British at last began negotiations for admission to the EEC. By this time, the British gross national product had fallen much behind West Germany's and West Germany had replaced Britain as the United States's main European partner in NATO. In 1967 the British withdrew from Aden, and a year later Britain announced that within three years it would evacuate all military and naval bases east of Suez. De Gaulle, who had vetoed the original British application to the EEC, died in 1970. His demise signified the end of an era. In 1973 the British finally secured membership in the EEC in a settlement achieved through personal talks between British premier Edward Heath, a conservative, and French president Georges Pompidou, a Gaullist.

Nevertheless, British and continental interests continued to diverge. This was particularly true in the field of agriculture, where the British were among the most efficient producers, and resented having to pay excessively high prices for food, to subsidize continental, especially French and German, farmers. The British consistently complained of making a disproportionately large financial contribution to the EEC's budget. Britain in essence demanded to renegotiate the terms on which it had first been admitted.

There were other problems. EEC policy was in practice determined by a Franco-German entente, solidified by close personal relations between German chancellor Helmut Schmidt (in office 1972 to 1982), and French president Valéry Giscard d'Estaing (in power 1974 to 1981). The British accession to EEC left EFTA as a rump, with Switzerland as its financially most powerful member. Political defeats left the EEC weak until 1969–1972 when the idea of a European union was revived. After the Hague Summit of the Council of Ministers, national governments became somewhat more willing to give the EEC more political powers but no fundamental changes were made until 1986.

"The Community's Dark Age"

Stanley Hoffmann, in an excellent essay, styles the period 1973 to 1984 "the Community's dark age."[11] There was the oil shock of 1973, and experts suddenly forecast an everlasting shortage of energy. The economics of Western Europe experienced a downturn; the "twenty-five golden years" after

World War II ended. The rise of mass unemployment led governments to give priority to national interests—this at the EEC's expense. Traditional industries such as steel, textiles, and shipbuilding declined; yet Europeans discovered that they were being outdone in high technology by the United States and Japan. "Euro-pessimism" was in the air. Europe seemed to fall behind. It was in the late 1960s that Jean-Louis Servan-Schreiber's book, *Le défi américain*, translated in 1968 as *The American Challenge*, came to stand on many a senior European civil servant's bookshelf. Eighteen years later, the author published a more cheerful work, *Le retour du courage*, translated in 1987 as *The Return of Courage*.

In 1972 the EEC said it wanted a political union by 1980. A report (1975–1976) by Belgian prime minister Leo Tindemans pointed out the many difficulties preventing political union, in particular that political union would not "automatically follow from economic integration." Even in the economic sphere there were many failures. Tindemans also criticized intergovernmental cooperation as a method of gaining political union; the community's institutional machinery would have to be strengthened to do the job. The report set out an agenda for reform: to strengthen by direct elections the European Parliament's powers to discuss, initiate, and pass legislation, even of matters not covered by the Treaty of Rome. Tindemans would also have given the Council of Ministers the right to decide by a qualified majority and would have given the European Commission more power. The 1980 date for union was not met, but most of Tindemans's ideas were later included in some form in the "Single European Act" of 1986.

The 1970s, however, were not simply a barren epoch. In 1973 Denmark and Ireland as well as Britain joined the EEC. Only Norway stayed aloof, after a bitterly fought referendum in 1972, the second instance, with Britain, where EEC membership turned into a passionate political issue. Parliamentary governance returned to Portugal and Spain after a long era of authoritarian rule. This peaceful changeover facilitated the admission of these two countries to the EEC in 1986, following Greece's adherence in 1981. In 1975 the EEC set up a Regional Development Fund and a Regional Development Committee to give assistance to the EEC's own "backward areas." In 1979, as we have seen, the EEC was further strengthened by the first direct election of the European Parliament.

More important, perhaps, in 1978 Helmut Schmidt and Giscard d'Estaing created as their joint brainchild the European Monetary System (EMS), with its own currency, the ECU ("ECU"—both an acronym and the name of an ancient French gold coin). The EMS was designed in part to deal with the problems arising from the U.S. decision to scrap the postwar system of fixed exchange rates and to replace it with floating rates. The EMS aimed at a tighter system, but in practice became, in Hoffmann's formulation, "a Deutschemark zone."

In a more general sense, the late 1970s witnessed a general disenchantment with Keynesian policies, increasing distrust toward the regulatory state, state direction, and the real or assumed imperfections of the welfare state. (Even in Sweden, the very homeland of welfarism, the 44-year rule of the Social Democrats was temporarily broken in 1976 by a "bourgeois" coalition.) Free enterprise economics became intellectually respectable. In 1977 Milton Friedman received the Nobel Prize and in 1979 Margaret Thatcher became prime minister of Britain, determined to turn her country into an enterprise state. (She was re-elected in 1983 and 1987.) In the United States, Ronald Reagan moved into the White House (1981), replacing a Democrat, Jimmy Carter, and stayed for two terms, thereby continuing a period of Republican domination over the executive branch of government. In West Germany, Helmut Kohl stepped into the chancellor's office in 1982, heading a CDU-FDP coalition. In the same year, François Mitterrand assumed the presidency of France. Mitterrand was a Socialist who had invigorated the Socialist party. Nevertheless his election also signified a shift away from the extreme left, as the Socialists, in 1978 for the first time since 1936, had garnered more votes than the Communists.

The Atlantic economies (especially that of the United States) began to recover; oil became plentiful. The winds of change were now blowing from the right. Even Communist leaders (such as Santiago Carrillo in Spain and Enrico Berlinguer in Italy) were calling for ideological revision of their respective parties' doctrines—a remarkable reassessment that paralleled far-reaching shifts in the Soviet Union itself.

"Le retour du courage"

Europeans had other reasons for a return of courage. Within the Atlantic Community itself, the relative standing of the United States declined. Between 1983 and 1989 the United States turned from being the world's largest creditor to being the world's biggest debtor, accumulating a $700 billion current account deficit as imports and capital flowed from Europe to the United States. The United States had traditionally run a comfortable trade surplus with the EEC, but between 1980 and 1987 the surplus gave way to a $25 billion deficit as imports and capital flowed from Europe to the United States. The Soviet Union fared much worse. The one-time "homeland of the workers" appeared to turn into the "sick man" of Europe—a process that culminated in 1990 when the once almost deified Communist Party of the Soviet Union (CPSU) relinquished its fundamental claim to being the country's sole guiding force.

The Europeans, by contrast, did well—despite widespread unemployment with its attendant social problems. The EMS, for instance, performed more effectively than its critics had imagined. The British cooperated with the EMS, even though they did not, for the time being, join the system. The EMS further advanced intra-European trade. When the EMS first came into existence, all

NETH = NETHERLANDS
BEL = BELGIUM
LUX = LUXEMBOURG
SWITZ = SWITZERLAND

ICELAND

Atlantic
Ocean

North
Sea

NORWAY

SWEDEN

FINLAND

USSR

DENMARK

NORTHERN
IRELAND

SCOTLAND

REPUBLIC of IRELAND

UNITED
KINGDOM

ENGLAND

WALES

NETH.

BEL.

LUX.

GERMANY

POLAND

CZECHOSLOVAKIA

FRANCE

SWITZ.

AUSTRIA

HUNGARY

ROMANIA

ITALY

YUGOSLAVIA

BULGARIA

PORTUGAL

SPAIN

ALBANIA

GREECE

Mediterranean Sea

NORTH AFRICA

EUROPEAN FREE TRADE ASSOCIATION

THE EUROPEAN COMMUNITY

The European Free Trade Association and
the European Community, 1991

members, apart from West Germany and the Netherlands, had stringent capital controls. Between 1985 and 1990, these controls disappeared. (The gaps between domestic and European rates for the French franc and the Italian lira largely closed.) Yet the EMS showed no signs of strain, and by 1990 the system looked stronger than ever.[12]

In 1984, the Europeans somewhat reformed CAP to make it less expensive (CAP had absorbed about 70 percent of the Community's budget), and to make CAP more acceptable to the British, and less wasteful. Priority was given to the reduction of those "lakes of wine" and "mountains of butter" whose existence consumers in Socialist countries would have envied. In addition, the EEC, in 1985, set up an Integrated Mediterranean Program to help its backward southern periphery, and Italy, in particular, stressed its "Mediterranean vocation."

The extension of the EEC (known as the EC after 1986) went with a new challenge that none had considered at the time the EEC had been formed. By 1989 Japan had become one of the richest nations in terms of per capita income. Japan enjoyed a trade surplus of $20 billion with the EC. The composition of the trade troubled Europeans as much as the size of the deficit. Europe bought from Japan the most advanced industrial products available—cars, computers, video-cassette recorders, and the like. As Chalmers Johnson put it, the movement toward unity in Europe entailed "a clearcut trade strategy aimed at recapturing competitive ability from Japan, and, to a lesser extent, the United States."[13]

Western Europe as a political entity has failed so far to become a superpower equal to the United States or the USSR—despite the Western Europeans' potential standing in the world arena. By 1984, forty years after the Normandy invasion (and before Spain and Portugal joined), the EEC's gross domestic product amounted to about two-thirds of the United States's ($2,400.4 billion as against $3,627.9 billion). Its population was larger than that of the United States (272 million as against 232 million). The EEC's export values were larger than those of the United States ($227.2 billion as against $217.88 billion). The EEC's members between them maintained as many men under arms as the United States (2,109,000 as against 2,350,000). The Europeans, however, remained unable to translate their economic strength into equivalent diplomatic and military might. The drive for an economic and monetary union operational by January 1993 hoped, however, to transform all of that and make the EC the largest single market in the world. But full economic and monetary union is not likely to be achieved; even phase two is not likely to be acceptable to the Germans and Dutch by 1993.

Indisputably, however, the West European states both became more firmly integrated into a wider Atlantic community, and at the same time drew more closely together. The EEC became not merely a permanent fixture, but continued to expand. More important, a Franco-German war, or conflicts of a kind familiar to earlier generations, had become inconceivable. West Germany remained firmly cemented into the European community, linked to its Western neighbors by NATO, trade, tourism, and by a great variety of ties through civil servants, trade unionists, academics, and businessmen from different countries. The EEC likewise created new bonds between politicians faced with new tasks that often transcended traditional divisions within their own countries. As a Belgian parliamentarian put it, "in all our countries religion is terribly important. It binds together every Catholic party in Europe, both leftists and conservatives, simply because they are Catholics. . . . In Europe people can sort themselves out on different lines."[14] A Socialist such as Spaak would find his best allies in the European Assembly among people such as Heinrich von Brentano and Pierre-Henri Teitgens (German and French Catholics, respectively).

By the 1980s, the wrangling over minor advantages, the inconclusive nature of so many EEC meetings, EEC's bureaucratic complexity occasioned at best boredom, and at worst disgust. According to its critics, the EEC by the 1980s lacked a foreign policy, and adequate mobility of people and capital. The technology gap between the EEC on one hand, the United States and Japan on the other, kept widening. Above all, the Europeans had still failed to set up a genuinely free market equaling the great internal market of the United States. As the British *Economist* put it:

> Any European tempted to think that the absence of tariffs within the European community makes it a common market should think again. Listen to the lorry driver who has to fill out 27 forms to drive between West Germany and Italy; border delays alone cost Europe $10 billion a year in higher-than-necessary costs. Ask the telecommunications-equipment makers who, because of national favoritism and different standards, can just about forget selling in one member country the switchboard they make for another. Ask the airline entrepreneur who would like to carry passengers between London and Frankfurt for a fare lower than Europe's airline cartel will approve.[15]

Nevertheless, it is necessary to stress the enormous difficulties faced by the EEC's architects at that time and now. Europe lacked, and continues to lack, the United States's relative homogeneity. National markets within the EEC varied enormously because of differences in size, language, tradition, and habits. Products proved hard to standardize in a continent where consumer habits differed enormously.

> For example, the wool industry in each country makes eight to ten different sizes of blankets, which are not the same from one country to another. The German consumer is strict about the maximum dimensions, for he does not want to tuck the blanket under the mattress; the French consumer is strict on the minimum size for he does not want his feet or his hands to become uncovered while he sleeps. The Germans and Italians prefer twin beds, which the French and Belgians regard with horror. Sizes of sheets, pillow and beds themselves vary from one country to another; blanket sizes cannot be stan-

The Council of Ministers

The Council of Ministers is the principal decisionmaking body of the EC. Its members are ministers from the member-states who represent their countries at the Council. Most meetings of the Council are in Brussels, where the General Secretariat (1,900 officials) is situated. Council meetings are also held in Luxembourg and in the nation holding the rotating, six-month presidency.

The Council holds periodic meetings with member ministers, varying according to the subject under discussion. Foreign ministers attend more meetings than, say, agricultural ministers or environment ministers because they discuss political and institutional matters of the EC and foreign affairs. The Council is helped in its deliberations by a Committee of Permanent Representatives (COREPER). Senior officials of COREPER come from the member-states and have played a major role in the effective operation of the Council. In recent years COREPER officials have had to take a back seat to member-state ministers, and national representation has damaged somewhat the community spirit. COREPER was better able to coordinate negotiations on a community basis on policy matters between the Council, the Commission, and other community institutions.

Decisions are not reached on a one-vote, one-state basis, and major decisions must be unanimous, whereas others may be made by qualified majority. The more powerful states have more votes than do the smaller states. West Germany, France, Italy, and Britain have ten votes; Spain has eight, and Belgium, the Netherlands, Portugal, and Greece have five each. Denmark and Ireland have three, and Luxembourg has two. Voting procedures were changed by the "Single European Act" of 1986 to a qualified majority instead of unanimity on most issues.

The European Council (Summit) developed after 1974 at the suggestion of French President Giscard d'Estaing and German Chancellor Helmut Schmidt. The leaders (heads of state, foreign ministers, and the president of the European Commission) of member-states started to meet directly two or three times a year. These Summit meetings have become a regular part of the system since 1986 and provide guidelines from the heads of state to the Council of Ministers and Commission for action by them. Summits are useful for their informality, which allows flexibility in setting guidelines, making important decisions, and resolving disagreements. It is a quicker, more flexible device for decisionmaking than the Council of Ministers; the Council is useful for exchanging views. The Summit leaders had feared that the EP, once it was elected by popular vote, would become a supranational assembly. The European Council then is a means of protecting the sovereignty of the nation states. All its decisions must be unanimous.[16]

dardized without taking account of these differences. The specific weight demanded in each country is different. Design, absence of design, borders and colors are the subject of national tastes. Six greens exist (German green, French green, Swiss green, etc.), each one of which is accepted only in one or two countries at any one time.[17]

Far more significant, however, are differing specifications in telecommunications and electronics.

Moreover, the EEC continued to suffer from grave functional flaws. The ECSC Treaty had transferred national decisionmaking in the fields of coal and steel to the independent High Authority. The EC, by contrast, turned the European Commission into the guardian of the treaty. Within the EC's framework, final power rested with the Council of Ministers, the only Community institution whose members represented national governments. The Council coordinated national and Community policies, and made most of the final decisions in Community affairs, its deliberations being prone to endless procrastination. The Council's work was prepared by a Committee of Permanent Representatives (COREPER), consisting of ambassadors appointed by member governments. COREPER in turn developed into a major power center whose members were faced with an almost impossibly difficult task. In a former member's words, a permanent representative "requires a number of skills touching on the miraculous." [18] He had to be able to grasp in a minimum of time the maximum information contained in the files related to every individual article of the EEC's founding treaties. He had to impose his authority on a numerous staff of top-level civil servants in his mission, recruited from a multitude of departments at home. He had to supervise these staff members, and coordinate their activities in numerous bodies subsidiary to COREPER. He had to attend countless meetings in his own capital—and so the list continued.

Under these circumstances, the EEC did a remarkable job. Young Europeans today may have forgotten Monnet and his coadjutors—but only because their achievements in breaking down accustomed barriers on trade and travel are now taken for granted. The first step was to eliminate all customs duties levied on imports and exports between member-states. This was done by a fixed timetable: The last customs barriers came down in 1968. In the same year, the EEC established a common customs tariff (CCT). In addition, quantitative restrictions disappeared, as intracommunity trade was gradually freed of quota restrictions (designed to keep down imports by imposing limits on their value or volume). These liberalization measures did not do away with impediments of a more indirect kind that member-states imposed on their competitors to protect declining industries (especially steel, shipbuilding, and textiles). The various European states unfortunately developed a great deal of ingenuity at this particular game. This started at the frontiers, with a host of vexatious formalities, and continued thereafter through a host of equally burdensome bureaucratic devices—rules and regulations created in the real or supposed interest of health, safety, consumer protection, and such like. (For example, beef, pasta, and brandy were held up at various ports and borders.) [19]

Nevertheless, overall intercommunity commerce greatly expanded, although free trade was not practiced with the United States or Asia. The EEC went a long way in assuring the free movement of workers within its boundaries. The treaties guaranteed Community workers equality of treatment in terms of employment, wages, and other working conditions. The movement of capital was liberalized. The Community developed a comprehensive policy regarding research and technology.

The EC also profited again from strong leadership in the late 1980s. Jacques Delors, president of the EC Commission, was a man cast in the Monnet mold. Delors had started life as a banker, later rose to be chief of social affairs in the *Plan Monnet*, a Socialist cabinet minister, wedded to that blend of Christian democracy and social reformism that had provided the Community's original inspiration. Delors stood resolved both to improve the EC and to extend its scope.

A Single Europe by 1993

Altiero Spinelli (as a member of the European Parliament) is credited with spearheading the drive for a federal Europe from 1980 to 1984. His efforts led to the Mitterrand–Kohl call for the European Union Treaty of 1984 and a much watered-down Single European Act of 1986. The EUT made the European commissioners' term five years instead of four, and they were to be chosen after the European Parliament elections, to increase the informal influence of the Parliament.

The European Commission

The European Commission members are appointed by the twelve governments. The Commission has a president and five or six vice-presidents who are appointed for two years. There are currently seventeen Commissioners (two each from the larger EC states—West Germany, France, Britain, Italy, Spain—and one each from the rest). All are nominated by their national governments and appointed by the Council for a four-year term. Decisions within the Commission are, when necessary, taken by a simple majority. The Commission implements decisions taken by the Council, and also has the power to enforce EC treaties and derivative legislation. No nation's decisions can interfere with EC policies. The Commission has a large staff (15,055 Eurocrats) and they are divided into 27 departments or directorates. The Commission has been likened to a cabinet which institutes policies and studies that are then sent along to the Council of Ministers who make policy. A Commission proposal can only be amended by unanimous vote.

Over time the EEC has developed into a kind of federal system. The Commission's proposals, if accepted by the Council, are binding on the member-states. Voting in the Council has shifted from unanimity to qualified majority in most matters.[20]

From June to December 1985, the Intergovernmental Conference (IGC) met to work out reforms of the EC treaties for the Luxembourg meeting of the European Council that wrote the Single European Act. The European Council thus has led the drive for a unified internal market. In 1985 it asked the Commission to put forward a proposal for achieving a unified internal market by 1992. A few months later the Commission published a 93-page report with over 300 specific suggestions to remove restrictions with dates for council approval before December 1992. "Completing the Internal Market: White Paper from the Commission to the European Council" (Milan, June 28–29, 1985) became the basis for the "Single Market Act, 1986." The Commission then set up a research project to determine the "costs of non-Europe." The project director, Paolo Cecchini, wrote a popular account called *The European Challenge, 1992: The Benefits of a Single Market* (published by Wildwood House in London, 1988). The detailed results of this research were published in sixteen volumes as *Research on the Cost of Non-Europe*, 1988.

The White Paper called for the elimination of various restrictions that remained in the EC. These comprised, among many others, vexatious border inspection of goods in transit; restrictions on the movements of people; differences in national product norms; problems connected with differential taxation; patents; standardization in service industries; complex issues connected with the standardization of computers, communications, and such. In 1986 the EC promulgated the Single European Act (entering into force on July 1, 1987—a date that future generations of European schoolchildren will probably have to memorize for their history examinations).

The Single European Act made many changes in legislative procedures, brought better political cooperation in foreign policy matters (European Political Cooperation, EPC) within the framework of the European communities, and, most important, worked for futher economic and monetary union and extended policy areas of concern beyond the legal basis of the 1957 treaty. The main effects of this act were, first, to speed up decision making by EC institutions in most policy areas and, second, to impose stricter limits on agricultural subsidies, which had consumed much of the EC budget and, finally, to increase the Community's budget base. These changes reduced quarreling among members and speeded up decision making, thus encouraging members to take on new responsibilities.

The act formed a milestone toward the creation of a European superpower. The Treaty of Rome in 1957 had drawn its main inspiration from bureaucrats, intellectuals, politicians, and magnates of heavy industry. The program for 1992, the new target date, by contrast received support from corporate capitalists engaged in a broad range of enterprises that had already extended the scale of their operations through massive transfrontier mergers. The 1992 program was backed likewise by professionals with transnational outlets for their respective skills, and by those who wanted a united Europe for its own sake; they were generally a confident group. Arrayed against them stood the pessimists, derived mainly from the ranks of small farmers, small employers, unskilled workers, and the indigent who looked toward their own national governments for relief. Above all, there was the great host of those who feared the submersion of their respective national cultures in a new Europe of plate glass and concrete, computer networks, *Gastarbeiter*, and Euro-bureaucracy.

The 1992 program was designed to create an economic and monetary union and to sweep away the remaining obstacles to free movement of people, goods, capital, and services within the Community. This was an immensely complicated process. It seemed unlikely that the entire task could be completed by the target date. The program, to be exact, required 279 measures. By the beginning of 1990 about 60 percent had been implemented by all the national states except Italy. Even when member-states did introduce the right laws and procedures, these were often ignored in practice. The Commission only has a small investigatory staff that oversees enforcement (15 by 1990). There was also the difficult problem of making sure that national laws did not actually conflict with the goal of a single market. Small technicalities in this sense could have a major effect on business. (For instance, West Germany objected to a French law regulating the size of caravan windows. Had this law been enforced, West German caravans would simply have been excluded from the French market.) As a last resort, there was the European Court of Justice in Luxembourg. But cases might take between a year and a half and three years to decide. And some governments simply ignored court rulings, with Italy again at the top of the list.[21] (Britain, though the least "federalist" of the EC member-states, actually had the best enforcement record.)

A great many issues moreover raise wider political questions. Outstanding among them is the abolition of all border controls, resisted by—among others— Margaret Thatcher, who believed such controls to be required in the fight against international drug dealers and terrorists. A treaty was signed in Schengen in June 1990 to lift all frontier controls on the movement of people between five European states (Germany, the Netherlands, Belgium, Luxembourg, and France). The five national parliaments must approve the free travel agreement, but that should be done by the end of 1991. The agreement lifts border controls among the five states, sets up a common visa policy for member-states' citizens, avoids passport controls at airports for Schengen states, grants the right of asylum, and establishes police and judicial cooperation through a computer setup in Strasbourg.[22]

The unification of indirect taxes presents difficult problems, as does the coordination of social policies. The unified market moreover will require a centralized monetary system. (Existing plans provide for the consolidation of the EMS by 1992–1993, with the former absentees, Britain, Portugal and Greece,

---

Court of Justice

The Court of Justice (thirteen members) deals mostly with cases brought by the Commission or member-states, and interprets Community law to national courts. It sees itself as the interpreter of the Community's treaties and legislation. In addition to the Court of Justice for hearing cases, there are also four chambers of three to six judges for less important matters. In 1986 a Court of First Instance was set up to relieve the main court of some routine cases.

The Court of Justice, like the American Supreme Court, has become very important in interpreting Community legislation and, by its decisions, promoting EC policy and integration. The Court forced Italy to accept German pasta, for example, and overruled a French ban on milk-substitute products. The Court now has the power to cut off Community funds to nations that ignore the Court's rulings. The Court is located in Luxembourg. Six advocates-general comment on the main points of each case in relation to EC law and how to interpret that law.

---

participating in one currency and a central bank.) The Germans will want to see this central bank run on lines similar to their own *Bundesbank* in Frankfurt, resistant to inflation, sheltered from political shifts. Whatever solution is adopted, disputes over its power are almost certain to arise.

How far, again, should the EC go in adopting a common social policy? Delors and his like are convinced that unfettered competition between great conglomerates must be balanced by joint action for social justice. Thatcher and other free traders, by contrast, looked to free trading in Europe in which bureaucratic interference will be kept to a minimum. As Stanley Hoffman puts it, "What is at stake is the future of the nation-state in Western Europe. Delors' logic is ultimately that of the construction of a federal state . . . legitimacy would be provided by universal suffrage, expressed in the election of the European Parliament."[23] In this respect, Thatcher—before leaving No. Ten Downing Street in 1990—had actually taken over the Gaullist legacy. It would prove a heavy burden for her, as the Tory party divided over the issue and as "Euro-Tories" in the European Parliament diverged from her leadership.

The major concern of the EC in its march toward 1992, however, has been economic and monetary union (EMU). A committee was established in 1988, chaired by Jacques Delors, president of the European Commission, to propose specific steps to achieve EMU. This resulted in the 1989 "Report on Economic and Monetary Union in the European Community," known as the Delors Report. Delors, an energetic visionary with long experience in the French government, depends, as do the other sixteen commissioners, on a small corps of advisers (cabinet). His cabinet has people of high caliber: forceful, authoritative, and well-trained. Although the president of the European Commission is supposed to have limited powers, Delors, by using his advisers, has centralized power in his office. He aims not only for EMU, but also for major constitutional changes in the EC.

Political union will thus increasingly dominate the EC's agenda. France and Germany, at the time of this writing, stood out as its chief advocates. In 1990, at a meeting of the European Council in Dublin, Mitterrand and Kohl thus presented the other EC leaders with new proposals that would not merely speed up monetary union but would also bring about political union. Of all the Western European countries, Thatcher's Britain had remained most opposed to far-reaching new commitments—Italy, Belgium, Holland, Spain, and Portugal less so. British reluctance was likely to end, however, with the resignation of Thatcher as head of the Conservative party in late November 1990.

Political union also raised the question of parliamentary control, and the future powers to be conceded to the European Parliament (EP). According to Kohl, one of the chief spokesmen for closer union, the EC suffered from a "democratic deficit." Unlike any other democratic parliament, the EP could neither levy taxes nor make laws. Nonelected officials made most of the key decisions in the EEC. The EP will probably be given more power as 1992 approaches. Parliament was left out of the 1985 conference that enacted the Single European Act; thereafter, the EP called for a preconference meeting with the European Commission and the Council of Ministers to talk about constitutional reforms. The EP also intends to discuss the reform agenda with each national parliament.

The Commission had other ideas, but did not publish a "blueprint" for a federal Europe. Instead, the Commission suggested building on the precedents of the Single European Act. The EP was to receive more power and the Council of Ministers' work was to be speeded up by basing decisions on majority rule, mostly, and not on unanimity. Delors also wanted social and environmental legislation and some tax laws to be passed by majority decision, which will in practice give more power to the EP. Delors believes Parliament should have more say in choosing the European Commission; this would make the Commission more democratic and more responsible to the elected Parliament.

Other reforms proposed by the Delors Report would make the Commission more political and less technical in its work, and would reduce the influence of the Council of Ministers in the many committees that oversee the work of the Commission. These committees slow up the work of the Commission as they give national governments oversight of the Commission's work.

Perhaps the most controversial of the reforms would give the Commission more say in foreign and security policy. At present, foreign ministers do coordinate their policies within the EC, but they are free from control of the Commission and of the Council. Since 1990, the Commission has reacted more quickly than national governments in responding to events in Eastern Europe and coor-

The European Parliament

The European Parliament is the EC's only directly elected body. It has been called the democratic conscience of the EC. The Parliament must be consulted by the Commission and the Council of Ministers, and the Parliament questions their activities. (In the Single European Act, the EP is called the European Assembly.) The first elected EP was in 1979, and since then it has tried to increase its legislative and supervisory powers. The Single European Act won the EP the power of veto over agreements between the EC and other nations; and the EP now has control over enlarging the EC. Many analysts think the EP should develop along the lines of the American system of three branches of government with the Court of Justice becoming the Community's Supreme Court and the Council of Ministers becoming the Executive branch of the EC.

The EP's structure is complex and diffuse. The Secretariat, about 2,900 officials organized into seven divisions, is in Luxembourg. Monthly meetings of Parliament are held in Strasbourg, and committee meetings take place in Brussels. Some foresee all these activities being centralized in Brussels. For the moment, the EP's effectiveness is impaired by constant moves and, even more, by lack of strong legislative power. The EP has genuine functions concerning the budget, but in legislative matters the EP is only consulted—and can be ignored.

Today the EP has 518 members, elected every five years by member-states, but grouped not as representatives of nations but by political affiliation—that is, Socialist, Christian Democrat, Conservative, Liberal, and Communist. Before 1979, members of the EP were appointed by national governments apt to use the EP as a place of exile for discarded politicians. Once members were directly elected, however, work in the EP became increasingly attractive, and the EP turned into a much more dynamic institution than hitherto. The EP further gained from the vigor of its president, Enrique Barón Crespo, a Spanish scholar and a moderate Socialist who believes in the creation of a European federal state along the model of the United States. The EP meets once a month for a week in plenary session. Debates are over commission reports, major current issues, statements of other EC bodies. Since 1986 the EP has had more power—for example, it can veto international agreements and amend EC laws related to 1992.[24]

dinating aid programs there. Reformers suggest merging the Commission's foreign trade work with political cooperation to form a specialist diplomatic service.

There are other concerns. The EC has developed an ever-growing bureaucracy. Its expansion, however, should be seen in perspective. By 1990 the personnel of the EC numbered no more than 20,000—compared to 50,000 employees on the payroll of the U.S. Department of Commerce alone. (The EC does not operate directly on populations; the national bureaucracies are responsible for enforcement. Hence the EC bureaucracy should remain relatively small.) There are more serious disputes concerning the internal distribution of

Politics in Western Europe ———————————— 408

political power within the EC itself; for example, the belief that the Council and the Commission have too much power and its elected Parliament has too little.

The EC, an Enlarged Germany, and Eastern Europe

On October 3, 1990, the two German states were reunified—on West German terms. Once the merger has become fully effective, German economic influence within the EC will become even more striking. Admittedly, the GNP of even a unified German state will be considerably less than that of Britain and France, or of France and Italy, combined. Furthermore, West Germany will have to rehabilitate East Germany, a country wracked by forty years of Communist mismanagement, this at tremendous cost and the possible risk of inflation. In March 1990, during the first free elections held for more than forty years in East Germany, the CDU won a striking—and unexpected—victory. After reunification has been technically achieved, and once East Germany has recovered economically, a united Germany will be even more powerful than before. The German capital may shift from Bonn, an unassuming Rhenish city, back to Berlin, a metropolis not known for the modesty of its civic culture. Fortunately for Europe, Germany has undergone profound political and psychological changes since the bad old days of Nazism. (German respondents to public opinion polls have consistently favored European integration by a large majority; ever since 1953, moreover, the CDU has managed to gain a larger share of the national vote than Hitler did in the not-so-free election of 1933.)

Given the EC's success and given the decline of communism in Eastern Europe, the EC has become the model for the former Warsaw Pact countries. For Eastern Europe, 1989 was the year of revolution. For the moment, the EC is unwilling to accept other new members. (The EC has thus not been prepared to admit as full members Austria, a neutral country, or Turkey, a relatively backward state with a high demographic growth rate.) Even as it stands, the EC already forms part of a wider network with external associates in the Middle East, Africa, and the Caribbean. Western Europe's trade, commercial, and cultural links are of age-old standing: The EC's influence is certain to spread rapidly beyond the Elbe. Early in 1990, for example, the EC and various other governments set up a European Bank for Reconstruction and Development—known by its French acronym, BERD. Its object is to promote political pluralism and a market economy in Eastern Europe. The only other agency linking Eastern and Western Europe at the time of this writing was the Conference on Security and Cooperation in Europe (CSCE). This body consisted of 35 members belonging either to NATO or to the Warsaw Pact. It was an informal body without a secretariat or permanent headquarters. Its deliberations had begun after the Helsinki Accord of 1975, with successive conferences centering on three key issues—security, economics, and human rights. It seems likely that the CSCE will take on a more permanent shape and expanded functions.

The European Commission office (Berlaymont) in Brussels had to prepare quickly, in August 1990, a 200-page report on the United Germany and the EC. The report describes how the GDR (East Germany) will be integrated into the twelve-member EC after it is joined to the Federal Republic (West Germany). All EC laws, rules, and regulations will apply to the GDR and it will have access to various Community funds. This will, of course, be expensive for the EC budget. The GDR will be integrated into the Community in three stages. Stage one began on July 1 when the two states established an economic and monetary union; it terminates in December when the states fully merge. During stage one, the GDR will have to adapt its legislation to West German and EC standards but will be able to apply for loans from the European Investment Bank and for funds from Phare (EC support program) and from Eureka (for research). The second stage starts once there is a united Germany and all Community laws apply to East Germany, with some exemptions during transition. The European Commission will propose any exemptions and transitional arrangements, and these must be approved by the Council of Ministers.

In the third stage, Community law will apply without exemption. When this will happen is not known; but the European Commission is anxious to have the whole process completed by January 1993, when the single internal market begins to operate. Three areas—agriculture, foreign trade, and environment—make this target date unrealistic. A longer transitional period for agriculture will be necessary if GDR farmers produce only goods that the Community already has in surplus. Curbing production and buying surplus output will be expensive, at least DM 20 billion, of which the EC will have to provide half. Too many workers are in the farming sector (10.8 percent), and the fishing fleet may have to be scrapped. Foreign trade agreements will have to be carried out by Brussels, not the GDR; these do not fit free-market arrangements, but probably will not be renegotiated until they run out in the year 2000.

Now that it is united to West Germany, the GDR has to meet EC and GATT regulations and follow the Lomé Agreement for aid and trade preferences to the Third World. The biggest hurdle for the GDR will be conforming to EC environmental standards. A transitional period will be needed, or most GDR industries would have to be shut down. All together the EC will have to pay heavily for German reunification even though Chancellor Kohl promised this would not happen.[25] The sixteen German *Länder* (states) will also face threats to their autonomy from the EC, whose institutions are increasing in power. Certain aspects of *Land* sovereignty are being given up to EC bodies.

A New NATO?

By 1990 the Warsaw Pact had distintegrated, and the future of NATO had become a matter of dispute. Suddenly, the military scene became completely transformed—this in a manner that no NATO planner had anticipated. Without firing a shot, the Soviet forces prepared to pull out of Hungary and Czechoslovakia. In 1990, the Soviet Union signed a treaty with West Germany providing for the unification of the two Germanys, the continued membership of a united Germany within the NATO alliance, and the gradual withdrawal of the Red Army from East Germany. Within the Soviet Union, the long-standing crisis of Marxism-Leninism deepened, regional separatism became a powerful force from the Ukraine and the Baltic to Soviet Asia; and the Communist party structure weakened. Even the Red Army faced serious morale problems, as ethnic dissensions grew within its ranks, as the returning army of occupation in the Eastern European countries had difficulties in finding adequate accommodation at home, as antimilitary sentiment grew within the Soviet Union, and as subaltern and field-grade officers disagreed with generals and colonels on the merits of *perestroika.*

NATO's bloodless victory seemed as complete as it was unforeseen. Success, however, produced tensions of its own. Even though its foreign commitments were eliminated, the Soviet Union remained a great power; its army continued to be modernized; its rocket forces and anti-ballistic missile defenses remained imposing in extent and technological sophistication. How should Europe or, indeed, NATO as a whole respond? NATO's forward defense strategy will have to go; it is not politically feasible to put eight army corps on the Oder-Neisse line. A large number of tanks, planes, and heavy weapons will probably be destroyed during the 1990s as the Soviets pull back from Central and Eastern Europe. The American dominance of NATO will decrease as a united Europe and a reunited Germany face a weakened Soviet Union and reassert their political and economic weight in NATO's councils.

The German-Soviet treaty of 1990 provided for the future reduction of the united German military to 370,000 troops, as opposed to 494,000 in West Germany's active military forces, and 173,000 in the now badly shaken East German forces. United Germany will neither manufacture nor deploy "ABC" (atomic, bacteriological, chemical) weapons. The British in 1990 decided to cut their regular forces by 18 percent and to withdraw half their troops from West Germany. The French announced they would withdraw 40,000 troops. The United States likewise contemplated far-reaching military reductions—in part as a response to the breakdown of the Warsaw Pact, in part as a means of reducing the U.S. budgetary deficit, and thereby profiting from the "peace dividend."

The Future of the EC

The existing members of the EC will move toward even closer association than at present. Once a single market has been achieved, by January 1993, there will be even greater pressure from outsiders to join the union. New arrangements will have to be made with the members of EFTA, all of them prosperous European states. In addition, the formerly Communist states of Eastern and Central Europe wish to adhere, to rebuild their wrecked economies. The sudden inclusion of so many new members could make the Community almost unworkable. In the long run, however, Western European unification will surely turn into a pan-European project, with Western Europe at its core and Eastern and Central Europe as its periphery. Having endured for nearly half a century, the Yalta settlement arrived at by the Big Three in 1945 will have finally been terminated.

The drive for economic and monetary union by 1993 or 1994 will force many changes not only on EC members, but also on its neighbors and the United States. Eastern Europe and EFTA will seek closer association with the EC, if not membership. Everyone is going to have to become more efficient and competitive. The EC leadership appears determined to cooperate with EFTA and Eastern Europe to make all of Europe one economic region. The aim is to apply market freedom—that is, free trade in goods, services, manpower, and capital—to all of Europe. There will have to be negotiations over freedom of competition, environmental protection, and cooperative research. The EC and EFTA are today each others' main trading partners (50 percent of EFTA's exports go to the EC and over 60 percent of its imports come from the EC). The EC trades more with EFTA than with the United States.

Preliminary negotiations began in June 1990 to apply market freedoms throughout each area. EFTA countries raised objections, for example, on the mutual right of abode, takeover bids, land and property purchases. EFTA states

---

Community Finances

Community finances up to 1970 were dependent on grants from member-states, which limited the Community's independence. Since 1970, the Community has secured its own funding from import duties on industrial and agricultural goods. The Council decides how the money should be spent.

The Court of Auditors (established in 1975) is a major EC institution; its function is to audit the accounts of Community bodies. It has twelve members who serve for six years and sit in Luxembourg. The Court of Auditors assists the Council and the EP to maintain control over the budget.

have high levels of health, safety, and environmental protection, and they do not want these lowered.

EC regulations (*acquis communautaires*) are numerous and onerous, and the EC bureaucracy large and intrusive. EFTA, on the other hand, has few regulations and a small bureaucracy. (By 1990, the EC employed 20,000 civil servants; EFTA, 71.) Concessions will have to be made on both sides. Most difficulty will arise over EC laws that impinge on national sovereignty. EFTA is concerned entirely with free trade and its members have not given sovereignty to supranational authorities. European economic and monetary union, however, will force EFTA to change and to join in the Community's decisionmaking procedures. The EC and its organ will have to develop consultative processes, and EFTA will have to conform to the EC's economic and monetary norms.

Unification, even in its narrow West European sense, affects everybody—industrialists, labor unionists, merchants, and professional people. Unification in the political sense goes with a host of nonpolitical links. For instance, under "Project Erasmus," 80 educational institutions from twelve member countries have agreed to recognize one anothers' degree courses. As in medieval Europe, a student can once again work successively at a British, German, Italian, French, or Spanish university until he or she obtains a "Euro-degree."

Future efforts to rebuild Eastern Europe will be aided by the OECD, which can play a leading role in the transition to market economies in Eastern Europe. It certainly has the experience, expertise, and statistical methods to help the former Communist bloc. In addition, the OECD can play a useful role as a forum for exchanging views, plans, and information. As a center for microeconomic research on Eastern Europe, the OECD can find a new, progressive role for itself.

Relations between the United States and the EC have changed from the "patron-client" era of the 1950s and 1960s to greater EC independence. Most disagreements have been over trade, agricultural subsidies, monetary policies, and foreign policy issues. Overall, both Europe and the United States should benefit, despite numerous differences of opinion that divide the partners on both sides of the Atlantic. Between them, the United States and the EC form the largest trade partnership in the world, which underpins the entire world economy. The United States, moreover, is by origin a European state. Today, something like four-fifths of all U.S. citizens trace all or most of their ancestors to Europe; however, this figure will dramatically change by 2010 as a result of millions of Asians and Hispanics pouring into the United States. The U.S. and European economies are interdependent, and becoming even more so. The EC is by far the largest commercial partner of the United States. According to current estimates, some 20,000 U.S. companies now operate in Europe, employing about nine million people. Total U.S. exports to the EC, shipments by U.S. subsidiaries within the EC, and total company sales by 1989 amounted to more than 800 billion dollars per year—almost three times as much as U.S. sales to

Canada, and four times as much as U.S. sales to Japan. Between 1987 and 1988, U.S. exports to the EC went up by 5 percent; the U.S. trade deficit with the EC fell by 50 percent to 12.8 billion dollars, 11.5 billion dollars lower than in 1987.

After 1992, the EC may become stronger and richer than the United States. Some Americans fear the EC will become protectionist against all those outside of Europe. After the Treaty of Rome, many U.S. multinationals went into Europe to avoid being shut out of the EC; today, U.S. firms are investing billions in the EC to forestall being shut out of the market after 1992.

There are major difficulties for those outside the EC as 1992 approaches. The United States and Canada, for example, are not sufficiently involved in the standard-setting process for manufactured products; this could cause their goods to be shut out of the European market. EC procurement regulations favor EC products in certain sectors, such as telecommunications and electrical equipment, so that U.S. exporters cannot sell to EC states. Local content requirements could reduce the number of U.S. television programs and movies shown in the EC. The demand for EC content also will limit U.S. exports in such items as computer chips. To forestall or limit these restrictions, the United States will need to have an agency or department to watch the EC and to coordinate and negotiate relations with the EC's institutions.

U.S. investments in Europe, however, will benefit from a strong European economy. U.S. subsidiary companies incorporated in Europe will profit from the removal of barriers in the same way as will European companies. U.S. companies are already accustomed to operating both in a global and in a large domestic marketplace; hence they may have less difficulty in adjusting to the new order than many indigenous European companies. Instead of facing twelve different sets of norms, standards, and certification procedures, U.S. firms will be selling in a single market with uniform requirements.[26] The United States can only gain by association with a market in which the value of private consumption now by far exceeds that of the United States itself. Above all, the 1992 program represents an astonishing vindication for those farsighted Americans who, after World War II, tried to cajole the various West European states into a political and economic union. Both Europe and the United States have a common stake in the success of "1992." It is to be hoped that the European and erstwhile American founding fathers of the EC will not be disappointed.[27]

The Approach to 1992 and After

The EC Summit in Dublin in May 1990 called for a treaty meeting on one currency for Europe before the end of 1992. The Dublin summit also called for a conference on possible changes in the Treaty of Rome to foster more political interdependence. A push for political union failed, but efforts were in-

Other EC Organizations

Another important Community group is the Economic and Social Committee, whose 189 members are nominated by member governments to serve for four years and advise the Commission and the Council of the views of interest groups—employers, workers, and various others. The Committee's work is organized by a Bureau into nine sections dealing with agriculture, industry, social and cultural affairs, environment, and so forth. Reports or opinions (more than a hundred) are presented in Brussels to ten plenary sessions a year. If a report is accepted, it is sent to the Commission and the Council. A similar body advised the ECSC.

tensified to make the EC more efficient, more democratic and consistent in its internal and external policies. The summit further called for a better way of making foreign policy and internal security policies. There was considerable pressure to democratize EC institutions; that is, make them more responsive to the European voters.

The Rome summit of the European Council in December 1990 began a new chapter in the history of the Community; it laid the legal groundwork for European economic and political unity by the year 2000. The object is to create a political as well as an economic and monetary union. The new political union therefore will be able to deal with foreign and security matters.

A European Central Bank seems likely, but not by 1993, and the development of a common foreign policy seems probable. The EP will be strengthened, but not at the expense of national parliaments, according to many critics. Euro-law should be democratized, according to many critics, especially in the Council of Ministers (the proto-senate of the Community). Council meetings should be more open, and matters decided by simple majority. The EP is likely to be given more power over communal laws and legislation; a veto over the president of the Commission and the ability to remove commissioners sent to Brussels would greatly strengthen the EP.

There are residual worries about the new EC of 1992 and its aims: a single market, monetary union, a social charter, and the rebuilding of Eastern Europe. There is special concern over the facts that civil servants, not elected officials, run the EC; that economic, not social, concern drives the EC; and that the centralized EC reduces national sovereignty.

The Belgian foreign minister, Mark Eysken, foresees four tests for the EC in the coming years: democracy, efficiency, political coherence, subsidiarity. For greater democracy in the Community, he suggested that the EP's power should be increased, especially in being able to modify Community legislation, treaties, and Commission votes on resource allocation. The EP should be able to veto Council directives and to ratify appointments. The EP should also be able to initiate legislation if the Commission fails to do so. There should be investigative and subpoena powers in the EP, according to Eysken.

Efficiency, for Eysken, means going beyond the Single European Act and making, for example, majority voting the rule in the Council of Ministers (except for treaty matters). The Court of Justice should be strengthened, to be able to compel member-states to comply with Community laws and treaties.

To achieve political coherence, the EC needs to have a common foreign policy, to be able to speak with one voice in the UN, the CSCE, and other such bodies. The EC also needs a common foreign policy to ensure a strong position in rebuilding and restructuring Eastern Europe. The European Political Cooperation Group (EPC) has its limitations. The General Affairs Council and COREPER should be revitalized and help in executing Community policies toward Eastern Europe. Experts on Eastern Europe should be added to the EPC and closer coordination should be sought between EPC, the Council Secretariat, and the Commission. Finally, Eysken insists that there should be no distinction between Community affairs and political cooperation in world affairs.

Subsidiarity, many observers feel, should be used in matters of cultural and social legislation. Member-states should be granted the right to seek redress against the Community through the Court of Justice. In spite of these problems, the future of the new EC of 1992 looks bright.

By mid-1990, 60 percent of the 1992 plans were adopted. Member-nations' commercial firms have had to change ways of doing business and have set up cross-border relationships. Already trade between member-states has grown, and this has encouraged them to push toward monetary union with one currency.

Outsiders have been forced to react to this drive for economic and monetary union. EFTA has been talking to the EC about forming a European Economic Space (EES) to achieve a free movement of capital, goods, and people. The United States has begun to upgrade its relations with the EC instead of relying only on bilateral relations with the twelve member-states. With the upsurge in Eastern Europe, the EC has become the dominant force in restructuring the former Communist bloc countries. The United States of America finds itself once again encouraging the creation of a United States of Europe. Indeed, The Economist calls President Bush and Secretary of State Baker "the second generation" of American leaders encouraging the creation of economic and monetary union among the nations of Europe. The Bush administration also forged new institutional connections with the EC, and has encouraged the EC to restructure the way it acts in foreign affairs. The speed of change in Eastern Europe has forced the EC to take stands not only on economic affairs, but also in foreign policy matters. The reunification of the two Germanys has been a further stimulus for Community changes and reforms—economic integration and political integration are being speeded up. There has been no slacking off from the goals set for 1992, however. As noted earlier, border controls were dropped between France,

Germany, and the Benelux nations; the single market plan is on schedule. It is events outside the EC that call for planning and negotiation, not the least of which are relations with the United States.

The United States welcomed the new initiatives of 1989 and 1990 and encouraged the EC to be the major player in Europe. It was President Bush who recommended that the European Commission coordinate aid for Poland and Hungary. Pressure from the United States pushed the EC into trying to reconcile its economic role and its lack of a foreign policy. The European Political Cooperation (EPC), a network of the foreign ministries of EC member-states, took the lead in coordinating efforts. In December 1989, Secretary Baker suggested new institutional links between the United States and the EC. (He did not want the EC to make foreign policy decisions before consulting the United States.) The EPC has been acting on its own and this has piqued the United States, which wants a seat at the table; the French often question the right of the United States to be involved in purely European matters. The response to Secretary Baker's initiative is the inauguration of twice-yearly meetings between the president and the Commission, between the U.S. president and the president of the European Council, and between the U.S. secretary of state and EC foreign ministers. The next appropriate step is the appointment of a U.S. ambassador to the EC for coordination on political and foreign policy matters, much as the U.S. ambassador to NATO coordinates security and military matters there.

The United States then has encouraged and stimulated European integration and wants a stronger, stabler Europe to govern itself with only limited help from the United States. Problems remain, especially, in areas of agriculture (EC subsidies to its farmers) and in security matters. The United States does not want to see NATO weakened or ignored. The United States would welcome the Western European Union as a support group in NATO and in consulting with the United States. "No consultation, no nuclear umbrella," advises former Assistant Secretary of State Rozanne Ridgway.

For the EC, a major question for the future is the number of members—12 or 24? Many nations are queuing up for membership—Austria, Sweden, Norway, Turkey, Cyprus, and Malta. Delors, president of the European Commission, wants no new members before 1993. To EFTA he offers the European Economic Space (EES) plan, which would link EFTA's six to the EC's twelve by negotiating on decision-shaping of laws affecting EES. EC and EFTA ministers and judges would meet for discussion and planning. The European Commission fears, however, that consultation would slow up the making of decisions.

According to EC bureaucrats, EFTA will have to make some concessions and settle for informational exchanges, but not a seat in EC institutions. EFTA may have to establish a larger bureaucracy and speak with one voice, not six, to be able to initiate and enforce decisions. Finally, Delors feels EFTA demands too many exceptions to Community laws. EFTA members have many disagreements among themselves and with the EC; it is hard to see them taking a united position toward the EC. The potential rewards of association with the EC in the EES are so great, however, that difficulties may disappear as the benefits are perceived.

Meanwhile, the EC, while denying membership to Eastern European countries, continues to make association agreements with them. In Central Europe, Austria has made new headway since East Germany was accepted as a special case, and with the end of the cold war the argument against neutral states has weakened.

The EC's program for Eastern Europe, the G-24 or Phare program, is working well in coordinating aid. The EC also is making bilateral agreements with Eastern European nations and association agreements for free trade into the EC while allowing protection for a period of time for Eastern Europe. Associate status could lead to political cooperation as well. Programs are being developed to help Eastern Europe, and some aid is coming in. The nations of Eastern Europe must, however, develop market economies and democracy before significant aid will be forthcoming.

An EMU by 1993?

The economic and monetary union (EMU) is the major event for the EC, since it takes monetary sovereignty from the nation-state and gives it to a European central bank (Eurofed). The EMU also gives more power to the European Commission. The EMU statutes were to be discussed at the December 1990 conference, but in fact a decision was delayed. The United States sees the ECU, along with the dollar and the yen, as governing the world monetary system. Having one currency in Europe will greatly help policy coordination there.

The Eurofed will be independent, as the Germans want, and will set interest rates to ensure price stability. Banks will be supervised by national authorities, not by the Central Bank of the EC. Eurofed will have a twelve-member governing board and an operating board of four members. As a check on Eurofed, the Council of Finance Ministers (Ecofin) will attend meetings as nonvoting members. The EP will be sent annual reports by Eurofed and could put questions to the central bank.

One debate over EMU revolved around two alternatives: Should EC currencies be fixed at set exchange rates or should they replace national currencies? The Germans wanted to keep their mark; the others preferred the ecu-symbol. The other debates concerned inflation and budget deficits. Germany and Holland wanted the central body to set national budgets; Britain and France wanted each nation to set its own budget. The agreed-upon solution was "binding procedures" with each state having to get approval from Ecofed for its own budget. If states do not comply, EC funds will be shut off. Three phases are laid out: free capital movement and economic and monetary cooperation; Eurofed operates but national governments set monetary policy; and, finally, in phase three, fixed exchange rates and set interest rates and a kind of economic union coordinated through member-states. Ecofed will have power to make regular recommendations to EC states and set three-year guidelines. The European Commission is seen as an executive branch to balance Eurofed.

The momentum toward economic and monetary union (EMU) slowed during late 1990. The EC states, with the exception of Britain, were for a single currency controlled by a central banking system. Formal treaty negotiations were to begin in December 1990, but uncertainties developed: High oil prices, German unification, the slowing-down of economic convergence, and the failure of some EC states to balance their budgets and reduce inflation have made EC countries cautious about the pace of EMU.

The Delors plan for a three-stage move to EMU is still on the drawing boards, and questions remain about how long a transition period will be required before a single currency is in place. France, Italy, Belgium, the European Commission, Denmark, Luxembourg, and Ireland all want to go ahead to phase two to establish an embryo system of central banks (ESCB) to take over from national central banks but not be subordinated to the ESCB until phase three sets up Eurofed. This, they claim, can be done while EC members try to reduce inflation as well as their budgetary deficits.

The go-slow states were Britain, Portugal, and Greece. Britain was against a single currency and opposed shifting more resources from the haves to the have-nots. Portugal and Greece feared they could not survive EMU. In the late 1980s the Germans and the Dutch were the ones who were really slowing up EMU by calling for perfection. *Bundesbank* president Karl Otto Pöhl spoke out (September 1990) repeatedly against full EMU until member-states had similar inflation rates, budget deficits, and trade imbalances. Budgetary discretion for individual states was still necessary, Pöhl argued, given different contributions to Eastern Europe. Full EMU will require subordination to community budget rules and a lasting anti-inflation policy. Pöhl, therefore, sees a "lengthy transitional process toward full EMU." Within the German government there is disagreement. Chancellor Kohl now sides more with the *Bundesbank*; but German foreign minister Hans-Dietrich Genscher favors moving to stage two on January 1, 1993. The argument may be won by Pöhl, the head of the *Bundesbank*, as Kohl now favors 1994 as the beginning of stage two.[28]

Two conferences were held in December 1990 in Rome: one to finalize EMU and the other to move toward European political union if the Commission has its way. Some EC members are trying to curb the Commission dominated by Delors. For example, France wants to strip the Commission of its veto powers over the EP and allow only the Council of Ministers to accept or reject acts of the

EP. Others want to take away the Commission's exclusive right to initiate Euro-law or to allow the Parliament to fire Commissioners. Delors opposes all these efforts: He wants a strong Commission to become the executive branch of the EC. He also desires the EC to have a common foreign policy but fears the EMU is getting more difficult. Delors wants stage two by January 1993 and is pushing Germany hard on this—he sees EMU as binding Germany irreversibly to Europe.

Reformers in the EC want to revise the constitution. There is concern over the democratic deficit; that is, EC officials are not elected and national parliaments control the EP. There is concern about how the EMU can be made accountable. There is the problem of who to admit—how many and when. There is a fear about the lack of institutions to carry out an EC foreign policy. The fall of an independent East Germany forced rapid readjustments and new ideas on EC governance. Mitterrand wants more and quicker integration (à plusieurs vitesses) and Mitterrand and Kohl called for "European Union," that is, political union, by January 1993. Kohl has now retreated from that early date. Many others in the EC now also hesitate over full EMU so quickly.

Other differences, moreover, have developed between the German view and the French view. The French want to increase the power of the European Council by appointing the president for several years, not for six months. Heads of state would meet more often and make the important foreign policy decisions. The French also want the members' national parliaments to play a bigger role.

A major continuing concern of the EC is how to get a better, more responsive foreign policy apparatus. The European Political Cooperation, begun in 1970, was strengthened by the Single European Act. Leadership of EPC is rotated every six months, so there is a lack of continuity, and the EPC has become ineffectual and unresponsive to EC interests as opposed to national interests. Reform suggestions would reduce national influence and give more power to the European Council and the Council of Foreign Ministers.

NATO will have to change in light of the new situation in Europe. For Germany's allies, a newly united Germany within the EC suddenly seems a potential threat; hence there is widespread support for a continued U.S. presence in Europe—not only to provide a nuclear deterrent but also to balance German strength. Others call for the reactivation of the WEU (Western European Union).[29] During the 1970s and early 1980s, the WEU had slipped into lethargy. Since 1984, however, interest in the institution began to revive—in part because the WEU was not tied to the defense of a specifically Atlantic security zone, as was NATO. There was increased European consultation on "out-of-area" problems affecting Europeans. Should NATO weaken further, the WEU could well increase its functions. Another suggestion calls for a European Security Community (ESC) as a part of NATO. The EC bureaucracy would ultimately like to control defense policies, and not leave them to NATO where U.S. control remains supreme. The EC commissioners want the Conference on European Security and Cooperation (CSCE) to remain a weak, consultative organization. (The CSCE comprises 35 countries on both sides of the former Iron Curtain.) Others want the CSCE to be upgraded, partly to contain Germany, partly to develop an institution in which the Europeans and the two superpowers are both represented.

The gulf war of 1991 likewise posed old problems in a new form. The Suez venture of 1956 did not merely set the United States against its British and French allies; the expedition briefly divided Britain—spouses quarreled and life-long friends parted company over the issue—as it had not been split since the 1930s. The French, in contrast, were united when the Algerian war was continuing; Egypt supplied aid to the Algerian revolutionaries. By 1991, the position was reversed. The gulf war turned out to be even more popular in Britain than in the United States. Britain supplied the second-most important expeditionary force; the "special relationship" between London and Washington, long derided by critics, suddenly seemed to have been restored. The Danes and the Dutch firmly backed Britain (as they would over many economic issues); the French were more divided, even though some French troops participated. In contrast, the Italians were mindful of their profitable relationship with the Arab world, and the Germans were reluctant to quarrel with Gorbachev as long as Soviet troops remained in East Germany. There were other cleavages. Smaller countries such as Spain and Holland resented the implicit Franco-German predominance in the EC. Britain gained new stature with the departure of Margaret Thatcher from 10 Downing Street and her replacement by John Major. Major was more courteous and flexible; Major also got on well personally with Helmut Kohl, and the two shared similar right-centrist political views. Yet Germany and Britain disagreed on a variety of economic and constitutional issues. Given these rifts, the EC remained unable to speak with one voice on foreign policy.

The Western European Union (WEU) received new attention during the gulf war because of the EC's failure to develop a common response to the gulf war. NATO, of course, could not respond to the out-of-theater war in Kuwait, but the WEU was to be a bridge between the EC and NATO. The crisis with Iraq erupted too suddenly for the WEU to respond positively, partly because of U.S. opposition to the WEU as an alliance within NATO that could act independently of Washington. The United States thus got bilateral support from France and Britain to send military forces and from Germany to send money. But the poor showing of the EC in the gulf crisis will probably spur the WEU to strengthen its handling of out-of-NATO-area problems.

The future forms of European unification obviously remain uncertain. Clearly, the cold war has ended with a Western victory. Economic cooperation between the West European states has immeasurably improved over the past generation. The drive for political integration could likewise gain in strength. In all likelihood, the EC institutions will be granted more responsibility and power.

Eastern Europe and EFTA will press for admission to the EC and to the European Security Commission. All of this will pose severe problems, but perhaps there need not be total compliance to all EC institutions, laws, regulations, and procedures at all times by all members. The reality of European culture and its shared values, within an economic and monetary union, therefore point to a loose European confederation in the not-so-distant future.[30]

The United States and the New Europe

Chancellor Kohl correctly calls for even closer cooperation between Europe and the United States in the future. Europe is developing into a United States of Europe, Kohl believes; it needs to keep the United States involved and to have even more intense political coordination than in the past. Europe's leaders obviously want the United States to take part in the economic reconstruction of Central and Eastern Europe. The Atlantic Alliance, in the eyes of Europe's leaders, is the best guarantor of freedom and prosperity in Europe, but the alliance must change its form and expand its agenda. The EC should not be a closed unit of only twelve members; it should be opened to others to create a United States of Europe.

The United States has three roles in Europe: first, in the Atlantic Alliance, second, in cooperation with the EC, and third, by participation in the CSCE process.[31]

Neither the USSR nor the Europeans want NATO to disappear nor the United States to leave Europe now. Views with regard to the long term differ, however. Future solutions include the following:

1. An Atlantic community in which the United States leads the old-line Western democracies.
2. A European–North American Commonwealth in which the Soviet Union and the United States each leads its respective allies toward trans-global cooperation.
3. A consortium of three superpowers: United States, USSR, Europe.
4. A universe of nation-states run according to traditional precepts.

The future is obviously difficult to predict. We should, however, plan for the reduction of U.S. forces in Western Europe and increased military specialization among the NATO allies. NATO should not simply be dismantled. A minimum of ten years is needed before NATO and Warsaw Pact forces can be reduced by negotiations to a state of parity—say, one-third of their present level of nuclear warheads, and one-half of their present conventional forces.

In the coming decade, Atlantic cooperation should increasingly stress societal and environmental issues, as against defense. Science and technology should be promoted and security redefined, to include ecological issues. The Conference on Security and Cooperation in Europe (CSCE) should play a crucial part in the future of Europe; CSCE will need an extended machinery to carry out its tasks. The EC likewise has a major role to play, but a modified NATO is the first requirement. To divide the world into competing trading blocs would be a disaster for all. We should therefore strive for free trade worldwide, not just inside the EC; we should preserve the shared values of NATO and keep a U.S. presence in Europe in a partnership that will continue to benefit all its members.[32]

Notes

1. Richard Schwartz, "U.S. Interest in Europe's 1992 Process: An Analytical Survey," *Washington Quarterly*, Summer 1989, pp. 205–13; also *Economist* (London), July 8, 1989, p. 6.

2. On early unification efforts, see Sergio Pistone, in *The Federalist*, A Critical Review 30, no. 2 (1988). Walter Lipgens and Wilfried Loth have written the definitive four volumes on European unification: *Documents on the History of Integration, 1939–1950* (Florence: European University Institute, 1989).

3. See Dick Leonard, *Pocket Guide to the European Community* (London: Basil Blackwell and The Economist Publications, 1988), pp. 154, 156. See also Lewis H. Gann, ed., *The Defense of Western Europe* (London: Croom Helm, 1997).

4. See, for instance, Robert S. Jordan and Werner J. Feld, *Europe in the Balance: The Changing Context of European International Politics* (London: Faber and Faber, 1986), pp. 50–79. See also Jürgen Schwarz, *Structural Development of the North Atlantic Treaty Organization* (Munich: Hochschule der Bundeswehr, 1982).

5. Figures from Frederic N. Smith, "The North Atlantic Treaty Organization: A Brief Description," in *Defense and Foreign Affairs Handbook 1989* (Alexandria, Va.: International Media Corporation, 1989), pp. 1287–94. See also Gann, ed., *The Defense of Western Europe*.

6. For history of U.S. involvement in postwar Europe, see Peter Duignan and L. H. Gann, *The Rise of the West: The Americanization of Western Europe, 1945–1958* (London: Basil Blackwell, 1991).

7. G. W. Keeton and George Schwarzenberger, eds., *The Uniting of Europe* (Stanford, Calif.: Stanford University Press, 1958), p. 377, table 2.

8. Richard Mayne, ed., *Handbooks to the Modern World: Western Europe* (New York: Facts on File Publications, 1986), p. 643. See also, by the same author, *The Recovery of Europe* (London: Harper and Row, 1970).

9. Jordan and Feld, *Europe in the Balance*, p. 276.

10. Anthony Sampson, *The Changing Anatomy of Britain* (New York: Vintage Books, 1984), p. 232.

11. Stanley Hoffmann, "The European Community and 1992," *Foreign Affairs*, Fall 1989, pp. 27–47.

12. "The EMS Without a Safety Net," *The Economist* 27 (January 1990), p. 71.

13. Chalmers Johnson, "Their Behavior, Our Policy," *The National Interest* 17 (Fall 1989), pp. 17–27.

14. *Economist*, November 24, 1984, p. 13.

15. Ibid., p. 14, and Jan Hendrick Lubbers, "New Horizons in Postwar Diplomacy," *Washington Quarterly*, Winter 1984, p. 19.

16. Tony Burgess, "The Structure of the European Economic Community," in Mayne, ed., *Handbooks to the Modern World*, pp. 568–778.

17. When the Council approves a proposal, it is published in the "L" series (Legislation) of the *Official Journal* as a regulation, directive, or decision. The majority of this legislation relates to day-to-day management of agricultural and customs matters.

18. Ibid.; Lubbers, p. 17. For a detailed account of the EEC's administrative structure, see Emil Noël, *The European Community: How It Works* (Brussels: European Perspective Series, 1979).

19. Roy C. Macridis, "The European Economic Community: Political and Economic Union," in Roy C. Macridis and Robert Ward, *European Politics* (Englewood Cliffs, N.J.: Prentice-Hall, 1972); and Ian Thomson, *The Documentation of the European Communities: A Guide* (London: Mansell, 1989). Stanley A. Budd, *The EEC: A Guide to the Maze* (London: Kogan Page, 1987).

20. The texts of the Commission's proposals, which are available to the public, are referred to as COM documents (identified by a document number consisting of the date and a sequential number, e.g., COM (90)45) and are among the most important of Community documentation. When the Commission completes a proposal, it is sent to the Council and other Community institutions in the form of a "COM final," designated by the document number followed by the word "final." The texts of proposed legislation also appear in the "C" series (Information and Notices) of the *Official Journal of the European Communities*. The *Official Journal* is published daily and is the principal source of information on Community legislation. See Noël, *The European Community*.

21. "Policing Europe's Single Market," *Economist* 20 (January 1990), pp. 69–70.

22. *Financial Times*, June 19, 1990, p. 11.

23. Hoffmann, "The European Community," p. 41.

24. The European Parliament refers legislative proposals to one or more of its committees for a report that forms the basis for debate by the full Parliament. These reports appear as European Parliament Session Documents, Series A. The European Parliament's debates are published verbatim in an annex to the *Official Journal*. The full text of the Parliament's adopted resolutions and official opinions are recorded in the "Minutes of Proceedings" in the "C" series (Information and Notices) of the *Official Journal* and later appear in *Texts Adopted by the European Parliament*. Two small periodicals, *EP News* and *The Week*, describe what took place at the European Parliament's most recent plenary session and are helpful for monitoring current developments. See Noël, *The European Community*.

25. See *Wirtschaftewoche*, Dusseldorf, July 27, 1990.

26. Youri Devnyst, "The United States and Europe, 1992," *World Competition* [Geneva] 13, no. 1 (September 1989), pp. 29–42.

27. "Europe Without Borders: Answers to Some Questions," *Europe*, October 1988, pp. 15–17.

28. *Financial Times*, September 21, 1990, p. 10.

29. Alfred Cahen, *The Western European Union and NATO* (London: Brassey, 1989).

30. "The European Community: A Power in Its Own Right," *Economist*, July 7, 1990, pp. 5–40.

31. *Die Welt*, June 8, 1990.

32. James E. Goodby, *Future Atlantic Cooperation and Cooperative Institutions: Meeting the Challenge*. Washington, D.C.: Atlantic Council of the United States, Occasional Paper, Feb. 1990.

Index